The Scientific Investigation of Mass Graves: Towards Protocols and Standard Operating Procedures

This book describes the detailed processes and techniques essential for the scientific investigation of atrocity crimes. It includes methods for the location, evaluation, excavation, recovery, and recording of mass graves and the analysis of human remains and other evidence in order to establish the identity of victims and the cause and manner of their deaths. This volume establishes protocols and standard operating procedures to guide standards and approaches that can be used in both judicial and humanitarian contexts. The procedures for field and mortuary application are flexible and can be used to meet specific project aims, constraints, and contexts.

The phases of activity and detailed methodological approaches set out in this book describe components of a complex scientific process. Chapters examine the evaluation of possible sites, scene of crime management, health and safety, key roles, excavation of graves, forensic sciences, mortuary management, analysis of human remains, and antemortem data collection. Recommended recording forms are included on the accompanying CD.

Professor Margaret Cox is visiting professor at the University of Southampton and chief executive of the Inforce Foundation. Her forensic work has taken her to France, Belgium, Kosovo, Rwanda, Iraq, and Cyprus, and she regularly undertakes domestic casework in the United Kingdom. She is the author of numerous peer-reviewed publications and several books, including *Forensic Archaeology: Advances in Theory and Practice* (coauthored with Professor John Hunter) and *Health and Disease in Britain: Prehistory to the Present* (coauthored with Professor Charlotte Roberts).

Ambika Flavel is a forensic osteoarchaeologist with the Inforce Foundation. She has worked for many different international organisations and been involved in numerous international mass grave investigations in such places as the Former Yugoslavia, Guatemala, and Iraq. She has also contributed to training and capacity building programmes and in teaching field and laboratory techniques to university students, professionals, and law enforcement agencies.

Ian Hanson is a lecturer in forensic archaeology at Bournemouth University, UK. His experience in working on mass grave investigations and exhumations has taken him to Bosnia, Croatia, Guatemala, the DR Congo, the United Kingdom, the United States, Cyprus, Egypt, and the Sudan. He has worked as a professional archaeologist in Europe, Africa, the United States, and the Middle East and has served as a consultant to various agencies such as the ICTY, UN, FAFG, Kenyon International, and the police.

Joanna Laver is a crime scene investigator for Dorset Police, UK. She has worked as a professional archaeologist in the UK, South America, and Cyprus. Her experience as a forensic osteoarchaeologist has taken her to such places as Kosovo, Cyprus, and Iraq, and she has contributed to domestic cases in the UK. She has been involved in training and capacity building programmes, teaching field and laboratory techniques to students and professionals.

Roland Wessling is forensic science and operations manager for the Inforce Foundation. He has worked as a consultant for numerous organisations on atrocity crime investigations and exhumations in the Balkans, Cyprus, and Iraq and on domestic cases in Germany and Britain. He regularly contributes to capacity building and training programmes for students and professionals.

The Scientific Investigation of Mass Graves: Towards Protocols and Standard Operating Procedures

Margaret Cox
Inforce Foundation

Ambika Flavel
Inforce Foundation

Ian Hanson
Bournemouth University

Joanna Laver
Dorset Police Service

Roland Wessling
Inforce Foundation

CAMBRIDGE
UNIVERSITY PRESS

CAMBRIDGE UNIVERSITY PRESS
Cambridge, New York, Melbourne, Madrid, Cape Town, Singapore, São Paulo, Delhi

Cambridge University Press
32 Avenue of the Americas, New York, NY 10013-2473, USA

www.cambridge.org
Information on this title: www.cambridge.org/9780521865876

First published 2008

Printed in the United States of America

A catalog record for this publication is available from the British Library.

Library of Congress Cataloging in Publication Data

The scientific investigation of mass graves : towards protocols and standard operating procedures /
Margaret Cox . . . [et al.].
    p. ; cm.
Includes bibliographical references and index.
ISBN   978-0-521-86587-6 hardback
1. Forensic sciences – Standards.   2. Autopsy – Standards.   3. Criminal investigation.
4. Crime scene searches.   5. Mass burials.   6. War crimes.
I. Cox, Margaret, 1950–
[DNLM: 1. Forensic Anthropology – standards.   2. Autopsy – standards.   3. Exhumation – standards.
4. Homicide.   5. War Crimes. W 750 S4165 2008]
RA1053.S33   2008
614′.1 – dc22   2007013561

ISBN   978-0-521-86587-6 hardback

This book is dedicated to all those who have pioneered the application and development of the forensic sciences and crime scene processes to mass grave investigations since the 1940s.

Contents

I Protocols for the location, excavation, and analysis of remains from mass graves and other deposition sites

2 Protocols for the investigation of mass graves • Alison Anderson, Margaret Cox, Ambika Flavel, Ian Hanson, Michael Hedley, Joanna Laver, Alison Perman, Mark Viner, and Richard Wright   **39**

II Standard operating procedures

3 Health and safety • ALISON ANDERSON, IAN HANSON, DAVID SCHOFIELD, HENDRIK SCHOLTZ, JEANINE VELLEMA, AND MARK VINER   **109**

6 Mortuary procedures I – Pathology, radiography, and the role of the anatomical pathology technologist • Alison Anderson, Hendrik Scholtz, Jeanine Vellema, and Mark Viner

8 Mortuary procedures III – Skeletal analysis 2: Techniques for determining identity • CAROLINE BARKER, MARGARET COX, AMBIKA FLAVEL, JOANNA LAVER, MARY LEWIS, AND JACQUELINE McKINLEY 383

9 Forensic sciences • MARTIN HALL, TONY BROWN, PETER JONES, AND DEREK CLARK 463

List of Figures

List of Tables

Acknowledgments

While aspects of the process and procedure described in this book originated with the experience of some of the authors and editors while working with ICTY's forensic teams in the Balkans, and elsewhere, the idea and impetus for this book developed from the Inforce Foundation's Protocols (Version 4) (Inforce, 2004a) and Standard Operating Procedures (SOPs) (Inforce, 2004b). This book is adapted and much expanded from those documents. The Inforce protocols and SOPs were developed to guide the forensic investigation of mass graves and the analysis of human remains and other evidence from mass graves. These documents were a product of the expertise and contributions freely given by many people from around the world, many of whom are or have been Inforce Scientific Advisors. They have been vitally important in our collective endeavour to improve the manner and effectiveness of the use of the forensic sciences in the investigation of atrocity crimes and mass fatality incidents.

The guidance presented in this book is adapted and expanded from these contributions, which have been drawn together, heavily contextualised, added to, and edited into a cohesive format by the editorial team under the leadership of Professor Margaret Cox. This book is the cumulative effort of many individuals to whom we are extremely grateful. The list begins with the many attendees who took the time to comment on the initial and relatively short draft protocol documents circulated at the 2002 Inforce Conference and Workshop, and on the more detailed versions that were circulated later. The early contribution of these experts is acknowledged. While they are too numerous to name individually, we would particularly like to thank Jon Sterenberg (ICMP, Bosnia). We are particularly grateful to the following contributors to the Inforce Protocols. Michael Hedley and Dr Andrew Tyrell (JPAC, US) acted as key contributors and coordinators to their areas of specific expertise in preparing the protocols. Each contributed much expertise and time. Andy Tyrell is also thanked for commenting extensively on earlier versions of Chapters 7 and 8 of this book. Also deserving a special mention are Alison Anderson, Paul Cheetham, Tim Loveless, Romina Manning, Steve Naidoo, David Oxlee, Alison Perman, Amanda Reddick, Professor Guy Rutty, Mark Viner, and Professor Richard Wright. We are grateful to Dr Thomas Holland for his permission to base part of the anthropology protocol and SOPs on the CILHI Laboratory SOP of circa 2002/2003.

The development of the Inforce SOPs has involved considerably more work than the protocols because this is a significantly more comprehensive document. We are particularly grateful to the following individuals, who have contributed to the development of the SOPs and so to this book: Alison Anderson, Professor Caroline Barker, Tony Brown, Paul Cheetham, Dr Derek Clark, Sarah Donnelly, Dr Martin Hall, Major Tim Haynie, Michael Hedley, Dr Peter Jones, Dr Mary Lewis, Dr Louise Loe, Romina Manning, Jackie McKinley, David Oxlee, Alison Perman, Margaret Samuels, David Schofield, Dr Hendrik Scholtz, Dr Andrew Tyrell, Dr Jeanine Vellema, Mark Viner, and Professor Richard Wright. Tim Loveless is thanked for both his editorial pen and his photographic expertise.

That all of the individuals and organisations mentioned here have contributed to the development of the Inforce Protocols and SOPs should not be taken to infer that they necessarily endorse all aspects of those documents or this book. Ultimate responsibility for the content of this book lies with its authors and editors.

We gratefully acknowledge the support of the British Foreign and Common-wealth Office and Bournemouth University in funding some of the development of the Inforce Foundation Protocols and SOPs, and of Bournemouth University and the Inforce Foundation for financial support while preparing this book.

All royalties resulting from the sale of this publication will go to the Inforce Foundation (registered UK charity no. 1097435).

List of Contributors

Alison Anderson National Health Service, Greater Glascow and Clyde, Scotland/Association of Anatomical Pathology Technologists, UK

Caroline Barker International Independent Group of Eminent Persons, Colombo, Sri Lanka

Professor Tony Brown School of Geography, Southampton University, UK

Paul Cheetham School of Conservation Sciences, Bournemouth University, UK

Dr Derek Clark Freelance Consultant

Professor Margaret Cox Inforce Foundation, UK

Sarah Donnelly Freelance Consultant

Ambika Flavel Inforce Foundation, UK

Dr Martin Hall Department of Entemology, The Natural History Museum, London, UK

Ian Hanson School of Conservation Sciences, Bournemouth University, UK

Major Tim Haynie Freelance Consultant

Michael Hedley Gloucestershire Constabulary, UK (retired)

Dr Peter Jones Freelance Consultant

Joanna Laver Dorset Police, UK

Dr Mary Lewis Department of Archaeology, University of Reading, UK

Dr Louise Loe Oxford Archaeology, Oxford, UK

Tim Loveless Freelance Consultant

Romina Manning United Nations

Jacqueline McKinley Wessex Archaeology, Salisbury, UK

David Oxlee Kalagate Imagery Bureau, St Neots, Cambridge, UK

Alison Perman City of London Police, UK

Margaret Samuels Department of Psychiatry, Duke University, Durham, NC, US

David Schofield School of Conservation Sciences, Bournemouth University, UK

Dr Hendrik Scholtz International SOS Pte Ltd., Singapore

Dr Jeanine Vellema Division of Forensic Medicine, University of the Witwatersrand/Gauteng, Department of Health, Forensic Pathology Services, Johannesberg, South Africa

Mark Viner Inforce Foundation, UK/Bartholomew and the Royal London Hospitals, UK

Roland Wessling Inforce Foundation, UK

Professor Richard Wright Emeritus Professor, University of Sidney, Australia

1

Introduction and context

Margaret Cox, Ambika Flavel, and Ian Hanson

1.1 Rationale

The development of this book exploring the establishment of protocols and standard operating procedures (SOPs) contributes towards the creation of an adopted suite of methodologies and helps ensure a consistent and appropriate quality of process and practice. The protocols and SOPs discussed here are specifically developed for application to the scientific investigation of crime scenes, particularly to sites of the deposition of multiple human remains (e.g. mass graves[1] and surface and other deposition sites). They are designed to guide standards and approaches that can be used to satisfy both judicial and humanitarian needs resulting from the multilayered legacies of such heinous crimes as genocidal massacres, war crimes, crimes against humanity, and mass murder. Much that is contained herein can also be applied or adapted to the recovery and identification of individuals who have died as a consequence of recently occurring mass fatalities, whether they relate to terrorist attacks (e.g. 9/11, the Bali bombings), natural disasters (e.g. the Asian tsunami), or other disasters (e.g., aeroplane or train crashes, fires in enclosed spaces).

It is our intention that by adopting and applying these protocols and the underpinning SOPs, any team of experienced and qualified forensic scientists and scene of crime examiners (SCEs) can investigate an alleged incident to an acceptable and agreed standard. Our aim is to establish processes and methodologies that are of a high enough standard to satisfy the evidentiary requirements of any court or judicial process, whether international, national, or local, and to satisfy the humanitarian

---

[1] These protocols are primarily intended for use on mass grave or deposition sites containing the human remains of a number of deceased and the associated scene of crime. The process and principles are, however, equally applicable for small or single graves and, in such cases, some aspects will be less complex than for larger graves (e.g., deposits survey and data processing).

need to locate and identify the dead and to be able to reconstruct histories and past events. These procedures are designed to be used flexibly so that they can be applied, as appropriate, to meet specific project aims and objectives, constraints and contexts.

We believe that the highest possible standards should pertain, dependent upon given circumstances, regardless of whether a site is investigated for judicial or humanitarian purposes. There are several reasons why the use of recognised procedures is becoming increasingly necessary. History has shown that global, regional, and national priorities and circumstances can change, reflecting international and more local pressures for justice and the identification of the Missing. Such circumstances might be the revocation of amnesty laws and the democratisation of formerly repressed peoples, as has occurred in parts of Central America and Southeast Asia (e.g., Cambodia). The nature of the investigation of interment sites, such as mass graves, involves processes that are destructive and usually cannot be repeated. Evidence can only be collected once, and it is rare to be able to reexamine physical evidence in later years. Consequently, there is a moral imperative to undertake such work to the highest possible standards particularly with the variety of uses that the evidence may be put to over time (see section 1.6). If we fail to do so, we do both the dead and the living victims of such crimes a serious disservice and further disempower them.

The adoption of common approaches will ensure the maximum recovery of safe evidence, regardless of whether the end use is initially perceived as judicial or humanitarian. It is a truism that the fundamental right to the best evidence and all available evidence is one that must be common to all, whether the goal is the safe trial and conviction of a perpetrator, the repatriation of the dead to their families and communities, or both. The families of missing persons have an absolute right to the establishment of an integrated approach to all aspects of investigation, including the establishment of the identity of the deceased. Without personal closure and a sense of justice in post-conflict scenarios, effective reconciliation, healing, or rebuilding of society cannot be achieved. The expectations of families and communities of the Missing for positive identifications will further increase as technologies such as DNA analysis are seen as being increasingly available. Because the same evidence can serve two distinct but entwined goals, scientists and SCEs have a dual responsibility to achieve the highest possible standard of scientific recovery, analysis, reporting, and evidentiary process and management.

For simplicity, we have written this book as if all applications of the protocols and SOPs are for judicial contexts. Thus, once any material has been recovered and is deemed to be of relevance to the case in question, it is seized as evidence and becomes an exhibit that is handled in a specific way to ensure its scientific and evidentiary integrity and the chain of custody. Although the terminology for such processes will be different in a humanitarian context, the same rigorous handling of recovered materials is required to ensure that the Missing are properly identified and that their possessions are correctly assigned to them.

1.2 Scope, background planning, and flexibility

The phases of activity and detailed methodological approaches set out in this book describe components of a complex scientific and scene of crime management process undertaken to fulfil judicial and humanitarian objectives within a broader investigation. These protocols and SOPs are concerned with the recovery and analysis of physical and contextual evidence from scenes of crime, which will include mass graves and other deposition sites. It must, of course, be remembered that recovery and analysis are components of a wider investigation and humanitarian process and that we work on such cases with numerous other specialists from a variety of organisations and agencies. The development of the comprehensive range of protocols and SOPs required for this work has been complex and iterative and remains so. The protocols and SOPs presented here will undoubtedly be subject to change as methodologies and new technologies develop and our collective experience grows.

This book is fundamentally concerned with scene of crime and evidence management, scene of crime location, evidence recovery, recording and analysis, antemortem and postmortem data collection, and associated data and reports. With such a complex operation, there are requirements for organisational structures and processes outside the scientific and legal aspects of an investigation. These pertain to such issues as wider mission planning, logistics, security, and development. Individual organisations undertaking such work will have their own internal procedures for these and other aspects that they must consider when embarking on forensic investigations. These protocols and SOPs sit alongside individual organisations' procedures that must also include a code of conduct and ethical guidance (see 1.9 for an example), health and safety procedures and mitigation strategies (see Chapter 3), report structures and equipment lists (see Tables 2–1 and 2–2 in Chapter 2), and data handling and management. Recommended recording forms for use with these protocols and SOPs are provided on the accompanying CD. An introduction to the forms and guidance in how to use them is situated in 1.11.

More specifically, matters that fall outside the remit of these protocols and SOPs that must be considered before any deployment and provided for include predeployment reconnaissance (authority/community liaison, climate and weather analysis) and feasibility and strategy studies (security requirements, scale, time, costs, resources, equipment, access, infrastructure). They must include administrative functions, overall project management, project support and development (including financial, technical, and resource support), and travel to the mission area. It is imperative to understand and comply with requirements determined by the legal status of the site and relevant authorities. Personnel matters such as medical prerequisites, contact and next-of-kin information, contracts, and insurance must also be addressed. Security requirements are extremely important and include security provisions for personnel and equipment on site, in accommodations, off site, and in transit. Operational risk assessment, local community impact assessment, team organisation (and, if appropriate, rotation), staff induction, staff welfare, communication needs, and emergency medical requirements are all essential issues. Equipment and logistical procurement is vitally important to get right, as is the involvement of and cooperation with other agencies, community liaison, provision for the repatriation of human remains, and death certification. Any organisation adopting these protocols and SOPs will need to consider and provide for these and other areas as appropriate.

What we have endeavoured to achieve with this book is to present the basis of the Inforce Foundation protocols (Inforce, 2004a) and SOPs (Inforce, 2004b) and embed that text within an overall framework of discussion, specifically of areas that are complex, undergoing development, or are particularly contentious. Although aspects of this text can be readily adopted and used by forensic organisations involved in recovering the dead from atrocity crimes and, indeed, in mass fatality response contexts, much of the text is designed to provoke thought and debate around the process. Some areas are discussed in more detail than others, particularly where research around the specifics is still ongoing or required. If an SOP is needed for a specific area of the process, we bring it to the reader's attention. In essence, our challenge is significant. We aim to set out protocols and SOPs that will be useful to other organisations, and set those two key elements within a context of discussion and considerations that are based on our collective experience and that will provoke debate and consideration.

Section I of this book (Chapter 2) covers the protocols, and the three components of the scientific process are described. These comprise Phase 1, Site Assessment; Phase 2, Excavation and Recovery; and Phase 3, The Mortuary. These components are designed as a sequence of processes occurring within the timeline of a mission, leading from one to the next. However, the three phases may be carried out independently if appropriate and may also be carried out concurrently (i.e., Phase 3 can commence once Phase 2 has begun) or in parallel (e.g., a prolonged operation with several grave sites). In this chapter, each phase of activity is preceded by a phase summary and includes flowcharts showing process and personnel typically involved. If the organisation undertaking the investigation of the mass grave site(s) is not dealing with other aspects of the investigation (e.g., witness interviews, antemortem data collection), then it is imperative that the scientists collecting biological information (postmortem data) work closely with the other agencies involved (Keough et al., 2004). This is essential to ensure that the resultant data sets are compatible and that appropriate and relevant ante- and postmortem data are collected (see Chapter 10).

It should be understood that within the phases of activity described, not all elements may be necessary or appropriate in all cases and, in some, even more elements may need to be added. What is described is a full range of scientific and scene of crime/evidential procedures that are commonly conducted during mass grave excavations. These procedures have a proven track record of being successful in recovering safe and sound evidence and for use in judicial and humanitarian processes. They are drawn on what has been learned during international experience over the past fifteen or more years and were trialled, with subsequent modification, in both the field and the mortuary, in simulation exercises undertaken in 2005 and 2006 and in investigations in Iraq and Cyprus from 2003 to 2005.

The protocols are process driven and set out the organisational and management requirements for successful forensic missions. By establishing a process to be followed or adapted as appropriate, we are providing a framework that is particularly useful when dealing with complex teams comprising personnel from various backgrounds in terms of experience, education, and scientific and crime scene management traditions and with various cultural traditions and expectations. The design of the protocols and SOPs eases the reader from a description of what should be done (i.e., the protocols) to a more complex discussion of the detailed methodologies involved (i.e., the SOPs). Further to this, it provides several levels of guidance. For those with significant levels of skills and experience, reference to the protocols alone may be adequate, while the less experienced or less well trained should refer to both. The protocols can act as an essential guide for those with less experience, while a recent graduate will need to absorb not only the guide to process that the protocols provide but also the detailed methodological information in the SOPs (Section II). The experienced practitioner in a specific field who lacks direct experience of this context may use the protocols as an *aide memoire* and guide to the less familiar working environment of the mass grave or temporary mortuary. Those with extensive forensic experience can use this text to provide a process and methodological framework that facilitates effective quality assurance and the ability to undertake work that follows acknowledged and high standards, an ever-increasing requirement of the judiciary.

When following the protocols, it must be remembered that usually the scale of all aspects of resource requirements (e.g., personnel, logistics, financial, equipment, time) is larger and more complex for Phase 2 than for Phase 1. The aims and objectives of an investigation, as well as deployment of available resources, will be crucial in determining what can be achieved. The key to employing these protocols and SOPs successfully is flexibility and basing decisions on available site or case information. For example, the investigation on behalf of a nongovernment organisation (NGO) of twenty accurately located single graves known to contain skeletonised human remains may mean that several elements of the assessment and mortuary phases might be omitted (e.g., geophysical survey or refrigeration of all human remains), and that the scale of equipment and personnel deployed might be limited. Alternatively, an investigation funded by an organisation such as the United Nations (UN) or the International Criminal Court (ICC) of a mass grave suspected to contain 400 people in a waterlogged environment may require the full range of analyses using all three phases and a full complement of field and mortuary staff. Flexibility around the basic sequence of process is essential.

1.3 Structure of this book

This book is divided into three sections of unequal length. This first chapter provides a brief introduction to the historical, political, and legal context within which this work is framed. This is followed by Section I, which contains the protocols set out in Chapter 2. Section II presents the SOPs. This section, with its detail and discussion underpinning the process defined within the protocols, is much more complex and much longer. It comprises eight chapters. Chapter 3 deals with health and safety in both the field and the mortuary and is set within the United Kingdom's (UK's) legal framework. Because the standards underpinning this framework are relatively high when compared to some parts of the world, it is unlikely to prove insufficient for the legal needs of a team practising internationally. However, as with all areas of activity, specific enquiry as to the legal and regulatory requirements must be made for all aspects of an operation wherever they may take place. As with Chapter 3, Chapter 4 – with its discussion of scene of crime processes and management – underpins the following chapters. Again, as for health and safety, the legal framework within which this process and detail is embedded is that of the UK. As stated previously, the standards imposed in the UK are high enough and detailed enough to satisfy the needs of most judicial authorities, but all due care and diligence is necessary to ensure that they are appropriate for the proposed context and application. The roles of the photographer and data entry clerk are also described here.

Following the generic principles and methodologies of the former two chapters that apply to both field and mortuary, and those that are specifically focussed, the attention moves first to the field. Chapter 5 provides the detailed methodologies to be applied to the search and location of sites, for site assessment and confirmation, and for excavation and recovery. Chapter 6 moves to the mortuary, providing detail for the pathologist, anatomical pathology technologist, and radiographer. Chapter 7 focuses on those methods employed by forensic anthropologists examining hard tissues. It deals with the preliminary processes and basic anthropological criteria. Chapter 8 provides anthropologists with detailed methodologies designed to provide estimates that can contribute to the determination of a presumptive identification. The forensic sciences most commonly deployed during mass grave investigations are discussed in Chapter 9, and there we include DNA analysis, forensic odontology, entomology, and environmental analysis. Chapter 10 explores issues surrounding interaction with communities and the collection of antemortem data. Various appendices, including equipment lists and legislation are generally found at the end of the chapters to which they pertain. As stated previously, all terminology used is, for the sake of consistency, that which would be applied in an investigation undertaken for judicial purposes.

1.4 Historical context

The deliberate taking of another individual's life is a crime that is described variously – for example, today as murder or homicide, or more specifically as patricide or infanticide. It is a crime that seems to have been part of human behaviour from our earliest days, and its longevity is evidenced by reference to the stories of Cain and Abel and Lemech as described in the Bible in Genesis (4: 1–15, 19–24), by Joshua's conquest of the town of Ai (Joshua 8: 2–25), the killing of Apsu by Ea in the Babylonian *Enuma Elish* (Speiser, 1969), and the murder of Agamemnon by Clytemnestra in Aechylus's *Oresteia*. These texts describe killings that reflect rivalry, self-defence, and revenge, acts that may or may not be impulsive or based on deliberation and premeditation. Physical evidence of murder and violent death predates evidence from literary sources and suggests that such acts have been with us since the beginning of our species (Thorpe, 2003). Indeed, we are not the only species to deliberately kill other members of our group as attested by the behaviour of chimpanzees and by many animal species where males kill the young fathered by their predecessor. The deliberate mass murder of groups of individuals would appear to have an equally ancient pedigree (Roper, 1969) and is generally considered to reflect deliberation and contemplative thinking (Bhalla, 1968). Mass murder, whether it is what we would today call war crimes, genocidal massacres, ethnic cleansing, or crimes against humanity, generally reflects aspects of 'identity,' a complex concept in its own right. Detailed reviews of this topic can be found in Chalk and Jonassohn (1990) and Charny (1999).

One of the earliest examples of what appears to be mass murder that has been interpreted as Neolithic genocide[2] was excavated in Talheim (Bavaria, now southwest Germany). An excavation of a settlement revealed a single large pit containing thirty-four contorted skeletons, seemingly killed by stone axes and cudgels. They comprised men, women, and children, but no infants. This has been interpreted as most of the population of a village and may indicate that this community was largely slaughtered by those aiming to take control of the village and its resources, and assimilate the infants into their group (Taylor, 1996). An explicit account of what we would call genocide, occurring in the twelfth century B.C., can be found in the Bible in Numbers (31: 7–12, 15–18). This account is replete with descriptions of slaughter, ideological justification, the transfer of children to the group of the perpetrator, and the enslavement of those not murdered (Smith, 2001). Accepting that modern perspectives of the past are subjective, telling us as much of the present as the past, and that many writers in history were equally as subjective, we find descriptions of events that we would describe as genocide, war crimes, or crimes against humanity in historical sources that date from the Bronze Age to the present day. The wholesale massacre of the population of Jerusalem by the Romans in A.D. 70,

---

[2] The term *genocide* was coined by Raphael Lemkin (1944). It is a relatively new word for an ancient and persistent pattern of behaviour.

described by Josephus, and again during the First Crusade (A.D. 1099) would today be classified as war crimes. An account by William of Malmesbury, written around A.D. 1120, describes how Britons were forced from Exeter in the reign of the Saxon King Athelstan (A.D. 895–939) in an episode of what would today be described as ethnic cleansing. This was clearly a political act that was part of a strategy to form a single English kingdom (Mynors, 1998).

These few examples serve to illustrate that human behaviour, in this case, mass murder, has not altered through time, but that how mass murder is defined and perceived has. Despite the longevity of such crimes, it was not until the British plans (in 1919) for a trial to investigate the alleged Armenian genocide that the international community began to formally object to such behaviour – in some instances. The phrase 'never again' was used following the Holocaust, but subsequent events have clearly shown that this concept only applies to specific peoples and specific contexts; persecuted peoples such as those in Cambodia and Rwanda were clearly not included and neither, apparently, are those in many areas of Africa and Asia today. However, in the twenty-first century, ever-evolving and developing international legal and other responses to atrocity crimes clearly demonstrate that we are now less willing to accept such behaviour and grant impunity to those perpetrating such crimes. It is in the context of the current movement to formulate and regulate international responses to both prevent and prosecute atrocity crimes that we present this text.

The term *genocide* was coined to describe the Holocaust, which has become emblematic of the term (Goldstone and Fritz, 2002). In reality, however, the Holocaust was just the tip of an iceberg that was the shame of the twentieth and now the twenty-first century. The scale and frequency of such crimes in the long-term past is immeasurable, but it has been estimated that the *democide* (genocide and mass murder) of the twentieth century alone witnessed the unlawful death of in excess of 170 million people, mostly civilians (Rummel, 1997). Notable genocides, war crimes, and crimes against humanity from the past century include the extermination of the Herero people of southwest Africa by German colonists in 1904[3]; the alleged genocide of more than a million Armenians in Turkey in 1915 (Rittner et al., 2002); of millions of Jews, Roma (200,000–500,000), Sinti, and Slavs by the Nazi regime from 1939 to 1945 (Brearley, 2001); and more than a million Cambodians by the Khmer Rouge in the late 1970s. The 1960s witnessed the slaughter of members of post-1960s revolutionary movements (Doretti and Fondebrider, 2001) in Central and South America, and the 1990s saw genocidal massacre in the Balkans and Sierra Leone. Astonishingly, it seems that Communist regimes may well have murdered about 148 million civilians – with Mao responsible for some 77 million between 1923 and 1987 and almost 62 million dying in the Soviet Union between 1917 and 1987, leaving Hitler's regime far behind with 21 million between 1933 and 1945 (R. J.

---

[3] According to the UN Whitaker Commission in 1985, this was one of the first genocides of the twentieth century (Rittner et al., 2002).

Rummel, personal communication, 28 November 2005). This places Stalin's well-known comment that while 'one death is a tragedy a million is but a statistic' into a hideous reality. Perhaps the most shameful and avoidable of all such recent events was in 1994 with the 100 days of genocide in Rwanda. The sequence of lies, deceit, complacency, and neglect that lead to the murder of 1 million Tutsis and moderate Hutus was paradoxically facilitated by both the actions and the lack of intervention of the Western powers and the UN (Melvern, 2000, 2004).

In the twenty-first century, innocent civilians continue to die in Liberia, Cote D'Ivoire, the Democratic Republic of the Congo, and the Darfur region of Sudan, and in politically inspired 'disappearances' elsewhere. For examples, visit the web-sites of Amnesty International, Human Rights Watch, Genocide Watch, and the Campaign to End Genocide. Other geographical areas of concern include Burundi, Angola, Algeria, Nigeria, Colombia, North Korea, Indonesia, Kashmir, Sri Lanka, Myanmar, Afghanistan, Chechnya, and Israel/Palestine. The international community often labels countries where such atrocities occur as 'failed states' and the conflicts 'tribal' or 'civil war' (e.g., Rwanda) (Melvern, 2004). By doing so, they avoid their responsibility to intervene inherent under such mechanisms as the Genocide Convention, which require appropriate action to be taken upon recognition that genocide is occurring. Today, globalisation and the extended reach of terror networks are forcing many states with previous isolationist tendencies to recognise their international responsibilities. Self-interest is creating a climate where solutions are being sought and interventions made, although not all of them either timely or appropriate (e.g., Iraq). Where previously there was a culture of impunity, there is now a consensus that applying a rigorous legal process acts in the interest of justice (Cox, 2003). The continued development of forensic archaeology, anthropology, crime scene management, and other forensic sciences in the investigation of such atrocities is set within this dynamic and thought-provoking context.

1.5   Semantics

The politics of the definition of such crimes as genocide is itself a complex and controversial topic (see Roth, 2002). Equally complex, the terminology used in cases of mass murder is often only understood by those with a background in international criminal law. This is indeed an unfortunate situation because those most often reporting on atrocities committed around the world[4] are frequently journalists or aid workers, and they are generally not trained or well enough informed to be able to interpret accurately what they are witnessing. Similarly, deciding what is and what is not a mass grave is complex and has not been defined to international agreement.

---

[4] It is often the reports of journalists, human rights observers, and aid workers that determine international awareness and responses. In Rwanda, in particular, the descriptions of the genocide as tribal conflict by journalists was particularly not helpful and was exploited by those politicians wanting to avoid an intervention (Melvern, 2000).

Mass grave is a term widely employed in the media and elsewhere, often without any clear understanding or broader contextual definition. For the purpose of this text, this term merits discussion and previous academic definitions are worth reviewing here. Skinner (1987) suggested that a mass grave should contain at least six bodies that are tightly packed and indiscriminately placed, while Mant (1987) described a mass grave as one in which two bodies were in contact with each other. Haglund (2002) rejected both, saying that all graves are different and should not be subject to oversimplifying descriptions, but should instead be defined by the number of deceased that they contain. Jessee and Skinner (2005) considered that graves containing multiple dead from armed conflict or mass fatalities are not mass graves, and, by doing so, they imbue a mass grave with the characteristic or intent of concealment and the unlawful taking of life and clandestine burial. What is clear is that mass graves (i.e., features containing multiple deceased) can have a wide variety of characteristics and can result from many different contexts, some being criminal in nature and some ranging from practical solutions to crises. An example of the former might be the place of concealment of victims of atrocity crimes and the latter a mass grave containing victims of a pandemic or natural disaster. It is also clear that the public and media use the term with a wider meaning, and narrowing its definition to a focus on unlawful actions will not gain acceptance. Consequently, a necessarily simple definition is that a mass grave is a demonstrable place of deliberate disposal of multiple dead within the same grave structure. It is our view that the term cannot be applied meaningfully without additional contextual definition.

Popular culture has also played a role in the use and abuse of some legal and other terminologies (Cox, 2001a) in forensic applications. The media have constructed a variety of terminology to describe regimes that kill their own civilian populations and the particular nature of their actions. These range from 'death squads' in Brazil, Peru, and Central America; to 'scorched land or earth policies' in El Salvador and Guatemala; and to 'famine as a weapon of war' in Mengistu's Ethiopia and the Sudan, where some consider politicide to be occurring (Committee on Conscience, 2001). 'Forced disappearances of persons' are often applied to crimes occurring in Central and South America (Doretti and Fondebrider, 2001). Although the use of such terminology can characterise obvious particularities of some crimes, legal definitions also exist and are important because they define the frameworks within which forensic scientists often work and within which scene of crime scene officers almost always work (Cox, 2001b).

Demonstrating the evolving concept of crime and contemporary perceptions of its seriousness, mass murder enacted for reasons of group identity was not labelled 'genocide' until the mid-twentieth century. *Genocide* is a term that was coined by Raphael Lemkin in 1944[5] and is today much misused in the media,

---

[5] Lemkin's (1944) book, *Axis Rule in Occupied Europe: Laws of Occupation, Analysis of Government, Proposals for Redress*, was the first published description of genocide. Lemkin coined the term *genocide* to describe the destruction of essential foundations of the life of national groups, with the aim of annihilating the groups themselves (Rittner et al., 2002).

where it is often used to describe the mass murder of civilians in times of war or peace. Genocide, as legally defined today, is a crime under international law, although not under the national law of every state (Kittichaisaree, 2001). It involves a denial of the right of existence of part of or the whole of a human group as characterised by nationality, ethnicity, race, or religion (ibid.). This most heinous of crimes is contrary to moral law and to the spirit and aims of the United Nations. (International Court of Justice, 1951. Article 38(1) see also http://www.armenian-genocide.org/Affirmation.227current_category.6/affirmation_detail.html). It can be committed by acts of omission and with *mens rea* (criminal intent) (Kittichaisaree, 2001). Genocide was described in the Convention on the Prevention and Punishment of the Crime of Genocide of 1948 (in force from 1951) and can include one or more of the following elements: killing members of the group, causing them serious bodily or mental harm, deliberately inflicting conditions of life calculated to bring about their physical destruction in whole or in part, imposing methods intended to prevent births within the group (the birth rate in Chechnya has fallen by 50 percent since the conflict there), and forcibly transferring children to another group (ibid.). Systematic mass rape is now considered as an important manifestation of 'biological genocide' following the seminal decision of the International Criminal Tribunal for Rwanda Trial Chamber in *The Prosecutor v. Akayesu* (1998), in which it was held that rape could constitute both bodily and mental harm for the purposes of genocide (Schabas, 2000; Rittner, 2002). Genocide can be committed in the context of peace and armed conflict (Kittichaisaree, 2001) and includes politicide. Although there are still some problems with this definition, it is the one that is generally subscribed to.

Crimes against humanity are defined as acts that can occur for a variety of reasons and within various contexts but do not focus on the denial of the right of existence of a human group. Such crimes can include murder, mass murder, extermination, deportation, or other widespread or systematic attacks knowingly committed against members of a civilian population, as well as persecution based on political, racial, or religious grounds (ibid.). Following from the Nuremberg Code (1947) (Kittichaisaree, 2001) the Nuremberg Tribunal treated crimes against humanity interchangeably with war crimes.

War crimes are those committed in violation of international humanitarian law applicable during armed conflicts (ibid.) by any rank within the armed forces under military command. The basic rules of international humanitarian law within the context of armed conflict, as defined by the International Committee of the Red Cross (ICRC) (1987), include protection and respect for those not directly involved; respecting the right to life and health of those who surrender; caring for the wounded and sick, and medical personnel and establishments; respecting the right of life and dignity of captured civilians or combatants; not inflicting torture and corporal punishment; and not attacking civilians and civilian property. War crimes and genocide contravene many of the basic principles also enshrined within the Geneva Convention (1949), which also include the right of the dead to a marked, individual grave. As with crimes against humanity, war crimes do not focus on the denial of the *right of existence* of a human group, although they may target specific human groups.

Because these protocols and SOPs are likely to be used in investigations of the crimes briefly described herein and possibly others, a generic term for these most heinous crimes is required. The terminology proposed by David Scheffer (2001), former U.S. Ambassador at Large for War Crimes Issues, cannot be bettered: 'Just as the term genocide will forever describe the Holocaust and what happened in Rwanda and Bosnia and Herzegovina during the last decade, we need a term that encompasses a wider range of mega-crimes. I propose that we begin describing this cluster of heinous, barbaric acts, which include genocide, as "atrocity crimes"' (p. 8). For simplicity's sake, in this text, the terminology that we use is 'atrocity crimes,' while 'mass graves' serves to describe the place of burial or disposal of a number of victims of such crimes.

1.6 Political and legal context

This book sets out processes and methodologies for key areas of forensic sciences and crime scene management in their contribution to the investigation of atrocity crimes. Any investigation requires an appropriate sociopolitical-legal context and the availability of adequate resources. Any contribution can only take place within the context of willingness for such investigations. For example, in recent Balkans cases, this has occurred relatively quickly within the context of international support for the mandate of the International Criminal Tribunal for the Former Yugoslavia (ICTY). Elsewhere, however, this has often been dependent on factors such as a change of priorities in international politics. An example is Iraq, where the killing of civilians was ignored by the West, who indeed supported the regime responsible at the time. However, these same killings became a crux on which political decisions and reputations were justified once it was politically expedient to remove a dictatorship. What is clear is that engagement with human rights issues may be driven and funded by economic and geo-political strategy rather than concern to prevent or stop the crimes themselves. A change of government or democratisation (Cox, 2003) can also shift priorities. In these contexts, there can be a marked incongruence between the needs of truth and justice, as sought by victims' relatives and the more progressive sectors of society, and in the imperatives of post dictatorship governments and investigating authorities (Doretti and Fondebrider, 2001).

Ignoring humanitarian imperatives in such investigations occurred in the forensic work undertaken in the Balkans in the late 1990s. Here, the ICTY's mandate excluded identifying victims solely for humanitarian reasons. In the case of international criminal tribunals (e.g., former Yugoslavia and Rwanda) or special courts (e.g., Cambodia or Sierra Leone), the motivation behind such investigations is always likely to be judicial. It may focus on demonstrating that certain crimes occurred, collecting evidence clarifying their nature, and linking the parties involved (i.e., victims and perpetrators) to facilitate indictment and successful and just prosecutions. In 'older' cases, the rationale for an investigation is often humanitarian, with such factors as amnesty laws or current political expedience (e.g., Cyprus) preventing a judicial element. Many investigations have been undertaken to provide closure for survivors and to allow the deceased the right of being laid to rest in a marked grave. To date, it has been rare indeed for an investigation to provide evidence in a way, and to standards, that satisfy the needs of both judicial process and human rights. We suggest that to fail to do so at the very least further disempowers both the deceased and the survivors; it also fails to fulfil the requirements of the Geneva Convention and may lead to the destruction of evidence that could be vital for justice to be served and identifications to be made. It cannot be denied that limited mandates and aims detract from justice in its broadest sense.

Another important consideration for those involved in such investigations, regardless of the primary aim accorded by the investigating authority, is that it is beholden upon us all to recognise that 'justice' means different things to different peoples (Cox, 2003). International courts and tribunals serve the needs of international structures and Western concepts of justice, while on a more local level communities need a form of justice of relevance to their own ideologies. The Gacaca system of Rwanda is far more meaningful to Rwandese seeking the solace of a sense of justice being done, following the genocide of 1994, than what they perceive to be the expensive and ineffective International Criminal Tribunal for Rwanda (post-1994). Another aspect of retributive justice can be seen in the actions of the Holocaust Restitution Movement in the United States (established in the late 1990s). This organisation invokes the concepts underpinning the restitution payments following the two world wars and is a consequence of 'victor's justice' (i.e., Germany paid for the rebuilding of numerous European cities following World War II but received no such labelled aid to rebuild such devastated cities as Dresden). In 2002, more than $8 billion had been paid (Bazyler, 2002); the seeking of monetary damages for historical wrongs is one that is generating much debate. Such civil damages can, of course, serve to remedy the theft of property that almost always accompanies genocides. For some, they may have a symbolic significance if it is perceived that money can repair injustices and that such payments can be a component of retributive justice.

The ratification of the Rome Treaty in April 2002 and the establishment of the ICC in The Hague in July 2002 demand a cohesive and effective process of forensic investigation of crimes falling within its mandate. The ICC has the power (if not the resources) to exercise its jurisdiction over the most serious crimes of international concern and is complementary to national legislation (Kittichaisaree, 2001). It has the legal capacity necessary to exercise its functions and fulfilment of its purpose. The ICC makes no distinction between military and civilian jurisdictions and has jurisdiction over genocide, crimes against humanity, war crimes, and crimes of aggression, where a state is either unable or unwilling to investigate such crimes. In this context, it is both timely and essential to build on the forensic investigations in the Balkans and in Rwanda in the 1990s, and to contribute further to the development and adoption of scientific and scene of crime protocols and SOPs. Further to the role of the ICC, national courts with jurisdiction to try such crimes also merit the best investigative process to underpin their role and authority. Likewise, in postconflict areas where reconciliation and unification are sought (e.g., Cyprus, Guatemala), recovering and identifying those missing from previous periods of conflict can assist this process, as well as be an aim in itself. At the time of this writing, the ICC has yet to become operational in the field, but it may be the case that the mandate of the investigating authority for the ICC will be limited to judicial matters, and that mandate will restrict what can be undertaken, as will resource constraints. In such cases, however, the work that is done must in no way jeopardise future investigation, and it must facilitate humanitarian remedies (i.e., identification and repatriation of remains). As stated previously, in humanitarian investigations, all work should be of a standard that could eventually be used by a court, and all records pertaining to humanitarian efforts should be securely kept for future use, if required. Ethical and moral dilemmas for forensic organisations occur when such an approach is clearly unwelcome by the politicians involved in belated attempts to recover and identify the dead from historical crimes. For present-day political reasons, ascertaining how people died and passing on such information to relatives may be considered so inflammatory to present-day political parties and governments as to preclude intervention by an independent team. Indeed, exhumations that do not record evidence of torture, restraint, trauma, and the cause and manner of death, where such exists, may be used as a way for authorities, or members of authorities complicit with crimes, to effectively destroy evidence (by not recovering and recording it) under the guise of humanitarian identification. This approach denies survivors access to the truth about their loved ones' deaths and also prevents reconciliation processes based on truth. It also prevents accurate histories from being reconstructed. Pressure to be part of recovery processes that conceal the truth about how people died may be hard to resist under some circumstances, but to do so is to be complicit in the crime.

International criminal and humanitarian law structures and frameworks are developing and providing a context in which gross human rights abuses can be heard. The political, legal, and ethical climate has changed and continues to change. If accountability through the courts has a new role in the emerging world order, then a robust legal process is needed to dispense justice. The ICC and other courts will require safe and reliable forensic evidence relating to the circumstances surrounding state-sponsored illegal killings. Such evidence must be robust, that is, collected and interpreted using sound scientific and legal principles. Although the existing UN guidelines (UN, 1991 and 1999) were a valuable beginning, the courts will demand an increasingly rigorous approach to the investigation of mass graves (Cox, 2003) as the physical and contextual evidence presented as part of trial processes becomes subject to ever-increasing legal scrutiny and cross-examination.

1.7   Forensic science and the investigation of mass murder, disposal, and concealment

The early twentieth century saw material evidence as secondary to eyewitness and confessional information (Snow, 1982); it did not take on a significant role in, for example, the United States until after the 1950s. This reflected the development of Supreme Court's constraints on the use of witness testimony and confessions. After this time, the value of material evidence began to increase, and the forensic sciences developed apace (Buchli and Lucas, 2001). Similar developments followed in the judiciary and policing in the UK and perhaps inevitably, given the obvious place of archaeology and anthropology as investigative tools in the recent and more distant past, there has been a gradual adoption of both sciences within criminal investigation (Hunter et al., 1996; Hunter and Cox, 2005). This change of focus in the value of physical evidence in the developed world is not, however, universal, and in such countries as Rwanda, the current judicial system cannot presently admit physical evidence other than documents and relies extensively on witness testimony (Inforce Foundation, 2003). That does not mean, however, that states will not change their law to allow a better and fairer process of justice.

The mass grave containing the concealed remains of victims of atrocity crimes and the wider forensic landscape[6] has then become a focus of investigation because it is here that the evidence of such crimes will survive. The recognition, definition, and analysis of the physical manifestations of these crimes will hopefully contribute to the prevention of such crimes in the future as the ability to carry out mass killings will be hampered not only by a lack of impunity for such crimes, but also by the threat that evidence-backed legal processes will lead to successful investigations, indictment, and safe prosecutions. In addition to the potency and threat of investigations acting as a deterrent, evidence from investigations must also be considered as a tool to refute revisionism. For example, the numbers of dead, scale of killing, and reasons for the Srebrenica massacre have been subject to speculation, propaganda, denial, and estimation in the media, on websites, and in court. This will continue until the tally of bodies excavated, evidence of experts and witnesses, and admissions by perpetrators in the trials at The Hague provide evidence to the contrary. Physical evidence and its imagery help dispel conspiracy, denial, and assumptions about events. Forensic investigations contribute to the historical record and provide evidence for identification and criminal prosecution. In this sense, the role and responsibility of investigators and scientists in such cases is at least as great as, if not greater than in other murder investigations.

Examination of a scene of crime by SCEs and forensic scientists aims to recover evidence that will allow the interpretation and reconstruction of a sequence of events through time of (usually) a single physical episode such as a murder and link that

---

[6]   This may include execution sites or body processing sites and evidence of the movement of the deceased to the grave and their deposition into the grave (Hanson, 2004).

evidence to persons, other events, and locations. Forensic archaeology contributes to this process by recovering a similar sequence of (usually) a single event from (in most cases) a buried context (Hanson, 2004). It differs from many traditional archaeological excavations in this respect. Archaeological excavations (even a simple test trench) usually find evidence of events, cultures, and their sequence of change representing extended periods of time. Only a small number of traditional excavations reveal 'time capsules' (Gamble, 2001), events sealed by burial concerning a time frame of a single day or a few hours. Significantly, however, almost all forensic excavations fall into this category. It is important to recognise that this latter scenario is in fact the common experience of the forensic archaeologist. It is on the usually buried surfaces of these time capsules that forensic evidence and human remains are most often recovered.

The use of forensic archaeology and anthropology in criminal investigations is relatively new, developing in the UK in the 1990s (Cox, in press 2007), although anthropology has been regularly employed in the United States since the work of Hrslička and Stewart for the FBI between 1936 and 1969 and since the large-scale repatriation of American war dead took place following the Korean War. In forensic investigations, in North, Central, and South America, archaeology has traditionally provided only limited, but nevertheless valuable, contextual information for recovered human remains (Connor and Scott, 2001a). Since the mid-1980s, there has perhaps been a concentration on the recovery and interpretation of artefacts and human remains themselves, rather than recording and interpreting the context of such evidence. Archaeological sciences in the past have been used primarily as a search technique. Forensic archaeology within the UK has, however, taken primacy over forensic anthropology (Cox, 2001b; in press 2007) and its major contribution lies in its role in a multidisciplinary approach to search and recovery. Both disciplines have been employed in the investigation of mass murder in Central and South America since the 1980s, and in central Europe and elsewhere since the mid-1990s (by such organisations as ICTY – see Sterenberg, 2001; Wright and Hanson, in press 2008), with anthropology being most used. The past few years have, however, seen the value of archaeology become more widely recognised as an investigative tool, providing evidence linking victim, scene, and perpetrator and ruling out areas of unrelated anomaly. Perhaps surprisingly, there have been no recognised methodological or recording standards in any aspect of the forensic sciences applied within this context other than a short UN document, the Minnesota Protocols (United Nations, 1991). The same holds true for scene of crime examination, and it is now increasingly recognised that it is imperative to successful and safe trial processes that the most rigorous of controls, evidential processes (i.e., chain of custody), and control and documentation of evidence is implemented (White, 1998). The same evidential control is also imperative for humanitarian recovery and secure identification of the deceased.

In the past and all too often in the present, it has not been unusual to find forensic practitioners appearing to work in technical and intellectual isolation from others, frequently repeating already acknowledged mistakes and reinventing wheels. The employment of scene of crime examination and management, forensic archaeology, anthropology, and other sciences within the context of the investigation of mass murder or mass fatality incidents represents the interests of justice and human rights, both of which are entitled to the rigorous and professional application of the highest standards and ethical considerations.

There are several NGOs working in the area of the forensic investigation of atrocity crimes, and each has developed and evolved differently, reflecting its particular genesis and context. The rationale underpinning the existence of the Guatemalan Team (Sanford, 2003) is more akin to that of the Argentine Forensic Anthropology Team (http://www.eaaf.org/) than of, for example, Physicians for Human Rights (http://physiciansforhumanrights.org/), Centre for International Forensic Assistance (http://cifa.ac/index.html), or Inforce (http://www.inforce.org.uk/), who are all in turn different from each other. Equally, the role of the scientists involved in ICTY (not an NGO – http://www.un.org/icty/) is radically different again and reflects the mandate and the environment within which each organisation evolves and operates (Cox, 2003).

The Inforce Foundation was born of the reaction of concerned practitioners to the well-intended but ill-considered deployment of numerous national teams, each with different levels and types of expertise and different methodological approaches into post conflict regions in the late 1990s (Cox, 2003). A varied quality of response deployed within an inadequate framework of deployment and operation. A similar uncoordinated response threatened to descend on Iraq in 2003–04[7] and has had an impact on the countries affected by the Asian tsunami in 2005 (Rutty et al., 2005). This reflects an uncoordinated and ill-considered response characteristic that has been described by a leading practitioner[8] as a 'forensic feeding frenzy.' The deployment chaos inspiring the formation of Inforce reflects that there is often no overriding authority directing international forensic responses to atrocities and natural disasters around the world. In a judicial context, such work, all of which may be well intended and conducted by able professionals, is limited by the lack of any commonly adopted approach, standards, and consistency to the process and methodology required to maximise safe evidence recovery. This potentially threatens legal cases because the confidence of a court in the forensic evidence may be weakened and challenged by the defence. Inforce was also born from recognising that too many investigations worldwide focussed on body recovery, while neglecting to recover evidence of the wider forensic landscape and the evidence of execution sites and mode of interment that these can reveal. It was our concern that such approaches could prove inadequate in terms of recovering all available and relevant evidence and of providing evidence of a consistent standard that could be used

---

[7] This has been prevented by increasingly serious security concerns that have deterred such teams from engaging.

[8] Dr William Haglund.

in court and, as important, provide evidence for making identifications. One of our principle aims has been to develop a multidisciplinary strategy to mass grave investigations supported by appropriate protocols and SOPs.[9] These methods and standards must be flexible enough to be appropriately applied by any team comprising qualified and experienced practitioners. This flexibility does not extend to any substantial compromise regarding evidence handling or scientific methodology. The protocols and SOPs are intended to aid practitioners, not to restrict them. This should ensure that future international responses work to the recognised standards and use common methods and approaches. This will not only facilitate sound court processes but also enable investigating authorities to plan appropriately.

In some countries, those working in forensic sciences are guided, to various extents, by theory, standards and regulations, codes of conduct, and protocols adopted and adapted over many decades of practice and set out by their particular professional body. Although adaptation and even innovation is acceptable in unusual contexts, generally there is little divergence from accepted procedures. However, as mentioned previously, the key to successful integration of forensic sciences into the mass grave context is to retain knowledge of everything one would normally practice, as a toolkit of options (Cox, 1995), and to bring to bear whichever of these is appropriate to any particular forensic context. Although this book sets out protocols and SOPs for forensic science and crime scene management used in investigating mass graves, it has to be recognised that the direct implementation of these may not be practically possible in all contexts and that flexibility of application is paramount. If given approaches are not directly appropriate then it may be necessary to modify procedures while maintaining appropriate standards. In such cases, it is essential to record any diversion from the SOPs and the rationale behind such change. This will ensure that evidence collected in investigations can still be used in legal proceedings by helping practitioners to justify their operation in court. The challenge in devising an appropriate strategy reflects the aims and the mandate of the investigating authority and applying principles and methods as appropriate. Similarly, such factors as cultural dictates, terrain, time constraints, health and safety issues, the presence of military rule and its oppressive machinery of arms and personnel, fear, insecurity, dislocation, and emotionally charged environments will generally influence procedures and practice (Cox, 2003). The ability and willingness to act expediently and employ lateral thought are essential skills of the forensic scientist and investigator working in the context of mass murder.

At the time of this writing, there is no published textbook on the use of forensic science in mass grave investigations. Some published papers exist, and these are mentioned throughout this discussion. A particularly useful chapter on forensic

---

[9]   The development of which has been funded by the UK Foreign and Commonwealth Office and Bournemouth University, UK.

archaeology is by Wright et al. (2005) and on forensic anthropology by Simmons and Haglund (2005). Detailed protocols (version 4) and SOPs (version 2) for use in investigating mass graves have been prepared by the Inforce Foundation[10] (2004a, 2004b). These include all aspects of mass grave investigation from scene of crime management to forensic pathology and photography.[11] This book is based on and derived from these two documents.

1.8 Mass murder and disposal scenes

A principle difference in locating and excavating sites of mass murder and disposal (as differing from individual and usually shallow graves as often found in domestic police crime scenes) lies in the difference in size, depth, and original methods of digging the graves. Further to this are the particular challenges and conditions arising from the inclusion of large numbers of victims within a grave (which can be hundreds), and the taphonomic conditions arising from what will, in such circumstances, often become an anaerobic environment – either in whole or in part (Haglund, 2002).

The scale of such graves, often dug with heavy machinery to accommodate the large numbers of victims, necessitates using excavation techniques most often used by archaeologists working in rescue/salvage excavations on commercial construction sites. To excavate a deep mass grave dug by a mechanical excavator into ground possibly below the water table is complex and logistically challenging. In the former Yugoslavia, this has resulted in the use of engineering and logistics as crucial components of a multi- and interdisciplinary approach to such work. Mass grave investigations will require machine operation to facilitate essential needs such as access and drainage trenches, sumps, safety stepping and battering, control, and placing of spoil (see Chapters 3 and 5). Area and sump pumping may be required to control water ingress, and care must be taken to avoid pumping contaminated pumped water into water courses that might contaminate drinking supplies. Tenting and shelter may be needed to protect from climatic excess. Without these techniques and facilities, context of evidence, evidence itself, and human remains can be lost, damaged, or destroyed on sites that can range from quagmires to scorched deserts.

The impact on staff may also be considerable when working in extreme conditions. With appropriate engineering and health and safety solutions, there is no

---

[10] These are available in English and Arabic.

[11] The Inforce Protocols and SOPs have been developed by experts in international criminal law, scene of crime management, and forensic sciences, including archaeology, anthropology, entomology, odontology, palynology, pathology, photography, and radiography. Also involved have been specialists in anatomical pathology technology, DNA analysis, database management, mortuary management, remote sensing, conservation of materials, and logistics.

reason why a grave should not be excavated in almost any reasonable scenario throughout the year. Perhaps the greatest perceived problem (in international cases) with excavating such sites has been access and movement of heavy equipment to and from remote sites. That the disposal of victims may also be in such challenging contexts as wells (e.g., Cyprus, Guatemala), latrines (e.g., Rwanda), and caves (e.g., Bosnia), or may be left on the surface and hence dispersed by weather and faunal activity, adds to the complexity of this challenge.

Issues of scale, identification, alteration, and protection of the range of evidence that the forensic scientists identify and process also present challenges in respect to scene of crime and evidence management (see Chapter 4). It is rare to find such complexity and scale in normal domestic police work, although recent terrorist attacks in heavily populated contexts are providing a comparable scale of challenge and complexity (e.g., 9/11; the Madrid, Bali, and London bombings). Standardisation of recording, survey, labelling, packaging, storage, processing, and analysis at crime scenes are concepts that SCEs are used to, and their requirements, processes, and contribution to mass grave investigations are being increasingly recognised, whether for judicial processes, to ensure safe evidence, or to humanitarian recovery operations to ensure that as many individuals as possible are identified.

Excavation of complex sites obviously requires considerable logistical support, which means appropriate levels of resources and funding. Health and safety requirements are also considerable where machine operation, earth moving, excavation, contact with live munitions and mines, and contact with water and human remains may occur on a large scale (see Chapter 3). Although legislation governing health and safety is a national issue, by and large, international large-scale forensic excavations have only dealt with these requirements to a limited extent (Wright and Hanson, in press 2008), with the greatest emphasis being placed on safety and unexploded ordnance. Security of personnel is of the utmost importance in postconflict areas where perpetrators may remain at large, and their supporters and communities are antagonistic towards investigative aims.

One of the reasons that mass grave sites are considered so complex is not only the scale and nature of the graves themselves but also the fact that these features are usually part of a much wider pattern of evidence and contextual association. Consider that victims are brought to a site by the criminals involved in their detention and murder; they may have been killed elsewhere or may be killed near or in the grave. Vehicles are used for transporting them to site; earth moving machines are used to construct graves and for post interment landscaping. Soil and material from the excavation, and possibly from the execution, is left around the grave; artefacts such as shell cases are dropped and spread. Crushed and broken vegetation, pollens, spores, and valuable entomological evidence are located in and around such sites and await appropriate sampling and analysis. All organic and nonorganic materials associated with the victims and the crimes are subject to subsequent taphonomic and diagenetic alteration, and understanding of the implications and ramifications of such are essential skills of the forensic scientists involved. Evidence may have been taken from one site and deposited at another, either deliberately or accidentally, sometimes in an exaggerated version of Locard's principle of exchange of evidence and contact (Jackson and Jackson, 2004). To complicate matters even further, some graves may be primary, but others will be secondary or even tertiary and will inherently also contain evidence from previous interment sites and of the subsequent exhumation process (see 5.3 in Chapter 5). These are all examples of physical evidence that should be recovered in an environment associated with the creation of a grave. Together they represent the wider sequence of events within the forensic landscape (Hanson, 2004). The forensic landscape is the surviving topography, alteration, deposits, artefacts, and materials left in the natural and/or cultural landscape within a given time frame, concerning and related to specific unlawful events. The SCE and the forensic archaeologists must be qualified through education, training, and experience to recognise such evidential patterns and may call on the assistance of other specialists, such as botanists and palynologists to recover and record evidence of this wider landscape. They, and others, are at the core of a multidisciplinary approach that is developing as the most effective way to successfully conduct mass grave investigations.

1.9 The ethical context

"The word 'ethics' is derived from the Greek *ethos* (character) and from the Latin *mores* (customs). Together, they combine to define how individuals choose to interact with one another. In philosophy, ethics defines what is good for the individual and for society and establishes the nature of duties that people owe to themselves and to one another" (Legal Information Institute, 2006, http://www.law.cornell.edu).

It is imperative that an ethical code underwrites all aspects of the work of forensic scientists in all contexts, including that of investigating atrocity crimes. This is particularly important when working in areas with differing cultural and religious norms. Ethics are discussed in depth in Hunter and Cox (2005), and this section is derived in part from that work. Ethical codes are systems of values that have implications for all aspects of our lives — professional and personal, private and communal. In all human cultures, some, but not all, aspects of what might be deemed to be ethical issues are reflected in legal systems, regulatory codes, and religious doctrine. Most branches of the forensic sciences work to agreed 'best practice,' which may implicitly contain ethical values in terms of behaviour and professional conduct. Protocols and SOPs such as these will inevitably contain implicit underlying moral reasoning.

Since the abuses of human rights recognised as a consequence of the genocide carried out by the Nazi regime and revealed to the world at the end of World War II, a moral imperative to work within acceptable codes of ethics has developed. As a consequence, such directives as the Nuremberg Code were developed in 1947 (Kittichaisaree, 2001) (modified in 1968 and 1983) and, in 1964, the Declaration of Helsinki (modified in 1975, 1983, 1989, and 2000) (Declaration of Helsinki, 1996). These directives provided the benchmark for later guidance developed by the UN's International Covenant on Civil and Political Rights (1966). Individual countries have also responded by developing national initiatives.

In providing evidence for the courts, forensic scientists are contributing to the process of justice and to human rights and humanitarian issues. Our professional careers bring us face to face with aspects of judicial processes and systems, and into areas of experience that involve interaction with humans at their most vulnerable. Forensic scientists work not only with the recent dead but also with the bereaved whose rights and needs, as well as their religious and cultural norms, must be considered. The mortal remains of victims of atrocities must be recovered in a manner that will balance practical difficulties, evidential requirements, and the dignity of the individual – both the dead and the survivors. Most victims will have lost their lives unlawfully, in many cases in a manner that is abhorrent and often following periods of incarceration and torture. In political killings, particularly where victims are interred and hence concealed in mass graves, injustice may be exacerbated by a denial of basic human rights, and the lack of an individual marked grave, as defined within the Geneva Convention (1949). The requirements of justice and judicial processes provide fundamental operating frameworks within which these various issues are constrained, according to the national, regional, religious, and/or political climate. This makes it all the more imperative to work to a wide-reaching ethical code of conduct, in terms of both practice and research.

A number of ethical principles guide and inform decision making when dealing with human remains (Department of Culture, Media and Sport, 2005). These include nonmaleficence (doing no harm), respect for diversity of belief (religious, spiritual, cultural), respect for the value and contribution of science, solidarity (furthering the understanding of humanity through cooperation and consensus), and beneficence (doing good). When making decisions about human remains, the following principles apply: rigour, honesty and integrity, sensitivity and cultural understanding, respect for communities and individuals, responsible communication, openness and transparency, and fairness (ibid.).

An issue with ethical ramifications that should be, but is in fact rarely integrated into mass grave investigations, is the assessment of the impact of the operation on the community amidst which this activity is occurring, and, if different, the impact on the community otherwise affected by the crime being investigated. 'Impact assessment is the systematic analysis of the lasting or significant changes – positive or negative, intended or not – in people's lives brought about by a given action or series of actions' (Roche, 1999, p. 21).

Community impact assessment is something that criminal investigators and forensic scientists have to recognise, limit, and manage (Association of Chief Police Officers and Centrex, 2005) in both domestic and international crime. Because each case and context will be different, these have to be assessed and mitigated for on a case-by-case basis. Community impact assessment is, of course, more complex when working in unfamiliar contexts, internationally and amidst potentially vulnerable groups with a completely different cultural background to that of the team involved. Best practice in this area should be adopted from one of the NGOs familiar with working in the same geographical and cultural background, and preferably where they have experience interacting with local or effected communities that are in some way victims of the case being investigated (e.g., ICRC, Médicins Sans Frontiéres). Such organisations should have well-developed processes for avoiding the pitfalls of such engagement and will have a better understanding of how best to mitigate against unnecessary adverse impact than most forensic organisations. Aid agencies, such as ActionAid, also have well-developed impact assessment strategies (ActionAid International, 2006).

It is vitally important to integrate impact assessment with the forensic organisation's strategic planning function. Operating with a disjointed process, where the organisation's activities and its impact are not integrated, must be avoided. It is essential to ensure that the priorities of affected communities are considered at an early stage and that the organisation overlays participatory techniques and interactions with empowering processes, where possible, to ensure that community needs are met. For an organisation to manage an intervention, it has to examine its anticipated outcomes and impact, as well as the presence of the team and its activities. Although a forensic organisation must be sensitive to the needs of the bereaved, it would be unusual for them to be the *lead* agency for the recovery process, and it is the lead organisation that the community generally directly interacts with.

Impact assessment is the focus on short-, medium-, and long-term, wider-ranging changes beyond the immediate results of work that is undertaken in a project or programme. This 'impact' has the potential to include expected, unintended, positive, and negative consequences. All planning, monitoring, and evaluation activities of any kind should consider the implications of the programme (i.e., the 'impact') (Roche 1999; Save the Children, 2003; Wallace and Kaplan, 2003; Chapman et al., 2005; Banos Smith, 2006). It is generally considered that impact assessment should be a system that creates the possibility for honest, transparent, empowering relationships between the effector, its partners, and the people with whom they work (see, e.g., ActionAid International, 2006).

The ethical code of conduct of the Inforce Foundation is set out below and further developed in Hunter and Cox (2005). It is strongly recommended that all organisations undertaking work of this nature should have an overarching ethical code within which to resolve both everyday and more unusual ethical dilemmas. We believe that ethical guidance can be broken down into several broad areas, including overriding concerns that govern component parts.[12]

---

[12] These ethical guidelines are developed from those set out in Hunter and Cox (2005). We are grateful to Professor John Hunter (University of Birmingham, UK) for his contribution to their development.

1.9.1   Overriding code of conduct

- to at all times uphold respect for human life and dignity;
- to act with integrity and honesty in all circumstances;
- to be apolitical;
- to provide confidential, informed and impartial advice;
- to practice within relevant current legal and regulatory frameworks;
- to respect the cultural and religious values of the host country, community or society;
- to uphold rules of confidentiality and, where appropriate, of sub-judice;
- to promote the improvement of standards and services through the development and adoption of protocols, and standard operating procedures, as well as professional bodies, education, research and best practice;
- to keep up-to-date with developments in field and/or laboratory techniques as appropriate;
- to refrain from issuing statements which appear to represent the position of the organisation as a whole without the specific authority to do so;
- to refrain from issuing statements which appear to represent the position of the relevant profession as a whole without the specific authority to do so;
- to prevent and outlaw malpractice;
- not to accept core or programme funding from any organisation considered to be inappropriate in any given context.

1.9.2   Contractual and operational involvement

- to provide services to the highest standards of excellence within the organisation's and the individual practitioner's field of competence;
- to uphold the terms of service agreed at the outset of any contract;
- to work within defined resource constraints (time, personnel, financial);
- to set 'reasonable' fees consistent with those charged by other forensic scientists, or other relevant professionals; these will reflect any given security situation or other specific considerations in overseas missions;
- to refrain from undertaking work on a contingency fee basis;
- to refrain from taking instructions from any party or organisation that is legally unacceptable, or that conflicts with our organisational values and ethics, or which precludes good scientific practice;
- to recognise and advise on techniques from an informed basis only;
- to maintain the highest level of objectivity in all cases and to accurately present the facts involved based on the limitations of the evidence itself;
- while adhering to the Inforce Protocols and Standard Operating Procedures where possible, to accept the need to adapt methodology when warranted by particular circumstances[13];

---

[13] When it is agreed as necessary to vary, however, the rationale and process must be logged.

- to ensure appropriate reporting and archiving/storage of findings and data;
- to refrain from working with non-police or other informal investigative agencies or to jeopardise on-going police or other formal enquiries.

1.9.3   Treatment of human remains in investigations, analysis, and research

- to accord human remains decency, dignity and respect under all circumstances;
- to accord survivors and relatives respect and have due regard to their emotional, religious and cultural needs;
- to make all possible efforts to obtain the consent of communities and families for tissue sampling, where to obtain such is possible;
- to refrain from removing samples from human remains for forensic or research purposes unless commensurate with legal, religious and cultural dictates where such a judgement is possible;
- to ensure, wherever possible, that all human material taken for sampling, or removed in the process of sampling, is ultimately interred with the remains;
- to refrain from undertaking research using material or data derived from unethical contexts;
- to undertake research based only upon sound scientific principles, such research should be based upon research designs approved by the Inforce Executive;
- to disseminate, where possible, the results of research and fieldwork which may increase knowledge or provide beneficial information for future work;
- to respect the fieldwork, research, and intellectual property of others;
- to refrain from undertaking research using animal remains outside of current legislation and regulation and without due regard to the environment and public health;
- to adopt and adhere to international, and relevant national and local regulations and legislation governing the use of human remains in research.

1.9.4   Acting as an expert witness

- to offer opinions only on matters within one's own area of specialism and competence;
- to explicitly state the limitations of the evidence itself;
- to explicitly state the limitations of the methodologies employed;
- to make every effort to use language and terminology that can be understood by the court;
- to clearly differentiate between scientific results and expert opinion;
- to disclose all findings, irrespective of their implications;
- to comment on the work of another expert in good faith, objectively and not maliciously;
- to recognise our over-riding duty to the proper administration of justice.

1.9.5   Education and public liaison

- only to use human remains in teaching if their provenance is acceptable both legally and ethically;
- to avoid using human remains in education in any way that might detract from the value of human life and dignity;
- only to use illustrative material of human remains when necessary in publication or lecture irrespective of the level of the intended readership or audience;
- to make efforts to ensure that illustrative material will not be offensive from any legal, political, cultural or religious point of view;
- only to use shocking, horrific or explicit illustrations where such is beneficial, and only to professional audiences;
- to include tuition on ethics in forensic practice in programmes at all levels of education.

1.10   Concluding remarks

We have prepared this text as a move towards what will be a long and iterative process – the establishment of internationally accepted protocols and standard operating procedures for the scientific examination of mass graves, similar crime scenes, and mass fatality incidents. They are intended for other practitioners to use as they see fit, within an ever-changing political, economic, legal, and humanitarian context. This context is multifaceted and complex, comprising our past and the present. The future will judge the worth of our endeavours in the dynamic social, political, ethical, and scientific world, which all people have the right to inhabit without fear of being detained, disappeared, or unlawfully killed, and our remains concealed.

1.11   Inforce Foundation recording forms

1.11.1 Introduction

The Inforce recording forms can be found on the CD that accompanies this book. They are intended for use in the field and mortuary as a primary data collection tool for humanitarian or forensic investigations. They can also be used for training and educational purposes. Some of them have been adapted or developed from forms widely used for field and laboratory work such as archaeological recording, anthropology recording or crime scene recording. Many are based on a standardised and general format found within various professions. We are very grateful to the following organisations as their forms have inspired one or more of ours (noted on the form): Museum of London Archaeological Service, Physicians for Human Rights (Cyprus) and ICTY. The radiography forms were developed in conjunction with the Association of Forensic Radiographers, UK. They are collated here as examples of the data recording forms that are required for this work and how this might be approached. Flexibility in recording may be required and forms and logs may vary between organisations or different projects as requirements change.

Standardisation of recording forms ensures that data is collected in a comparable format across and between missions. Using a standard format aids cross referencing, quality control, and statistical analyses of data. The layout of the forms is designed to ensure that all fields are completed. Data can be collected simultaneously at different sites within one mission or in long standing missions regardless of changes in personnel and supervisors. Data entry is generally simplified by standardised terminology and the use of tick boxes rather than large blocks of text where possible. This also improves the quality, consistency and accuracy of recording in multi-lingual teams.

There are two formats for data collection provided here; forms and logs. Usually logs are overviews of such data as evidential numbers that have been issued, data readings, or records of collections of forms. Forms are templates designed to allow detailed, systematic recording of essential primary data in a standardised manner. They are designed to aid in collating data that can be electronically processed into relevant databases and subject to necessary analyses. Logs and forms should be backed up (paper copies or electronically) and all paperwork should be kept securely at the end of each working day.

1.11.2 Selecting the correct form

The CD that accompanies this volume contains recording forms for the field and mortuary. It is important to remember that the forms are flexible in their utility, and are intended to help rather than hinder the recorder. Consequently, recording forms may be interchangeable between phases of activity, and may be adapted and used in a way that best suits the situation. For this to be successful it requires a detailed knowledge and understanding of the forms and the information required from the investigation. Familiarity with the forms prior to deployment is therefore essential.

There are more forms on this CD than would ordinarily be required on any single mission. This is necessary as the recording forms are designed to anticipate any potential circumstance that might occur frequently enough to require a standardised method of data collection. Therefore, it may not always be necessary to use or complete all forms provided, or even all sections within each form. There are often multiple versions of each recording form. For example, several different forms are provided to record human remains during the excavation phase, depending on such factors as type of survey or the state of preservation. Some forms are designed for bodies which are saponified and others for skeletonised remains. When bodies are encountered that are partly skeletonised and partly saponified the decision as to which recording form should be used will be at the discretion of the senior anthropologist on site.

The recording forms provided can be used in their current format or modified for specific project and organisational use.

1.11.3 The recording forms

Field forms

General

Code	Title	Recorder	Description
FA00F	Notes Form	General	In infrequent or unusual circumstances where one-off data needs to be collected or where there is not enough space on another form, this 'extra notes' form can be used; these are blank pages where explanations, notes, or sketches are recorded.
FA14R	Personnel Entry Register	SCE	A daily record of security staff, personnel, and visitors entering and exiting the site. Individuals must sign the register; time in and out is also recorded. Essential to prove site integrity.
FA17F	Field Handover Form	SCE	A generalised chain of custody form for items permanently leaving the field. One form must be created for each container, box, or other storage medium; the items handed over are recorded individually.
FA11L	Site Evidence Log	SCE	A centralised list of all evidence recovered from a site. This is the master numbering system for evidence, artefacts and bodies/body parts. Here descriptions (including remarks, associated evidence numbers and ID details), photos, and location are recorded. This log is managed by a scene of crime examiner (or equivalent) and backed up at the end of each working day.

Assessment

Code	Title	Recorder	Description
FA01F	Site Assessment Form	Archaeologist or scene of crime examiner or manager	A multiple page form used to record preliminary information about a site during the assessment phase of an investigation. The form should be used as a reference prior to and during subsequent investigation. One form should be used for each new site assessed.
FA02F	Site Risk Assessment Form	Archaeologist or health and safety officer	A multiple page form used to identify potential hazards and risk to personnel, property, and evidence and mitigation strategies. The form should be used as a reference prior to and during subsequent investigation. One form should be used for each new site assessed.

Geophysics

Code	Title	Recorder	Description
FA03F	Geophysical Surveying Form	Geophysical operator	A multiple page form used when assessing a site using proven geophysical surveying methods (resistivity, conductivity, magnetometry, and/or ground penetrating radar).
FA03RF	Geophysical Surveying Data Analysis Form	Geophysical operator	This form allows the geophysical operator or analyst to report results in a systemised manner.

Survey

Code	Title	Recorder	Description
FA04LB	Site Survey Log: Bearing Survey with Dumpy Level	Surveyor	A single page (of which multiple copies can be made), on which all manual site survey data is recorded. Each point taken is recorded. The log also serves as a reminder for points that have to be taken later in the excavation process out (of context).
FA04LT	Site Survey Log: Total Station or Grid Survey	Surveyor	A single page (of which any number of copies can be made), on which total station site survey data is recorded. Each point taken is recorded. The log also serves as a reminder for points that have to be taken later in the excavation process (out of context).

Photography

Code	Title	Recorder	Description
FA09LD	Site Digital Image Log	Photographer	A list of digital images taken; a new log is started for each download session or working day, whichever comes first.
FA09LN	Site Negative Film Photograph Log	Photographer	A list of negative film images taken; a new log is started for each film roll or working day, whichever comes first.
FA10LD	Site Digital Video Log	Photographer	A list of digital video clips; a new log is started for each download session or working day, whichever comes first.
FA10LN	Site Video Log	Photographer	A list of video clips; a new log is started for each tape used or working day, whichever comes first.

Archaeology

Code	Title	Recorder	Description
FA05F	Context Recording Form	Senior archaeologist or site supervisor	A single, double sided form; used to record information about a single archaeological context (deposit or cut). Museum of London Archaeological Service Archaeology Site Manual descriptions are required. Context numbers are taken from the Site Context Log FA05L.
FA06F	Surface Recording Form	Archaeologist	A single, double sided form; used to record all surface features of an archaeological surface context. Context numbers are taken from the Site Context Log FA05L.
FA05L	Site Context Log	Senior archaeologist	A list of each context; it serves as the master numbering system for contexts (FA05F and FA06F). Description and location of the context can be recorded, also if plans, sections, and samples were taken.
FA07L	Section Log	Archaeologist or scene of crime examiner	A list of all section drawings that relate to a particular site. It serves as the master numbering system for sections.
FA08L	Plan Log	Archaeologist or scene of crime examiner	A list of all plans drawn that relate to a particular site. It serves as the master numbering system for plans.

Human remains

Code	Title	Recorder	Description
FA12BH	Body Location, Attitudes, and Properties (without total station)	Archaeologist or field anthropologist Relevant archaeologist	A single double sided form used to record contextual information about a body or body part that displays soft tissue, including associated clothing, personal effects, evidence, relationship to other bodies or features, and three dimensional provenance. One version is for hand planning (triangulation); the second is for total station recording. The body number must be taken from the Site Evidence Log FA11L.
FA12BT	Body Location, Attitudes, and Properties (with total station)		

Code	Title	Recorder	Description
FA12SH	Skeleton Location, Attitudes, and Properties (without total station)	Archaeologist or field anthropologist	A single double sided form used to record contextual information about a skeletonised body or body part, including associated clothing, personal effects, evidence, relationship to other bodies or features, and three dimensional provenance. One version is for hand planning (triangulation) the second is for total station recording. The body number must be taken from the Site Evidence Log FA11L.
FA12ST	Skeleton Location, Attitudes, and Properties (with total station)	Archaeologist or field anthropologist	
FA12BP	Assessment Phase Inventory Form: Scattered and Commingled Skeletal Remains	Field anthropologist	A multiple paged form used to record bones or bone fragments found in disarticulated contexts. A new form should be used for each section, however divided (e.g. quadrants or layers). This form can also be used in the laboratory if required.

Sampling

Code	Title	Recorder	Description
FA13F	Sample Recording Form	General	A form to record contextual information about samples; biological, entomological, geological, etc. It also allows for descriptions of packaging and storage requirements for each sample, and analysis required. A new form must be completed for each sample. Evidence numbers are obtained from the Site Evidence Log FA11L.
FA13L	Field Sample Log	Archaeologist	A centralised list of all samples taken. It serves as an overview of all samples taken in the field.
FA15L	Dry Sieving Log	Archaeologist	A list of all evidence collected through dry sieving for each context.
FA16L	Flotation Summary Log	Archaeologist or environmental archaeologist	A list of all evidence collected through wet sieving for each context.

Mortuary

General

Code	Title	Recorder	Description
MG00F			In infrequent or unusual circumstances where one-off data needs to be collected or where there is not enough space on another form, this extra-notes form can be used. These are blank pages where explanations, notes, or sketches are recorded.
MG01L	Booking in Log	Scene of crime examiner	A list of each piece of evidence (body, body part, or artefact) entering the mortuary.
MG02F	Mortuary Risk Assessment Form	Mortuary manager or health and safety officer	A multiple page form used to identify potential hazards and risk to personnel, property, and evidence and mitigation strategies. The form should be used as a reference prior to and during subsequent investigation. One form should be used for each new site assessed.
MG04F	Mortuary Handover Form	Senior scene of crime examiner or mortuary manager	A generalised chain of custody form for items permanently leaving the mortuary. One form must be created for each container, box, or other storage medium; the items handed over are recorded individually.
MG05F	Mortuary Cover Sheet	Senior scene of crime examiner or mortuary manager	Each body or body part should be accompanied at all times by this single, double sided form. The SCE or mortuary manager is responsible for its completion, recording the names, and obtaining the signatures of all experts undertaking specific tasks sign completion of the relevant forms and/or logs.
MG07R	Mortuary Personnel Entry Register	Scene of crime examiner, security staff, or mortuary manager	A daily record of personnel and visitors entering and exiting the mortuary. Individuals must sign the register; time in and out is also recorded.
MC10L	Case Record: Mortuary Investigation Team	Scene of crime examiner	A log maintained by the SCE of personnel undertaking each part of the post-mortem investigation for each case.
MC11L	Mortuary Case Evidence Log	Scene of crime examiner	A list of all evidence first encountered in the mortuary from a case, managed by the SCE (or equivalent).
MC12F	Case Identification Form	Senior scene of crime examiner or mortuary manager	The collation of all evidence that may be useful for identification of an individual collected either in the field or in the mortuary, such as results of post-mortem examinations and presence of identification documents.
MC13L	Mortuary Evidence Log	Scene of crime examiner	A list of all evidence first encountered in the mortuary, managed by the SCE (or equivalent), this is the master numbering system for evidence collected in the mortuary.

Photography

Code	Title	Recorder	Description
MG06LD	Mortuary Digital Image Log	Photographer	A list of digital images taken; a new log is started for each download session or working day, whichever comes first.
MG06LN	Mortuary Negative Film Photograph Log	Photographer	A list of negative film images taken; a new log is started for each film roll or working day, whichever comes first.

Sampling

Code	Title	Recorder	Description
MC14F	Mortuary Sample Recording Form	General	A form to record data on samples taken in the mortuary for further analysis, including packaging and storage requirements and analysis to be undertaken. Evidence numbers must be obtained from the Site Evidence Log MG13L.
MC14L	Mortuary Sample Log	General	A centralised list of all samples taken. It serves as an overview of all samples taken in the mortuary.

Radiography

Code	Title	Recorder	Description
MR21L	Radiation Dose Record	Radiographer	A log of the radiation dose used in each case.
MR22F	Radiographic Survey Form	Radiographer	This form is best treated as a booklet consisting of a cover page and internal pages. These pages comprise 3 sections corresponding to the primary, secondary and tertiary surveys and the relevant pages should be completed for each survey undertaken. (Pages should be left blank if a specific survey is not performed.) Upon completion of analysis the pages are numbered consecutively and bound. The cover page records the site code, case number, and number of completed pages in the booklet as well as the signatures of the analyst(s).
MR23L	Radiography Log	Radiographer	A list of every case examined in the mortuary together with details of the radiographs taken during each examination.

Pathology

Code	Title	Recorder	Description
MP31F	Post-Mortem Examination Body Recording Form	Pathologist	The post-mortem forms are best treated as a booklet consisting of a cover page and internal pages which will vary in number
MP32F	Post-Mortem Examination Body Part Recording Form	Pathologist	depending on the case. Upon completion of analysis the pages are numbered consecutively and bound. The cover page records the site code, case number, and number of pages in the booklet as well as the signatures of the analyst(s). Each section of the form provided can be used discretely or discarded when not applicable, additional notes pages, drawings etc can be added when required. For example in skeletonised remains the section relating to soft tissues can be removed from the form. There are two versions of this form, one for complete (or near complete) bodies, and one for body parts. The pages within each form can be used interchangeably if necessary.
MO33F	Dental Chart	Odontologist or other appropriate person	A standardised post-mortem form for recording human dentition, for comparison with ante-mortem data if appropriate.

Anthropology forms

The anthropology forms are best treated as a booklet consisting of a cover page and internal pages which will vary in number depending on the case. Upon completion of analysis the pages are numbered consecutively and bound. The cover page records the site code, case number, and number of pages in the booklet as well as the signatures of the analyst(s). Each section of the form provided can be used discretely or discarded when not applicable, additional notes pages, drawings etc can be added when required. There are currently six versions of this form:

Code	Title	Recorder	Description
MA41F	Individual Adult Skeleton	Anthropologist	This form is for the skeletonised or mostly skeletonised or heat modified remains of
MA42F	Individual Non-Adult Skeleton	Anthropologist	a single human individual. Potential for full anthropological analysis is provided for, including biological profile, pathologies and trauma. There is the possibility for additional human and non-human bone, and other objects to be recorded. There are two versions of this form; adult and non-adult. The pages within each form can be used interchangeably if necessary. For example, late adolescent individuals may in some cases be assessed for sex and stature.
MA43F	Multiple Heat Modified Adult Remains	Anthropologist	This form is designed for heat-modified remains of multiple disarticulated bones which cannot be separated into discrete
MA44F	Multiple Heat Modified Non-Adult Remains	Anthropologist	individuals. It allows the analyst to separate bones into body parts (arms, legs, head, torso) and determine an MNI from the fragments. Age, sex, trauma and pathology information can also be summarised. It is anticipated that analysis will be done at an assemblage rather than individual level in these cases. There are two versions of this form; adult and non-adult.
MA45F	Skeletonised Body Parts Recording Form	Anthropologist	This form is intended for use to record elements of a single body part. Each bone that makes up that body part can be assessed for biological profile, pathology and trauma.
MA46F	Individual and Commingled Skeletonised Remains	Anthropologist	This form allows the analyst to record all bones which cannot be associated to a body or body part. Each bone can be assessed for biological profile, pathology and trauma.

Protocols for the location, excavation, and analysis of remains from mass graves and other deposition sites

2

Protocols for the investigation of mass graves

Alison Anderson, Margaret Cox, Ambika Flavel, Ian Hanson, Michael Hedley, Joanna Laver, Alison Perman, Mark Viner, and Richard Wright

2.1 Standards and personnel

These protocols represent the minimum scientific and crime scene/evidentiary management procedures to be considered when undertaking forensic investigations of mass graves and associated sites. During an investigation, forensic teams should always employ the best possible protocols for evidence gathering and processing for the circumstances of the investigation. Such an approach will satisfy current or foreseeable judicial requirements, irrespective of whether work is undertaken primarily for judicial or humanitarian reasons. More in-depth guidelines for each of the three phases described in these protocols can be found in the following chapters of this book, which detail the standard operating procedures (SOPs) that underpin these protocols. To reiterate, the protocols set out *what* is required, and the SOPs describe in detail *how* to achieve these requirements (i.e., common methods and techniques used in the process). The forms, logs, and registers mentioned in these protocols are located in the CD accompanying this book and guidance in using them is located in 1.11. In many investigations, aspects of the information recorded on the forms will also be entered directly into an evidence database by a data entry team or by the scientists or scene of crime examiners (SCEs), creating an electronic history for each case. Organisations will have their own database systems, and it is imperative that these are capable of effectively correlating evidence.

These protocols provide a range of methodologies for consideration. It is recognised that in certain circumstances and locations it may prove impossible to adhere to all aspects of these. In such cases, the most appropriate protocols will be implemented after consultation with the initiating authority and organisational management. What is imperative is that in any given circumstances, the highest possible standards are applied because the concept of best practice is central to the application of these procedures. Where variation to procedure is agreed, the circumstances, rationale, and process involved are comprehensively recorded.

These protocols are intended to be applied under the overall command of an experienced criminal investigator by experienced scientists and SCEs. Their aims are to locate, recognise, recover, record, and process evidence, whether for production in an international court of law (with a view to prosecuting those responsible for acts of genocide, war crimes, or crimes against humanity), or another legal or humanitarian authority.

An important matter meriting mention here is the issue of limited mandates in some investigations. As a matter of principle, wherever human remains are recovered, whether primarily for judicial or humanitarian reasons, we have a moral responsibility to attempt to record and interpret all contextual, biological, and material evidence that can contribute to the identification of as many of the victims as possible. This is a humanitarian imperative relevant to the basic human rights of both the victims and the survivors. Although it is recognised that DNA analysis may not always be possible or appropriate, every effort must be made to collect all information (whether biological or derived from other evidence) that can contribute to determining presumptive identifications.[1] Where survivor communities and authorities agree and appropriate storage is possible, taking a dental or osseous sample for possible future DNA analysis should be considered. Scientific teams should work closely with appropriate organisations to ensure that the evidence recovered and analysed fulfils requirements for identification in a given investigation, and that the evidence is collated in such a way as to be appropriate and relevant to other authorities involved with repatriating human remains.

To satisfy the requirements of courts and build confidence in the process for relevant authorities, organisations, and communities, it is essential that all personnel involved at a senior level in the processes described in this book have appropriate qualifications, expertise, and experience in relevant aspects of forensic sciences or scene of crime management and analysis. These credentials can be established by reference to statutory registration requirements, existing occupational standards, and recommendations by professional bodies. However, we must recognise that we are working in a relatively new area of scientific endeavour that is consequently a developing and expanding field, and specific qualifications do not exist. There are, in fact, only a small number of individuals who have significant experience in this area, bringing their considerable expertise to this specific and often unfamiliar

---

[1] Identification (ID) can be attempted on several levels. Positive IDs can only be made where DNA, odontology, or fingerprint matching is possible. Presumptive IDs are where biological data suggest that an individual might be a person whose identity is indicated by other factors.

context from a variety of professional backgrounds. These protocols and SOPs set in place the basic methods involved and therefore provide those with minimal experience with a procedural and methodological framework within which to engage effectively. Furthermore, these guidelines also allow those entering the profession to gain experience through effective mentorship. To ensure best practice and high standards, it is strongly recommended that, at the recruitment stage, all personnel working within these processes should be contractually bound by the commissioning organisation to become familiar with and adhere to the protocols, associated SOPs, health and safety regulations, risk mitigation strategies, ethical principles, and related confidentiality issues as set out in organisational documents. As such, these then become contractual obligations, and if operatives fail to comply, they can be removed from the team. It is also important that all personnel are effective team players. All personnel should be fully familiar with the protocols and SOPs before deployment, as well as their role within the overall team structure.

One matter requiring further clarification here is the role of the health and safety officer for any or all of the three phases of operation described in this document. Ideally, health and safety matters should be addressed by a qualified and experienced occupational health officer or equivalent who is trained and certified to appropriate standards for all aspects of health and safety and risk assessment involved in the investigation of mass deposition sites of forensic or non-forensic importance and concern. Appropriate prior knowledge may be gained in such professional contexts as hospitals, mortuaries, archaeological excavations, construction sites, or factories. In some cases, this may not be considered appropriate or practical. However, it must be stressed that whoever is designated to undertake this role (e.g., the chief anatomical pathology technologist [APT] for the mortuary phase of activities) must have appropriate training, experience, and competence in health and safety issues in the relevant area of activity, and be fully cognisant of the current legislative position in respect to health and safety management.

2.2 Phase 1 – Site assessment and evaluation

The aim of a site assessment is to precisely locate and define sites, and to determine the nature of the site as to whether it is a grave or graves containing human remains and other evidence. The stages set out here provide guidance to accomplish this.

Whenever practical, suspected mass grave and associated sites will be assessed and evaluated prior to undertaking any major invasive site activities. Assessment and evaluation by forensic teams will aim to locate, recognise, examine, survey, plan, record, and recover evidence, as well as deduce both quantitative and qualitative information about graves and human remains. Activities occurring within the assessment phase are varied and may involve many different specialists working together as a multidisciplinary team. In this section, we organise the protocols

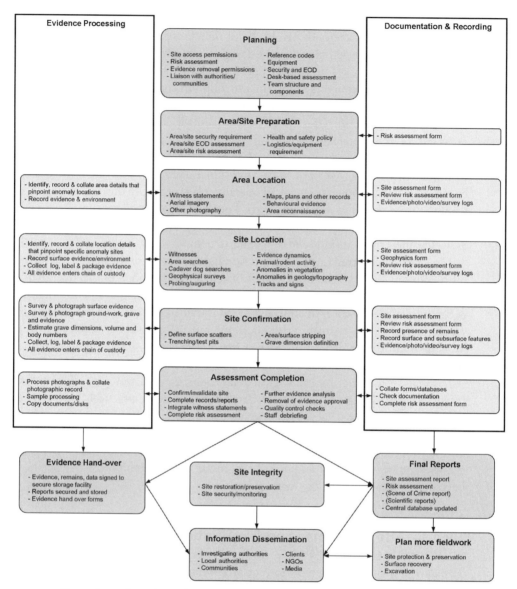

Figure 2–1. Flow chart of the site assessment process. *Source:* Inforce Foundation.

in a manner reflecting the step-by-step practical processes. The relevant associated evidence processing, documentation, and recording requirements are used throughout the process; they are described separately in 2.2.4, 2.2.5, 2.3.2, 2.3.3, and 2.4.3 to 2.4.6. The structure and organisation of the assessment process provides for an efficient and consistent operation. This is illustrated in a flowchart summarised in Figure 2–1. An indicative list of equipment required for Phases 1 and 2 is listed in Table 2–1 (see 2.5).

2.2.1 Planning

Effective preplanning is crucial to determining the success of any forensic investigation, and to this end the input and involvement of the investigatory or governing authority will be sought at each stage during the planning and eventual exhumation and analysis process. Site assessment involves a small team locating and confirming sites of forensic interest, be they mass graves, clustered graves, execution sites, or other places where evidence may potentially have been left or concealed. All necessary equipment requirements and costs will be determined before ground operations begin. This includes requirements for transport and logistics.

A number of elements must be considered before commencing the practical element of an investigation. It is vital that necessary permissions should be sought for access to prospective areas and sites. These may vary in nature from those obtained from local, regional, or national authorities. It is usually necessary to inform all local authorities, groups, and communities that have an interest in an investigation, as well as suspected areas and sites, of the aims and objectives of any mission. Whenever possible, guidance will be sought from the investigating authority. It may be necessary to remove evidence that is threatened with loss or damage, or to collect samples (e.g., to determine chemical contamination) during the assessment phase. Permission and cooperation must be sought from the relevant authority before ground operations begin.

It should be stressed that where other forensic or humanitarian teams are employed on the same investigation, it is imperative to communicate with each other and cooperate as far as may be possible.

A health and safety risk assessment will be required and must include such issues as security, unexploded ordnance (UXO), and infectious disease. An appropriately qualified and experienced health and safety officer will be appointed to oversee the assessment phase. To carry out assessments, appropriately qualified and experienced staff will be appointed, and it is imperative that their inductions include such matters as security and ID badges, a case briefing, and a health and safety briefing. Clearly, they must be familiar with the implication of these protocols. The requirements of the investigating authority, or client, will determine some aspects of the approach taken to the assessment. The assessment must be carried out within the rule of law and particularly with regard to rules of evidence; the scene of crime officer will ensure that necessary requirements are met. If the investigating authority does not issue reference codes for the project, then the scene of crime manager (SCM) will establish appropriate codes.

All personnel working within the assessment team need to be aware that they are personally responsible for updating their vaccinations/immunisations and for ensuring that they are fit to travel. Many organisations will expect prospective personnel to undertake and pass a general medical examination and possibly to provide a DNA sample (usually a buccal swab) for exclusionary purposes. The organisation employing personnel, or to whom they are contracted, must provide appropriate advice for each mission. Those working within the assessment team must be aware of the findings of any risk assessment and comply with all health and safety policies and mitigation strategies.

A desk-based assessment should be undertaken before any field assessment to assist in the efficiency of ground operations (see 5.2). Such an assessment will (as for most archaeological projects) include the collation of all relevant documentary, cartographic, and photographic information (Hunter et al., 1996; Hunter and Cox, 2005). Further to this, the investigating/governing authority (where such exists), or nongovernment organisation (NGO) or other client, will be asked to release any available information about the area under investigation and the circumstances of the enquiry. This request will include the release of any investigator reports and relevant witness statements (anonymously as necessary) or such information as intelligence data, collation of media reports, NGO and human rights organisation reports, judicial findings, and police reports, as well as satellite and aerial imagery, other remote sensing output, and historical archive material. Communicating with organisations already involved in an investigation will assist with this. The collated results will, as far as possible, be used to inform an efficient and targeted site evaluation phase. A thorough and well-executed, desk-based assessment before deployment is cost and resource effective.

The composition of the assessment team will be determined to some extent by the investigation requirements and also by what is revealed during the desk-based assessment. The flowchart of personnel (Figure 2–2) provides a guide to an ideal team makeup, assuming a judicial component to the task. However, individuals with multidisciplinary skills and adequate experience may fulfil more than one role in an assessment, thereby reducing the number of individuals required on a team. Conversely, when larger teams are required, more than one individual may be necessary to fulfil a single role. The team may have the following elements and possess the associated skills. The management component should include a project manager, senior archaeologist, and logistician. Some of the same roles are also involved in the field phase and these comprise a SCM, a SCE, photographer, senior archaeologist, surveyor, anthropologist, and geophysicist.[2] The SCM will coordinate the implementation of protocols in the site assessments, and authorise and record deviations from the protocols as necessary. Evidence handling will be the responsibility of suitably trained and experienced SCE(s). They will process, log, record, and retain the integrity and chain of custody of evidence recovered (and records produced) during an investigation. They will also be responsible for providing or arranging suitable labelling, packaging, conservation, security, storage, and transportation of all evidence and human remains. The project manager will ensure compliance with the health and safety risk assessment recommendations and application of appropriate mitigation strategies, and carry out necessary investigation

[2] Although geophysical survey may not be useful in all circumstances, it should be used as appropriate. The value of these methods could be determined as part of the desk-based assessment.

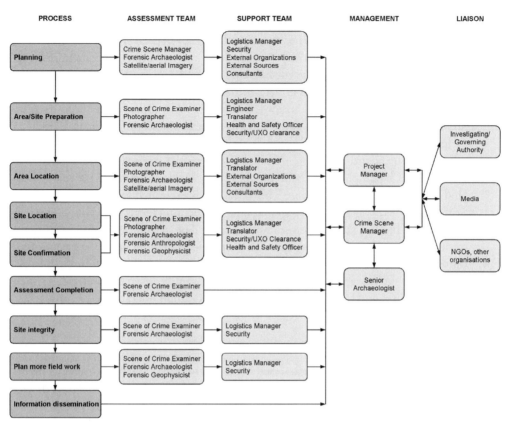

Figure 2–2. Flow chart of personnel associated with the site assessment process. *Source:* Inforce Foundation.

and project liaison. Determination and procurement of equipment, logistical, and communication needs is the responsibility of the logistician, who will liaise with others to ensure that equipment needs are met. A senior archaeologist will direct scientific matters concerning search, location, confirmation, and recovery of evidence and human remains.

The roles in an assessment team should reflect the investigative requirements as far as they can in the planning stage. The team structure shown in Figure 2–2 is a multidisciplinary scientific and crime scene management resource that provides contingency for what will always be, to a certain extent, evidential and logistical unknowns until after the assessment stage is complete.

In some assessments, crime scenes are well known and documented; in others, limited information may be available, and these sites have to be located. With this in mind, the procedures for site assessment provide a sequence of steps to focus investigation in space and time. They are designed to guide the examination of an initially large area and then to narrow down the search to a specific scene or site. If appropriate, it might be useful to define an area by its geographical, topographical, or cultural character (e.g., a river valley or communally defined zone) and a site as a more specific unit of space and functionality (e.g., mass grave, surface scatter, or execution area), as defined by the assessment. The concept of site assessment provides general stages to define sites according to a stepped process. First, acquire general information on an area that will help in the planning and execution of fieldwork, such as seasonal rain patterns, and whether a river valley is accessible for four-wheel drive vehicles. If information about a site is limited, examining at an area level can help pinpoint area anomalies[3] – this is *area location*. Second, once these anomalies of interest are identified, more detailed and extensive approaches for search and location can be employed. The anomalies can then be pinpointed on the ground and defined – this is *site location*. Third, the site is examined to determine whether it is a grave – this is *site confirmation*. This process provides a logical and efficient method of finding and assessing crime scenes. The site location and assessment process is important because it provides essential information including background information about an area that will be useful in planning and executing field work. This might include information about weather conditions and other factors such as access routes and conditions that might impact upon operations.

2.2.2   Area or site preparation

Any area or site location to be assessed needs appropriate preparatory arrangements to ensure safe and efficient deployment of an investigating team. Assessing an area or a suspected site may require security precautions, depending on the mission location and circumstances. Under no circumstances should assessments be undertaken without adequate security arrangements, and all areas and sites through which the assessment team will move must be assessed for mines, other types of UXOs, and any other recognised threats by qualified personnel or organisations (e.g., explosive ordnance disposal [EOD] personnel in the case of UXOs). All locations will undergo a continuing risk assessment, with appropriate forms completed and filed by the project manager before and during the ground operations. The organisational health and safety policy guidelines will be applied to all ground operations in the assessment phase. First aid–trained staff will be present within the excavation team, and, if appropriate, a trained medic should be present. All staff will receive a health and safety and security briefing before assessing an area or site. These briefings will be updated and repeated to account for changes to risks and security. Risk assessment will be ongoing, and all personnel must take responsibility for ensuring that mitigation strategies are adopted as indicated. Specific requirements to assess locations will be needed before groundwork commences (e.g., off-road vehicles, geophysics equipment, carried water supply, global positioning system [GPS] or procurement of specific maps, aerial or satellite imagery). A list of equipment that

---

[3] Anomalies may be archaeological, anthropogenic, structural, faunal, botanical, geological, topographical, or geomorphological in nature and represent areas that are observed to be in some way abnormal or irregular.

is practical for Phases 1 and 2 can be seen in 2.5 (Table 2–1). A Site Assessment Form (FA01F) (see CD) is used to guide the Phase 1 process.

2.2.3   Area location

The geographical area that is likely to contain a suspect site will be defined before any detailed search and location activities can be undertaken. To reduce the size of the suspect area to a more accurate search area, all relevant intelligence relating to site location will be consulted, assessed, and used. Required resources are varied and are briefly described here; further information and discussion of such methods can be found in greater detail in Hunter et al. (1996) and Hunter and Cox (2005). With a smaller or more accurate geographical search area, the amount of resources required to pinpoint the exact location of a grave will be less.

Information from witnesses, either written testimonies or accompanied site visits, can be useful in helping to locate suspect areas and sites. Witnesses may be the main sources of information for defining areas of interest. However, they have to be treated with extreme caution because the accuracy of recollection often diminishes and landscapes change with time, making recognition of precise locations difficult. Further to issues of recognition, some witnesses will have been profoundly disturbed by their experiences and may not provide accurate information, albeit unwittingly (Cutler and Penrod, 1995). Alternatively, there may also be those calling themselves witnesses whose agenda is to mislead and waste time. The rule applied by the experienced investigator is to initially accept the evidence of all witnesses and by the process of the investigation corroborate or bring into question that evidence.

Aerial imagery (e.g., satellite images) is often taken in regions where armed conflict is underway and where it is suspected that war crimes or other atrocity crimes are occurring. These may exist in various archives and can be obtained through appropriate authorities such as governments and commercial organisations (although they can be expensive) (see 5.3.1). In some cases, images may be difficult to procure from government agencies because of the particular sensitivities of their political and economic agendas and the sensitivities of the operation during which the images were taken. If obtained, they can be extremely useful in defining areas, especially where there are no witnesses, as well as corroborating evidence of activities and timing of events. Other forms of photography may also be used. These can include journalists' images or video footage taken during the massacre and those taken by various human rights organisations (e.g., Human Rights Watch, Amnesty International) with teams on the ground during the investigation. It is increasingly common for the media, NGO personnel, perpetrators, and members of the public to carry cameras (even if only in their mobile phones) and to use them in times of crisis and human rights abuse.

Various forms of cartography may be used where they exist. It must be remembered that detailed and accurate maps are difficult to obtain in some regions, and in others they may be very basic. Whatever the level of detail, maps may not always be particularly up to date. Plans (e.g., services) and other records such as land boundary records may also be used. In some parts of the world, conservation, environmental, and other agencies may hold maps or aerial images recording such detail as vegetation and access points.

Such approaches can provide effective planning information as components of a desk-based assessment, and be checked and verified by area reconnaissance, which may also employ other approaches to the search. Aspects of psychology[4] (Miethe and Drass, 2002) and/or forensic geography (Godwin, 2001) and may be useful in locating mass graves. For example, analysis of the repetition of recognised scene of crime characteristics, patterns of grave placement (e.g., the distances of graves from roads), patterns of vehicle movement, and the observation of Naismith's Rule (Naismith, 1892) may all focus attention on the most likely areas in which a crime scene may be located.

It is vitally important that all parts of the assessment process are accurately and fully described and recorded. Details that pinpoint locations of anomalies will be recorded and collated using the appropriate recording forms. This will include recording detail of all potential evidence and the nature of the environment around such evidence and anomalies. It is best practice to produce an assessment report that summarises, displays, and analyses the initial area and site assessment and makes recommendations for fieldwork that will pinpoint site location. The procedures required to survey, photograph, record, label, package, and store evidence and human remains are described in 2.2.4.

2.2.4   Site location

Site location is the recognition of specific features on the ground within a wider area of interest, employing physical examination, observation, and proximate sensing of anomalies. Suitable site preparation will be carried out before ground investigations commence. The health and safety risk assessment conducted before work commenced will be reviewed, adapted if and as necessary, and then used for this stage of the operation. It may be necessary to place a scene of crime perimeter/cordon around a site, and provide delimited access corridor(s) to control movement of personnel and visitors at the site. There are several noninvasive (or minimally invasive) methods and approaches that archaeologists can use to locate specific sites of anomaly in a given area. They include witnesses; cadaver dog searches (Rebmann et al., 2000), whose use has potential but has yet to be demonstrated in mass grave contexts; and geophysical surveys (for further detail of methodologies, see Gaffney and Gater, 2003; Watters and Hunter, 2004; Cheetham 2005). Probing or auguring has a role to play and can be used to locate the presence of disturbance and decaying material with minimum intrusion. An understanding of a site's history is

---

[4] This is sometimes known as psychological profiling and geographical profiling, respectively.

vital to recognising what is and is not relevant to an investigation. An appreciation of site formation processes and the sequence and impact of taphonomic change is imperative to meaningful interpretation. Evidence dynamics is the recognition of influences that change, relocate, obscure, or obliterate physical evidence, regardless of intent (Chisum and Turvey, 2002). Brought together, these approaches greatly assist in the detection of sites and the wider pattern of related crime scenes that are often created when atrocity crimes occur. The pattern of sites can be said to exist within a forensic landscape (Hanson, 2004). An example might be where surface bone scatters are reflecting that a grave has been robbed (in which case the remains have been largely removed and taken elsewhere for disposal), and/or that surface bone has been scavenged and dispersed in an area wider than the immediate grave site. Bones on the ground surface at the bottom of a slope may have been transported down the slope by gravity and weather when the actual grave is situated further up or at the top of the slope. The recognition of the potential forces acting on a site assists greatly in predicting the location and survival of evidence. Finally, faunal or avian activity can disturb, damage, destroy, or relocate evidence, and the impact of such activity must be recognised and identified to causal agent.

Field skills is also useful in more precisely locating sites. This includes recognising anomalies in vegetation (e.g., unusual concentrations of plant species, atypical plant species, stressed vegetation, or absence of ground cover on disturbed ground). Observation of tracks and signs in the landscape is possible even long after events have taken place (e.g., vehicle and or animal tracks leading to and from specific areas). Recognition of anomalies in geology and topography is important (e.g., recent landscaping, mounds and slumping in ground surfaces, rubbish or spoil tipped over large areas, unusual soils or rock types on the ground surface). Surveys recognising and recording such information can assist in the location of subsurface anomalies, define size, and help confirm the character of the anomaly. Wherever possible, multiple and complementary approaches will be employed at a site to obtain more accurate information prior to further investigation. For example, the identification of surface evidence may be followed by geophysical survey, reevaluation of the relevant aerial images, and a search for the boundaries of ground disturbance. Section 5.3.2 should be consulted for details of the application of individual methods.

Accurate recording, labelling, packaging, and storage of any evidence collected is crucial in this process, and the procedures described here are applied to evidence recording and processing in each step of the activity. Evidence that pinpoints sites of anomalies will be identified, recorded, and collated. Any surface evidence and the nature of the environment around potential evidence and anomalies will also be recorded. It may be necessary to collect and log evidence that is at risk of loss or obliteration before site confirmation and excavation and recovery can occur. Survey-relevant evidence numbers and codes (issued by the SCE) will be used to label corresponding survey data. The surveyor will establish a main datum point for planning. This will act as an origin for an appropriate system for the recording of any necessary point in the area of investigation in three dimensions. The surveyor will use a global positioning system (GPS) to locate the site regionally when possible; in many regions, accurate location of datum is limited by a lack of permanent and easily recognised survey points and maps. All surveys should be made from fixed datum points that can be referenced to fixed features (e.g., roads or buildings) or (if available) grid references for acknowledged survey points or benchmarks.

At this point, it is a valuable lesson for future assessments to review the health and safety risk assessment and mitigation strategy and amend these if necessary. The procedures required to survey, photograph, record, label, package, and store evidence and remains are described in 2.2.4 and 2.2.5.

2.2.5   Site confirmation

Once an anomaly has been investigated with the methods described previously, it must be validated through physical evaluation and confirmed or discounted as a mass grave or associated site. Site confirmation will involve one or more of the following activities. It is crucial that any surface scatters[5] are defined and recorded. Evidential materials and objects (referred to here as 'artefacts'), such as cartridge cases, identity cards, jewellery or clothing, and human remains visible (or partly visible) on the ground surface, are referred to as 'surface scatters'. Once a surface scatter has been identified, its extent in terms of spatial dispersion and intensity of material must be determined, photographed, recorded, and surveyed. Taphonomic processes (for a more detailed discussion, see 7.3) directly influence the extent and intensity of surface scatters, the most significant impact being deliberate human intervention (Skinner et al., 2002) and time since deposition. These will be further exacerbated by anthropogenic forces (traffic, farming practice) and environmental factors (weather, terrain slope, faunal, and avian activity). As a result, surface scatters may be moved, become buried, or be subject to scavenging (faunal, avian, or insect). Further search(es) of the area through techniques that are both non invasive (i.e., metal detection) and invasive (i.e., excavation) may therefore be necessary to identify the extent of the surface evidence.

Probing[6] or auguring[7] can be used to locate the presence of artefacts, or human remains, or simply be used to help detect the odour of soft tissue decay and decomposition. Augers, in particular, should only be employed by those with experience,

---

[5] Surface scatters may reflect a deposit that extends below the ground and that has been exposed by erosion or similar activity.

[6] Probing is the insertion into the ground of a 'tile probe' (a rod with a small metal ball welded to the end that is just larger than the shaft of the rod) to detect changes in the firmness of soils or sediments. Some practitioners also smell the end of the rod for indications of decomposing tissues.

[7] Augering is the collection of a core from beneath the ground in order to examine the sediment. An auger can also be used in much the same way as a probe (i.e., for assessing changes in resistance to pressure from above). There are many different types of auger, a Dutch auger being the most versatile for forensic work. Auger transects (at, say, 1-m intervals) can be used to plot the potential extent of graves.

and both should be used with great care. To confirm the presence of a grave, invasive and potentially destructive methods are unavoidable; these include trenching, test pits, and/or area stripping. However, initial test excavation is often considered necessary to rapidly define deeper graves, especially if soil or other material has been imported for concealment. A remote test trench, dug to determine the natural geological or manmade stratigraphic sequence of the immediate area, as well as the hydrological regime, may be appropriate. This will provide a guide in interpreting the stratigraphy of the grave itself and may be used to collect soil and water samples to use for testing for contaminants. An experienced environmental archaeologist can use an auger to investigate the stratigraphy of the substrate using a Russian (500-mm chambered) auger. Where mechanical diggers are used in this process, experienced archaeologists will guide machinery at work at all times heeding health and safety issues and taking appropriate precautions. Trenching involves cutting a narrow trench across the anomalous area manually or by using machinery. The trench is used to identify changes in the soil below the surface and human remains that may be uncovered. The initial focus of trenching will be delineating the grave or anomalous area based on soil change rather than 'chasing' human remains or clothing. The minimum amount of trenching should be undertaken to confirm the presence of a grave and human remains. The potential of trenching is that the various types of information may be rapidly determined with limited excavation. These include depth of evidence, the difference between natural stratigraphy and disturbance, and the presence of (multiple) human remains and their condition.

When no grave structure can be observed from the ground surface, even after removal of vegetation or debris, then area or surface stripping is a useful method to provide a wider definition of a grave structure (the walls and upper limits of the grave contents) with limited disturbance. Care should be taken not to disturb surface scatters or a grave structure that may survive, in whole or in part, in the topsoil. Area or surface stripping involves removing surface vegetation, material, and soil in a narrow band to expose atypical, often mixed or disturbed soil that represents the grave area in plan. It is, in effect, shallow trenching that does not penetrate observed archaeological deposits or the sub-soil horizons (as defined by such authors as Brady and Weil, 2002, and O'Connor and Evans, 2005). Human remains or clothing may be visible if they lie close to the upper surface of a grave, and when exposed by stripping, this will limit the need for deeper destructive trenching. Surface stripping allows the orientation of potential graves to be pinpointed and their extent to be delineated without serious disturbance of the fill (the backfilled or accumulated soil within a feature such as a grave, and the human remains and other evidence) and structure of the grave itself. It may involve removing natural layers of topsoil or landscaped and 'made-ground' deposits of a site to reveal the subsoils or anthropogenic layers of the soil profile beneath. The topsoil layer is constantly changing and moving due to the actions of temperature flux, frost, plant roots, microbes, worms, insects, animals, and human activity (e.g., ploughing, logging, landscaping, drainage), and over time the visual structure of a grave or hole that is dug through this disturbed ground may be lost. The visible grave is usually retained most clearly in the more stable subsoil. Earth moving machines can be used efficiently to strip site areas and expose the discernable grave structure provided that the machine operator is suitably experienced and skilled. If appropriate, stripped topsoil will require sieving or sorting to establish if evidence is present, and further excavation will be required to confirm the presence of multiple human remains. This can occur once the dimensions of a grave are revealed in plan, a small trench being dug from the external side of the grave edge. This proceeds to a depth where the presence of human remains is confirmed and the depth of human remains, as well as the depth of the grave structure, can be assessed (if this has not been determined by other means, e.g., auguring or geophysical survey).

All identified evidence will be planned, surveyed, and photographed. All examinations and groundwork to locate and confirm the presence of evidence, human remains, and graves at suspected sites will be fully documented through photography, video, records, plans, and survey by the senior archaeologist, assisted by other team members. Although it should generally be avoided in an assessment, evidence may need to be recovered during this phase to prevent destruction or allow verification. This should only be undertaken when a judicial process is in place to carry forward the investigation. Such evidence will be checked, collected, logged, conserved, and stored appropriately. The procedures required to survey, photograph, label, package, and store evidence are discussed in 2.2.4 and 2.2.5.

2.2.6   Evidence processing

For each of the previous steps, all evidence recovered (e.g., cartridge cases) and created (e.g., plans and records) from this phase of activity must be appropriately documented and recorded, and all such documentation and evidence must be appropriately packaged and stored. The SCE will assign a number to each item of evidence, and codes are also issued to categorise evidence. Human remains are now traditionally[8] annotated by the letter 'B' for body and 'BP' for body part. Artefacts are annotated by the letter 'A'. Whatever code is applied, it must be used consistently. Effective and well-managed evidence processing limits errors, standardises recording, ensures consistent treatment for evidence, it demonstrates and enables competent and thorough crime scene control, and management and integrity of evidence, ensuring a tightly controlled and rigorously controlled chain of custody.

Numbers and codes generated from survey will be used to label corresponding survey data. Photographic evidence numbers and codes will be used to identify

---

[8] These conventions were introduced in 1998 by the forensic field team during the investigative work of the International Criminal Tribunal for the Former Yugoslavia.

photographs and video footage taken will be orally dubbed, with a description of what is being recorded. The photographer will also ensure that the name of site, relevant evidence numbers, date, and time are incorporated into the filming. Any surveys undertaken, such as area searches or geophysical survey, will be planned and recorded, and all evidence will be recorded and logged in the photo, video, and survey logs. All records of the survey, including survey data files, will be copied daily for security and will be recorded in the survey register. Photographic images will be recorded in the photographic log, and digital images will be downloaded and copied daily. Once film and videotape have been completed, they will be labelled with the time and date of completion, site name, and relevant evidence number and initialled. They will then be signed over to the SCE. Relevant logs will be completed. Soil or water samples will be collected for testing if necessary (e.g., for contaminants), and any evidence or samples collected will need appropriate labelling and packaging by the SCE. All recovered evidence, samples, film, and data disks will be entered into the chain of custody by the SCE. If the presence of human remains is suspected, this will be confirmed and recorded by the anthropologist. If a grave or graves are located, the senior archaeologist will estimate the grave dimensions, volume, and potential number of bodies in the grave to assist in planning for the excavation, should it be decided that this is the appropriate follow-on strategy. If geophysics has been used, then a geophysics survey form and the photo, video, and survey logs will be completed.

2.2.7 Documentation and recording

The forms used in this scientific process are comprehensive and include the Risk Assessment Form (FA02F), the Site Assessment Form (FA01F), photograph/video/survey logs (FA04LB, FA04LT, FA09LD, FA09LN, FA10LN, FA10LD), and the geophysical survey forms (FA03F, FA03RF). As with any crime scene or archaeological excavation, it is the thorough recording of context and evidence that allows maximum interpretation and reconstruction of events. It also allows cross-referencing of information that finds and deals with errors. Many of the forms used here are adapted from appropriate professional contexts.

2.2.8 Assessment completion

To conclude the assessment process, the site assessment form will be completed by the senior archaeologist and collated with any supporting notes, such as information from investigator reports. In all aspects of an investigation, basic principles about note making must be maintained. These include that all forms must be signed, dated, and written or completed in permanent blue ink, and any changes must be single line, crossed out (to be transparent in process), and initialled and dated as prescribed by organisational house style. The material generated will enter the chain of custody. Security copies will be made and secured, and copies of relevant material made for use in preparing reports. Text and sketches for all logs and notes will be written or drawn in permanent ink and placed in a designated tamperproof bound field logbook with initialled and numbered sheets. Plans can also be made in ink or pencil on suitable paper (e.g., tracing paper with a grid marked on it). Any plans or sketches that are not drawn to scale must specifically be marked as 'Not to Scale'. Any mistakes or alterations will be crossed out and initialled. If considered appropriate by the investigating authority, or in a humanitarian mission, copies of any witness statements may be integrated into the site assessment report. In some cases, it may be necessary to send evidence collected from the site for scientific analysis. Permissions to do this must be sought from the investigating authority; transport, export, and import regulations in all countries must be observed; and agreements must be reached with specialists to examine evidence. The process of assessment that has been undertaken will be reviewed and verified by the SCM. Any improvements and changes to procedure that can be undertaken for future assessments will be made. Checks for consistency of coding, recording, and data entry will also be made. An administrative review will be made of the associated mission planning requirements.

All photographic images, both film and digital, will be processed and filed. The photographic record will be checked and collated with relevant photographic logs. Any samples taken will be processed, and documents and disks will be copied for security purposes. Such copies will be securely stored in a different location than the originals. At this stage of an operation, all forms and databases will be reviewed and collated, all other documentation will be verified and cross-referenced, and the risk assessment form and the site assessment form will be completed and signed. An assessment report summarising findings should be produced, regardless of the evidence (or lack of evidence) identified or recovered and the requirements of the investigation. The senior archaeologist will produce the report. The report will be structured to set out the following: aims and objectives, methods (and rationale for approach) and equipment used, results, interpretation of the results, and recommendations for further work. Further to this, specialist reports on specific aspects will be included in, or appended to, the main report. These could include the geophysical survey report or reports of soil analysis or contamination. Responsibility for collecting completed reports from specialists lies with the SCM. At this stage, if there is a central database for assessed sites, this will be updated. The organisational database will also be updated.

It is extremely important to debrief all personnel involved with any phase of an investigation into atrocity crimes or humanitarian programmes. This serves several purposes, including reducing the risk of post traumatic stress disorder among personnel, providing an opportunity to reiterate contractual issues such as confidentiality and *subjudice*, and a chance to obtain feedback into process and management that may be beneficial for future operations. If possible, this should be done prior to personnel leaving the mission area to avoid unnecessary travel for team members who do not live in the city/country in which the organisation is based. In the same way, detailed briefing may be done on arrival. However, contractual and pre-deployment information should always be provided well before this briefing.

2.2.9 Site integrity

To ensure site integrity and security after an assessment and prior to any further works (if planned), the following measures will be undertaken. The site must be left in a safe condition and, as far as is possible, restored to its previous condition with any evidence protected where possible. In some circumstances, it may be appropriate to delineate, secure, or guard a site after assessment, or monitor its integrity at regular intervals. It may also be considered necessary to recover any surface evidence, particularly if site security cannot be guaranteed and where conditions suggest that tampering could occur. The collection of surface evidence is described in 2.3.5.

2.2.10 Information dissemination

The dissemination of any case papers and reports produced in any operations will only be disseminated to the investigating authority(s). This will usually be contractually regulated between the commissioning authority or 'client' and the forensic organisation undertaking the work on their behalf. When this is agreed, political and practical matters have to be considered. For obvious reasons, where there is a legal mandate involved, the judicial power and authority in the investigation will need to receive copies of all reports and papers arising from an assessment. These will inform their decision about further proceedings and inform any further forensic work on that site. In investigations that are primarily humanitarian, a number of groups, including family associations, local community groups, human rights or humanitarian groups, or NGOs, may be included in the dissemination of information as appropriate and as contractually agreed and subject to confidentiality agreements. What is clear is that all information and reports are confidential and that none can be distributed without the consent of the investigating authority (if appropriate) and the commissioning organisation. In some circumstances, and with agreement from the investigating authority (if relevant), client and other authorities, organisations, and advisors, it may be appropriate to release case information to a wider audience. It is advised that forensic organisations should consider delegating such responsibility to the investigating or commissioning authority. This might include that authority passing information to the media, and in such cases, the forensic organisation must consider its own position and the benefits of being buffered from direct media contact, especially in light of any publicity concerning human rights cases, which will almost certainly have mixed consequence. In any event, all forensic teams should have a designated press officer. This role may be undertaken by a liaison officer or be undertaken or delegated by the project manager. Staff working on such sites must abide by rules of confidentiality, and this important issue should be set out in employment or consultancy contracts.

2.2.11 Evidence handover

All evidence will be entered into the chain of custody, logged, stored, and transported to a suitable and secure facility by the SCE. Evidence and data will be signed over to the relevant secure storage facility, and copies of all reports will be secured and stored as set out previously. All documents and disks will be copied for security purposes and copies kept in a secure facility that is separate from the main secure evidence facility.

2.2.12 Summary: Phase 1 – Site assessment and evaluation

Whenever practical, suspected mass grave and associated sites will be assessed and evaluated prior to undertaking any invasive site activities. Assessment and evaluations teams will, if necessary, locate, recognise, examine, survey, plan, record, and recover evidence to assist in forensic or humanitarian identifications and criminal investigations. This protocol represents the minimum set of scientific and crime scene management procedures to be considered when undertaking assessments of forensic investigations of mass graves and associated sites.

Site planning. A health and safety and UXO risk assessment will be undertaken for the activities proposed in the mission area. This and appropriate mitigation strategies will be continually reviewed and adapted as necessary throughout the assessment process. All site access permissions will be sought, and all available area and site information gathered and assessed for significance before ground investigation begins.

Team structure. The management element of the assessment team will coordinate and take responsibility for the implementation of protocols, risk assessment requirements, equipment, logistics, and communications needs and carry out liaison. Evidence handling and chain of custody issues will be the responsibility of the SCE(s). A senior archaeologist will direct scientific processes.

Area location. The geographical area that is likely to contain a suspect site needs to be defined and assessed before any detailed search and location activities can be undertaken.

Site location. Physical examination and observation of defined areas and proximate sensing of anomalies will pinpoint specific features on the ground within the wider area of interest. These can then be subject to further investigation. Suitable site preparation will be carried out, including setting up adequate site perimeters. Wherever possible, multiple and complementary evaluation and examination approaches will be employed.

Site confirmation. Anomalies will be assessed through physical evaluation and identified or discounted as a mass grave or associated forensic site. When a feature proves to be of forensic relevance, the extent and nature of surface evidence will be delineated. Buried features will be defined through trenching and/or surface stripping, and comparative local stratigraphic sequences established. Test samples may be necessary.

Grave dimension definition. The dimensions and volume of a grave will be revealed in plan and in depth where possible. The presence of multiple human remains and their condition will be confirmed as appropriate.[9]

Documentation and recording. Any potential evidence, anomalies, and the nature of the adjacent environment will be recorded, using photography, video, survey, and written notes as necessary. All surveys should be made from fixed, referenced datum points where possible. A site assessment form will be completed, together with any other relevant registers and logs. A site assessment report will be produced.

Any evidence and human remains recovered and data produced will be signed over to a relevant secure storage facility, reports secured and stored when completed, and documents/disks copied. All necessary further analysis will be arranged.

2.3   Phase 2 – Site excavation and evidence recovery

Excavation and evidence recovery recognises, defines, recovers, records, secures, and analyses sites, human remains, and other evidence that are of interest to an investigation and can aid in determining the identity of any human remains recovered. These processes pertain whether that investigation is directed towards judicial proceedings or humanitarian relief.

Whenever practical and appropriate, taking into account social, humanitarian, political, and judicial considerations, mass graves and associated sites will undergo detailed examination and analysis to assist in forensic or humanitarian identifications and judicial and/or humanitarian investigations. Activities occurring within the excavation and recovery phase are varied and involve many different specialists working together as a multidisciplinary team. As for Phase 1, we have organised

---

[9] Some graves may be primary or secondary graves that have subsequently been disturbed, with victims' remains being removed. In such cases, there are almost always bodies or body parts remaining and evidence pertaining to the original interment and subsequent exhumation process.

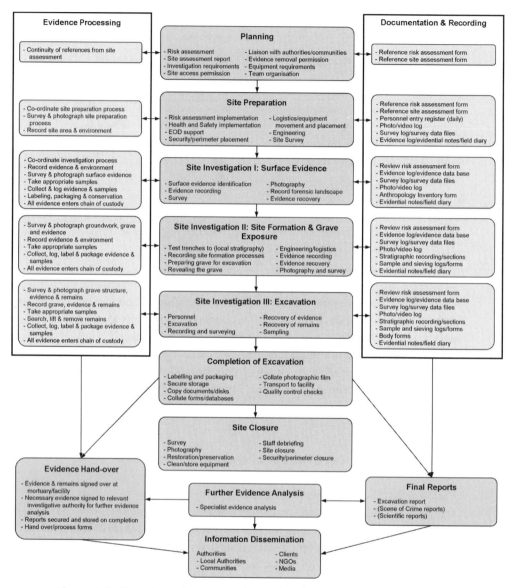

Figure 2–3. Flow chart of the excavation and evidence recovery process. *Source:* Inforce Foundation.

the protocols in a manner reflecting the step-by-step practical processes involved. The relevant evidence processing, documentation, and recording requirements are used throughout the process. The structure and organisation of the excavation process provides for a professional and consistent operation that is summarised in the flowchart depicted in Figure 2–3. An indicative list of equipment required for Phases 1 and 2 is listed in Table 2–1.

2.3.1 Planning

The site excavation process described here involves a team of scientists and SCEs defining, exposing, recording, recovering, and storing evidence and human remains from sites of forensic interest. These could be mass graves, clustered graves, single graves, execution sites, or other places where evidence has been left. The field investigation team is assisted in this process under the command of the SCM and with the support of the logistics team manager. A first step in any forensic operation is staff induction, which should include a security briefing; issuing ID badges; a project and health and safety briefing and ensuring familiarity with these protocols; and, if appropriate, any site-specific modifications. The risk and site assessment forms and reports that were completed as part of the assessment phase will be reviewed and used as a guide in planning the next phases of activity. If a site code has not been issued by the investigating authority, or established by the site assessment, the SCM will allocate an appropriate reference code for the site. If one was issued previously, it will continue to be used. Where possible, all references and codes used in the assessment phase will be continued in the excavation phase for consistency and to reduce the potential for confusion.

The requirements and objectives of the investigating authority or client will determine the aims of the excavation and will, to some extent, influence planning. In some cases, the project manager and SCM will liaise and inform interested local authorities, groups, and communities of the work to be undertaken by the excavation team. Alternatively, another agency may undertake this. Arrangements for access to the site, information releases, or accommodation of religious practice[10] during the investigation will need to be assessed and agreed on. Relevant access permissions for the scientific and crime scene management team (in judicial cases) acquired during the site assessment phase will need to be reevaluated, renegotiated, and agreed on. This is important considering that new information may have been acquired during the assessment and that the scale of site access will be greater in the excavation phase. If no assessment phase was required or undertaken for the site, then access and other permissions must be sought at this stage. On most sites that are excavated, a great deal of evidence will be removed from both surface and buried locations. Permission for this will be sought from the relevant authority. Special licenses or judicial orders are often required for disturbance of human remains and must be obtained as appropriate prior to their disturbance. Specifically, the removal, handling, transport, and storage of human remains may have to be authorised in writing by the relevant judicial authorities. Such an authorisation may have to overrule existing legislation that governs human remains recovered from domestic crimes. All necessary equipment requirements and costs will be determined before ground operations begin. This includes requirements for transport and logistics. For

---

[10] For example, for those of Islamic faith, the implications of Ramadan on working practice should be catered for.

large mass graves, this forms a considerable part of the required resources and costs planning, and the cost and time involved in logistics should not be underestimated.

The size of the excavation team will be determined on the basis of the investigation requirements. The flowchart of personnel (Figure 2–4) provides a guide to team makeup and structure. Again, team members with a broad range of skills give the greatest and most cost-effective range of expertise in relatively small excavations.

The project manager will implement risk assessment and health and safety mitigation strategies and requirements; determine equipment, logistics, and communications needs and carry out liaison. He or she will take overall responsibility for the mission. In the field, the team is always under the overall control of the SCM, who will liaise closely with the project manager and other senior scientific staff. The SCM has an extensive role and will impose processes designed to ensure the integrity of evidence and the chain of custody. The SCM will oversee evidence collection, processing, and storage, as well as manage issues of discipline, personnel, administration, resources, and security. Coordination of the implementation of protocols in the field is also the SCM's responsibility, and he or she will coordinate and supervise the conduct of the investigation. The SCM will draw on the expertise of a multidisciplinary team of forensic specialists to uncover, examine, and report on their findings in the course of forensic excavation and subsequent analysis. Evidence handling at all stages of an investigation will be undertaken by suitably trained and experienced SCEs. They will process, log, record, and retain the integrity of all evidence recovered (and records produced) during an investigation. The provision of suitable labelling, packaging, security, storage, and transportation of all evidence and human remains is their responsibility. An assistant SCE/data entry clerk will enter information into the evidence log and database. As part of the field investigation team, a surveyor will survey the site, and a photographer will take photographs and, if required, video footage, at the direction of the senior archaeologist, excavation supervisor, or SCE.

The senior archaeologist will direct scientific matters concerning search, location, confirmation, and recovery of evidence and human remains. He or she will coordinate the excavation process and organise the recording of this process. All evidence, human remains, and the grave structure will be recorded. The senior archaeologist will direct the archaeologists, photographer, and surveyor as appropriate, and will coordinate and direct all archaeological processes and evidence identification within the designated crime scene (demarked by scene of crime tapes). For large excavations where a number of excavating staff are employed, the senior archaeologist may appoint one or more archaeologists as excavation supervisors. The excavation supervisor will, where necessary, assist the senior archaeologist in managing the archaeologists, anthropologists, and machine operators within the grave. For the excavation of smaller sites, the positions described previously can be combined where appropriate multiskilled individuals are available. For example, one suitable individual might carry out the role of senior archaeologist, excavation supervisor,

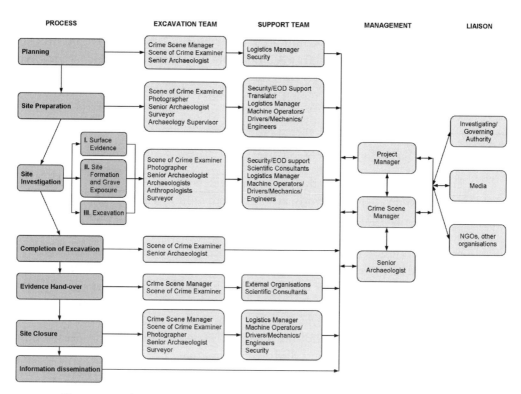

Figure 2–4. Flow chart of personnel associated with site excavation and evidence recovery process. *Source:* Inforce Foundation.

and surveyor. For large sites, staff numbers may be increased; for example, several SCEs may be required where complex or large amounts of evidence (e.g., thousands of cartridge cases) need to be processed and packaged. If available and appropriate (i.e., where soft tissue survives), a pathologist will be present to provide advice on matters concerning confirmation, recovery, and care of human remains. A senior anthropologist will oversee the exhumation, recording, care, and removal of human skeletal remains where necessary.

The logistics manager will be responsible for coordinating support with machine operators, mechanics, engineers, drivers, and technicians. He or she will manage the support team in its role of providing all necessary equipment, communications, supplies, shelter, storage, necessary site clearance, engineering, machine operation, maintenance, haulage, site restoration, and other logistical assistance to the management and investigation teams. The level of support will reflect the scale of the site; these tasks may be undertaken by one person on very small sites or by several with a fleet of vehicles on the largest sites. First aid–trained staff will be present within the excavation team and, when possible, a trained medic will be present.

The roles in a field investigation team should reflect the investigative requirements of maximum evidence location and recovery. This includes determining the site history, as relevant, which allows a reconstruction of the sequence of events that occurred and subsequent identification of the human remains. The team structure shown in Figure 2–4 provides a multidisciplinary scientific and evidence recovery team of experts. This reflects the evidential requirements in controlling the complexity and the scale of the mass grave analysis and optimises evidence identification and recovery.

2.3.2   Evidence processing

For each step described in this section, all evidence recovered (e.g., cartridge cases) and created (e.g., plans, records) arising from this phase of activity must be appropriately documented and recorded, and all such documentation and evidence appropriately packaged and stored. The SCE will assign a number to each item of evidence, and codes are also issued to categorise evidence. Human remains are traditionally[11] annotated by the letter 'B' for body and 'BP' for body part. Artefacts are annotated by the letter 'A'. Whatever code is applied, it must be used consistently. Effective and well-managed evidence processing limits errors, standardises recording, ensures consistent treatment for evidence, and demonstrates and enables competent and thorough crime scene control and management and integrity of evidence, ensuring a tightly and rigorously controlled chain of custody.

Numbers and codes arising from survey will be used to label corresponding survey data. Photographic evidence numbers and codes will be used to identify photographs, and video footage taken will be orally dubbed, with a description of what is being recorded. The photographer will also ensure that the name of site, relevant evidence numbers, date, and time are incorporated into the filming. Any surveys undertaken, such as surface scatters, or body recording will be planned and recorded, and all evidence will be recorded and logged in the photo, video, and survey logs. All records of the survey, including survey data files, will be copied daily for security and will be recorded in the survey log. Photographic images will be recorded in the photographic log, and digital images will be downloaded and copied daily. All initial evidence photographs will include the evidence number, a scale (to show dimensions of the item to be collected), and an arrow pointing to the north; subsequent detail photographs may not necessarily require these. The photographer will keep a photographic log with roll and frame numbers showing the evidence number and a brief description of the item or scene photographed. Photographs and video footage will be taken of the grave at the beginning and end of each working day to record continuity. Once film and videotape have been completed, they will be labelled with the time and date of completion, site name, and relevant evidence number, and initialled. They will then be signed over to the SCE. Relevant registers will be completed. Soil or other samples will be

---

[11] These conventions were introduced in 1998 by the forensic field team during the exhumation work of the International Criminal Tribunal for the Former Yugoslavia.

collected for testing if necessary, and any evidence or samples collected will need appropriate labelling and packaging by the SCE. All recovered evidence, samples, film, and data disks, will be entered into the chain of custody by the SCE.

2.3.3 Documentation and recording

The forms used in this scientific process are comprehensive and include the risk assessment form, photograph/video/survey logs, and a variety of archaeology and anthropology forms and logs. As with any crime scene or archaeological excavation, it is the thorough recording of context and evidence that allows maximum interpretation and reconstruction of events. It also allows cross-referencing of information that assists with finding and dealing with errors. Many of the forms used here are adapted from appropriate professional contexts.

Appropriate personnel will complete all forms, registers, documents, photographic record, maps, drawings, databases, and reports. This information will ultimately be copied and collated by the SCE for the review of the SCM. The senior archaeologist will produce a final report related to the results of the examination and excavation. Documents, evidence, and human remains will be signed over to the mortuary facility and/or investigative authority as appropriate.

2.3.4 Site preparation

The results of the risk assessment will guide and inform site preparation and planning. The assessment phase may inform measures implemented to reduce health and safety and other operational risks specific to the site. New risks may become apparent during ongoing ground operations, such as machine operation or deep excavation, and these will be accounted for, and the risk assessment amended as an ongoing process. The overarching health and safety policy guidelines will be applied to all ground operations in the excavation phase. Flexibility to some areas of policy may be necessary due to local circumstances.[12] A first aid station will need to be established, trained staff will be present within the excavation team, and, when possible a trained medic will be present. All personnel will need to be aware of medical evacuation and other procedures. If necessary, the whole area of an excavation and the broader forensic landscape will be assessed, checked, and cleared of UXO by qualified EOD staff or organisations. If required, EOD support will be in place and remain for the duration of the excavation to deal with any UXO issues that arise during the process. The site may require security precautions, depending on the mission location. Excavations will not be undertaken without adequate security arrangements. Any other risks such as chemical contamination or medical waste will be dealt with as appropriate by specialist personnel, and the site made safe

---

[12] Examples are a review of hard hat policy in hot climates or of high-visibility vests if there is a threat of sniper activity.

for work. A secure outer perimeter to prevent access, and a perimeter to protect evidential integrity will be placed around the defined site area under investigation and around any logistics/equipment areas. Once site security perimeters and access corridors are in place, a personnel entry register will be used to record all personnel and visitors to the site. Adequate security for the team will be provided on site, during transportation to and from the site, and at their accommodation. Site and evidence security will be 24 hours a day, 7 days a week, regardless of whether or not the team is working on site, until the site is officially closed.

Requirements for the location of equipment, stores, storage of spoil, and engineering works will be determined with reference to the site and the health and safety risk assessments. All logistics hard-standing and storage space will be within a secure perimeter, will be adequate to avoid disturbing evidence, and will be efficiently placed to allow movement between work, storage, and clean areas. Any remedial engineering works will be carried out to prepare the site for excavation at the direction of the senior archaeologist in collaboration with the logistics manager. These will avoid disturbance to evidence, and may, for example, include water storage, drainage, construction of a hard-standing area for vehicles and containers, maintenance of clean areas, and requisition of water.

Before any work occurs on site that might affect the landscape or substrate, a topographic and landmark survey will be undertaken, in addition to surveys that may have been carried out in the assessment phase. Any changes made to the area and site, such as vehicle parks and drainage ditches, will also be surveyed as part of the site record. Any security and scene of crime perimeters and access corridors will also be recorded by survey. All surveys will be made from fixed datum points that can be referenced to known features or (if available) grid references and acknowledged survey points or benchmarks. If not already established as part of the site assessment, the surveyor will establish a main datum point for the site. This will act as the origin for an appropriate system for recording (in three dimensions) any necessary point in the area of investigation. The surveyor will use a GPS to locate the site regionally when possible and locate all plans within the local landscape so the site can be pinpointed in the future. All site preparation works will be photographed (e.g., EOD clearance or perimeter establishment) to provide an explanatory record of the investigation process and surveyed. The SCM and the senior archaeologist will coordinate the site preparation process, and organise the recording of this, where appropriate. He or she will record relevant aspects of the site area and environment that may be altered by the site preparation process. All forms and the evidence log for this phase of work will be collated by the SCE. Once surveying and photography have begun, the survey log and photograph log will be used to record images and data taken. Survey data files and digital photo images will be downloaded and copied daily for security. The senior archaeologist will begin a field diary and make evidential notes at the outset of this operation. A brief summary of the procedures required to survey, photograph, record, label, package, and store evidence and human remains are found in 2.3.2 and 2.3.3, and more detail is located in Chapter 5.

2.3.5 Site investigation I: Surface evidence

The senior archaeologist will direct the location and recovery of surface evidence and associated scientific processes. The position and type of all evidence and human remains will be determined and recorded, and then the evidence itself will be recovered and processed. This process will be carried out by the field investigation team and supported by the logistics team. The full extent and nature of any surface evidence will be determined. This may comprise artefacts such as cartridge cases, human remains such as bone scatters, or changes to the environment such as disturbed soil and vehicle tracks, or damaged, altered, or unusual vegetation. Ground vegetation or debris may need to be cleared as part of the search process, and upper soil horizons searched or surveyed. Sieving of disturbed topsoil may be required. Any patterns and sequences of surface evidence deposition should be identified, and all identified evidence should be flagged or marked in order to visualise potential patterns and to record such findings with photographs.

All relevant evidence, including human remains, will be logged and recorded *in situ* by note taking, form completion, survey, photography, and video, where appropriate. The surveyor will undertake an area plan and topographical survey, surveying any relevant surface features and evidence in three dimensions. The surface area, environment, and evidence will be photographed (and video recorded where required). Scales and north arrows will be included where necessary. The methodology and procedures undertaken will be photographed to provide an explanatory record of the investigation process. Video and static photography of the site should take place at the start and end of each day to maintain a full record and to demonstrate the integrity of, and lack of interference with, the site outside working hours. If there are multiples of similar evidence (e.g., hundreds of cartridge cases at an execution site), each logged and collected item will be surveyed and photographed, up to a number agreed by the SCM with the SCE and the senior archaeologist. After that, each item will only be surveyed. The items will not be individually photographed unless they are of significant or renewed evidential importance. Photographs should not only be of individual items but also of the context in which they are recovered and the wider landscape in which they were deposited. It should always be considered that the scene of crime may extend beyond the area of the grave. For example, vehicle tracks, execution sites, landscaping, evidence moved by natural or human intervention, and evidence that has been dropped while being brought to or taken from a site may be located within the adjacent area or wider forensic landscape around a site. The senior archaeologist will examine and record the history of this environment. All identified evidence will be recovered systematically under the supervision of the SCE. Once all visible, recognised evidence is recovered, the identified area of surface evidence will be searched again, with attention paid to searching within the topsoil for evidence that may have moved from the surface. Deliberate landscaping to conceal graves (Figure 2–5), or natural processes such as land slippage and erosion on slopes or in valley floors, may have buried relevant land surfaces; this possibility must be considered and catered for.

Figure 2–5. A multiple mass grave site in the Former Yugoslavia where imported material was dumped in piles across a grave site presumably to disguise the graves. *Source:* Margaret Cox.

As described in 2.3.2, the SCE will coordinate the surface evidence recovery process and organise the recording of this, as appropriate. All relevant environmental factors will also be recorded. The SCE will assign a number to each item of evidence. The procedures required to survey, photograph, record, label, package, and store evidence and human remains are also found in 2.3.2. It will then be signed over to the SCE to enter the chain of custody. Appropriate samples such as soil or botanical samples will be taken. All evidence, samples, film, and data disks will be collected and logged under the supervision of the SCE, who will undertake evaluation of and oversee any conservation requirements to preserve evidence and samples. Wherever possible, trained conservators will carry out agreed on, appropriate passive conservation measures, and these will comprise the use of appropriate packaging materials. Once conservation and packaging is complete, all such evidence and samples will, under the supervision of the SCE, be entered into the chain of custody.

All recording forms used during this exercise and the site evidence log will be collated by the SCE. The risk assessment and mitigation strategies will continue to be reviewed and amended, where appropriate; a practice that should take place regularly, regardless of the stage of an operation. The site evidence log and all other records will be entered into the evidence database being employed. All records of the survey, including survey data files, will be copied daily for security reasons and will be recorded in the survey log. Photographic images will be recorded in the photographic log, and digital images will be downloaded and copied daily. Any human remains recovered will be listed in a Body Location, Attitudes and Properties Form. As mentioned previously, the senior archaeologist will keep a field diary and evidential notes, and notes may need to be taken by the SCE or a forensic scientist if specific evidence needs specialist investigation. These also enter the chain of custody at an appropriate point in time.

2.3.6 Site investigation II: Site formation and grave exposure

The senior archaeologist will examine and record the history of the environment, site formation processes, and stratigraphic sequence of the grave and area under investigation. He or she will be assisted by the field investigation team. If a test trench has not been dug during the assessment phase, it should be dug now for the reasons cited in 2.2.5 and situated adjacent to the grave location (but not disturbing evidence). The sequence of events of the site and environment around the grave will be recorded. These processes may predate and/or postdate any relevant criminal events, but may have relevance to or influence the interpretation of the evidence of those events. Geophysics may have a value in the excavation phase. This might be by providing more precise detail of grave dimensions (ground-penetrating radar) and locating evidence (metal detector). The latter can be useful both prior to and after excavation. Area stripping by machine will be used (see 2.2.5) to remove layers of overburden or topsoil until archaeological deposits are revealed. All archaeological deposits will be stratigraphically excavated whenever practical to do so. Experienced archaeologists will guide the machine operator at all times. If a grave has been disturbed there may be archaeological deposits containing human remains and evidence above and around the surviving structure of the grave. These will be excavated, and all evidence recorded, collected, and processed. Excavation will proceed to determine the highest visible surviving grave outline in plan or associated archaeological deposit or human remains by recognition of contrasting soils, structure, inclusions, and artefacts.

In some conditions, remedial engineering work may be required to render the environment of the grave safe, devoid of ground water, and suitable for excavation. This may be in the form of trenches dug to divert ground water, drainage trenches or sumps, access trenches or ramps, stepping, battering, or shoring. This is especially relevant to deep graves or graves that penetrate the water table. Some graves may not be deliberately dug structures but may be within preexisting structures such as wells, buildings, or cesspits, or natural features such as caves (Simmons, 2002) or swallets. These may require specialist engineering such as parallel shaft construction and pumping and equipment such as ladders, shoring, lighting, and platforms to allow safe access. Where human remains have been buried or dumped in deep holes or shafts, particular care must be taken to test for methane gas within the feature. All evidence of the stratigraphic sequence in such deposits should be recorded. All human remains and other evidence found will be logged and their position surveyed; they will then be recorded and recovered. Analysis of evidence such as body position or tool marks in grave surfaces will be undertaken *in situ* before recovery. This is necessary because they may be lost once evidence is moved. All identified evidence will be recovered systematically under the supervision of the SCE. If deposits are removed, sieving may be required to recover loose artefacts and other evidence.

Evidence of relevant site formation processes will be photographed (and video recorded where required). Scales and north arrows will be included where necessary, and all relevant deposits and features will be photographed. The grave exposure process should also be photographed to provide an explanatory record of the excavation methodology. The surveyor will record the position of all relevant evidence and the extent of deposits in three dimensions, as mentioned previously. Recording of sections may be appropriate in both test pits and across buried deposits. The senior archaeologist will coordinate the collection and recording of site formation evidence and grave exposure. He or she will record information and process in a field diary, along with other contemporaneous evidential notes. As in the surface evidence survey (described previously), if there are multiple pieces of similar evidence, each item will be logged, collected, and packaged separately up to a number agreed by the SCM, and thereafter they will be surveyed only. The procedures required to survey, photograph, record, label, package, and store evidence and human remains are found in 2.3.2 and 2.3.3. Any disarticulated human remains recovered will be listed in the Scattered and Commingled Skeletal Remains Form, and any anatomically associated sets of human remains will be described on a Body Location, Attitudes and Properties Form.

2.3.7   Site investigation III: Excavation

The field investigation team will carry out the process described here, supported by the logistics team. In mass grave investigations, it is vitally important that all archaeologists involved in excavating, recording, and recovering human remains are trained in human bone recognition. Archaeologists with no experience in recovering human remains should not be involved in such work. The role of the archaeologists/anthropologists is to locate and uncover human remains and other evidence within the grave context. They will carefully clean, record, and lift all human remains. SCEs will undertake necessary evidence analysis (e.g., taking casts) and advise on controlled evidence removal. EOD personnel will be present throughout the excavation on sites with an UXO risk. They will assist in checking suspect surface objects, items in deposits and items on, between, and under bodies; and any other suspected location.

As far as is practically possible, deposits and features will be excavated and recorded using stratigraphic principles and methods that do not destroy stratigraphic boundaries or interfaces (for the rationale for this approach, see Tuller and Duric, 2006). If this is not possible, the reasons for applying a different methodology, and the method itself, must be recorded. Deposits should be removed by machine or by hand in stratigraphic sequence. Removal of deposits will be carried out systematically to avoid movement and damage to evidence and human remains, and to maintain the *in situ* position and integrity of evidence and human remains. Deposits will be

Figure 2–6. Careful excavation around the edges of grave sites can reveal important evidence such as tyre tracks associated with transporting bodies to graves. This example is from a grave site in Former Yugoslavia. *Source:* Margaret Cox.

removed carefully from around human remains. Human remains will be examined to determine a systematic order in which they may be removed and, if possible, their sequence of deposition. At the end of each working day or during extremes of weather, the grave and any exposed areas under examination, such as tyre tracks (Figure 2–6), will be sheltered with appropriate covers. Once bodies and/or fill (matrix) are removed from the original grave cut, the walls and floor of the grave will be carefully cleaned and analysed. A metal detector will be run over the bodies, deposits, and bottom and walls of the grave to locate ordnance dropped, fired into, or exploded in the grave. The senior SCE will maintain a log to allow management of the distribution of evidence numbers among archaeologists. The photographer will photograph items of evidence *in situ* when requested, using the evidence number assigned to the archaeologist by the SCE. The procedures required to survey, photograph, record, label, package, and store evidence and human remains are found in 2.3.2 and 2.3.3.

All initial photographs will include the evidence number, a scale (to show dimensions of the item to be collected), and an arrow pointing to the north; subsequent photographs may not necessarily require these. The photographer will keep a photographic log with roll and frame numbers or digital image number showing the evidence number and a brief description of the item or scene photographed. Photographs and video footage will be taken of the grave at the beginning and end of each working day to record continuity. The surveyor will survey the precise location of all items of evidence, when requested, using the evidence number assigned by the SCE. He or she will also map the grave in plan, as well as its surrounds and all relevant points. A survey log will be used to facilitate management and tracking of the distribution of evidence numbers among excavators by the SCE.

When bodies and body parts are exposed, the excavator will be allocated an evidence number by the SCE. The excavator will complete the appropriate Body Location, Attitude and Properties Form before removal. The forms should only be filled out and signed by the excavator of those remains described in the form. All bodies and body parts will have the anatomical landmarks listed in the Body and Skeleton Location, Attitudes and Properties Form and Scattered and Commingled Skeletal Remains Form (FA12BH, FA12BT, FA12SH, FA12ST, and FA12BP) and surveyed where present. All bodies and body parts will be photographed to provide a fully illustrative record (e.g., of state of preservation, taphonomic processes, body or part position, presence/absence of clothing, ballistics). If film photography is used, additional digital photographs will be taken immediately in certain circumstances for the purpose of illustrating and documenting significant evidence or features of human remains (e.g., tattoos, ligatures, or blindfold position). Such images will also be taken if digital photography is the primary mode of documentation. These will record *in situ* evidence in danger of alteration by decomposition or the recovery process, and will also be used to provide images that can be passed on to the mortuary to inform the scientists involved in the analysis of those remains. Isolated bones that may assist identification (e.g., a mandible or foot in a shoe), or may form an identifiable associated pattern, should be identified by the anthropologist. Their position will be surveyed, recorded, and logged, and they will be annotated as body parts by the SCE. Potential associated human remains will be linked when possible and their possible relationship recorded.

Bodies, body parts, and clothing will be checked by the SCE in conjunction with the archaeologist for evidence, personal effects, and documents. These may be numbered, recorded, and removed for further examination, photography, and conservation, if appropriate. Once recorded, bodies and body parts will be removed under the supervision of the SCE, who will ensure proper labelling, packaging, and storage.

Disassociated clothing, personal artefacts, or bones that have an *in situ* context or recognisable relationship to other evidence within the grave, may be collected in a general bag or box (which receives a specific log number issued by the SCE). They will then be surveyed and recorded by appropriate area coordinates. In such cases, overall survey points of individual bones or scatters (if recording a surface scatter) may be recorded, and photographs of an area rather than individual bones may be appropriate, depending on circumstances. This is often a practical necessity when a grave has been robbed and redeposited evidence is found in the backfilled disturbed soil. Any isolated bones will be listed in a Scattered and Commingled Skeletal Remains Form and any anatomically associated sets of human remains will be described on a Body or Skeletal Location, Attitudes and Properties Form (form codes are as described previously).

During the excavation, a metal detector, used by an experienced operator, may be employed to locate metal items not easily visible and lightly buried (e.g., ordnance). In sites where UXO is suspected or known to have been used, bodies and clothing will also be checked before removal for possible ordnance by the SCE with, if necessary, advice from EOD personnel. They will also assist in checking suspect surface objects; items in deposits and items on, between, and under bodies; and any other suspected location.

At appropriate times in the overall process, the senior archaeologist and the SCM will guide the mortuary staff around the excavation site to familiarise them with the crime scene, explain methodologies, and indicate and explain important issues (e.g., taphonomy), which may impact the interpretation of their observations in the mortuary. This will feed into process review and ensure mutual understanding. Reciprocal visits are advisable if the field and mortuary process run concurrently.

At any stage of the examination, and in consultation with the SCM, the senior archaeologist may recommend the appointment of other scientific experts or specialists (e.g., entomologists or palynologists) to carry out specific on-site examinations to assess, identify, collect, and analyse evidence falling within their particular area of expertise. Samples will be taken of materials of potential evidential, contextual, and forensic interest (e.g., insects, plant remains, soil) at appropriate times during an investigation. The SCM will coordinate sample processing by appropriate forensic experts.

Sieving of excavated soils or other deposits may be undertaken if necessary to recover further evidence. During and after completion of the excavation of a grave, the walls and floor will be checked for trace evidence, ballistic tracks, and tool marks. Any such evidence located will be recorded, surveyed, and photographed where appropriate. The SCE will sample and process trace evidence such as hair, fibers, paint, or fingerprints (if appropriate). They will preserve tool marks, footprints, tyre tracks, or other impressions found at the grave floor or walls or in the surrounding forensic landscape by casting them in plaster or another appropriate material. Ballistics evidence will be excavated and recovered from the grave surfaces and processed appropriately. The empty grave will be surveyed to record the grave dimensions, and a topographical survey will be undertaken to record the final grave dimensions and elevations. The empty grave and areas from which evidence and human remains have been removed will be fully photographed, including tool marks.

The senior archaeologist will continue to maintain a field diary throughout and make evidential notes. Notes will also be taken by the SCE or a forensic scientist if specific evidence needs specialist investigation. The senior archaeologist may delegate note taking, in-the-field diary, and evidential notes, if absent from the place of investigation for a length of time.

2.3.8 Completion of excavation

In all aspects of an investigation, basic principles about note making must be maintained. These include that all forms must be signed and dated, written and completed in ink, any errors should be crossed out with a single line, and any changes should be initialed. All material generated at any point of the process must ultimately enter the chain of custody, and security copies made and stored separately. Text and sketches for all logs and notes will be in ink in a designated bound field book with initialed and numbered sheets. Plans can also be made in ink or pencil on suitable paper (e.g., grid-lined tracing paper), but as with forms, any mistakes or alterations must be crossed out (to be transparent in process) and initialed.

All evidence and samples will require appropriate labelling, packaging, and storage under the supervision of the SCE to protect the evidence during transport to a mortuary or storage facility. At all times on site, prior to transportation to a central holding facility or designated mortuary, all evidence, records, and human remains must be stored in a locked and secure storage facility within a secure perimeter on the site. The SCE will hold the keys to all locks. Fleshed or partially fleshed human remains and some evidence such as documents may require refrigerated storage. Databases, digital film, and data disks will be copied and collated under the supervision of the SCE. Documents, logs, and forms must all be copied for security purposes and so the SCE can take the originals into the chain of custody. All documentation will be checked and collated, and all other documentation must be checked and cross-referenced, with all forms completed and signed. Copies will be securely stored in a different location than the originals. The SCE will collate digital printed images for use in the mortuary with the Body Location, Attitude and Properties forms FA12BH and FA12BT. All photographic images, both film and digital, will be processed and filed, and the photographic record will be checked and collated with relevant photography logs and records. It falls to the SCE to ensure photographic film is developed in a secure, appropriate facility, and they will also ensure that all evidence and human remains are secure and safe to be transported to a mortuary or appropriate facility. Shipment containers will be secured, locked, and sealed. The SCE or a designated person will escort the shipment to the facility, as will appropriate levels of security staff.

It is extremely important to debrief all personnel involved with any phase of an investigation into atrocity crimes or humanitarian programmes. This serves several purposes, including reducing the risk of posttraumatic stress disorder among personnel, an opportunity to reiterate contractual issues such as confidentiality and *subjudice*, and a chance to obtain feedback into process and management that may be beneficial for future operations.

2.3.9   Site closure

Upon completion of the examination/excavation, a comprehensive record will be made of the site employing still and video photography. This should be undertaken both before and after site restoration. The grave will then be refilled. Under exceptional circumstances, where a site may require further examination, if the grave walls and floor have detailed tool marks or vehicle tracks, then it may be appropriate to preserve the surfaces under a permeable membrane. Any large items of evidence that are considered impractical or unnecessary to move and take into storage (e.g., bulldozed trees, building materials, motor vehicle parts) can be wrapped and placed within the grave before backfilling. The grave and site must be left safe, and any necessary remedial measures must be undertaken. These might include backfilling the grave; controlling water flow and drainage across the site; dealing with compaction; and removing waste water, rubbish, or fuel spills. The site, as far as possible, is to be returned to a safe and tidy condition. Any requests or requirements by authorities or by communities concerning the site will be accommodated whenever practicable. These might include aspects of site restoration or religious ceremonies.

Under the control of the SCM, all equipment will be thoroughly cleaned after the excavation is finished and stored to be ready for transportation. Cleaning should be documented and be of a standard to ensure that the possibility of cross-site contamination cannot occur. Once all of these tasks have been completed, then the SCM will declare the site investigation/excavation closed. Once the site is closed, the storage containers, equipment, and vehicles will leave the site, and the perimeter and access cordons will be removed. In some circumstances, it may be necessary to formally hand the site back to an appropriate authority.

2.3.10 Off-site analysis

Evidence and samples that requires further analysis will be signed over to the relevant investigative authority, scientists, or approved external laboratory. Such analyses may include ballistics, soils, geological samples, botanical samples, and entomological samples. Appropriate security and transport of evidence to facilities will be undertaken.

2.3.11 Final reports

In large projects, it is usually considered appropriate for the senior member of any team of specific experts (e.g., archaeologists) to act as a conduit and collator of all relevant written and photographic evidence in that area of expertise. In such cases, the senior archaeologist will produce the report of the location, the nature and attributes of the site, the sequence of activities undertaken during the excavation, and an interpretation of the site and the history of the sequence of events. The drawing together and synthesis of material produce the final field report. In addition to this, specialist reports on specific aspects may be included in the main report, possibly as appendices. They might include specific stand-alone reports from the SCM or from specialists such as the forensic botanists or palynologists. Responsibility for receiving completed reports lies with the SCM.

2.3.12 Information dissemination

Upon completion of the excavation, all appropriate information will be passed on to the investigation and mortuary management teams (MMTs). At the appropriate point in time and in line with legal and moral responsibilities and requirements, the relevant documentation and reports, and all attachments will be disseminated to the appropriate organisations, which may include some or all of the following: investigating authorities, local authorities, commissioning clients, local or affected communities. This will be agreed in the commissioning contract.

2.3.13 Evidence handover – Check

Upon completion of an excavation, the process and results should ultimately be reviewed and checked by the management team. Checks for consistency of coding, recording, and data entry will also be made. An administrative review will be made of the associated mission planning requirements. Subsequently, a record of any methodological or structural improvements and changes to procedure that could enhance the process for further excavations will be made.

The handover of evidence for further examination or storage will be undertaken by the SCE who will sign it over to an appropriate person at a mortuary or other appropriate facility. The SCE will assist mortuary staff in checking and organising the evidence handover, and investigate any discrepancies. Appropriate security and transport of evidence to facilities will be undertaken. Relevant forms for handover of evidence and human remains will be completed under the supervision of the SCE. Where the mortuary process follows consecutively from the site investigation, a briefing will be prepared by the senior archaeologist describing the methods of excavation and recovery used, as well as other pertinent detail such as taphonomy.

2.3.14 Summary: Phase 2 – Site excavation and evidence recovery

Whenever practical, mass grave and associated sites will undergo detailed investigative and scientific analysis to assist in forensic or humanitarian identifications and criminal investigations. Site investigations and excavations will, as appropriate, locate, examine, survey, plan, record, and recover all evidence of a case, including human remains. The guidelines or protocols set out in this chapter present the minimum set of scientific procedures to be considered when undertaking forensic investigations of mass graves and associated sites.

Site planning. A risk assessment will be undertaken, determining security and health and safety requirements in the mission area. This will be continually reviewed, and mitigation strategies modified accordingly. Investigation requirements will guide planning, and the site assessment report and local contacts will be consulted. Site access and evidence removal permissions must be arranged, and site codes will be established or continued. All necessary equipment and logistical needs must be established and addressed.

Team structure. The project manager will coordinate the following activities: health and safety risk assessment requirements; equipment, logistics, and communication needs; and carry out liaison. The SCM will facilitate implementation of protocols and will assume overall control of the scene of crime or site under investigation. He or she will delegate direct evidence handling issues and chain of custody and continuity to the SCE(s). The senior archaeologist will direct scientific matters working in collaboration with the SCM, who will in turn direct nonscientific examination and process and ensure site and evidential integrity. The senior archaeologist will appoint a survey and grave supervisor where necessary, and coordinate the scientific investigation team. The logistics manager will manage the support team (machine operators, mechanics, engineers, drivers, and technicians) who provide all necessary logistical assistance.

Site preparation. Risk assessment, health and safety, and logistics/equipment require-ments will be implemented before groundwork begins. Excavations will not be undertaken without adequate security arrangements, including the assessment by qualified EOD staff of all areas accessed by the team. Safe areas will be clearly demarcated. Engineering requirements will be met, and a secure perimeter will be established. A site survey will be carried out, and all relevant activities and features will be photographed and recorded.

Site investigation – Surface evidence. The senior archaeologist will examine and record the history of the forensic landscape and environment. This will involve full assessment and interpretation of the extent and nature of any surface evidence and determination of any sequences of surface evidence deposition. All evidence will be systematically recovered, fully recorded, surveyed, and photographed.

Site investigation – Site formation and grave exposure. Test trenches will be dug to determine local stratigraphy, check the hydrological regime, take soil profile sam-ples, and check contamination where necessary. The history of the environment, site formation processes, and stratigraphic sequence of the grave and area under investigation will be examined and recorded. The grave will be prepared for excava-tion, exposed in plan, and made safe for work through engineering measures. Any evidence exposed during this process will be recovered and fully recorded, surveyed, and photographed.

Site investigation – Excavation. Archaeologists and anthropologists will excavate the grave and its contents, including human remains, following stratigraphic principles as outlined in this protocol. The team will be aware of the possibility of UXO within the grave. A detailed record of stratigraphic boundaries or interfaces, the position of human remains, and other evidence will be taken to accurately record and reproduce the grave and its contents in three dimensions. Consistent documentation, records, surveys, and photographs will achieve this. Specialists may be required to collect and analyse samples. Human remains and other types of evidence will be uncovered, labelled, photographed, surveyed, documented, lifted, appropriately packaged, and stored to maximise conservation requirements and evidential value and potential. Similarly, tool marks, tyre tracks, and other evidence not within the grave but within the wider forensic landscape will be sampled, documented, and recorded. Once the grave fill has been removed, the grave walls and floor will be examined manually and with metal detection devices for further evidence.

Documentation and recording. Appropriate personnel will complete all forms, logs, documents, the photographic record, maps, drawings, databases, and reports. This information will be copied and collated by the SCE for the review of the senior archaeologist and SCM. The senior archaeologist will produce a final report relating to the results of the examination and excavation. Documents, evidence, and human remains will be signed over to the mortuary facility and/or investigative authority as appropriate.

Site closure. Once the grave and forensic landscape have been surveyed and photographed, exposed areas can be filled in, perimeter and access cordons removed, and the site left in a safe and visually acceptable state. Equipment can then be cleaned and transported, staff will be debriefed, and the site declared closed.

2.4 Phase 3 – The mortuary

Whenever practical, mortuary operations will carry out detailed pathological, anthropological, radiographic, forensic, and investigative analysis to assist in judicial and/or humanitarian identifications. Mortuary investigations and analyses aim to identify, record, recover, and interpret evidence of cause and manner of death. They also record data that will assist in establishing the presumptive identity of the deceased, including, if appropriate, assessment of ethnicity, biological sex, age at death, and stature, as well as evidence of antemortem trauma, disease, and other individuating characteristics. Examinations will also recover, record, and analyse other forensic evidence.

This section sets out protocols for the mortuary phase of activity in a manner reflecting the step-by-step processes of an investigation. This commences with planning and moves on to site preparation and commissioning, mortuary operation, postmortem examination, mortuary closure, and information dissemination. The relevant evidence processing, documentation, and recording requirement are used throughout the process. They are described in sections 2.4.3 to 2.4.6 for clarity. These mortuary operations protocols represent the minimum set of scientific procedures to be considered when undertaking forensic investigations of mass graves and associated sites, and they should be followed where practically possible to do so. However, local conditions may require aspects to be modified. Where variation is agreed, the rationale and process must be documented in detail. The protocols for the mortuary phase have been summarised in Figure 2–7.

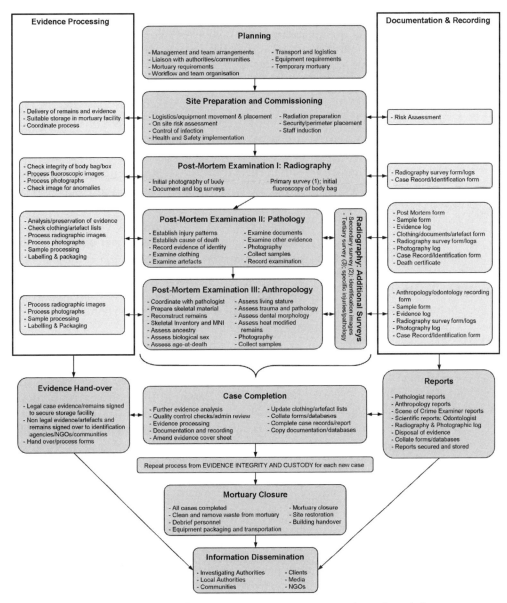

Figure 2–7. Flow chart of the mortuary process. *Source:* Inforce Foundation.

2.4.1 Planning

The organisation of mortuary facilities established in the planning, site preparation, and commissioning of the mortuary provides for a professional and consistent operation. Establishing an effective mortuary operation helps ensure the scientific, legally sound, and efficient investigation, identification, and return of human remains and personal effects to the legal next of kin and contributes to the judicial process. On confirmation of the requirement to undertake a mortuary operation, the MMT will be established under the leadership of the senior pathologist or the senior anthropologist. This will reflect the predominant state of survival of the human remains. Subject to the size of the operation, the management team will consist of the senior representative from each professional group involved, together with the senior investigating officer and senior logistician. The staffing structure is illustrated in Figure 2–8. The MMT will agree on the precise protocol to be used within the mortuary, and will agree and log any agreed variations to these procedures.

A mortuary manager will be appointed who will report to the MMT, and who will be responsible for liaison with the field team and local authorities; planning and commissioning of suitable premises; staffing, including rostering and induction; all matters pertaining to health and safety, security, equipment, and supplies; workflow; and decommissioning. It may be necessary to use appropriate existing buildings within the local community to set up the mortuary, temporary or otherwise. The mortuary manager will liaise with the authorities and the communities to facilitate a formal agreement for this to occur. The MMT will liaise with and agree on a policy on procedures for sampling, retention of samples for analysis, the requirements for obtaining antemortem data (as appropriate), and the repatriation of human remains and the personal possessions and clothing of the deceased.

The mortuary manager in consultation with the MMT and radiation protection advisor will select a suitable site for the mortuary, if no preexisting mortuary facility is available. A number of different criteria will be considered when selecting a suitable location and type of property. The location of the mortuary is of crucial importance for a variety of reasons, including services and logistics. Ideally, it needs to be relatively close to the mass grave(s) or scene(s) of crime and practically suitable for the transportation of human remains from the grave. Ease of access for supplies and staff arriving from other locations should be considered, and it needs to be sited in a secure location where access for those not officially involved is difficult both by day and night. Proximity to staff accommodation is also important and nearby parking for vehicles is an asset, if for no other reason than security. If it is possible to accommodate staff near to the mortuary, that saves resources in terms of time and removes an unnecessary security concern. The supply of essential and reliable services is critical. These include electricity (which needs to be compatible with equipment if possible), hot and cold running water, and sewage disposal. An appropriate heating and/or cooling and ventilation system is required. Clinical waste disposal is a matter that must be catered for by an appropriate licensed authority. Radio, telephone, and other communication links are also important. These essential services can be portable, and installed and maintained in most areas.

Within the mortuary structure, it is essential that there is a large open area sufficient in size to accommodate the proposed workflow through the different stages of postmortem examination. Adequate space is required for the examination of evidence, taking into account the rate of exhumation and workflow variation within the mortuary. It is important to ensure that there is sufficient storage for

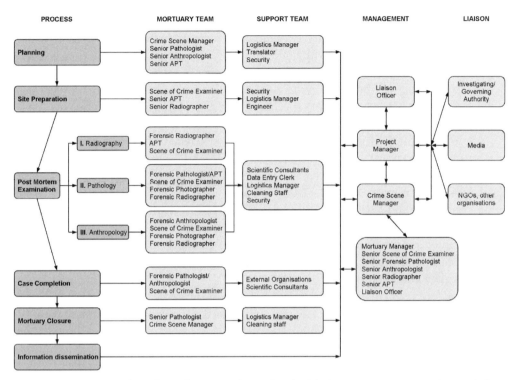

Figure 2–8. Flow chart of personnel associated with the mortuary process. *Source:* Inforce Foundation.

predicted volume of evidence. Good natural light is preferred, but where this is not possible, natural daylight bulbs ('full spectrum light bulbs') should be used to ensure a safe working environment for staff and maximum analytical capacity and efficiency during the working day. In any event, avoid lighting that produces unwanted heat.

A number of separate and distinct functional areas will be required within the mortuary location. These include separate (male and female) changing areas with shower and toilet facilities and a staff rest area with a beverage point. Locker facilities are useful but not essential. These can be situated in a separate area within another building or in a separate area within the mortuary.

A body holding area is essential. This provides an arrival point for human remains and room for temporary storage prior to mortuary examinations (e.g., portable refrigerated storage units that are shelved). A body processing area is required for the recording of unique identification numbers, photography, and other logging procedures, and a property examination area is necessary for recording clothing and such personal items as documents and jewellery. Regardless of whether a conservator is available for a mission, conservation of evidence (e.g., ID cards, photographs) is crucial, and for this to take place there must be a work table and sufficient space for drying and other remedial actions.

A large proportion of the mortuary space will be dedicated to the postmortem examination of human remains. An essential segregation between wet and dry areas must be accommodated within the mortuary. However, the proportion of space allocated to each will depend on the percentage of skeletonised versus soft tissue remains that will be entering the mortuary. The postmortem examination consists of several phases, each having specialist space and equipment requirements.

The use of radiography is essential in a mortuary, and designated space must be provided for fluoroscopy and/or x-ray to be undertaken. This requires an appropriately shielded area with sufficient space for a mobile C-arm fluoroscope and monitor cart, cadaver on trolley, and a worktop. Further to this, an area is needed for taking x-rays. This must also be a suitable shielded area with sufficient space to allow for required examination, which may include dental and whole body radiographs. A designated space is required for each aspect of postmortem examination. The radiography area can be made secure either by lead shielding or by establishing a suitable exclusion zone around the working area. The required distance will be determined by the radiation protection advisor.

The pathologist will require space for autopsy tables, a dissection area, and a clothes examination area (to be multiplied with respect to the number of pathologists present). The APTs require suitable space for tables to hold their instruments and equipment. A separate 'clean' workstation should also be available. The anthropology area must have suitable space for preparation and examination tables for each operative. If an odontologist is involved, sufficient space for examination and casting will be required. Photography is a crucial component of the work of the mortuary, and for this the photographer will require sufficient space for a table and lighting equipment. If the return of bodies to families is integral to the mortuary operation, then there must be a designated body release area, and possibly embalming and coffining facilities. If relatives are likely to come to view bodies then a relatives' reception area is needed. This should include both a waiting area and a separate viewing area.

Mortuary equipment and consumables must have dedicated and appropriate storage space and cupboards. Similarly, there should be appropriate space and shelving or similar for secure evidence storage and refrigeration. The mortuary office needs to be adequate in size to allow for collation, digital recording, and preparation of forms and reports. To avoid contaminating clean areas, mortuary staff must be discouraged from entering the office and will be given their own PCs within the mortuary confines. These will be networked. If the operation is complex enough and the space available is sufficient, there will be a separate mortuary manager's office. This must have telephone, radio, and other appropriate communications. In some operations, the field investigation team may also have some office capacity within the mortuary complex, as may the overall project management function.

The allocated and demarked areas described previously need to be appropriately sized for the anticipated workflow and for the number of personnel involved. This will be assessed and agreed on by the MMT, prior to the selection of suitable premises. There must be a clear demarcation or, if possible, a physical boundary

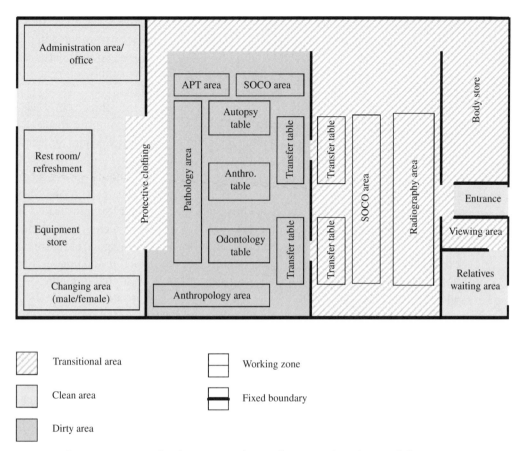

▨	Transitional area	⊟ Working zone
▤	Clean area	▬ Fixed boundary
▦	Dirty area	

Figure 2–9. Example of a mortuary layout demonstrating clean and dirty areas. *Source:* Alison Anderson.

between areas that are considered 'clean' from those that are 'dirty'. The boundaries promote awareness and ensure that no cross-contamination occurs between each area; colour coding the areas works well and traditionally red denotes 'dirty', green denotes 'clean', and yellow 'transitional' areas. An example of an effective mortuary layout is shown in Figure 2–9.

2.4.2   Site preparation and commissioning

The equipment required for operating a mortuary will depend on the likely condition, completeness, and number of bodies passing through on a daily basis. However, the mortuary should be well equipped and flexible enough to operate effectively if alterations are made to the process. The equipment required for the mortuary is listed in 2.5 (Table 2–2).

In cases where temporary mortuaries are the only available option, the requirements described previously remain the same. The components needed to achieve the requirements may have to be specially manufactured. For example, the building may consist of a tent or portable cabins. However, the available space must still be divided into the required functional areas, and workflow must be considered in this arrangement. Security is of paramount importance to any investigation undertaken, and the basic services must be installed, including electricity supply, running hot and cold water, and appropriate sanitation and sewage facilities.

The personnel involved within the mortuary phase fall into three teams, each of which will have appropriate expertise. The MMT should comprise the senior pathologist, senior anthropologist, senior radiographer, senior APT, senior SCE, and logistics officer. The mortuary investigation team can include any number of pathologists, radiographers, forensic anthropologists, SCEs, APTs, photographers, a cultural anthropologist, and a conservator (or SCE or similar with conservation skills), and possibly an odontologist and data entry staff. The mortuary support team will include one or more mechanics, engineers, drivers, logisticians, technicians, clothes washers (the deceased's), and cleaners. The number of each category of personnel will reflect the anticipated size of the operation. The team structure and organisation for each part of the process within the mortuary phase is illustrated in Figure 2–7. Similarly, the integration of individual team members is illustrated in Figure 2–8.

Calculations will need to be made regarding the capacity of the mortuary team needed to process the human remains from the grave site(s). This will determine the room sizes and layout required. The MMT will decide the daily workflow, depending on the nature of the work. It is the dual responsibility of the senior pathologist and the senior APT to oversee the organisation of workflow within the mortuary on a day-to-day basis. Where there are no fleshed bodies, there may be no pathologist involved (other than to undertake death certification). In such cases the mortuary may be managed by the SCM, or senior anthropologist; the MMT will make this decision.

Once a suitable site for the mortuary has been established, then the necessary consumables, equipment, facilities, plant, services, and logistical functions must be procured and installed. The commissioning team will be small in number and could be the MMT. They will travel to the site a sufficient period of time before the full team to set up the equipment and commission the mortuary. Prior to commissioning the mortuary, a comprehensive health and safety risk assessment will be undertaken on the buildings, equipment, chemicals, and duties associated with the mortuary operation. Risk Assessment Forms (MG02) (see accompanying CD) will be completed and filed by the mortuary manager. The mortuary manager will be responsible for ensuring that appropriate health and safety regulations and local rules and procedures are in place and adhered to. They will ensure that all staff working in the mortuary read and sign all local and organisational health and safety rules prior to working in the mortuary. First aid–trained staff will comprise a certain percentage of the MMT, and, when possible, a trained medic will be present.[13] Health and safety policies (see Chapter 3) will need to be in place, including the following, some of which are legislated for and some of which will be the organisations' internal policy

---

[13] Some forensic pathologists will be able to undertake this role.

documents: Health and Safety Policy and Local Rules, Radiation Protection Policy and Local Rules, Security Policy, Fire Regulations, Emergency Evacuation Procedures, Policy for Handling Munitions and Unexploded Devices, Control of Infection Policy, Manual Handling Policy, Control of Substances Hazardous to Health Policy, Environmental Protection, and Waste Disposal Policy.

The senior APT will act as health and safety officer reporting to the mortuary manager. He or she will be responsible for advising and overseeing all health and safety issues within the mortuary on a day-to-day basis. A radiation protection advisor (normally an appropriately qualified radiation physicist) will be appointed. He or she will be responsible for preparing a radiation protection policy, and together with the senior radiographer, for the local radiation rules that will be adhered to within the mortuary. The senior radiographer on duty will act as radiation protection supervisor and will be responsible for all matters relating to radiation safety within the mortuary on a day-to-day basis. All staff working within the mortuary have the responsibility for maintaining strict hygiene procedures to control and minimise the spread of infection and prevent transmission to the wider community. They must all provide evidence of up-to-date immunisation appropriate to the area of operation and will agree to follow any special procedures that may be determined by the senior APT, senior pathologist, or senior anthropologist. The control of infection procedures within the mortuary will be determined by the senior APT. Areas within the mortuary will be designated as clean, transitional, or dirty areas as described previously, and appropriate protective clothing worn within each is detailed within 3.5.3.

A member of the MMT and a deputy will be responsible for the integrity and security of the mortuary facility, and both should be advised by mortuary security staff on appropriate measures to maintain this. They will be the first to arrive and the last to leave the facility each day, and will amend the personnel entry register accordingly. Both will hold keys for the facility and will be responsible for locking doors and setting alarms upon leaving. They will also check regularly that the security team is in attendance day and night. Depending on circumstances, it may be necessary to establish a perimeter fence around the mortuary (if none already exists) for security purposes.

Staff induction includes issuing security and ID badges, going through contractual formalities, overseeing the health and safety briefing and induction, and ensuring that staff is familiar with the security status of the area. It is vitally important that all personnel are familiar with the use of these protocols and SOPs and that they will apply them. Immunisation and vaccination records must be checked, and staff should be inducted in all areas of their work and the overall mission.

2.4.3   Evidence management, integrity, and custody

All radiographs will be uniquely identified with case number, date of examination, radiographer's initials, and anatomical markers using an actinic marker or another photographic method prior to development. Digital images will have this information recorded electronically at the time that the image is taken. The radiographer will note any possible identifying features on all survey record sheets and recommend any further imaging examinations as necessary.

All photographs will be taken in either negative or digital format, and where it is deemed necessary, both types of images will be taken. Digital images will have this information recorded electronically when the image is taken. The MMT, with their colleagues from the field operation, will have to decide if film or digital photography will be the primary method to reflect relevant legislation and regulation and practical considerations. Details of photographs taken will be entered into the photographic log by the photographer.

All anthropological samples that are taken will be checked to ensure that the bags have metal or other appropriate tags bearing the case number that corresponds to the anthropologists' records. The anthropological samples form must be completed and the exhibits placed into secure storage. Any DNA samples will be refrigerated at $+4°C$ for short-term storage or frozen at $-80°C$ for longer-term storage. If a freezer is not available, alternative storage methods are discussed in Chapter 9 (9.3.5). Other biological samples must be stored in a refrigerator. The samples will be handed over to the appropriate scientific organisation for analyses, and the transfer documented and signed off.

All evidence and clothing will be packaged following the instructions described in 4.3.2, following UK Forensic Science Service best practice. If the original packaging is badly soiled or damaged, then the item will be placed into a new exhibit bag or other container together with the original packaging and the label complete as appropriate. After the mortuary examination is complete, bodies and body parts will be returned to the same store, but placed in a new location designated for completed cases only. If there are sufficient individual refrigerated stores, then a separate one may be retained for this purpose.

Upon the conclusion of the examination, the anthropologist will complete the anthropology recording forms (adult or subadult) (MA41–46), and the pathologist will complete the pathology forms (MP31 and MP32). The sample recording forms and logs (MC14F and MC14L) will be completed by the SCE, as will the case and evidence forms and logs (MC10L, MC11F, MC12F, MC13L, and MC15L); and the radiography forms and logs (MR21–23) will be completed by the radiographer. To ensure that quality is controlled and that recording standards are consistent, the senior anthropologist will review each case after examination by the anthropologist has been completed. They will also periodically review the case materials and analytical notes. The appropriate area on the case identification form will be completed. A copy of the anthropological report and any photographs will be attached to the mortuary-based SCE's papers.

The senior SCE will collate and collect the documents and will pass them to the data entry clerk for processing. Each anthropologist will complete the summary pages of the anthropology form. These will be checked and signed off by the senior anthropologist who will collate the individual summaries to produce the overall anthropology report. This will be passed to the senior pathologist who will produce the final mortuary report for each individual and the combined group of the deceased. The radiography and photographic log, negatives, and digital hard copies will all be stored as appropriate.

The role of the cultural anthropologist (and possibly the conservator) is to provide specific descriptions of such materials as clothing, which may be unique culturally or regionally. These descriptions should be added and collated with the lists of clothing and artefacts that are used to categorise evidence in the mortuary. This is often an ongoing process as previously undescribed item types are logged. The original paperwork generated for each individual case and updated forms and databases will be collated and collected by the senior SCE and entered into the chain of custody. Digital hard copies of photographs and radiographs will also be placed within the file. All electronic sources of data must be logged and stored as evidence. Once a case in the mortuary has been completed, a check will be made by the senior SCE to ensure that all documentation has been completed in full. The documentation will be kept together by treasury tag or other appropriate means and the file handed to the data entry clerk to update the computerised entry. Once the computerised entry of documentation has been undertaken, the evidence cover sheet will be amended accordingly. When all the case papers are completed, a copy will be made and passed to the investigator for further dissemination to the organisation who will be conducting an investigation for missing persons. The original paperwork should be packaged and labelled accordingly. All databases should have security copies made that should be stored in a separate location from the originals. It may be relevant to copy paper or imagery documents by photocopy or scanning for security/data safety reasons.

Effective organisation of the postmortem processing of human remains and other types of evidence ensures the proper collection and preservation of human remains, personal effects, and other types of evidence within the mortuary. Evidence from the field will arrive at the mortuary in various types of secure containers and be accompanied by a SCE. On arrival from the site, appropriate members of the MMT and SCE will check the containers carrying the evidence to ensure the integrity of the seals and/or locks. If they are secure, the container will be opened, and the senior pathologist, anthropologist, and SCE will check each body, body part, artefact, general clothing and bone bags, or other evidence. The evidence will be removed individually, checked against the handover form, and signed for. If there are any inconsistencies, they will be noted and investigated immediately. A copy of the signed sheet will be handed over to the accompanying SCE for reference purposes. If any seals and/or locks are found to have been tampered with, then the damage will be recorded and a photograph taken before they are opened. Inconsistencies will be dealt with immediately.

If an item is received in an original exhibit bag, it will be left in the bag or returned to it after examination, unless the bag is soiled or damaged in a way that will affect the evidence. On returning the evidence to the bag, it will be signature sealed, secured with clear adhesive tape or a heat sealer, and the label amended accordingly. For each case, an evidence cover sheet will be generated by the data entry team from the information received from the site. A copy will be attached to the mortuary SCE's case papers for every body, body part, site artefact, and general clothing and bone bags received. Upon delivery, bodies, body parts, artefacts, and general clothing and bone bags received from the site will be placed in a secure store, refrigerated where necessary, until processing. After processing, the evidence and/or human remains are then placed into either the original (as above if clean) or new individual exhibit bags and boxes and put into appropriate secure storage to which the SCM or senior SCE hold the keys.

It is essential that when using any form of refrigerated space, the human remains will be placed on appropriately spaced shelves. If fleshed human remains are not separated from each other by the use of shelving, the refrigeration facility may fail to slow down decomposition and, in any event, human remains may be damaged or compromised by the weight and proximity of others. The same applies to other types of fragile evidence or evidence in poor condition. Disarticulated skeletons will always be boxed rather than placed in bags.[14] Where skeletal remains are recovered within clothing, it may be necessary to separate the body accordingly. In such cases, particular care must be taken to examine damage to or disarray of clothing that might relate to trauma (i.e., ballistics, blade, or blast injury) and to record this *in situ* because during packaging and moving to the mortuary, the human remains and restraints and/or clothing may separate. In any event, clothing and human remains should not be deliberately separated prior to examination in the mortuary. As a precaution, it is advisable to attach 'Fragile' labels to both the front and the back of exhibits, which may require highlighted labelling during storage and handling.

The exhibit labels on each item will be checked against the handover sheet to ascertain that the information is correct. Items will be dealt with one item at a time. When booking exhibits and human remains for examination, specific procedures must be implemented. Items should first be removed from the store, and all details entered on the booking form and evidence cover sheet. For human remains, it is essential to enter the case number on the appropriate workflow chart. The mortuary team will adopt the numbering system generated by the field-based SCM. This will then be issued by the mortuary-based SCE for continuity of evidence. Artefacts from a specific body will be given a new unique evidence number from a group of numbers allocated to the mortuary and entered onto the artefacts form. Descriptions will be taken from the established artefacts list, providing uniformity in description and ensuring that data entry and searching are consistent. A number of specific forms and logs, controlled by the SCE, are to be completed appropriately and handed to the data entry clerk for processing and entering onto the mortuary database. It will be

---

[14] Boxes should be adequate for controlled temperature storage of skeletal remains. In the unlikely event of needing refrigeration for skeletal remains, an alternative packaging medium may be required.

the responsibility of the senior pathologist, anthropologist, and SCE to ensure that, on a daily basis, all staff complete the personnel entry register, and they must sign the sheet to show that it has been completed correctly. In addition, they must ensure that only essential personnel will be admitted to the mortuary. Official visitors will sign in and out of the facility, entering the details onto the mortuary entry register. The evidence handover form will be generated by the site database and will be maintained by the site/field-based senior SCE. This form will be signed and handed to the mortuary-based senior SCE, and a copy will be given to the site/field-based senior SCE. The evidence database should be initiated, incorporating the database from the field and following the database SOP (see 4.5).

2.4.4   Postmortem examination

The aim of a postmortem investigation is to establish the cause and manner of death and to record evidence needed for establishing either a positive or a presumptive identification.[15] The step-by-step process of the mortuary operation is divided into a number of sections within these protocols. Evidence integrity must be maintained throughout the postmortem examination, specifically radiography, pathology, odontology, and anthropology; and also, case completion. Maintaining the mortuary operations described in these protocols helps ensure that a quality assured postmortem examination can occur. Full descriptions of each stage of postmortem examination are provided in Chapter 6. Each mortuary operation will undoubtedly require different approaches regarding the postmortem examination, reflecting the varying degrees of decomposition and preservation of human remains and evidence. Further to this, there may be cultural or religious imperatives that influence this decision, making discussion with family or community representatives necessary. In light of this, it is the responsibility of the senior pathologist to decide which method of analysis or identification is most appropriate for each context. Ultimately, such decisions are also likely to be influenced by resources and mandate.

Postmortem examination I – Radiography. Radiography is a vital early step in processing human remains. There are three types of radiographic survey. These are described as follows and in more detail in Chapter 6 (6.5).

Following initial photography of the unopened body bag, the body(ies), body parts, and any other evidence requiring definition will be x-rayed prior to visual examination and autopsy while still in the packaging. This is in accordance with the radiography SOP described in Chapter 6 (6.5.2). This is the primary level of radiographic survey, and it is absolutely essential in all cases involving any type of explosion, when a gunshot injury is suspected, or with bodies that are decomposing. Its purpose is to establish the nature of the human remains contained within

---

[15] A positive ID relies on such definitive evidence as fingerprints or DNA and, occasionally, dental records. A presumptive identification is based on less specific and unique characteristics.

the body bag or box to determine the presence or absence of ordnance (UXO), to identify metallic and other artefacts, to identify and locate bullets, shrapnel and other projectiles, and to determine any features that are potentially useful for identification. Any unique identifying features seen during the primary survey (e.g., dental treatment, previous healed fractures, congenital abnormalities) will be noted for possible further investigation as part of the tertiary examination.

X-ray fluoroscopy is currently the method of choice for this 'primary survey', although both direct digital x-ray and CT scanning techniques can also be used for this purpose. If resources are limited, and a fluoroscope or digital x-ray unit is not available, plain film radiography of the entire body bag could be undertaken as a substitute.

A secondary survey may be necessary to acquire standard radiographic information that may be used to determine the identity of the deceased (e.g., full dental survey). The exact imaging examinations to be undertaken will be established for each case by the senior radiographer in consultation with the senior pathologist, senior anthropologist, and odontologist.

Further radiographic examination (the tertiary survey) may be undertaken to record unique identifying features seen during the primary survey and at the request of the pathologist, odontologist, or anthropologist in order to record specific injuries or pathology, establish the path of projectiles, and record unique identifying features and/or other supplementary information as required by the investigating team. Radiographic examination of artefacts may be undertaken at the request of the pathologist, anthropologist, odontologist, SCE, or conservator. Direct digital, computed radiography, or plain film radiography are currently the methods of choice for the secondary and tertiary surveys.

Recording is as described in 2.4.3. The radiographer will note any possible identifying features on all survey record sheets and recommend any further imaging examinations as necessary. The radiographer will complete a radiography survey record form for each case. Exposure factors, radiation dose, screening time, and number of images taken will be recorded in the examination log within the radiography room. The pathologist, anthropologist, odontologist, and radiographer will make a detailed note of any findings together with a permanent record either in the form of a thermal printout, conventional radiograph, or digital radiographic image. These images must be logged as exhibits by the SCE. The appropriate logs and forms having been completed as appropriate will be coordinated by the SCE and handed to the data entry clerk for processing and entering onto the mortuary database. These forms and logs comprise the Case Identification Form (MC12F), the Radiography Log (MR23), and the Photography Log (MG06LD and MG06LN).

Postmortem examination II – Pathology. Confirming the identity of the deceased is critical to the investigation. It also serves the basic humanitarian need of survivors for closure and gives the deceased their right (under the Geneva Convention of 1949) to an individual identified grave. The pathologists, other mortuary-based scientists, and external specialists will aim to provide a positive or presumptive identification[16] in order to issue death certificates and assist with judicial and humanitarian issues and to notify the legal next of kin. The pathologist will aim to establish the cause and manner of death, which might be of relevance to an international or national court of law seeking to establish the nature of a possible crime. The pathology investigation will be completed with the maximum degree of thoroughness, coupled with minimum delay, and always maintaining continuity of the chain of evidence. For further detail of the process described, see Chapter 6 (6.3).

Following the primary survey by the radiographer, and where soft tissue is present, the body will be transported to the autopsy table together with the radiography log, which will be handed to the pathologist. If the remains are completely skeletonised, they will be handed over directly to the anthropologist. Where possible (i.e., as dictated by condition and completeness), the pathology examination will include all of the components described here. To recognise and record evidence of injuries and cause and manner of death, a detailed postmortem examination will be carried out on each body or body part. All injuries and any pathological abnormalities due to natural disease, evidence of previous surgery and/or trauma, and the presence of prosthetic devices will be recorded. Evidence of perimortem trauma will also be recorded to assist in establishing the cause of death. Photographs will be taken to record pathology and/or trauma. To record evidence that may aid in determining identification, a detailed description of the general identifying characteristics of each of the deceased must be made and recorded. Photographs will be taken of key characteristics, including the following (if present and relevant): length, colour and texture of hair, any distinguishing marks, circumcision, evidence of antemortem disease and/or trauma, tattoos, decorative piercing, scars and patterned scarring, height, and an estimate of physique (if it is not possible to assess weight). Personal items, including prostheses, may be identifiable, and therefore will be photographed, with a copy of the photograph attached to the mortuary-based SCE's papers. The appropriate area on the identification form will be completed. The same process of recording and logging is also followed for recording such characteristics as tattoos, marks or scars, or evidence of skin disease (e.g., psoriasis) that may still be visible. If during the postmortem examination it is evident that fingerprint detail remains, an attempt will be made to take a record of these. Any fingerprints recovered will be laminated and attached to the mortuary SCE's papers. The appropriate area on the identification form will be completed.

The pathologist will want to view the clothing and other evidence and complete the records as to the description and colouring, amending the case evidence form. After examination by the pathologist, all clothing and artefacts will be removed. Each item of clothing will be checked for adhering evidence. The actual examination of

---

[16] One approach to this is to adopt a system similar to that used in the UK where an identification commission is established, consisting of such specialist input as that of the pathologist, odontologist, anthropologist, fingerprint expert, and/or biomolecular geneticist chaired by a coroner.

the clothing and additional artefacts and documents falls to the SCE. The pathologist will examine clothing both before and after it has been washed and dried to reconcile evidence of wounds on the body with those on clothing. Personal effects such as watches, jewellery, medication, and money will be examined and documented appropriately. A case evidence form and an evidence cover sheet will be completed for each separate item. If a document is recovered that bears a form of written identification, it will be photographed and/or scanned in detail, on both sides if appropriate, and the case identification form completed with as much detail as possible. If the document is soiled or wet, it will be photographed as soon as possible before attempting to clean and dry it. Any item believed to be relevant to the investigation will be bagged separately and labelled accordingly. The bagged and labelled item will be placed in the evidence store for forwarding to the investigating authority.

A secondary radiographic survey (full dental and/or full skeletal) may occur if necessary after the body or body part has been cleaned. The requirement for routine secondary surveys will be dependent on the nature of the case. It may be that in most cases it will only be necessary to perform a full dental survey. However, in cases where systematic antemortem beatings or torture are suspected, a full or limited skeletal survey may be of benefit to the investigation. The precise process to be followed for each case will be determined in consultation with the MMT and the secondary survey taken following pathological examination. With recent improvements in DNA testing, where resources exist facilitating DNA analysis and where access to a surviving appropriate relative is available, it is recommended that a full skeletal survey for identification purposes be limited to those cases where identification is likely to prove difficult to determine by these and any other means. A tertiary radiographic examination may be requested by one or more of the pathologists, anthropologists, or odontologists to record specific injuries or other pathology, to establish the path of projectiles, and to record unique identifying features or other supplementary information for the investigation team.

The body bags or boxes will be photographed after opening, and bodies and body parts will be photographed fully before and after undressing. Once the body is unclothed, any visible signs of injury will be fully photographed and documented onto a body sketch as part of the pathology form. All evidence pertaining to identification and cause and manner of death will be photographed. When photographing exhibits that may be useful in determining the identity of an individual, they will be in digital and/or negative format and the photographic log completed. A printed hard copy of the digital photograph should be attached to the mortuary-based SCE's case papers.

The sampling policy for a particular investigation will be agreed in consultation with the relevant local authority and community. The pathologist will consult relevant mortuary personnel as to which samples, if any, should be taken. Any samples taken for the purpose of identification by DNA profiling will be entered on the sample log and on the appropriate sample recording form. All samples will receive an evidence number issued from the mortuary evidence log. Other biological samples such as entomology or hair may also be collected after consultation with the appropriate scientific specialists. All samples are to be signed over to the SCE who will record them in the sample log and on a sample recording form. In addition, the pathologist must record the location from which the sample was taken. The pathologist may take tissue samples from bodies that are fleshed. Examples might be formalin-fixed tissues from all major organs if required for histological examination; unfixed tissues for frozen section identification of fat embolism; or tissue from the trachea, bronchi, or lung for evidence of inhaled smoke or diatoms.

All evidence (artefacts and clothing) removed during the postmortem examination will be labelled and processed immediately with the appropriate reference code by the SCE.

The SCE will also undertake an evaluation of the need for the conservation of evidential material samples in consultation with appropriate experts. Trained conservators will carry out agreed, passive conservation measures, and appropriate packaging materials will be used in all cases to assist with the preservation of evidence and avoid causing unnecessary damage through the use of inappropriate materials. The SCE will, after conservation measures have been implemented, number, package, and store all artefacts individually. In addition to digital photography, a computer scanner should be available as a backup to assist in the production of an electronic record of documents recovered. Scanning will only be used if the process will not damage the item. After conservation, all documents will be photographed in negative and/or digital film formats. Broken or damaged items will be photographed in this condition, and if repaired or reconstructed to recover more information, then once again after this process is complete. The photographic procedure detailed in the SOPs in Chapter 4 (4.4) will then be followed. When the artefacts are fully documented on the artefact log, they will then be put into the appropriate packaging.[17] Each item of loose clothing collected without association must be labelled using a metallic label or adequate equivalent with the labels completed and then placed into secure storage. The SCE will make a detailed description of each item of clothing and artefact using the preselected or appropriate clothing/artefact list, and then complete the appropriate form. The clothing/artefact list will be adjusted to accommodate ethnic, cultural, gender or biological sex, regional, and other typologies and variations in any given mission area. A note will be made of any clothing labels and identifying details.

Sampling for DNA will only be taken after examination by the pathologist and anthropologist and after any reanalysis has been undertaken. An agreed-on protocol for sampling will be determined by the MMT, and any laboratories that will be testing samples will be consulted in advance of this process. All exhibits will then

---

[17] Packaging must adhere to evidential requirements and be selected from the perspective of conservation (e.g., do not put damp items into a sealed plastic bag). Packaging guidelines can be drawn from such sources as the UK Forensic Science Service (FSS) Scenes of Crime Handbook (FSS, 2004), but consideration is needed of both practical application and theoretical ideals.

be handed to the SCE dealing with documentation and storage. All samples will be placed into appropriate containers, and then sealed in self-seal evidence bags or nonseal bags using evidence-sealing tape with an appropriate label bearing the case number. The case number will also be written on the outside of the packaging in large letters with a waterproof freezer pen and stored appropriately. All artefacts and clothing will be packaged following the SOP described in 4.3.2. If the original packaging is too soiled or damaged, then the item will be placed in a new exhibit bag together with the original packaging and the label completed as appropriate.

Postmortem examination III – Anthropology. This section applies to the analysis of human skeletal remains in a mortuary. The human remains may have been recovered as skeletons or as cadavers with some, or all, soft tissue surviving in any state of completeness or putrefaction. The anthropologist will aim to provide information contributing to the determination of a presumptive identification of the human remains. Skeletal features will be examined to develop a biological profile to assist in personal identification and determination of the circumstances surrounding death. For each case, the anthropologist will work in conjunction with the pathologist to examine skeletal remains. The anthropologist will have access to the expertise of an APT, and he or she may request additional x-ray examination and photography. For further detail of the processes outlined in this section, see Chapters 7 and 8. For a guide to which recording forms should be used when recording human skeletal analysis, refer to Figure 8.35.

Pretreatment. Where it is absolutely necessary to do so, human remains may have to be defleshed for specific analysis to take place. Out of respect for both the dead and their relatives, no unnecessary defleshing will be undertaken. Where it is possible to do so (i.e., some methods destroy the soft tissues), removed soft tissue will be retained with the human remains for reburial. In the preparatory phase, the anthropologist will separate bone from other nonosseous material, which will be bagged and labelled accordingly. In most cases, osseous human remains can be distinguished from nonosseous materials and nonhuman bone on the basis of differences in structural and developmental morphology. Remains (and nonosseous materials) will be determined to be either human or nonhuman. Fragmentation of skeletal human remains, if encountered, is the result of either peri- or postmortem forces; therefore, identification of the cause of any fragmentation should be attempted. Reconstruction of human remains is a procedural step that may assist in subsequent analyses. As such, reconstruction will be undertaken only when it is deemed useful, or potentially useful, for deriving analytical results. It will not be undertaken where bone is obviously misshapen because of peri- or postmortem pressure. Photographs of the human remains should be taken before and after reconstruction. The anthropologist or odontologist engaged in reconstruction will exercise care not to obscure evidence of perimortem trauma or hinder other subsequent analytical procedures.

Whenever possible, reconstruction should be reversible (achieved by using reversible or water-soluble adhesive).

Skeletal inventory and minimum number of individuals. Where remains are skeletonised, an inventory of all skeletal elements (complete, fragmentary, or absent) will be completed, including recording the condition and preservation of each skeletal element. Any additional human bone and nonhuman bone will be listed separately. Analysis of human remains to determine minimum number of individuals (MNI) is undertaken after osseous remains have been determined to be either human or nonhuman and after any cleaning and reconstruction, but prior to the assessment of the biological profile.

Assessment of demographic characteristics.

Assessment of ancestry. If assessment of ancestry is deemed appropriate, relevant, or critical to the analysis (see Simmons and Haglund, 2005), such assessment is undertaken after any necessary cleaning and reconstruction of the cranium. Assessment of ancestry will be done before the assessment of biological sex, age, and stature because some methods for determining these characteristics are ancestry specific. If a computer programme such as FORDISC 3.0 is to be used, then sex identification will need to be done first. In the assessment of ancestry, biological sex, age, and stature, feedback from each process is necessary. See 7.4 for further detail.

Assessment of biological sex. Where the human remains are established as being those of a single individual, determination of biological sex[18] is carried out while they are laid out in the anatomical position. In cases of commingled human remains where a direct association/relationship to other bone elements or fragments within the assemblage cannot be made, sex determination will be undertaken on individual bones. Remains that have been extensively fragmented, cremated, or subjected to other taphonomic processes that render analysis impossible will be recorded as indeterminate in cases of both single individuals and commingled remains. Biological sex cannot be established for infants and juveniles (before puberty) except by DNA analysis. See 7.5 for further detail.

Estimation of age at death. Analysis of age at death is undertaken after any cleaning and reconstruction has been completed and after ancestry (where appropriate) and sex have been established. Radiographs may be useful for age estimation in juveniles. Consultation with the odontologist may be necessary for a final age estimate for any individual with dentition present, depending on the methods used. See 7.7 for further detail.

---

[18] The term gender must not be used when determining biological sex; gender is socially constructed and an entirely different mode of categorisation based on aspects of human behaviour and values.

Estimation of parity status in females. With the well-preserved skeletal remains of adult females, parity status will be assessed using the extension of the pubic tubercle as an indicator. Care must be taken when recovering and cleaning skeletal remains, and for this type of analysis, it is imperative to treat the pubic bones with extreme care at all times. See 7.6 for further detail.

Assessment of individuating characteristics.

Estimation of living stature. Living stature will be assessed where possible when the appropriate formulas are available. However, it will be recognised that determination of metrical stature has little or no significance in many cultures for several possible reasons (i.e., in some societies, stature is not measured). In many homogenous groups, there is little divergence from the 'norm', so in such groups it may be sufficient to designate someone as unusually short or tall in respect of the majority. Where this is so, such judgment will be based on metrical observation and comparisons. See 8.2 for further detail.

Assessment of handedness. Handedness similarly is a subject that has more value in some cultural contexts than in others. The freedom to express side dominance within populations is not widespread, and prior to assessment of this characteristic, the merit of the work should be undertaken in consultation with a social anthropologist. The assessment of handedness and measurements used for this process will be described on the appropriate recording form. See 8.6 for further detail.

Assessment of skeletal pathology and trauma. The anthropologist will work in conjunction with the pathologist to identify and record evidence of any existing pathologies (i.e., evidence of disease) or trauma expressed on the bone. The latter may be ante- or perimortem. Ante-, peri-, and postmortem trauma, including taphonomic change, will be assessed and recorded separately.[19] Additional x-rays may be requested as a tertiary radiographic examination; this is discussed in more detail in a later section. The relevant inventory will be completed and the presence of trauma and/or pathology will be described and represented on the recording form, and the photographer will take detailed photographs as required by the anthropologist. All key identifying criteria and all characteristics to determine cause and manner of death will be photographed. See 8.3 for further detail.

Assessment of dentition. The anthropologist will undertake the initial examination of the dentition, including an inventory and description of any existing

---

[19] Cause and manner of death will be determined by the pathologist and/or the anthropologist. The findings of the anthropologist regarding perimortem trauma will be considered by the pathologist when determining cause and manner of death.

anomalies or pathology, trauma, and reconstruction, in accordance with the odontology SOP (see Chapter 9), which may include a secondary (dental) radiographic survey. All subpubescent dentition will undergo radiographic survey. If the anthropologist deems it necessary, and if extant dental records exist and are available, an odontologist will be consulted. See 8.4 and 9.4 for further details.

Assessment of postmortem influences. Assessment of all taphonomic change should be undertaken. This will include recording evidence of such factors as weathering, postmortem fractures, faunal or avian scavenging, temperature flux (e.g., freeze–thaw) fracturing (see Figure 7.1), rootlet or mycorrhizal leaching, or burning. A photographic record of such changes will be made. The impact of taphonomic change on analyses will be considered during such analysis. See 7.3 for further detail.

Assessment of heat-modified human remains. The methodologies for the analysis of burnt or cremated human bone are largely the same as those used in the analysis of unburned human remains. It is recommended that, where possible, cremated and burnt bone is examined by an anthropologist with particular experience in the analysis of burnt or cremated human remains.[20] The following data will be recorded and assessed on the appropriate recording form and photographs taken as necessary: quantification (weight and particle size), inventory and MNI, biological profile, pathology, nonmetric variation, trauma, and formation processes (e.g., colour, fragmentation patterns). See 8.5 for further detail.

Radiography survey. As mentioned previously, the requirement for routine secondary surveys will be dependent on the nature of the case. It may be that in most cases it will only be necessary to perform a full dental survey. However, in cases where systematic antemortem abuse and/or torture are suspected, a full or limited skeletal radiographic survey may be of benefit to the investigation. The precise approach adopted for each case will be determined by the MMT, and the secondary survey taken following the pathologist's or anthropologist's examination. At the request of the anthropologist, a tertiary radiographic examination may be undertaken to record specific injuries or other pathology, to establish the path of projectiles, and to record unique identifying features or other supplementary information provided by the investigation team.

Photography. The photographer will photograph clothing and personal effects using negative and/or digital format. The anthropologist will enlist the expertise of the photographer to produce a photographic record using conventional 35-mm colour negative film and/or digital imagery. The following will be photographed: the

---

[20] This refers to familiarity with, and expertise in, patterns of distortion and shrinkage of skeletal material and the effect of both on standard anthropological techniques.

skeleton or remains in the anatomical position; characteristics pertaining to ancestry, biological sex, and age; details of significant pathologies; detail illustrating ante- and perimortem trauma; significant taphonomic processes; frontal and occlusal views of the dentition; and other identifying features.

Sampling. Samples will only be taken after examination and analysis. Where samples are taken by the anthropologist, they must sign appropriate forms to that effect. Assistance of the APT may be required to extract some samples. Other biological samples such as hair, entomology, and botany may also be collected after consultation with the appropriate scientific specialist. All samples are to be signed over to the mortuary-based SCE and the sample log and sample recording form filled in. All samples will receive an evidence number issued from the mortuary evidence log.

2.4.5   Completion of the postmortem examination

Upon completion of the postmortem examination, the human remains will be prepared for storage. Fleshed bodies and body parts will be placed into a new body bag or box that will be labelled accordingly, in full. The original body bag or box can be retained for evidential purposes if it is thought relevant by the senior pathologist on consultation with the SCE. Where there are bones with no adhering flesh or tissue, they can be placed into the original skeleton box or packaging if it is clean and undamaged, and the continuity label amended accordingly. Once repackaged, the bodies, body parts, and skeletal human remains will be placed into appropriate storage to await notification of permission to repatriate, in accordance with the respective judicial or authority guidelines.

Upon the conclusion of the postmortem examination, the pathologist and/or anthropologist will complete a report of their findings, including a cause of death if one can be ascertained. If the cause of death is not ascertained, then the pathologist or anthropologist will report this fact. If there is a name or an identification number associated with an individual, it will be checked against any missing persons' register that may be available. Determination of the cause of death remains the responsibility of the pathologist who conducts the postmortem examination, and it will be their duty to pronounce a cause of death and sign a death certificate, in the appropriate manner, for the local authorities. The senior SCE will collate and collect the case evidence form, case identification form, and radiography log, and will pass them to the data entry clerk for processing. The pathologist will also provide all documents that facilitate the appropriate handover or deposition of human remains and personal effects according to the wishes of the bereaved. All reports will be typed following a standard format, and a hard copy of the report will be generated and passed back to the pathologist for careful checking. If the information contained in the final typed report is correct, the pathologist will sign and date the postmortem report.

2.4.6   Final reports

The final reports will follow a consistent format and will include all the information from the relevant recording forms. Both the documentation and the photographic record will be handed to the data entry clerk on completion. The reports will include all handwritten documents and any electronic data. These will be generated by each area of expertise within the mortuary and include the pathologists' (postmortem examination) reports (including radiographer's reports), the anthropologist reports (again including the radiographer's reports), and the SCE's reports. Other specialist reports such as odontology reports will also be completed. The reports produced by external scientific organisations or experts on samples taken for further analysis (e.g., DNA, biological samples) will be integrated into or appended to the final reports. Completion and return of such reports may occur after the mortuary has closed. The case summary and lists of other evidence obtained from the SCE will be completed and signed by all forensic staff involved in the analysis. The purpose of such records is to facilitate completion of the final report, and allow checks and quality control to be undertaken.

2.4.7   Case completion and closure of the mortuary

As with any such process, analysis is not complete until all evidence has been examined and recorded. Reports concerning evidence (e.g., biological samples and ballistics) that has been sent to analytical laboratories may not be received until after the mortuary has closed. Quality control checks and an administrative review will be undertaken during and at the end of the mortuary process or at appropriate intervals in longer-term projects. As cases within the mortuary are completed, the MMT should review and refine the process to provide and maintain the highest possible standard of evidence collection and procedure under the given circumstances. Checks for consistency of coding, recording, and data entry will also be made.

Although this will occur regularly during each working day, prior to closing the mortuary, a thorough cleaning and disinfecting of the autopsy room and associated areas should be carried out, and all equipment and instruments should be thoroughly cleaned and decontaminated. Several types of cleaning solutions and disinfectants can be used in the mortuary, and local policy must be established to control which types and dilutions are necessary for which situations. Further information on the appropriate use of disinfectants and in which situations they should be used can be found in 3.5. Disposal of waste produced as part of the mortuary analysis is another area where strict adherence to local protocols to control segregation, containment, and disposal must be followed to minimise the potential risk of contamination. All waste should be considered as potentially infective clinical waste and treated accordingly, as detailed within the SOPs (3.5.5). Clinical waste includes effluent waste, which relies on an adequate drainage system, and solid waste such as disposables, paper, and some equipment. Such waste should therefore be separated into two main groups: waste for incineration, and waste that can be disposed of into foul water drains. The building and/or its surrounding area should be thoroughly cleaned and disinfected, made safe, and restored to its previous state (as appropriate) before it is handed back to the relevant authorities.

It is necessary to decommission all equipment and buildings used in an investigation. This will involve packing and transporting equipment and unused consumables, returning plant facilities (if hired) or transporting them back to base if owned, and the building/area handover.

It is extremely important to debrief all personnel involved with any phase of an investigation into atrocity crimes or humanitarian programmes. This serves several purposes, including reducing the risk of posttraumatic stress disorder among personnel, an opportunity to reiterate contractual issues such as confidentiality and subjudice, and a chance to obtain feedback into process and management that may be beneficial for future operations.

2.4.8 Information dissemination

As regulated contractually, the case papers and identification forms and their attachments will be disseminated to the appropriate organisations, which could include the investigating authorities, local authorities, commissioning agencies, and local or relevant communities. Exceptionally, and with careful consideration and agreement from the investigating authority and other relevant authorities, organisations, and advisors, it may be appropriate to release case information to a wider audience.

2.4.9 Evidence handover

Evidence of significant legal value and all human remains must be signed over to a central secure storage facility under the custody of a SCE and the relevant authorities. This may include physical evidence such as personal effects, bullets, documents, and any other relevant items that may be required in court proceedings or that require further testing. Digital photograph records, photographic logs, videotapes, handwritten evidence logs, and discs of computer data will also be transported to a secure central storage facility under the custody of a SCE. The photographic negatives (if present) will be couriered to an accredited laboratory in appropriately sealed and labelled packaging in the custody of a SCE. All items must be signed for on receipt. Copies of signed receipts must be handed to the senior SCE for retention.

Antemortem data provided by an appropriate external organisation is vital to the positive identification of the deceased. Where a positive identification has been made, the antemortem data should be integrated with the appropriate mortuary records during the mortuary process when possible. Evidence and human remains that have been recovered and analysed for nonlegal reasons will be signed over to identification agencies, NGOs, or communities as appropriate to each case. The human remains and any personal items will be returned to the families or the local authorities or identifying agency upon a signature, under the custody of the SCE and other interested parties. Bodies will only be released to families on the instructions of the investigating authority after consultation with the families' representatives, where possible. It may be possible to release a body immediately after the post-mortem examination is complete, but the simultaneous release of all the deceased from a particular gravesite to the identified families or to the local authority may be more appropriate in some circumstances.

When a positive identification is made, the next of kin must be informed that the investigating authority or the delegated agency has samples and personal possessions belonging to the deceased. If any personal item relevant to a court proceeding must be detained, then the family must be informed. The next of kin must receive a copy of the retention form for the human remains and property and will have the opportunity to decide on the subsequent form of funeral (e.g., burial, cremation) for the human remains. The next of kin must be asked to sign the retention form, a copy of which will be attached to the case papers. Case files will then be transported to a secure central storage facility awaiting handover to the appropriate authorities. Where remains are not identified, they will be handed over to the relevant authority taking responsibility for them. Regardless of whether identified, a signature will be required to document the handover of the body recovery reports, photographs/negatives, radiographs, thermal and digital images, digital cards, photographic logs and videotapes, handwritten evidence logs, and discs/CDs of the computer data. A copy of the case papers and identification forms and their attachments will be handed over to the investigating authority upon signature.

2.4.10 Summary: Phase 3 – Mortuary process

Goal. Where appropriate, forensic evidence and human remains recovered in areas under investigation will undergo detailed investigative and scientific analysis to assist in forensic or humanitarian identifications and criminal investigations. These protocols represent the minimum set of scientific procedures to be considered when undertaking forensic investigations of human remains and associated evidence.

Planning. Before setting up a mortuary, the SCM, senior pathologist, senior anthropologist, and liaison officer will consider and determine the investigation parameters. Following this, they will assess the necessary requirements in terms of equipment, facilities, and personnel (type and numbers). They will ensure that health and safety and security risk assessments are undertaken and mitigation strategies developed. They will also identify suitable mortuary premises. To complete these tasks, it will be necessary to communicate with local authorities and communities and access relevant antemortem data or records.

Site preparation. The necessary logistics, equipment movement, and siting activities identified during the planning phase will be implemented by the MMT prior to commencement of mortuary operation processes (the team includes a mortuary manager, senior pathologist, senior SCE, senior anthropologist, radiographer, and senior APT). Risk assessments and mitigation strategies will be reevaluated continually throughout this process.

Evidence integrity and custody. All evidence and human remains entering and leaving the mortuary facility will strictly follow custody procedures as specified by these protocols. All material will be suitably packaged, stored, and documented to maintain its evidential integrity under the responsibility of the senior SCE.

Postmortem examination I – Radiography. Body bags brought to the mortuary will undergo a primary survey in order to locate any UXO, metallic, or other radiopaque material. Further surveys may be necessary during later stages of the examination.

Postmortem examination II – Pathology. Fleshed or partly fleshed human remains and other evidence will be examined for evidence of cause and manner of death and identity. Appropriate sampling, photography, documentation, and recording will be undertaken. Coordination between the pathologist, radiographer, and anthropologist will precede examination and any final report.

Postmortem examination III – Anthropology. Human skeletal and burnt human skeletal remains will be examined to determine the minimum number of individuals and to reconstruct a biological profile (ancestry, biological sex, age at death, parity status, living stature, handedness, trauma, pathology, and dental morphology) as appropriate for each individual. Appropriate sampling, photography, documentation, and recording will be undertaken.

Documentation and recording. All processes within the mortuary are accompanied by recording forms, logs, and lists, which will be completed by appropriate personnel. A digital and/or negative format photographic record of relevant information will be kept. Copies of all documentation will be made and kept by the SCE. Data entered onto such forms will be entered into an electronic database.

Identification data. All information derived from this process that can contribute to identifying the deceased must be collated in such a way to allow that data to be passed on, as appropriate, to the relevant authorities, NGOs, and communities. The data must be presented in a manner that is compatible with data collected by other organisations responsible for collecting antemortem information. It is essential that prior to the collection of antemortem data, full consultation should take place between the relevant scientists and the psychosocial experts working on the case to ensure that the data that are most relevant to biological identification (presumptive identification) are collected in the most meaningful and useful form.

Case completion. A case is considered complete when all records and reports have been written, and other documents copied and entered into appropriate databases. All necessary quality control checks and administrative reviews must also have been made.

Mortuary closure. When all cases have been complete, the premises cleaned and disinfected, waste removed, personnel debriefed, information disseminated, evidence handed over, and equipment packed and removed from site, the mortuary can be closed by the MMT, and the building can be handed over to relevant authorities.

2.5 Appendix: Equipment lists

Table 2–1. *Field equipment*

Personal Protective Equipment

- Paper coveralls
- Overshoes

- Rubber boots
- Disposable masks

- Heavy-duty gloves
- Work gloves

- Surgical gloves
- Safety glasses

Survey Station

- Survey flags
- Grid pegs
- Survey spray paint
- Line string & level
- Half prism set

- Permatrace
- Drawing boards
- Compass
- Tape measures
- Planning frames

- Ranging poles
- Probe
- Scale rules
- Total station & Tripod

- SDR logger
- Survey software
- Dumpy level
- Site logs
- GPS

Geophysics Station

- Earth resistivity meter

- GPR Ground-penetrating radar

- Ground conductivity (electromagnetics)

- Magnetometer
- Metal detector

Excavation Station

- Paint brushes
- Scalpels
- Wooden tools
- Plastic tools
- Spoon

- Hand pick
- Hand shovel
- 4" WHS trowel
- Shovel
- Spade

- Long-handled spade
- Mattock
- Pick
- Flat blade hoe
- Machete

- Secateurs
- Plastic buckets
- Plastic colanders
- Wheelbarrow
- Tube/pump

SCE Station

- Scene of crime number set
- Self-sealing evidence bags

- Metal evidence tags
- Waterproof labels
- Evidence sealing tape

- Evidence seals
- Plastic bags
- Paper bags

- Body boxes (skeleton)
- Body bags

Photography Station

- Photo boards & numbers
- Photo scales

- North arrow
- SLR film camera
- Film & Videotapes

- Digital video camera
- Digital photo software

- 1GB Memory cards

Stationary and General

- Medical kit
- Hazard tape
- Duck tape
- Masking tape
- 6-in. nails
- Flight cases
- Tables & chairs

- Laptop
- Printer & scanner
- Power converter
- Power boards
- Extension cables
- Two-way radios
- Electric fans

- CD-Rs & DVD-Rs
- 200GB External HD
- 1GB Flash Drives
- Stationary
- Permanent markers
- Paper
- Notebooks

- Poster carrier
- A4 lever arch
- Clipboards
- Folders
- Batteries & charger
- Cling film
- Cool boxes

Cleaning and Cooking

- Water containers
- Washing brushes
- Soap/liquid soap

- Cleaning products
- Mops/brushes
- Blue paper roll

- Toilet roll
- Portable cooker
- Refuse sacks

- Kettles/pans
- Cooking utensils
- Eating utensils

Table 2–2. *Mortuary equipment*

X-Ray Receiving and Office

- Laptop PC running MS Office and printer
- Trestle table

Fluoroscopy Station

- C-arm fluoroscope (image intensifier), digital c/w two-monitor trolley, last image hold, large hard disk storage, CD writer or zip drive, and thermal printer
- Carbon-fibre fluoroscopy table
- Lead rubber apron (0.25 mm lead equivalent) – protection at front and back
- Lead rubber thyroid shields (0.35–0.5 mm lead equivalent)
- Lead protective glasses
- Lead protective screens
- Lead rubber gloves – pair (0.5 mm lead equivalent)
- Trestle-style table
- Illuminated viewing box

X-Ray Station

- Portable (not mobile) high-frequency x-ray machine, kV range: 40–110 kV, 80–100 mAs max complete with stand; high-specification veterinary unit may be suitable
- Lead protective screens
- A & E emergency trolley incorporating x-ray cassette tray
- Portable direct digital x-ray unit with computer viewing station
- Foam pads – assorted for positioning
- Small sand bags – assorted for positioning
- Lead rubber apron (0.25 mm lead equivalent) – protection at front and back
- Trestle-style table

Dental X-Ray Station

- Dental x-ray machine
- Direct digital dental x-ray system
- Patient/cadaver trolley
- Foam pads – assorted for positioning
- Small sand bags – assorted for positioning
- Lead rubber apron (0.25 mm lead equivalent) – protection at front and back
- Trestle-style table
- Paralleling dental film holders
- Dental film forceps
- Actinic light marker

Film Viewing

- Trestle table
- PC with 17-in. high-resolution monitor

Pathology Examination Equipment

- Trestle-style tables
- Autopsy knives (PM40)
- Scalpel no. 22
- Disposable brain knives
- Forceps (toothed)
- Forceps (toothless)
- Lion-toothed forceps (for removing teeth)
- Rib shears
- Rib knives
- Bags
- Scissors, 4 in. & 6 in.
- Steel probes
- Handsaw
- Electric oscillating saws
- Chisel
- Rulers/tape measures
- Mallet
- Head blocks
- Dissecting boards
- Ladles
- PM needles/string
- Syringes/needles
- Stretchers
- Cotton wool
- Basins
- Body bags/boxes
- Coloured tape (3″ duct tape yellow/red/green)
- Waterproof labels for clothing
- Sharps bin

(cont.)

Table 2–2 *(cont.)*

Anthropology Assessment Equipment

- Sliding calipers (0.01 mm)
- Spreading calipers
- Osteometric board
- Tape measure (plastic, flexible without metal ends)
- Acetone soluble adhesive
- Acetone
- Sieve 8.00 mm
- Sieve 4.00 mm
- Sieve 2.00 mm
- Sieve 1.00 mm
- Weighing scales (0.001 mg)
- One table per anthropologist, plus two extras (white or blue tops, alternatively a white or blue cloth)
- Work station/table

- Plastic colanders
- Plastic trays, flat-bottomed bowls
- Paint brushes
- Toothbrushes
- Wooden tools
- Wooden kebab skewers
- Plastic tools
- Dental tools
- Tweezers – plastic
- Probes
- Dissecting set
- Dissecting dish
- Rotary saw
- Hack saw
- Hack saw blade

- Bone cutters
- Low-power microscope
- Lens cleaning tissue
- Magnifier with light source
- Container of glass beads or sand
- Casting materials
- Defleshing equipment: large pot (15–20 L), heat source, muslin or net bags, biotox/bleach, scalpels, forceps, tweezers, large knife, trays
- Relevant anthropology assessment forms and logs
- Checklist

Anthropological Reference Material

- Reference books
- Mckern-Stewart pubic symphysis plastic cast set (manufactured by Darrell Van Buren, Inc.)
- Suchey-Brooks pubic symphysis plastic cast set for males
- Suchey-Brooks pubic symphysis plastic cast set for females

- Lovejoy et al. auricular aging techniques photographic set (produced by the Department of Sociology and Anthropology, Kent State University)
- Iscan-Loth sternal rib end plastic cast sets for females and males
- Plastic human skeleton

- Resin human skeleton
- Human skeleton poster
- Human musculature poster

SCE-SCE

- Folding Magnifier
- Compass (Directional)
- Torch and spare batteries

- Tape measures, 5 m & 30 m
- Sterilised trowels (for soil sampling)

- Cling film
- Fingerprinting kit
- Relevant evidence forms and logs

Protective Clothing

- Theatre suits/scrubs
- Disposable plastic aprons
- Disposable Tyvex suits/gowns
- Heavy-duty gloves
- Surgical gloves

- Disposable masks
- Safety glasses
- Needle/sharp proof gloves
- Rubber boots
- Arm protectors
- Protective hats

- Overshoes
- First aid kits
- Clogs

Storage and Labelling

- Chest freezer
- Refrigerator
- Evidence trunks – lockable
- Padlocks and keys
- Flat pack boxes

- Plastic sample pots (universals/histology)
- Clear sealable polythene bags
- Freezer tape
- Retractable needle syringes, 5 ml & 10 ml

- Metal evidence tags
- Adhesive labels
- Biohazard labels or tape
- Ladders/steps
- Fire extinguishers

- Evidence bags – plastic
- Evidence bags – paper
- Body box – skeleton
- Body bags

- Fluoride oxalate bottles
- Evidence sealing tape
- Numbered seals

- Fire blanket
- Bag sealer

Photographic Equipment

- Camera and associated equipment
- 55-mm micro lens
- Ring flash
- Film
- Photo scales
- Photo board and numbers

- Flash unit
- AC mains adapter
- Reflective umbrellas
- Sync cord
- Shutter release cable
- Electronic light meter
- Tripods

- Light box
- Blue tack (nongreasy)
- Background fabric (several colours)

Office Equipment

- Tables
- Chairs
- Adhesive tape
- Stationary
- Guillotine

- Clipboards
- Plain paper
- Notebooks
- Report files
- Folders

- A4 lever arch folders
- White board
- Board markers

Computer Hardware and Consumables

- PC work stations preloaded with evidence recording database and evidence forms
- Printer
- Scanner

- Toner cartridges
- Laminator
- Laminator cartridge
- Power cables, electricity extension cables, adaptor plugs

- Floppy discs
- CD-Rs
- Batteries

Cleaning Equipment

- Washing up bowls
- Sponges
- Multipurpose cloths
- Scourers
- Washing brushes
- Blue paper rolls
- Toilet rolls
- Industrial washer/dryer

- Disinfectant (halogenated tertiary amine)
- Buffered formaldehyde
- Mop and bucket
- Hand soap
- Forensic drying cabinet
- Detergent (Teepol)
- Air freshener/deodoriser

- Self-sealing refuse bins
- Refuse bags
- Ethanol
- Clothes line
- Plastic pegs
- Clinical waste bags
- Cable ties (sealing waste bags)
- Fly spray or equivalent

II

Standard operating procedures

3

Health and safety

Alison Anderson, Ian Hanson, David Schofield,
Hendrik Scholtz, Jeanine Vellema, and Mark Viner

3.1 Introduction

Every phase of the investigation of an atrocity crime incurs a number of potential risks to the 'safety' of team members. In this chapter, unless indicated otherwise, 'safety' refers to the management of injury, health, psychological, and security hazards. It is vital that all aspects of these risks are assessed before an investigation takes place and that they are constantly reviewed during the investigation. Risks must be mitigated against in a responsible and practical way, and safety strategies have to be dynamic because some risks can change or arise for the first time during the course of an investigation. Risks are often highly specific to the circumstances and conditions of the work and the environment in which it is carried out (Schofield, 2004). Generally, most aspects of risk assessment and related safety matters will be dealt with during the mission planning phase of an investigation and will not be discussed in detail in related operating procedures. These rules for safety are based on current best practice (UK) and use guidelines designed for the specific risks of investigations into atrocity crimes. When working with other agencies, governments, and the military, it is recommended that any higher standards should always be adopted, but lower ones should not. This chapter begins by setting out a typical statement of intent that an organisation might make as required by the Health and Safety at Work etc. Act 1974 (S2[3]). This is followed by an 'organisation section' or 'who does what', allocating functions to logical parties, and an 'arrangements section' or 'how to do it', in which personnel are guided on how to carry out those functions to ensure that they maintain the highest standards and ensure consistency. In this chapter, the word 'wet' is used to denote areas that are also known as 'dirty' or 'contaminated' as distinct from dry and clean.

3.1.1 Statement of intent

The statement of intent of an organisation should recognise that its most important resource is their employees, or those specifically contracted to work with them on particular projects. Ensuring the health and safety of employees is an integral part of all work activity, and organisations should be committed to having a systematic approach to health and safety management. This should focus on compliance, as far as is reasonably practicable, with all relevant enforcement agencies. They should work with external bodies to further their understanding of health and safety management and practice. Safe working practices and systems, based on risk assessments, are central to all operational activity. An organisation should ensure that there are effective procedures for consultation on health and safety with all employees and their safety representatives. Health and safety concerns from employees, and others involved in or affected by operations must be taken into account. Those contracted to deliver services as a component of any project should be required to demonstrate their health and safety competence. It is essential to ensure that buildings that are to be used for work provide a safe and healthy work environment. Managers, at all levels of an organisation, must be responsible and accountable for visible and proactive leadership in implementing this policy, issuing appropriate advice and information and maintaining adequate supervision. Employees also have a critical role to play, through active partnership, in developing and complying with systems introduced to keep them safe. The responsibility for health and safety is a shared one. All employees have a responsibility to comply with health and safety policies and procedures, to take care of themselves and colleagues, and to bring to their employer's notice health and safety concerns that may lead to accident or injury. The employer must allocate appropriate resources for the implementation of its health and safety policy, with emphasis being placed on the education of employees in health and safety matters. Progress in compliance in achieving these goals should be measured by appropriate proactive and reactive monitoring, through the use of review mechanisms and by independent auditing.

3.2 General policy

An employing organisation must, as far as is reasonably practicable, comply with the provisions of all relevant health and safety legislation. Specifically, they must provide, within the framework of law and good practice, safe and healthy working conditions, equipment, and systems of work and safety equipment for all their employees, consultants, contractors, visitors, and others. They also have a responsibility for the health, safety and welfare of other people who may be affected by their activities. All employees should be aware of their responsibility under legislation, to work in a safe manner to prevent accidents to both themselves and others. Health and safety issues should be on the agenda at all management meetings, supervisory meetings, union liaison meetings, staff and any special meetings that may be called to cover particular health and safety topics, and specific health and safety training and induction meetings. These meetings may also serve as a forum for staff to voice concerns and to make recommendations for improvement.

The recommendations contained in this chapter should not be considered to supersede statutory or any other regulations and codes of practice that are relevant to those working in the investigation of atrocity crimes around the world. All paid staff members, consultants, volunteers, or other people working on any forensic investigation missions or projects must be directed to the organisational health and safety policy, and they are required to read it prior to commencement of any work. In addition to the designated health and safety officer's (HSO's) responsibilities, all paid staff, consultants, volunteers, and visitors must exercise personal responsibility for their own and others' safety in all places of work. It is the duty of all staff to cooperate with the organisation's management in implementing this policy and to do everything possible to avoid injury to themselves or others. Health and safety considerations must take precedence in all instances of conflict with regard to working practices. If volunteers are involved in projects, then they are subject to the same rules and procedures as employees.

To comply with legal and regulatory requirements, an organisation must maintain a safe facility, one or more safe means of access, and a safe working environment. It must also provide safe systems of work, and safe storage facilities. The organisation must also prepare and review a written statement of safety policy, provide all other suitable information and instruction, and provide appropriate training and supervision. Employees are required to take care of their own and other people's safety and to cooperate with the management and others to allow them to comply with their statutory obligations. Staff must not intentionally or recklessly interfere with or misuse anything provided in the interest of health and safety or welfare. It is ultimately the responsibility of the organisation's chief executive officer (CEO), who will decide on resource allocation and action regarding the health and safety of staff. The CEO may delegate this authority to the senior safety adviser (SSA). The SSA will assist investigation teams in assessing and preparing for investigations prior to travel. If required, the SSA will visit sites in the initial stages to assess local risks and will liaise with safety staff of any other agencies involved in the investigation. The SSA is responsible for the selection and communication of arrangements of this policy. Other functions include safety performance monitoring, support of operations, staff consultation, communication (external and internal), ensuring general safety competence, control of contractors, and designing safe systems of work.

For every operation, one member of the excavation management team and one of the Mortuary Management Team (MMT) will be appointed as site HSOs. They will advise on the local implementation of legislation, policy, risk assessments, and maintenance of safe working practices. HSOs will keep in regular contact with the SSA and seek guidance and assistance where necessary. In circumstances where x-ray or other equipment employing ionising radiation is to be used, it is essential to appoint a qualified radiation physicist as radiation protection advisor (RPA). The senior radiographer, reporting to the HSO, will have responsibility for all matters relating to radiation safety and will act as radiation protection supervisor. He or she will take advice from the RPA, undertaking risk assessments and advising the HSO on the local implementation of radiation legislation, policy, and maintenance of safe working practices.

HSOs can be consulted on any safety-related matters and will ensure that all designated responsible person(s) and all staff follow safe working practices and maintain a healthy work environment. It is the role of the SSA to ensure that the health and safety policy is implemented and followed by all members of staff. The HSO is responsible for ensuring that safe working practices are exercised in the course of investigations, and that all members of staff are aware of the health and safety policy and all safety aspects of their own operations. All site and mortuary supervisors are responsible for ensuring that all staff, consultants, volunteers, and visitors (where applicable) are aware of all instructions and relevant information relating to the use of tools, equipment, and materials at their workplace.

Prior to commencement of site or mortuary operations, the management team responsible for setting up the project will address any safety issues in the planning stage in consultation with the SSA and HSOs. A method statement will be prepared where necessary, and the site supervisor will be informed of all relevant safety issues. Site and mortuary management teams will provide site-specific inductions to all staff, consultants, volunteers, or visitors before they start work or gain access to a site. This must be consistent with the skills and experience of the visitor. Any staff, consultants, volunteers, or visitors who require clarification of safe working practices should, in the first instance, discuss the matter with the site supervisor. If the matter is not resolved at this point, it should be discussed with an HSO, and in case of an unsatisfactory resolution, the matter can be taken up with the overall project manager who will arbitrate after seeking advice from the SSA.

In advance of the commencement of work, a risk assessment will be carried out for each site. This will be undertaken by the individual with overall responsibility for safety at the site or mortuary, usually a member of the management team. He or she will, if necessary, liaise with another experienced HSO on any specific problems. A copy of this risk assessment will be provided for the HSO. The HSO will ensure that risk assessments are completed and implemented and that after a site is closed, the risk assessment documentation is retained for monitoring and for the organisation's health and safety archive. Copies will be submitted to the SSA for checking.

Specific areas that the HSO is responsible for include carrying out any Control of Substances Hazardous to Health (COSHH) assessments required for an operation. They will also supervise and manage manual handling issues and the investigation and reporting of any accidents, incidents, or dangerous occurrences. It is the responsibility of the project manager to ensure that sufficient resources are available to deal with all relevant safety issues as required for a particular site. A copy of the current organisational Health and Safety Policy, risk assessment, and a copy of the 'Health and Safety Executive Health and Safety Law poster (1999)' will be prominently displayed at the organisation's UK base (if relevant) and, where practicable, at other places of work. All staff are encouraged to report all safety issues to their HSO, and if no satisfactory resolution is found, to the overall management and, ultimately, the CEO. No members of staff, consultants, volunteers, or visitors will be allowed access to any site without prior agreement and knowledge of the HSO and the project manager. Any accident or incident will be investigated by the HSO and/or the SSA, and all injuries or accidents must be entered into the site accident book; this is kept by the HSO at each site. Serious accidents will be immediately reported to the SSA, who will decide on action regarding the 'Reporting of Injuries, Diseases and Dangerous Occurrences Regulations 1985'. In addition, on completion of fieldwork, the site accident book will be checked by the HSO, and any incidents occurring on the site will be recorded and kept on file for future reference. Yearly accident and incident statistics will be compiled by the organisation. To comply with the Health and Safety (First Aid) Regulations (1981), and the associated Code of Practice, the HSO will verify that there are adequate first aid facilities at all sites. It will be the role of the HSO to ensure that a first aid kit is available and that a qualified first-aider (with an up-to-date HSO-approved certificate) is assigned to every project. The SSA will ensure that a sufficiently large number of staff is trained in first aid to cover all sites.

The HSO is responsible for the maintenance and issuing of any and all safety equipment used on site. They will ensure that all equipment is in good working order and that it is only issued to personnel who have been trained in its use and have the appropriate and up-to-date certificates. All equipment will be regularly inspected by qualified staff or independent contractors to ensure its continued safe operation. All new equipment will be assessed for any associated risks before being used. Any member of staff asked to use new equipment will be instructed in its use and informed in how to operate the equipment safely. The SSA will review staff training at least annually. In addition, extra training requirements will be reviewed on a project basis. All HSOs and management will receive formal training from the SSA or other specialists to allow them to carry out their roles as specified in this policy.

Any contractors involved in forensic investigations will be asked to provide the contracting organisation with a copy of their health and safety policy, and will be provided with a copy of the contracting organisation's health and safety policy. Subcontractors will also be required to provide a copy of their site-specific risk assessment and will be provided with a copy of the contracting organisation's risk assessment. Liaison will take place between those responsible from each organisation. Any contractor will be required to provide copies of their COSHH, if appropriate, and general risk assessments. Any contractor not operating safely as determined by the HSO will have their contract reviewed. No subcontracting should be allowed without the express permission of the contracting organisation. Every site should have at least one designated fire warden.

Statutory safety requirements are the starting point for all staff and visitors, and the incumbent safe operating practices and procedures should be adopted as organisational policy. All staff should be aware that some local contractors and their personnel may have a lower awareness and practice of safety than is required. Taking into account the practical problems encountered during field operations in post war countries (e.g., running out of supplies or electricity shortages), it should be recognised that it may not always be possible for the working environment to be made safe to a satisfactory level. In such cases, staff should leave the area of danger and immediately report the conditions to the HSO (or the site supervisor). Staff must never engage in any activity or enter any area that is patently unsafe. They must report their concern to the person in charge of the workplace. Individuals should never be allowed or required to work while their ability or alertness is impaired by fatigue, illness, or other causes that might expose the individual or others to injury. Anyone known to be under the influence of alcohol and/or recreational or other drugs, which impair their performance, should not be allowed to work while in that condition. Working hours should be set by the management teams, based on practical needs, environmental circumstances, and the health and safety of personnel. Regular breaks will be set and enforced by the management teams and/or HSOs.

Only qualified, competent, and authorised personnel are permitted to operate plant, machinery, and other equipment (including chain saws) or repair and service any equipment. Defective equipment must be taken out of use and reported to the person in charge of the workplace. Where reasonable, all plant equipment must have relevant certification, and operators must have appropriate licences. The HSO should inspect licences and certificates prior to a machine being permitted to operate on any site. Where staff are likely to work in proximity to plant, the implications of this must be covered in the site risk assessment. Personnel will work with the appropriate personal protective equipment (PPE) and, where required, a lookout or 'banksman' will be designated. Staff must be aware of the movement of heavy mobile site plant. When approaching such plant, they must assure that the driver has seen them and signal their intentions. When such plant operates in an excavation area, the archaeological supervisor should appoint a person to act as banksman to assure drivers are aware of the presence of others and to warn of dangers caused by the plant. Vehicle or plant access and egress points must be marked as such.

Lone working on site is not permitted under any circumstances. On some projects, it may be acceptable for a lone representative to carry out a 'watching brief' as long as another individual (e.g., a contractor) is working with that person. In all circumstances, one person should remain in a position where a clear view of nearby machinery is maintained. Volunteers or members of the public are not allowed into mortuary sites or associated offices unless accompanied by a staff member. Staff working on sites where contractors are present must ensure that the contractor's personnel are aware of their presence and of the work they intend to carry out. Contractors are to be asked about the work they are carrying out and how this might affect forensic staff.

All staff on site or in the mortuary must wear appropriate PPE. Any conventional safety concerns must be considered in light of security matters (e.g., highly visible vests may not be advisable if staff members are potential targets for snipers). When dealing with PPE, extreme climatic conditions have to be taken into consideration (e.g., hard hats in hot conditions). Safety levels must always be kept at their highest, but the rules must be appropriate and practical for specific site or mortuary conditions. All staff must maintain a high standard of personal hygiene, including regularly washing their hands and any other exposed parts of the body that might have become soiled while working. Site welfare facilities must include access to safe drinking water, adequate changing facilities, and suitable and sufficient toilet and washing facilities, including warm and cold running water. In addition, there must be suitable and sufficient eating and resting facilities.

3.3   Legal requirements

The organisational safety policy will, as a minimum, comply with UK statute where relevant and other national statutory requirements when working abroad. A summary of some of the relevant legal obligations can be referred to in *Health and Safety in Field Archaeology* (Allen and St John Holt, 1997). Apart from commenting on the legislation, this guide also outlines the responsibilities of employers and employees in planning, executing, maintaining, and analysing health and safety rules before, during, and after excavations. A summary of relevant UK statutory instruments is found in 3.7 and includes the following: Workplace (Health, Safety and Welfare) Regulations 1992; Health and Safety Information for Employees (Modifications and Repeals) Regulations 1995; Construction (Health, Safety and Welfare) Regulations 1996; Carriage of Dangerous Goods (Classification, Packaging and Labelling) and Use of Transportable Pressure Receptacles Regulations 1996; Fire Precautions (Workplace) Regulations 1997; Lifting Operations and Lifting Equipment Regulations 1998; Management of Health and Safety at Work Regulations 1999; Ionising Radiations Regulations 1999; Ionising Radiations (Medical Exposure) Regulations 2000; Personal Protective Equipment Regulations 2002; Chemicals (Hazard Information and Packaging for Supply) Regulations 2002; Health and Safety (Miscellaneous Amendments) Regulations 2002; Control of Asbestos at Work Regulations 2002; Control of Lead at Work Regulations 2002; Control of Substances Hazardous to Health Regulations 2002; Dangerous Substances and Explosive Atmospheres Regulations 2002; Control of Substances Hazardous to Health (Amendment) Regulations 2003; and Management of Health and Safety at Work and Fire Precautions (Workplace) (Amendment) Regulations 2003.

3.4   Health and safety in the field

Health and safety for excavation processes is based on international health and safety guidelines (Allen and St John Holt, 1997; Kneller, 1998; Kneller, 1999, Office of the United Nations, n.d.; many of the UK statutory instruments are mentioned in 3.3 and described in more detail in 3.7) for archaeological work, construction, dealing with human remains, and related topics. Some other publications are relevant to this area (e.g. Roberts, 1999; Wisner and Adams, 2002). Risk assessment for field investigations covers the same areas encountered in archaeological sites but also includes concerns that are specific to international investigations and postconflict zones. Staff dealing with particular issues will be directed to specific codes of practice, either written by their employing organisation or adopted/adapted from other recognised sources. Discussion of some practical problems of health and safety on mass grave sites (field) are considered in Wright (2005) and Wright and Hanson (in press 2008). The following are examples of hazards that can be encountered in forensic excavations and should be considered, assessed, risk-rated, and mitigated against: security; terrain; accidental injury; infectious disease; hygiene; water ingress; travel; unexploded ordnance (UXO); poisonous and dangerous flora and fauna; deep excavation; equipment; climatic extremes; hazardous materials (e.g., contaminated land and garbage); and posttraumatic stress disorder (PTSD) (Office of the United Nations Security Coordinator, 1998; National Centre for Post Traumatic Stress Disorder, 2001a and 2001b; Wisner and Adams, 2002; World Health Organization [WHO], 2004).

Security is always of paramount concern when working in areas being investigated for atrocity crimes or when providing assistance for humanitarian reasons and mass fatality incidents. Security helps provide a safe working environment. Each team will have a designated security officer, usually the HSO. Security may be needed for personnel protection, evidence integrity, and contamination control. Security for field teams is the responsibility of the management and must be assessed before deployment. In some circumstances, team security may be provided by an investigating or governing authority; however, in such cases, the organisation involved should have such a provision assessed by independent specialists. Scenarios giving rise to security concerns are likely to be those where an investigation may encounter local political opposition or may be situated in a geographical area where the local populace, or parts of it, do not want investigations to occur. To prevent incidences of protest or violence, site access may need to be limited and controlled. Security staff may be purposely contracted to prevent loss of, or interference with, evidence and to maintain the chain of custody of evidence. Security for personnel should allow team members to work, live, and travel without unacceptable risk. Security for a site will protect the nature, attributes, and content of the site while investigations and examination are underway. Security for evidence will maintain integrity at a site before and after recovery, and during transport and subsequent storage.

A risk assessment of potential hazards to health and safety will be carried out for every investigation. Assessment should begin before ground operations start and continue as necessary. Each team will have a designated HSO. Risks will be identified, rated, and mitigated against by the application of appropriate strategies whenever possible (e.g., use of protective clothing, masks, safety glasses, and gloves while handling human remains). The investigative strategy on site should be flexible and respond to both security and health and safety issues. The health and safety risk assessment, including mitigation measures, will be disseminated to all staff members before groundwork begins. All staff and visitors to a site will be given a health and safety induction specific to that site. All other organisations involved with the site works should exchange health and safety documents with the lead organisation and come to agreement on specific and acknowledged risks.

Adequate medical facilities and trained first aid staff will be available on site. Location, contact numbers, and journey method and times to emergency treatment facilities should be assessed for each site. Medical evacuation insurance and contracts should be in place. Prospective team members will be informed of the medical requirements of the mission and given sufficient time to implement them. This usually concerns physical and medical fitness levels, inoculations, and preventative medication. The medical requirements aim to allow personnel to efficiently complete allocated tasks with minimal risk to themselves and other team members.

Explosive ordnance disposal (EOD) officers will be available for investigations that have a risk of UXO to teams and associated personnel in, on, or around a site and/or the routes of travel and place of work or rest. Areas of a site assessed or in use must be made safe before any team works are carried out. EOD officers should be available for the whole process of these site works. All team members will undergo an ordnance induction course where relevant to an investigation.

Grave sites and places of disposal for clandestine burials may also be rubbish tips and waste ground that is, or has been, used for dumping refuse. Some may have been subsequently deliberately littered with metal waste by the perpetrators of the crime to prevent adequate EOD identification procedures (as witnessed in Kosovo). Ground hazards might include materials such as medical and chemical waste, sharp objects, and building materials such as asbestos. To work on a site known as the 'Old Firing Range' brings with it associated hazards that may extend beyond the obvious. One such site in Kosovo also had evidence suggesting that it had been used for chemical weapons testing (Figure 3–1) prior to the crimes under investigation. Services may also run through sites, and these need assessment. Procedures must be amended appropriately to deal with these.

Many international forensic sites are in remote locations in climates that may be unfamiliar to team members. Working on steep slopes or in humid tropical environments may expose team members to increased risk of heat stroke or physical injury. These risks will be assessed and work procedures amended appropriately by the management team. Extremes of heat and cold and those aspects of the environment that can be managed (i.e., clothing, work rate, fluid and electrolyte intake) need to be considered. Managers will distinguish between thermal stress and thermal discomfort, the former being likely to affect health. Measurement of the environmental 'envelope' (air temperature, air movement, and relative humidity) will be carried out. Where practicable, staff will be acclimatised with light duties in the first instance.

Figure 3–1. Evidence recovered during the investigation of a mass grave site in the Former Yugoslavia strongly suggested that the area had previously been used as a chemical weapons testing site. *Source:* Margaret Cox.

Injury can occur in any environment that involves manual labour, deep and shallow excavation, and heavy machinery use. Excavating mass graves is in many ways similar to a commercial construction site. All site staff will be shown proper use of tools and behaviour around machinery by the designated HSO. Depending on geology, soils (especially sandy soils and gravels) may be unstable in section at as little as 70 cm in depth. Redeposited, water-soaked, or dry soil can be unstable at any depth. Any excavation that is more than 50 cm deep should be assessed by the senior archaeologist, HSO, and logistics officer. Appropriate stepping and shoring measures may be introduced at an appropriate depth to prevent collapse and slumping. Heavy machinery and transport often operates on forensic sites. All staff should be familiar with how this equipment operates and how to behave in its proximity. Specialist equipment should only be used by those with the specialist training, and such training should be provided if necessary. Staff should be clear as to the proper use of hand tools and other site equipment. All equipment should be used for its proper function, kept clean, maintained, and stored properly. Cleanliness is also essential to avoid contaminating sites and evidence with material from other contexts, and should be built into normal working practice; all cleaning processes should be logged to demonstrate that contamination could not have occurred.

Risks of disease may be heightened in some mission areas and on some sites. Environment may bring risk of disease due to geographic location combined with latitude and other environmental parameters. This can include such conditions as malaria, meningitis or bilharzia. Sites may have biohazards from organic rubbish or medical waste. Forensic evidence and recent human remains may bring risk of diseases such as hepatitis, although a recent report suggests that corpses do not pose a serious risk of spreading disease and infection (Ball, 2005). Appropriate programmes of vaccination and immunisation must be implemented and certified prior to deployment. Obtaining clean drinking and washing water is vital to avoid such conditions as gastric infection, associated gut parasites, or bacterial infections (e.g., of the ear). It is common in some environments to be exposed to toxic and poisonous plants and dangerous mammals, rodents, and insects on forensic sites. Team members should have appropriate protection in terms of clothing, repellents, and medication. Awareness of potential hazards should be researched, and the team briefed.

Post-traumatic stress disorder (PTSD) can affect anyone working in a stressful environment at any time. No one is immune to this condition, which can arise as a result of significant triggers, whether they are apparently traumatic or otherwise (i.e., PTSD may be incremental). Measures to deal with and mitigate stress and trauma incurred during and after operations will be implemented. This may be in the form of work breaks or holidays and will include regular debriefings (discussed further in 10.6). Advice should be sought from psychologists specialising in this area and is likely to include appropriate interview techniques, peer counselling, and self-awareness training.

Forensic scenes, especially if they contain human remains, should be examined using strictly enforced and high standards of hygiene. Measures must be taken to minimise health risks to staff and visitors, to prevent risks within and without the site, and to prevent evidential contamination. Separate mess and food storage facilities must be available to maintain hygienic food and water supplies and a hygienic environment maintained for the preparation and consumption of meals. Personnel should not contaminate the living or 'clean' working areas with soiled boots, clothing, equipment, or evidence. Appropriate protective clothing, ablution, and disposal facilities must be available to prevent contaminated and soiled equipment and clothing from leaving the site and to allow for the safe removal of waste. Clothing, boots, and equipment must be cleaned, stored, or disposed of appropriately. Some contaminated material will have to be disposed of as clinical waste. This is an expensive process, and it must be adequately resourced at the planning stage. Suitable water for use on site for ablutions and other needs should be made available. This may mean shipping in water or authorising collection from local water sources. Equally, potentially contaminated water pooled from ground flow or surface run-off may have to be removed. It may be necessary to obtain permits to clear site water into drains or natural waterways. This issue should also be addressed at the mission planning stage.

Perhaps the greatest threat to staff working on many international forensic investigations is travel. Local road traffic provides the highest risk of accident. Care should be taken during team movement to and from investigative locations by all forms of transport. Team drivers will, when possible, have experience (and training) in convoy driving and the local driving environment. For security reasons, routes and times of departure should be modified periodically.

3.5 Health and safety in the mortuary

This guidance is primarily directed at health and safety risks in postmortem examination practice and aims to provide advice for mortuary managers. This section includes a number of specific and related areas. For comprehensiveness, it includes considerations relevant to the more recently deceased and to decomposing human remains, where death occurred weeks or months before the investigation. It is essential to identify and assess the risks of infection to which persons entering the mortuary facility may be exposed and to take appropriate precautions to ensure that such health risks are either avoided or adequately controlled. Comprehensive protocols and procedures must be prepared. These will detail the precautions to be taken by all permanent or temporary staff, contractors' staff, and visitors while in the mortuary facility, and they will also define the organisation and arrangements needed to carry them out. Appropriate personnel will help prepare local rules to cover the principal work activities undertaken in the mortuary and postmortem examination room. They will ensure that all persons likely to be exposed to the assessed risks can easily use and follow the local rules that must be regularly reviewed and revised as necessary and brought to their notice.

Risk assessments must be undertaken in all circumstances where employees or others may be exposed to hazardous substances at work. The assessment must also identify the appropriate measures needed to control these risks. These assessments should identify any potential risks, whether immediate or delayed, from substances hazardous to health arising from a work activity. Although such substances are generally classified as being very toxic, toxic, harmful, corrosive, or irritant, they also apply to microorganisms hazardous to health, which may arise from work activity. Reportable accidents include all those that result in inability to carry out normal work for more than 3 days as well as all fatal and major injuries. Certain incidents, diseases, and dangerous occurrences have to be recorded and reported directly to the health and safety executive (HSE) via the SSA. As well as conforming to the specific requirements of the regulations, a record should be kept of all injuries, diseases, and dangerous occurrences that take place or are associated with the work of the mortuary or autopsy room. The appointed record keeper must be fully authorised to follow up all such occurrences or incidents as necessary and report them to the nominated mortuary manager or authorised deputy so suitable action to prevent recurrence can be taken. All members of staff who work in a mortuary are required to take reasonable care for the health and safety of themselves and others who may be affected by their acts or omissions at work. The responsibility for health and safety is extended to all persons working in the mortuary; this is not only for protection of people at work, but also for the general public who may be affected by the work activity. Safe working practices will require the provision of autopsy and mortuary facilities in a location with adequate working space, body storage, ventilation, water supply, sewage, and lighting.

Periodically, staff immunisation regimes should be reviewed. A useful guide is the latest edition of the *International Travel and Health* (WHO, 2004). Accurate health records must be kept for all members of staff and more detailed records kept for those who may be regularly exposed to a high risk of infection (e.g., mortuary staff in regular contact with blood or body fluids). It is important where hazards exist that employers are able to monitor regularly the health of their staff and note and act on occurrences of work-related illness. Employers must ensure that occupational health arrangements include agreed immunisation procedures for all members of staff. Selected immunisation procedures should be implemented as soon as possible after staff are appointed, and ideally before they start work.

Specific risks to consider can include some infectious diseases. Tuberculosis is one such risk, and any recently deceased cadavers infected by *Mycobacterium tuberculosis* bring with them the risk of exposing staff to pulmonary tuberculosis by the airborne route. It is important that all mortuary staff should, on appointment, be provided with tuberculin testing and chest x-rays where appropriate. When indicated, BCG immunisation should be offered. The method and frequency of subsequent monitoring for tubercular infection must be decided locally. Immunisation with tetanus toxoid should be routinely maintained for all staff working in the mortuary or in the field, and it is recommended that all mortuary staff should receive immunisations against the hepatitis B virus (HBV) and meningococcal meningitis (Tetravalent ACYW135 polysaccharide vaccine). The incidence of undiagnosed infection in most communities worldwide with pathogens such as human immunodeficiency virus (HIV) is expected to increase, presenting additional risks to mortuary staff. The risk from unconventional agents, such as those causing Creutzfeldt-Jakob disease, also remains. Because of the possible risk of unexpected infections, a high standard of safe working practice applying 'universal precautions' should be adopted on the assumption that all cases are potentially infectious.

To facilitate reporting of occupationally related illness, employers should supply medical contact cards to all staff employed in the mortuary, including those employed for ancillary fieldwork. The following details should be provided on the cards: employee's name, home address, and telephone number; and the work address, nature of employment, immunisation record, and a brief statement of the hazards involved. Further information should include a contact telephone number and/or address for the employee's medical aid scheme and general practitioner. A duplicate copy of the card should be available at the place of work.

Smoking, drinking, and eating must not be permitted in any work or 'wet' area within a mortuary facility. Such activities should only be permitted within a designated restroom or canteen situated well away from wet areas. Hands must always be washed with appropriate antiseptic soaps before leaving any of the designated wet work areas in the mortuary. Used protective clothing must be discarded in the appropriate container in accordance with local rules and must never be worn outside the wet areas of the mortuary facility.

Under normal circumstances, postmortem examinations should be performed during normal working hours. They should never be rushed because this considerably increases the likelihood of an accident. The number of people present in the examination room should be kept to a minimum, although there should never be fewer than two persons working on an examination. Safe working in a mortuary facility requires a high standard of vocational training and education. For the purpose of infection control, the mortuary complex may be seen operationally as comprising clean activity areas, transition areas, and potentially wet activity areas. Any unauthorised entry to the mortuary or movement between the clean and wet areas should be controlled at all times. Operational practice should ensure that all work with bodies, organs, and unfixed specimens is strictly limited to the potentially dirty activity areas. The workflow within the mortuary and postmortem examination room complex should be organised to minimise or avoid unnecessary movement. Where possible, the need for movement of people and materials from potentially dirty activity areas (postmortem examination room and wet utility room, soiled protective clothing discard area, and, to a lesser degree, the body store) to the clean activity areas (reception, waiting and viewing rooms, offices, general stock and linen store, and observation area) should be reduced to a minimum. Changing and shower facilities are necessary in a transition zone located between the postmortem examination room and clean activity areas.

Specimens should be brought out of the postmortem examination room only in suitable containers and only after these have undergone appropriate surface cleansing and decontamination. The methods for keeping and transferring specimens within the mortuary facility and their subsequent transport to the laboratory should be subject to the requirements of local rules. Anyone entering the body storage area, postmortem examination room, and specimen store, and particularly those persons handling bodies and/or specimens, may be exposed to infection risks. Staff working in these areas and all visitors to them must take precautions to protect both themselves and others whom their activities might affect. The degree of risk will depend on the sort of work they do and the manner in which they observe the safety guidelines specified by the relevant controlling organisation.

Infections and infectious diseases may be acquired by a number of mechanisms. These include breathing airborne droplets or particles contaminated with infectious microorganisms; hand-to-mouth contact; introduction of infectious material direct into the bloodstream via cuts, abrasions, or puncture wounds; or liquid splashing onto the mucous membranes such as the eyes. Any cuts, grazes, dermatitis, or other forms of skin defect, especially on the hands, should be referred for assessment by an occupational health specialist (usually a nurse or medical practitioner) under arrangements set out in the local rules. Similarly, any skin defects on individuals working in a wet work area must be protected by a water-proof dressing before work begins. Despite the use of dressings, individuals working in the mortuary facility with open wounds or any active skin lesions (e.g., dermatitis) should not come directly into contact with 'high-risk' specimens or bodies clearly labelled 'Danger of Infection' (3.5.4). If they are allowed to enter in any capacity, the wounds must first be assessed by the occupational health officer and adequately covered by water-proof dressing. More generally, all actions that can bring the hands (gloved or otherwise) into contact with the face and mucous (eyes, nose, and mouth) must be avoided (e.g., the adjusting of safety glasses and contact lenses). Hygiene procedures, detailed in local rules, must be strictly observed before moving from wet to clean areas, and appropriate protective clothing (PPE) must always be worn.

Although the risk of transmission of some pathogens from less than recent cadavers is unlikely, it is prudent to be cautious because the risk of accidental transmission of, for example, Tuberculosis, HIV and HBV cannot be ruled out. To minimise the risk of infection, it is important that mortuary staff are fully briefed of any possible risk associated with a particular body. This information will enable the potential danger of all cases to be assessed. Cases with known infectious or other risks should normally be dealt with last, or separately, when a number of examinations are to be performed. Similarly, staff must be fully briefed of any possible risks associated with UXO and 'booby-trapped' remains. These are normally detected during the primary radiographic survey (6.5.2), but caution is nevertheless advised. Appropriate precautions must be made, including waiting for an EOD expert to inspect the remains before any examination can take place. Notwithstanding the above, all cases should be regarded and handled as potentially infectious, employing 'Universal Precautions'.

3.5.1 Radiological safety in the mortuary

In addition to the guidelines set out above for safe practice in the mortuary, the following rules will apply to all areas where x-ray equipment is in use. These rules comply with the UK Ionising Radiation Regulations (1999) and the Ionising Radiation (Medical Exposure) Regulations (2000), which could meet or exceed the requirements of national regulations in other countries. Where no national regulations exist, International Atomic Energy Agency (IAEA) basic safety standards should be complied with (IAEA, 2004).

A radiation physicist will be appointed as radiation protection advisor (RPA) and will be responsible for all matters relating to radiation protection. The senior radiographer will act as radiation protection supervisor (RPS), as defined by the Ionising Radiation Regulations 1999, and will report directly to the HSO in relation to health and safety matters. The RPA and RPS will ensure that an initial risk assessment is undertaken and that local radiation safety rules and agreed schemes of work are in place.

During the initial risk assessment, the RPS, in consultation with the RPA, will define the extent of the controlled radiation area, which will exist whenever the x-ray equipment is switched on. Only those personnel whose presence the RPS considers to be essential for the conduct of an imaging examination will be permitted to be present in the controlled area. For radiography and dental examinations, this will normally be the radiographer alone. For fluoroscopy, this will normally be the radiographer, either the pathologist or anthropologist, and one another person. All personnel must wear protective lead aprons at all times while in a controlled area. Lead rubber aprons and lead-equivalent barriers of no less than 0.25 mm LE will be used.

X-ray and other imaging equipment will only be operated by persons who have received appropriate training in the use of ionising radiations. This must meet the level required of a 'practitioner' as defined by the Ionising Radiation (Medical Exposure) Regulations (2000). Each radiographer (and attendee) will be monitored for exposure to radiation, and records of doses received will be kept. These records will be copied to the radiographer's dosimetry service at the base hospital. During examinations, exposure factors and screening times for all x-ray examinations will be recorded on the radiography examination log. All protective equipment (e.g., lead aprons) will be stored according to the agreed protocol and checked annually, with records kept. For internal processes, records of the following will be maintained: equipment details, serial numbers, and dates of purchase; equipment maintenance record; annual quality and radiation checks on imaging and protective equipment; annual checks of protective equipment; and personal radiation dosimetry. All radiation incidents will be reported according to the agreed health and safety protocol and reported to the RPA.

3.5.2 Supervision of safety procedures

The responsibility for safety in a mortuary rests with the individual employer and, in practice, the designated senior pathologist. It is strongly recommended that such individuals appoint HSOs or supervisors to oversee the implementation, on a daily basis, of safety standards and requirements of local rules. HSOs and safety officers or supervisors will be pathologists or senior anatomical pathology technologists (APTs). For matters of radiation safety, the RPS will be the senior radiographer. All safety officers and supervisors must have appropriate training in safety procedures and requirements, delegated authority, and sufficient free time from other commitments to carry out their duties in this respect. The duties of individual HSOs or supervisors, in relation to line managers, must be set down in writing by the employer and include provision for a number of factors. These include the adequate, supervised safety training of all new members of staff in accordance with local rules. Time must be made available for the preparation and introduction of programmes for the training and familiarisation of staff with new work techniques and for regular updating of training programmes. Written procedures for dealing with incidents (e.g., accidental spillage) must be prepared and made available, preferably prominently displayed. Policies must be implemented for safe working practices, effective decontamination and disinfection, and the safe collection and disposal of waste.

The HSO is also responsible for the preparation and regular updating of written instructions for safe systems of work and, where appropriate, the operation of 'permit to work' systems for use by staff, maintenance, and service personnel. These must ensure that adequate supplies of protective clothing and safety equipment as specified by local rules are available and kept in good order and that periodic inspections are carried out to detect and identify any unsafe work practices or items of equipment and to see that any faults are promptly corrected. They are also responsible for ensuring that all hazardous materials are labelled, handled, stored, and disposed of safely and that an effective system for liaison with infection control staff, the occupational health service, the fire protection officer, and appointed safety representatives is established and maintained. The HSOs' responsibilities also include ensuring that all staff, including those working outside normal hours, are properly supervised and that arrangements are made for a responsible person to be available at all times, in case of incidents or accidents. They must also ensure that all visitors (including equipment service and maintenance personnel, undertakers, police, and relatives) while in the mortuary facility are either accompanied or closely supervised by a staff member who advises them of the appropriate safety measures.

HSOs and safety officers (or supervisors) should participate in any safety committee or meeting related to the risks of infection present in the department. In light of the above, it is essential that HSOs or supervisors are readily identifiable and recognised by all persons entering the mortuary or postmortem examination room. The wearing of easily seen badges is one method used successfully.

All staff must receive adequate instruction and practical training in dealing with the risks encountered in their work. The MMT must not assume that new staff are familiar with the safety standards and techniques needed for work in a mortuary. They must check and provide training and information where gaps in knowledge and/or experience are found to exist. This will normally mean placing the newcomer with an experienced member of staff for a specified period of training. Staff should not work with bodies or specimens where an infection risk is indicated until they have demonstrated adequate skill and understanding of the risks involved. Staff must be competent to deal with emergency procedures before they are declared fully trained. Mortuary staff will have access, at all times, to a copy of the Health and Safety Policy Statement. They should also have direct access to, or have in their possession, copies of all safety directions and literature circulated or displayed by the relevant person or the safety supervisor (i.e., local rules). Adequate opportunity must be provided for staff to familiarise themselves and become competent in dealing with new methods or techniques. Safe working within a mortuary demands high standards of training and education. All APTs should be encouraged to obtain an appropriate qualification (e.g., in the UK, the Royal Institute of Public Health's certificate or diploma of anatomical pathology technology).

There should never be fewer than two persons engaged on a routine examination, for example, the pathologist and an APT. If the circumstances demand it, further personnel may have to be present (e.g., anthropologist, radiographer, scene of crime examiner, or second APT).

3.5.3   Personal protective equipment

Anyone entering the mortuary must do so via the changing rooms where they will be required to put on the protective clothing specified in the local rules. In the case of visitors not using an observation area to view either examination procedures or specimens, protective clothing will normally consist of a gown or laboratory coat (or shirt and trousers) over their clothing together with plastic overshoes or boots, surgical masks, and head covering. For observers close to the examination table, a full-length gown, mask, and eye protection should be worn, along with water-proof boots.

On entering the wet areas, overshoes, or rubber boots must be worn as required by local rules. Boots should extend to about midcalf level and have nonslip soles. Prescribed footwear must be worn by all persons who enter any designated wet area, even though they may not be engaged actively in postmortem examinations. If there is a known risk of infection, a total change of clothing may be necessary. Staff working on postmortem examination procedures must change completely, removing their outdoor clothing and replacing it by a short- or long-sleeved surgical shirt, gloves, trousers, water-proof boots, gloves, masks, safety glasses and a hat or hood that completely covers the hair, or as otherwise specified in the local rules. Aprons must be worn in accordance with agreed local standards and procedures. When dealing with cases that have been designated 'high risk' (i.e., where the presence of pathogens in Hazard Group 3 is either suspected or confirmed, or when the identity and medical history for a body is not known), a long-sleeved 'jumpsuit' made from water-proof materials should be worn instead of the surgical shirt and trousers. Additionally, a full-face visor must be worn at all times when splashing can occur.

In wet areas, other staff members (e.g., photographers or odontologists) who may need to be in close proximity to the body while it is being examined must also wear protective clothing in accordance with the requirements of local rules. Several categories of observer may need to be present at a postmortem examination (e.g., clinical or medical staff, legal representatives). If there is a properly designated observation area, there may be no need for protective clothing to be worn. If an observation area is not available, essential observers may be located away from the examination table within the postmortem examination room. On such occasions, they will normally be required to wear a cap, mask, gown (back or side fastening), and overshoes over their own clothing. When they need to observe a case where the body has been labelled 'Danger of Infection', they must change fully into the protective clothing specified in local rules and take any additional precautions deemed necessary by the pathologist at the time. Afterward, they will be required to shower before dressing.

The protective clothing worn in other designated wet areas in the mortuary (i.e., the body store or specimen store), and in the postmortem examination area after it has been decontaminated, will not be the same as that required during postmortem examination procedures. The standard selected will be specified clearly in the local rules, and any person entering such areas must comply with the agreed requirement. Normally, a long gown and overshoes worn over the outdoor clothing will be satisfactory, but there may be local exceptions. Gloves should always be worn when bodies are handled.

As noted previously, staff working on the examination will normally wear a complete change of clothing, but they may, for short visits (when postmortem examinations are not in progress and when the area has been cleaned and disinfected), use the type of protective clothing normally prescribed for visitors. However, before commencing a postmortem examination, staff must change into the protective clothing. For the pathologist and APT, this will normally consist of a long-sleeved surgical shirt and gown, together with gloves and plastic sleeve protectors to protect the arms against accidental injury, as well as surgical trousers and water-proof boots. Alternatively, a long-sleeved water-proof jumpsuit may be worn. A head covering, mask, and eye protection should also be worn.

The protective clothing that should be worn includes full-length, disposable or washable aprons, extending to the level of the ankles; these should be worn by all those present at the examination table and by any observers who stand close by. Caps or hoods that completely cover the hair should be worn by all persons participating in the examination, and a surgical face mask and eye protection should normally be worn to guard against splashing. When band saws are used, ear protection may also need to be worn.

In high-risk cases, a plastic face shield or visor must be worn. During cutting operations, particularly sawing, eye protection should always be worn, particularly where an infection risk is either suspected or known to exist. The visor must cover the entire face and neck region and any facial hair (e.g., beards). There is, at present, no general agreement on the best form of protection for the hands. Protection may be provided by double gloving, in which, for instance, an inner latex glove is covered by a thicker outer glove, which extends beyond the cuff of the gown sleeve. Heavy-duty gloves of elbow and shoulder length are available, as are plastic sleeve covers. When there is a danger of infection, heavy-duty neoprene, latex, nitrile, or butyl gloves should be considered, although it is recognised that there will be some loss of touch sensitivity. Stainless steel mesh or cut-resistant safety gloves should be used during high-risk and blind postmortem examinations. When using hand saws, the user should wear stainless steel mesh gloves. Before touching any human remains where a risk of infection is suspected or known to exist, disposable gloves, masks and a protective overall will be worn. If there are open wounds or lesions through which blood or body fluids may flow, it is imperative to wear rubber boots, a head covering, and a face mask and eye protection.

When undertaking fluoroscopy, all personnel must wear protective lead aprons at all times while in the area. All protective equipment (e.g., lead aprons) should be stored correctly and checked annually, with records kept of the equipment details, serial numbers, and dates of purchase.

During cleaning and disinfection of the mortuary, many cleansing/disinfecting agents are strong irritants. They give off toxic vapours and as such are subject to COSHH and Occupational Exposure Standards. Occupational health legislation and regulations require that where exposure to substances hazardous to health may occur, suitable PPE (e.g., respirators) should be used if other suitable control measures are not available or do not adequately control exposure. If a full-face respirator is to be worn, a good fit must be ensured, and the appropriate canister fitted to the respirator.

3.5.4   Health and safety during postmortem examinations

On each day that postmortem examinations are to be carried out, and before examinations begin, the examination room must be prepared and equipped in accordance with the instructions set out in the local rules. This will usually require APTs to ensure that an adequate supply of basic protective clothing both for staff and visitors is available throughout the day. This will include disposable water-proof aprons, gloves, visors, and masks, and heavy-duty rubber gloves and aprons. In terms of services, the APT must ensure that the air supply and extract systems are functioning satisfactorily, drains have been cleared and disinfected, and the water supply is functioning correctly. Lighting must be properly adjusted and functioning correctly, and dictation and communication systems should be tested and functioning correctly. From a hygiene perspective, adequate supplies of liquid soap, freshly prepared disinfectants, detergent solutions, paper towels, swabs, and specimen containers must be available, as must mops, buckets, disinfectants, and detergents for cleaning floors and work surfaces during and between examinations.

Tools and equipment required during postmortem examinations must be clean, ready for use, and set out as required at examination tables and dissecting benches. For example, knives must have been sharpened after thorough cleaning and disinfection, and electrically operated tools and the integrity of splash-proof power sockets must have been regularly checked by a competent electrician. The regularity of checks must be specified in the local rules, and the electrician's findings recorded in a logbook. Any abnormalities must be reported immediately to the safety supervisor and dealt with before work can proceed. The safe supply unit for the specially protected electrical circuits in the mortuary must be trip tested, and details of these and all other checks must be recorded, with any abnormalities brought immediately to the attention of the safety supervisor. He or she must then decide whether work can proceed before the fault is dealt with. The required equipment and sets of instruments for a postmortem examination must be decided locally, taking account of the projected workload and any specific circumstances.

Infections may be acquired in the mortuary by inhaling airborne droplets or particles contaminated with microorganisms; by hand-to-mouth contact; by infection directly into the bloodstream via cuts, abrasions, puncture, or other open wounds; or as a result of splashing contaminated material onto the mucous membranes or into the eyes. Anyone wearing contact lenses must wash their hands and leave the wet area before cleaning or adjusting the lenses. Examination techniques must ensure that liquid dispersion, splashing, and vaporisation is minimised, and that all instruments and exposed bone fragments likely to cause puncture wounds or cuts are handled appropriately. Instruments must never be passed hand to hand during an examination. They must be set out on a table for selection in accordance with the pathologist's preferred practice and taken from the table as required. Receptacles containing an appropriate disinfectant solution (usually phenolic based) must be available for holding instruments not required for further use during a particular examination after they have been rinsed in detergent solution. No attempt must ever be made to arrest the fall of a dropped instrument. To help prevent accidental falls, instruments must not be laid down indiscriminately after use. If no longer required, instruments should be placed directly into the container of disinfectant. All cutting operations, particularly sawing, will produce vaporised and liquid droplets and splashing and should be guarded against using PPE, particularly where an infection risk is either suspected or known to exist. Band saws must not be used unless they are either fitted with local exhaust ventilation or used within an exhaust-ventilated enclosure.

During the postmortem examination, all procedures likely to cause splashing (e.g., washing down with high-pressure hoses, squeezing organs that have been removed from the body), must, where practicable, be avoided. Where appropriate, evisceration should not be undertaken until an external assessment has first been carried out by the pathologist responsible for the case. In general, an 'en bloc' type (Ghon) evisceration in which 'blocks' of anatomically related organs are removed is generally safer than an 'en masse' (Letulle) total evisceration technique (Sheaff and Hopster, 2005). The latter has more risk of accidental injury and also of splashing with blood and other body fluids. However, the pathologist should consider all the facts when deciding what procedure must be followed and is personally responsible to make (or cause to be made) as adequate an evisceration and dissection as the circumstances require. With recent remains, when pulmonary tuberculosis is suspected, the lungs should be perfused with formalin before commencing the pulmonary dissection. It is further recommended that the use of an electrical oscillating saw should be avoided in cases where tuberculosis, meningitis, and prion (CJD) infections are suspected.

In opening the rib cage, hand cutters should be used on the costal cartilages. The cut ends of the rib cage and any other exposed bones should be covered by a surgical towel to prevent accidental contacts that may cause cuts or puncturing of the dissector's gloves or skin. During the dissection of the body, care should be exercised with sharp instruments present on the body and the dissection table. Blunt-ended scissors should be used whenever practicable. If needles used for the collection of blood or body fluids need to be removed from a syringe, forceps or other approved devices must be used. Used needles must be discarded safely, immediately after use, into a 'sharps' container. Needles must not be resheathed unless local rules specify a safe method. When dealing with cases where a high risk of infection is known or suspected, spare instruments should be kept readily available. When required for use by the pathologist, the instruments should be placed on a side table where they can be picked up. Throughout the postmortem examination, procedures involving the use of a sharp instrument must be announced in advance so other members of the team are adequately forewarned. Special care should be exercised when scalpel blades are changed. One or more spare scalpels will normally be required within the clean instrument area. Used blades must immediately be disposed of in the designated 'sharps' container. It is the responsibility of the person using the scalpel to personally remove and dispose of the blade appropriately, on completion of the postmortem examination.

Where appropriate, dissection of the organs after evisceration should be carried out either at the postmortem examination table on a suitable nonslip surface or at a side bench. Organ dissections should be carried out on an impervious surface. Synthetic resin boards are most satisfactory. All organs must be weighed, and the weighing of organs should ideally be undertaken in close proximity to the dissection area. Great care should be exercised to avoid splashing and droplet dispersion. Water-proof electronic scales are recommended, and equipment should be selected that provides for easy cleaning with no traps for infected material. Wall-mounted or hanging balances are preferred. Intestines should normally be opened under water in a deep sink provided for this purpose, but not under a running tap. Blunt-ended enterostomy scissors should be used where practicable.

If appropriate, particular care should be exercised when opening the skull for removal of the brain. All saws will produce droplets and cause splashing. Air-powered oscillating saws are available with remote exhaust ports and are preferable to the conventional 100/200-V oscillating saw. The traditional handsaw is often cleaner and less traumatic to the dura and underlying brain, and is less likely to generate droplets. A disadvantage in using a handsaw is the greater risk of accidental trauma to the operator so appropriate PPE must be used.

To minimise the period of exposure to any airborne droplets generated during work, the skull should be opened at the end of the postmortem examination, except in cases where otherwise indicated, such as bloodless neck dissections. In high-risk cases, it is possible to enclose the entire head within a large plastic bag during use of the bone saw. The bag is fitted over the head and neck of the cadaver and the saw and hands are introduced through a hole in the bag, which may then be sealed by tape as necessary.

If appropriate, tissue specimens for histology should be placed in appropriately sized containers, which will allow them to be totally submerged in at least ten times their volume of fixative solution. Care should be taken to ensure that the outside of these containers is properly decontaminated before placing them into a plastic bag for transportation to the laboratory. Large specimens (e.g., brains, hearts) should be retained in a secure area of the mortuary until temporary formalin fixation has been attained, prior to dispatch to the appropriate referral centre. When fresh, unfixed tissue or body fluids are to be sent to the laboratories (e.g., for microbiological or toxicological analysis), they should be placed in a sealed leak-proof container, and then placed inside a transport bag and labelled according to local rules. Biohazard or similar warning labels must be affixed to specimens taken from high-risk cases. The guidelines for labelling, storage, transportation, and reception of specimens should be strictly followed.

Bodies where infection with organisms or chemicals with high hazard ratings is known or suspected must be treated as high-risk cases and labelled 'Danger of Infection' or 'Biohazard'. Whenever practicable, infected bodies should only be examined under carefully controlled conditions. Bodies suspected of being infected with hazard group 4 pathogens should never be examined routinely, but only when a special need for a postmortem examination is identified (Royal College of Pathologists, 2002). If the conditions for postmortem examination of these cases cannot be met, arrangements should be made to transfer the body to a mortuary where appropriate conditions are available. All staff (medical, scientific, and technical) working in the postmortem examination room during the postmortem examination of very high-risk cases must be fully trained in mortuary techniques and safety procedures. When risk of infection is deemed to exist, the body must be placed inside a leak-proof disposable plastic body bag. Any spilled blood or fluids must be treated with disinfectant according to local rules. If one does not know how to deal with spillage, make sure that someone with specialist knowledge deals with it as soon as possible. The number of persons involved in such postmortem examinations must be limited to two and consist of the pathologist and an assistant. The pathologist should be solely responsible for the opening and removal of organs and examination of the body. The APT should remove all excised material for later attention, as indicated by the pathologist. They should not handle sharp instruments or tools unless specifically instructed to do so by the pathologist. The pathologist and APT must not both handle sharp tools and instruments at the same time. The APT should, so far as is practicable, remain uncontaminated. If the clothing becomes soiled, they must be changed at once. The pathologist and APT may occasionally be required to perform duties normally carried out by other persons, such as photography; removal of specimens in containers; and communication, recording, and observation. They will constantly be on the lookout for any risks associated with the presence and use of sharp tools, instruments, spillage, and splashing. Danger warnings issued by a member of the postmortem examination team must be instantly obeyed by all present in the postmortem examination room, including observers. Work must cease until the matter has been dealt with. In high-risk cases, it may be preferable to complete the dissection of organs only after adequate fixation with 10 percent buffered formalin. If this procedure is to be adopted, preliminary slicing may be undertaken to ensure adequate penetration of the fixative. Steps must be taken to guard against exposure to formalin vapour in dangerous concentrations. At the end of the postmortem examination, the APT must be responsible for ensuring that all clothing worn during the postmortem examination is disposed of correctly or treated as infected linen. This responsibility must be designated as specified in appropriate local rules.

A common, easily identifiable warning label must be used on all bodies or human remains to alert staff to the possible presence of pathogens. Pathology recording forms (6.7) accompanying the body should provide sufficient clinical information to enable experienced staff to know what special precautions are necessary. Information about the presence of pacemakers or other prostheses or the existence of radiation or chemical hazards, as well as any risk of infection, must be provided. Although warning labels must be conspicuously placed on the body, the accompanying clinical information need not be available to anyone other than the mortuary staff. Local arrangements must, so far as is reasonably practicable, ensure that steps have been taken to minimise exposure to leakage of body fluids before being delivered to the reception area in the mortuary. Local rules must ensure that the senior APT is informed of any cases where an infection risk is believed to exist before a body is delivered to the mortuary. This will enable mortuary staff to make any special arrangements for dealing with a particular form of infection or contamination and, where necessary, seek specialist advice.

Where a reception area is not provided, unauthorised/untrained persons must not enter the body store unless they have first received permission from the designated mortuary staff. They will be required to wear whatever protective clothing is prescribed for that purpose.

Accidents that occur in the mortuary, especially when risk of infection exists, must be dealt with immediately and medical advice sought. All accidents must be recorded in the incident book kept for that purpose. The reporting of injuries should follow relevant regulations, ideally the F2508 format (Reporting of Injuries, Diseases and Dangerous Occurrences Regulations, 1985). Details of the accident should be entered in the book with information about actions taken (a) to treat any wound or the effects of splashing, and (b) to avoid a repetition of the incident.

3.5.5   Disposal of waste

Most of the waste arising from postmortem examination can be defined as clinical waste and falls into two distinct groups and four subcategories (see Table 3–1). Waste in both groups is a potential risk to health for those required to deal with it prior to incineration. There must be a strictly administered policy to control the

Table 3–1. *Overview of waste disposal*

Waste for incineration	Disposal to drain
Disposable, generally single-use items such as paper shrouds, swabs, dressings, protective clothing, and gloves	Discarded chemicals, such as fixative solutions and disinfectants
Human tissues and body fluids	
Discarded syringes, needles, and other disposable 'sharps', which must be placed in a 'sharps' container immediately after use	

segregation, containment, and disposal of waste. Adoption of the system of colour coding is strongly advised for all containers used for waste disposal (see Table 3–2) because strict adherence to this will help ensure against the dangers resulting from infectious waste finding its way into the general refuse stream. The colouring of bags or containers is preferred to the attachment of coloured tags that can fall off or become illegible.

Any nondisposable protective clothing worn in any workplace in the mortuary and/or postmortem examination room should be treated as infected linen. Protective clothing used with high-risk cases must be autoclaved before laundering, and protective equipment such as rubber boots, reusable gloves, and visors must be cleansed with detergent and disinfectant before being presented for reuse. Metal reinforced safety gloves should be disinfected and cleaned in accordance with the manufacturer's recommendations. Disposable equipment such as gloves or aprons must be sealed in a correctly colour coded bag before being placed in the bin for disposal or incineration. Bags for waste destined for autoclaving should be made of a material suitable for this purpose and should also carry an indicator to show whether they have been subjected to this treatment (e.g., autoclave tape). Outer containers for waste destined for autoclaving must be capable of withstanding the heat/pressure cycle to which they will be repeatedly subjected. Disposal

Table 3–2. *Recommended colour coding for containers for clinical waste*

Colour of bag	Type of waste
Black	Normal household waste: not to be used to store or transport clinical waste
Yellow	All waste destined for incineration
Red or yellow with black banding	Waste (e.g., home nursing waste), which preferably should be disposed of by incineration, but may be disposed of by landfill when separate collection and disposal arrangements are made
Light blue or transparent with light blue inscriptions	Waste for autoclaving (or equivalent treatment) before ultimate disposal

stations in the workplace must be clearly marked to indicate the type of waste catered for.

3.5.6 Mortuary specification

Mortuary layout is also discussed in detail in 2.4.2. The engineering services required for a temporary mortuary should include heating, lighting and other electrical supplies, ventilation, and adequate drainage for the disposal of large quantities of liquid waste. The guidance provided must be followed, or an equivalent standard of safety achieved. Specially protected electrical equipment will be required in areas such as the postmortem examination room and body store, where splashing with water jets can occur. The standards for such installations must be rigorously applied. Electric saw and other power-operated equipment must be checked frequently by a competent electrician, and the results of all checks should be recorded in a logbook that will be regularly inspected by the safety supervisor.

The mortuary, consisting of such designated areas as a body store, examination room, wet utility room (including biological waste), and staff changing rooms, should, if possible, have a dedicated supply and extract ventilation plant. Similarly, any specimen store will also need continuously operating air extract ventilation. Although natural ventilation may be appropriate for areas in the mortuary that workers visit infrequently and that are designated as being clean (e.g., the body viewing room and access corridors), controlled mechanical ventilation is preferred. Special consideration needs to be given to drainage. The primary objective is to provide an internal drainage system that uses the minimum of pipe work, remains water and airtight at joints and connections, and is easy to maintain.

Clean and wet areas in the mortuary. The mortuary facility must be clearly demarcated (by either a physical barrier or a red line on the floor) in line with health and safety regulations into 'wet' or dirty (potentially infectious) and 'dry' or clean areas; the wet areas must be designated as access-controlled areas. Areas in the mortuary facility where there may be a risk of acquiring an occupationally related infection should be designated as wet areas. Warning notices should be positioned at the points of access to and exits from the wet areas. Where barriers are in use, these must be clearly visible to avoid accidents. Whatever form of demarcation is adopted, it should be adequate to deter casual entry by unauthorised persons. Staff working on postmortem examination procedures must change completely, using PPE as described in 3.5.3.

The pathologist will decide who can and cannot enter the various wet areas in the mortuary. Standards should be specified in local rules. Smoking, drinking, eating, chewing, or applying cosmetics is forbidden anywhere in the mortuary or postmortem examination room. Personal belongings, unless specifically approved in local rules (i.e., spectacles, hearing aids), must not be taken into areas designated 'dirty' unless they can be thoroughly cleaned afterward. Everyone leaving a wet area must always thoroughly wash their hands and all unprotected skin surfaces. Spectacles worn for work must also be thoroughly cleansed before leaving the area.

Protective clothing worn in a wet area must be removed in the transit zone on the wet side of the barrier or demarcation line in the changing area. Discarded clothing must be placed in the appropriately labelled receptacles. Contaminated clothing, especially when dealing with 'high-risk' cases, must be changed as soon as possible after the case is completed and not left until the end of a work period. If the presence of Hazard Group 3 or 4 pathogens is suspected, the clothing must be autoclaved before being sent for laundering. Perforated or split gloves must be changed immediately. The hands must be thoroughly washed before putting on the new pair. The gloves should be washed frequently during periods of work and whenever they become heavily contaminated with blood or other body fluids to prevent them becoming slippery. Individuals who have been closely involved in postmortem examination or handling bodies categorised as high risk must shower before putting on their outdoor clothing. People not required to shower by local rules must wash their hands after removing protective clothing and before crossing to the 'clean' side of the changing room.

3.5.7 Other personnel

Staff who are not fully conversant with the local rules developed for the mortuary must not enter the changing area, postmortem examination room, and body or specimen stores without first seeking the advice of the pathologist, senior APT, or HSO. They will not be allowed to enter any areas that have been classified as wet (i.e., areas where the risk of serious infection may be present) without first changing into the protective clothing prescribed for them (described in 3.5.3). They must be made aware of and conform to any special precautions specified for persons entering these areas. While in the mortuary and, particularly, when entering any of the wet areas, they must be prepared to follow any safety instructions issued by the pathologist, senior APT, or HSO. At the end of the visit, they must remove any protective clothing and equipment worn (e.g., full-face visor) and deposit it in the bins provided in the changing room. They must then wash their hands and, if required to do so, shower, before putting on personal or other clothing removed before entering the wet area. Clothing worn in wet areas must not be taken from the mortuary. Even when entering a 'clean' area, they may still be required to wear overshoes as well as a protective coat or gown.

Cleaning staff will not be required to work in the designated wet areas of the mortuary (i.e., areas where a serious risk of infection may exist), unless the area has first been decontaminated. Nevertheless, staff may accidentally come into contact with potentially hazardous materials and must observe certain precautions. Staff who have not received instructions about hygiene and safety at work, especially in the mortuary, must not work there. They must be properly trained and aware of the dangers that can be present. Cleaning staff must never enter the mortuary until they have made sure that it is safe to do so by asking their own supervisor or senior APT. If they also clean other facilities, before entering the mortuary, they must remove their outdoor coat of the overall worn for other work, and replace it with the special overall, overshoes, and gloves provided for use in the mortuary. Staff must only enter those parts of the mortuary that they have been instructed to clean by their supervisor or senior APT. When work in the mortuary has been completed, they can take off their protective clothing in the designated changing area, dispose of it as instructed, and then, very thoroughly, wash their hands before putting on personal clothing. Items of protective clothing should never be taken from the mortuary because they could spread infection. The clothing must be deposited in the bins provided for that purpose.

Service and maintenance staff may be required to visit the mortuary, usually when it is not in operation, to repair or maintain equipment. Mortuary staff must ensure that the equipment concerned is cleaned and decontaminated. Service and maintenance staff will not, knowingly, be required to handle infectious items. They may, however, accidentally come into contact with infectious materials and must always follow certain instructions. Before commencing any work in the mortuary, service and maintenance staff must ensure that appropriate cleaning and decontamination procedures have been carried out by mortuary personnel. They must wear and use the protective equipment deemed necessary by the senior APT, and they must follow the instructions issued before they start work. If they are unsure about anything, they must ask for advice from the senior APT. All tools or test equipment used in the mortuary must be inspected afterward by the mortuary staff. Before they can be taken back to the workshop, they may need to be properly decontaminated. Joints, seals, and connections on equipment must not be opened or broken unless advice about the possible contents has first been obtained from the mortuary staff or safety supervisor. Wherever practicable, all connections will have been drained and decontaminated before any service or maintenance work is begun. If material (liquid or solid) is found when joints are broken, it must not be touched. Joints must be immediately resealed or covered, as appropriate, and the incident reported to the senior APT as soon as practicable. They will decide what further action should be taken. Any equipment that must go to the workshop or be sent away for maintenance or repair must be clearly labelled to record what action has been taken to clean and decontaminate it; special precautions may be necessary. Service maintenance staff must adhere closely to any special advice or precautions that are issued by the safety supervisor or their own supervisor in connection with the equipment.

3.5.8 Health and safety and the arrival of remains at the mortuary

On arrival of human remains at the mortuary, it is essential to ensure that any infection risk labels on bodies are identified and brought to the attention of mortuary staff. When delivering a body, it should be left at the designated reception area with the SCE and other relevant mortuary staff. Those responsible for transporting remains must not enter other parts of the mortuary (i.e., postmortem examination room or body store) unless instructed to do so by the staff. Additional safety precautions will be required in the other parts of the mortuary, and they will be advised as to what is required. After delivering remains, any protective clothing that has been worn should be removed and disposed of safely according to local rules. Hands must be thoroughly washed after handling a body and before leaving the mortuary. If personal clothing has become contaminated with fluids when handling 'infection risk' cases, it may be necessary to shower and change clothing. Mortuary staff will provide advice.

3.5.9 Decontamination and disinfectants and disinfection of the mortuary

Housekeeping standards must be observed throughout the mortuary. The spillage of any material likely to cause infection must be dealt with by either direct disinfection or cleansing with detergent followed by decontamination. The law requires employers to control exposure to hazardous substances to prevent ill health; therefore, *all* chemicals used must be subjected to a COSHH assessment (www.coshh-essentials.org.uk).

Dried blood or body fluids should be softened with diluted bleach or detergent disinfectant before being scraped off to prevent the dispersal of potentially infectious material. Some disinfectant solutions are harmful to health and must always be handled in accordance with the supplier's instructions. Unhindered access to a small steam steriliser within the mortuary is essential. At the end of each working day, the examination room and associated areas must be decontaminated.

The term 'disinfection' is commonly used to mean the destruction of microorganisms but not usually bacterial spores. Disinfectants do not necessarily kill all microorganisms but rather reduces them to a level that makes the disinfected object safe to handle and decreases infection risk. A disinfectant is a chemical agent, which under defined conditions is capable of disinfection. Disinfection is commonly used where sterilisation (i.e., rendering items free from all living microorganisms) is considered unnecessary, impractical (e.g., due to an object's size), or may cause damage. However, disinfection is not synonymous with sterilisation.

Specific surfaces require specific approaches. Tables and benches (both dissecting and side) must be washed with detergent solution then rinsed off with water before disinfection. Walls must be rinsed with a disinfectant at the end of each day. Floors, as well as being thoroughly cleansed and disinfected at the end of each day, will also require swabbing with a disinfectant solution to remove blood and other spillage during and between cases. Daily cleansing and decontamination must include attention to all floor drains and floor drain baskets. Additionally, two or three times each week, at the end of a day's work, floors should be systematically and thoroughly cleansed, preferably using a rotary scrubbing machine. However,

Table 3–3. *Types of disinfectants and their application*

Disinfectant	Contains compatible detergent	Active against				
		Vegetative bacteria (e.g., *Escherichia coli*)	Mycobacteria (e.g., tuberculosis)	Bacterial spores (e.g., anthrax)	Fungi (e.g., aspergillus)	Viruses (e.g., HBV)
Phenolics	Yes	Yes	Yes	No	Yes	Variable
Hypochlorites	No	Yes	Limited	Limited	Yes	Yes
Quaternary ammonium compounds	No	Yes	No	No	No	No
Higher-grade blended quaternary ammonium compounds	Yes	Yes	Yes	Variable	Yes	Yes
Halogenated tertiary amines	May contain some	Yes	Yes	Yes	Yes	Yes

because some floor surfaces are known to be damaged by such cleansing methods, a suitable alternative method must be used.

Instrument kits must be thoroughly cleansed, disinfected, and/or autoclaved. Items that cannot be washed, such as electrical equipment, must be thoroughly wiped with noncorrosive disinfectant (e.g., 70 percent alcohol solution). Sufficient sets of instruments should be available to enable technicians to cleanse and disinfect the wet items in rotation during the working day. A policy for the safe handling and disposal of sharps must be in operation.

Protective equipment such as rubber boots, aprons, reusable gloves, and visors must be cleansed with detergent and disinfectant before being presented for reuse. Metal reinforced safety gloves should be disinfected and cleaned in accordance with the manufacturer's recommendations.

The postmortem examination room, equipment, and instruments within it present a serious challenge to all disinfectants. Any disinfectant must be effective against a wide range of potentially pathogenic microorganisms. Care must therefore be taken in the selection and use of disinfectants. Effective disinfection depends on three main factors: activity, contact, and time. There are many different disinfectants available, and their efficiency is varied. It may be appropriate to use more than one type of disinfectant in the mortuary, depending on the biological agent anticipated; however, choosing a single disinfectant that has a wide microbiocidal spectrum will reduce mistakes in application. The common types of disinfectants and their applications can be seen in Table 3–3. In addition, the disinfectants will be affected by other factors such as the presence of organic material, incompatible soaps and detergents, chemicals, the surface of the material being treated, pH, temperature, dilution, and time elapsed since the preparation of the working solution.

Instruments should be thoroughly washed with a disinfecting detergent solution before total immersion in an appropriate disinfectant. Working surfaces may be initially washed with a phenolic disinfectant containing a detergent; however, thorough cleaning is the most important decontamination procedure. Adequate time should be allowed for the disinfectant to perform its function. This will vary according to the type and usage of the disinfectant. It is therefore imperative to select a suitable disinfectant; use it correctly; and ensure that discard containers, mops, and cleaning materials do not adversely affect the disinfectant or act as a reservoir of potentially pathogenic microorganisms.

Disinfectants should be used in accordance with the manufacturer's instructions. Full details of the effectiveness, use, dilution, stability, compatibility, and safe handling of a particular product must be obtained from the supplier in the form of a material safety data sheet (MSDS).

Appropriate precautions must be taken by all persons using disinfectants. Bar or liquid soap, with or without an antiseptic, is usually sufficient for cleaning the hands; however, should the skin become contaminated with potentially hazardous material, it should be thoroughly cleansed and disinfected with 70 percent alcohol or a 2–4 percent Sodium Hypochlorite solution. Aqueous formulations containing chlorhexidine or povidone iodine can be used on broken or damaged skin. Gloves must always be worn when disinfectants are handled, and plastic aprons and visors if splashing can occur. Safety spectacles, goggles, or full-face visors appropriate to the task must be worn by everyone handling strong disinfectants (particularly when dilutions are being prepared from concentrated stock solution). Some disinfectants (e.g., glutaraldehyde, formalin) are strong irritants that give off toxic vapours. Disinfectant vapours must not be inhaled. Most disinfectants are unstable chemicals and should therefore be freshly prepared before use. Appropriate control measures or PPE will be adopted as described. If more than one disinfectant is used, care must be taken to ensure compatibility between them. Care should also be taken when cleaning the postmortem examination room. Low-pressure hoses should be used and care taken to minimise splashing and generation of liquid droplets.

3.5.10 Clinical waste management

For waste to be classified as clinical, it must contain pathogens with sufficient virulence and quantity so exposure of a susceptible host to the waste could result in an infectious disease. This may be any waste capable of producing or potentially producing an infectious disease or condition. Alternatively it could be any solid waste that is generated in the diagnosis, treatment, or immunisation of humans or in research projects or any solid or liquid waste that may present or potentially present a threat of infection to humans and the environment. Most of the waste arising from postmortem examination can be defined as clinical waste and falls into two distinct groups and four subcategories.

The first of these is clinical solid waste, which can be disposable and is generally single-use items such as paper shrouds, swabs, dressings, protective clothing, and gloves. Alternatively, it can be human tissues (and body fluids) or discarded syringes, needles, and other disposable 'sharps' that must be placed in a 'sharps' container immediately after use. Second, clinical liquid waste is that which comprises discarded chemicals, such as fixative solutions and disinfectants. In the case of recyclable chemicals (e.g., those used in radiography), it is essential to comply with the provisions of the COSSH or similar hazardous chemical substances regulations. Third, hazardous chemical substances are any toxic, harmful, corrosive, irritant, or asphyxiant substance; a mixture of such substances for which an occupational exposure limit is prescribed; or a mixture of such substances for which an occupational exposure limit is not prescribed, but that nevertheless creates a hazard to health. Waste in any of these categories is a potential risk to health of those who are required to deal with it prior to disposal.

There are additional 'wastes' that should be evaluated to determine whether they may pose a health hazard because of potential infectiousness or toxicity. These include, but are not limited to, contaminated equipment, wastes from surgery and postmortem examination, and miscellaneous laboratory waste. There must be a strictly administered policy to control the segregation, containment, and disposal of all waste. It is recommended that the HSO evaluate these wastes to determine which should be managed as clinical waste and supervise the in-house control of waste. Procedures for the segregation, collection, storage, labelling, and movement of waste must be documented. Staff handling clinical waste must be familiar with health and safety procedures.

The first element of a clinical waste management plan is to specify which wastes are to be managed as clinical. As designated previously, the two categories of waste treated as clinical must be strictly adhered to. Provision should be made for clinical wastes with multiple hazards (i.e., injury and infection) because, if not separated from the general waste stream, these can pose a double injury factor to those handling the waste. There are three golden rules in managing clinical waste. First, when in doubt, put it in a red bag. If unsure of whether waste is 'general' or 'clinical', place the item in the red bag (unless it is categorised as 'sharps' in which case it must be placed in a sharps container). The second rule is consideration of all people in the chain of disposal. Clinical waste must be collected and transported to the disposal site or stored appropriately until it can be disposed of properly. It is essential to consider the danger to mortuary personnel collecting the waste from the facility and placing it in the appropriate containers, storage, and collection area. It is crucial to take measures to avoid injuries to contractors collecting general waste; this can happen if medical waste and general waste are not segregated. Injuries to contractors collecting medical waste, due to containers not being sealed or being overloaded, must be avoided, as must injuries to contractors due to sharps not being placed in the correct container (i.e., placed in red bags instead of sharps container). It is essential to avoid creating hazards at refuse sites to local people and faunal or avian

Table 3–4. *Recommended containers for waste*

Characteristics	Rigid plastic	Flexible plastic	Fibre board and liner
Bulky low weight	Yes	Yes	Yes
Bulky high mass	Yes	No	Yes
Average volume + mass	Yes	Yes	Yes
Wet or liquid	Yes	Yes	No
Dry	Yes	Yes	Yes
Sharp	Yes	No	No
Soft	Yes	Yes	Yes
Ordinary medical waste	Yes	Yes	Yes
All other categories	Yes	No	No

scavengers that may search among general waste for recyclable items or food/nesting, respectively. The third rule is not to put objects in clinical waste that do not belong there.

All wastes should be segregated at the point of generation (i.e., at the point that the material becomes waste). This is best accomplished by those who generate the waste because they are best qualified to assess the hazards associated with it. Disposal stations in the workplace must be clearly marked to indicate the type of waste catered for, and the containers that are used to isolate medical waste must be carefully chosen. It is crucial to use the right container for the right application. These containers should be marked with the universal medical symbol (or biohazard sign); all bags should be distinctively coloured and marked with the biohazard symbol. Table 3–4 indicates the recommended types of container to use for different categories of waste. Adoption of the system of colour coding recommended internationally is strongly advised for all containers used for waste disposal; this system can be seen in Table 3–2. Strict adherence to a colour coding system will help ensure against the dangers resulting from infectious waste finding its way into the general refuse stream. Using coloured bags or containers is preferred to the attachment of coloured tags, which may become detached. Bags for waste destined for autoclaving should be made of a material suitable for this purpose (i.e., capable of withstanding the heat/pressure cycle to which they will be repeatedly subject) and should also carry an indicator to show whether they have been subjected to this treatment (e.g., autoclave tape).

It is preferable to treat clinical waste as soon as possible after generation, but this may not always be possible or practical. In such cases, it may be necessary to store the waste, and four important factors must be considered in this instance. The integrity of the packaging must be ensured and the storage temperature (if possible, mechanically ventilate or refrigerate the medical waste area) appropriate to the stability of the materials. The anticipated duration of the storage will influence the adopted storage strategy, as will the available location and design of the storage area; it should be in the wet area, washable, drained, and secure.

Liquid waste may be generated in the following wet areas: body reception area, body storage area, postmortem examination room, wash bays (trolley and vehicles), medical waste storage area, and the laundry facility. Liquid biological waste may consist of blood, body fluids, and solid elements such as bone dust and tissue removed during unavoidable defleshing procedures, all of which may be mixed with water or chemicals. The liquid waste, which will contain large amounts of contaminated water, must be discharged directly into the sewer system (if such is available) via trapped drains. The waste may not be discharged into the storm water drain. If no sewer is available, tanks should be available in which to store such liquid waste until it can be appropriately disposed. The trap baskets may contain solid medical waste (e.g., sharps), and occupational safety precautions must be implemented in handling these baskets.

In handling minor or major spills of any and all hazardous substances, the important elements are common sense and a practised contingency plan. The procedure for managing spills must include evacuation of the immediate spill site; appropriate protective equipment; readily available information concerning the specific substance spilt; having an established procedure for the disposal of the waste spill (if possible, flushing into the sewer with copious amounts of water); and detailed documentation of the incident. Following due process, all work must cease until the HSO declares the area hazard free. Any employees exposed to the spill must be monitored and treated, if necessary.

3.5.11 Observation of postmortem examinations

For legal reasons, nonessential staff or visitors should be kept to an absolute minimum. While in the observation area, staff must conform to local safety rules and use PPE as appropriate and at the direction of the senior APT. If an observation area is not available, staff may not be present when infection risk cases are being examined or unfixed high-risk case specimens are being dissected, unless conforming to the requirements of local safety rules (i.e., suitably protected and attired). Next of kin and representatives of religious orders may want to see the body(ies). They should, however, be discouraged from making close contact if there is a risk of infection, especially if the deceased was classified as a 'Danger of Infection' case (i.e., the presence of Hazard Group 3 or 4 pathogens suspected or confirmed). In 'Danger of Infection' cases, the relatives or representatives of religious orders should be told of the risk and advised against physical contact with the body. If they insist, contact should be brief, and the person concerned must be encouraged to wash his or her hands immediately afterward. Kissing should be strongly discouraged. When, for religious purposes, there is a requirement to wash the body, those concerned must be clearly warned of any risk that may exist. They will be required to sign a disclaimer form if the ceremony goes ahead. In such a case, the participants in the ceremony should be advised about the precautions they must take to help reduce the possibility of their contracting an infection or passing it on, and must be made to understand the possible consequences to themselves and others with whom they

Table 3–5. *Safe operations list*

Security	Occupational	Operational	Forensic processes	Hazardous materials
• Explosive remnants of war (EOD) • Booby traps • Terrain • Travel • Self-protection	• Infectious disease • Hazardous flora and fauna • Deep excavation • Hygiene – general • Hygiene – food • Water • Hazardous materials – general • Climactic extremes • Equipment – general	• Accidental injury • Posttraumatic stress disorder	• X-ray • Fluoroscopy • Plain film	• X-ray processing chemicals • Sterilising agents • Disinfectants • Clinical waste

may subsequently come into contact. It will be necessary for all persons entering wet areas in the mortuary to change into appropriate protective clothing. Types of clothing and protective equipment to be used will be specified in local rules for the various locations.

3.6 Documentation and recording: Risk assessment forms and logs

Forms for use when undertaking the health and safety risk assessment are FA02F and MG02; the former for site work and the latter for use in the mortuary. These forms can be located on the accompanying CD and guidance as to their use in 1.11.

Table 3–5 lists the issues for which an organisation must devise a safe operating procedure. These will detail specific roles, resources, arrangements, and references to ensure operations are safely carried out. Safe operations procedures are broadly divided into security, including travel and accommodation; occupational safety involving general activities such as lifting; and use of plant and forensic safety, including specialist techniques, situations, and equipment. The list is as comprehensive as practicable but should be added to as and when necessary.

3.7 Appendix: Health and safety legislation

Health and Safety at Work etc. (1974). This is the main UK act of Parliament, and it requires general and particular duties of employers, employees, and third parties to protect their own health, safety, and welfare, and the health, safety, and welfare of others. More detailed regulations are made under this act.

Workplace (Health, Safety and Welfare) Regulations (1992). SI-No: 3004 – These regulations impose requirements with respect to the health, safety, and welfare of persons in a workplace, in particular, with respect to subjects like maintenance, ventilation of enclosed workplaces, temperature indoors, lighting (including emergency lighting), or cleanliness of the workplace.

Health and Safety Information for Employees (Modifications and Repeals) Regulations (1995). SI-No: 2923 – These regulations modify the Health and Safety Information for Employees Regulations of 1989 (S.I. 1989/682) by (a) applying the 1989 regulations to certain premises and activities outside Great Britain, and (b) adding provisions to the 1989 regulations that enable the HSE to approve posters or leaflets that are specific to particular classes of employment, so that employers in those classes may display or provide those specific posters or leaflets rather than those of a general nature. The regulations also repeal a number of provisions in health and safety legislation related to the display of notices or posters and the provision of information.

Construction (Health, Safety and Welfare) Regulations (1996). SI-No: 1592 – These regulations impose requirements with respect to the health, safety, and welfare of persons carrying out construction work and of others who may be affected by that work.

Carriage of Dangerous Goods (Classification, Packaging and Labelling) and Use of Transportable Pressure Receptacles Regulations (1996). SI-No: 2092 – These regulations impose requirements and prohibitions in relation to the classification, packaging, and labelling of dangerous goods for carriage by road or on a railway. The regulations repeal and re-enact with modifications the Carriage of Dangerous Goods by Road and Rail (Classification, Packaging and Labelling) Regulations 1994.

Fire Precautions (Workplace) Regulations (1997). SI-No: 1840 – These regulations give effect in Great Britain to (a) article 8(1) and (2) of Council Directive 89/391/EEC on the introduction of measures to encourage improvements in the safety and health of workers at work; and (b) article 6 of, together with paragraphs 4 and 5 of each of the annexes to, Council Directive 89/654/EEC concerning the minimum safety and health requirements for the workplace (OJ No. L 393, 30.12.89, p. 1), in so far as those provisions relate to fire precautions and in so far as more specific legislation does not make appropriate provision. The regulations also give effect to certain other articles of the directive, in so far as they concern the substantive provisions.

Provision and Use of Work Equipment Regulations (1998). SI-No: 2306 – These regulations impose health and safety requirements with respect to the provision and use of work equipment. The regulations revoke and reenact the Provision and Use of Work Equipment Regulations 1992, which gave effect to the minimum health and safety requirements for the use of work equipment by workers at work. This was with respect to Great Britain, except in relation to certain matters, to Council Directive 89/655/EEC – OJ No. L393, 30.12.89, p. 13.

Lifting Operations and Lifting Equipment Regulations (1998). SI-No: 2307 – These regulations impose health and safety requirements with respect to lifting equipment. The regulations place duties on employers. Regulation 3 (application) places those duties on self-employed persons and certain persons having control of lifting equipment; of persons at work who use, supervise, or manage its use; or of the way it is used to the extent of their control.

Management of Health and Safety at Work Regulations (1999). SI-No: 3242 – These regulations define the need for employers to carry out a suitable and sufficient assessment of the health and safety risks to which employees are exposed while they are at work. It also requires the same in respect to the health and safety risks of persons not in the employer's employ that arise out of, or in connection with, the conduct of the employer's undertaking, for the purpose of identifying the measures the employer needs to take to comply with the requirements and prohibitions imposed by or under the relevant statutory provisions.

Ionising Radiation Regulations (1999). SI-No: 3232 – The Ionising Radiation Regulations supersede and consolidate most previous regulations concerning ionising radiation in the workplace. The regulations emphasise the duties of employers to protect their staff and the general public from ionising radiation (including radioactive substances) arising from work environments. The regulations also imposes certain duties on employees.

Ionising Radiation (Medical Exposure) Regulations (2000). SI-No: 1059 – The Ionising Radiation Regulations are an addition to the 1999 (No. 3232) regulations and deal with specific aspects of ionising radiation during medical exposure (International Atomic Energy Agency, 1996).

Personal Protective Equipment Regulations (2002). SI-No: 1144 – These regulations consolidate with amendments the Personal Protective Equipment (EC Directive) Regulations 1992 (S.I. 1992/3139; as amended by S.I. 1993/3074, S.I. 1994/2326, and S.I. 1996/3039 and extended by section 2(1) of the Economic Area Act 1993, c. 51). The basic health and safety requirements applicable to a particular class or type of PPE are set out in Schedule 2. There is a presumption that the relevant basic health and safety requirements applicable to a class or type of PPE are met if the PPE complies with transposed harmonised standards.

Chemicals (Hazard Information and Packaging for Supply) Regulations (2002). SI-No: 1689 – These regulations revoke and reenact with amendments the Chemicals (Hazard Information and Packaging for Supply) Regulations 1994 (S.I. 3247). These regulations, as respect Great Britain, implement (a) Council Directive 1992/32/EEC (OJ No. L154, 5.6.92, p. 1) amending for the seventh time Council Directive 67/548/EEC (OJ No. L196, 16.8.67, p. 1), in so far as its provisions relate to the classification, packaging, and labelling of dangerous substances; (b) Council Directive 1999/45/EC (OJ No. L 200, 30.7.99, p. 1) on the classification, packaging, and labelling of dangerous preparations; (c) points 29, 30, and 31 of Annex I to Council Directive 76/769/EEC (OJ No. L262, 27.9.76, p. 201) as most recently amended by Directive 2001/41/EC of the European Parliament and of the Council (OJ No. L194, 18.7.01, p. 36); and (d) Commission Directive 91/155/EEC (OJ No. L 76, 22.3.91, p. 39) on the provision of safety data sheets.

Health and Safety (Miscellaneous Amendments) Regulations (2002). SI-No: 2174 – These regulations amend the regulations relating to health and safety at work that are specified later in this section, to give effect to European requirements in Great Britain. They also contain drafting changes. Regulation 2 amends Regulation 2 of the Health and Safety (First-Aid) Regulations 1981 to require that a first aid room be easily accessible and sign-posted. Regulation 3 amends the Health and Safety (Display Screen Equipment) Regulations 1992. Regulation 4 amends the Manual Handling Operations Regulations 1992 by adding regulation 4(3). It specifies factors to be taken account of in determining whether operations involve risk. It gives effect to Annex II to Council Directive 90/269/EEC (OJ No. L156, 21.6.90, p. 9) on the minimum health and safety requirements for the manual handling of loads where there is a risk particularly of back injury to workers. Regulation 5 amends the Personal Protective Equipment at Work Regulations 1992. Regulation 6 amends the Workplace (Health, Safety and Welfare) Regulations 1992 to variously give complete, or clearer, effect to the following provisions of the Workplace Directive.

Control of Asbestos at Work Regulations (2002). SI-No: 2675 – These regulations reenact, with modifications, the Control of Asbestos at Work Regulations 1987 (S.I. 1987/2115) as amended. The 1987 regulations imposed requirements for the protection of employees who might be exposed to asbestos at work and other persons who might be affected by such work. They also imposed certain duties on employees concerning their own protection from such exposure.

Control of Lead at Work Regulations (2002). SI-No: 2676 – These regulations reenact, with modifications, the Control of Lead at Work Regulations 1998 (S.I. 1998/543). The 1998 regulations imposed requirements for the protection of employees who might be exposed to lead at work and other persons who might be affected by such work. They also imposed certain duties on employees concerning their own protection from such exposure.

Control of Substances Hazardous to Health Regulations (2002). SI-No: 2677 – These regulations impose duties on employers to protect employees and other persons who may be exposed to substances hazardous to health. They also imposed certain duties on employees concerning their own protection from such exposure, and prohibited the import into the United Kingdom of certain substances and articles from outside the European Economic Area.

Dangerous Substances and Explosive Atmospheres Regulations (2002). SI-No: 2776 – These regulations impose requirements for the purpose of eliminating or reducing risks to safety from fire, explosion, or other events arising from the hazardous properties of a 'dangerous substance' in connection with work.

Control of Substances Hazardous to Health (Amendment) Regulations (2003). SI-No: 978 – These regulations amend the Control of Substances Hazardous to Health Regulations 2002 (S.I. 2677) by adding (a) a definition of 'mutagen' and amending references to 'carcinogen' to also include 'mutagen', thereby implementing paragraphs 2 to 4 of article 1 of Council Directive 1999/38/EC amending for the second time Council Directive 90/394/EEC on the protection of workers from the risks related to exposure to carcinogens at work; and (b) 17 polychlorodibenzodioxins and polychlorodibenzofurans to the list of substances in Schedule 1 to which the definition of 'carcinogen' relates.

Management of Health and Safety at Work and Fire Precautions (Workplace) (Amendment) Regulations (2003). SI-No: 2457 – These regulations amend the Management of Health and Safety at Work Regulations 1999 and the Fire Precautions (Workplace) Regulations 1997. These regulations make a small number of amendments that rectify minor defects in the 1999 regulations. In addition, they replace regulation 22 of the 1999 regulations (which provided that breach of a duty imposed by the regulations could not confer a right of action in any civil proceedings), to the effect that employees may bring civil claims against their employers where they are in breach of duties imposed by the 1999 regulations (however, in respect to claims by nonemployees, the exclusion of civil liability for breach of duties imposed by the 1999 regulations remains). They also make amendments to the 1997 regulations to achieve the same effect in relation to breaches of duties imposed by Part II of those regulations and regulations 1 to 5, 7 to 12, and 13(2) and (3) of the 1999 regulations in so far as those regulations impose requirements concerning general fire precautions to be taken or observed by an employer.

Additional Health and Safety Regulations and Guidelines. Other guidance on specific topics (e.g., explosive remnants of war [EOD], disease) and more detailed guidance on machinery and PPE will be found in supporting documentation specified in safe operating procedures designed by the organisation undertaking the work. These will relate to particular investigation activities.

4

Scene of crime examination

Sarah Donnelly, Michael Hedley, Tim Loveless, Romina
Manning, Alison Perman, and Roland Wessling

4.1 Introduction

It is necessary to begin this chapter by reiterating a point made in 1.1. Not all
mass grave or mass fatality investigations are undertaken for judicial reasons. Some
may be primarily intended to recover the mortal remains and other possessions
of the Missing; to identify the Missing and to ultimately allow their remains to be
returned to their families for appropriate funerary rites; and to help facilitate closure
and reconciliation processes. However, even in the latter context, there is always the
possibility that future needs may require a previous recovery and identification
process to serve a belated judicial function (see 1.1). As such, it is crucial that
the process of recovery, recording, and analysis is done to an appropriate standard
and in a manner consistent with the confident association of human remains and
other materials, and detailed recording of context and other information to ensure
correct identification. In this chapter, the terminology used is consistent with that
appropriate to a process serving a judicial function, where the scene of deposition
is believed to be a crime scene and where everything recovered from that scene,
including the human remains, is considered to be evidence and treated as such.
That said, the processes and principles described and set out in this chapter equally
well serve missions with a humanitarian goal, and if considered appropriate, different
terminology may be used to diffuse a potentially difficult situation. All recording
forms or logs referred to in this chapter can be found located on the CD that
accompanies this book. Guidance in their use can be found in 1.11.

During the course of any investigation that examines a scene of crime, the scientists (and examiners) involved will locate, record, and seize material, or evidence,
which will be in a physical, documentary, biological, or other material format.
Once seized, material and subsequent records become potential 'exhibits' that may

be presented in a court (White, 1998). Further to that, the excavation, recording, recovery, and analysis processes will themselves create further documentation that is in itself evidence and has to be treated in the same way. During the entire field and mortuary processes, ensuring continuity and a secure chain of custody through an effective and rigorously controlled and documented process (Association of Chief Police Officers [ACPO] and Centrex, 2005) is paramount. Not all evidence recovered and recorded will be used in the trial, and some may be discarded later in the analysis process. All such decisions are made by the investigator with the relevant (i.e., field or mortuary and judicial) management team. All exhibits and records generated in their recovery, recording, analysis, and storage must be processed in a manner that ensures their integrity and their provenance (ACPO and Centrex, 2005). Management of this process is the responsibility of the SCM, and he or she will delegate responsibility as they see fit to scene of crime examiners (SCEs).

For simplicity's sake, in this book, all of the evidence collected and recorded, as well as all reports that are produced, are referred to as 'exhibits'. However, under UK law, an item of evidence recovered from a crime scene only becomes an exhibit when it is formally produced by a witness in court or admitted formally in court. Human remains are described more explicitly, although still generically as set out in this chapter.

4.1.1   Scene of crime manager

Depending on the scale of operations, there may be SCMs for both the field and the mortuary, or one SCM with overall responsibility for both, but who for one site may delegate day-to-day authority to a senior SCE, who will effectively also be the exhibits officer. In practice, this delegation is most likely to take place within the mortuary where processes are more predictable and controllable than in the field. In all investigations of the kind with which this text is concerned, it has to be remembered that probably the most important role of all is that of the SCM. If they fail to control the way evidence is managed then the whole process may be challenged in the court process and invalidated. He or she must therefore be very experienced in this role and must also possess first rate process and people management skills.

In both the field and the mortuary, the teams are always under the overall control of the SCM, or his or her delegate. They will liaise closely with the project manager and other senior scientific staff. The SCM(s) have an extensive role and will impose processes designed to ensure the integrity of evidence and the chain of custody. They will oversee evidence collection, processing, and security. The SCM will call on the expertise of a multidisciplinary team of forensic specialists to uncover, examine, and report on their findings in the course of forensic excavation and subsequent analysis. Coordination of the implementation of scientific protocols in the field and the mortuary is, however, the responsibility of the senior scientists, and they will coordinate and supervise the scientific process of the investigation. The SCM may delegate actual tasks connected to site/mortuary and evidence continuity and integrity, but will be ultimately responsible for both.

4.1.2   Scene of crime examiner

Evidence handling at all stages of an investigation will be undertaken by suitably trained and experienced SCEs. They will process, log, record, and retain the integrity of all evidence and exhibits recovered (and records produced) during an investigation under the supervision of a senior SCE. The provision of suitable labelling, packaging, security, storage, and transportation of all evidence and human remains is their responsibility. An assistant SCE/data entry clerk will enter information into the evidence log and database.

It is desirable that SCEs be present at all stages of the investigation of an atrocity crime that have the potential to yield physical evidence. It is the SCE's duty to ensure this continuity and integrity from the moment any exhibit is brought to their attention, throughout the time in their custody and control until it eventually passes to the next stage of the evidence chain. During this time, evidence needs to be assessed, recorded *in situ*, documented, recovered, prepared for packaging, analysed, conserved, stored, and otherwise correctly handled. All of these processes are conducted under the overall control and management of the SCE, even if they are carried out by various experts, ranging from the archaeologist, who excavates and records the material, to the DNA expert, who extracts the genetic profile of the deceased from soft or hard tissues. In this chapter, all aspects of the SCE's role in the field and the mortuary will be discussed in detail. Some conservation and packaging processes for specific types of sample are not discussed in this chapter but can be found elsewhere in this book (e.g., Chapter 9).

4.2   Field procedures

There are three components to the evidential element of any field operation: the integrity and continuity of the site, the integrity and continuity of the evidence recovered and seized, and the integrity and continuity of the records and documentation produced throughout the recovery and analysis process (i.e., logs, forms, photographs and other original notes).

4.2.1   Site integrity and continuity

Personnel entry control. To document and preserve site security and integrity, the personnel entry register will be maintained at all times. At the start and close of every working day, all field staff must sign in and out, and the name, date, and time of arrival and departure of every member of staff will be registered by the field management team or a designated nominee. On arrival, any visitors to the site must obtain authorisation from the SCM, or, in the SCM's absence, the designated member of the field management team, and be checked out on departure. Visitors must state the reason for their presence on site (using form FA14R – personnel entry register). Anyone who does not have a legitimate reason for attending should be refused entry.

At the beginning and end of the day, the senior SCE or the SCM will be the first to arrive and the last to leave and will complete the register accordingly.

Scene contamination. During the forensic examination of a crime scene, soil, geological, and/or environmental samples may be taken from that scene for comparison with samples taken from other suspected scenes to ascertain whether a connection between them exists. If subsequent scientific analysis of samples establishes a connection, it will be necessary to satisfy a court of justice that no possible physical link existed between the two scenes, other than that established by the actions of the perpetrators during the commission of the crime. It is vitally important to prevent any possibility or suggestion of contamination between sites. Teams carrying out exhumations within a particular theatre should be aware that contamination between sites can occur by transference of material carried by, for example, excavating implements, plant machinery, personal baggage, footwear and clothing, and vehicles. To preclude and negate any allegation of contamination, practical but positive steps should be taken to prevent any cross-transference of materials. To ensure this, personal protective equipment worn during the excavation process (e.g., overalls or gloves) should be disposable and not used elsewhere or on more than one site. Working boots should not be worn off site, and will be washed and cleaned before being worn on a subsequent site. Personal tools and equipment must be thoroughly cleaned at the completion of a site. Such cleaning should be scrupulous and logged. All equipment, including that which is hired, borrowed locally, or bought for the purpose of the grave exhumation, should be thoroughly cleaned and inspected before being introduced on site. Containers, vehicles, and plant machinery will be power washed and thoroughly inspected, inside and out, for adhering material that could be deposited at a subsequent site. It is imperative that the method of cleaning be adequate to remove microscopic as well as more superficial materials. In the preparation stages of the exhumation, a member of the management team, in most cases, the SCM, will examine all personal and issued tools, equipment, and machinery for the presence of potential contaminants. The SCM should hold an inventory of all plant and equipment held and used on site, and record details of the cleaning process. This inventory will be a disclosable evidential document and will be made available to prosecuting counsel during case preparation.

4.2.2 Evidence integrity and continuity

Through delegation of powers from the SCM, the SCEs have responsibility for all of the evidence and exhibits, and its handling, on site and for the safe custody, preservation, and continuity of all evidence in his or her possession. In terms of physical

Figure 4–1. Tarpaulins are effective and useful temporary protective covers for mass graves. *Source:* Inforce Foundation.

evidence at deposition sites, this will include human remains and other exhibits. The SCE will ensure that no one enters the cordoned site unless they are directly involved in the exhumation process. At the conclusion of the working day, if the site is not protected by a tent but protection is deemed necessary, the grave will be covered with tarpaulin sheets (Figure 4–1) to prevent intrusion of vermin, scavenging animals, or displacement by adverse weather. The site will then be handed over to the officer in charge of security. Upon commencement of the next working day, the SCE will inspect the site for disturbance. The photographer will, under the direction of the SCE, take a video recording of the site at the end of each working day and at the commencement of the next (using form FA10LD/N) (see 4.4.1). This will also be undertaken at various stages throughout the day if necessary, such as before placing and after removing covers protecting the exposed exhumation area during downtimes (see 4.4.1). Any breach of continuity will be recorded and investigated and a report, with findings, submitted in evidence.

Material evidence, having passed to the custody of the SCE, will be housed in a secure lockable cargo container or an appropriate equivalent. Recovered bodies and body parts will be secured in a shelved, refrigerated container with lockable doors, the keys to which will only be held by the SCE. If deemed necessary, a tamper-evident seal will be placed on the doors of the containers at the end of each working day, in the presence of the officer in charge of the security detail protecting the site and containers. Any subsequent breach of the integrity of a seal will be recorded and investigated.

Exhibit logging. A key role of the SCE is to advise and assist forensic archaeologists on evidence/exhibits handling methods. The SCE will maintain a Site Evidence Log (FA11L) recording every body, body part, and exhibit retained during the course of the assessment and exhumation. Upon receiving a request for a number from the evidence log, the SCE will ascertain whether it is for a body (B), a body part (BP), or an exhibit (A). In the case of a body or body part, that number will be written in indelible ink onto a suitable tag and handed to the person who will be responsible for the removal of that body or body part and who will then ensure that the tag is securely fastened to a limb or major bone of that body or body part. All references to the evidence number (including on logs, documents, and labelling) will also display the initials (or other identifying mark) of the person finding the evidence (e.g., an archaeologist), the initials or other identifying mark of the SCE controlling custody of the evidence, and the appropriate date. The Site Evidence Log (form FA11L) will show details of the evidence, including the name of the issuing SCE and the scientist who recovered the evidence, if different. The SCE and archaeologist/anthropologist will later confirm that the number on the issued tag corresponds with the number on the prepared body container and the body/body parts recovery report form before the remains are placed in that container. The only exception to this labelling requirement concerns individual bones, discovered out of context, which will, for large sites, be collected in a 'general bone bag'.

In the case of an exhibit, a suitable evidence bag will be selected and all relevant details, together with the Site Evidence Log number, will be written on that bag for the later collection of the exhibit by the SCE. Every exhibit will be photographed *in situ* (form FA09LD/N) upon issue of a number from the Site Evidence Log. That same number will be displayed in the photograph adjacent to the item being photographed, together with an appropriate scale and an arrow indicating the north cardinal point. The surveyor will record the precise position of that item on a body, within the grave or at that scene. If a body is being recorded, then this will be recorded using a sequence system (Tables 5–1 and 5–2).

Evidence relating to the date, time, and relative chronology of events following the death of the recovered victim or victims may be revealed during an exhumation. This may be indicated by documentary evidence in the form of dated script and evidence such as day and date features on, for example, kinetic wrist or pocket watches as were recovered during investigations relating to the Srebrenica Massacre (ICTY, 2001) (see Figure 4–2). In addition, entomological evidence adhering to

Figure 4–2. The day and date recorded from Seiko automatic watches served as strong evidence in dating events in the Srebrenica Massacre. *Source:* ICTY/Tim Loveless.

the cadaver may provide indicators such as time between death and interment, and associated botanical evidence (see 9.1) may indicate month or season of death and/or interment. The SCE will seize and record such evidence for analysis by an appropriate specialist. If the circumstances require it, soil or geological samples will be collected and recorded. Where a secondary grave (not the original or primary site of interment) is suspected, samples can be compared with samples collected from a previous or subsequent grave(s) excavation. The importance of taking a comprehensive range of control samples cannot be overstated. Sampling strategies will be in accordance with the specific requirements of the analysis to which it will be subjected (see 9.2) and recorded using the sample recording form (FA13F). For the purposes of recording all relevant information of an individual victim's excavation, the 'Body Location, Attitude and Properties Form' will be completed by the anthropologist or archaeologist responsible for the excavation and subsequent removal of those particular human remains (see forms FA12BH, FA12BT, FA12SH, FA12ST, and FA12BP which are located on the accompanying CD).

Before excavation procedures start, the overall management team has to establish whether bodies are to be searched for identifying features and explosive ordnance devices (EODs) in the field or in the mortuary. In the interests of health and safety and to prevent further deterioration caused by exposure to air, it is advisable to undertake this first in the field, and for this purpose the SCE will be responsible for searching the clothing of all excavated bodies and body parts *in situ*. The SCE will record in detail any identifying documentation associated with the body or body part. Identifying features remaining on the body or body part (e.g., tattoos, prostheses) will be photographed and recorded. Where ordnance is suspected, the SCE will enlist the assistance of an EOD officer. Reasons for deciding whether to search bodies in the grave or in the mortuary are presented in Table 4–1.

Table 4–1. *Reasons for body search in the field and in the mortuary*

Reasons for searching in the grave	Reasons for searching in the mortuary
• Unearthing human remains often restarts or at least accelerates the decomposition process, which will continue even in cold storage. This decomposition process can affect or even destroy evidence such as identification papers.	• The mortuary is a controlled environment in which a search can be conducted more thoroughly and efficiently, due to proper cleaning facilities, better lighting, and the use of radiographs.
• Bodies may be booby-trapped by the perpetrators. This endangers personnel in the mortuary, where usually there is no EOD expert present.	• Evidence can be processed more efficiently. Documentation, conservation, and analysis of evidence are easier than in the field.

At the end of each day, the SCE will make an inventory of all numbers issued that day against the exhibits in their possession. Those exhibits will then be held in a place of secure storage only accessible by the SCE. If logs have been completed by hand (rather than directly onto computer), the assistant SCE will, under the supervision of the SCE, be responsible for transferring the data from the handwritten evidence and photographic logs to the site computer preprogrammed with an evidence-recording database (see 4.5.3). The SCE will be responsible for the retention and safekeeping of all bodies, body parts, exhibits, evidential logs, completed body recovery reports, exposed film, videotapes, and any other evidential item until the eventual handover to the evidence-processing unit.

Exhibit packaging. For the purpose of packaging some nondegradable exhibits and samples, standard 'Police' heavy polythene evidence bags will be the most suitable. The bags will be preprinted and will have an adhesive, tamper-evident seal. The polythene will be suitable for writing on with black, permanent, and waterproof pens. The preprinted detail on the bag will include sections for the site name and code, evidence log number, time and date, description of the item, location of the find, person finding the exhibit, and person receiving the exhibit. They will also have 'continuity' areas on them (i.e., handover signatures) and cater for laboratory handling with a preprinted section for the name of the person opening the bag. The manufactured bags will vary in size to accommodate the anticipated range of materials to be recovered. Preprinted, permeable, acid-free, synthetic bags containing the same details will also be available for packaging and preserving perishable exhibits. Small rigid plastic containers should be used within these bags to protect vulnerable or sharp exhibits that will not deteriorate in an impermeable environment (a health and safety warning should accompany this latter type of exhibit). Occasionally, extremely large and heavy exhibits will be recovered that the investigator may not consider feasible for removal from site (e.g., metal girders, quarry stone). On-site examinations may be required involving the taking of precise measurements, paint or other samples, representative samples, and castings. These will be carried out by the SCE and comprehensively recorded by photography (a supplementary statement of evidence will be submitted to the investigator by the relevant SCE). With the exception of explosives, live ordnance, and loaded firearms, exhibits positively associated with a body or body part will not normally be separated at exhumation. The investigator may request removal of specific items to expedite a certain aspect of the enquiry; the SCM will rule upon each request based on the information submitted but such associated materials or exhibits will normally be separated at autopsy.

For bodies (B) and body parts (BP), the site code and evidence number issued to each will be indelibly marked onto a suitable tag and fixing. That tag will be securely attached, as appropriate, to an item of clothing or alternatively to a limb or major bone (if attaching to a bone, do not use metal ties because they can cause damage and corrode; plastic ties are preferred). Whenever remains are fully skeletonised, bones will be wrapped in acid-free tissue and packed and suitably cushioned in a crush-resistant box. In such cases, the box will be labelled with the body part number, the site name, and the name of the person recovering (e.g., an archaeologist) and receiving the evidence (the SCE). The box will be sealed with a tamper-evident adhesive tape.

Storage and transportation of evidence, bodies, and body parts. Human remains that are recovered during an excavation will normally be stored in appropriate containers in suitably racked and secured refrigerated containers to preserve and protect them for subsequent examination. Bodies or body parts with soft tissue will be placed in body bags. To prevent the build-up of heat from decomposition of fleshed remains, ventilation around the body bags should always be ensured. The temperature should be kept around 4°C to 6°C, which is low enough to slow down further decomposition, but high enough that bodies do not freeze. Freezing can damage soft tissue and alter bone microstructures (Micozzi, 1991).

Once an item is recovered and packaged, it should be transported to the mortuary as soon as is practicable. If there is a delay, this could cause wet or damp items to further decompose and would therefore adversely affect any subsequent forensic examination. Under these circumstances, it is acceptable to place items temporarily into permeable bags and store them in a cool location until they reach the mortuary, where they will be immediately examined, recorded, and preserved.

General or nonassociated bones. During assessment and/or exhumation, teeth, bone fragments, or small bones may be unearthed that cannot be positively associated with particular bodies. Execution sites may have many bone fragments scattered over the area, these having been dislodged by impacting bullets, bladed or blunt instruments, deliberate acts of dismemberment, or exploding ordnance. Similarly, sites of secondary graves, robbed graves, and body processing may contain numerous bones or bone fragments both on the surface and/or within graves (Figure 4–3). If such items have no contextual value, they will be placed in a general bone

Figure 4–3. The unscientific excavation of mass graves will always fail to recover all evidence. Material may be left *in situ*, dropped in the backfill, or dropped as surface material. This was seen and recorded by Inforce personnel working in Iraq. This site had been excavated by the local community in 2003. *Source:* Inforce Foundation.

collection container (known as 'general bone bag'), having first been recorded *in situ* but not photographed unless it is nevertheless deemed to have evidential value.

Collections of general bones with no contextual value are given a single evidence number. Whenever necessary, each item will be wrapped in acid-free tissue and placed in a paper bag. In the case of an associated group of small bones, these would be wrapped and bagged as a group, and then placed in a container designated as 'general bone'. When the container is sufficiently full, the container will be sealed and labelled. Where bones are recovered that have the potential to be reassociated with other remains, their location should be recorded, and each bone (or collection of associated bones) should be given a number (BP).

General exhibits. During mass grave exhumation, it is not unusual to recover a large amount of footwear and significant amounts of clothing that cannot be associated with any particular body or body part. These will be placed, without individual listing, in bags that have been given an exhibit number and described as a 'general clothing bag'. An exception to this would be where clothing contained an item that identified the wearer (e.g., an identity document). Under these circumstances, the article of clothing and the identity document should be given a single exhibit number and dealt with accordingly by the SCE. General clothing bags will be handed over to the mortuary evidence unit so the contents can be further examined, laundered and processed.

Bearing in mind that the surface search of a suspected gravesite may be a considerable time after an event, the initial search may reveal items that are initially assessed as not being evidentially relevant to the enquiry. Similarly, there will be items found in the infill of the grave that may be declared by the investigator as evidence of less significance. These items should, however, be retained and logged under a single exhibit number until the excavation is complete. Then, in consultation with the investigating authority, a final decision will be made to discard or retain any or all of these items. Retained items will subsequently be handed over to the evidence-processing unit. Authority for on-site disposal will be entered against the evidence log entry pertaining to the general exhibit bag as authorised by the investigator. Photographing and surveying these items on recovery would be at the discretion of the senior archaeologist, SCE, and/or investigator.

Evidence handover – The field. The SCE will remain with the excavation or investigation team until the site is reinstated after the excavation is completed. Upon completion of the exhumation, the SCE will compare the inventory of the bodies, body parts, and exhibits in his or her custody against the detail in the evidence log, the exposed film against the photographic logs, and the body recovery reports against the evidence logs (see CD for these logs). Any discrepancies should be investigated and a report of the findings submitted in evidence. Handover sheets will be prepared from the site computer evidence database. The exhibits will then be handed over, upon signature, to the evidence processing unit or an investigator; exposed film and videotapes will also be dealt with in this way. Bodies, Body Parts and Body Location, Attitude and Properties Forms and all logs will be handed over to the senior mortuary SCE or, if appropriate, the mortuary SCM, upon signature. Copies may be made for the production of reports by the SCE, SCM, or others for whom they are relevant.

For the purpose of continuity, the SCE should accompany the evidence to its destination and be present while the person receiving the evidence checks each item against the Field Handover Form (FA17F) and against the evidence number affixed to the item. That person will comply with the chain of custody process by acknowledging receipt of each item in appending their signature against that item on the handover documentation. The completed Body Location, Attitude, and Properties Forms will be listed by evidence number, handed over in the same manner, and acknowledged by signature of the receiving officer. Although the film processing unit may be separate from the mortuary facility, handover of exposed film, photographic log sheets, and videotape will follow the same procedure. The handwritten Site Evidence Log and a copy disc of the computer-generated data log will be handed over to the processing unit, again, upon signature. The site SCE will retain a copy of the handover documentation bearing the signatures of the SCE handing over and the receiving SCE. A copy of the handover documentation will be supplied to the senior investigator.

4.3   Mortuary procedures

As with the field operation, there are three elements to the evidential side of any mortuary operation: the integrity of the mortuary itself, the integrity of the human remains and other evidence, the integrity and continuity of the records, and documentation produced throughout the investigation process (i.e., logs, forms, photographs).

4.3.1   Mortuary integrity and continuity

Personnel entry control. At the start and close of every working day, all mortuary staff members will sign in and out using the personnel entry register. Any visitors to the mortuary, after being authorised by members of the management team, will also sign in and state their reason for attending the mortuary. Anyone who does not have a legitimate reason for attending will be refused entry. At the beginning and end of the day, the senior SCE or a designated mortuary manager will be the first to arrive and the last to leave, and will complete the personnel entry register accordingly.

4.3.2   Evidence integrity and continuity

The integrity and continuity of evidence starts in the mortuary with the handover of evidence to them by the field investigation team.

Evidence handover – The mortuary. Upon arrival at the mortuary, the refrigerated vehicle or storage containers carrying exhibits must be checked by the senior SCE to confirm the integrity of the seals and locks. If any are found to have been tampered with, before they are opened, the damage will be documented, a photographic record made, and a full investigation carried out and reported upon. When the containers are opened, the senior SCE will then check every exhibit within the container separately and mark the handover sheet accordingly. This form is generated from the site database, which is maintained by one of the site SCEs. This should be undertaken for the bodies, body parts, and all site exhibits. Once the SCE is satisfied that all the exhibits are accounted for, they should sign the form as received. A copy of the completed form is then handed back to the SCE who is accompanying the containers from the site for record purposes. The senior SCE will also sign to demonstrate the handover of the Body Location, Attitude and Properties Forms, photographs and negatives, photographic logs and videotapes, the handwritten evidence logs, and the discs of the computer data, upon checking. The electronic history of information gathered from the site will be handed to the data entry team, who will later collate and integrate the site data with the mortuary data.

The mortuary team will adhere to the numbering system adopted by the field team for the continuity of evidence. When mortuary and field operations are working simultaneously, it may be necessary to begin numbering in the mortuary, from an arbitrary number such as 5001 (i.e., field operations would be numbered 0–5000 and mortuary 5001–10,000). Every new exhibit is allocated a unique number. So that recording of exhibit types and clothing are consistent, a list of possible items has been produced and should be adhered to. This list can be amended at the start of every mission to include items that may be culturally or geographically specific to that particular location. If unusual garments are encountered once the investigation has begun, then they should be added to the list at the first encounter and not subsequently (i.e., do not wait for it to be repeated before adding it to the list).

Associations of exhibits to a body (e.g., a bullet found in a body) can be made on the evidence log. Links can therefore be made between several objects. For example, a ligature tying two bodies together will have its own evidence number and can then be linked to both bodies in the evidence log.

Drying, packaging, and storage of evidence. Any object, sample, or material that needs to be stored for any length of time must be subject to appropriate passive conservation techniques. This will ensure that the material can be held in a stable condition so the processes of degradation are halted or significantly slowed down. Material collected from the postmortem, dental, or anthropological examination will vary in nature and conservation requirements. The approaches to treatment and storage of these materials must be passive in nature so no alteration to the material can interfere with its evidentiary nature. Detailed recording and photography of the material in its original state must be made. Active conservation methods must only be used when no passive method can be applied, and in such cases, this must be fully documented. For treatment and storage of specialised and organic material, such as biological samples, see the appropriate SOP. For all other sensitive material, advice from a suitably qualified and experienced conservator must be sought.

So that an exhibit does not further decompose during storage, it is usually essential to dry it thoroughly before it is stored. Paper documents and photographs should be dried to prevent the growth of mould. This should be done with the advice of a conservator. When documents are folded, rolled, or stuck together, they should be separated and dried on a flat, absorbent surface. The surface of the document should never be wiped. It is preferable that items are slowly air dried with no form of heating (including sunlight). In certain conditions, this may prove difficult, especially if the mortuary is located in a cold climatic area or one with high relative humidity. Potentially, an item may take days to dry and therefore many exhibits may be left to dry at any one time. In these circumstances, exhibits could accidentally be misplaced, transferred to another case, or lose their labelling. Each item therefore has to be clearly and securely labelled, as described in 4.2.2. It is recommended that a dedicated drying cabinet should be used. Documents, in particular, should be dried in the cabinet because even a small amount of moisture left in them will cause them to degrade and disintegrate. They and other damp or wet organic material should not be stored in plastic evidence bags while there is any possibility that they still retain moisture.

Once an exhibit is completely dry, if it is badly soiled it should not be placed into the original packaging. The original packaging should be signed by the SCE and placed into a new bag, separate from that containing the exhibit, which should be documented accordingly. If resources are limited and it is likely that the original packaging would be reused, it should be signed by the SCE and then resealed using a signature label and tape. Packaging guidelines (Tables 4–2 to 4–4) should be adhered to once the items are dealt with at the mortuary.

When bodies and body parts are delivered to the mortuary, they will be in body bags or, if skeletonised, in acid-free cardboard boxes until the postmortem examination. If soft tissue is present, the refrigeration unit must have a racking system inside so the cold air can circulate around the bodies. This will help delay any further decomposition of the bodies and body parts. When bone and teeth are recovered in a stable state, they can be cleaned with a soft brush. If it is necessary to wash bone, it should not be immersed in water because to do so can cause damage. When bone is washed, it should then be allowed to dry naturally. When bone has associated trace evidence such as blood or metallic fragments, it should be dried but not washed. Bone, regardless of whether it has been washed, should be placed in suitable ventilated containers that are clearly labelled and placed in an environment that is cool with low humidity to slowly air dry. It should not be exposed to sunlight to dry.

Examined bodies are to be kept separate from those yet to be examined. Once the bodies have been examined, they should be returned to a different area within the refrigeration unit or to a different refrigerated unit if resources permit. The refrigeration unit must be fitted with a suitable lock so the continuity of evidence is maintained. Keys should be kept by both the senior SCE and another relevant senior person (e.g., the senior anatomical pathology technologist [APT] who may become the *de facto* mortuary manager), and never left in the mortuary when it is unattended. The exhibits that are received from the site should arrive in a locked container. This must remain at the mortuary; once the items have been examined, they should be returned to a different container, or a different part of the original

Table 4–2. *Items to be packaged into plastic evidence bags*

Evidence category	Treatment and packaging
Ballistics and firearms	Items should be dry (or dried), wrapped in polythene, and then secured within a rigid container. This should then be placed into an exhibit bag. Once dry, firearms should be securely tied into an evidence box and then into an exhibit bag.
Currency: coins or bank notes	Once thoroughly dry, they should be placed into a clear dry plastic exhibit bag.
Personal items such as watches, tobacco tins, jewellery, and eyeglasses	Personal items commonly found on bodies can range from metal, organic, and plastic, and often combinations of these. A conservator should be consulted for the treatment and handling of specific items. Reference material may be consulted for suggested conservation techniques. Once dry, they should be packaged in an appropriately sized container. If an item is believed to be fragile, then it should be placed in a rigid container with a suitable soft acid-free packing medium, such as acid-free tissue paper, before being put into an exhibit bag. Otherwise, they can be placed directly into an exhibit bag.
Documentation, including photographs, letters, and other items	Once thoroughly dry, they should be placed into a clear plastic exhibit bag. If they are in a fragile state, they may be protected in a cardboard box before being put into the exhibit bag.
Films	Loose dirt should be gently brushed from the film on advice of a conservator. Wet film can be placed in a plastic bag and frozen. Dry film should not be exposed to water.
Video- and audiotapes	Loose dirt should be gently brushed from the film on advice of a conservator. Wet tapes must be drained of water and kept in a cool place (not frozen).
Vinyl discs	Loose dirt should be gently brushed from the sleeve on advice of a conservator. Wet discs can be gently rinsed with distilled water or clean tap water and dried with a lint-free cloth (do not rub the surface).
DVDs and CDs	Loose dirt should be gently brushed from the cover on advice of a conservator. The cover can be wiped with a damp cloth. Dry discs can be gently brushed to remove loose dirt; however, the label side should not be scratched.

container, which is then locked. As with the keys for the refrigeration unit, these should never be left unattended in the mortuary.

Exhibits from bodies. The pathologist may recover exhibits from the bodies during the postmortem examination. These are handed to the reporting SCE and may vary from bullets to items of jewellery. Each exhibit will be given a consecutive number that is unique and will be noted on the Mortuary Evidence Log (MC13L). When an exhibit is discovered broken, it should be photographed in this state. It should not be 'glued' (or similar) together because this may affect any subsequent forensic examination. The item should be cleaned, dried, and packaged as all other exhibits. Some exhibits may be destroyed within the mortuary. This may only occur if they

Table 4–3. *Items to be packaged into rigid or other type containers*

Evidence category	Treatment and packaging
Sharp-edged instruments (e.g., knives, hatchets)	If they fit, these items can be placed into rigid 'knife tubes', and then placed into exhibit bags. Alternatively, they can be tied into a rigid container such as a cardboard box and placed in an exhibit bag.
Plants and leaf samples	Plants should be air dried and then wrapped in acid-free tissue in a cardboard box. Leaves should be treated similarly. Both should then be placed into an exhibit bag.
Tyre mark casts, tool mark casts	These should be placed into a rigid container and secured. They can then be placed into an exhibit bag.

are believed to be of no evidential value, no monetary value, or no sentimental value to the family or friends of the deceased. A list of items to be destroyed should be agreed on by the investigator prior to the commencement of the investigation. This may include items such as tobacco in a tin (the tin would be kept) or cigarettes. If the item is destroyed, it should be included on the Mortuary Evidence Log, and a record made of why it was destroyed (e.g., condition on finding).

Bullets, bullet fragments, shell casings, and other ballistic items should all be visible on the x-rays that are taken by the radiographer and will then be removed by the pathologist or anthropologist during the postmortem examination. When the exhibit is identified on the x-ray, or when it is removed from the body, the precise anatomical location should be recorded on the appropriate section of either the pathology or anthropology form. This is to assist pathologists, anthropologists, and SCEs when they are completing their later reports and/or forms. Once the whole examination has been completed and all bullets, fragments, or other ballistic items have been recovered, the form can be handed over to the SCE and the cleaning and documenting process can begin.

Table 4–4. *Items to be packaged into paper evidence bags*

Evidence category	Treatment and packaging
Dry clothing, shoes, and material	Clothing and textiles comes in a variety of materials, synthetic, organic, and often a combination of both. These should not be removed from bodies until they have been analysed by the crime scene examiner and pathologist. Washing of clothing should only be undertaken if they will be displayed to families for identification. In all cases, clothing should be separated by item and naturally dried to prevent mould from developing. Each item should be placed flat in its packaging (paper or plastic as appropriate). Any bones or metallic fragments must be removed from the clothing while damp because they will stick to clothing when dry, increasing the chances of damaging them on removal. Once thoroughly dry, they should be placed into a paper exhibit bag and the exterior noted with the evidence number.
Blindfold and ligatures	These should be packaged as for dry clothing.

When it is decided that exhibits should be washed (i.e., where no chemical or microscopic examination or sampling is anticipated), they should, ideally, be photographed first. Items to be washed should be cleaned individually, dried thoroughly, and then photographed again. No hard probes or brushes should be used to clean the exhibit because this may damage the surface of the item and therefore affect any later examination that may take place. Soft and hard tissues and fluids must be cleaned off the exhibit, after recording their presence, because they may affect the surface of the material during long-term storage and therefore any subsequent forensic examination. Prior to washing, however, a pathologist should be consulted because he or she may require samples to be collected from the items. When the exhibit is photographed, it should be placed onto a neutral background, next to a label showing the evidence number and a scale. The photographic log should be completed in full. Each exhibit is then placed into an appropriate evidence bag and the label completed in full, showing, in particular, the evidence number. The Mortuary Evidence Log should be completed and the exhibit then placed into secure storage as discussed previously.

Other items that are recovered from the body or body part are to be placed into a bowl or similar receptacle and kept with the body. Once the pathologist or anthropologist informs the SCE that there are no more items to be recovered, they are removed from the examination area, recorded, and cleaned. Care must be taken to ensure that the items are kept together and not mixed with exhibits from another case. They should be examined visually first to determine that there is no fragile evidence present. If believed to be appropriate, photographs can be taken at this stage. The item(s) can then be washed carefully, preserving any evidence that may be contained in or on them. The item(s) must be dried thoroughly either by natural means or by drying them with a clean, dry paper towel. Once the items are dry, they should be photographed, and the Photographic Log must be completed. The items are then to be placed into the appropriate packaging, as described in Tables 4–2 to 4–4.

Blindfolds and ligatures are treated as exhibits from a body, so care should be taken in removing them. During removal, the knot should not be untied. If the blindfold cannot be removed intact, it should be cut and both ends should be tied to a piece of string. This method ensures that evidence of the knot is preserved. Hair may be attached to the blindfold and should be removed and preserved for further tests prior to any treatments of the item. The blindfold or ligature can then be treated as other items of clothing. Prostheses and implants of any type (e.g., dental, surgical, implants, IUDs) should be treated as any other exhibit.

Clothing from bodies. During the postmortem examination, the SCE is present throughout. The APTs will label each item of clothing with a metallic tag or appropriate equivalent with the evidence number written on it. When written with a stylus or ballpoint pen, it will indent the metal and therefore be permanent. As each item is removed, it will be carefully checked for further evidence that may have adhered to it or may be located in pockets, seams, or folds of material. They should be placed into a receptacle, containing clothing only related to that particular case. The clothing will then be passed to the clothes washers (washing will aid preservation of materials and make it more appropriate for photographing for relatives to identify or view), and any exhibits are passed to the SCE. The method of washing will depend on the state of the clothing and the nature of the soiling. Some clothing can be cleaned by dry brushing, whereas other clothing may have to be soaked. The use of washing machines and tumble dryers is not recommended because the physical damage to the clothing is likely to outweigh the benefit of the automated washing process. Detergents should only be used if unavoidable. When each item is completely dry, it will be laid out on a plain background with an exhibit label and a scale rule (if the background sheet is large enough) and photographed. At this stage, the pathologist and/or anthropologist who completed the postmortem may want to view the clothing and complete his or her record. A clothing form is then completed by the reporting SCE (Clothing and Personal Effects Associated with Individuals [MC11L]). This will include a full description of each item also using the descriptions of clothing as relevant for each case. The manner in which items of clothing are classified will have been ascribed by the cultural anthropologist. This will prevent any confusion in the way an individual describes or names an item. This list can be amended as appropriate for cultural norms for any particular location. All labels in clothing should be checked carefully for identifying marks such as name tags. If any significant bullet holes, tears, or cuts are found on the item, they can be photographed at the pathologist's or anthropologist's request. If interpreting such damage accurately is relevant to the investigation, specialist examination is recommended, especially when dealing with degraded material. These photographs would include all relevant site code and evidence numbers and scales. When dealing with each case, any item of clothing that is believed to be particularly relevant to the investigation should be packaged separately in a paper bag and labelled accordingly. All other items will be folded and placed into one large paper bag and again labelled. These bags will then be placed in secure storage.

Biological samples from bodies. Biological samples can be taken for various reasons, including DNA and other submacroscopic analysis, and those required for assessment of age at death and other anthropological analyses. Samples should only be taken when absolutely necessary. When removed from the body, they should be placed into a plastic evidence bag and the details on the bag completed with the case details. Also in the bag should be a metallic or plastic case tag, showing the case number and date. Care must be taken to ensure that this does not abrade the sample. The samples are then passed to the SCE, who will check the samples taken against the anthropological records to confirm that they are correct. The Mortuary Sample Recording Form and Log (MC14F, MC14L) can then be completed by the reporting SCE. Once all documentation is complete, the samples should be placed into appropriate storage facilities, such as refrigerators for bone for anthropological

Table 4–5. *Scene of crime examiner's mortuary forms*

Code	Forms and logs
MC10	Case Record: Mortuary Investigation Team
MC11L	Mortuary Case Evidence Log
MC12F	Case Identification Form
MC13L	Mortuary Evidence Log
MC14F	Mortuary Sample Recording Form
MC14L	Mortuary Sample Log

analysis and freezers for DNA samples (see 9.3). With the exception of DNA samples, if more than one type of sample is taken per case, they should be kept together during storage for ease of location at a later date. For DNA sampling, see 8.6 and 9.3 for specifications on sample collection and storage. (Table 4–5 shows the scene of crime recording forms).

If bones, teeth, and tissue are taken from a body during the postmortem and that body is subsequently identified, the family or friends of the person have the right to know what samples have been taken. When the family is interviewed by the investigator, they should be informed of this and handed a copy of the Mortuary Sample Recording Form (MC14F). The form should be duplicated so the next of kin may retain a copy. The investigator should have completed the form with the relevant details of samples, and the next of kin should be asked to complete the part of the form concerning relatives' wishes for the handling of samples. This will then be attached to the final case papers.

Forms of identification. Many characteristics, such as personal possessions, an injury to the body, evidence of an operation that affects bone, documents, and tattoos, have the potential to contribute to identifying the deceased and may be extremely important to the overall investigation. In all cases, the relevant area of the Case Identification Form (MC12F) should be completed.

Documents should be photographed and/or scanned as soon as possible; they may be soiled and wet, but they should nevertheless be photographed as a matter of urgency. This is undertaken in case the drying process causes the details to fade or deteriorate. They should also be photographed again when they are clean and dry. All readable details should be recorded on the Case Identification Form, and a hard copy of any photograph(s) should be attached to the case papers. The relevant area on the form should be completed. If a name is discovered, then a check of any relevant 'missing persons register' should be carried out. If a tentative 'match' is made, then the reference number should be noted on the identification form. However, the discovery of identifying documentation and personal effects should not be considered as definite proof of that individual's identity for various reasons, including that they may have been passed from one victim to another prior to death. That said, personal items such as jewellery, tobacco tins, and keys, including handmade or hand-altered clothing, may be unique to an individual and therefore be identifiable by the family and friends. Depending on the level of decomposition of a body, the pathologist may comment on the presence of tattoos, marks, or scars on the victim. If so, the area must be photographed and described in detail. When the pathologist is carrying out the postmortem examination, he or she should consult with the SCE as to whether there are fingerprints present on the body or body part. If there are and it is believed that they can be recovered, the SCE should attempt to retrieve the prints. A fingerprinting kit should be available for this purpose and contain all the relevant equipment for taking fingerprints from cadavers.

Dental prostheses should be recorded on the Odontology Forms (MO33), which will be completed by the odontologist or anthropologist and should be attached to the SCE case papers. If dental prostheses are found, these will be treated as exhibits, and should be photographed and described in detail. During the examination by the anthropologist, it may become apparent that the victim, during his or her lifetime, has had surgery, a fractured or dislocated bone, or a congenital, genetic, or acquired condition affecting the hard tissues. If so, the area or bone should be photographed, described in detail, and radiographs taken. A hard copy of any photograph(s) and or radiograph(s) should be attached to the case papers. Where a prosthesis is present, it will be treated as an exhibit but may be used as a contributing factor towards assigning a presumptive identification.

Once all the case papers regarding identification are completed, a copy should be made and kept so it can be passed to the investigator for further dissemination to such organisations as the International Committee of the Red Cross, local authorities, or any other organisation who may be conducting an investigation for missing persons.

Exhibits from the site. Depending on the location of the mortuary, the facilities, and the staffing levels, it may be appropriate to process the exhibits recovered from the site at the mortuary. This decision may also be influenced by the condition of exhibits when they are recovered. The exhibits that are received from the site will arrive in locked and sealed containers. Once the contents have been checked at the handover, the cleaning process can start. Only one exhibit should be dealt with at a time to prevent any accidental mixing. The exhibit should be checked against the handover sheet from the site to confirm that the description is the same on the label and the handover sheet. Once this is done, the item can be examined and, if required, the item can be removed, checked to see if there is any evidence adhering to the actual item, and then cleaned as already described. Once this has been done, the item should again be photographed and the Photographic Log (MG06LD and MG06LN) completed accordingly. If appropriate, the exhibit should then be returned to the original packaging, which should be resealed and the continuity label amended showing by whom and when the exhibit was initially inspected. If the original packaging is not suitable, then the instructions given in Tables 4–2 to 4–4 should be followed. If an exhibit is found to be broken, then it should be dealt with as outlined previously. Once the exhibits have been dealt with, they will be returned to a lockable storage box and kept within secure storage until the evidence handover, postexamination.

General clothing bags or containers contain items of clothing not associated with a body. Upon opening, each item shall be labelled with a metal tag or appropriate equivalent, containing the evidence number and the initials 'GC' for general clothing. Each item will be visually checked for evidence, and then washed and dried. The items should be photographed as groups if they were recovered as such; otherwise, they should be photographed individually. The clothing will then be folded and placed in one or more large paper bags on which the evidence number is written and placed into storage.

Data entry. Once each case is dealt with and the forms have been collated, they can be handed over to the data entry team. The data entry team will update the mortuary database with all relevant information, and on completion, they will sign the cover sheet to confirm this has been done. The SCE case papers will then be attached to the postmortem report, anthropological reports, and any others submitted for each case for computer entry and filing. They will then be placed in storage for the final handover to the investigating authority.

In the future, some, most, or even all of the data gathered during the different stages of the mortuary investigation may be entered directly onto a computerised database system, practically eliminating the 'data entry team'. Instead, there will be a role for a monitor to ensure accurate data entry and quality control. Electronic data entry is likely to replace traditional paper form recording in the fullness of time.

Postexamination evidence handover. When all the work for each individual site has been completed, the evidence should be handed over to the appropriate authorities. Hard copies of the exhibit records should be generated from the database and checked as each item is located, identified, and then signed for accordingly. The signatures should be that of the person(s) receiving the exhibits and the senior SCE. A copy of the signed form must be handed to the SCM responsible for the mortuary. The evidence should be distributed as shown in Table 4–6. If any personal effects, such as items of jewellery or spectacles, that belong to a deceased person who has been identified, are required to be kept for court proceedings, then relatives should be informed of this. If the next of kin wish to have the property returned to them after any court proceedings, then this needs to be recorded and passed onto the relevant authorities. This record should be duplicated, and a copy attached to the final case papers.

4.4 Forensic photography

This section is concerned with general photographic applications, rather than giving specific guidelines for how individual groups of finds are photographed, such as the

Table 4–6. *Evidence handover guide*

Evidence category	Appropriate authority
Human remains and personal items	These are to be handed to the relevant authority.
Physical evidence	This includes items such as bullets, personal effects, and/or documentation and any other evidence that may be required in court or that requires further testing. Physical evidence should be stored, and then transported to the central storage facility awaiting action. It must be signed for, and copies of the handover sheet must be given back to the senior crime scene examiner.
Biological and DNA samples	These exhibits are kept for identification purposes only, as an aid to determining the age and identity of the deceased. Where it has been agreed that bone, teeth and tissue might be disposed of then detailed documentation including permissions must accompany the case file. They should be transported to and stored in the central storage facility.
Photographic negatives, photographs, videos, digital cards, and photographic logs	All items are to be transported to the central storage facility for retention.
Case files	All documentary evidence such as postmortem reports, evidence logs, and crime scene examiner case papers should be transported to the investigating authority for retention. Copies should be retained in hard and soft copy.

angles and distance at which a skull injury should be documented. Most objects will have unique circumstances, and the photographic parameters will vary. This section will, therefore, outline concepts and leave detail to the discretion of photographers, based on the specific needs of the investigators or scientists. Photographs should always be taken after consultation among the scientist, SCE, and photographer. Although the scientist or SCE identifies what information needs to be documented, the photographer has the specialist knowledge to create an accurate record.

Photographic equipment is constantly developing and improving so specifications can change rapidly. It is therefore impractical to give detailed lists of recommended equipment or manufacturers, although all cameras, 35 mm or digital, must be single lens reflex (SLR) and fitted with zoom lenses with focal lengths of at least 28 to 70 mm (or the digital equivalent). The photographer should be consulted during the project planning phase when the management team is aware of the conditions, scale, and requirements of individual projects. From this advice, the right equipment can be acquired and regulations drawn up to accommodate the conditions that teams are likely to encounter in the field and mortuary or laboratory.

A photographer should be present at all stages of the evidence gathering process, from site assessment, excavation, and recovery and throughout the mortuary phase. The primary purpose of forensic photography is to provide an accurate record of specific evidence as identified by the forensic scientists, and the methodology applied by them, to be used in a court of law. However, on large-scale investigations, the photographer must be aware of a wider, historical context and may want to consider the additional use of larger-format cameras and different films. During the planning phase of the mission, the management team should consult investigators and obtain relevant legal advice, whereby an appropriate photographic format (or multiple formats) will be agreed on by all parties. If 35-mm film is used, the first frame of each film used must show the site code and film number, and a detailed log should be kept for each roll of film used.

If digital photography is used, the camera-assigned file name should be recorded in the photographic log. When using digital photography, the file number rather than the image number should be used for recording in the photographic log. During the download process, each image will be allocated a file name. This is usually comprised of a prefix (three to four letters) and a serial number. Most digital cameras can show this file name immediately after the image has been taken in the LCD screen and can be set either to start the numbering system anew after each download or to keep numbering the images consecutively, regardless of downloads (starting at 0 after reaching 9999). It does not matter which system is adopted, but the same system should be used throughout the operation on all digital cameras.

4.4.1 Photographic processes

During the site assessment phase, still and video images will be taken of the suspected site before any other work has taken place. Subject to explosive ordnance device restriction, it may be impossible to gain initial access to the suspect area. It will therefore be useful to take photographs from other vantage points. It is helpful to use topography, or even to work from the top of a vehicle, to gain elevation. In cases where aerial photographic evidence or specific witness testimony is available, it may be possible to identify features of greater interest to the investigation. These should be photographed in detail and within the wider context of the whole area. In cases where specific testimony is lacking, any physical anomalies such as changes in vegetation or disturbances in the ground surface should be recorded in detail. Scales and north arrows will be used in all photographs. Video footage will be orally dubbed with the name of the site and direction of view. As the assessment progresses, all evidence and applied processes will be photographed (i.e., geophysics, survey, test trenching). In certain situations, the assessment team may not go on to undertake the excavation phase, and their reports may be required urgently. In these situations, and given that film processing facilities are unlikely to be readily available, the use of additional digital photography is recommended.

When photographing large spaces such as meadows, ranging rods of 1 to 2 m should be placed perpendicular to the field of view and at intervals in a straight line extending away from the photographer and into the subject area. Where access is restricted or when the suspect area is very large, this may be impracticable. The scale may be too small, relatively, to give a meaningful impression of the size of the area. Using human scales within a photograph or including parked vehicles on the perimeter of the area, will give the viewer an immediate sense of proportion.

As with the assessment phase, during the excavation and recovery phase, the site will be photographed before any excavation work begins. During the excavation, a full record will be made of methodology and equipment using a separate, dedicated camera. This will include 'working shots' of personnel showing how each task is performed. Where film is used, these films do not require a written log, but the site code will, as usual, be identified in the first frame. If the film has not been fully used, when work at the site is completed, it will be rewound and a new film started before beginning work at another site. Similarly, if for any reason the photographer is replaced, all films will be rewound – whether completed or not, new films will be started and any empty lines on the photography log crossed out.

Each body will be photographed. The photographer must ensure that, wherever possible, the complete body is visible. If, for good reason, this is not possible, the explanation for that decision will be noted in the photographic log. It is the photographer's responsibility to ensure that each body or body part has been sufficiently cleaned. If the photographer does not believe that the body is clean enough, he or she must request further cleaning from the archaeologist or anthropologist responsible for that body. There will be circumstances where it is feared that (further) cleaning may destroy trace evidence such as fragmentary ballistics. In such cases, the decision to discontinue cleaning will be at the discretion of the archaeologist or anthropologist and the photographer will abide by that decision.

For each body, the first frame must include the evidence number assigned by the SCE, scales, and a north arrow. Note that the scales can be used to delineate the outline of the body or, in some cases, flagging tape may be used. In a small, well-defined grave, it may be possible to establish a fixed point outside the grave from where a series of photographs will be taken. Thus, each body will be photographed in detail and also in relation to the whole grave. Subsequent photographs of the same body may be taken without numbers, scales, or arrows, as appropriate. This is of particular importance when photographing small details such as bullets or trauma because too many numbers and scales may obscure the actual evidence. It is, however, useful to include a small arrow pointing to the detail and to photograph the detail itself and its position relative to the complete body. Body parts will be photographed where they might assist in identification.

Detailed photographs will be taken of all blindfolds and ligatures as they are found (i.e., *in situ*) (Figure 4–4). Other evidence types such as bullets and shell cases will be photographed *in situ*, although on a large site it may be considered sufficient to photograph a limited number unless the position in which such evidence is discovered is believed to be significant. If resources allow, a separate camera should be set up under shade, adjacent to the grave with a tripod and cross-arm (additional flash equipment may be needed), to photograph any documentary evidence such as identification cards and driving licences. These will be taken as soon as possible after recovery to avoid deterioration.

Archaeological evidence, such as grave cuts, machine wheel, and tooth marks identified by archaeologists, will be photographed using scales and a north arrow.

Figure 4–4. Blindfolds can trap hair in the knot. They can loosen from the head during decomposition. As well as thoroughly recording blindfolds *in situ*, care should be taken during excavation, lifting, and transportation so the blindfold is not detached. If it does become detached, it may be viewed during autopsy as a 'knotted cloth'. *Source:* ICTY/Tim Loveless.

Other evidence such as botanical or geological samples also identified by the senior archaeologist or other experts will be photographed. When the grave has been fully exhumed, a series of photographs of the grave will be taken using ranging rods as scales. The last photographs will be taken when all work has been completed and the site has been restored.

All completed films and photographic logs will be handed to and signed over to the SCE who will place them in individual evidence bags and assign each film an evidence number. During the excavation, the films will be stored with other exhibits in a cool, dry environment and will be signed over to the mortuary facility at the completion of the site. If a separate facility is used for film processing, the films may be handed directly to that facility at the discretion of the SCE. The same forms and processes will be used as when handing evidence to the mortuary.

If resources allow, in the mortuary, the photographer will have three cameras set up and will work under the supervision of the SCE and pathologist or anthropologist. One camera will be dedicated for use at the pathologist's or anthropologist's table to record the complete body and related evidence as directed by the SCE, pathologist, or anthropologist. A second camera will be set up in combination with flash units and tripods to photograph detail of trauma, pathologies, and so on, as directed by the pathologist or anthropologist. The third camera will be used to photograph clothing and related personal items, which will be displayed in a clearly comprehensible manner. If deemed appropriate by the mortuary management team, a colour photograph of the face of all saponified or well-preserved bodies should be taken. The photograph must be printed, and the number of the body must be entered above the photo in an appropriate log. A register of all photographs taken of each body must be kept at the mortuary facility. The register must have the following headings: date (when photograph was taken), photograph and case number, and date of identification of the deceased (if appropriate).

If decomposition or damage is not extensive and the face is potentially recognisable, a clear photograph of the face of the deceased can be taken for viewing by relatives. The following information must also be noted and made available: how, where, and when the body was found, and a full description of the clothing, scars, and tattoos on the body or any other special identifying feature. The body must be cleaned before the photograph is taken and covered with a clean sheet so only the face is showing. No identifying number, wounds, or blood must be shown. The photograph of the body must not be taken in the dissecting room or on the dissecting table.

Video recording will be used mainly for the purpose of proving the integrity and continuity of the crime scene or to document working processes. For example, the photographer will video the covered excavation area at the end of each working day and before work starts the next morning. This way, the integrity and continuity of the excavation is documented. During filming, the photographer should add audio comments so date, time, site name, and any other relevant information is recorded with the visual images. If possible, video filming should be done using a tripod for clearer and more stable images.

It would be useful to have film processing and scanning facilities available on site to process film from the mortuary team and the field teams as they are taken, and thus to ensure consistent quality control. This way pathologists or anthropologists will also be able to see photographs of the body as found *in situ* before they begin their analysis. Digital photography can also be used for this purpose. If film processing cannot be carried out in the field, it should still take place as soon as possible after the photographs have been taken. During field and mortuary operations, negative film material should always be kept in a cold, dark place to protect it from any kind of radiation that could alter the film. Photographic material should also be kept in a safe location to guarantee the integrity and continuity of evidence. It is recommended that initially film be processed only (i.e., not printed) and then scanned. The scanned image will be stored on the chosen storage medium (see 4.4.2) and thus will be easily available to view. When photographs are selected for display in court or other purposes, photographic prints will be made from the original negative.

4.4.2   Digital image capture and handling

The photography of recovered forensic evidence using a digital format is becoming more frequent within the forensic field as a whole. It is a format that is currently being used by police forces and other agencies around the world. Where it is not possible to have film processing facilities on site, it may be appropriate to use an equivalent SLR digital camera. If such use is considered feasible, the digital camera should be of sufficient quality to be comparable to 35-mm film. The circumstances regarding the image itself as an item of evidence may differ from country to country; therefore, relevant legal advice regarding the use of digital photography must be obtained during the planning phase. The photographer should undertake the following precautions and methodology to minimise the risk of image corruption, and to produce images that are 'true' and not tampered with and that will therefore be considered unadulterated 'negatives'.

All photographs should be taken on a digital SLR camera of sufficient resolution for the intended purpose. The camera should remain with the photographer at all times, until the images can be safely downloaded. Photographs are taken and logged using the same procedures that are already in operation (described in 4.4.1). These include the use of scales, evidence numbers, and so on, details of which are recorded on a pro-forma paper log. Recorded images should be downloaded as soon as practicable and burned (copied) onto nonreusable storage media such as CR-R or DVD-R. If available, downloading equipment that burns directly from the camera or memory card to the CD-R or DVD-R, without the use of a computer, should be used. During this process, the SCE should be present at all times or undertake the downloading themselves. This process is described in more detail in 4.5. This master CD-R or DVD-R can then be labelled, signed, and sealed into an evidence bag or container with signed tamper-evident adhesive. As with all recovered exhibits, the disc should be secured at all times throughout the operation, preferably stored in a lockable room.

Consideration must be given to the choice of file format. Digital photographs can be captured in various formats, and the intended use of the photograph should dictate what format is chosen and also the level of file compression used, if any. Photographs that are intended to be used for comparison purposes or that are subject to image processing should be captured in an uncompressed format (e.g., RAW or TIFF uncompressed), or using lossless compression (where the original image data can be restored, e.g., TIFF LZW). For photographs that are to be used merely as visual aids, lossy compression formats (where original image data are permanently discarded, e.g., JPEG) may be more efficient and convenient. System validation tests should be carried out in advance to ensure suitability of the image format and quality level for the intended purpose. This can range from a simple visual assessment to a detailed analysis of image resolution data. At no stage should digital photographs be intentionally or unintentionally deleted because file deletion may be subject to legal challenge (Police Scientific Development Branch, 2002).

4.4.3   Protection of digital photographs

Captured photographs should be archived as soon as possible in their original state, for instance, by transferring the photograph to nonreusable media such as CD-R or DVD-R, or an alternative designated storage medium (see 4.5), at the conclusion of each day.

Records of this transfer must be kept, including when and by whom the process was carried out in the Digital Image Log (MG06LD). This 'master' reference must be immediately assigned a unique evidence number, and then sealed and stored appropriately. Once the master is defined and stored, all further access and use of the photographs should be made from a 'working copy'. A working copy is a binary copy of the master and may be produced simultaneously or immediately following the creation of the master. It is also necessary to ensure the images contained on the master and working copy are authentic (i.e., are binary duplicates). One example of an authentication technique involves the use of software that generates the unique 'hash value' for the image. Any pixel changes will cause the hash value to change. The reusable media (this will normally be the camera's 'memory card') should be reformatted at the beginning of each day in preparation for reuse (deleting the content of a memory card is not sufficient).

No digital photograph is to be opened in an image-processing programme before the master has been created, defined, sealed, and stored. Only the working copy may be used to access digital photographs. The digital photographs may be printed or otherwise circulated to relevant parties. Quality control and chain of custody needs to be maintained at all stages. If any enhancement or processing is performed on a photograph, this must be recorded in such a way that a third party could produce the same results. All processing steps must be based on sound scientific and validated techniques and applied in an appropriate manner. All equipment used in digital image processing must be operated in accordance with the manufacturer specifications, and an end-to-end system check carried out regularly. All storage media should be stored in a clean, dry environment specifically devoid of light, chemicals, and magnetic fields.

4.5   Data storage and security

This section aims to set out key concerns for establishing and managing the data arising from both the site and the mortuary. Database implementation can be generally divided into two stages; the first stage corresponds with site assessment and excavation, and the second stage with the mortuary process. These will be referred to as the 'site database' and 'mortuary database' hereafter. The mortuary database is, in fact, an extension of the site database, and site data are imperative for the mortuary database to commence. Consequently, the site database must be compatible with the mortuary database to enable data transfer from one to the other. The site database can operate independently of the mortuary database but not vice versa; they may, however, operate simultaneously.

Under the direction of the SCM, the SCE acting as the data entry assistant is responsible for the data processing, maintenance, and management of the site database and hard copy filing systems responsible for cataloguing all potential evidence collected and for ensuring chain of custody of computer data. This includes, but is not limited to, assisting forensic archaeologists, anthropologists, and scene of crime teams, if required. All personnel working directly or closely with electronic data should be computer literate and have experience with software such as Microsoft (MS) Access, MS Word, digital image software, and video editing software (multimedia systems).

4.5.1   Hardware and software

The only viable solution for housing the site database is a laptop computer. The components of the system (e.g., memory, operating system, ports) have to be suitable to record the database, download digital images, download video footage as a backup to the original tape, and back up the database itself with ease and speed. The laptops have to be suitable for the environment that they are used in (e.g., with extra strong cooling systems and dust filters in desert environments). General peripheral equipment required includes a portable printer (preferably a colour laser printer) and a flatbed scanner. Software should include an office suite comparable to a current MS Office Professional Edition. This package includes Word, Excel, Outlook, PowerPoint, and Access. All computers should be equipped with the same operating system and office suite. Antivirus software is also crucial and should be from a recognised vendor such as Symantec Norton Antivirus. This will be for the scanning of unknown files on disc or any other media and outgoing files. Other optional software might include Adobe Photoshop, or a comparable image processing programme. Adobe Premiere, or a comparable image processing programme, is useful for the processing of copied video footage for presentation and past referral. The video camera should come with its own editing software. Adobe Acrobat, or a comparable PDF programme, is useful to protect and secure sensitive documents in PDF format. Software, vendor critical updates, drivers, and associated cables for peripheral equipment such as the printer, digital camera, and video must be installed and tested prior to deployment for compatibility and confirmation of workings. The site database and the mortuary database will use five or more computers between them, depending on the size of the operation. As an alternative to buying individual software for each computer, most software providers offer cost-effective licensing for multiple users. A user's guide and instructions outlining how to operate the database should be made available for quick reference.

4.5.2   Electronic data handling

Electronic data will be generated in several different forms. There are three main groups of data: digital imaging (photographs and video), electronic measurements (surveying and geophysical data), and database records.

Data compression. Although electronic measurements and database records can be stored uncompressed, digital photos and video will need some form of data compression in order to be of any practical use to the staff. Compression of data can result in a loss of quality, and in cases of extreme compression, in a loss of content. Some forms of compression can be qualified as lossless. When using a high resolution camera, for most circumstances, the medium setting is adequate. However, a setting that compromises the content is not acceptable.

When generating digital images or video, the level of quality can often be set. Usually, the higher the quality is, the larger the file size. The quality level should be set as low as possible but as high as necessary to create files that are as small as possible and therefore minimise the need for compression. The on-camera image quality settings should be set according to the intended use of the image (refer to 4.4.2). Generally, using the highest resolution/size settings is recommended.

Before any digital imaging data are collected, the project management team must consult with the local authorities and/or the local or international court system to become familiar with their policy. If certain compression of data is allowed, then the raw data collection may be undertaken in a compressed version. If compression is not allowed, data must be collected as a true representation format. These data can then be stored as the master version, and compressed files can be generated as working versions.

Some digital photo and video cameras store the images directly in a compressed format. Care must be taken during the project planning phase to ensure cameras are capable of capturing images in the appropriate format.

For digital still images, the most commonly used compression software is that of the Joint Photographic Experts Group (JPEG). Their original standard (the .jpg format) results in an irreversible loss of image quality and content. A new standard (JPEG2000) promises to be loss-free, compressing data up to 200 times. One of the most widely used compression vehicles for digital video is from the Moving Picture Experts Group (MPEG). There are a number of different evolutions of this standard available, and research is ongoing. All of these standards are ISO registered. Whichever software is used, its specifications must be documented, as must detail of how and to which level the original data have been compressed.

Data enhancement. Digital imaging data may need to be enhanced beyond compression to be useful. An image may be too dark or too light, the contrast may be too strong or too weak, or the image may show a lot more than is necessary and need to be cropped. All of these kinds of data enhancement have been acceptable in many national jurisdictions, as long as they do not alter the actual nature of the image, and as long as the enhancement is properly documented and therefore replicable by a third party. If such data enhancement is acceptable, an original version of the image must be stored separately, and the type and degree of enhancement must be recorded and documented in detail (e.g., contrast: +25; cropped: left 2 cm), including the software used.

Electronic measurement data will almost always need enhancement. Geophysical surveying data can rarely be published without running it through filters, which are designed to emphasise the results. All electronic measurement data will need some form of visualisation in the form of grey- or colour-scale diagrams. Such visualisation is, in itself, an interpretation by the software, directed by the user, and therefore a enhancement of the data. Any enhancement must be recorded and documented in detail, including the name and version of the programme. Most geophysical and surveying programmes record any enhancement in their case history. If the programme does not record this, it must be done manually. A raw data file must always be kept separately.

Data storage. When it comes to storing electronic data, a number of issues have to be considered: security, availability, longevity, and long-term accessibility. All of these topics are influenced by the fast speed of development in the information technology industry and can therefore not be dealt with definitively in this text. The basic principles will be discussed in this section, but with continual advances in hard- and software, the issues surrounding data handling will have to be reviewed before each operation.

Security. A number of measures must be taken to ensure that electronic data are only seen by designated personnel. Such measures range from limiting physical access to PCs or laptops, by password protection, by secure networking facilities, or by limiting the number of copies of certain files. It is essential that the number of copies of each file is not only restricted, but also known to the person in charge. If only two out of three copies are known to exist, the third one may not be protected at all. Hardware that is decommissioned must be cleaned of all data by an expert. Simple deletion processes will not be sufficient.

Availability. Electronic data are only useful if they can be accessed conveniently. Locking an external hard drive in a fire-proof safe or keeping a CD in a sealed police evidence bag may be very secure, but it is not necessarily practical. A good balance has to be achieved between security and practicality. It is suggested that one copy of all raw data always be kept securely, and a controlled number of copies are available for the staff to work with.

Longevity. There are presently two main ways of storing data that are perceived to be long term: optical storage media (CDs and DVDs) and PC/network storage. The question of how long data can be stored on CDs or DVDs without loss has no definitive answer at the moment. Physical and chemical degradation will lead to loss of data after a certain amount of time (a process accelerated by storing such media in the wrong environment and by physical damage). When it comes to hard drive–based systems such as direct-attached storage, network-attached storage (NAS), or storage area networks (SANs), the longevity, as well as the costs (substantially), are likely to increase. Before any operation begins, a comprehensive review of current storage media has to be carried out, and an equally comprehensive system has to be put in place for every element of the operation (field, mortuary, and management).

Long-term accessibility. Data are usually stored in a specific format such as a word processor document, spreadsheet, or digital image. This format is dictated by the software in which it is produced. Over time, while data in this specific format are stored, software changes and often this new software cannot access past formats. This can lead to total loss of data or to expensive data recovery operations. When storing data long term, care should be taken that they are either stored in a format that is likely to be accessible in the future, or that computer hardware and software from the time of storage be 'archived' as well. This will ensure that the data can be accessed by the original method of storage.

4.5.3   Postmortem database

The following will describe the minimum requirements in regard to the postmortem database system. It is based on the concept of paper forms being used as the primary data collection mode and then data being entered into the database. In the future, some, much, or even all data are likely to be entered directly into a database system (via barcode scanners or portable pocket PCs), and paper printouts will then be used as backup. But even when this technology is widely available, some operations with the most basic equipment will still operate in the conventional way of using the database as a secondary data entry tool.

   Site and mortuary databases should be designed in a widely used format such as MS Access, which ensures greater end user compatibility. If it is a specially designed database programme, it should at least enable the user to export the data into formats that can be read by commonly used software. The database used by the field investigation team should consist of sites designated with individual reference codes selected by the SCM. Each site code and evidence/case number will form a composite key (primary key) and will enable data to be collected for reports that relate to it. The site database must be relational, containing multiple tables that can be linked to produce combined output from all tables. Information gathered during site assessment and evaluation will form the basis for subsequent phases. During site excavation, a more detailed response to individual recovery of bodies, body parts, and artefacts from the site will be recorded on the database from the Site

Evidence Log (FA11L). The negative films will be entered separately, and associated roll and exposure numbers will appear on the appropriate site evidence record on the database. The data from the site laptop should be backed up at the end of each day onto more than one removable disc. The SCM and senior archaeologist will each hold a disc in safe custody.

Predefined reports will be available on command selection. These will include a list of bodies and body parts by site code, case number, description, storage, date, and signed receipt for handover to the mortuary; a list of exhibits by site code, case number, description, storage, date, and signed receipt for handover to the mortuary; a list of photographic film images by site code, case number, roll number, exposure number (or file name for digital images), description, date, and signed receipt for handover for either processing or secure storage; and a list of bodies, body parts, and exhibits by case number, description, photo number, and date for site retention and referral (either daily or weekly).

Best practice and good housekeeping includes a number of routine measures. Prior to going 'live', the database should be tested thoroughly. Despite this, it should be anticipated that the database will go through a 'teething' stage, and as such, the author should be available to facilitate its implementation. This will ensure that any problems are dealt with immediately, and all requirements and expectations of its capabilities are delivered. A backup of programmes and files, repair disc, and defragging should be completed on a routine basis using the System Tools provided with MS Windows XP. If the circumstances require it, the laptop should have the following passwords: power-on password; CMOS password – known by the SCM and database administrator; and screen saver password – set and known only by user's administrator access. These should also be recorded in a safe place for access by the overall project manager. Laptops should not be available for use by unauthorised persons, and computers should not be left unsecured overnight. The SCM will be responsible for the security of the laptop outside working hours. On computers used for the database, the modem should be disabled prior to deployment. This will discourage extracurricular activities that could potentially harm the database. The SCM will be responsible for any updates required and given access (if Internet access is available) in the absence of the database administrator. Computers that are used for work, such as for accessing a database or downloading of optical or geophysical survey data, should be disconnected from the Internet and not be available for any form of recreational use. However, it should be ensured that team members have access to the Internet via other means so regular contact with friends and family is possible, especially during long missions in isolated areas.

At handover, the data recorded will be saved to a suitable storage medium while accompanying reports and receipts are printed. Subsequent upload will be compatible with the mortuary database. This database mainly records the case history of each set of human remains and exhibits. It will combine radiographic imaging, pathology, and anthropology data, as well as photographic records taken during the postmortem examination process. This data will be combined with any relevant data from the field investigation to form a comprehensive case history. The database may also aid the anthropologists in their skeletal analysis by processing metric and non-metric data. It could be designed to analyse (descriptive and other statistics) designated groups of data (e.g., percentage of victims with execution-style gunshot wounds, percentage of victims with blindfolds, number of projectiles per site).

Before starting any collection of data, the postmortem database has to be established and tested. Certain operations may force a modification of the database because different data sets need to be gathered. Care must be taken that the postmortem database is compatible with any antemortem database, which may be operated by a different organisation. This aspect of compatibility does not only concern the connectivity of the two software packages, but also the actual data stored in the database.

4.5.4   Laptop user policy and guide

This information is designed to familiarise laptop users with the terms and conditions of the use of project-designated laptops and should be imparted to appropriate personnel prior to receiving a laptop. When personnel have read and understood the following information, they should sign a disclaimer agreeing to the rules and regulations governing computer use. The physical security of all project laptops is crucial, both for their replacement value and, most important, for the sensitivity of the data they may contain. Lost, stolen, or damaged laptops and associated equipment represent a considerable loss in terms of replacement costs and proprietary information, as well as a decrease in productivity. Users must take note of all equipment and accessories and its condition, and adopt a high level of personal responsibility to prevent misuse or damage. Any circumstances where the user has been shown to have been consistently negligent and has ignored the appropriate warning procedure could result in the individual being held liable for loss and expense and/or the termination of employment. The protection of the privacy and integrity of all data is also a major responsibility. It is a condition that during and after employment, the employee does not disclose to any person any information concerning the work undertaken. The user must agree not to attempt any security modifications, system changes, or the loading of any other programmes unless approved. Under no circumstances should the original hard drive be substituted (even temporarily). Nor should any changes be made to the original hardware configuration, unless approved. Good housekeeping dictates that all laptop users must always ensure that the battery is in place and fully charged; this also applies to any secondary battery. It is sensible to use the AC adapter when it is possible.

Although laptops can withstand the rigors of portable use, they are delicate electronic machines and require care to ensure proper operation. The following guidelines are provided to help the employee get the most from the use of the laptop: Never leave the laptop exposed to excessive heat or sudden changes of temperature (e.g., avoid leaving in vehicles), the laptop should be turned off and placed in its folded position any time it is moved, always place the laptop in its carry case when moving, do not plug or unplug an external device without following the appropriate procedures (turning the laptop off or deactivating it from the hardware profile), and do not expose the laptop to magnetic fields that could damage the contents of the hard drive. Laptop LCD screens are fragile and should not be touched with fingers, pens/pencils, or any other object. Do not place drinks or food in close proximity to the laptop, and because the laptop's keyboard and touch pad are permanently attached to the rest of the system, hands should be clean before using them. When using the laptop, keep it on a flat, solid surface so air can circulate around it.

5

Search, location, excavation, and recovery

Paul Cheetham, Margaret Cox, Ambika Flavel,
Ian Hanson, Tim Haynie, David Oxlee,
and Roland Wessling

5.1 Introduction

This chapter has been prepared to provide a guide to the search, location, and excavation of mass graves during the investigation of atrocity crimes and for humanitarian recovery. The goal of such an investigation is to research, locate, evaluate and if appropriate recover and record all potential material and contextual evidence and human remains in a manner providing safe and secure evidence. Further to this, it seeks to determine, recover, interpret, and record the landscape and context in which all evidence is found, and to secure all evidence recovered for the appropriate legal or humanitarian authority (Hunter et al., 1996). These approaches are vital to the concept of 'total evidential recovery'[1] and to the efficiency and cost effectiveness of planning and successfully undertaking mass grave investigations. In recent years, archaeology has proven itself to be an effective tool among the forensic sciences (Hunter and Cox, 2005), and it is in the context of search, location, evaluation, and excavation that it is particularly useful as one of a suite of skills and disciplines working within an investigative process. These may be disciplines working for humanitarian goals or within the authority of the relevant judicial authority and the appointed scene of crime manager (SCM). Archaeologists have, in recent years, used the principles of their discipline to determine the location, attributes, composition, and context of buried evidence from graves and crime scenes (Hunter et al., 1996; Sterenberg,

[1] The concept of total evidence recovery refers to acknowledging the breadth of forensic sciences that now contribute to mass grave investigations. It is virtually impossible on large outdoor scenes to recover all evidence because it is not always recognized and new techniques to detect evidence is continually being refined and developed.

2001; Hunter and Cox, 2005). The multidisciplinary involvement and the wide scope of evidence recognition and recovery has gone far beyond the limited focus on human remains that typified many forensic excavations following World War II. This is a rapidly developing area, owing much to long established forensic sciences, but forensic archaeology, by virtue of its recent contribution to criminal investigations, now stands as a distinct discipline within the field of forensic science.

Forensic archaeology entails comprehension, recognition, control and interpretation of space, site history, and site formation. This includes the context and attributes of (usually) buried features and artefacts within a defined area and their recording, documentation, and processing. From a legal perspective, the context and nature of a scene in mass murder investigations has as much potential evidential value as a human body because it can help in the reconstruction of the sequence of events surrounding a crime, the disposal of human remains, and the identification of the dead. This applies equally whether a body is lying on the floor of a building or woodland, within a well or latrine, or in a purpose-built grave. While scene of crime examiners (SCEs) determine the context, attributes, and sequence of evidence that tends to lie on exposed surfaces, forensic archaeologists determine the context, attributes, and sequence of evidence from buried surfaces. The importance of forensic archaeology is heightened by its 'one chance only' character. Much evidence from forensic burials can only be recorded *in situ*, such as the position of skeletal human remains in relation to each other and the grave structure. Conclusions on the importance, value, or even identification of evidence can differ greatly when viewed either *in situ* or remotely. The characteristics of human remains and other evidence can often be changed or lost when they are moved and handled during a recovery process and subsequently examined at autopsy and in laboratories. This infers considerable responsibility on the archaeologist (Cox, 1995), who has to be extremely thorough and scientific at the scene during excavation, recording, and interpretation.

Archaeology has always needed a logical, flexible approach (France et al., 1992) to locating, excavating, recording, and interpreting sites of interest, and has always employed experts from a wide variety of sciences to assist in doing so. This multidisciplinary base gives it great strength as a contributor to forensic investigations. Forensic archaeological techniques and methods are appropriate for domestic and international forensic investigations, human rights investigations, mass disaster/accident scene recovery and investigation, recoveries from post disaster, disease and accident burials, historical investigations and battlefield graves, and cemetery and crypt clearances.

The broad scope of the approaches described here can be considered and applied to various scenarios requiring forensic investigation. These include the following: primary mass graves (variously defined [see 1.5], but usually two or more bodies); nonprimary mass graves (which might be secondary or tertiary); previously disturbed graves (possibly to clandestinely remove evidence, or other anthropogenic or taphonomic disturbance); single graves; serial graves (e.g., multiple single graves in cemeteries) (Figure 5–1); multiple-use graves (graves that may be used for depositing

Figure 5–1. In the Former Yugoslavia, some victims' remains were buried in local cemeteries. *Source:* Margaret Cox.

bodies on several occasions); bodies covered and buried on surfaces (burials in natural or anthropogenically created depressions such as quarries) (Figure 5–2); bodies disposed of in natural or artificial structures (e.g., houses, crypts, wells, caves) (Figure 5–3); surface scatters of human remains; mass fatality incident scenes; and buried and/or hidden structures or deposits (e.g., weapons caches).

These standard operating procedures (SOPs) recognise that there is a regional and cultural difference of approach in the nature and application of archaeology to forensic investigation. Furthermore, they also acknowledge the difference in position and emphasis of archaeology in relation to physical anthropology in North America compared with Europe. It should be remembered that despite frequent statements in academic papers that 'standard methods' (Hunter et al., 1996; Dirkmaat and Adovasio, 1997; Hoshower, 1998) are used during forensic excavations, there are no widely acknowledged and accepted international (and, in most cases, national) standards and protocols for forensic archaeology.[2] The aim of our work in developing these SOPs is to begin to remedy this lacuna.

5.1.1   Personnel and standards

All personnel involved in the processes described in this chapter should have appropriate levels and types of qualifications, expertise, and experience in relevant aspects

[2] The United Nations' *Manual on the Effective Prevention and Investigation of Extra-Legal, Arbitrary and Summary Executions* (UN, 1991), although now dated, has provided the only recognized widespread international guidance on archaeological recovery. A more detailed document, although less well known, is the *Protocolo Modelo para la Investigación Forense de Muertes Sospechosas de Haberse producido por Violación de los Derechos Humanos* by the Argentine Forensic Anthropology Team (EAAF) and Instituto Nacional de Medicina Legal de Portugal.

Figure 5–2. Sand quarry north of Najaf, Iraq. Local nongovernment organisations believed this quarry was used to hide bodies after the Shia Uprising in 1991. *Source:* Inforce Foundation.

of archaeological, forensic, and other related sciences or scene of crime management and examination. These may be set out by various registration bodies (e.g., American Academy of Forensic Sciences, Council for the Registration of Forensic Practitioners in the UK) but should concur with statutory registration requirements, existing occupational standards, and recommendations by professional bodies. It may be appropriate during some investigations to employ small numbers of less experienced personnel within a framework of close supervision to gain field experience and increase the currently small pool of experts. Time and resources for the proper supervision and training of the staff should be allocated as necessary. The fastest and most effective way for interns to gain useful experience is to pair them with an experienced practitioner. These requirements must never take precedence over the legal requirements of an investigation or in any way jeopardise standards of work. Although it is not desirable in legal cases, it may be appropriate during investigations to employ local staff for some auxiliary tasks. Time and resources for the proper supervision of these staff should also be allocated. Specialist training may be needed for personnel before beginning certain investigations, and qualified personnel should be contacted to assist when necessary. Training in site practice will be needed before commencing ground works, such as ordnance recognition and

Figure 5–3. The local community at Nyamata, Rwanda, recovered human remains from a backfilled latrine to a depth of 9 m. The equipment used for this process is visible in the image and comprised a tree branch, thick rope, and a leather bucket. *Source:* Margaret Cox.

health and safety procedures. All personnel should receive training in appropriate peer support and counselling before undertaking operations.

All staff should be familiar with the procedures and standards being employed in the investigation before it commences. These can be diverse, from which types of pen and ink colour to use on forms, to appropriateness or otherwise of the use of pencils, to awareness of the agreed conventions and descriptions for soils, botanical species, and so on. Forensic archaeologists must be fully aware of the principles of the broader forensic sciences that can be applied to mass grave investigation, of archaeological excavation, of the judicial framework, and of the recovery of human remains. A high standard of scientific ethics should be maintained (see 1.9). All methods and techniques of excavation should be justified on a scientific basis, and hypotheses should be demonstrable. This should be achieved through thorough recording of the methodological process. Effective team work is fundamental to the success of any operation, and regular and, as appropriate, *ad hoc* team discussion should be encouraged. Extreme care must be taken to prevent inappropriate allocation of credit, errors arising from negligence, and fabrication and falsification of results, records, and interpretation. Complaints or issues raised by excavation staff should first be brought to the attention of the supervisor and then the senior archaeologist.

These should be discussed between the senior archaeologist, SCM, SCE, and supervisor. Regular team discussions concerning site development, procedures, and issues such as health and safety should take place, including mortuary and investigatory staff where possible. Regular debriefing sessions should occur during and after an investigation, and, where possible, should be directed by an experienced trauma counsellor.

Archaeological excavation is destructive. Most methodologies of excavation rely on objective, thorough recording and subsequent interpretation by the archaeologist. This is paramount for several reason, including that it is often impossible for others to test results by reexamining the excavated site.[3] The archaeologist's results are, in the first instance, the main evidence. This places, as with the SCE, an ethical responsibility on forensic archaeologists for the highest level of honesty and integrity. This is greater on forensic than traditional excavations because of contemporary legal and human rights considerations. For a forensic excavation, which is, or may become, part of a legal investigation, validity of evidence and methodologies used should be justifiable in terms of accepted standards and sound scientific techniques, as exemplified by legal cases such as *Daubert v. Merrell Dow Pharmaceuticals* (Christensen, 2004). This case sets out four basic principles: that the type of evidence presented can be, and has been, tested by scientific methodology, and that the underlying theory or techniques have been subjected to peer review, and have been published in professional literature. *Daubert* (ibid.) asserts that it is essential to state how reliable the results are in terms of the potential error rate and, finally, acknowledges that general acceptance of an approach can be significant.

All protocols and SOPs employed in forensic archaeological investigations should be printed and made available to staff and all interested parties. A summarised site archaeological procedures document should also be distributed. Alterations to methodology during investigations must be recorded, explained, and disseminated by the SCM and the senior archaeologist. In this way, the rationale and methodology underpinning the work carried out by archaeologists should be transparent. The SCM and senior archaeologist are responsible for ensuring that team members are working to the required standard and are following procedures adequately. The SCE and supervisor will report discrepancies and monitor standards of work. The archaeological surveyor should check all exhibit numbers and the location of evidence and bodies personally before surveying, as should the photographer. The correct issue of exhibit numbers and correct labelling should be checked by the SCE. Use of exhibit numbers in the grave will be monitored by the supervisor, who will report to the SCE. Cross-referencing of evidence, survey, photo, and context logs should be carried out to eliminate errors. The supervisor and SCE will check all body forms (FA12BH, FA12BT, FA12SH, FA12ST, and FA12BP, see accompanying CD

---

[3] There are exceptions to this such as Ian Hodder's excavation at Catal Huyuk, Turkey, or the reexamination of the Lazete 2 grave site from the Srebrenica investigation, first exhumed in 1996 and then excavated again in 2000 (International Criminal Tribunal for the Former Yugoslavia, Krstic trial transcripts, 2001).

for all recording forms and logs referred to in this chapter, and 1.11 for guidance to their use) submitted by excavation staff before filing.

5.2 Approaches and phases

The archaeological and crime scene management processes described in the protocols (see 2.3) can be followed to successfully locate and excavate sites of forensic relevance. The first phase, site assessment and evaluation, defines three stages (area location, site location, and site confirmation). The process then gathers data as time passes and survey is undertaken, and focusses on a specific point of interest on the ground such as a grave, from an initial starting point of information, space, and time that may be as superficial as a news report of a massacre in a named province or nation state. The basic process includes defining a geographical area that is likely to contain the suspect site (see 5.3), and within that, defining specific areas of interest on the ground using physical examination, observation, and remote sensing of anomalies (see 5.3). This is followed by testing the location of potential anomalies to determine their nature and then to confirm or refute them as a suspect site through structure and content (see 5.4). The second phase is site excavation and evidence recovery (see 5.5). The purpose of this is to record, recover, process, and interpret human remains and other evidence. The successful location and excavation of any clandestine grave will always depend on using a combination of these structured phases. When less structured or more selective approaches are applied, the results are often false negatives. These may be caused by uncertainty as to the thoroughness of a survey within an area or site, lack of recognition of an area, or the fact that the site has not been fully evaluated. This ends with partial or misleading results.

Indicators and prerequisites for site location include initial information, desk-based research, field data, climatic data, environmental data, geological and topographical data, hydrological data, and, finally, adequate resources. Initial information is that which raises suspicion that there may be a scene of crime in an area. This may be provided by witness statements, the location of artefacts/evidence, 'tip-offs', and reports from journalists and the media. The accuracy of initial information will have a strong effect on time, cost, and resource factors in any investigation and all subsequent stages of a search. Information can often be confused, misleading, and erroneous, especially in scenarios concerning atrocity crimes or mass fatality incidents. The most resource-effective way to locate a suspect grave is to carry out effective desk-based research. Although aspects of this research such as purchase of aerial imagery may be expensive, staffing numbers, time, and resources can be saved by pinpointing the approximate location of a site from records and statements. The absence of maps, records, or photographs of a suspect area means that the investigation is 'blind', and the approach on the ground is inevitably more complex and has to be resourced more heavily.

5.2.1 Resources

The availability of field resources will directly affect the speed, efficiency, and result of any attempt to locate, evaluate, and excavate a suspect site. The outcome of any search depends on sufficient personnel, access to experts, and specialised equipment. Skilful management of these resources can increase the effectiveness of this phase of the process. With unlimited time to conduct a search, any area can be completely searched and either eliminated or confirmed as containing a suspect site. In reality, there is never unlimited time because time is directly linked to resources. However, the amount of time available will affect the efficiency and result of the search. Because the time required is probably the most difficult factor to determine in any investigation, initial planning of projects should budget for additional site location and recovery time. Any estimate of time should have a substantial contingency added. With unlimited funds to conduct a search, an area can be completely searched and eliminated or confirmed as containing a suspect site. As mentioned previously, this is an improbable scenario. In practice, the amount of money available will affect the efficiency and result of the search because cost is directly linked to time and resources. All possible budget lines for an investigation should be based up up-to-date costings and include contingencies, in the planning stages.

5.2.2 Climate and environment

Climatic extremes will have logistical consequences, which will alter time and resource requirements, ultimately affecting the cost factor. Seasonal rain, snow, or fire can physically prevent searches from taking place during certain times of the year. Extreme cold or heat can inhibit effective search efforts, whereas ideal climatic conditions may help in locating graves. Year round climatic conditions at any site of investigation should be determined and factored into the planning process before deployment. The physical environment of a suspect area may also have logistical consequences that affect resources. Geological criteria and hydrological regimes need to be determined prior to any ground search. Topographical features such as dense woodland, mountains, and ravines or bodies of water and swamps will slow or limit searches. Contrarily, topographic features such as prairie, farmland, and open woodland can make searches efficient and fast. Year round conditions and the nature of the landscape at any site should be determined before deployment.

5.3 Area and site location

It is necessary to begin this section by acknowledging that strategic, theoretical, and practical approaches to the search and location of sites of relevance in the investigation of atrocity crimes and in humanitarian recovery of the Missing have been relatively ill researched and undeveloped when compared to the investigation of domestic murder cases, for example, in the UK or the United States. In such domestic murder enquiries, considerable financial, logistical, and staffing resources are deployed. Consequently, a complex, sequenced multidisciplinary approach is adopted that is underpinned by psychological and geographical profiling and modelling prior to progressing to more practical approaches. That said, there can be little doubt that even in such countries as the UK, insufficient time and attention is spent determining the types and availability of documentary sources that can assist in search strategies in domestic cases (Simpson, 2005), and the same is true for international work, even though experience since the mid-1990s has shown us there is usually more evidential information available concerning international cases than domestic murders.[4]

With many atrocity crimes, the perpetrators do not expect to be held accountable for their actions (where they consider their power to be absolute or where a climate of impunity prevails), and so there are no real attempts made to 'conceal' the remains of the victims or their identity; instead, disposal is prompted more by the need to remove the remains of the victims from day-to-day proximity to the living, to add to the destruction of the victims' identity and existence, or for reasons of hygiene.[5] In other contexts, innocent people are coerced by the perpetrators into disposing of the remains, or the remains may be buried by relatives or postconflict agencies active in the affected region, as has been seen in Bosnia, Central America, and parts of Africa. Those issues aside, there is also postburial disturbance of remains to consider, and with that, possible reburial elsewhere. This is discussed in depth by Skinner et al. (2002) and includes such contexts as body trading during or after war. Examples include human remains recovered at Balinovac in West Mostar, Bosnia-Herzegovina, or El Kattoon in Iraq (where combat dead returned from the Iran–Iraq War were initially described to investigators as murder victims). This can also apply to mandated excavation of human remains with reburial during warfare (e.g., victims killed at Pakracka Poljana, Croatia), recovery and reburial by relatives (considered to be a common occurrence) (ibid.), and body relocations for concealment purposes (e.g., numerous sites in Quiche Province, Guatemala, or Tasovcici, Bosnia-Herzegovina).

Not all reasons underlying disposal are clandestine, and hence, the psychological motives and basic differences of intent underlying the disposal mode require a more complex range of psychological and geographical profiling models to be applied when attempting to find mass grave sites. Mass graves are more than clandestine repositories of the dead. Prior to excavation, they can function as political tools to intimidate survivors (Skinner et al., 2002) and be used as propaganda to infer the

---

[4] It is, however, often logistically more difficult and more resource intensive to recover these data and evidence.

[5] Hence, in Rwanda, remains were left on the street or were thrown into rivers and lakes, buried in gardens, wells, latrines, and conventional graves (Melvern, 2000).

guilt of accused groups. They can also be important as territorial markers of communities that have been ethnically cleansed and war memorials. Graves unrelated to particular episodes may be used to cast blame on accused groups and by communities to erroneously identify the locations of their dead. Graves can generate sources of aid and income for victim communities through reparations and as visitor attractions (Figure 5.4).[6] Furthermore, for relatives involved in the burial or who otherwise know the location of the grave, they are not clandestine other than in official terms (Sanford, 2003),[7] but are both public and private spaces representing memory and the certainty of loss; a relative luxury not afforded to many whose loved ones who are amongst the 'disappeared'. What these factors suggest is that more so than with domestic murder, there are often multiple direct or indirect witnesses to the location of grave sites, and there are often several sites or graves relating to one criminal episode. These are all detectable.

In locating mass grave sites and associated forensic landscapes, the first step is area location. This involves identifying and defining the geographical area that is likely to contain a suspect burial or disposal site, and confirming the general area of suspicion. There are several methods that can be used to identify possible areas of interest in the investigation of atrocity crimes, and they are described in this chapter. Suitable planning and preparation should, of course, always be undertaken before ground investigations begin.

Unlike domestic crime situations where witness testimony is considered only as collateral evidence (Association of Chief Police Officers [ACPO] and Centrex, 2005), in mass grave investigations, witness testimony can be a vitally important component of both area and site location and often provides the initial information that informs a broader search strategy. With atrocity crimes, witnesses' experience of the events may reflect a number of scenarios. They may have survived the crime (which happened at several Srebrenica Massacre sites[8]), witnessed an incident occur, seen the incident location after occurrence, been a perpetrator or a member of a perpetrator group,[9] heard or been informed of a crime or event, found artefacts of which they are suspicious, or found a site of which they are suspicious (journalists such as David Rohde [1997] often film grave sites). It must also be remembered that in some cases such witnesses may have malicious or well-intended motives. In some contexts, witnesses are so by virtue of being the individual or one of a group of

---

[6] As is the case in parts of Rwanda (e.g., Nyamata), where the local survivors derive an income from such visitors; this is a very divisive practice.

[7] In Guatemala, many rural clandestine graves were clandestine only by virtue of official negation of their existence and the silence imposed on communities by perpetrators (Sanford, 2003).

[8] See, for example, ICTY (2001, 2003, 2004) trial transcripts for Krstic, Blagojevic and Jokic and Obrenovic, and Blagojevic and Jokic.

[9] Such as Drazen Erdemovic, a member of the 10th Sabotage Detachment Bosnian Serb Army, who testified to carrying out executions at Branjevo Military Farm of victims from Srebrenica in 1995 (ICTY, 2001).

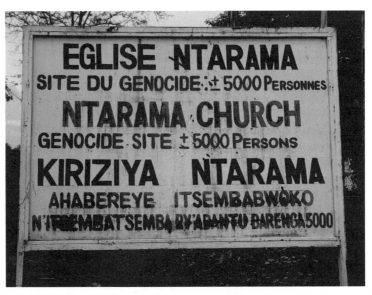

Figure 5–4. In Ntarama, Rwanda, the massacre site has become a focus for genocide tourism. In such contexts, a few villagers will gain financially from such sites. This practice is clearly divisive and not to be encouraged. *Source:* Margaret Cox.

individuals who were coerced into participating in the events being investigated. These may include transporting victims to execution or grave sites, or elsewhere (e.g., bus drivers made to drive Srebrenica victims to execution sites [United Nations (UN), 1999]); to disposal of the dead, such as local people at Serniki, Ukraine (Bevan, 1994); or killing the victims (e.g., same bus drivers mentioned previously). They may also be relatives of such a person passing on second-hand information (common in Guatemala, where rural communities share information readily). A reliable witness can give information that leads to the rapid and accurate location of a suspicious site. However, information may be so vague that a site cannot be accurately located without supplementary information. Therefore, taking and interpreting evidence from witnesses is a skilled procedure and requires careful and precise evidence gleaning and extraction, which must be considered carefully before it is acted on. Detailed analysis of all available witness statements by criminal investigators can also guide and corroborate the physical examination of a scene. However, it must be remembered that witnesses can also provide inaccurate information that can hinder and lead a search astray.[10] Similarly, informants may make statements that conflict with conclusions from physical examination of the scene. Witnesses have often experienced events under traumatic circumstances, and this can affect their

[10] In more than one case in Bosnia, witnesses appeared when investigation teams arrived on the ground, providing information that ranged from accurate (from a victim who escaped execution) to spurious (a local farmer who 'knew' a grave was located nearby because he had been told so).

Figure 5–5a and b. Photographs have been taken of the dead, mass graves, and excavations since cameras were developed. They provide identity and actions of victims, perpetrators, and chains of events. *Source:* http//www.law.umkc.edu/faculty/projects/ftrials/nuremberg/einsatzshoots.jpg

reliability in assisting investigations (Gilbert, 2003). Furthermore, the accuracy of witness statements lessens over time.

The use of documentary sources when locating grave sites has, in many cases, been ill developed in this field of enquiry. It should be remembered that in many parts of the world, particularly where graves might be located in urban contexts, there is an abundance of documentary information related to land use that can contribute useful information about possible areas of interest that both pre- and postdate the incident in question. Documentation might relate to planning and development control legislation and regulation, refuse and waste disposal regulation (Simpson, 2005), and other land-use activities such as mineral extraction and conservation strategies. One source that is proving increasingly useful in the search, location,

Figure 5–5. *(cont.)*
Source: http://userwww.sfsu.edu/~rhernand/Wounded%20Knee.htm

and analysis of mass graves is photographic documentation. When atrocities take place, the media may be present to film, record, or write about events and the aftermath, and this information is often available to investigators. Civilians with cameras and camera phones increasingly record events that they witness in passing or by chance (e.g., the Petrovic video of the Kravica warehouse massacre, Bosnia [ICTY, 2003; ICTY, 2004]). With the growing availability of affordable video and digital cameras, atrocity events are becoming increasingly filmed by, or with agreement of, the perpetrators, which then end up in investigators' hands (e.g., footage of the Serbian militia Scorpions executing Srebrenica victims, which came to light in 2005). This is not a new phenomenon. Bodies being put into mass graves have been photographed since Wounded Knee in 1890 and killings in the Ukraine by the Nazis in 1941 (Figure 5–5). These film documents not only provide evidence of the atrocities themselves and the perpetrators but also the location of the events and the identities of victims.

Archived materials, such as images and elevation data recorded by satellite; archived photographic images of killings; and documentary records of witnesses, perpetrators, receipts, and logs of the logistics involved in mass murder, all provide an evidential record that, if it can be accessed, provides a ready source of comparative, evidential, and mission planning material. Comparison of such material with new remote sensing surveys can provide information on areas to search, site location, the dating of graves, and postburial site formation activity. Physical site inspection confirms the location and nature of graves indicated by research and sensing. Documentary evidence about an area and data on its geological, geomorphological, topographical, and land use history, together with surveys on the ground, can be collated in a geographical information systems (GIS) analysis, which can provide data to pinpoint potential grave locations and to indicate how these may become more or less detectable remotely and on the ground over time. A good example of this approach is the search for mass graves associated with the Jasenovac World War II concentration camp in Croatia/northern Bosnia (Babic et al., 2000). An important part of such search techniques is remote sensing combined with ground examination.

Area reconnaissance is a vital tool in site location and involves examining the area in a structured way, using information gathered. It is also useful in planning site location activities. A trip by vehicle through an area can give information on vehicle access, deployment scale, cost and time requirements, geology, landscape, vegetation, local population, security, and risks. Appropriate use of the methods described in this chapter to investigate the area of a suspect site should be made if such resources are determined to be available during an investigation.

5.3.1   Remote sensing and imagery

Air imagery. Air imagery is an integral part of area or site location search strategy. After the interviewing of witnesses, air imagery has perhaps, since the mid-1990s, provided the most important source of data used to locate mass graves. It also provides collaborative dating evidence on the creation of graves and captures events of forensic interest at crime scenes. Usefully, many organisations regularly take images from the air to check such factors as topography, mapping, boundary assessment, tax assessment, land management, vegetation change, geological survey, archaeological survey, and climate change, and for military monitoring. Some satellites (e.g., LANDSAT) constantly take images that are archived, representing global coverage every 18 days (Gibson, 2000), and these are available for public purchase. This has provided a consistent worldwide source of imagery back to the 1970s, which may pinpoint grave sites and their creation. Archived imagery that may be relevant for mass grave investigation dates back to World War II often comprises military air surveys. Analysis of Luftwaffe reconnaissance photos of the Smolensk area, including the Katyn Forest taken from 1941 to 1944, provided collaborative images concerning Soviet excavations at the site of the massacre of Polish officers (Fox, 1999). In addition, imagery may be specifically taken to record events that lead to massacres (e.g., NATO imagery concerning the fall of Srebrenica) (see Figure 5.6). This imagery can show recent or past changes to the landscape that may indicate ground disturbance and even physical events taking place, such as grave excavation or the immediate aftermath of executions. Imagery supplied by the U.S.

Mass Burial at Branjevo Farm
Donje Pilica Area,
Bosnia and Herzegovina

5 Jul 95

before burial

17 Jul 95

burial activity

(a)

Figure 5–6a and b. Aerial imagery taken by NATO for military reconnaissance purposes over Srebrenica in July 1995. These recorded execution and burial sites and were released by Madeline K. Albright in August 1995. *Source:* http://www.globalsecurity.org.

State Department to ICTY was used by tribunal investigators and the forensic field team to pinpoint a series of primary and secondary grave sites from 1998, which provided enough detail to enable the exact area to be approached and recognised, the grave locations being corroborated by other evidence such as vegetation change

Figure 5–6 (cont.)
Source: http://www.globalsecurity.org.

and visible soil disturbance[11] (Figure 5–7). These sites were then confirmed by physical testing. Ground disturbance affects soil, vegetation type and growth, drainage,
contour, snow cover, and ground temperature. These effects can be seen from the
air using the right cameras and in the right conditions, providing a pinpoint guide
to the location of disturbance or land use change, even on a small scale. In addition,
these systems can be used to review an area already subject to ground search in order
to find anomalies that may have been missed by the human eye.

Air imagery must be acquired with sufficient inherent detail to enable the imagery,
on analysis, to provide information on mass graves or other relevant sites to an evidential standard. There are three definable stages in acquiring this sort of information
from the air, each with a minimum resolvable scale. These stages are the detection,
recognition, and identification of potential graves. In providing the requisite air
imagery, it is imperative to follow the three stages if air imagery is to be the primary
sensor in the search. Thus, initial cover would be at a scale of 1:10,000 for a large

---

[11] This imagery also showed heavy machinery operating on sites, digging and robbing graves, and the victims
grouped before and after death. (For examples, see ICTY [2001, 2004] trial transcripts Blagojevic and Jokic and
Krstic.)

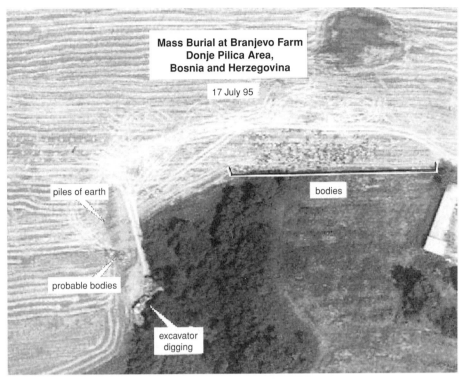

**Mass Burial at Branjevo Farm
Donje Pilica Area,
Bosnia and Herzegovina**

17 July 95

piles of earth

bodies

probable bodies

excavator
digging

Figure 5–7. Imagery released in August 1995 showing machines excavating graves at Branjevo Farm, dating the Srebrenica Massacre. *Source:* www.globalsecurity.org

area search. Alternatively, if a suspected site is already established by other means, a pass at 1:5,000 should be followed by a number of such passes at a scale of 1:1,000, depending on the overall size of the site (Oxlee, 1997a). To achieve sufficient inherent ground resolution (clarity) to meet an evidential standard, the imagery must be taken to obtain the following rating against the internationally recognised Imagery Interpretation Rating Scale (IIRS), defining the criteria for detection, recognition, and identification of various scenes and items (ibid.). In the context of mass graves, the requisite resolution is in the order of a scale of 1:1,000. To enable accurate air imagery interpretation, vertical stereoscopic cover must have a minimum forward frame overlap of 60 percent (Hamshaw-Thomas, 1916). Moreover, to maintain complete coverage, there should be a lateral overlap of 30 percent between passes.

Comparative analysis and change detection is fundamental to the exploitation phase of imagery analysis. As a consequence, the earliest available cover of the site under investigation must be obtained, together with any intermittent imagery. Air imagery should not be considered alone if any ground photographs are available. If possible, images of the site under investigation taken prior to the incident in question should be compared with those taken subsequent to the date of the incident. The prime sensor must be in natural colour. However, if possible, imagery from beyond that part of the electromagnetic spectrum should be acquired to assist exploitation (ibid.). The optimum mix as far as the detection of graves is concerned is described by Oxlee (1997b). Cover should be recorded with a time interval to provide a permanent record of events from start to finish. Care must be taken to determine optimum timing with respect to sun angle and imaging aspect. It is sensible to include some low-angle oblique views and vertical cover (Wilson, 1982). The record should also include night coverage, if practicable.

All images, of whatever type, must have certain information recorded on them. Such information is vital to the photogrammetric factors permitting accurate measurement on the imagery. The following is the minimum to be recorded: frame number, taking unit identifier, focal length of the sensor, aircraft altitude, and size of frame. A report of the analysis must be compiled in accordance with the provision of specialist expert evidence to a court. It must include a signed and dated witness statement, and an appropriate designation. As with an expert witness report from any expert in any field, it should also include the following information: on whose instruction the report was compiled, the purpose of the report, a statement as to the image quality, information on the methodology used, good quality illustrations, conclusions, a list of the exhibits, and details of the qualifications and experience of the author.

It is imperative that the original imaging medium (negative film and video) is reproduced onto a master copy. This initial reproduction should be done digitally, if possible. The original must then be placed into suitable secure long-term storage to guarantee the integrity and continuity of evidence. It must then be stored in conditions designed to avoid degradation and under secure circumstances. A master copy should be given to the image analyst and used in the production of the report. This master copy must be kept and secured in the same way as the original. It is advisable for a further working copy to be made for consultative/demonstration purposes.

Parts of the electromagnetic spectrum other than traditional air photography can also be extremely useful in search operations. These include near-infrared false colour photography limited to daytime exposure and thermal infrared systems that may be used at night to determine areas with differences in surface temperature due to heat emission from decomposing material (Simonett, 1983).

Commercial satellite imagery. Commercial satellite imagery can be obtained from a number of private commercial companies. This imagery can be used for many different purposes, including site mapping, visual and situational awareness, archived information to document change over time, and spectral and interferometric analysis. Because there are many different types of sensors, spatial resolutions, and spectral resolutions, no one sensor is ideal for the detection or analysis of mass graves. Each has its own particular capabilities and limitations.

It is not unusual for imagery vendors to maintain a library of satellite data collected over time. Satellite imagery collected over a particular area during a specific time frame may assist in the detection of changes to an area, provide historical information about a particular site before and after events occurred, or provide additional information not readily observed in a more recent collection. Recently collected satellite imagery is ideal for creating image maps for planning and marking grave locations. Typically, high-resolution satellite imagery is most suited for this type of mission because of its ability to identify subtle features within a site and to provide a larger overhead view for general studies. Any competent GIS-trained person can create image maps from these data and derive vector layers to emphasise critical information to untrained users. By analyzing the spectral colour and near-infrared bands of a particular scene, it is often possible to obtain information about the site that is not easily discerned by the naked eye. Spectral imagery analysis and interferometric analysis of commercially available Synthetic Aperture Radar (SAR) data can be used in conducting vegetation health analysis, anomaly detection, and disturbed soils analysis. Such an analysis was undertaken in June 2003 by specialists with U.S. Army[12] at the behest of the Coalition Provisional Authority for Iraq and the Inforce Foundation. This analysis recognised the value of available aerial imagery as a resource (*The Eagle*, 2004), after a series of graves near Musayib in Iraq, dating to massacres related to the uprisings after the first Gulf War in 1991, were identified. The local communities had already located and were excavating the sites. Analysis of archived LANDSAT images from 1991 showing the site before and after ground disturbance were used to corroborate witness statements that the graves were created in the spring of that year. Contemporary imagery also showed that a military defensive berm had been placed over the grave site, perhaps to deter local interest. Spectral analysis was recognised as helpful in dating these Iraqi grave sites because it detected disturbed areas where the digging of graves brought subsurface deposits of gypsum (common in this area of the Middle East) to the surface, creating a specific recognisable signature (ibid.).

Nearly all commercial imagery, both new collections and archived imagery, can be obtained by contacting the imagery vendors directly. At the time of writing, prices normally range from $11 to $12 per km^2 for high-resolution imagery and $250 to $600 per scene for low-resolution imagery, depending on the vendor and type of satellite imagery requested. Before contacting vendors, it is imperative to know the following information:

1. It is essential to know the location of the site(s) in terms of latitude and longitude. Most sites can be identified as a single point, while larger sites may require identification of the four bounding corners that include the entire site to be examined.

2. The time frame of the event(s) is also crucial and will help determine whether a new collection is required or whether the mission can be completed with an archived image.

[12] U.S. Army Space and Missile Defence Command provides, among other capabilities, satellite coverage analysis. The use of military aerial imagery began archaeology aerial imaging (Wilson, 2000). Application of contemporary military imagery for a number of human rights and civil aid uses are increasingly being recognised (see the Federation of American Scientists 'Public Eye' program); for example, software algorithms used to identify 'dug in' military targets can also be applied to identify similar disturbance caused by the digging of mass graves or support planning for relief efforts during natural disasters (Cloutier, 2005).

3. The size of the objects or features to be detected will determine the spatial resolution of the imagery needed to discern them. Typically, grave site analysis requires high-resolution imagery to discern information in the site. Current high-resolution commercial imagery vendors can provide imagery with pixel sizes ranging from 2.5- to 0.6-m spatial resolution (NIIRS ratings roughly from 3 to 5). Spectral (colour) imagery is typically lower in resolution than panchromatic imagery.

4. It is important to consider the project time frame and required turnaround time when ordering commercial imagery. Although an archived scene can be delivered in a few days or weeks, a new acquisition could take significantly longer (weeks to months, depending largely on the weather and satellite availability).

5. Information defining the level of processing and/or file format needed must be provided to the vendors when ordering commercial imagery. The vendors are typically flexible in providing data in a variety of formats, levels, or georectification, and map projections. It is essential to select an imagery format that best suits the specifications of the type of system and software used to manipulate the imagery. Satellite imagery files are very large (file sizes range from 10 MB to 1 GB), which makes electronic delivery often impractical. It may be prudent to order the imagery on CD or DVD and have it shipped to the mission planning headquarters via mail service (e.g., FedEx, DHL).

Currently available satellite imagery sources include the following different resolutions available via various satellites. High-resolution (small area coverage) imagery is available from Space Imaging (IKONOS), DigitalGlobe (QuickBird), and OrbImage (OrbView). Medium-resolution (large area coverage) imagery can be obtained from SPOT Image, EROS satellites, and Indian Remote Sensing (IRS) satellites. Low-resolution (large area coverage) imagery is available via the LAND-SAT, ASTER, and Earth Observer 1 (EO-1) systems. There are a number of software applications that can be used to examine satellite imagery. They range in ease of use from those suitable for those with low-level information technology skills to those requiring high-level analysis skills and extensive training. The more common software packages used to view satellite imagery include Adobe Photoshop or similar image manipulation packages. For image map compositions or spectral imagery analysis, widely used packages include ERDAS Imagine or RSI's ENVI (Environment for Visualizing Imagery).

Satellite imagery can be used in various stages of mission planning and during operations to plan site access or to reconstruct past events. There are a multitude of spectral imagery analysis applications that could be used to improve situation awareness or to provide information about an area. Analysis of spectral imagery goes beyond interpreting the data with the human eye and allows the software to classify pixels according to their composition. By doing so, specific materials or groups of materials, such as road surfaces or heavy machinery, may be identified purely because of their signature and not because they can be visually identified.

5.3.2 Geophysical survey

Because little geophysical survey work has been performed on multiple and mass grave sites, the following guidelines are based on publications and research of limited applicability and theoretical approaches. As such, these are embryonic procedures that are expected to evolve rapidly through further discussion and future research outcomes. For further discussion, see Cheetham (2005). Proximate surveys to locate graves using ground-based geophysical survey techniques help define areas of potential by locating geophysical anomalies. These anomalies result from contrasts in physical properties of the materials that comprise the ground substrate. Different techniques measure different properties and so are, in general, complementary, but may also be confirmatory. The benefits of surveys can be to reduce the size of an area to be physically tested by highlighting anomalies of potential interest. It is also useful for visualising anomalies in areas where there may be prohibitions or disadvantages to physically disturbing the ground, and to providing an assessment of the depth and volume of graves without extensive physical probing, to aid in the logistical planning of excavations. The requirement to move systematically across a survey area can make some techniques problematic in areas where the potential presence of unexploded ordnance (UXO) makes ground survey difficult, such as in Iraq or the Balkans.[13]

Only those techniques that have a proven record of success in grave detection should be employed as primary search methods. At least one other proven technique should be used to corroborate the presence or absence of anomalies within a particular area. Only when proven techniques have been employed should any less well-researched methods be used.[14] Specialists who are experienced in the theory and practice of geophysical techniques for grave detection should advise on the appropriate techniques and survey methodology (Figure 5–8). Geophysical techniques that have been successful in locating graves are ground-penetrating radar (GPR), electromagnetic (EM) systems, earth resistivity (geoelectrical area survey and electrical imaging), and, in special cases, magnetometry. Little relevant evaluation has been undertaken that is in the public domain, using any of these systems for the detection of multiple and mass graves, and much of the published work on the detection of individual graves in a forensic context has been limited in its general applicability. Because of this it would be unjustified, at this point in time, to limit the range of techniques that may be applicable, although techniques that have been shown to be successful should be the primary techniques employed.

Geophysical survey is potentially destructive to ephemeral surface evidence, so it must be carefully sequenced with other potential grave location techniques such as a

---

[13] For many ICTY assessments, the placement of many mass graves in Croatia and Bosnia made the use of geophysical survey too impractical as an assessment tool in the years following the end of the war.

[14] Searching for mass graves near Musayib, Iraq, Inforce employed resistivity, GPR, and magnetic survey to pinpoint anomalies. The arid ground conditions meant some techniques were more useful than others, and use of multiple surveys provides a data contrast across a designated area.

Figure 5–8. Inforce personnel using GPR in Iraq to search for anomalies that pinpointed potential grave sites in an area indicated by local witnesses. *Source:* Inforce Foundation.

topographic or vegetation survey and after other surface evidence is recorded and/or removed. For geophysical survey, all survey grid points or traverse end points should be located to within ±10 cm of the true position on the local or site coordinate system in use. To ensure this level of accuracy, electronic survey instruments should normally be employed. Where possible, all such points should be located and georeferenced by using a differential global positioning system (DGPS). Where survey grid and traverse end point location has been undertaken, using a local or site coordinate system, a minimum of three site coordinate datum points should be georeferenced using a DGPS, or if that is not available, referenced to features on scale maps or aerial imagery. If a survey instrument has a DGPS capability, then the use of such a system will allow individual readings to be fully georeferenced without reference to any local or site coordinate system. For the detection of single adult graves, a reading interval of 0.5 m along and 0.5 m between traverses is the maximum separation that is likely to resolve such features. For the detection of larger multiple or mass graves, the reading interval along and between traverses may be increased, but as a consequence the loss of detail may result in features of interest not being detected. Where instruments are capable of acquiring data at greater resolution along the line of a traverse, then greater resolution should be employed. However, intervals of less than 10 cm are unlikely to increase the chances of defining a grave if the distance between traverses is 0.5 m. The spatial resolution (reading intervals) of the survey must be documented.

Only experienced specialist operator(s) should perform the survey.[15] The operator(s) should be familiar with the geophysical response characteristics of each technique, in general, to near-surface natural and cultural features and, specifically, to the likely response characteristics of graves. Such knowledge and experience should be obtained by a system of practical field survey mentoring. Survey data should be recorded digitally in the instrument manufacturer's proprietary format. Where data are to be recorded manually on paper, they should be recorded on prepared data logging sheets that allow detail of the survey type and instrument used, value of any instrument configuration, and survey parameters to be included on each sheet. At suitable intervals, copies of the downloaded data should be saved to a suitable high-quality storage medium, such as a recordable compact disk (CD-R) and one copy sealed in appropriate packaging as per other primary evidence.

All steps employed in the processing of the raw data to enhance it for the purpose of effective analysis must be fully documented. Many proprietary geophysical processing packages will log a processing history, and such facilities should be employed whenever possible. Otherwise, this information must be recorded manually and documented in a report. If the most appropriate processing cannot be achieved on site within the survey fieldwork period, then such processing should be completed immediately after fieldwork, dependent on the results before any further exploration is undertaken.

A report must be prepared that includes all details concerning the survey type, the instrument used, the value of any instrument configuration, the survey parameters, and environmental conditions. The geo-referencing data should be presented in both numerical and map form, and it should indicate the location of survey grids and survey traverses. Plots of raw data and processed data appropriate to the survey technique should be included with interpretations. These should be provided either annotated onto the plots (wherever possible) or as separate diagrams. Because of the possible poor quality of reproducing such reports, digital copies of the report (including all plots) should be included in an accompanying suitable storage medium. Full details of the software used to process the data and the file formats of the digital data must be documented. Where possible, ASCII data files should be created and included in the report in digital form on a suitable storage medium, along with copies of the raw data in the instrument's proprietary format. Paper records should be dealt with as any other such material.

Ground truthing, or proving of geophysical anomalies that may represent graves, is more fully described in 5.4. It is the geophysicist's role to inform the forensic

---

[15] Staffing efficiency means that a geophysical operator employed on mass grave investigations will almost always have another professional skill such as field archaeology.

archaeologist of the position, size, orientation, and estimated depth of the feature that the anomaly represents. The geophysicist should be available during ground truthing to assist in the identification and analysis of the source of the anomaly, thus improving their interpretation experience.

5.3.3   Other methods

Maps, plans, and records can also play a role in search strategies, and a detailed review of these sources of information can help eliminate areas from a potential search. Geological and topographical maps are particularly useful in this respect Maps can show areas that may or may not match witness description; they are also useful to identify areas that for geological, hydrological, or other reasons could or could not be used as sites in which to dig mass graves, that present potential hazards to a search, that show access routes to an area, and that indicate site history and the effects this may have on interpreting other methods of locating graves.[16] Such documents are a cost- and time-effective way of verifying preliminary information.

Forensic psychologists and geographical profilers are familiar with patterns of predictable habits and behaviours of people and have assessed how they can be used to help determine possible locations of graves. Several patterns of behaviour have been identified that may be useful. It is generally the case that a person will not carry an adult body more than 50 feet from a car or road because of weight-bearing difficulties (McLaughlin, 1974; Killam, 1990). Naismith's Rule is also useful in that it sets out that the speed and distance moved in a given time will decrease over difficult terrain and at night (Kennedy, 1998). Along the same lines, the 'principle of least effort' suggests that victims may be moved a certain distance from the place of murder (Zipf, 1950). Following different principles, 'winthropping' relates to the identification of locations within, and movement across, a landscape by using prominent landmarks or features as guides to route selection (Hunter, 2000). Figure 5–9 illustrates the features in the forensic landscape that are typically searched for during investigations. Research also indicates that bodies buried in exposed locations may be buried at a shallow depth because the perpetrator fears discovery while at the site. The factors of time and distance are important (Keppel and Weis, 1994). Experience shows that mass graves may be located in areas with deep deposits of easily dug soil such as river valleys and that many bodies or graves are deposited in places of habitual or convenient garbage disposal, such as rubbish tips, wells, or caves (Rossmo, 1999; Lundrigan and Canter, 2001a, 2001b).

The traditional method for locating forensic sites, especially in remote locations, is area search using a team such as law enforcement officers, search specialists, and occasionally volunteers (Hunter et al., 1996). In such an approach, search patterns

---

[16] The link between the Srebrenica grave site of Orahovac/Lazete and its secondary graves along the Hodici Road was initially made by the ICTY forensic team consulting regional geological maps. From these, they pinpointed the origin of a rare geological stone found in the secondary graves that could only have come from a volcanic outcrop above the Lazete grave site, where matching samples were subsequently found.

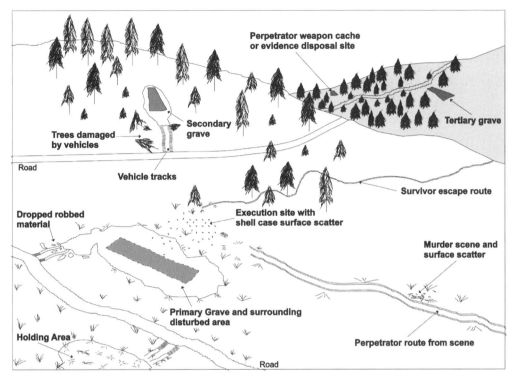

Figure 5–9. Forensic landscape – features in the landscape often have significance to perpetrators. The scenes associated with atrocity crimes may be numerous and reflect the sequence of events undertaken by perpetrators. *Source:* Inforce Foundation.

and grids must ensure all areas are adequately covered. Search teams should contain experts such as trackers and ecologists who can determine changes to plants, soil, and atypical natural habitats. They should be managed to ensure that all topographical features are explored from different approaches. Any search area should be assessed by specialists only (i.e., not unskilled volunteers), photographed, surveyed, and videotaped before a main search causes potential damage and contamination. Area searches are labour intensive, expensive, alter the ground at a scene dramatically, and can be destructive while seeking to locate anomalies and evidence. All of these combine to make it an undesirable method; consequently, it should only be used if other methods have failed. Despite this, an area search may still yield positive results. For exemplar methods of area search, see Skinner and Lazenby (1983) and Galloway et al. (2001).

Cadaver dogs and handlers have been used for some time to find not only decomposing bodies and body parts but also skeletal remains and human fluids such as blood and urine. Dogs can be used to cover a large area of search. They should follow specific search patterns to ensure the ground is covered (Rebmann et al., 2000). Dogs are not always reliable, and their effective use in searches for mass graves has yet to be demonstrated.

Field craft was first described as a forensic method by Hunter et al. (1996). It involves the recognition of tracks and signs (Brown, 1999), faunal patterns, human activity, topographical patterns, and geological states causing discernible alterations to the environment. A broad knowledge of natural sciences and the life cycles of ecosystems, flora, and fauna can assist in differentiating between activity that may be clandestine or that of the local anthropogenic and natural environment. Changes and alterations noted should be fully recorded and documented, including location and contrast with the normal environment. Such an approach must be applied systematically to ensure that all areas are considered.

Awareness of the dynamics of evidence is crucial in recognising influences that change, relocate, obscure, or obliterate physical evidence, regardless of intent (Chisum and Turvey, 2002). Skills in observing and identifying change are essential to recognising the sequence of processes and events affecting physical evidence, whether buried or above ground. Examples include predicting the location of surface bones moved down slope by gravity over time or by the water action of a fast-flowing stream.[17] Such skills are important in recognising what may be potential evidence related to a sequence of events. For further examples, see Manhein et al. (2003).

Evidence of scavenging of human remains is common in surface scatters and shallow burials, and it is important to be aware of indications of scavenging in site location. Animals, such as rodents and birds, have been known to remove human remains and relocate them both close to, and far from, the area of primary deposition. Bone elements within a grave may be repositioned by burrowing animals and then misinterpreted during excavation. Animals and rodents may dig up human remains and leave them scattered on the surface; identifying these bones can indicate the presence of graves. Animals, rodents, and birds may, however, return with remains to their burrows, nests, and dens. Animals and insects may change their pattern of behaviour in the proximity of remains, and this can be observed. Animal tracks and paths may have been used by missing persons or perpetrators to move through difficult terrain. For examples of scavenging, see Haglund and Sorg (2002b).

Modified areas of vegetation caused by soil disturbance can remain visible, in some cases, for a number of years. Observations can include complete absence of vegetation, stressed or scorched vegetation, dead vegetation, retarded growth, accelerated growth, or change or concentration in species across a site. Factors that affect the reaction of plants to soil disturbance include the length of time since the site has been disturbed, the moisture and air content of the disturbed soil, changes in soil composition, contents of the grave, climate, vegetation growth rates, and anthropomorphic factors. Post disturbance, some plants may colonise the disturbed soil faster than others and dormant seeds may germinate in altered soil conditions. Concentrations of these species can indicate anomalies (see Figure 5–10). Soil that

---

[17] Bodies from the Kravica warehouse massacre were dumped from a track down a steep slope at Ravnice, Bosnia (ICTY, 2004). At the base of the slope was a winter stream, the prediction that bones would have moved downhill and then be moved by water action resulted in several skulls being found some 200 m from the original deposition site.

Figure 5–10. Vegetation growth over an area of soil disturbance following the creation of a mass grave. Note the concentration of camomile (white flowers) in the sparsely vegetated area, which also demonstrated the difference in plant growth rates over disturbed areas. *Source:* Inforce Foundation.

has been dug can have a different compaction rate and can consequently hold more or less moisture than surrounding soil. Depending on soil characteristics, growth rates of plants in disturbed soil will react to moisture levels and may be taller or shorter than surrounding plants. This can be observed on the ground and especially in aerial photography, during the growing season. Changes in species succession seen on burial sites commonly occur naturally. Plant growth is affected by time of year in certain climates. In lush tropical environments, plant growth is so profuse that differences caused by digging can soon be lost. Buried plant material can indicate movement of materials from primary to secondary sites, as well as seasonality (Figure 5–11) (Wright et al., 2005). Alkaline conditions reflecting proteolysis can also affect plant growth and colonisation (Janaway, 1996).

Awareness of animal and other tracks is also useful in site location. Care should be taken not to misinterpret animal tracks and other modifications. For example, dispersed freshly dug soil may indicate burrowing by badgers rather than the presence of a grave. Differentiating between paths made by large omnivores, other animals, and people is necessary to correctly interpret the area. Consideration of the loss of visible evidence on a ground surface due to leaf fall or movement of vegetation litter should be born in mind. Observations, predictions, and awareness of seasonal

Figure 5–11. Plants growing in a quarry used as an execution site in Bosnia were crushed beneath victims. The flowering heads provided evidence as to the season in which killings took place. *Source:* ICTY/Tim Loveless.

change and habits of faunal species should also be considered. For more examples, see Rackham (1994) and Rezendes (1999).

An understanding of the underlying geology of an area is important for determining excavation requirements and in spotting potential anomalies. Bodies or vehicles that are moved out of the area may carry atypical soils with them. This can link primary and secondary sites. Local geological and hydrological knowledge and relevant maps can be used to predict stability, depth, and location of graves. Sampling the soil stratigraphy through core samples and test trenches or pits can indicate such impacts as what effects digging particular soils will have on the appearance and visibility of graves, and the potential for water logging. Pollen and mineral ratios can also indicate atypical soil presence at a site when analysed by palynologists and geologists.[18] See O'Connor and Evans (2005).

[18] The secondary graves from Srebrenica were matched to the primary sites by analysis of the soils and their pollen content by Professor Tony Brown (see 9.2, Brown, 2006, ICTY [2001, 2004] trial transcripts of Krstic and

5.3.4   Key points

In concluding this section, the following points are worth noting. Archaeologists should be skilled at differentiating local natural features or old archaeological features that may mimic the after effects of excavating a grave (e.g., ground cracking, slumping, mounding). Topographical knowledge and understanding is important and can indicate if there are natural features such as caves or gorges where bodies could be hidden. Prior reading and research are useful in this process and in understanding topography and geology.[19] This can simplify the organisation and carrying out of search patterns, and can help in predicting areas that are more or less likely to be of significance. Further to this, understanding the topography of the area in question can help predict movement of remains due to faunal, gravity, and water forces. Similarly, topographical knowledge and understanding of hydrological and sedimentary processes can indicate whether a particular area may be prone to flooding or erosion and so determine what appropriate steps need to be taken in the search and recovery methodology to account for this. Finally, understanding of topographical anomalies can help indicate graves from the surface. Appropriate use of one or more of the methods described in this chapter should help pinpoint the sites of anomaly in a suspect area and should be employed during an investigation.

5.4   Site confirmation

Site confirmation is the identification or elimination of a specific anomaly or site of forensic interest to an investigation. Suitable site preparation should be carried out before ground investigations begin.

5.4.1   Surface scatters

Surface scatters are the easiest of human remains deposits to locate and identify simply because at least some of the remains will be visible on the surface. Once artefacts, evidence, or human remains have been recognised, the challenge lies in determining the extent of a scatter (both horizontally and vertically). Archaeologists term the systematic and mapped search of the surface material of an area (on foot) as field walking. Closely connected to this, and equally as important, is determining

Blagojevic and Jokic). The accuracy of the predicted source of these secondary grave soils allowed a focus of the most likely primary sites on which to carry out comparison tests.

[19] The primary grave of Kozluk, Bosnia, relating to the Srebrenica Massacre was located through analysis of a secondary grave (found by aerial imagery) containing robbed bodies and material from the parent site. The foreign soil in this grave consisted of typical river terrace gravels, sands, and clays for this region, indicating that the primary grave should be close to a river bank. Addresses on labels on bottle glass mixed in this soil narrowed the search to the Drina River at Kozluk (ICTY, 2004; Wright et al., 2005), the primary grave being found some 20 m from the river course.

how long the remains have been present and what taphonomic effects have acted on the remains. An understanding of the likely taphonomic effects involved will allow a judgement to be made on how large an area to search for the remains. It is unlikely that all of the elements of a human skeleton or skeletons will be located from a surface scatter. Evidence and remains may move into the upper soil horizons and become buried, or represent a deposit that was buried and has subsequently been exposed by such action as erosion. A single search may reveal some evidence but often not all. Repeated area searches may be necessary.

It pays dividends to have specialists at the site, when possible, who can assist in any of the aforementioned tasks. Surface scatter recovery methods are described in 5.5. Taphonomic processes directly affect the extent and intensity of surface artefacts, the largest variables being human intervention and time since deposition. This will be further affected by environmental factors. As a result, scatters may become buried or be subject to scavenging. Further search of the area through techniques that are both noninvasive (e.g., metal detection) and invasive (i.e., excavation) may therefore be necessary to identify and recover as much of the evidence as possible. Once artefacts such as shell cases, clothing, and human remains have been located, their extent (in terms of spatial dispersion) and their density can be defined. They must be photographed, recorded, and surveyed (see FA06F for details of the Surface Recording Form).

5.4.2   Site assessment

There are four physical methods that can be used in evaluating a suspect area. These are augering or probing (useful indicators), field walking, trenching, and area or surface stripping (more positive means of assessment). These methods are useful if no grave structure can be observed from the ground surface, even after removal of vegetation or debris. Care should be taken not to disturb surface scatters or a grave structure that may survive in the topsoil (upper soil horizons).

The confirmation of anomalies and decaying matter can be made with minimum disturbance. Intrusion by both probes and augers can, however, damage human remains if undertaken by inexperienced personnel. A blunt tile probe is recommended because it is easier to insert into the ground and is less likely to cause damage. Only hand-turned augers should be used to assess anomalies and detect changes, rather than petrol engine-driven models. This will limit the chance of damage to human remains. For details on the methodology of probe use, see Owsley (1995). Such techniques must be employed in a systematic way using a grid.

Field walking is a useful and noninvasive method. It can be used to identify the presence, distribution, and extent of human skeletal material exposed at the surface, other associated materials (e.g., shoes, clothing), and evidence of the killing and/or disposal of the victims (e.g., cartridge cases or vehicle tracks).

Trenching is one of two more destructive and invasive techniques used to assess anomalies, most of which can only be confirmed as graves by initial test excavation. A remote trench or test pit , dug to determine the natural geological or manmade

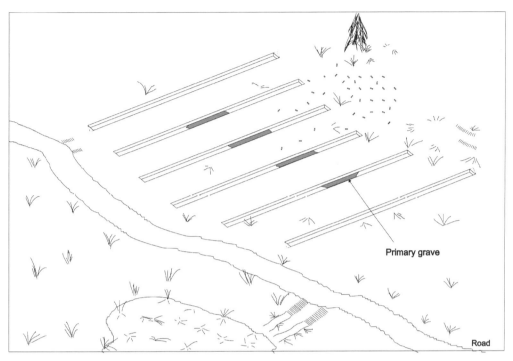

Figure 5–12. Trenching to locate graves – this is the fastest way to locate the structure of the grave. Trenches should be close enough in series that the sought feature will not be missed. *Source:* Inforce Foundation.

stratigraphic sequence of the immediate area, and the hydrological regime, is a useful prerequisite for testing the anomaly. Such a trench or pit (as well as auguring) may also be used to collect soil samples. Where mechanical diggers are used in this process, experienced archaeologists will guide the machine operator at all times. Trenching entails cutting a narrow trench across the anomalous area either manually or using machinery. The trench is used to discern changes in the soil below the surface, and human remains or other evidence that may be revealed. The focus of trenching should be to delineate the anomalous area based on soil change and stratigraphy and human remains or clothing. Determinations should include the depth of the feature, the difference between natural stratigraphy and disturbance through soil changes, and the presence of (multiple) human remains and their condition.

The disadvantage of trenching is that by excavating a feature to any depth, it is possible to destroy part of it before fully understanding its nature. Furthermore, it is easy to miss small but important subsoil features due to the narrow nature of the trench, which limits the area under investigation. Additionally, it may be difficult to see features within a narrow trench due to shadow and angle of view. Systematically examining a suspect area by trenching may require the use of several appropriately spaced trenches (Figure 5–12) to locate a grave and then determine it size. Heavy machinery can be used to demonstrate the presence of a grave rapidly; an area the size of a football pitch can be checked in a day by an experienced supervised operator. Trenching is also a rapid method for sampling a small area to confirm or eliminate the presence of anomalous soils and human remains.

The second of the more destructive and invasive techniques used to locate graves is area or surface stripping. This method involves removing surface vegetation, material, and soil to expose atypical, often mixed or disturbed soil areas, which represent the shallowest detectable manifestation of a grave area in plan. It is usually shallow trenching that does not penetrate observed forensic deposits. Surface stripping allows potential graves to be pinpointed and their extent delineated without serious disturbance of the fill and structure of the grave itself. It may involve removing natural layers of topsoil, landscaped, and 'made-ground' deposits of a site to reveal subsoils or archaeological layers of the soil profile beneath (Figure 5–13). The shape of any features such as graves, burrows, pipelines, and construction trenches, and natural features such as silted streams, can then be seen in plan within the revealed horizon and the stratigraphic sequence identified. Anomalies and potential graves and their sequence can be pinpointed without serious disturbance of the fill of the grave. The soil within mass graves is often visible because of the gleying resulting from biochemical processes. Human remains or clothing may be visible if they lie close to the upper surface of a grave and are exposed by stripping. This will limit the need for deeper destructive trenching, although this may still be necessary to determine the depth of the grave.

A grave or pit dug through the ground will often remain visible in subsoil layers. Subsoils frequently differ in colour, texture, and compaction from topsoil. A feature containing mixed topsoil and subsoil contrasts with the outline of a grave in undisturbed subsoil and can often be seen clearly when the overlying soil is removed. The feature will, in most cases, remain visible perhaps for thousands of years. However, grave visibility is retained most clearly in the more stable subsoil deposits that are sealed beneath the topsoil and made ground. The topsoil layer is constantly changing and moving due to bioturbation (e.g., plant roots, microbes, worms, insects, animals) and human activity (e.g., ploughing, logging, landscaping, drainage). Consequently, the visual structure of a grave or pit that is dug through this disturbed ground may be lost over time. It should be remembered that on recent graves the grave structure and evidence may be retained in the topsoil and vegetation layer, and this should be fully recorded before removal. If removal by stripping is necessary to analyse an anomaly and the anomaly proves to be a grave, the stripped topsoil will require monitoring, sieving, or sorting, as appropriate, to recover evidence that may be present. All topsoil should be checked by metal detector for evidence if required after stripping. It must be remembered that evidence recovered during sieving has lost its context.

Excavating machines with a toothless bucket can be used to strip the topsoil.[20] Surface stripping is the best way to clearly expose the anomaly in plan. It exposes the

---

[20] A toothless ditching bucket should always be used to carry out such work because it acts as a giant trowel to clean the soil surface, and does not gouge or disfigure the soil profile.

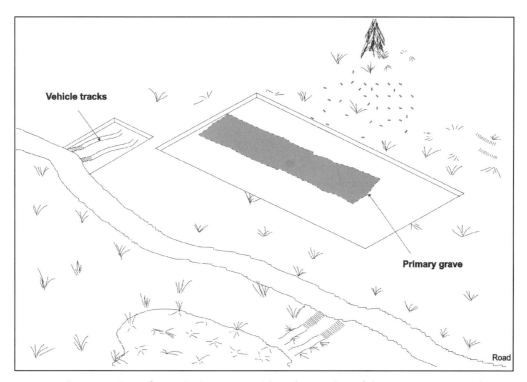

Figure 5–13. Surface stripping can provide a clear outline of the grave structure without intrusive trenching. In environments with shallow top soils, only 0.10 m of material may need to be removed to reveal a grave. Care must be taken to search for and remove all surface evidence before stripping. *Source:* Inforce Foundation.

complete surface area of an anomaly, allowing size to be determined, and therefore the next stage of an assessment can be planned. It is also a useful way to determine stratigraphy within a mass grave. A robbing episode affecting a grave can often be determined by revealing a secondary series of deposits in plan. With machinery, a large area can be stripped quickly with limited intrusion into the grave. Identifying and determining the nature of subsurface features requires experience in the recognition of soil alteration and change.

It is, of course, essential to demonstrate that an anomaly is in fact a grave (i.e., that it contains human remains) and then to determine its extent, and, if possible its depth, before planning any further work.[21] If it cannot be determined that an anomaly is a grave by surface analysis, test pits or small trenches sited at strategic points over an anomaly will be required to confirm this. To determine approximate feature depth, we recommend a test pit be dug adjacent to the outer edge of the grave, thus limiting disturbance to the contents (if geophysics cannot provide these data).

---

[21] Many features (e.g., disused defensive berms in Iraq) are made in the same way and closely resemble mass graves in plan; only the necessary degree of test excavation will prove a grave from a similar, but non-charnel, feature.

All site assessment and confirmation ground work should be thoroughly recorded (the Site Assessment Form [FA01F]).

5.5 Forensic archaeological excavation

Throughout this text, the process of archaeological examination and recovery of evidence from mass graves is described as a process of excavation. This describes both the process of investigating and revealing the context of the burial and the scientific recovery of human remains and associated evidence. The term 'excavation' is used to differentiate the process of scientific recovery of evidence from 'exhumation', which is simply the recovery of buried remains (Connor and Scott, 2001b; Juhl, 2005).

There are several basic principles that are axiomatic to the successful application of archaeology in forensic cases. Foremost of these, as discussed in 5.1, is that any forensic or human rights investigation has the potential to be (or become) a legal case and, consequently, that all work should be conducted to an appropriately high standard. This will ensure that the results will meet the evidential standards of the most demanding and rigorous court process, as well as satisfy humanitarian objectives.

The standard of archaeological investigation, excavation, recording, and interpretation of forensic scenes should be high enough to allow scientifically verifiable and independent analysis, reinterpretation, and auditing of any records and conclusions. These should concern the history, formation, nature, and stratigraphic sequence of a site; the character and position of all relevant artefacts and features; and the methodologies and management structures employed throughout the process. The methodologies employed should optimise the evidential identification, location, recovery, and recording for an investigation, while minimising the loss of potential evidence and standardising of the process. To accomplish this, these methodologies should include single (and multiple) context recording of deposits and features, the three-dimensional (3-D) survey and planning of all contexts, the recording of the identified stratigraphic sequence of a site as a Harris Matrix (Harris, 1979),[22] and the use of standardised recording forms and logs for forensic archaeological contexts, human remains, plans, sections, and samples (see 5.10).

As stated previously, archaeological excavation in a forensic context is a destructive and unrepeatable evidence collecting process. The archaeological excavation carried out should ensure high standards of *in situ* evidence retrieval and interpretation from all forensic archaeological contexts, including layers, soil fill, cuts, deposits, structures, and interfaces. These may include ground surfaces, and natural, structural, and artificially dug buried surfaces (see Harris, 1979, for definitions of these terms).

---

[22] The aim of using these methods is to ensure evidential recovery, and they reflect what is considered by Inforce as demonstrable of maximising this potential (see Barker, 1987; MoLAS, 1994; Roskam, 2001; Institute of Field Archaeologists, 2004).

All forensic archaeological excavations should be carried out with an understanding of, consideration for, and observance of the laws of archaeological stratigraphy. The idea that the features (contexts) of an archaeological site are to be found in a stratified state, one layer or feature on top of the other, is of first importance in their investigation by archaeological excavation. Whenever possible, excavation should be carried out using stratigraphic principals and methods that do not destroy stratigraphic boundaries or interfaces. If this is not possible, all stratigraphic relationships should be recorded before boundaries or interfaces are removed (Hanson, 2004). Deposits should be removed and recorded in their stratigraphic sequence as single identified contexts whenever possible. Removal of identified deposits will be carried out systematically to understand the sequence of evidential deposition; avoid movement and damage to evidence and human remains; and maintain the *in situ* position, context, and integrity of evidence and human remains. All records produced and all evidence recovered from a forensic scene must enter a chain of custody and be processed, sampled, stored, and conserved in a stable and secure environment that will not compromise further analysis or the investigative evidential process. Archaeologists have a distinctive skill in identifying a wide variety of both buried and landscape evidence and advising which specialisations are appropriate to deal with potential evidence. Forensic archaeologists should work as part of a multidisciplinary team. Specialists, when appropriate and possible, should be present during excavations to contribute to *in situ* evidential identification, recovery, sampling (if appropriate), analysis, and interpretation.

The archaeological approach to forensic investigation should be scientific, ethical, objective, and independent. Archaeologists carrying out forensic investigation should be aware of their archaeological expertise and its limits. Methodology should be archaeologically mundane. "It is as an archaeologist that expert testimony will be given. The touchstone of the expert testimony is that at the mass grave what was done, would normally be done on an excavation" (Wright et al., 2005: 157). Forensic archaeologists should have a clear understanding of the investigative and research questions being asked when approaching specific projects, and what may be required to answer those questions before beginning fieldwork.[23] An archaeologist's skill also lies in having a wide knowledge of evidence and context identification and excavation techniques and methods that he or she can employ as a 'tool kit' (Cox, 1995). This ensures suitable evidence location, excavation, recording, recovery, and interpretation from a forensic landscape and archaeological contexts. This is essential given the inevitable constraints of time, resource, cost, security, climate, and politics. As such, archaeologists working in forensic investigations should have appropriate levels of qualification, skill, and experience in fieldwork and in the excavation of

---

[23] This may mean delaying the start of fieldwork until it is assured that logistics and sufficient background information is in place to allow an effective operation, or it is ascertained whether the investigative requirements can be met. A great deal of time can be lost and negative publicity generated by premature deployment. At the same time, it may be negative results in the field that demonstrate to a client that insufficient preparatory works have been undertaken for successful outcomes.

human remains. Such forensic archaeologists should support, assist, encourage, and develop standards of archaeological theory, technique, and methodology used in forensic work worldwide.

5.5.1   Forensic sites and archaeology

In a forensic context, archaeologists will work as part of a team that can effectively and appropriately recover evidence and human remains from any potential crime or humanitarian scene. Such scenes are often in 'outdoor' settings and can be very large, complex, and subject to a multitude of taphonomic actors. Many crime scenes and human rights cases requiring archaeological excavation, in national and international cases, have been disturbed after initial deposition.[24] The longer a scene is left before investigation, the greater the taphonomic effects that can alter the scene leading to additions, changes, and loss of evidence and human remains that may consequently need a greater variety of experts for identification, recovery, and analysis. For example, skeletons in soils that have fluctuating water tables and acidic pH, such as around Lake Izabal in Guatemala, provide an excellent environment for bacterial decay of bone and may, after 20 years, have lost almost all tissues (Figure 5–14). In such a case, to determine trauma and potential cause of death and confirm the presence of human remains, it may be necessary to use specialists in radiography, chemistry, and isotope analysis (because of extreme taphonomic effects) to determine what an anthropologist alone might normally conclude. The team investigating a mass grave site must collectively have a wide knowledge of natural sciences, the landscape and environmental and ecological sciences, and a basic understanding of cultural anthropology. The skill of the archaeologist often lies in identifying and understanding the wide variety of potential evidence that can be recovered from such sites (Barker, 1987). Working alongside the SCE, the team's success also relies on an understanding of when and which experts to bring in to contribute to evidence identification, recovery, analysis, and interpretation.

A team of archaeologists investigating a site must collectively have the range of practical skills and understanding necessary to adequately carry out forensic investigations. These include relevant legislation, scene of crime procedures, and how to work within a tightly regulated chain of custody. A team of forensic archaeologists needs to include among its collective skills a basic understanding of a breadth of issues, including forensic sciences; logistics and equipment deployment and management; risk assessment and health and safety implementation; time, resource, and cost management skills; working with heavy plant; search and location techniques; site assessment techniques; excavation techniques and methods;

---

[24] Reasons for disturbance vary. Many sites in the Balkans were tampered with by perpetrators hiding evidence; in Guatemala and Iraq, graves have been sought and exhumed by communities looking for the Missing; and sites in Cyprus and Bosnia have been found and disturbed by road construction.

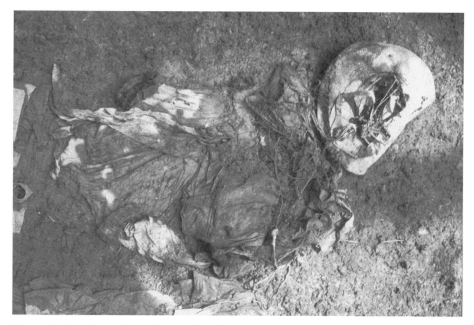

Figure 5–14. The survival of materials in this grave demonstrates the variability of preservation that can occur. At this FAFG exhumation in Guatemala, after 20 years in the ground, all traces of a coffin and soft and hard tissue have disappeared. However, natural clothing fibres survive. *Source:* Ian Hanson.

stratigraphic principles and site formation processes; survey and planning; site recording; documentation and photography; artefact and evidence recognition and recovery; human remains recognition and recovery; faunal and avian remains recognition, differentiation, and recovery; sampling and sieving strategies; conserving, storing, and archiving of records and materials; report writing; and presentation and information dissemination for nonexpert client and community groups. Individuals making up the team must be effective team players and must be in tune with archaeological and scientific ethics.

5.5.2 Survey

The basic principle of survey in mass grave investigations is to identify and record all evidence and points of interest in three dimensions. Site survey aims to provide a set of maps and coordinates that clearly depict the location of any given site at several scales. There are several principle aims of survey within forensic settings. These are to provide a mapped plan, contour map, and 3-D image of an excavated grave and the area around a grave/crime scene. Survey is also used to establish points and description for articulated bodies, body parts, and individual bones that can be used to produce two-dimensional (2-D) and 3-D plans of all human remains in and around a grave/crime scene. Similarly, it is essential to record points for all

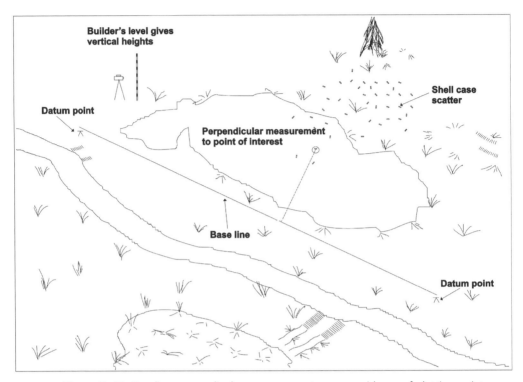

Figure 5–15. Baseline perpendicular measurements are a rapid way of plotting points. *Source:* Inforce Foundation.

artefacts (e.g., shell case scatters) found in and around a grave/crime scene (including execution surfaces). Geographical reference points must be established so the plans of the graves, bodies, and artefacts can be located on available aerial photographs and grid maps. The information collected should, as with all other data recorded, be treated as exhibits that can serve to provide representations of the grave/crime scene for reports. It can also be used as a visual guide for presentation during court proceedings. The wider considerations for survey as an archaeological application are considered in detail by Banning (2002).

As a rule, all measurements should be taken in three dimensions; be in the same format and units; and record all relevant points that provide position of evidence, topography, landscape, and structures. All measurements should be associated to a set datum point that can be related to 'real' coordinates on maps or satellite images, and be measured and related to a known benchmark or mapped feature, whether the grid is arbitrary or real (see also grid location in 5.5.2). This should all be recorded on relevant survey forms (FA04LB and FA04LT) and on the body (FA12BH, FA12BT, FA12SH, FA12ST, and FA12BP) and context recording form as appropriate (FA05F).

Survey methods include baseline perpendicular measurement, baseline triangulation, grid measurement, and distance and angle measurement using a surveyor's

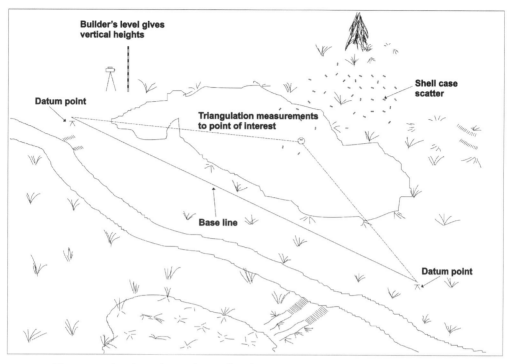

Figure 5–16. Triangulation from a baseline is a more accurate method for rapidly plotting points. *Source:* Inforce Foundation.

level and total station survey. Baseline perpendicular measurement is a simple form of measurement that is particularly useful when time and resources are limited. It involves placing a baseline (between two datum points) parallel or adjacent to the grave, and measuring to points of interest with a tape measure perpendicular to the baseline (see Figure 5–15). Vertical measurements can be taken by using a line level and string from which to measure a depth from the horizontal height of the baseline or with a surveyor's (dumpy) level (with a 5-m extendable staff). Baseline triangulation is a similar method to baseline perpendicular measurement. The accuracy can, however, be slightly greater because the distance to the point of interest is measured from two points on the baseline, thus triangulating its position. The horizontal height measurement is again taken as mentioned previously (see Figure 5–16). Baseline methods do not interfere with ground works or vehicle movement. The limitations of these methods are that accuracy over distance diminishes accuracy, and that the accuracy of a plan or errors are not observed until it is drawn out from measurements, which is usually not contemporary with excavation of the measured features and artefacts. Grid measurement is an accurate method often used on archaeological excavations. A grid is accurately laid across the site using tape measures to triangulate squares of the same size. Alternatively, a theodolite, total station, or DGPS can be used. The grid is marked with protected pegs

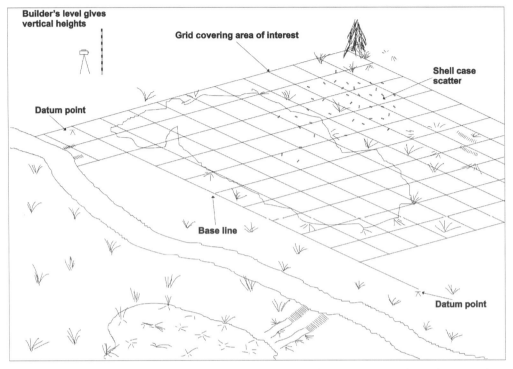

Figure 5–17. Grid measurement allows accurate and systematic recording of an area, but is difficult to apply when heavy machinery is in the area. *Source:* Inforce Foundation.

or with lines if the grid is suspended. A problem with this method is that having a grid on site can impede movement of vehicles, personnel, and equipment. Measurements are taken by measuring to the point of interest from the easting and northing lines of the relevant grid square (see Figure 5–17). The points can be planned on gridded paper.[25] This method allows accurate planning while excavating to depth. Horizontal heights are taken with a surveyor's (dumpy) level, and the measurements are accurate. Distance and angle measurement using a surveyor's level is a method that requires two determined datum points. Both are outside the area of activity but as close to the grave as is possible. These points provide a baseline to which all points can be referenced. The subsidiary datum should preferably be to the north of the main datum, but any bearing measured by compass will suffice (see Figure 5–18). This method uses the surveyor's (dumpy) level to record bearing and distance as well as height. The level requires tachometric hairlines, rotating on a 360-degree base. For the manual survey methods described previously, a form (FA04LB) recording bearing and distance is required.

[25] Commonly used in the UK by commercial archaeological organisations are transparent, waterproof, pregridded sheets of drafting film, commonly known as 'permatrace' by archaeologists, that allow scale plans (conventionally at 1:20) with a capacity to plan 5 m² per sheet at this scale. They allow plans to be made in real time, detecting and limiting error as excavation proceeds. They are designed for long-term archiving.

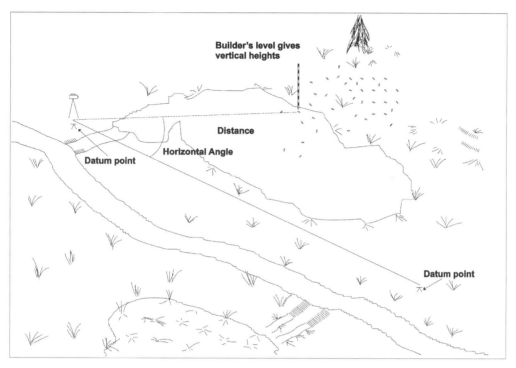

Figure 5–18. The surveyor's level provides a remote station for reading heights to augment baseline 2-D survey, and can be used to measure distance and angles. *Source:* Inforce Foundation.

Team members needing information and procedures for electronic surveying equipment (namely, data collectors, total stations, and GPS systems) should refer to the user manuals, user guides, and field books that are supplied with the equipment. This section is designed as a guide to electronic surveying methodology and recording in the field and postexcavation data processing for forensic field teams. The procedures summarise the information and methods team members will need to apply to complete necessary surveying for a forensic context. The designated team surveyors should ensure all reference materials are available in the field, stored properly, and kept in good condition.

For the most accurate readings using a total station, the prism staff should be held vertically; the prism facing the survey station. If there is a lot of background noise or distance between the grave and the survey station, a radio can be used to communicate. When points are taken on an articulated body or body part, they should be taken in a standard order by anatomical landmark, if possible (Figure 5–19). Following this sequence makes it easier for the surveyor to recognise and correct errors immediately, as well as later during editing. It also allows for easier data processing at the map production stage. The order can be altered if, for example, an arm is under a body, and some points cannot be taken until the body is moved or turned over. The specified list of points to survey (see Table 5–1) will allow a 'stick figure' image

Table 5–1. *Data entry codes for articulated bodies*

Data entry code	Description
CRAN	Centre of what is visible of the cranium/skull/head
LSHO	Left shoulder
LELB	Left elbow
LWRI	Left wrist
RSHO	Right shoulder
RELB	Right elbow
RWRI	Right wrist
PELL	Left pelvis (lateral ilium)
PELR	Right pelvis (lateral ilium)
LKNE	Left knee
LNKL	Left ankle
RKNE	Right knee
RNKL	Right ankle

of an articulated body to be produced (Figure 5–20a and b), which provides a supplement for photography and allows all related body positions to be planned in 3-D. Although the suggested list is only a guide, following it can reduce errors. If parts of the anatomy (e.g., the right wrist) are missing or there are disarticulating

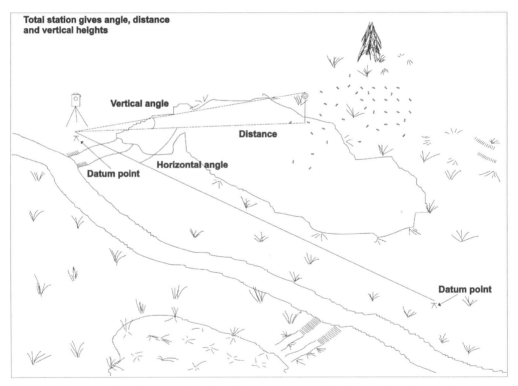

Figure 5–19. Using a total station allows remote, rapid 3-D surveying. *Source:* Inforce Foundation.

(a)   (b)

Figure 5–20. Survey of anatomical landmarks allows simple 'stick figure' representation for 3-D survey manipulation. It supports the data provided by a 2-D photograph, illustrated by this recording of a skeleton from a Roman period cemetery in Egypt. *Sources:* (a) Ian Hanson. (b) Inforce Foundation.

fractures, then alternative codes can be used (see Table 5–2). Before taking the points, the surveyor must be given information that should include a description of the body, including the exhibit number and any missing or disarticulated parts for bodies. If some anatomical points cannot be taken immediately, the 'point giver' needs to inform the surveyor of this, and they both need to come back to the body and obtain the remaining points when practicable.[26] The surveyor must be aware of the grave context and know at all times which team members are excavating which bodies and artefacts. This can be achieved by constant consultation at the grave. This is the method that will have the greatest impact on reducing errors in taking readings.

The code entered to identify each body point or artefact should begin with the site code (e.g., QQ01), followed by the relevant exhibit number (i.e., body: B001, body part: BP001, or artefact: A001), followed by the relevant code from the given list for bodies, body parts, or artefacts. Total stations handle data in folders (called 'jobs'), and a separate 'job' can be set up for each site or grave, keeping survey data discreet. Tables 5–3 and 5–4 show example entry codes. There is room for

---

[26] Points that are delayed in being taken should be noted on the body form and survey form. With fleshed bodies, the intertwining of limbs may mean that points cannot be taken until some hours or days have passed, and without noting the delay, it is easy to forget to record points.

Table 5–2. *Additional data entry codes for bodies and body parts*

Data entry code	Description	
CRAF	Cranium that is fractured but intact	
CFRG	Fragments of cranium	
MAND	Isolated mandible	
NECK	Most superior cervical vertebrae present (when cranium is absent)	
RHUM	Proximal/distal end of disarticulated/fractured humerus	
RRAD	Proximal/distal end of disarticulated/fractured radius/ulna	Replace R with L when surveying the left arm
RHUM/RRAD (2 points)	Both proximal and distal ends of a completely disarticulated humerus or lower arm	
SPNt	Top of thoracic vertebrae in a disarticulated skeletonised body/body part	
SPNB	Bottom of lumbar/thoracic vertebrae in a disarticulated skeletonised body/body part	
TRST	Top of thoracic vertebrae in a disarticulated saponified body/body part	
TRSb	Bottom of thoracic/lumbar vertebrae in a disarticulated saponified body/body part	
RFEM	Proximal/distal end of disarticulated/fractured right femur	
RTIB	Proximal/distal end of disarticulated/fractured right tibia/fibula	Replace R with L when surveying the left leg
RFEM/RTIB (2 points)	Both proximal and distal ends of a completely disarticulated right femur, tibia or fibula	
MASS	Jumbled and disarticulated body or body part; 4 or 5 points taken around mass	
RHAN	Disarticulated but intact right hand	Replace R with L when surveying the left hand or foot
RFOO	Disarticulated but intact right foot	

Any individual bone with an agreed four-letter code

LRIB	Left rib	
LCLA	Left clavicle	
RSCA	Right scapula	
SACR	Sacrum	

sixteen characters and spaces on the entry screen in many data collectors and total stations, so codes are abbreviations. The given list of points for bodies (B) in order of preference is shown in Table 5–1. All codes are entered as uppercase letters for consistency and ease of reading screens in the field. In addition to the codes listed previously, other codes are used if there is disarticulation, fractures, or individual bones. These are described in Table 5–2. Artefacts (A) that are surveyed are given an abbreviated code to describe them in the relevant survey file. It is sensible to coordinate artefact codes with field and mortuary teams. Examples are described in Table 5–4. More codes can be added as necessary (e.g., specific shell cases). For points

Table 5–3. *Example entry codes for data collectors such as the SDR33*

Data entry code	Description
QQ01 B001 RS	Site name QQ01; evidence number 001 for a body; surveying the right shoulder (RS)
QQ01 BP001 LFOO	Site name QQ01; evidence number 001 for a body part; surveying the left foot (LFOO)
QQ01 A001 762S	Site name QQ01; evidence number 001 for an artefact; surveying a 7.62-calibre shell case (762S)

taken for surveys of the grave outline, the code OUTLINE is used. Points should be taken in either clockwise or anticlockwise sequence returning to the starting point because this makes processing the data and plan production straightforward. Points should ideally be taken every 20 to 30 cm, but if time is limited on site,

Table 5–4. *Data entry codes for artefacts*

Data entry code	Description
762S	7.62-calibre shell case, short type
762L	7.62-calibre shell case, long type
765P	7.65-calibre handgun shell case
9MIL	9-mm handgun shell case
556N	5.56-calibre shell case NATO
ROND	Bullet/bullet fragment (normally 7.62)
R765	Bullet with calibre description
PRPG	Part of rocket propelled grenade
FRAG	Grenade \ mortar \ shell fragment
LGTR	Wrist/ankle/neck ligature
BLND	Blindfold
CGBX	Cigarette box
POCH	Tobacco or other pouch
BAGS	Any variety of bag
WLLT	Any personal wallet
PPRS	Any personal papers or documents
I.D.	ID documents
DENT	Any kind of dental prosthesis
JCKT	General
COAT	Clothing
CTHS	Descriptions
BEAD	Prayer beads
SOIL	Any soil sample taken
PLNT	Any plant sample taken
STNE	Any stone/geological sample
PACK	Any packet such as food/medicine
STRE	Stretcher
TINS	Any food tin/container
PROS	Any prosthesis such as false limb

Any other artefact can be described using an agreed four-letter code

fewer points can be taken and points can be duplicated in the data processing stage. This allows a 2-D plan of the exposed grave to be produced. For contour surveys, the code CONTOUR is used, and points should be taken across the whole grave surface (sides and bottom). This should pay special attention to the top and bottom of breaks of slope and changes of slope angle. Points should be 20 to 30 cm apart on slopes to produce the best outline and 3-D images. Points can be duplicated in the data processing stage off-site if time is limited on site for a contour survey. This allows a 3-D plan of the grave to be produced in CAD software packages. Points taken to allow grave and crime scene location area planning should be coded so they can be identified later from maps or aerial photographs, and should be obvious fixed features such as houses or road edges. Avoid using structures that may be removed. Many data loggers use standard codes that allow automatic plotting of topographic plans. A paper (hard copy) survey log (see FA04LB and FA04LT) should be kept to list bodies and artefacts that are currently being recovered and require surveying to reduce error.

A handheld receiver yielding data from the American Global Positioning System (GPS), the Russian GLONASS system, or, from 2008, the European GALILEO system is designed for general-purpose position location and navigation. This is a useful survey tool to locate sites that are indicated on maps and aerial photographs,[27] and to record site positions and detail once located. The scale of maps available for some areas may not be less than 1:50,000. In such cases, it renders the precise location of a grave (which may be a few metres wide) on such a map an exercise that does not provide enough detail for courts or those who may need to find the grave at a later date. It is useful to make an area plan of the site of the grave/crime scene and to take GPS readings that allow the triangulation of arbitrary datum points, allowing any plans to be linked to 'real' global coordinates. It will be necessary to use larger-scale maps and aerial photos to provide a set of maps and coordinates that clearly depict the location of any given site at several scales. The straightforward instructions to use GPS to produce a reading are found in the relevant user manual. Handheld GPS can now fix a location to within 15–30 metres. More accurate professional DGPS that has an accuracy of centimetres is available and can work, if it is possible, to set up a receiver over a fixed known local datum for comparative readings. Unfortunately, many countries do not have blanket coverage of such points. The forthcoming GALILEO system should, in theory, provide far more accurate readings (to within 1 m) for cheap, handheld systems. Coordinates can be downloaded from the receiver using manufacturer's software or noted from the receiver screen. The appropriate datum for the area or country of investigation and the specific coordinate system used (easting and northing or longitude and latitude) should be recorded.

---

[27] In Iraq, suspected grave sites that had been noted from aerial images and by personnel on the ground were described by eight- or ten-figure grid references. Handheld GPS and 1:50,000 scale maps were then used to successfully guide assessment vehicles to these locations.

Figure 5–21. Munitions such as cluster bomblets will regularly fail to explode on impact and are dispersed in areas that are marked as free from munitions on military plans. They become a hazard for local communities and investigative teams on the ground. *Source:* Inforce Foundation.

5.5.3 Grave preparation and protection

Any ground investigation requires site preparation to determine an area or site location, to confirm a site as being of interest, or to recover evidence from a site. All health and safety procedures must be followed, and staff must be aware of them. Any ground work of a potential evidential nature will require the area under investigation to undergo a degree of initial survey and photography. Secure, permanent survey datum points should be established so the location of any evidence, structures, and the position of the site itself can be determined in a wider geographical area. Secure, permanent photography and video points should be established to allow standard repeated photography from the same position. These points can be marked with surveyor's pins or fluorescent spray paint. Necessary works to make an area safe and suitable for scientific surface and forensic archaeological investigation should be carried out. These include clearance of UXO[28] (Figure 5–21) and other

---

[28] Team must allow EOD specialists to clear any suspected site before they access it; in war zones, sites should always be presumed to have a UXO threat. In Bosnia, mined sites were often unmarked or locally marked with

hazardous materials (e.g., chemical waste). Team members should be aware of the likely presence of any potential dangerous fauna and flora (identified as part of the risk assessment). Vegetation may have to be cleared (after checking for evidence) to expose the site and surface evidence. It is also essential to mark, fence or infill holes, obstacles, and any other dangerous features. Drainage pipes, storm drains, or services may run across sites, especially in urban settings. These should be located and made safe (see Figure 5–22). It is important to construct and maintain works to control groundwater and surface water before work begins. Engineering work for drainage and other purposes is often required at sites under investigation. This may require ditches or berms to control surface water ingress, and sumps or drains to carry away groundwater (see Figure 5–23). Access, storage, and parking areas may need to be drained, levelled, and/or metalled. To control access, it is necessary to delineate safe access routes and, where necessary, to position walkways. Site cleanliness is vital in forensic investigations. The provision of rubbish disposal receptacles and regular emptying of such, along with providing means of safe disposal of rubbish and foul water, is essential. For staff hygiene and comfort, latrine and ablution facilities are required.[29] Scenes of crime should be screened from public view, where necessary, and means of controlling public access provided. Health and safety and directional notices, in all relevant languages, must be posted, and suitable shelter must be provided. Space must be cleared and the site layout designed to ensure that there is adequate and suitable space, particularly where heavy plant is operating. Space is also required during the site preparation phase; as well as defining the suspect area, adequate space must be provided for the volume of potential spoil from an estimate of area and depth of any grave. For a mass grave, this will normally be an area that is far greater than that of the area on plan of a grave (perhaps 3:1). Considerable space is also required for equipment storage and installation. This may require clearance or placing of hard-standing. Space may also be required for visitor access, media viewing, and potentially an emergency helicopter extraction landing zone.

The excavation of mass graves almost always necessitates associated engineering. Drainage ditches may be needed to prevent groundwater from entering a grave. These should connect to any necessary access trenches or sumps around a grave (which allows removal and exposure of large, entwined masses of bodies) to allow water to be drained away from a grave. An alternative to drainage ditches taking water away by force of gravity is the removal of water from smaller sumps by diesel or electric pumps. This is likely to be less damaging and intrusive to a grave and is, in any event, the only effective method of removing water from deep excavations

---

upturned basins or pots on sticks. In Iraq, some aerial munitions threats were not mapped (see Figure 5–21a). Munitions used to kill victims, placed as deterrents, or carried by victims may also be found within graves, and specialists need to be available to assist throughout an excavation (see Figure 5–21b).

[29] In built-up areas, mobile ablution units may be available. In remote areas without access to facilities, cess pits, burning pits for rubbish, and sump pits for foul water drainage may need to be dug and positioned in locations that prevent groundwater contamination. Water may need to be brought in by bowser and sterilised.

Figure 5–22. Perpetrators do not normally check for services before digging a grave. Teams need to be aware of potential hazards (e.g., severed electrical cable) caused by damage to these. *Source:* Inforce Foundation.

and wells. Sumps may be a more suitable method of water removal, especially for deep excavations. An adequate length of pump hose should be available to remove water from the sump to an appropriate remote area. It may be necessary to excavate holding or relay pits to store wastewater. Pumps should have sludge filters available and automatic activation devices to prevent water buildup at night. Deep trenches may require stepping or sloping of edges to make excavations safe. Shoring of graves is not often practical but may be necessary in some scenarios such as shafts or wells. Any grave can be excavated in most climates and all seasons, as long as there is

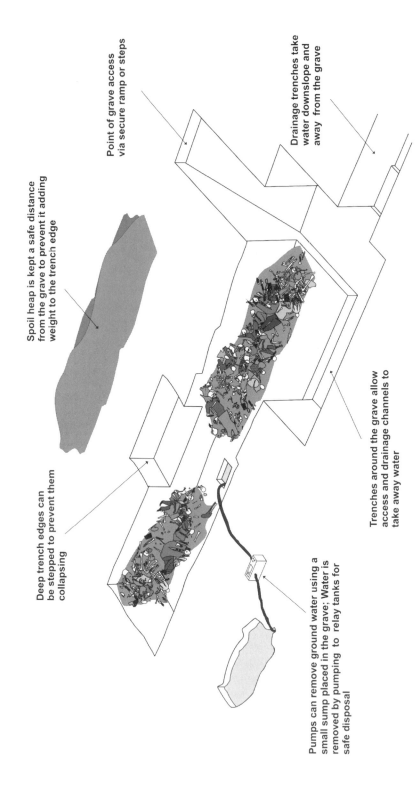

Point of grave access via secure ramp or steps

Drainage trenches take water downslope and away from the grave

Spoil heap is kept a safe distance from the grave to prevent it adding weight to the trench edge

Deep trench edges can be stepped to prevent them collapsing

Trenches around the grave allow access and drainage channels to take away water

Pumps can remove ground water using a small sump placed in the grave; Water is removed by pumping to relay tanks for safe disposal

Figure 5–23. A deep grave showing the ground works and engineering that may be required to safely excavate a mass grave. Sumps, pumps, and drainage channels take away groundwater and surface water from the grave. Trenches allow access and provide drainage. Sloping and stepping the grave edge provides safe access and prevents steep sides of deep holes from collapsing. All works altering the grave should only be carried out after fully recording what is to be removed. *Source:* Inforce Foundation.

suitable drainage, cover, and temperature control. It should be remembered that access and drainage trenches excavated in certain subsoils, such as clay and sand, may collapse after time, especially during rain; they should be monitored regularly. Disturbed silts also take on quicksand-like qualities when deep and waterlogged. Platforms and ramps may be required to allow access into a grave, and to allow access and recovery of evidence and human remains. Duckboards, shovelling boards, and plank wheel barrow runs are essential in many (especially wet) conditions to allow safe and efficient access around the site and removal of spoil.

Covers and tents may be required for the grave. Transparent or bespoke 'scene of crime' tents are preferable because they let in as much natural light as possible, allowing colour contrasts in soil to be ascertained. Tents or covers also act as screens, and are required to shelter equipment and paperwork on the SCE and photography tables and in the survey station, and to provide shelter for the team during breaks and in extreme weather. In severe climatic conditions, air conditioning or heating may be required within tents so work can proceed when it would otherwise not be possible. Tarpaulins should be used to cover surface stripped areas and the grave during periods of inactivity, during rain or snow, and at night[30] (see Figure 4.1).

Adequate electricity supplies for communications, logging and survey computers, and lighting are required (usually by petrol generator). Strong lighting (halogen lamps) is required for deep excavations, covered sites, structures such as caves and wells, and night work. All lights in working areas should be 'cold'. Sites require good communications, such as radio communications and satellite phones. Fuel is required to run generators.

For many large and deep sites, site preparation and recovery cannot be undertaken efficiently (i.e., in given time frames) without heavy machinery. This in part reflects that the graves were themselves dug with heavy machinery by the perpetrators. Excavating plant must be adequate for the site requirements[31] (Figure 5–24). It is essential that staff are experienced in the direction and safety procedures for heavy plant use. Backhoe loaders have the advantage of an excavating bucket and a front bulldozing blade but can become bogged down in wet conditions. Tracked excavators (also known as '360s') are useful because they can reach further than backhoe loaders, are more accurate, and are very mobile in wet conditions. They may, however, require a support vehicle such as a backhoe to move spoil on large sites (see Figure 5–25). The logistical support for a field team requires adequate

---

[30] Ideally, tents should cover graves, but logistically they can be expensive and difficult to move. Inflatable tents are a cheaper and effective alternative, with the advantage that they can easily be moved around site once erected. Waterproof tarpaulins are just as effective at protecting a site from rain when drawn over a grave (in the same way that tennis courts are protected during bad weather), but they do not protect the team while working or limit visual access from outside the site when they are pulled back.

[31] At the "Dam" site near Petkovci, Bosnia, the ICTY forensic team found a backhoe inadequate to remove several-ton rocks from a grave dug into the plateau of a masonry dam, so it brought in an 8-ton excavator to accomplish the excavation (see Figure 5–25).

Figure 5–24. Small 360 excavators are useful for operating in and around a grave; backhoes are useful for moving spoil and site preparation. *Source:* ICTY.

and qualified personnel to move, run, drive, and service equipment and vehicles. These include engineers, machine operators, mechanics, electricians, refrigeration technicians, and drivers. At the end of an excavation, a site should be restored adequately with respect to the health and safety of the public. There must not be piles of unstable soil or sediment, open pools of water, or sludge that may have a quicksand-like property.

Adequate hazard barriers and warning signs should be set out at least 1 m away from the edge and around any excavation and associated works. Special measures should be taken for deep trenches. The sides should be stepped or sloped as appropriate. Clear points of entry and exit for the excavation team should be made. It is dangerous to approach an excavation from a steep edge; therefore, steps and ramps may be required for safe access. Contamination of the site with materials from outside the trench must be prevented. Any soil fill from the grave must be separated from surrounding soils when excavated and stored if sampling and sieving strategies are employed. If these soils are mixed, the contextual integrity of evidence will be lost (see Hanson, 2004).

5.5.4   Excavation

Excavation involves the identification, definition, recording, recovery, and interpretation of features, evidence, and human remains from a surface or burial site.

Figure 5–25. The ICTY excavation at the 'Dam' site near Petkovci; a larger machine was brought in to deal with the heavy masonry blocks filling the grave. *Source:* Ian Hanson.

Suitable site preparation should be carried out before investigation on the ground begins. The risk assessment for the presence of ordnance, hazards, location of equipment, and so on must be regularly updated throughout this phase (see 3.4). The crime scene extent must be established and a perimeter set. It may be necessary to carry out surface recovery on some sites before an excavation begins. A further outer perimeter must be established to enclose parking, storage, and space for spoil. Recovery should be controlled in a systematic way within a defined 3-D space. For each item of evidence, human remains, or forensic archaeological context, the following ten-stage sequence of procedures ensures suitable standards of recovery and recording:

1. Cleaning and identification (evidence, human remains, or context)
2. Recording I (exhibit numbers issued, see 4.2)
3. Photography (photographs in necessary format, logs completed)
4. Recording II (recording logs and forms, planning and survey started)
5. Excavation (observing stratigraphic sequences)
6. Recording III (if necessary, additional exhibit numbers, photography, planning, survey)
7. Recovery and removal (controlled by SCEs) followed by re-evaluation of the context

8. Sampling and sieving (necessary exhibit numbers issued, and forms and logs completed)
9. Cleaning (to reveal and identify further evidence, human remains, or context)
10. Recording IV (completion of logs, forms, notes, and records; cross-referencing; checking records and packaging)

This process should be repeated for all features and evidence. It may not be necessary, in certain cases (e.g., recording tool marks), to carry out all steps in this recovery and recording process. This will be determined during the ongoing multidisciplinary interpretive process and discussion with SCEs that should parallel the steps outlined.

All procedures for site recovery should be carried out after full consideration of the protocols (see 2.2 and 2.3). Divergence from the protocols and SOPs may be necessary in some circumstances and where this is the case the rationale and change of process must be fully documented. Nevertheless, appropriate standards must always be applied. The SCE will maintain a log noting the distribution of exhibit numbers allocated to archaeologists and anthropologists within the crime scene. The supervisor should liaise with the SCE concerning the removal, labelling, transport, and storage of exhibits and human remains. The surveyor or supervisor (if more than one surveyor is involved) should maintain a survey log (FA04LB or FA04LT), listing any evidence surveyed and details of survey codes, monitoring and managing all survey. The surveyor should communicate with the supervisor and the SCE to ensure conformity of exhibit numbering and description. The photographer should maintain relevant photographic logs (FA09LD, FA09LN, FA10LN, and FA10LD) listing all photographs taken in all formats and specific information as set out in 4.4. Photography should be requested by team members through the supervisor and by the SCE for evidential details. Photographs should cover all aspects of site location, evidence and human remains location, attributes and detail, contexts, and features (e.g., sections) and include working shots of methodology and process, such as the techniques of archaeological excavation.[32] Circulation of information and details of evidence and exhibits should be continuous between the SCM, senior archaeologist, supervisors, and SCEs throughout a field investigation. They should closely monitor the excavation and update the field team when process and interpretation are updated. Team members should inform the senior archaeologist, supervisors, and SCE of any potential points of evidential interest or dispute throughout a field investigation. These management steps provide an effective system for efficient, controlled examination, and recovery.

---

[32] The archaeological methods and techniques of the process should be recorded for four reasons: to allow cross-referencing of photographs, to assist in reducing error, to allow auditing of the scientific process, and for use in the courtroom, if required.

The structure and stratigraphy of the grave needs to be assessed, revealed, and analysed to determine the best method of excavation. Examination of a grave may reveal the structure of the grave if visible at the ground surface. This is often the case in graves of recent date that have not been subject to the effects of bioturbation that can remove clear indications of the grave from the topsoil, or graves dug through inert deposits such as decayed sandstone. In these cases, the definition of the extent of the grave and the removal of soil from the grave can be carried out in a straightforward manner from the ground surface. All surface evidence should be identified and dealt with before excavation begins.

If the grave structure is not initially visible from the ground, then the designated area should be carefully and systematically stripped of the surface layer, plant material, debris, and topsoil until an outline of contrasting soils or structure can be seen. In some deposits, contrast between the fill of a grave and surrounding area may not be visible in initial stripping. In these cases, controlled removal of arbitrary 'spits' of soil (by machine, spade, or hand tools) is carried out until the first features or contexts are recognised.[33] This is one of the few occasions when the arbitrary removal of soil should be carried out on a forensic excavation (Hanson, 2004). Backfilled soils should be excavated with an understanding of the stratigraphic sequence. In most cases, the extent, context, and sequence of forensic deposits can only be fully understood when excavated stratigraphically.[34] Accuracy of excavation and more effective recovery of remains are achieved in this way rather than using the pedestal method (Tuller and Duric, 2006).

The engineering works described previously to control water and protect the grave must not remove evidence of the forensic sequence until it is identified, understood, and recorded. It may be necessary to excavate one or more trenches around part of the grave (this will remove the graves walls) to gain access to the human remains and/or to provide drainage. This should only be undertaken after recording of the wall to be removed (Figure 5–26). At one extreme of this approach, a perimeter trench is constructed that destroys the walls of the original grave, while the other extreme is to excavate entirely within the confines of the original grave and avoid the use of trenches at all (Figure 5–27). Limited trenches of varying lengths and location take the middle ground of possible action. If it is decided to dig a trench then it is important not to create one that is so deep that it destabilises the mass of

---

[33] Graves in countries with warm climates and zones with active soil, fauna, and flora, such as Guatemala or the Democratic Republic of Congo, may have no evidence of grave structure in the upper soil zones left after 5 to 10 years. This does not mean the position and nature of the grave cannot be detected by other means such as geophysics and analysis of the infrared spectrum. Obscurity of grave structure may also be because the area has been landscaped. Graves in Bosnia such as Glogova were landscaped and covered with soil or imported material, in some cases up to a depth of 2.5 m, to hide the presence of other graves.

[34] Many mass graves contain separate deposits of soil and bodies that have different origins and are stratigraphically distinct. Careful removal of dumped and backfilled soils can reveal sealed ground surfaces and the surfaces within graves, exposing a great deal of evidence, including tool marks, tracks, and trace evidence.

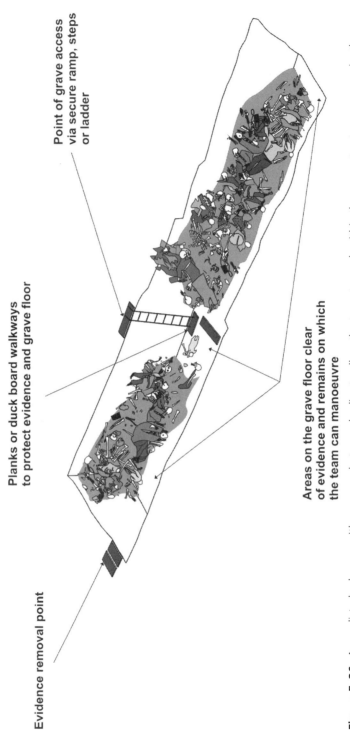

Planks or duck board walkways to protect evidence and grave floor

Point of grave access via secure ramp, steps or ladder

Evidence removal point

Areas on the grave floor clear of evidence and remains on which the team can manoeuvre

Figure 5–26. An undisturbed grave with no space between bodies to allow the team to work within the grave structure may require the removal of one or more grave walls. Clearing soil covering the bodies allows an assessment to be made of whether walls need to be removed. All walls should be fully recorded before removal, including a survey to facilitate 3-D representation of the grave. *Source:* Inforce Foundation.

**Planks or duck board walkways
to protect evidence and grave floor**

**Point of grave access
via secure ramp, steps
or ladder**

Evidence removal point

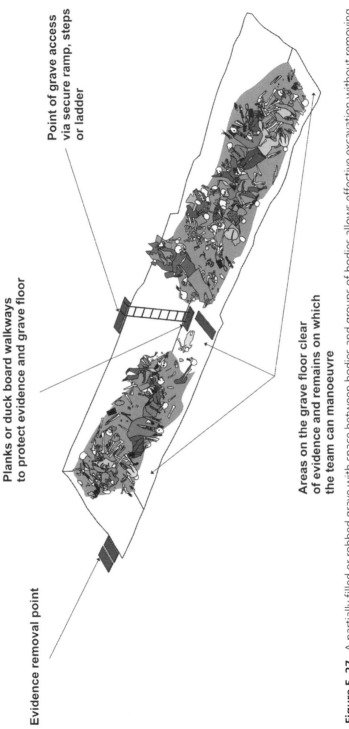

**Areas on the grave floor clear
of evidence and remains on which
the team can manoeuvre**

Figure 5–27. A partially filled or robbed grave with space between bodies and groups of bodies allows effective excavation without removing walls or damaging remains. Clearing backfilled soil covering the bodies allows an assessment to be made of whether there is room on the grave floor for the excavation team to work without damaging the grave structure or treading on the remains. *Source:* Inforce Foundation.

239

bodies. It is safer to keep the depth of the trench just slightly deeper than the surface of the bodies being currently excavated (Wright et al., 2005). The nature of each grave will reveal what potential excavation strategies can be applied. For example, in cases where a grave is robbed, excavation of the soil backfilled over the robbed area will reveal space within a grave that excavators can then use and stand in to excavate the remaining original fill of the grave and the grave structure, without the need to remove walls.

A trench may be required under certain circumstances. These circumstances include unstable deposits (e.g., sand); problems of surface water control (inability to channel all surface water away from grave in rainstorm); groundwater problems (penetration of an aquifer or a recharge hydrological context); and deep deposits. They also include circumstances where there are multiple workers (who need to get better access to bodies to prevent unnecessary downtime), where there are only opportunities for a short excavation period (generating a need for greater access to bodies to meet deadlines), where there are no requirements to preserve the original grave cut or where it is not feasible to do so, and where access to bodies or artefacts is otherwise impossible (Wright et al., 2005).

Uniform backfills of soil within a grave can be removed carefully in arbitrary spits, using an excavating machine and under supervision. This should only take place within the limits of a single recognised context (see Figure 5–28). Failure to do so destroys stratigraphic boundaries and the surfaces that hold much evidence (Figure 5–29). Due to the size of many mass graves, it is practical to remove fill by machine until the field team can carry out hand excavation using a spade, mattock, and then trowel, as proximity to bodies or surfaces increases. Careful cleaning of evidence, surfaces, clothing, tissue, or bones should be carried out with 'soft' tools such as wooden spatulas and sculpting tools. Soft brushes can be used to remove dislodged soil. Cleaning should be adequate for recognition of evidence and detail in photographs, but not so intensive that trace evidence such as ballistic fragments are removed. After emptying a grave, the bottom and side surfaces that were sealed under bodies, should be cleaned and recorded. Metal detectors should then be used to check for ballistics embedded in the grave walls and floor (it must be remembered that some graves are also execution sites). A grave should never be declared excavated until the sides, walls, and floor of the grave have been completely checked, and until the feature has been completely recorded. The intact structure of any grave or surface at the end of the excavation may be protected by covering it with a permeable membrane and then backfilled. This will help facilitate future investigation of the site, if necessary. Any evidence too large to remove from a site can be covered and buried in the empty grave,[35] if this is approved by the investigating team. The excavation considerations described here, while describing mass grave

---

[35] At the Glogova site, Bosnia, evidence was brought with the bodies to the grave from the execution site at Kravica warehouse, including building materials, car parts, and steel beams. These were too large to ship to the permanent storage facility and were wrapped and reburied in the grave after recording.

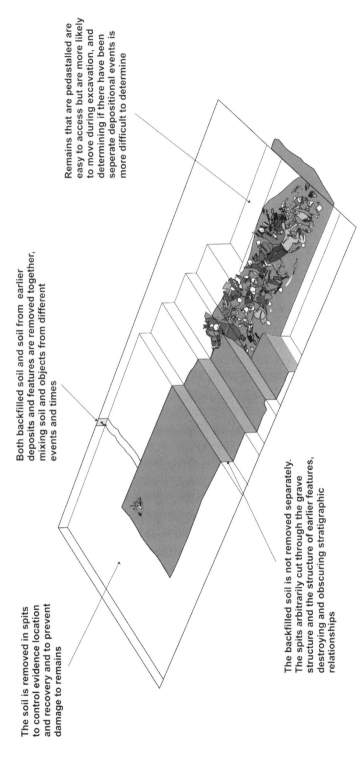

The soil is removed in spits to control evidence location and recovery and to prevent damage to remains

Both backfilled soil and soil from earlier deposits and features are removed together, mixing soil and objects from different events and times

Remains that are pedestalled are easy to access but are more likely to move during excavation, and determining if there have been seperate depositional events is more difficult to determine

The backfilled soil is not removed separately. The spits arbitrarily cut through the grave structure and the structure of earlier features, destroying and obscuring stratigraphic relationships

Figure 5–28. Stratigraphic excavation maximises evidence recovery and stratigraphic understanding. Once the grave outline has been identified, the backfilled soil can be removed, ensuring that integrity of the stratigraphic boundaries are maintained. The soil is removed within the grave to preserve its structure and evidence on the grave surfaces. Single contexts of depth can be removed in spits to control evidence recovery and allow observation of proximity of remains. Backfilled soil can be removed by machine until some 20 to 30 cm is left over the bodies; it is then removed by hand. *Source:* Inforce Foundation.

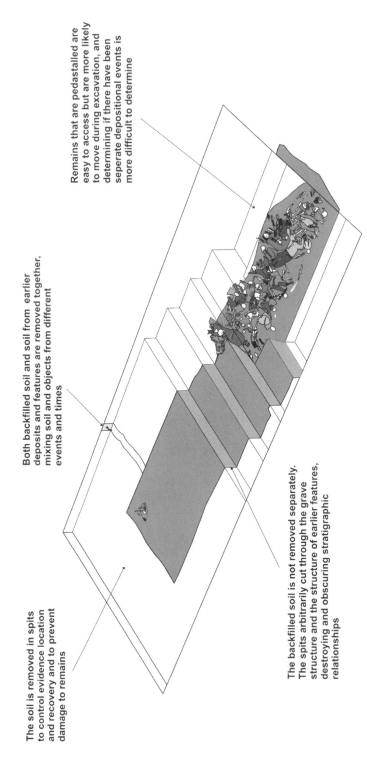

The soil is removed in spits to control evidence location and recovery and to prevent damage to remains

Both backfilled soil and soil from earlier deposits and features are removed together, mixing soil and objects from different events and times

Remains that are pedestalled are easy to access but are more likely to move during excavation, and determining if there have been seperate depositional events is more difficult to determine

The backfilled soil is not removed separately. The spits arbitrarily cut through the grave structure and the structure of earlier features, destroying and obscuring stratigraphic relationships

Figure 5–29. In forensic cases, when the grave outline has been identified, the backfilled soil is removed in arbitrary spits. While controlling soil removal laterally, this assists in finding objects and preventing damage to remains. Such an approach to soil removal within and outside the grave can destroy the grave structure and mix the evidence, soils, and samples from different events and times. Furthermore, it can prevent stratigraphic understanding. The context of the evidence may be compromised, as may the ability to record accurately. Such methods, when used without consideration of contextual boundaries, have been shown to destroy evidence. However, it is possible to combine the stratigraphic and spit methods effectively if recording links evidence to context rather than spits. *Source:* Inforce Foundation.

sites, are also applicable as basic principles for any forensic excavation. Variation from this sequence may be required for certain scenarios.[36]

5.5.5 Recovering forensic evidence

In the same way as evidence of a homicide may be left on the floor, walls, and furniture of a room in the form of a body, body materials, objects, and impressions (Gerberth, 1996), similar evidence types can be left on the subterranean surface (the walls and floor) of a grave during the burial of a body (Figure 5–30) (Hanson, 2004). Digging a clandestine grave creates a new surface, below ground, onto which a body is placed. More than that, it is a surface on which perpetrators may move and work, but in any event on which they will leave evidence of their activities. The acknowledgment of surfaces within the stratigraphic sequence is essential to their identification and exposure and to maximising the potential for evidence recovery from a grave. The recognition and careful recording (by planning, survey, scanning, and photography) of the walls and floor of a grave should be considered a powerful tool in criminal evidence recovery (ibid.).

Often overlooked in past investigations, wheel tracks, bucket marks, and other machine tool marks are common in machine excavated mass graves. When these are initially dug, the teeth of the excavating bucket (and wheel tracks in ramped graves) leave compressed negative impressions in the new surface of the excavation. They become sealed and protected beneath bodies and backfilled soil. Upon sequenced removal of the soil fill and bodies, these negative impressions are revealed (ibid.).[37] The tool marks of hand tools such as mattocks and spades can also be found. The quality of impression varies, depending on the composition of the deposits through which the grave has been dug. For deep graves, this will usually be 'natural' geological deposits. Sands, 'soft stone' (chalk and sandstone), and clays take bucket impressions easily, so each tooth can be observed and measured (Figure 5–31). Gravel by its nature will not retain smaller detail, but it may retain the shape of a large machine bucket or general wheel shape (ibid.), depending on particle size. As well as tool marks, trace evidence and human hair and tissues can be left on the grave wall and floor surfaces. This is especially significant in robbed graves. Stratigraphic excavation can reveal a sequence of activity when bodies have

---

[36] For example, excavation of deep, multiple single graves in a cemetery may require reduction of the ground surface to coffin height across a wide area if there is no room to dig trenches around each grave. Bodies disposed of in solid structures such as concrete cess pits or caves cannot have trenches dug around them; they must be excavated from above using suspended platforms and swings.

[37] These impressions can reveal individual traits of an excavator bucket. These have been used to show that the same machine was used to create different graves (in a series of secondary graves) during attempts to hide evidence from the Srebrenica Massacre along the Hodici Road, Bosnia (ICTY, 2003). This demonstrated planning and organisation in mass murder.

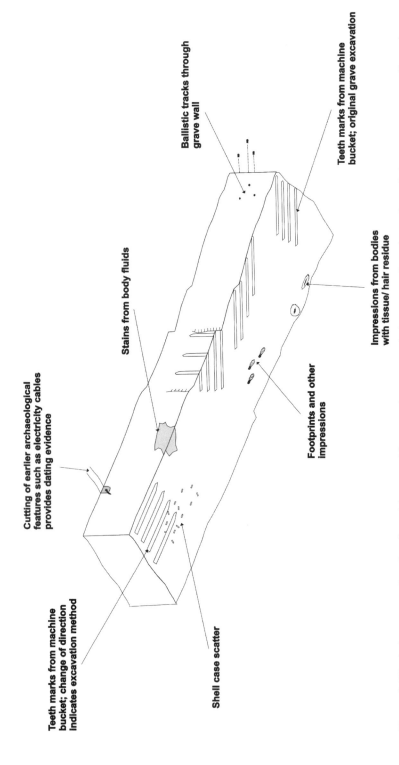

Teeth marks from machine bucket; change of direction indicates excavation method

Cutting of earlier archaeological features such as electricity cables provides dating evidence

Stains from body fluids

Ballistic tracks through grave wall

Teeth marks from machine bucket; original grave excavation

Impressions from bodies with tissue/hair residue

Footprints and other impressions

Shell case scatter

Figure 5–30. A deep grave showing the evidence and features that are regularly preserved on the surface of the grave structure. From the careful recognition and exposure of grave walls and floors, the type of vehicle used to excavate the grave can be determined, evidence of victim and perpetrator can be recovered, and sequence of events reconstructed. *Source:* Inforce Foundation.

Figure 5–31. Recovery of machine tool marks can provide data on the make and type of machine, as well as individuating the machine used itself. *Source:* ICTY/Tim Loveless.

been deliberately removed (including a second cut truncating original backfilled soil).

Removal of a body always leaves some evidence behind. Locard's principle of exchange (White, 2004) applies as much to buried evidence as it does to evidence elsewhere. In clay and sandy soils, impressions of body parts (sometimes no longer surviving, e.g., soft tissue), such as the head, may remain in the sides and floor of graves. Hair, fibre, skin, bone, and ballistic fragments can be left in these impressions, especially when loosened by trauma and decomposition at the time of movement. Bone and tissue fragments from the back spatter of close-range gunshot wounds to the head will heavily contaminate nearby surfaces (Burnett, 1991). Small bone fragments can be recovered from surfaces if the soil fill adhering to the surface is levered, peeled, and lifted away carefully with a trowel or small tool. Shots fired into a grave can pass through the walls and floor into the surrounding soil, and careful examination of soils and surfaces can reveal the entry holes of ballistic tracks, especially in sand and clay. In a robbed or disturbed burial, fluids and other by-products of decomposition left in the grave can signify the removal of a body. Rough movement of a body during robbing can detach adipocere, hair, or body parts and leave it adhering to the grave surface. Organic-rich soils forming the surfaces can be stained by decomposition (Mant, 1950), and soils can be altered by biochemical processes associated with decomposition (including gleying). Biomarkers such as volatile fatty acids from a decomposing body can penetrate the soil of the surface interface (Vass et al., 1992). The ratio of trace elements in soil adjacent to the place of deposition of a skeleton may assist in the sourcing of bones that are found away from the burial site (Trueman, 2004).

Seasonal and flowering plant material, including pollens, can survive between and under bodies, either having fallen into a grave at the time of burial, or because they were growing in depressions such as quarries and pits used to conceal bodies. They can be used to infer seasonality of burial for considerable periods of time; both pollen and plant macrofossils survive for millennia in archaeological contexts. Bodies can act as a stratigraphic layer protecting the plants lying on the ground surface (Hanson, 2004; Wright et al., 2005). The interface between grave surface and fill can also reveal the point where plant roots were severed by the digging of the grave and any subsequent growth (Willey and Heilman, 1987).

5.5.6   Excavation techniques

Careful excavation can reveal fine stratigraphic boundaries, allowing control of exhibit recovery and stratigraphic recording. It should be remembered that in the forensic time frame, perhaps after several years, the grave wall may visibly extend down from the ground surface it was cut through and be traceable (e.g., in a turf line). Over time, however, the clarity of a cut edge and the upper zone of a soil fill may become obscured. This is caused by the physical and biochemical breakdown and movement of the near surface organic material and soil layers. Plant root growth, animal burrowing, plough action, and the action of earthworms, for example, all cause extensive bioturbation of these organic soil horizons (Hanson, 2004).

When the uppermost contexts of the grave have been exposed and identified, and the controlled removal of fill from a grave begins, care should be taken in the few centimetres where the fill has an interface with the grave wall. If a 10-cm depth of fill is removed, the soil immediately against the surface should be left until last so it can be levered away and have room to 'fall' from the grave wall. Sometimes in very wet or dry conditions the soil fill will separate slightly from the grave wall, accentuating the stratigraphical boundary and forming a crack. A trowel can be used to gently nudge or lever the fill away from the wall, revealing the intact surface. In 'sticky' clay soils, this levering action may remove clumps of soil fill that pull away trace evidence such as hair or fibres from the surface. The interface should be carefully observed during this action, and any 'clump' so removed should be checked for adhering trace evidence. The soil fill will usually be looser than the truncated deposit against which it lies, and in very loose and sandy fills this can simply be encouraged to fall away from the wall of a grave with the tip of a trowel (ibid.). This action also works when removing soil from around a body or skeleton and maximises the chances of recovering trace evidence on human remains; it limits any damage to the human remains and clothing. Ballistic fragments, plant material, and other trace evidence adhere to tissue, clothing, and bone, but also adhere readily to the soil covering them; if this is removed without due care, then unrecorded evidence will be removed with it. Detailed photography should be carried out to record this procedure. Once the surface is revealed, the traditional trowelling action that archaeologists use to clean surfaces should not be used until after a careful examination is made. This action will destroy trace evidence and fine tool marks.

Disturbed graves usually have a more complex stratigraphic history than undisturbed graves. It is imperative that the sequence of events is determined; a disturbed grave will contain more than one stratigraphically separate soil. The complete robbing of a grave is almost impossible. It requires the excavation of an area larger and deeper than the total volume of the original grave to accomplish this. Invariably, there is a great deal of evidence from the original burial episode left in and around a disturbed grave (see Figure 5–32).[38] The senior archaeologist should first concentrate on excavating the deposits associate with the disturbance event to expose its limits. Removal of backfill from a robbing event within a grave often allows space inside, providing access to the remaining primary material without having to remove the original grave walls. Care should be taken when excavating disturbed backfilled soils, particularly when they are waterlogged; they can take on quicksand-like properties and represent a significant health and safety hazard.[39] Loose unassociated bones and other evidence are frequently mixed in such disturbed soil.

Any soil or matrix separating layers of bodies should be sampled and described. Similarly, if sampling and sieving strategies are employed, soils recognised as being from separate episodes of grave use should be excavated and stored separately. If

---

[38] All 'emptied' primary graves can still retain considerable human remains and associated evidence (body parts, clothing, tissues, artefacts, and other evidence of decomposition) on the floor, walls, and around the edges, as well as 'dropped' or impressed along a route of removal, as described by Walsh (1996), where remains from a robbed grave site in Brcko, northern Bosnia, were dropped on a road beside the grave.

[39] Ill-considered activity in a partly robbed primary grave in Kosovo could easily have resulted in the serious injury of the SCEs concerned. If it had not been for the quick intervention of the plant operator, the outcome could have been fatal.

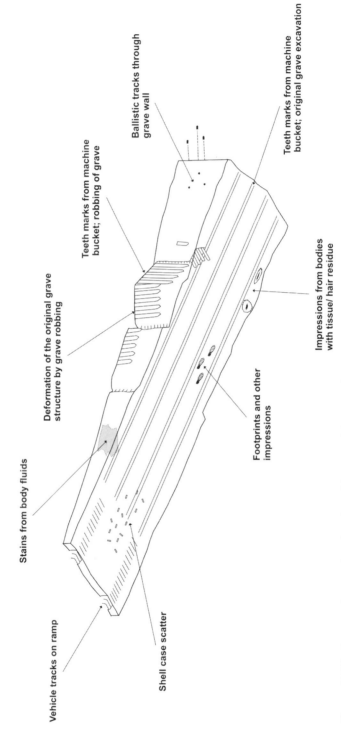

Figure 5–32. A ramped grave showing the evidence and features that are regularly preserved on the surface of the grave structure, as well as what can be left behind after a grave is robbed. From the careful recognition and exposure of grave walls and floors, the type of vehicle used to rob the grave, and the method of robbing can be determined. *Source:* Inforce Foundation.

248

Figure 5–33. Suspending planks within or over a grave allows workers to remove fill and clean remains without disturbing them. Foot plates for moving over crime scene fulfil the same principle. Photograph of an Inforce training simulation. *Source:* Inforce Foundation.

these soils are mixed, evidential contextual integrity will be lost. Sections across a grave may display the episodes of burial in detail. The limits of disturbance should be photographed and surveyed appropriately.

As with disturbed graves, multiple-use graves have a more complex stratigraphic history than a single deposit grave. These graves may have been left open and then filled episodically (Tuller and Duric, 2006), or they may have been repeatedly reexcavated and had more bodies added. Such activity gives them a complex stratigraphy and sequence of use that can be revealed through careful excavation. The more complex the potential sequence of events, the more appropriate the use of stratigraphic excavation to reveal the stages of burials. Repeated disturbance to graves may make it appropriate to use specialists such as entomologists and palynologists to assist in understanding the detail of the burial sequence, including seasonality, exposure to insects, and origins of material.

Shallow single graves can be the simplest burial type to excavate due to their depth, size, and straightforward stratigraphic sequence. To prevent contamination of evidence, it is desirable to separately recover backfilled soil and surrounding soils, whose deposition predates the burial event. Subject to depth, it is usually possible to excavate a single grave within the limits of the grave structure (sides and base) by removing the grave fill first. Single graves with limited access may be excavated by assembling a plank-and-strap suspended platform (see Figure 5–33 for plank use in a larger grave) so an archaeologist can safely remove the grave fill without damaging the body or grave structure, negating the need for access trenches. Where

Figure 5–34. A deep single grave is accessed by removal of a section of one wall (left) in Guatemala. *Source:* Ian Hanson.

this is not practical, single graves of more than 80 cm depth may be difficult to excavate other than by using such a trench and removing part of the grave walls.[40] See Hunter et al. (1996), Hunter and Cox (2005), and Figure 5–34 for examples of different approaches. The removed wall should be photographed and recorded

---

[40] Access trench requirements in any grave often depend on body position. There is often room to stand within a grave (on foot platforms to prevent damage to the remains and grave structure) between limbs or to one side. Working within limited spaces also depends on the fitness and size of the excavator. Preservation of evidence must be balanced against practicality.

before destruction. Excavation strategies that do not accurately locate, recognise, record, or interpret the structure of the grave will not provide a standard of contextual evidence suitable for investigations that may have a legal bearing. This point is valid for all forms of grave and burial site.

Staff involved in evidence recovery should be aware of the potential evidence types and recovery, handling, and storage procedures for these. Protocols for scene of crime examination (see 2.3) should be consulted to coordinate evidence recovery and recording. Pathology and anthropology protocols (see 2.4) should be consulted for procedures for the recognition and recovery of human remains. Other evidence types that are commonly encountered are trace evidence (e.g., hair, fluids, paint from tools); personal effects (e.g., clothing, jewellery); documents (e.g., identification papers, photographs); weapons and associated evidence (e.g., shell cases, bullets, ballistic fragments); botanical remains (e.g., pollen, spores, leaves, flowering plants); soil and geological evidence (e.g., atypical soils, foreign stones); entomological samples (e.g., puparia cases, insect exoskeletons); indented surfaces (e.g., tool marks, footprints, handprints); topographical surfaces (e.g., wheel tracks, structure comparative samples – tiles, brick); and garbage and debris (e.g., datable tin cans, packages, building material). Relevant specialists may be required to recover and process specific evidence types. If appropriate specialists are not available during excavation, then the procedures described in Chapter 9, or relevant professional standards, should be consulted for the appropriate procedures for the recognition and recovery of specific evidence types. Where no procedural standard exists, the senior archaeologist and SCE should determine procedures for a specific evidence type based on the principles of recording *in situ*, evidence preservation, and conservation. Any item can and may constitute physical evidence. Excavation team members should be aware of the potential for unfamiliar types of evidence in a given investigation.[41]

On a large site, there is a rapid requirement for the issue of exhibit numbers, photography, and surveying. The speed of the recovery process will usually be governed by the speed with which the photography can be accomplished. One photographer can usually provide a sufficient service for up to fifteen excavating staff. If there are multiple graves being recovered simultaneously at one location, it may be necessary to have an assistant SCE, photographer, surveyor, and multiple supervisors. This requires greater quality control checks to ensure that preventable errors are minimised. A total station, electronic distance measurement device (EDM), or surveyor's level can survey for an excavation staff of fifteen to twenty. More than one may be appropriate or required for larger sites. It is a useful practice during recovery to pair off excavation staff and periodically rotate pairings. This is helpful in terms of

---

[41] At Gologova grave, Bosnia, the knowledge that the victims had been killed in part by rocket-propelled grenades meant that, in addition to such evidence, other fragments that later were identified as vehicle or refrigerator parts were initially kept; they were stored in temperature-controlled containers along with ordnance evidence to preserve potential explosive residue and surface characteristics until they were discounted.

complimenting different skills such as anthropology and archaeology, and sharing differing experience levels and exposure to varied international backgrounds. The fastest way for interns to gain useful experience is to pair them with an experienced practitioner.

Notes, plans, and records will be required to adequately describe the location, nature, attributes, and properties of evidence. Archaeologists and SCEs should make sequenced plans and take photographs during the exposure and recovery of evidence to demonstrate the methodology and recovery sequence. Numbering and recording of forensic contexts should reflect the distinctions noted between separate layers. Such recording is important for evidence recovered from a soil-filled context. Soil clinging to objects or materials can obscure the true nature of an artefact until after complete excavation has been carried out. It may be necessary to change the description of an exhibit or human remains from that applied at first exposure to another at full excavation. Team members should be aware that some evidence (e.g., photographs, identity documents) will not survive recovery and packaging without the risk of substantial change.[42] The fullest recording (including photography) of such evidence should be taken at the earliest opportunity in the excavation and recovery process and prior to such alteration, but within the context of evidence handling procedures. Scientific team members should liaise with the SCE who will allocate numbers, and control the packaging, movement, and storage of exhibits after recovery.

5.5.7   Other forensic contexts for mass disposal of human remains

In some cases, bodies are not buried but placed in natural or anthropogenic depressed features such as quarries, gullies, or roadside slopes and soil is bulldozed over them.[43] They may also be placed on flat surfaces and covered over. This creates a grave that does not have cut edges in the normal manner of a dug grave. To determine the extent of burials, the limits of the exposed preexisting feature and the limits of the dumped covering soil, or other matrix, should be determined and fully recorded. Careful removal of the dumped soil is most easily achieved by clearing from one edge of an identified uncovered ground surface to the opposing edge. Progressively removing a deposit from such a starting edge will reveal buried land surfaces and all bodies and associated evidence in an *in situ* position (Figure 5–35). Covering bodies with soil by machine may cause damage to bodies and other evidence on the periphery of such a grave. Such potential postmortem movement should be taken into account when excavating because human remains and other evidence may have been moved

---

[42] Seiko 5 automatic watches, which were recovered from numerous graves around Srebrenica, were photographed *in situ* to record the time and day/date on the watch face before they were touched or lifted. This evidence was important to corroborate time of death (see ICTY, 2003; Wright et al., 2005); in some cases, the watch motion started again on lifting, immediately altering their evidential nature.

[43] An example of this was seen at al Hilah in Iraq by the Inforce team. Here, perpetrators deposited bodies at the base of an ancient tel (man-made mound) and then bulldozed a side of the tel to provide spoil to cover them.

Figure 5–35. Removal of overlying deposits from a defined edge revealed *in situ* bodies at an execution site from the Srebrenica Massacre at Kozluk, Bosnia. *Source:* ICTY/Tim Loveless.

by this action into the covering spoil. Removal of the covering spoil by context in controlled spits will allow spatial control of any evidence or human remains encountered. In these cases, access trenches will not normally be required because the human remains and other evidence are usually on an approachable surface. If water logging or flow of groundwater is a problem, it may be appropriate to dam this at a suitable point to redirect the water. To excavate the site, a sump should be placed in an evidentially clear area of the grave floor to allow water to be pumped out.

Sites of body disposal commonly found in forensic situations include wells, caves, swallets, cisterns, latrines, and tanks (see Figure 5–3). The nature of such structures (that are often deep) will, as with all graves, require detailed health and safety risk assessment and may require specialist advice. Health and safety considerations (see 3.4) come before the need to recover evidence and bodies. Particular care must be taken to check the base and shaft of wells and other similar structures for methane gas, and gas monitoring devices must be used. Due to the nature of such structures, it is only rarely possible to extend access to the sites by trenching. Access must often be from above, although in some cases digging an adjacent shaft and working from that is an effective option. There is no doubt that the excavation of deep and usually narrow shafts is extremely complex and requires a significant level of resourcing, including appropriate expertise and engineering. If there is no room on the floor of a structure to accommodate working team members, it may be necessary to provide ladders, cages, and platforms from which recovery can occur from a suspended or raised position (Simmons, 2002). The excavation of wells or latrines dug through subsoil can be achieved by excavating a parallel shaft that allows access to the contents of the well from one side. It is also recommended that the entrance to the well be stabilised with brickwork. Retaining the stability of the shaft is paramount. Ladder and rope access will be required, and pumps may be needed to remove water. Specialist training, such as in abseiling (e.g., Industrial Rope Access Trade Association [2001] qualification), will be required in such circumstances and additional specialists and training for relevant staff members may be needed to complete some recoveries.

5.6   Excavation of human remains

During the site location and assessment phase or during the surface evidence recovery of the excavation phase, the team may encounter scatters of skeletonised human remains on or exposed at the ground surface. Depending on the length of exposure (see 7.3), human remains may have undergone some degree of taphonomic change and may be incomplete, fragmentary, and mixed with other assemblages of human or nonhuman bone (e.g., see Lyman, 1979). Therefore, experienced anthropologists are required to identify and analyse scattered bone on surfaces.

Anthropologists may be required to perform a number of different tasks in the field. During the assessment phase of an investigation, it will be necessary to recognise the presence of multiple individuals for a site to be confirmed as a mass grave, disposal, or execution site. In such circumstances, the anthropologists will be required to identify osseous material; differentiate human from nonhuman remains; and recognise, quantify, and inventory bones (often via major skeletal landmarks). A minimum number of individuals (MNI) will be established from the skeletal inventory. If the human remains are not to be removed from the site for analysis in a laboratory during this phase, it will be necessary to complete as much of the appropriate recording form (see forms MA41–46) as possible. An anthropologist may be required to take biological samples (see Chapter 9) such as DNA (tooth or bone), hair, and fingernails (for tests such as isotope analysis). It is, of course, always preferential to analyse human remains in the mortuary, but it may not always be possible. The decision to take samples should be decided by the management team in conjunction with the governing authority and/or representatives of the local communities. (See the Sample Recording Form [FA13F] and the Field Sample Log [FA13L].)

Anthropological skills are obviously essential in the excavation phase of an investigation, especially when skeletonised or partially skeletonised human remains are encountered. These skills are paramount when assessing secondary or robbed graves because human remains are often disarticulated and/or commingled, and it may be necessary to determine associations and nonassociations between separate body parts. In this phase, anthropologists may be required to assist with excavation of human remains from graves and subsequent mortuary analysis. However, the anthropologist may be required, in certain circumstances, to undertake analyses in the field. This may occur when there would be a substantial loss of information or damage to the human remains if they were moved, where remains are on the surface and there is no permission for removal, when a grave is opened but the human remains are not to be exhumed, or where destruction or alteration of the site is imminent and all remains cannot be removed before this occurs.

The process of anthropological assessment in the field should mirror assessment in the laboratory, and the anthropology recording form(s) (MA41–46) can be used for this task. Analysis can involve any or all of the following: assessment of ancestry; assessment of biological sex; assessment of biological age; estimation of stature; recording dental anomalies, stage of development, disease, restorations, and prostheses; assessment of antemortem trauma, distinguishing features, anomalies, and pathologies; assessment of perimortem trauma; assessment of postmortem trauma and taphonomy; and taking biological samples. Chapters 7 and 8 set out procedures for the completion of the following forms, which can be used to record skeletal material as appropriate: the form for heat-modified human remains (for multiple human remains in adult and nonadult versions; MA43 and MA44); the form for commingled and individual bones (for single unassociated bones; MA46); the form for body parts (for more than one articulated bone; MA45); and the form for single individuals (adult and nonadult versions, burnt or unburned; MA41 and MA42).

Anthropologists with archaeological skills, and archaeologists with good faunal and human bone recognition skills, may also be required occasionally to undertake basic analyses in the field. Aside from those mentioned previously, these could include identifying individual bones or fragments, siding bones (left or right) or fragments, determining the biological sex and age of bones or fragments, determining relationships and articulations between bones to link single individuals, and differentiating the anatomical position of skeletal material to identify individuals and their elements in multiple burial contexts. The anthropologist may be asked to assist other team members with specific or general queries, including identifying postmortem trauma and taphonomic changes, recognising possible ante- and postmortem trauma, and recognising associated prosthetics and medical aids.

5.6.1   Excavation of human remains procedures

Because of the variation in the mode of burial and consequent taphonomic change, procedures for excavating human remains must be flexible, and guidelines can be followed. Once the soil and material over human remains is removed (see 5.5.4) and the remains have been partially exposed, a metal detector may be used by EOD staff, when appropriate, to check for metal objects and UXO. Prior to the recovery of human remains, bodies and body parts should be completely exposed, when possible, prior to recording so the complete anatomical associations and position of the body can be observed. To achieve this, the body or body part should be cleaned using methods appropriate for the soil type (i.e., brushes work well in sand, wooden tools are better in clay) and reflecting the condition of the human remains (i.e., leaf trowel for saponified bodies, soft brushes for bones subjected to heat modification). The important point is that a body is cleaned well enough for it to be clearly defined in a photograph but not overcleaned so as to remove details, dislodge bones, or lose forensic trace evidence. Assessing this balance requires experience. In cases where bodies within graves are tangled or entwined and cannot be completely exposed, recorded, or recovered at one time, it may be necessary to leave a limb beneath another body.[44] In this situation, the body part(s) temporarily left behind must be separately tagged and labelled (with the same evidence number as the relevant body). This will be noted on the appropriate body form, site evidence log, and survey log to avoid doubling up on exhibit numbers and omitting to survey the remains. As a conservation measure, it is recommended that if blindfolds, bindings, or other loose evidence are exposed *in situ*, they are first photographed and then secured in place with cling film to avoid them being displaced during transport and handling.[45] This is also true for any other element that may move or be damaged during lifting and exposure such as fractured bones. Similarly, saponified and skeletonised hands and feet may be bagged to keep them together. The use of bags or cling film, as with any other conservation technique, must be recorded on the appropriate recording form (skeletal or body). Photographs should be taken both before and after this process to record the method.

For bodies with soft and saponified tissue, the soil close to the body should be removed as described in 5.5.4 and the stratigraphy of body placement determined, if possible. In mass graves, bodies that are pedestalled lose support and may collapse and disintegrate; this should be avoided (Tuller and Duric, 2006). It is sensible to work by cleaning from one end of the body to the other or from the centre of the body outward, following the contours of the body to allow soil to be channelled away to ensure that areas already cleaned are not soiled. Such soil can be collected using hand shovels and buckets, and kept separate for sieving to screen for evidence.

---

[44] This was a common occurrence in mass graves in Bosnia, where excavations of primary and secondary graves could not continue unless limbs were left behind, such was the degree of entanglement. This was especially true of bodies where the remains appear to have been bulldozed into graves.

[45] Such movement occurred with blindfolds in Bosnia between recovery from field and arrival at mortuary, leading to issues of continuity of evidential description. Digital photographs were taken before and after wrapping, and these images were printed and attached to recording forms for the body (noting conservation measures) that travelled to the mortuary to inform pathologists.

The human remains should be left *in situ* but exposed as fully as possible without causing movement or loss of material. Care should be taken with skeletonised human remains, especially hands and feet, because small bones can easily be dislodged if too much supporting soil is removed; these should be lifted first when possible to prevent accidental loss.

With skeletonised or partially skeletonised bodies or body parts, trowels, leaf trowels, wooden sculpture or pottery tools, modelled chopsticks, spoons, and brushes of various sizes have all been used to remove soil from between bones. Picks and mattocks should never be used to clean soil around bones because they may cause damage. Less experienced anthropologists and archaeologists should not use metal implements because they may cause damage that could mimic peri- or postmortem trauma. It is more likely to find small objects like bullets or ballistic fragments in the soil close to skeletal remains because they represent evidence that was in or on soft tissue that has now decayed. It will be necessary to sieve (wet or dry) the soil to recover such evidence around bones and within the area of the torso and abdomen. Enough of the bone should be cleaned that they remain *in situ* but are exposed enough to allow assessment and recording. The underside of a bone can be left supported within the soil because this will act as an 'anchor' to support the bone during photography and recording. Care should be taken with skeletonised human remains because facial bones are particularly fragile, especially the orbits and maxillary-nasal region. Excavation of human remains can only continue when the recording and surveying of major points of the body and any associated evidence has been undertaken (see 5.5.2). Further soil removal may be necessary for the recovery of human remains to be efficiently undertaken. It is essential that bodies or bones are not 'pulled out' from surrounding soil because this may result in breakage and loss of association with other bones and artefacts. Bones must always be fully exposed prior to lifting.

Commingled human remains are those human remains that potentially represent more than one individual and where a direct association or anatomical relationship between the bone elements or fragments within the grave cannot readily be made. Each element can be cleaned by a suitable method (as described in previous sections) and treated as either a 'body part' if articulated or an 'individual bone' if not articulated. All remains will be surveyed and planned (as described in 5.5.2) prior to lifting. A field recording form for body parts and individual bones (FA12BP) may be completed prior to excavation of human remains. This is undertaken if it is considered necessary to describe the position of bones, record associations to other body parts, evidence, or photography and survey information. Complete, partial, or commingled remains should be surveyed and described anatomically when possible.

The condition in which heat-modified human remains are found may range from slight burning or charring of the bone surface to complete fragmentation. A number of states of burning or cremation may be encountered in forensic cases.

Burnt remains may comprise complete bones or those that are complete enough to be identified as representing a single individual. They might be fragmentary bones where those of a single individual can be identified, fragmentary or complete bones, commingled but individual bones can be identified, or fragmentary and no individual bone can be identified. When heat-modified bones are encountered and can be identified either as bones of a single individual, body parts, or individual bones, they can be prepared for excavation of human remains as suggested in previous sections. Care must be taken not to dislodge fragments and teeth or to overclean heat-modified human remains. Small brushes, wooden tools, and leaf trowels are usually effective in removing soil.

When human remains are found to be highly fragmented (regardless of whether they are heat modified) and they cannot be identified as individual bones, the area of deposition can be split into quadrants for ease of location, recovery, recording, packaging, analysis, and interpretation of human remains. Small brushes, wooden tools, leaf trowels, and baby bellows or an air spray (as used by photographers to remove dust from lenses) may be useful to clean human remains, which will be surveyed, recorded, and collected by quadrant.

5.6.2   Documentation and recording responsibilities

Once the body or skeleton has been fully exposed, it is ready for further photography and survey. A pathologist may want to examine the human remains at this point to gather contextual information while the human remains are *in situ*. The appropriate forms (Table 5–5) for describing *in situ* human remains must be completed (including issue by the SCE of an exhibit number for the body). These include recording and describing the position of the body as found, the stage of decomposition and condition of the body, the general appearance of any visible clothing and personal effects that are present, and a plan of these. Caution should be exercised in describing the colour or design of clothing since it will almost certainly be altered by staining from the burial environment, body fluids, and such variables as staining from metals; it should be properly described only after washing. Caution should also be exercised in describing trauma in such a way that it may conflict with descriptions at autopsy. It is essential to record if any ballistics, blindfold, or other binding are recovered and to locate these on the drawing provided.

Any absent body parts, trauma, postmortem damage, and excavation damage visible at the time of recovery must also be recorded. It is essential to ensure that the anatomical points of the body are surveyed, either with a total station or manually (see 5.5.2), and to describe physical relationships to surrounding bodies, or features, and determine the stratigraphic position of the body, if possible, recorded within a Harris Matrix. Recording is crucial, and suitable photographs must be taken to record the body position clearly, illustrating the position and properties of the body and any specific evidential detail, with appropriate numbering, scales, and north

Table 5–5. *Field recording forms*

Code	Forms and logs
FA00F	Notes
FA01F	Site Assessment Form
FA02F	Site Risk Assessment Form
FA03F	Geophysical Surveying Form
FA03RF	Geophysical Surveying Data Analysis Form
FA04LB	Site Survey Log: Bearing survey with dumpy level
FA04LT	Site Survey Log: Total station or grid survey
FA05F	Context Recording Form
FA05L	Site Context Log
FA06F	Surface Recording Form
FA07L	Section Log
FA08L	Plan Log
FA09LD	Site Digital Image Log
FA09LN	Site Negative Film Photograph Log
FA10LD	Site Digital Video Log
FA10LN	Site Video Log
FA11L	Site Evidence Log
FA12BH	Body Location, Attitudes, and Properties (without total station)
FA12BT	Body Location, Attitudes, and Properties (with total station)
FA12SH	Skeleton Location, Attitudes, and Properties (without total station)
FA12ST	Skeleton Location, Attitudes, and Properties (with total station)
FA12BP	Scattered and Commingled Skeletal Remains
FA13F	Sample Recording Form
FA13L	Field Sample Log
FA14R	Personnel Entry Register
FA15L	Dry Sieving Log
FA16L	Flotation Summary Log
FA17F	Field Handover Form

arrow. The photographs should also demonstrate and record the methodology of excavation, exposure, and recovery.

5.6.3 Recovery of human remains

Once fully exposed and initially recorded, recovery of human remains can begin. Clothing and visible pockets may be searched for documents or other perishable or dangerous material that should be recorded and then removed immediately for photography and, if appropriate, for conservation or treatment. The removal should be noted on the body or skeleton recording form (FA12), including its exhibit number. A SCE undertakes this process.

Soft tissue and saponified bodies should be checked to determine and ensure that all elements and clothing are exposed, free of soil, and not 'trapped' under other bodies or features. This may require limbs to be moved to understand anatomical relationships, especially when bodies are pressed together and intertwined. Limbs will need to be moved slightly to verify that there is no UXO hazard beneath, and checked for any additional evidential details. When satisfied that all parts belong to a single individual and that the human remains are safe to move, the lifting method can be determined.[46] Subject to condition, the body can be rolled to one side (this is a more stable operation when undertaken by two people) and a body bag then placed beneath the body by a third person, if necessary. The rear of the body and back pockets can be checked at this point. The body can then be rolled back onto the body bag, which is pulled around and over the body from both sides. This operation is made easier when bodies are clothed. A second search for documents or other perishable material can be made using the techniques described previously.

Completely skeletonised human remains may be more complex to exhume than fully fleshed or saponified bodies and the technique to be used will depend on various factors. Skeletonised human remains may be recovered in differing states of preservation. These include well-preserved bone without clothing (or with fibres of clothing not strong enough to support bone) or well-preserved bone with clothing (clothing that will support the human remains during handling and transport). Equally, remains may be in the form of unstable bone with or without clothing.

The method of excavation of bones, clothing, and personal effects will vary according to the conditions in which they are found. Logically, bones should be removed stratigraphically (i.e., as an anatomically complete individual) and, where possible, should follow the guidelines set out by the Institute of Field Archaeologists (McKinley and Roberts, 1993; McKinley and Brickley, 2004). Each bone should be fully exposed and freed from the surrounding matrix prior to lifting. Even if bone is in good condition, it can fracture when pried or pulled out of the soil. Complete and stable bones can be gently loosened and then lifted; if they cannot be easily loosened, then more soil must be removed from around the sides of the element. Splinters of fractured bone can be temporarily stored in small containers until all fragments have been recovered. This may require sieving (or complete recovery) of the soil in the immediate area around the bone; fragments should be kept with the fractured bone. Highly fragmentary bone can be collected as a block by pedestalling the bone slightly and collecting the soil from beneath to stabilise it. In circumstances where bodies are tightly packed together or the soil is unsuitable (very sandy, muddy, stony, etc.), this may not be possible. Consolidation or casting of the bone is another option but often impractical. For instructions, see Cronyn, 1990; Museum of London Archaeological Service (MoLAS), 1994. Tightly packed and highly fragmentary heat-modified bone can be collected by softly brushing fragments, or gently using

---

[46] It has not been unusual in cases of closely compacted and well-preserved bodies in mass graves to get to the point of recovery only to realise, when lifting occurs, that the leg considered to be of the individual in question belongs to another. It can be necessary to apply some force to following limbs and clothing to determine the anatomical extent of an individual.

wooden tools to loosen the fragments. In some circumstances lifting the bone in a block is advised and the human remains are separated from the matrix under controlled conditions in the mortuary.

The conservation methods applied to the bones, clothing, and personal effects will vary according to the conditions in which they are found. In general, it is recommended that bones and other exhibits are kept in a similar environment to that in which they are found (Cronyn, 1990; MoLAS, 1994) until laboratory-based conservation measures can be undertaken. The overriding principle in forensic cases is that conservation should, if possible, be passive. That is, it should not alter the biochemical nature of the material being conserved because this may inhibit certain analyses and cause a loss of some types of evidence. Some general options are discussed here.

When skeletonised human remains are found heavily clothed (e.g., within a leather jacket or heavily wrapped), it should not be necessary to open clothing or remove bones from within them. This would depend on the perceived UXO threat, or necessity for further *in situ* recording of perimortem trauma, or of other evidentiary properties. A SCE will oversee this process. If removal of clothing or other bindings is not necessary, then the human remains can be lifted and stored within the clothing and taken to the mortuary in their approximate anatomical position; the torso and trousers can be placed directly within a body bag. Hands, feet, cranium, and other small bones should be bagged separately and labelled as described in 5.6.1. Where human remains are well preserved and in stable condition, and where there is no or only degraded clothing present, they can be removed and separated anatomically for packaging (although it is possible for all bones to be packaged and labelled individually where resources permit). In practice, bones are usually packaged according to anatomical part. This also aids the organisation and processing of the human remains at the laboratory. For example, the cranium (separate cranium and mandible), the neck (optional separation of cervical vertebrae, hyoid, and larynx), the thorax (thoracic vertebrae and sternum), the lumbar region (lumbar vertebrae), the ribs (left and right and bagged separately), the pelvis (innominatum, sacrum, and coccyx), the upper limbs (separate right and left, optional separation of hands), the lower limbs (separate right and left), and optional separation of feet. Feet should not be removed from socks or boots or hands from gloves. It is recommended that scapulae need careful packaging as individual elements because they are particularly fragile, and clavicles should be bagged with the ribs of the same side. Strong paper bags are suitable for packaging bone unless the bone is very wet because they prevent growth of mould that occurs in 'sweating' plastic bags. The general rule regarding the packaging of skeletonised human remains in boxes and rigid containers is that the more robust and heavy bones should be packed at the bottom. Bubble wrap may be used around and between layers for extra cushioning if required. It is recommended that pathological and fragile bone be treated separately and have extra cushioning by means of acid-free tissue paper, which can be wrapped around the bone. Ideally, bespoke postcranial and cranial boxes should be used, and packaging should be permeable.

It may be more convenient for badly preserved bone in an unstable state to remain within clothing because it can protect the human remains during handling and transport. However, when human remains are encountered in a brittle or unstable state, and clothing is not present, it is recommended that each bone (e.g., left and right innominatum) be first wrapped in acid-free tissue paper and then bagged separately. The soil beneath human remains may also be collected with the bone. If the bones are not expected to survive excavation and transport to a laboratory, conservation methods (e.g., described in Cronyn, 1990, or MoLAS, 1994) may be applied. Alternatively, or additionally, analysis can be undertaken in the field, and this should be accompanied by detailed photographs (with a scale).

It is recommended that the soil around broken bones should also be collected to facilitate recovery of bone fragments and splinters for reconstruction in the laboratory (especially perimortem trauma to the head and neck area). Unfused epiphyses, ballistics, and other associated evidence may also be recovered this way. Similarly, if bodies are clothed, the bones and soil within the clothing should be recovered together. In this case, attempts must be made to keep the human remains flat. This is most easily accomplished by lifting the clothing directly into a body bag, suitably sized box, or other rigid container (this will keep left and right bones and evidence separate until it reaches the mortuary) and carried on a stretcher to minimise movement.

Nonadult human remains may be excavated and stored in the same way as adult human remains, but special attention should be taken to collect teeth and unfused ossification centres (e.g., epiphyses). If infant and foetal human remains are encountered fully clothed or wrapped, they can be collected as they were found, taking care to place the human remains in a box so as not to disturb the anatomical position. If this is unavoidable (e.g., if there is a threat of UXO), removal of clothing may be necessary, and separation and bagging of bones by left and right side is the minimum requirement. Soil around an infant or foetal individual should be kept for sieving in the laboratory.

Heat-modified remains should be recorded and bagged as described for skeletonised human remains. If in stable condition, bones can be separated by body part; if bones are fractured or fragmented, they can be bagged by individual bone. Fragmented bones can be lifted in a block. When commingled bones are encountered, the method of lifting and bagging will be dictated by the way exhibit numbers are allocated. If individual bones or articulating parts are labelled as such, they can be lifted and bagged as separate units. When bones are not labelled separately, and they are in a relatively stable state, they can be bagged communally, either by quadrant or by site. The method of excavation will be the same for bodies or body parts. Dry stable bones can be bagged in paper bags and the skull in an appropriately sized and shaped box; all the bags can then be stored in a body bag or box. It is recommended that all packaging is acid free. Where body bags are used, they should be placed on separate shelves and not directly on top of another body bag. Dry clothing can be placed in plastic or paper bags so any small bones, bullet fragments, or other evidence is not lost. Stable but waterlogged bones can be placed in permeable (i.e., breathable) plastic bags. Paper bags should be secured with noncontaminated adhesive tape or, alternatively, folded and stapled (with stainless steel staples). Plastic bags can be tied with plastic ties or insulated electrical flex; alternatively, resealable bags can be used.

The bags must be labelled with a permanent marker (waterproof/indelible ink), and the label must contain the body number, excavator initials, date, and contents of the bag (i.e., left arm and hand). The bags can be given a consecutive number to ensure that a record of the number of bags associated with the body is created; this number can be placed within a circle in the top right corner. Labels should be written in the central part of the bag so they are not obscured, particularly once sealed. All bags relating to one individual can then be placed in an appropriate container (body bag or box). An inscribed metal tag should be attached to clothing (e.g., a belt) with a metal wire or to a long bone with a plastic tie to ensure that the bone is not damaged. This tag must clearly show the body number and the date and initials of the excavator. The bag or box can then be sealed and stored in suitable conditions. Any soil, bones, clothing, or other associated items will also be placed in appropriate packaging into the body bag (or container) before it is closed. The body bag will then be transported to suitable storage facility or refrigerated container. Appropriate conditions for storing body bags or boxes can vary according to conservation needs. Dry material can be stored on shelved facilities at constant room temperature and constant low humidity; wet material can be slowly dried (but never in direct sunlight) or stored in cold facilities under the supervision of a conservator. Storage facilities must always be secure to maintain evidential integrity.

5.6.4   Excavation of human remains: Summary

For surface remains, the extent of possible human remains on the surface must be determined and initial site photography undertaken. A grid, quadrant, baseline, or fixed datum point will be set up, and human remains and other evidence will be identified and flagged. These will then be allocated a number, surveyed onto the plan, and an inventory made. As appropriate, samples of dentition, bone, or other tissue types will be taken. Finally, the remains will be collected, packaged, and labelled as human bone (or suspected human bone) or associated artefacts.

For buried human remains, the grave fill will first be removed and the body(ies) and/or skeletal remains will be exposed. Before proceeding any further, a health and safety assessment must be undertaken, especially for UXO. The remains will then be numbered, photographed, and surveyed *in situ*, and the position and attitude of the human remains recorded. Perishable evidence will be recorded and recovered, and human remains will be exhumed, packaged, and labelled. Appropriate conservation and storage methods will be applied to all exhibits.

5.7 Sampling and sieving

Sampling of specific evidence types are dealt with in various sections of this text, particularly Chapter 9. If an appropriate specialist is not available, sampling should be carried out by the SCE and senior archaeologist (or a designated team member). When sampling, the process to be followed is as described in this section. All samples should be given sequential numbers and entered into the chain of custody by the SCE, but only after the *in situ* location of the sample has been surveyed and photographed with appropriate reference to scale and the wider context. All samples should be collected and packaged suitably to conserve them, avoiding further degradation. The samples must be appropriately labelled. Storage of samples should be adequate for their specific conservation requirements or necessary pretreatment, but they should be passed on to the relevant specialist laboratory for processing and analysis as soon as possible. This handover will be thoroughly documented to maintain the chain of custody and evidential security.

Sieving strategies should reflect the specifics of the case and the context. They should consider and specify what percentage of a deposit is to be sieved and how (i.e., gauge of mesh and wet or dry). If there are time constraints, deposits are measured in many tons, or no evidence is found after sieving a percentage of the sample and resources are limited, then the remainder may not be sieved. This must be agreed by the SCE, senior archaeologist, and investigator. It is imperative that whatever sieving strategy is employed, both strategy and rationale must be recorded. An example might be to recovering bullets from soil under bodies. Material types that can be recovered from sieving includes small body parts (e.g., unfused epiphyses, phalanges, teeth, and fingernails), objects that directly bear on the manner and cause of death (e.g., bullets, shell cases), and objects that bear on the identification of the victim or perpetrators. Moreover, there is a strong argument in favour of collecting all artefacts because it is not necessarily known what objects might bear on the case at the time of the excavation. Total collection is common practice at the forensic investigation of individual criminal graves because it is not known what may become exhibits, or be particularly important evidence, during the collection phase. Clearly, in many multiple-death contexts, the sheer scale or the context of the site makes this impossible both practically and in terms of resources involved. An example could be where a grave has been dug into a town waste dump containing an infill almost entirely of artefacts. Time and storage may preclude total collection, but in such cases careful observation of the surrounding waste will serve to identify objects that are out of character or anomalous (Wright et al., 2005).

Soil that is suitable for dry sieving has a low moisture content that will allow the soil to break into small particles that will reveal small items of evidence. Samples should be stored in spotlessly clean 'bins' with secure lids for small deposits, or strong plastic sheeting or tarpaulins for large deposits. They should be maintained in such a way as to avoid contamination and should be far enough away from the grave to avoid causing an obstacle to team and vehicle movement. Stored samples should be covered and sited down wind from a grave to prevent dust and debris from contaminating the grave, bearing in mind the prevalent wind direction for a specific area. Sieves on legs that work on a lever or shaking action are best for dry sieving. However, other recognised methods of dry sieving can be employed. Soil should be placed into the sieve and sieved through in suitable quantities (depending on the overall size and mesh size of the sieve). A see-saw action allows the small soil particles (spoil) to fall through the mesh grid. The sieve should be moved periodically because the spoil builds up beneath it. Care should be taken not to mix the spoil with the soil yet to be sieved. Sieve mesh size will depend on the soil matrix and the type of evidence anticipated. For example, small bullet fragments in sandy soil will probably require a 3- to 5-mm mesh size, whereas clay soils will block a sieve with small mesh. Trials may be necessary to determine the correct size. Information on natural soil type and local geology obtained from test trenches or pits dug during the assessment phase of the investigation may be useful. Upon collection in the sieve, any potential artefacts or evidence should be removed and placed in bags. When completed and checked, these should be labelled and sealed. The appropriate context recording form (FA05F) and the Dry Sieving Log (FA15L) should be filled in to record the sampling, and any evidence recovered from the sieved matrix should be numbered appropriately.

Wet flotation may be necessary to recover evidence from heavy and wet soils and sludge. This process may also be necessary to recover trace evidence, organic materials and burnt bone from dry deposits. Consideration should be made of the potential of this method to damage or alter evidence before it is undertaken. A suitable place for flotation must have a good clean water supply and run-off space, and an electricity supply will be needed to power a pump. For small-scale sieving, hand buckets may be used. Each deposit sieved should be recorded in the Flotation Summary Log (FA16L), and any exhibit numbered.

5.8   Site preservation and restoration

Any forensic site should be managed to provide preservation of structural evidence and other evidence that cannot be removed. Consideration of the imperative to return a site to a state of 'normality' so it does not pose a danger to the public or landowner is also essential. Obviously, if the site is within a mined area, then making the wider environment around a site safe is not the responsibility of the field team; the site itself will have been made safe to allow fieldwork to be carried out. Large holes, as many mass graves are, when backfilled can suffer from subsidence, and (especially if the grave penetrated the water table or is within a hydrological recharge regime) become waterlogged as the soil being backfilled is soaked with rising groundwater. This can lead to dangerous and unstable areas of ground. Remedial engineering works may be needed to landscape the area appropriately and sympathetically. Direction and flow of groundwater, or features such as streams or ponds, may need to be considered. This may result in having to clean silted field ditches or dig trenches specifically to redirect water and prevent ingress of water into the loose backfilled area.

All backfilling should be monitored and checked by archaeological staff and the logistics officer. In some cases, it may be necessary to compact the backfill in a grave with heavy machinery. Any works should be marked and fenced in some form, even after backfilling, and local authorities must be informed, for health and safety reasons, of the nature and location of the works, unless the aims of the investigation prevent this.

If surfaces and evidence are present in the grave when it is backfilled (e.g., tool marks in the grave floor), these may be covered with a permeable membrane and protected. Prior to backfilling with soil, sand should be poured over this surface to a depth of approximately 10 to 20 cm. If sand is not available, then fine soil should be immediately and carefully placed over the evidence (it must not be mechanically tipped) to protect it. The soil should not be stony.

5.9   Documentation and recording: Field forms and logs

Interpretation in archaeology occurs during excavation and postexcavation. As methodology effects interpretation, records should be kept that illustrate and describe the method and process of the work carried out. These should include notes, photographs, and video footage of the team at work, as well as descriptive images of the processes as directed by the senior archaeologist, SCM, or SCE. When recording the results of an excavation, the senior archaeologist may delegate record making to suitable staff; this may be the drawing of sections or description of soils. All records generated at the site must enter the chain of custody. The senior archaeologist, surveyor, and (potentially) others may process records and unite their papers off site after completion of the excavation. Security copies of all forms, reports, and any additional papers must be made. The SCE will control the distribution and monitoring of any records being used for report writing. The SCM will collate the reports. Archaeologists and anthropologists will complete appropriate body forms. These must be submitted to the SCE on completion, after being checked by the supervisor or senior archaeologist. Copies should not be retained by individual operatives under any circumstances and only exceptionally with permission. This is also true for other records.

The senior archaeologist will produce a report detailing the location, nature, attributes, properties, excavation methodology, sequence, events, and interpretation of the site. Further reports may be produced by the SCM and SCE concerning evidential matters. Specialist and laboratory-based reports concerning specific evidence and analysis, such as entomological or palynological reports will be produced by the specialists in question. For large sites with various complexities of evidence, containing numerous victims and/or evidential links to other sites, it may be relevant and necessary for pathologists and/or anthropologists to contribute to the interpretation of a grave site. For example, linking a primary robbed grave site with the secondary site by identifying conjoining body parts separated during the robbing of a grave.

6

Mortuary procedures I – Pathology, radiography, and the role of the anatomical pathology technologist

Alison Anderson, Hendrik Scholtz, Jeanine Vellema, and Mark Viner

6.1 Introduction

This chapter is intended to provide a standard method of practice for the pathologist, radiographer, and anatomical pathology technologist (APT) undertaking medico-legal and/or humanitarian work following atrocity crimes. It does not discuss the detail of various diagnostic techniques (see, e.g., Saukko and Knight, 2004) for making specific deductions but provides a process of work and detail of responsibilities. The role of the anthropologist in this process is discussed in Chapters 7 and 8, and that of the odontologist in 9.4. Details of the role and process employed by the pathologists as developed for the Inforce Foundation's standard operating procedures (SOPs) (Inforce Foundation, 2004b) have been revised and updated from the *National Code of Guidelines for Forensic Pathology Practice in South Africa* (Scholtz et al., 2007). Any variations of these standards should be made only if necessary to satisfy legal or safety differences when working on international missions. Alternative SOPs of equal or higher standard can only be used with the express permission or approval of the mortuary management team.

All mortuary staff must have access to this SOP prior to deployment and in the field. This document does not provide the legal framework for the mortuary activities or for the practice of forensic pathology. All personnel working in a mortuary associated with international forensic investigations must have the relevant qualifications, experience, and professionalism to perform their role with objectivity, impartiality, and scientific accuracy. All information and documentation produced at mortuaries is confidential and may not be disclosed to any unauthorised person or authority, except in cases where lawful permission is granted.

The aim of the medicolegal investigation of death is to establish the primary cause, mechanism, and manner of death, and to facilitate the administration of justice. Those involved in the analysis of human remains and associated exhibits must therefore endeavour to gather any evidence that may facilitate the administration of justice or humanitarian repatriation in their attempt to establish this. Any information or evidence accompanying the body that may be of importance in subsequent civil or criminal judicial proceedings should also be recorded and analysed. This must be undertaken by relevant experts either within the mortuary complex or in internationally accredited laboratories.

The decision as to whether the pathologist charged with the postmortem examination (PME) will or will not dissect the body or remove any part, organ, or contents for special investigation varies according to the context. In the UK, for example, the decision as to whether an open dissection is required is legally the responsibility of the coroner (Dorries, 1999), who would make that decision in conjunction with the pathologist, whereas in South Africa it is currently at the sole discretion of the forensic medical practitioner. In some mass fatality contexts, for example, the Asian tsunami and some terrorist incidents, it is assumed that the cause of death is known and so only a limited dissecting autopsy to establish identity is required. This responsibility is a most important one in a case for which some person(s) may be held criminally liable. Failure to conduct an adequate investigation may lead to the irretrievable loss of evidence that may later prove to be of great legal or humanitarian importance, thereby seriously compromising the administration of justice and human rights. For the purpose of this chapter, it is implicit that all human remains recovered are likely to have a cause of death that is 'other than natural'. All recovered bodies and body parts will therefore undergo an open, dissecting PME by the pathologist to determine the cause of death. Within this chapter, the term 'open, dissecting PME' is abbreviated to 'PME' and implies examination of fleshed, saponified, mummified, heat-modified, or skeletonised remains.

This chapter sets out best practice as applied to the more recently deceased, and some of what is included will not be applicable to mass graves where remains are mostly skeletonised. However, it must be remembered that the age of a grave does not necessarily indicate the state of preservation and that older graves can contain human remains in variable states of preservation, depending on substrate, numbers interred, water table, and other extrinsic variables that create different taphonomic zones of preservation/decomposition (as described by Haglund, 2002). All recording forms relating to this chapter can be found on the accompanying CD and guidance as to their use in 1.11.

6.2 Property and exhibits

When a body is received at a mortuary facility, and after it has undergone primary radiographic survey (see 6.5.2), all property and valuables (e.g., clothing, money, jewellery, firearms, bags) present or found on the body must be recorded on the form for Clothing and Personal Effects Associated with Individuals (MC11L). All evidence recovered from the body must be photographed *in situ* before it is removed from the body. Full particulars of the property found on a body must be logged and the chain of custody maintained. The entry must be signed by the mortuary-based scene of crime examiner (SCE) who receives the property and clothing, and by the field-based SCE who hands over the body and property. All objects and documents on the body must be appropriately conserved and placed in a tamper-proof bag. They should be placed in the appropriate packaging, with delicate items placed in rigid containers. This bag must be sealed and labelled with evidence numbers. The bag(s) must be kept safely in the evidence store under lock and key or in a safe until disposal. All property from one body must be kept together in a plastic bag, and numbers must be secured to the plastic bag containing the property (see 4.3.2). Perishable property or property that has no intrinsic, judicial, identifying, or potential sentimental value may be destroyed. In all such cases, the disposal must be documented by the SCE in the Mortuary Evidence Log (MC13L).

The clothing of the deceased must be left on the body for the pathologist to examine because clothing forms an important part of the medicolegal evidence in cases of death due to unnatural causes. It may aid in establishing the identity of the deceased and in deducing cause or manner of death. In cases where the pathologist has not seen the body before it was received at the mortuary, the body and clothing must be left in the same condition as when they were received. The clothing will be removed only after the pathologists have seen the body and have made their initial observations in their report.

Items of physical evidence, such as spent bullets or clothing, are handed over to the SCE, who must sign the evidence log to verify receipt. The SCE must be present when all evidence, clothing, and so on is removed, and these must be packaged immediately. All items of clothing should be carefully removed from bodies. They should not be shaken out before packaging them in correctly labelled paper bags. Soiled, bloody, or damp garments should ideally be air dried before being packaged. Plastic packaging bags are not recommended because they trap moisture, which can cause degradation of evidence by fungal or bacterial elements (Saferstein, 2004).

6.3   Role and duties of the forensic pathologist

6.3.1   Medicolegal postmortem examination

PMEs should normally only be carried out by forensic pathologists (or trained forensic medical practitioners), and a full examination will be undertaken on all bodies as soon as possible after recovery. The examination should always be supplemented by photographs of the body and injuries present at the time of the examination. A photographer or SCE will perform this task, which must never be performed by the APT because they are in effect 'dirty', and the camera must be kept clean to prevent cross-contamination. At the end of the examination, the pathologist should ensure that the dissected organs and tissues, except those retained for special investigations, are returned to the body. The pathologist should complete the Mortuary Personnel Entry Register (MG07) and Open Dissecting Post-mortem Examination Body Recording Form (MP31) or the Open Dissecting Post-mortem Examination Body Part Recording Form (MP32) in all cases, irrespective of the cause of death. A copy of the form and original notes should be kept and information entered into the mortuary database.

The pathologist may consult colleagues or specialists on any case and is urged to do so if any problems or unusual cases are encountered. The expertise of anthropologists will always be available and that of odontologists may be necessary where dental records exist. A team effort may be required especially when encountering heat-modified or skeletonised remains. Other specialist personnel may be requested, depending on the nature of the investigation, availability of resources, and time constraints.

The following objectives are particularly important in most cases. It is crucial to establish the primary medical cause and mechanism of death and to establish the manner of death. It is also important to establish other relevant information, such as secondary features of identity, which may, in the considered opinion of the pathologist or other specialists, become relevant or important at future legal or administrative proceedings. This will include appropriate sampling, and the collection and recording of other evidence as deemed appropriate. Regardless of the nature of the investigation, it is important to facilitate the categorisation of the manner of death as being murder, suicide, accidental, natural, or undetermined. It is important to consider that mass graves can also reflect fatalities resulting from epidemics and mass disasters – whether natural or anthropogenic.

No PME should be undertaken before the pathologist has been fully informed of the appropriate case history, where such is known (including circumstances of death). In the case of mass grave exhumations, the body recording form completed in the field and any accompanying photographs of the remains *in situ* should be consulted. When the mortuary facility is reasonably close to the grave site, the pathologist is encouraged to visit the site regularly. Even in cases when the mortuary is at a distance that precludes daily access to the exhumation site, a visit to the grave should be made at least once.

Prior to any dissection procedure, the pathologist should anticipate the probable outcome of the PME in terms of preparatory procedures (e.g., for photography, secondary, and tertiary radiography; external specimen collection; fingerprinting), specialised dissection techniques, and other special investigations that may be required (e.g., specimen collection for toxicological analyses, histological examination, and identification). The appropriate containers, preservatives, and so forth should be available prior to the onset of the PME.

It is the responsibility of the pathologist to ensure a number of matters, many of which may be delegated to the APT or other specialists. Prior to the PME, it is important that appropriate and functional dissection instrumentation is available and that appropriate health and safety measures and personal protective equipment (PPE) are in use. It is critical to ensure that appropriate identification criteria are recorded, and that adequate and scientific methods are used to identify bodies that cannot be reliably identified by routine methods (e.g., fingerprints). This is especially applicable in cases of severe mutilation, decomposition, charring, and so on. Dental examination, serology, DNA analyses, or radiological examination should be considered. The pathologist is responsible for ensuring that only authorised individuals may attend the PME and that the body is not released before, or until, they are satisfied that a complete investigation has been done and that all examinations, including specimen collections and sampling, have been adequately performed. They must also ensure that appropriate documentation has been completed, prior to commencement of the PME.

Although PMEs may only be conducted by a qualified medical practitioner (the pathologist), appropriately trained APTs may assist in the PME or dissection. However, they should at all times operate under the direct supervision and instruction of the pathologist. A complete PME consists of a number of elements. This includes a primary examination by x-ray fluoroscopy or radiography within the body bag in which it was received (see 6.5.2). A full external examination of the body must be undertaken, including assessment of its mass and height and a description of the clothing and any other accompanying items. Appropriate examination of the skeletal and soft tissues should be undertaken and recorded. The PME must include the opening of all the major body cavities (cranial, thoracic, abdominal), as well as the spinal canal where necessary, and the inspection of the internal organs *in situ*. Where necessary, all internal organs may be removed, and their individual dissection and examination will be undertaken according to recognised dissection protocols. The judicious selection and collection will be undertaken of such specimens and samples as may be deemed necessary for special laboratory investigation. In all stages of the PME and subsequent analyses, appropriate or relevant negative findings should also be recorded.

In a PME, all external injuries must be noted on a sketch of the body, and all abnormal internal injuries or changes observed should be fully examined and accurately and fully recorded. Where appropriate, the mass of all organs, which appear to be abnormal in size, should be determined and noted, and all abnormal collections of fluid in the body should be accurately measured. Detailed notes of the findings should be made at the time of the examination. All relevant findings (including identifying features, injuries, significant disease features, relevant clothing features, and medical or therapeutic interventions) should be noted on the relevant recording forms. This will facilitate the compilation of a comprehensive report, contributing to the administration of justice. All procedures, body manipulations, and sampling procedures must be performed within a framework of dignity, respect, and care for the deceased. All tissues and organs should be returned to the body unless sampled for further specialist analysis.

Factors to determine at PME are considerable and most can only be undertaken where postmortem interval, condition, and completeness of remains facilitate such analyses.

6.3.2 Features contributing to the identification of the deceased

The establishment or verification of the identity of a body is one of the objectives of a medicolegal investigation and usually the primary objective of a humanitarian mission. Only fingerprints, DNA, or dental records are currently internationally accepted as primary identifiers. However, presumptive identification of an individual may be assessed by reconstruction using biological features, including such biological criteria as ancestry, biological sex, age at death, and living stature. Such investigations can be undertaken by the pathologist or anthropologist subject to the condition of the remains. Identification can also be facilitated by comparison of postmortem examination findings with antemortem records and information. Methods used for identification by comparison may include fingerprints; dental records, including radiographs; medical and laboratory records, including radiographs; photographs; clothing; and special identifying features on the body (e.g., tattoos, scars, implants, prostheses). Information about the place where death occurred (e.g., the scene of death or disposal), any personal documentation present on the body, or information from the investigating authority pertaining to the subsequent investigation may also be useful in establishing the identity of the deceased.

In investigations of genocide, war crimes, or crimes against humanity, it may be desirable to hand responsibility for identification of victims to an appropriate specialised agency (e.g., the International Committee of the Red Cross or the Disaster Victim Identification Committee of Interpol) to undertake the process of identification of individuals. In this case, all autopsy information, including DNA samples, will be handed to the external agency. This will be undertaken at the discretion of the project manager after consultation with relevant interested parties. It is likely when investigating mass graves that the identity of individuals will not be readily forthcoming or may form part of a large register. Bodies will therefore be unidentified as they are analysed. Photographs of the bodies may be a useful method of assisting in the identification of less decomposed remains.

The estimated postmortem interval may be established by working in conjunction with the taphonomy specialist and anthropologist, within the context of the archaeological findings. The decomposition of human remains in mass graves is complex (see Haglund, 2002) and generally contradicts criteria applied in traditional medicolegal investigations. Only rarely, in the investigative time frame that usually applies in the investigation of atrocity crimes, are more traditional pathology criteria (see Saukko and Knight, 2004, for an overview of this subject) of relevance. Where appropriate, development of secondary postmortem changes (e.g., hypostasis, rigor mortis, putrefaction, skeletonisation) will be recorded. It is important to note that eye colour (iridium) must not be used to assess identification because autolysis alters this, turning pale-coloured eyes dark after death (Saukko and Knight, 2004). Postmortem eye colour does not reflect eye colour in life (Gomez, 2005), and the rate of change is influenced by such factors as relative humidity and temperature. Hair colour can also alter postmortem with hair oxidising in some burial contexts (Rowe, 1997). If hair appears red or reddish, do not automatically assume that was the original hair colour.

A very approximate age of the deceased is initially estimated by the pathologist from the victim's general appearance. In the young, including newborn infants, radiographic examination is vital, and age may be determined from the appearance of appropriate ossification centres, as well dental and general development. It is likely that anthropological analysis will prove to be of most value in this respect. If the body is that of a newborn infant, it is imperative to record such factors as whether the child has been washed or not; whether the umbilical cord has been cut, torn, or tied; the circumference of the head; if relevant, the presence and position of a caput succedaneum; and the nature of any wrappings in which the body was found.

Stature and body mass are important contributors to identification. Body length should be measured in millimetres, centimeters, or metres, and the value must always be accompanied by the unit of measurement used (e.g., 35 mm, 16 cm, or 1.75 m). If possible, the mass of the body in kilograms should be determined, measured, or estimated by the pathologist from the general appearance of the deceased. The unit of measurement should always accompany the figure (e.g., 2.50 kg). If the mass is estimated, the word 'estimated' should be endorsed in brackets immediately after the mass. Where decomposition has taken place, this must be stated alongside an estimate of body mass. Where condition facilitates such, the pathologist will describe, in general terms, the physique (e.g., muscular, normal, or frail) and the nutritional status (e.g., fat, normal, or thin) of the body.

A description will be made of any special identifying features, including scars, tattoos, and deformities. If the body has not been positively identified, special attention should be paid to all possible identifying features, which should then be fully described, photographed, and, where appropriate, sketched on the aforementioned recording forms.

6.3.3 Establishing the cause and manner of death

The primary medical cause of death is determined solely from the postmortem findings. If more than one cause appears to have been operative, where possible, state first the immediate cause, then the secondary causes, and, finally, any contributory causes and make clear the relationship of these causes to each other. This has not always proved possible in mass grave contexts because often there are multiple wounds, and the degraded and fragmentary condition of the remains in mass grave contexts renders untangling sequence and impact difficult if not impossible (Clark, personal communication). When no soft tissue survives, consultation with the anthropologist should be made to determine any injury to the bone that occurred around the time of death. When the cause of death cannot be determined with reasonable certainty from the postmortem findings alone, the cause of death can be recorded as 'based on the postmortem findings alone, undetermined'. Later at the court proceedings, it may be possible to determine the cause of death from the postmortem findings considered alongside other relevant evidence or from the results of any special laboratory investigations that have been carried out.

All external injuries or abnormalities of the body and all injuries or abnormalities of the limbs, must be clearly, fully, and accurately described on the recording form. This will include information such as the precise anatomical location (so as to be able to pinpoint this at a later date) of features or lesions, a description of lesions using terminology that is unambiguous and descriptive, a record of the distribution of any lesion, their classification, and an interpretation of their significance stating the degree of confidence of that interpretation.

The accurate dimensions of all injuries must be recorded, and reference may also be made to any sketches or photographs that have been made of the body and that are enclosed with the report. Such sketches or photographs should include a record of the case number allocated to the deceased, the date of the PME, a short appropriate description, and the signature of the pathologist. As noted previously, it is imperative to also record, package, label, and preserve any foreign objects or material found on the body or in any wounds. The pathologist must obtain from the SCE an evidence number so the object can be entered into the chain of custody.

When the body of a person who has died as a consequence of firearm injuries is received at the mortuary, the clothing must not be taken off and the body must not be washed prior to the PME. It must be handled as little as possible to prevent the loss of any propellant that may be on the clothes. (See 6.3.5 for evidence collection.) A clear colour photograph of the wound must be taken (with a scale). After the preliminary examination by the pathologist, the clothes must be carefully removed from the body. The clothing must never be cut off the body. If appropriate to the investigation, and if the entry shot is through clothing, the air-dried clothing item must be placed in a clean, labeled paper bag, keeping the area around the entry shot flat (to avoid creasing) before being dispatched for gunshot residue analysis. The body, but not the wound and gunpowder marks, may now be washed. The wound must be washed in the presence of the pathologist. While the water flows gently over the wound, it must be sponged carefully. To prevent gunpowder from being wiped off, a cloth must not be used.

Colour photographs must be taken of the body and the wound, these photographs must be registered on the Mortuary Digital Image Log (MG06LD), and Mortuary Negative Film Photograph Log (MG06LN) and/or the Mortuary Cover Sheet (MG05). Details of the photographs must be cross-referenced with the appropriate body recording forms (MP31 or MP32).

Photographs must also be recorded in the case file, and the photographs stored as discussed in 4.4. The wound and gunpowder marks must be clearly visible on the photograph. A probe must be placed in the wound to indicate the depth of the wound. A measuring scale must be used to indicate the size of the wound.

A complete PME must be performed. The body must be completely dissected, and the path of the bullet must be determined. A probe may be used to indicate the depth and direction of the wound track, but only after proper documentation of the wound appearance, including photography, has been done. In the case of head wounds, the hair may only be shaved after initial examination by the pathologist and documentation as to the presence of singeing. The hair absorbs gunpowder and also indicates burn and scorch marks. Only in serious and essential cases must the skin that has gunpowder marks be excised for further gunshot residue analysis. (See 6.3.5 for correct sample handling.)

The SCE is responsible for cleaning, handling, documenting, and conserving all evidence, either themselves, or with the help of conservators or other specialists (see 4.3).

When examining intracranial contents, it is necessary to note any abnormal odour present when the cranial cavity is opened and examine carefully the intracranial contents. Remove the dura fully to examine the base of the skull. Examine the eyes. The cavities need only be examined if special indications to do so are present. The mouth, tongue, and pharynx, as well as all the air passages, should be examined for the presence of any foreign material, and if such material is present, a sample, if necessary should be taken to determine its nature. If there is any suspicion that constrictive force may have been applied to the neck, carry out (preferably in a bloodless field) a careful flap dissection exposing the soft tissues of the neck layer by layer. Care should be taken to differentiate between antemortem bruises that may be present and any local effusions of blood into the tissues as the result of dissection. Take specimens for histological examination, if appropriate.

Open all chambers of the heart. Dissect the coronary arteries, and cut into and inspect the myocardium. Remove the stomach and duodenum after tying the ends with ligatures, or clamping them with clamps, and open in a clean dish. Note the presence of any abnormal smell, colour, or substance, as well as the nature and state of digestion of any food and the condition of the mucous membrane.

In some cases of suspected poisoning, though it may sometimes be deemed unnecessary to forward the intestines for toxicological examination, they should always be carefully examined. The small intestine should be removed, after tying with ligatures at the duodenal and caecal ends, placed in a clean dish and opened by splitting along the antimesenteric border. After examination of the contents, the mucous membrane surface should be washed in running water and then carefully inspected. A similar technique may be used for examination of the large bowel. The distance from the stomach that food is discernible in the duodenum will be noted.

In females in whom it is suspected that rape or sexual assault has occurred, condition of the remains permitting, the vulva and vaginal entrance, including the hymen, if present, should be carefully inspected prior to dissection. It is occasionally necessary for the pelvic organs to be removed en masse. This may be accomplished by dissecting downward from the abdominal cavity outside the peritoneum and close to the pelvic wall, starting above the false pelvis and continuing down to the pelvic floor. Dissection should then be commenced upward, to join the incision made from above, from an elliptical incision around the vulva and anus. The pelvic organs can thus be removed in a single block. They may then be spread on a dissecting board, dissected, and examined individually. If a fetus is present in the uterus, its degree of maturity may be estimated from its length and the development of ossification centres. In cases of suspected recent rape or sexual assault, swabs should be taken from the mouth, genitalia, vaginal fornices, and cervix for microscopic examination for the presence of spermatozoa and DNA analysis. Any other biological evidence present on the clothing, hair, skin, or fingernails including pubic hair combings, dried semen, or saliva samples, must be collected together with a control blood sample for comparative DNA analysis. (Refer to instructions in specialized biological evidence collection kits referred to in 6.3.5.)

The spinal column must be examined for possible fractures and dislocations by inspection, palpation, and manipulation after removal of all internal organs. If injuries of the spine are present or such injuries are suspected and it is desired to examine them in more detail, the spine and spinal cord should be exposed from behind. An anterior approach may be easier after evisceration. The spinal canal need only be opened and the spinal cord examined if there are indicators for doing so (e.g., injury to the spinal column).

6.3.4 Guidelines on issuing death certificates

Although rarely relevant in mass grave investigations, a natural cause of death is defined as being where death is solely and exclusively the result of a natural disease process, not precipitated by trauma, anaesthetic, or therapeutic mishap. The cause of death is the primary medical cause of death (i.e., the disease, incident, or injury that set in motion the train of diseases or morbid events leading to death). For example, a person with a myocardial infarction resulting from atherosclerotic coronary artery disease will be certified as having died of ischaemic heart disease due to atherosclerotic coronary artery disease, but not myocardial infarction alone. The primary medical cause of death is not the physiological mechanism of death (i.e., do not certify death as being due to renal failure, heart failure, cardiorespiratory arrest, cardiac arrest, liver failure, haemorrhagic shock, etc.). The primary medical cause of death does not take into account the external nonmedical factors precipitating the disease.

Nonnatural causes of death would include any death due to an extrinsic factor causing the disease process or injury (e.g., accidental, homicidal, or suicidal injuries), or where a new factor (such as a surgical procedure or anaesthetic), precipitated death. Cases where death occurred due to natural causes, but where possible negligence, either deliberate or incidental, on the part of a person by act or omission may be present, are also classified as nonnatural. Contributing cause of death is not the primary medical cause of death, but the condition contributing to an early death (e.g., diabetes may be a contributing cause of death in a patient who dies as the result of multiple injuries sustained from a motor vehicle accident or a patient who dies as the result of pneumonia). The terminal cause of death should be distinguished from the primary medical cause of death. Where the patient dies of terminal bronchopneumonia after months on a ventilator due to a spinal injury sustained in a motor vehicle accident, the death is nonnatural, and the primary medical cause of death is cervical spinal injury. A more complex example might be where death is from occupational exposure to certain substances (e.g., mesothelioma caused by asbestos exposure and pneumoconiosis caused by coal dust exposure). These are conditions that, if there is no occupational exposure, are considered to be natural causes, but occupational circumstances are considered unnatural and meriting an inquest. In such a case as this, death is certified as mesothelioma due to asbestosis due to occupational asbestos exposure in a mine. It is the last line of the cause of death formulation that determines whether or not a case is natural.

6.3.5 Specimen collection and sampling

The pathologist must state the nature of specimens retained, the test requested, the seal number of the specimen container where applicable, and to whom the specimen was handed. It is the duty of the pathologist, in consultation with the SCE, to ensure the correct and appropriate specimen or sample selection, collection, and submission for special analyses. In most cases, the pathologist has only one opportunity to collect these specimens. Pathologists should be well informed about the nature and scope of specialist analyses. They must ensure that adequate packaging of specimens and samples is undertaken, for the purposes of preservation of the integrity of the specimen, as well as with regard to biosafety considerations and for legal/custodial purposes. Detailed records of special analyses that have been requested should be included in the report.

Autolytic and putrefactive changes may develop rapidly after death and may obscure important findings. Pathology specimens for histology, microscopy, microbiology, serology, viral, or biochemical tests should therefore be collected as soon as possible after death and recovery and preserved in suitable fixative. Histological examination is not often undertaken in mass grave investigations, but it can be of great diagnostic value in demonstrating macroscopic lesions, determining more precisely the nature of lesions, deciding the age of lesions, and confirming macroscopic diagnoses. Where it is undertaken, specimens should be carefully selected from affected areas, and be sufficiently large and representative of normal and abnormal areas (~20 × 20 mm). Sections should be cut in thin slices with flat parallel sides and be 5 to 7 mm thick. Be careful to avoid sections that are too thick because these will not absorb fixative properly, and the centre of these lesions may become autolytic. Handle the specimens gently to avoid tissue distortion and expression of fluids from the tissue. Place specimens in wide-mouthed containers with watertight closures (e.g., plastic specimen jars). Add sufficient fixative (approximately twice the volume of tissue). A suitable fixative is 10 percent buffered formaldehyde; never use alcohol as a tissue preservative because it hardens the tissues. In certain instances, special fixatives may be required and should only be used after consultation with the relevant laboratory.

Specimens for microbiological analysis, where indicated, should be taken as soon as possible after recovery using aseptic techniques. Suitable material from organs should be collected by inserting a cotton wool swab into the organ through a sterile incision or taking a small tissue block (approximately 1 cm^3). A sterile incision in an organ can be produced by searing the surface of the organ with a heated metal object such as a knife, and then incising the area with a sterile scalpel blade. Fluid (e.g., blood, cerebrospinal fluid, effusions, pus) for microbiological examination should be aseptically collected into culture bottles, both aerobic and anaerobic.

Where the identity of the deceased has not been adequately or scientifically established, the following tissue specimens may be harvested: blood, bone (e.g., rib), muscle, or teeth. Virtually any biological material can be used for DNA analysis, if required (see 9.3). Because of the profound biochemical changes that occur in the body during the postmortem period, many biochemical tests of proven clinical diagnostic value in the living are of no definite diagnostic value when performed on postmortem specimens.

All containers used for specimens and samples must be chemically clean, and all those used for microbiological specimens must be sterile. Suitable types and quantities of containers for the various types of specimens (histological, microbiological, and biochemical) must be available in all mortuary facilities. When international missions are in isolated locations, containers should be procured in the UK or from the closest supplier to the mission area and transported to the mortuary. It is useful, however, to determine where containers are to be procured locally if a shortage is encountered. Clear and full labelling of specimen containers is imperative. Clearly label all containers of specimens for special laboratory examination for medicolegal purposes with the following particulars at the time the specimens are collected: site code and case number, sample number, nature of the sample, date of its collection, nature of investigation required, and name and signature of the responsible person.

Secure the seals on the containers firmly to prevent any leakage of contents. Pack each container in a stout cardboard, wooden, or metal box of suitable size that has been surrounded by sufficient cotton wool to minimise the chances of breakage during transit and to effectively absorb any escaped fluid if breakage does occur. All containers must be placed in exhibit bags before they are transferred to the laboratory. Secure the lid of the box firmly, wrap the box in stout brown paper, and effectively fix with string or adhesive packaging tape. The necessary biohazard warning label should be attached. Every specimen or set of specimens forwarded to a forensic chemistry laboratory for toxicological examination for medicolegal purposes in connection with a death must be accompanied, *inter alia*, by forms that have been fully completed by the pathologist who performed the PME for humanitarian cases and by the SCE in legal cases. Because it is impossible to be sure that an investigation originally undertaken for humanitarian purposes may not ultimately be of judicial relevance, we recommend that the SCE always complete the form. For more information on sample collection and handling, see Chapter 9. For specimens for toxicological analysis in cases of suspected fatal poisoning, the decision as to whether specimens are to be submitted for toxicological analysis should depend on a careful assessment of all available facts in respect to the death.

When selecting material for toxicological analysis, where poison is ingested and is absorbed from the stomach and upper portions of the small intestine, it is metabolised in the liver and is chiefly eliminated through the kidneys into the urine. The following specimens should routinely be submitted for analysis: blood (clotted 10–50 ml), the stomach and its contents, the liver (without the gallbladder), bile, kidneys, and urine. Perinephric fat may be collected for chemical analysis for substances such as butane.

Other specimens may be submitted in addition to those listed previously, depending on the circumstances. These can include specimens found at the scene indicating the type of poison. Subject to preservation and unlikely in mass grave contexts, vomiting is often an early sign of poisoning, and much of the poison that has been taken may be ejected in the vomitus in an unaltered form. Analysis of the vomitus may thus afford useful information as to whether poison was ingested and, if so, in what form. Only material vomited at a relatively early stage of the attack is likely to contain significant amounts of poison, and later specimens of material obtained at the end of repeated bouts of vomiting may show little or no poison. Stomach washings that are collected shortly after the onset of symptoms may also be of value in the detection of poisoning. Poisons are frequently concentrated and excreted in the urine, from which they may be readily isolated and identified. If upon PME the bladder is found to contain an appreciable amount of urine, this urine should be collected for analysis. In cases in which the principal action of the poison is on the nervous system (e.g., barbiturates), it may be desirable to submit the brain for analysis. Where cases of suspected carbon monoxide poisoning exist, blood should be submitted for carboxyhaemoglobin analysis. When arsenic poisoning is suspected, hair and nail specimens should be submitted in addition to the routine specimens mentioned previously. In cases of heavy metal poisoning, some of the poison may be excreted by the colon and cause erosions of its mucous membrane. In such cases, the intestines should always be removed and opened at PME, and their contents and mucous membrane surfaces should be carefully inspected for the presence of any abnormalities or lesions. Drugs or poisons may be administered by sniffing or injection into the subcutaneous tissues, muscles, or genital tract in cases of abortion. In such cases, the appropriate tissues or organ should be submitted for analysis. In all cases of suspected poisoning, due consideration should be given to taking specimens for histological examination.

Every mortuary should possess one or more toxicology boxes. They are large wooden boxes, each of which is packed with one large earthenware or plastic jar, one small earthenware or plastic jar, one 200-ml bottle, one 100-ml bottle, one 50-ml bottle, and one small 100-ml wide-mouthed jar. Before the boxes are issued by the relevant laboratory, the containers in them are chemically cleaned. An appropriate amount of sodium fluoride is also added to the 50-ml and 200-ml bottles (intended for blood and urine specimens, respectively) as an antienzymatic preservative agent. After the containers have been placed in the box, the lids are sealed at the laboratory with the official laboratory seal. Before a box is opened for the receipt of specimens, the seals should be inspected by the pathologist, and only boxes with intact seals should be used for packing toxicological specimens. The intact seals are evidence of the fact that the containers inside the box have been properly prepared for the receipt of specimens. The stomach and its contents should be placed in the small earthenware or plastic jar and the liver and kidneys in the large earthenware or plastic jar. The liver and other organs may be divided into several pieces to facilitate their placement in and removal from the jar. If other organs are to be sent for analysis, the small toxicology box may be opened and its jar used for the extra specimens. Urine specimen is transferred to the 200-ml bottle. If possible, fill the bottle. Blood specimen is transferred to the 50-ml bottle; shake well to dissolve the fluoride. Hair samples are packed in the 100-ml jar without any preservative, and nails are packed in an envelope.

The pathologist who conducted the PME is responsible for packing the specimens obtained at PME and adding the preservative. The SCE is responsible for the sealing, labelling, and dispatching of the specimens. As soon as written authority for a toxicological examination is received, the sealed box containing the specimens should be delivered to the approved forensic chemistry laboratory by the SCE.

At PMEs of cases where a firearm has been involved, the bullet is valuable evidence. When bullets or projectile fragments are found or removed from the deceased, their integrity must be maintained for successful subsequent ballistic investigations (Di Maio, 1999). Standard metal instruments such as forceps can scratch the jacket or lead of the bullet, producing marks that could hamper or prevent analysis of bullet striations and thus firearm identification. Russell et al. (1995) suggested using a 'bullet extractor' to accomplish the dual purpose of safe handling (in the case of bullets with jagged projections and sharp edges) and evidence preservation. The bullet extractor could be a standard artery forceps fitted with lengths of rubber as protective tips. The retrieved projectile should be examined for macroscopic trace evidence such as fibres and glass. If none is found, the projectile may be gently rinsed to remove excess blood or body fluids and then dried before wrapping in acid-free tissue paper and packaging in a bullet envelope or plastic container (ibid.). To scientifically demonstrate the presence or absence of powder in cases of suspected short-range shots, the skin portion surrounding the entrance wound ($\pm40 \times 40$ mm) must be excised. It is important to state to what degree clothing may have interfered with the transfer of powder. The skin sample must be packed as follows: It must not be placed in a preservative, but should be tautened, placed in a plastic container, and entered into the chain of evidence. It must then be stored in a secure freezer and not in a refrigerator. Alternatively, if a freezer is not available, a piece of cotton wool moistened (not soaked) with a few drops of formalin must be placed on the base of a sample container with a piece of dry gauze over it. The skin sample must be placed on top of this layer of gauze with the outer surface of the skin facing upwards and then secured with another piece of gauze over it, before closing the sample container. No further formalin should be added to the container. In the event of powder transfer onto an article of clothing, the article must be placed flat in a paper bag and sent to the laboratory after it has been allowed to air dry. (See 6.3.3.)

With biological samples, if the biological unit of the external laboratory has a standard specialised sampling kit available for the taking of samples, these should be procured before a mission and used as appropriate. Such kits should contain the necessary information and instructions for taking blood, semen, sputum, and hair samples for determining the identity and the connection of such samples to an individual.

6.3.6 Body and specimen/sample storage

Operational practice should ensure that all work with bodies, organs, and fixed and unfixed specimens is strictly limited to the 'wet' activity areas. Bodies and body parts will normally be stored in a refrigeration facility (body store) at a temperature of 4°C (Health and Safety Executive, 2003). However, in practice, a temperature of 6°C to 10°C is more appropriate. The body store should have adequate space to provide respectful storage of the remains, and ideally, there should be direct access to the PME room. Storage compartments should be designed to be easily accessible for the movement of bodies and for regular cleaning and maintenance.

Specimens and samples should be brought out of the postmortem room only in suitable containers after having undergone appropriate decontamination. They should be surface cleaned, wiped down with disinfectant, and stored in the designated area. If possible, a separate room or area should be set aside for the storage of organs and body tissues in fixative, usually formalin. The room should be provided with adequate and secure storage space. The room must be ventilated to ensure that concentrations of fixative vapour do not exceed the permitted levels (maximum exposure limit for formaldehyde is 2 ppm for any period of exposure). Mechanical ventilation would be the preferred option. If adequate ventilation is not achieved or achievable, then the appropriate respirator should be worn when entering this area. A warning notice should be posted on the specimen store door, alerting staff that they should not enter without the appropriate protective clothing.

6.4 Role and responsibilities of the anatomical pathology technologist

6.4.1 Medicolegal duties

As far as postmortems and the medicolegal work in mortuaries are concerned, APTs function directly under the supervision of the senior pathologist. When a body is received at a mortuary, the APT, working with the senior SCE, has responsibility for the remains and all associated property and evidence by signing the Mortuary Evidence Log as indicated in 6.2. The APT will arrange for a primary radiography survey to be undertaken on all incoming bodies (see 6.5.2). In cases where the pathologist has not seen the body prior to its receipt at the mortuary, the body and clothing must be left in the same condition as when they were received, until the pathologist starts the PME. This procedure is of the utmost importance for reasons outlined previously.

The duties of the APT are varied and of extreme importance. These include the enforcement of mortuary cleanliness and, in particular, the dissecting rooms and storage facilities. The APT is also responsible for cleaning, and disinfecting or sterilising postmortem instruments before, during, and after a postmortem and for the enforcement of health and safety procedures within the mortuary facility. He or she must ensure that reusable protective clothing such as boots are cleaned by personnel on removal. The APT is also responsible for receiving, collecting, inspecting, identifying, and storing the bodies, as well as all administrative duties and upkeep of the prescribed registers and forms. The SCE is responsible for all possessions and other exhibits (e.g., related to cause of death or evidence of coercion). The APT prepares bodies for PME, helps with the preliminary work (including the measuring and weighing of a body), and supplies all information at his or her disposal regarding the death to the pathologist. The APT assists with the examination of the body and the PME at the direction of the pathologist. He or she should prepare the dissecting room (including instruments and containers) for a PME, and ensure that all instruments are available and that they are clean, sharp, and ready to use. The APT must ensure that all supplies needed for the smooth running of the mortuary are in stock, that replacements are anticipated and ordered, that there is an adequate supply of basic protective clothing both for staff and visitors, and that there is an adequate supply of all consumables (e.g., waterproof aprons, gloves, masks) available throughout the day. He or she must ensure that sufficient containers and preservatives are available for specimens earmarked for pathological and toxic examination, and that all labelling, weighing, and so on is correct. The APT is responsible for the specimens of tissue and fluids earmarked for laboratory analysis and for closing, cleaning, and preparing bodies to be handed over to the relevant authority or family for burial or cremation. He or she must also ensure that the registers and forms, which must be completed by the pathologist who performs the postmortem, are available.

6.4.2   Reconstruction of the body

If appropriate to an investigation, the reconstruction of a body can be an important aspect of medicolegal work in the mortuary. It is a duty that is performed by the APT. The closing of a body is an art that can only be perfected by practice and experience. The quality of craftsmanship reflects the total competence and skill with which the duties at the mortuary are performed. There are various important points to remember following a PME. After the PME and before a body is closed, all fluids in the body cavities and skull must be drained as much as possible. Cotton wool must be placed in the pelvis and throat cavity to prevent the loss of any fluids that remain within the cavities. All organs that are not required for further examination must be placed in a plastic bag and returned to the body before closing. If the breastbone (sternum) is removed and cannot be replaced in position because the respiratory organs have been removed, it must first be joined to the ribs on either side before the skin is closed over the breastbone. Incisions in the skin are closed from the outside and from the opposite direction to that from which it was made (e.g., from the pubic area to chin so the primary incision is left until last). Postmortem twine (twine made of twisted linen threads) should be used to close the body, and this must be long enough to ensure that it does not have to be joined. The skin must be pulled tightly (first from the one side and then from the other) with one hand, and the needle must always be passed through the skin from the inside to the outside. The stitches must be pulled tightly and must not be more than 13 mm apart. This method ensures that the incision is closed tightly, that the area is smooth, and that it has a neat appearance. If the loose section of the skull does not fit properly, it must first be joined to the main section of the skull before the skin is closed over it. If necessary, small holes can be made in both sections and then tied together with wire or string.

6.4.3   Viewing for identification purposes

Most human remains from mass grave investigations will not be in a sufficient state of preservation to allow for visual identification, so the procedures that follow may not be necessary and the body can be returned directly to the storage facility. However, these procedures should be followed if human remains will be viewed by relatives or witnesses for identification purposes after the PME. After the body has been closed, it must be washed with water, dried, and transferred onto a clean sheet/shroud laid over a stretcher or trolley. The eyelids must be closed and pieces of cotton wool can be placed under the lids to help maintain them so. The arms must be in a vertical position next to the body and, if necessary, the hands can be placed under the hips to keep the arms in position. Before a body on which a PME has been performed is laid out for identification, it must be ensured that the body is properly sewn up and prepared in such a way that it will not cause offence. The body must be covered with a clean sheet so only the face is exposed.

Public relations are of the utmost importance, and care should be taken that the wishes and requests of the community or family should, as far as possible, be met. In the unlikely event that identification of victims is to be attempted by viewing, it must be remembered that identification witnesses are usually under tremendous emotional stress. Personnel on duty at mortuaries should ensure that mortuaries, and specifically the identification rooms, are always neat and tidy. If possible, there should be ample seating for witnesses, and fresh drinking water and toilet facilities should always be available. Personnel must be aware that next of kin/identification witnesses may be within hearing distance and, therefore, the utmost dignity and respect is expected at all times. To identify a loved one is an emotional and traumatic experience, and professional conduct is expected at all times from all personnel involved.

If viewing remains within the mortuary facility is appropriate and practically possible, access to the waiting room should be via a direct route from the outside of the building. Visitors should not have to enter other parts of the mortuary to reach the waiting room. If possible, the waiting room should have direct access to a viewing room from which the deceased can easily be seen. There should be means of access between the viewing room and the deceased to allow relatives to be close to the body if they so wish. However, contact with the body should only be allowed after the PME has been finalized, because of the risk of evidentiary contamination prior to collection during the PME. Families should be informed that contact restrictions will not apply once the body has been released. The mortuary manager should, however, advise relatives as to whether there is any health risk for them if they want to touch the body after completion of the PME. If the risks are considered to be significant, relatives should be actively discouraged from doing so. It will also be the mortuary manager's responsibility to ensure that the viewing room is cleaned as appropriate after visits and use. Visitors who have had physical contact with a body must be encouraged to wash their hands thoroughly before leaving the mortuary. If possible, a washbasin should be provided in the toilet adjacent to the viewing room or some alternative made available. If an observation area cannot be provided, observers may be allowed to enter the postmortem room, but they will first be required to put on appropriate protective clothing for the dual purpose of protecting themselves and preserving any forensic evidence. Where they will be allowed to stand and what clothing they must put on will be determined by the senior pathologist in relation to the local safe operating procedures and the potential level of risk.

6.4.4 Skeletonised remains

The APT will be responsible for preparing skeletonised remains for examination by the pathologist and the anthropologist. Skeletal remains should undergo primary radiographic survey, which will usually consist of the thorax and cranium, clothing, and any area of the body indicated by the field team as having fractures or firearm projectile injuries associated with it. This is important to remember if and when the APT is washing the skeletonised remains because small fragments are easily lost.

Small bones/bone fragments should be carefully placed in a colander and washed gently. The APT, after washing the bones (see 7.2.1 for details), should place them on the examination table, where they can assist the anthropologist to lay out the bones in anatomical order.

6.5   Role and responsibilities of the forensic radiographer

6.5.1   Personnel

The forensic radiographer must be a qualified, state-registered diagnostic radiographer with additional postgraduate training and/or experience in the medicolegal aspects of radiography. Diagnostic radiographers will have differing levels of experience in specialised techniques (e.g., dental radiography, skeletal image reporting), and the decision regarding the need for such specific skills should be agreed by the assessment group taking into account the advice of the senior radiographer involved. The radiologist must be a qualified, registered medical practitioner with formal postgraduate training and experience in the interpretation of radiographic and other medical images. Specialist radiological opinion will only be required by the pathologist, anthropologist, or odontologist in a small number of cases and can usually be sought remotely (by transmission of film or digital images).

These SOPs apply to the fluoroscopic and radiographic examination of cadavers and skeletal remains as part of the PME and identification procedures. The procedures will apply both to the examination of the remains of single and multiple individuals, both as part of forensic investigations and/or identification of the deceased. These procedures may be adapted to suit the specific requirements of the investigation in consultation with the senior pathologist. All x-ray examinations will be conducted in accordance with *Guidance for the Provision of Forensic Radiography Services* (The College of Radiographers, 1999) and local radiation rules conforming with prevailing national radiation regulations, or in the absence of such national regulations, the International Atomic Energy Agency (IAEA) basic safety standards (IAEA, 2004). The local radiation rules will be authorised by a qualified medical radiation physicist appointed as radiation protection advisor, and a senior radiographer will be designated as radiation protection supervisor (see 3.2 for details).

6.5.2   Examination procedure

Radiological examination of human remains may be undertaken in three phases as an integral part of the autopsy procedure: a primary survey; a secondary survey, which may include, or be limited to an odontological survey; and a tertiary examination of specific areas.

The primary survey will be undertaken in all cases. The purpose of the primary survey is to establish the nature of the remains contained within the body bag; check for unexploded ordnance; identify metallic and other artefacts; and identify

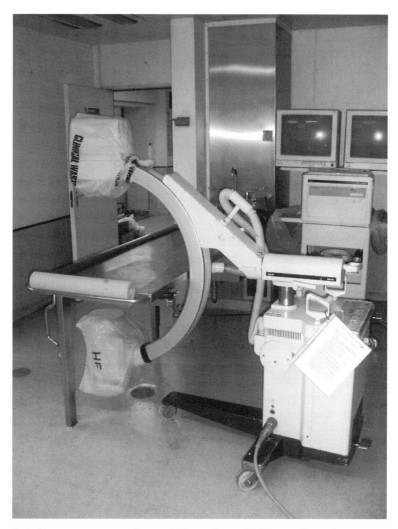

Figure 6–1. Fluoroscope c-arm for use in forensic work. *Source:* Xograph.

and accurately locate bullets, shrapnel, and other projectiles. Any unique identifying features seen during the primary survey (e.g., dental treatment, previously healed fractures, or congenital abnormalities) will be noted for further radiological investigation as a tertiary examination.

Wherever possible, the primary survey will be undertaken by means of fluoroscopy, either with a mobile c-arm image intensifier (Figure 6–1) or fixed installation fluoroscopy unit. In the absence of fluoroscopy, a series of 35.43-cm radiographs (either digital or film) will be taken, covering the entire area of the body bag.

The primary survey examination of human remains while still in a body bag will be undertaken by the radiographer, either operating with a forensic pathologist or anthropologist or with another radiographer or technician as circumstances dictate. The fluoroscopic survey will cover the entire area of the body bag and its contents.

The position of projectiles will be noted in relation to adjacent anatomical structures wherever possible, and a permanent record will be taken. This may be in the form of a thermal printout, conventional radiograph, or digital radiograph that is then stored on electronic media. For forensic cases, and where required by the pathologist, a film or paper print, or digital image file, must be made for inclusion in the postmortem report. Any possible identifying features will be recorded on the primary survey record sheet for further examination.

In the case of skeletonised remains, the penetrating power of the radiation will be low, due to the density of many of the objects being examined. This increases the potential radiation skin dose to operators. It is thus imperative that hands are kept away from the x-ray beam during fluoroscopy. If it is necessary to locate metallic artefacts, a long radiopaque probe should be used. This will require careful coordination between radiographer and pathologist to ensure that their hands are not accidentally exposed to radiation. Fluoroscopy times must be kept to a minimum. Prior to considerable time being spent attempting to locate or remove tiny fragments of metal, a check should be made with the senior pathologist to ensure that these will be essential to the case. If not, an image can be taken to show findings. A Radiographic Survey Form (MR22) will be completed by the radiographer and pathologist for each case. Exposure factors, radiation dose, screening time, and number of images taken will be recorded in the Radiation Dose Record (MR21) and details of the examination and images taken should be recorded on the Radiography Log (MR23) within the x-ray room.

The purpose of the secondary survey is to acquire standard radiographic information that may be used to determine the identity of the deceased. The need for a secondary survey and the exact imaging examinations to be undertaken will be established for each investigation by the senior radiographer in consultation with the senior pathologist, senior anthropologist, and odontologist. If dental surveys are required, the deployment of suitably experienced dental radiographers will be necessary. Because radiographs obtained as part of the secondary survey may be compared with antemortem records, it is important that standard projections are used, and that exposure factors replicate as closely as possible those that would have been used to take antemortem images. For this reason, the secondary survey should take place after the cadaver or remains have been cleaned, all clothing and artefacts have been removed, and the body has been examined by the pathologist. All radiographs must be uniquely identified with case number, date of examination, location, radiographer's initials, witnesses' initials, either electronically at the time of exposure (for digital images), or by using an actinic marker or other photographic method prior to development (for film images). All images should show the correct anatomical marker using lead or other radiopaque 'Left' and 'Right' markers in the primary beam at the time of exposure.

A standard survey series of dental and/or skeletal radiographs may be undertaken at this stage, and a suggested series is outlined in Table 6–1. However, this sequence is not necessarily appropriate in all contexts, and it is suggested that, generally, only dentition and the chest region should be x-rayed because these are the areas

Table 6–1. *Standard skeletal and dental radiograph series*

Skeletal survey		Dental survey
Skull	OF 20	L & R lateral obliques of mandible
	Lat	L & R bitewing views
	OM	Periapical views of all other teeth areas
AP chest		
AP abdomen		
AP pelvis		
Lat C spine		
Lat T spine		
Lat L spine		
AP humerus	left & right	
AP radius & ulna	left & right	
DP hand	left & right	
AP femur	left & right	
AP tibia & fibula	left & right	
DP foot	left & right	

most commonly x-rayed in a clinical context. If the context demands a different series, this should be discussed between the senior forensic radiographer, pathologist, anthropologist, and/or odontologist. In some cases, it may be appropriate to conduct a limited secondary survey in cases where systematic antemortem abuse or trauma is suspected (e.g., to show healing rib fractures).

Tertiary examinations may be undertaken in specific cases where it is considered that additional radiographic information may be of benefit to the investigation. The purpose of the tertiary survey is to undertake specific examinations to record particular injuries or other pathology, establish the path of projectiles, record unique identifying features, or supply other supplementary information as required by the investigating team. The need for such examinations will be established either during the primary survey (where abnormalities may be noted) or at autopsy. The precise nature of the examination to be undertaken will be determined by the pathologist, anthropologist, and/or odontologist in charge of the case, in consultation with the radiographer. In the case of antemortem fractures or surgical intervention, antero-posterior and lateral radiographs should be taken to cover the area of interest.

6.5.3 Equipment and storage

The use of appropriate equipment and the correct storage of the resulting medium and records are always vital to the success of any process. Primary surveys should be conducted using a fluoroscope or direct digital x-ray machine wherever possible. Hard copy images from the fluoroscopy primary survey should be printed on thermal paper or provided as a digital file for inclusion in the pathology report. A digital copy should be retained where possible and stored according to organisational or commissioning agency policy. Secondary dental surveys should be undertaken using a specialist dental x-ray tube and digital dental x-ray receptor where possible. Failing this, D-speed intraoral and occlusal film and high-definition 18.24 film/screen

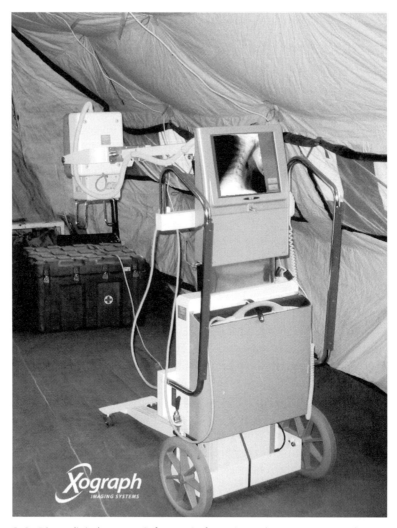

Figure 6–2. Direct digital x-ray unit for use in forensic work. *Source:* Xograph.

combinations will be required. Films should be numbered and retained as part of the odontology report. Digital images should be retained where possible and stored appropriately (see 4.5). Secondary and tertiary radiography surveys should be undertaken using a portable x-ray machine with maximum focal spot size of 1.0 mm. Direct digital technology should be employed wherever possible (see Figure 6–2). Failing this, fast (400-speed) and high-definition (200-speed) film screen combinations in all standard sizes (18.24, 24.30, 30.40, 35.43) will be required. Films should be numbered and recorded as items of evidence following completion of the pathology report. Digital images should be retained and stored appropriately (see 4.5).

If digital technology is not available, on-site film processing will be required (Figures 6–3 and 6–4). A field-deployable, large-film x-ray processor, dental processor,

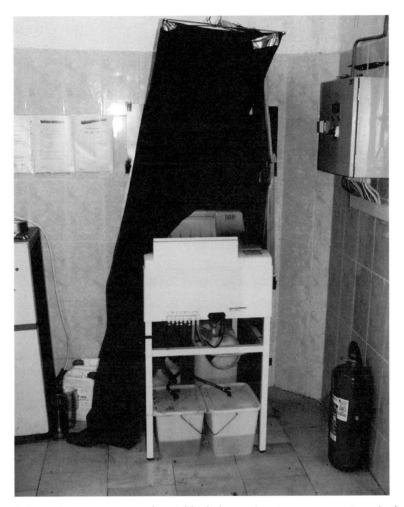

Figure 6–3. Desktop processor and portable darkroom in a temporary mortuary in the Former Yugoslavia. *Source:* Mark Viner.

and darkroom tent should be considered as standard equipment. The radiographer will be responsible for installing, commissioning, using, replenishing, cleaning, and decommissioning the processing equipment, and ensuring the quality of the development process. In extreme circumstances, manual processing may be deployed. In such cases, this should be agreed prior to the commencement of the mission as specialist radiographic expertise will be required.

6.5.4 Recording

A number of records will be made during this process. The Open Dissecting Postmortem Examination Body Part Recording Form (MR22) will be completed for each primary survey undertaken. These sheets will form part of the health and

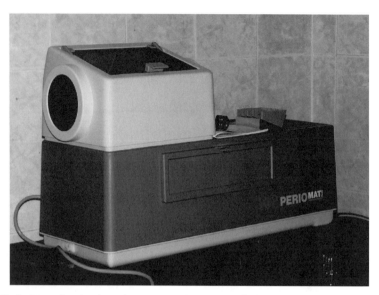

Figure 6–4. Example of a dental processor. *Source:* Mark Viner.

safety and workflow control record of the operation and will not be a direct part of the medicolegal investigation. The Radiography Log (MR23) and the Radiation Dose Record (MR21), will be completed for each primary or secondary survey, or tertiary radiography examination undertaken. These sheets will also form part of the health and safety and workflow control record of the operation and will not be a direct part of the medicolegal investigation. The Primary Survey sheets of the Radiographic Survey Form (MR22) will be completed for each primary survey undertaken. These sheets will be passed to the pathologist at the end of the primary survey and will form part of the postmortem report. The Secondary Survey sheets of the Radiographic Survey Form (MR22) will be completed for each secondary survey undertaken. These sheets will be passed to the pathologist or odontologist at the end of the survey and will form part of the postmortem report. The Tertiary Survey sheets of the Radiographic Survey Form (MR22) will be completed for each tertiary survey undertaken. These sheets will be passed to the pathologist, odontologist, or anthropologist at the end of the survey and will form part of the postmortem report.

6.6 Documentation and recording: Mortuary forms and logs

Postmortem recording forms are the Open Dissecting Post-mortem Examination Body Recording Form (MP31) and the Open Dissecting Post-mortem Examination Body Part Recording Form (MP32). As appropriate, one of these forms must be completed during the PME. A written report will be compiled as soon as reasonably possible after the examination from notes on the recording form that were made at the time of the examination. It is essential to preserve all notes because they

Table 6–2. *Radiology, pathology, and general mortuary recording forms*

Code	Forms and logs
MG01	Booking In Form
MG02	Health and Safety Risk Assessment
MG04	Mortuary Handover Form
MG05	Mortuary Cover Sheet
MG06LD	Mortuary Digital Image Log
MG06LN	Mortuary Negative Film Photograph Log
MG07	Mortuary Personnel Entry Register
MP31	Open Dissecting Post-mortem Examination Body Recording Form
MP32	Open Dissecting Post-mortem Examination Body Part Recording Form
MR21	Radiation Dose Record
MR22	Radiographic Survey Form
MR23	Radiography Log

may be required at a later stage. The recording form is divided into the following sections: case summary, PME records, clothing and personal effects, external examination, trauma and injuries, postmortem change, diagrams, internal examination, implanted devices and objects, specimens retained, notes on overall findings and interpretation, and cause of death. If the space allotted on the form is insufficient, additional description and/or sketches can be made on an analytical notes page. This separate page will display the site and case number, date, name, and signature of the pathologist. The page must also contain the section in the text to which it refers (e.g., skin). Similarly, a reference to this page must be made in the main body of the report (e.g., 'see attached analytical notes'). A list of relevant forms for use in the mortuary is shown in Table 6–2.

The pathologist will compile a comprehensive report for each case; these must be as detailed as possible. This report will be typed, and the pathologist will read the typed version and sign the document if satisfied it is an accurate version of the handwritten report. The report must contain a description of all injuries, abnormalities, and relevant negative findings. The observations should be brief but complete, accurate, and clear, using nontechnical terms as far as possible. Where there is no accurate nontechnical term, the technical term can be used, but should be followed by its meaning in brackets. Measurements and dimensions of injuries, the mass or measurements of all organs that appear abnormal in size, and the measurement of all abnormal collections of fluid should be included in this report. If a particular organ or tissue is not examined, 'not examined' must be clearly stated under the relevant heading so a false impression that a complete examination was performed is not created when only a limited or partial dissection was performed. When an organ or part appears normal, a brief description of the appearance of the organ is still necessary. Stating 'nothing abnormal detected' will not suffice. When an injury involves several organs or parts, it may be desirable to give a complete description of the injuries under one heading and to refer to the corresponding external injury description under following the headings (e.g., 'as described under paragraph 4').

The pathologist and other specialists may only discuss the findings of the PME and their significance with the following specified individuals. Clearly, they can communicate with those from whom they may officially seek advice or assistance in the investigation of the case (e.g., the anthropologist, odontologist, or specialist to whom specimens may be sent for special investigation). They can also communicate with those who are officially concerned with the investigation (e.g., the investigating officer of the relevant investigating authority), those who are officially concerned on behalf of the relevant governing authority in presenting the evidence before a court (e.g., the prosecutor), and other relevant official bodies. No copies of any recording forms, reports, or any other information concerning the PME may be divulged to any other person. It is important to note that private attorneys, family members, and insurance companies do not represent official bodies and must obtain a copy of the report via the relevant legal authority.

7

Mortuary procedures II – Skeletal analysis I: Basic procedures and demographic assessment

Caroline Barker, Margaret Cox, Ambika Flavel, Joanna Laver, and Louise Loe

7.1 Introduction

The purpose of examining skeletal remains from a forensic context is to assist in establishing the identification of the individual, or group of individuals, and, where possible, to establish cause and manner of death. The role of physical anthropology in both areas is limited, and the anthropologist is part of a larger team of specialists. It should be remembered that when attempting to identify individuals, anthropological analysis used in conjunction with antemortem data rarely produces an accurate identification (<40 percent in the Former Yugoslavia) (Simmons and Skinner, 2006). Such an approach rarely determines a positive identification. What it can do, however, is help construct a shortlist of possible identities and act as an exclusionary tool from which more specific and accurate tools such as DNA analysis can be used to establish a positive identification. In this respect, the wide confidence limits that are inherent with many aspects of anthropological analysis (e.g., age at death, stature estimation) can be both helpful and unhelpful.

Anthropological analysis is a component of a broad spectrum of approaches used to assess identification. The contribution of the anthropologist to such analysis supplements that of other specialists such as the pathologist, molecular biologist (where DNA analysis is undertaken), radiographer, and odontologist. The relative importance of anthropological input will vary according to the condition and completeness of the skeletal remains and the availability of resources for DNA analysis. In cases of fleshed, saponified, or mummified remains, a partial or parallel anthropological examination may be requested by the pathologist. In such cases, defleshing relevant areas of the remains may be necessary.

If resources permit, full analysis is expected in all investigations where skeletal remains are brought to the laboratory. Where resources are scarce, it may be that some aspects of the suite of approaches discussed in this chapter may be omitted in favour of those contributing to the specific information required to meet the aims and objectives of the investigation. Such an approach raises ethical issues and will lead to understandable dissatisfaction for surviving relatives. This is exemplified in the following quote: "In criminal cases involving genocide and crimes against humanity, the *ad hoc* international tribunals have placed greater emphasis on 'categorical identification' as opposed to 'personal identification' of victims. This approach has created a tension between the humanitarian needs of families of the missing and the evidentiary needs and mandate of international war crimes tribunals. On the one side are the families who wish to know the fate of their missing relatives and, if they have died, to receive their remains. On the other side are the *ad hoc* tribunals that have lacked the resources to undertake forensic investigations aimed at identifying all of the dead" (Human Rights Watch, 2004, http://www.hrw.org/reports/2004/iraq1104/4.htm).

The anthropology component of Section II of this book is extensive, and for ease of use, it has been split into two separate chapters. This chapter covers basic processes and demographic assessment, while Chapter 8 addresses other individuating criteria and criteria that contribute to understanding cause and manner of death. These chapters outline standard procedures for the analysis of skeletal tissue recovered as a result of single, multiple, or mass grave excavations. Where information is readily available elsewhere, we refer the reader to that text; where information is crucial to the analysis or not published in standard texts, it is included here as much as possible. Equally, where we consider inappropriate methods are used or appropriate methods underused, attention is paid to those areas. These chapters cover examination processes for skeletal remains recovered in both judicial and humanitarian operations. They are divided into sections reflecting the various types of analyses, and they are presented in the sequence in which it is advised that analysis of skeletal material should be undertaken. Anthropological analysis should follow a logical order with subsequent analyses being informed by the results of preceding methodological phases. When recording and reporting the results of analysis, it is important to use terminology appropriately. The term 'accuracy' is the degree to which an estimate conforms to reality, and 'precision' is the degree of refinement with which an estimate can be made (White and Folkens, 2005). Following this sequence allows the process of analysis to be standardised, leaving less room for inadvertent omission. The recording forms and logs relevant to this chapter are located on the accompanying CD, and guidance for their use is situated in 1.11.

Anthropological assessments will primarily be undertaken in a suitably equipped mortuary or laboratory facility. External factors may occasionally require assessments to be conducted in a field setting. In such cases, analytical notes, documentary photographs, and reported results will indicate and describe the circumstances that required skeletal analysis to be conducted outside the mortuary setting (see 5.6). Where anthropological assessments are undertaken in the field, the sections that follow can be used independently as appropriate, using the relevant recording forms (MA41F–MA46F).

At the outset of a mission, the mortuary management team (MMT) will decide which suite of analytical and investigative methods will be employed. However, in the mortuary or laboratory setting, it is possible to encounter circumstances that preclude the application of some procedures (e.g., collection of DNA samples, assessment of ancestry), and in such cases, the senior anthropologist will confer with the MMT to devise alternative procedures. These will be described and explained in the analytical notes and in the final report. This chapter is intended to provide an anthropologist with much of the information needed for effective analysis. We have, however, not replicated basic information that is described in other texts, except that which is crucial to the work with which we are concerned. Important reference works should be available within the mortuary, and it is suggested that charts, tables, and keys are reproduced on laminated card for ease of use and cleaning. Suggested reference collections and texts are provided in the text.

In these two chapters, we use the term 'skeletal remains' to describe skeletal and dental elements that have been identified as human. All skeletal remains will be handled in accordance with appropriate specimen handling procedures. There are normally no inherent health and safety hazards involved with anthropological analysis of skeletal remains (Kneller, 1998; Central Identification Laboratory, 2002/2003). However, bone with associated decomposing soft tissue and desiccated tissue will be handled with appropriate caution and personal protective equipment will be employed as appropriate (3.5). In addition, when working within the mortuary, the health and safety guidelines and risk assessment procedures outlined in 3.5 will apply.

When analysing skeletal remains, interpretations and conclusions must be supported by documented observations. Ensuring quality control will be the responsibility of the senior anthropologist who will review all cases for accuracy and consistency. The repeatability of all scoring methods advocated in this chapter should be assessed for intra- and interobserver error as a matter of routine.

It is imperative that prior to the commencement of any work in the mortuary, or any work with families and communities, an integrated approach to data collection similar to that described in Figure 10–1 is considered and adopted (Keough et al., 2004; see 10.2). This will ensure the most effective use of ante- and postmortem data, and will serve the best interests of survivor communities and the courts.

7.2 Basic procedures

7.2.1 Defleshing, cleaning, and handling human skeletal remains

The pathologist is required to make the primary assessment of any human skeletal remains brought into the mortuary, and this must occur before any soft tissue, clothing, and other artefacts are removed or altered in any way. The MMT will decide, on a case-by-case basis, whether removal of soft tissue from a body or body parts is justified to facilitate further analysis of hard tissue by the anthropologist.

Removal of soft tissue, or defleshing, is a process that should only be undertaken when it is not otherwise possible to determine the biological profile or other relevant information from the remains. For example, in decomposing remains, sufficient soft tissue may be left to determine sex through the presence of internal organs and external genitalia, and in such cases, defleshing for osteological sex determination cannot be justified. If determination of age, sex, and stature cannot be achieved by any other means (including x-rays and DNA profiling), it may be necessary to excise certain elements (e.g., the pubic symphyses or sternal rib ends) to enable a detailed examination. If it is deemed necessary to extract these elements, care must be taken to cause minimal alteration to the skeletal remains by removing the least amount of flesh possible. In the case of paired bones, both sides should be excised because it is known that the criteria assessed for such methods as age determination and parity assessment are not necessarily the same bilaterally, and their morphology may also reflect individual biomechanical stress (Cox and Scott, 1992).

In appropriate situations, all removed tissue should be labelled, retained, and returned to relatives or communities with the associated skeletal remains for appropriate funerary rites. Desiccation or other means of preservation of soft tissue (e.g., freeze-drying and vacuum packing) may be necessary when long-term storage is envisaged. Under no circumstances should this process be neglected. All removal of soft tissue must be documented, preferably using photography, but at the very least in the analytical notes.

Most methods for removing soft tissue require the requisite body part to be separated from the body. It is therefore imperative that the body part or bone is adequately labelled and that the label is maintained throughout the defleshing and analytical processes, until the excised element is returned to the body. To maintain the integrity of the chain of custody, and for ethical considerations, body parts and bones from separate cases or bodies (e.g., pubic symphyses), must never be collectively defleshed, especially when undergoing maceration or boiling. Separate containers must be used for different cases, and the label (metallic or plastic tags) must be attached to the remains at all times. The label must be resistant to degradation by the defleshing technique being used (e.g., some detergents are corrosive to metal, and some plastics are sensitive to high temperatures). There are several methods for defleshing available to the anthropologist or the anatomical pathology technologist (APT) who may undertake this work, and these are described briefly here (Reid, 2003; Simmons and Haglund, 2005). Each method has associated benefits and disadvantages, and the senior anthropologist will make the decision as to which technique should be applied to each individual case. It is essential that all samples intended for biomolecular and biochemical analyses are taken prior to any cleaning procedures. Each method must be subject to a detailed health and safety risk assessment, and mitigation strategies adopted and modified as necessary.

All techniques described in this section can be accelerated by first removing most of the soft tissue by hand. This can be undertaken using a scalpel, but as with all methods, care must be taken not to damage the underlying bone. Any such damage may potentially be confused with perimortem trauma. In some cases, the removal of decomposing or preserved soft tissue will be undertaken using appropriate wooden or metallic tools and water. For safety reasons, electric or hand-powered surgical saws and clippers used to expose the relevant skeletal area may only be operated by qualified technicians.

The technique of leaving fleshed or partially fleshed bones in water to soak until the flesh separates is the most passive of all defleshing methods. It does not require specialised equipment other than a lidded container, a water supply, and facilities for the disposal of biological waste (the liquid in which the remains have been soaking). If available, fume hoods may make the process less unpleasant for mortuary staff. Maceration of fleshed bones is relatively time consuming. Depending on the size of the bone and the degree of existing decomposition, it can take from weeks to months for flesh to be easily removed. It is often not possible to remove tendons, ligaments, and cartilage completely using this method. Most forensic missions are unlikely to use this method because it is too slow.

Boiling fleshed bones in water is another option that allows most of the flesh to be removed relatively quickly. This may take from several minutes to several hours, depending on bone size and decomposition stage, and as with maceration, tendons, ligaments, and cartilage are more resistant. The temperature of the water is crucial because vigorous boiling can result in damage to the bones as they hit the sides of the pot; thus, gentle simmering is advised. Placing the body part into a container or 'bag' will provide some protection during this process, and a variety of materials may be used for this, including plastic or metal screening material and mesh laundry bags. Containers should be of an appropriate size for the bones, and the water level should remain above them at all times to avoid damage. A hot plate or other constant heat source, such as a microwave oven (Simmons and Haglund, 2005) can be used to heat the water. This process is ideally conducted under a fume hood.

Generally speaking, it is recommended that bone should be placed in a weak solution of water and a degreaser such as a commercial enzyme detergent[1] or sodium borate (borax) (Fenton et al., 2003). This should then be gently simmered, ensuring that the water level is maintained. Potassium hydroxide can be added to this solution to act as a catalyst to the reaction. It may be necessary to remove the bones from the water at frequent intervals and gently remove loosened soft tissue until the process is complete. Finally, drain the water from the container into a sieve and collect all biological material for preservation; persistent ligaments and tendons can be gently pulled away from the bone with plastic tweezers (Simmons and Haglund, 2005). Boiling water or chemical agents must be handled in accordance with health

[1] Biotex, for example, is a readily available and inexpensive detergent.

and safety regulations (3.5). Care must be taken to collect all small bones, bone fragments, and epiphyses in cases of nonadult individuals.

A final option, but one that is not very practical in field missions, is to employ the dermestid beetle, which will consume flesh without damaging skeletal elements. However, colonies of beetles consume flesh at a rate that is usually too slow for most forensic cases. In addition, it is difficult in most temporary mortuary settings to maintain a colony of beetles for any length of time (Simmons and Haglund, 2005).

When dental and skeletal remains are in good condition, they are not easily affected by the routine handling associated with anthropological analyses, or by the ambient environment of a laboratory or mortuary. Special care should be taken in handling crania and mandibles to ensure that dentition does not become dislodged and that the fragile bones of the facial skeleton are not damaged. Care should be taken to ensure that skeletal remains that are fragile and unstable are kept in conditions that are similar to the environment from which they were recovered (i.e., stable temperature and relative humidity). Burnt bone, as opposed to cremated bone (see 8.5), may be fragile in nature, depending on the temperature and the duration of exposure involved. It can be adversely affected by routine handling, or by the ambient environment of laboratory or mortuary, and particular care is required.

Where human remains are skeletonised at the point of recovery, cleaning of any adherent soil or sediment should be undertaken prior to any analysis, unless the remains are so fragile or friable that any attempt to clean the bones will cause further damage. Skeletal remains are most easily cleaned as soon after recovery as possible, before soil and other sediments dry and adhere to the bone. With sandy soils, dry brushing may be all that is required to remove the matrix. As long as the bone is in good condition, water can be used to aid the cleaning process. Where the trabecular bone is exposed, avoid wetting these areas. Do not 'soak' bones in water because this may cause dissolution of the bone mineral. A light spray can be used to wet bone prior to soft brushing to remove any adhering matrix. Once clean, the water should be disposed of through a sieve, or a 'catch' should be used in the plug hole of the sink. Skeletal remains considered to be too fragile to be washed can be gently cleaned using a very soft brush over a sieve of mesh size 0.2 or 0.25 cm. Bone, regardless of its condition, must not be dried too quickly or it will deteriorate. Alcohol should never be used to clean bone, and consolidants should be avoided unless absolutely necessary because they will impede any future chemical and microbiological analyses. It is not necessary to mark individual bones with their identification number, unless very long-term storage is envisaged, or when dealing with commingled remains.

Any reconstruction of fragmentary skeletal elements should be undertaken in accordance with the detailed methodology set out in 7.2.3. During metrical analysis, care should be taken to ensure that no scratching or damage to the bone surface occurs when using metal callipers.

7.2.2 Distinguishing human from nonhuman skeletal and dental remains

This section establishes routine procedures for differentiating vertebrate hard tissues from nonosseous and nondental material, and also for determining whether skeletal and/or dental remains can be characterised and classified as human. Sections of this discussion are based on the Central Identification Laboratory *Standard Operating Procedures* of the Central Identification Laboratory (CIL, 2002/2003). The first step in all anthropology casework should be the establishment of whether the material presented is relevant to anthropological analysis. This requires that an anthropologist determine whether case material is bone or dental tissue, and if so, if it is human.

The majority of cases present no problem for anthropologists with training and experience in comparative vertebrate anatomy who can readily distinguish between human and nonhuman skeletal remains, although this is more problematic with extensively fragmented or burnt material. Care must be taken to avoid misclassifications when skeletal remains have been thermally altered or fragmented and deposited in conjunction with other resinous, crystalline, or finely layered, vesicular or granular materials. Low-power light microscopes, hand lenses, and graphic and physical exemplars of human and nonhuman bone should be available to anthropologists for comparative purposes.

The graphic and physical exemplars recommended for use are as follows:

1. Articulated adult human skeleton – preferably real, but a cast will suffice
2. Disarticulated adult human cranial and postcranial elements
3. Casts of human cranial and postcranial elements
4. Disarticulated nonhuman skeletal remains (various species and examples)
5. "Exploded" human cranium
6. Cast of an infant human skeleton
7. Cast of a juvenile human skeleton
8. Selection of vertebrate and human osteology texts
9. Key charts in a laminated form

There are two primary means of differentiating skeletal and nonskeletal remains that are based on the macroscopic and microscopic structural differences between materials and the gross anatomical differences between species.

There are a variety of nonbone materials that are quite frequently confused with skeletal remains by inexperienced practitioners. These include ceramics, rocks (particularly calcareous sedimentary rocks), flint nodules, shells, corals, plant remains, synthetics, and laminates (particularly after exposure to high temperatures). Bone has fundamental variations in architecture, at both the macroscopic and the microscopic levels. The basic macroscopic subdivisions of bone tissue are marrow, cortical, and trabecular bone. The associated marrow and cartilage are largely absent in most cases that are examined by forensic anthropologists. The mineralised parts consist of two distinct types – trabecular and cortical bone – and these are largely distinguishable in their macroscopic and microscopic appearance through the variation in their porosity (Martin et al., 1998). Trabecular bone has a high porosity of 75 to 95 percent. It is most commonly found in cuboidal bones and in the ends of long bones. Macroscopically trabecular architecture is in the form of a three-dimensional lattice of spicular plates and struts (called *trabeculae*). In load-bearing areas, the trabeculae are sometimes arranged in arrays; however, more often, the trabeculae appear as a randomly organised, quasiorthogonal framework. Cortical bone has a much lower porosity (5–10 percent) than trabecular bone, and hence is much denser. It is found in the shafts and outer surfaces of other bones forming their external cortex. Macroscopically, the cortex is a smooth layer of varying thickness that exhibits fine layers, which usually parallel the surface morphology of the bone.

Microscopic examination of cortical and trabecular bone reveals that each may contain two further types of bone tissue – lamellar and woven bone. Lamellar bone is slowly formed and highly organised – it is frequently encountered in the cortex of bone. Woven bone is deposited as part of the remodelling and healing processes. These are fundamental responses that are a component of bone homeostasis and impacts to the skeleton that result from other life events. Woven bone is formed quickly through the mineralisation of a rapidly established and disorganised network of collagen fibrils. This formation process gives it a fine, fragile, and lacy appearance macroscopically, and a uniformly chaotic deposit that has no layers microscopically. It is usually found in small quantities around trabecular spicules, but it may also be encountered in the subperiosteal and endosteal regions of the cortex. Constant remodelling will eventually result in woven bone becoming established as lamellar. The variation in relative proportions of cortical and trabecular bone and the overall structural morphology of an element are the result of different functional requirements. As such, they are factors to consider when identifying smaller fragments of bone as part of an individual skeletal element.

Bones have a distinctive anatomical morphology consisting of joint surfaces, muscle attachments, grooves, foramina, canals, and other bony landmarks. Bone-to-bone and soft tissue interactions are the major reason for an individual bone's characteristic landmarks and morphology. Bones articulate with other bones at joints of which there are several different types, and each has a characteristic appearance that can aid in the identification of a bone. Articulations associated with synovial joints are usually smooth, with a well defined area of dense, fine-grained cortical bone and a well-defined border that broadly corresponds to the insertion of the joint capsule. Less mobile joints, such as cartilaginous joints (synchondroses and symphyses) are typified by quasiparallel billows and striations with varying densities of small depressions and pits (e.g., pubic symphysis). Fibrous joints (synarthroses) are usually characterised by interdigitating suture lines of varying complexity (e.g., cranium). Nonskeletal materials lack these features.

Teeth, because of their highly specialised functions, have a distinctive crown and root morphology. They are pearlescent, hard, dense, and crystalline structures. Because they are such highly specialised structures, they have a distinctive morphology that, for complete teeth, can enable relatively easy macroscopic classi-fication between species. When complete, teeth are so distinctive that they are not easily confused with other materials. However, fragmented or thermally altered teeth may become hard to distinguish, especially from other hard, crystalline, ceramic, or vitreous materials. Teeth are made of three distinctive materials: enamel, den-tine, and cementum. Enamel thickness varies between about 2 mm and less than 1 mm. Enamel bands can usually be seen macroscopically with offset lighting, and in the case of adult molar teeth, these incremental bands are usually visible to the naked eye. The spacing and appearance of these perikymata (Hillson, 1996) can vary between individuals and populations. Enamel fragments, if large enough, may show distinctive fissures and cusps, which are also partially reflected in the underly-ing dentine. Dentine, although softer than enamel, is also banded, although these bands are much harder to see with the naked eye. Macroscopically, dentine can appear opaque and brittle, with conchoidal fracturing. When thermally altered or in certain burial environments, dentine and enamel can become chalky and white. Cementum is also banded, but it is not usually possible to see these bands except in ground section. Furthermore, cementum is almost always poorly preserved, except in cases of recent death. It often cracks and separates away from the dentine.

The morphology of the human skeleton is distinctive for largely functional rea-sons, primarily the requirements of bipedalism. Despite this, the generalised verte-brate form sometimes means that when an anthropologist is presented with frag-ments from other species, a determination of whether skeletal remains are human may be difficult to determine. This seems to be particularly true of the appendicular skeletons of medium-size quadrupedal mammals. The species most commonly con-fused with human skeletal remains by those with little experience are ursids, canids, suids, and bovids. Teeth are less frequently misclassified. Human skeletal remains exhibit articular surfaces and bony landmarks that are unique to the species. Simi-larly, human dental remains exhibit characteristic class features unique to humans. Comparison of skeletal and dental remains to exemplars of known human and nonhuman remains results in one of five professional opinions:

1. Match to human: the default category when skeletal remains demonstrably match known human exemplars to the exclusion of other reasonable possibilities
2. Consistent with human: when skeletal remains are consistent with known human exemplars, but not to the exclusion of other reasonable possibilities
3. Match to nonhuman: when the skeletal remains demonstrably do not match human exemplars, or alternatively, do match known nonhuman exemplars to the exclusion of other reasonable possibilities
4. Consistent with nonhuman: when the material is consistent with known non-human exemplars, but not to the exclusion of human skeletal remains
5. Inconclusive: when the skeletal remains lack sufficient morphological features to make an assessment; the skeletal remains may be subject to further chemical, microscopic, or radiographic investigation, if deemed necessary

All human skeletal remains will undergo further examination set out in the following sections. The remains of nonhuman skeletal elements will be recorded in 'Additional Skeletal Elements: Quantification' and/or in the additional notes section within the relevant recording form (see 8.9). Do not put nonhuman skeletal elements in the inventory or archive them with human remains. If they are of evidentiary value, a new evidence number can be allocated by the SCE. In contexts where the nonhuman bones are of no analytical or evidentiary value, they may be recorded and discarded.

7.2.3   Reconstruction of human skeletal remains

Human skeletal remains may become fragmented as a result of either perimortem or postmortem forces. Reconstruction of skeletal remains is a procedural step that may assist in subsequent analyses. As such, reconstruction should only be undertaken when it is deemed useful, or potentially useful, for deriving analytical results. Components of this section are based on the *Standard Operating Procedures* of the Central Identification Laboratory (CIL, 2002/2003). The anthropologist engaged in reconstructing skeletal remains should exercise care not to reconstruct skeletal remains in such a manner that may obscure evidence of perimortem trauma or hinder other subsequent analytical procedures. Where such skeletal remains are exhibiting diagnostic changes (e.g., of disease or trauma), it may be easiest and most useful to photograph the relevant areas and/or edges prior to reconstruction. Reconstruction of skeletal remains is normally undertaken after they have been determined to be human and after any cleaning, but prior to the assessment of the biological profile.

In cases where there are believed to be, or there is the possibility that, multiple individuals are present, then an assessment of the minimum number of individuals (MNI) should be made, and an attempt at segregation should be undertaken before reconstruction. However, this is a fluid process, and sometimes reconstruction of skeletal remains may assist in determinations of MNI.

All fragmented skeletal remains believed to originate from a single individual or from a common incident should be laid out anatomically on one or more examination tables. These should first be covered with a material that will protect them from damage on a hard surface (e.g., upside-down bubble wrap, which can also be cleaned between cases). Fragmented skeletal remains must first be identified to element (e.g., left femur), type of bone (e.g., long bone), or region of the skeleton (e.g., pelvis) prior to reconstruction. These determinations are made on the basis of the anthropologist's professional experience and knowledge of the human skeleton. For very small fragments, the anthropologist may need to compare the fragment(s) to the exemplars of skeletal remains. Once the unknown specimen has been identified, the anthropologist will examine the broken margins for variations in colouring or morphology that would indicate recent breakage. If such evidence is found, the anthropologist should search other fragments for similar features and attempt to match these margins. Fragments exhibiting similarities should be dry-fitted to test for congruence of fit. All three surfaces – internal, external, and marginal – should exhibit congruence, as should surface morphology. However, it should be remembered that colour and preservation can often exhibit marked differences if the two fragments had been subjected to differing microenvironments during the postmortem interval. Special care should be taken not to 'abrade' or alter the margins of the fragments while dry-fitting. Prior to fitting, the margins of bone fragments likely to be glued should be cleaned of any adherent soil, sediment, soft tissue, or other matter that would preclude a secure join or a secure mechanical fit. For fragments exhibiting no evidence of recent breakage, the anthropologist should look for similarities of colour, thickness, preservation, surface texture, staining, and surface morphology (e.g., grooves, ridges, articular surfaces). Special attention should be paid to similar and inverse fracture angles that suggest a fit.

When water has been used to clean bones, or where skeletal remains are wet or damp from their burial environment, if time and circumstances permit, the skeletal remains should be left to air dry prior to gluing. Clean, dry margins should be coated with a thin layer of acetone-soluble adhesive, and the fragments lightly held together until the glue sets. Fragments may be temporarily held together with masking tape, or they can be placed in sand or glass beads for support while the glue hardens. In some cases (e.g., fragile cranial reconstructions), small-diameter wooden dowels may be necessary to support reconstructed skeletal remains. As a general rule, smaller fragments should be reconstructed into larger pieces and then fitted together. Be sure to identify as many corresponding pieces as possible before gluing so as to have a mental picture of the outcome, and consider the effects of plastic deformation. In some cases, postmortem plastic deformation of the skeletal remains, especially cranial fragments, may preclude matching all broken margins accurately. Fragments should never be rebroken, filed, sanded, or otherwise altered to obtain a fit. Instead, the matching margins that approximate to the original shape and contour of the fragment should be reconstructed, and the other margins left unfitted. If the affected areas exhibit pathology or trauma, it may be best not to reconstruct them as a matter of course. The anthropologist should always consider what features are important to illustrate photographically and then reconstruct accordingly.

The reconstructed skeletal remains should be compared to exemplars of similar bones or teeth to ensure that the reconstruction is accurate. If the results indicate that plastic deformation of the bones has occurred, the osteometric landmarks affected by the deformation should not be used, and hence any measurements affected by these points should be eliminated. Where the skeletal elements have been reconstructed, the skeletal element will be marked with an asterisk (*) on the 'inventory' in the various forms (see 8.9).

7.2.4 Determination of the minimum number of individuals and the examination of commingled skeletal remains and body parts

The determination of MNI and the analysis of commingled skeletal remains and body parts from a single case, or associated multiple cases, have various applications in the investigation of human rights abuses. The determination of MNI itself provides the minimum number of individuals involved. A further consequence of this process can be the reassociation of body parts from individuals within a grave and individuals recovered from different contexts (e.g., primary and secondary graves). Correct identification and siding of elements is vital to the success of this procedure. Some of the discussion that follows is based on the *Standard Operating Procedures* of the Central Identification Laboratory (CIL, 2002/2003).

Disassociated and disarticulated human skeletal remains are frequently encountered in forensic investigations, whether as surface scatters or as commingled disarticulated elements within an interment site. Attempts to reassociate elements in the mortuary can provide important evidence in an investigation (e.g., leading to the association of primary and secondary graves, or execution and burial sites). However, unfortunately, the reassociation of every element in an assemblage to individuals by anthropological methods is rarely likely to be possible. Relationships between body parts observed in the field may assist in the rearticulation of individual and single bones. The use of genetic markers (DNA) for every element and fragment is usually cost prohibitive (exceptions are in highly politicised mass fatalities in wealthy countries, e.g., September 11 or the London bombings in July 2005). The anthropologist must decide at what point useful results from anthropological techniques diminish to the point of meaninglessness. Selective use of genetic markers may be beneficial to reassociate portions of skeletal remains that have been tentatively linked by other indicators. The use of DNA for this purpose, although it will ultimately produce sequence data, is resource dependent, and where resources are available, must be at the discretion of the senior anthropologist in consultation with the project manager. The reassociation of disassociated skeletal remains is imperative to the determination of an accurate MNI, although lesser accuracy in determination of an MNI can be based on the duplication of elements.

An inventory of the skeletal remains is the first step when determining MNI. All skeletal remains in a single case need to be laid out in anatomical order, with supernumerary elements being laid next to each other. In the case of multiple associated cases, these too should be laid out in anatomical order in an adjacent analytical location (either on the same table, if it is large enough, or on an adjacent table). It is essential to maintain provenance of individual elements during this phase (by using string tags or permanent marker). Such procedural steps must be determined from the outset by the senior anthropologist. All material from associated cases must remain separate until tentative reassociation of material is confirmed. Reassociation of material across case numbers needs to be tracked rigorously. Any amalgamations must be confirmed by the senior anthropologist. Notation must also be given to the evidence manager and/or the mortuary scene of crime officer and entered into the evidence log. Ideally, a written record of any amalgamation needs to remain with the evidence.

During the inventory phase, it is essential that anthropologists, pathologists, and APTs in the mortuary consult the Location, Attitudes and Properties Form (FA12BH, FA12BT, FA12SH, FA12ST, or FA12BP) on which field anthropologists or archaeologists have recorded possible relationships between bodies and other body parts. It is vitally important to ensure that all contextual information is understood, furthermore, it serves to double-check that the evidence is correctly numbered. A photograph should be taken of the skeletal remains once they are laid out in anatomical order. The inventory should be recorded on the appropriate forms (MA41F–MA46F). Skeletal elements will be recorded as Absent (A), Present >95 percent (P), Present but Incomplete 75 to 95 percent (PI), Large Fragment 50 to 75 percent (LF), Medium Fragment 25 to 50 percent (MF), Small Fragment <25 percent (SF), and an additional notation for reconstructed bone (*).

If there is no duplication of bone, teeth, or fragments, then the MNI is one. If elements, or morphologically diagnostic fragments (e.g., the left orbital rim), are duplicated or multiple, then the quantity of the component with the highest number of representations is given as the MNI. When very large numbers of individuals are present (e.g., through the analysis of multiple or mass graves), then it may become necessary to specify the use of a particular element for analysis of an MNI. The criteria for the selected element, or region of an element, is that it is robust, easily sided, and identifiable (e.g., petrous bone). Each bilateral element chosen should be counted on a single side (e.g., all left tali, all left tibiae). Anthropologists should consult the relevant recording form to identify possible neighbouring sets of skeletal remains to which the multiple elements may belong. Where a match cannot be found, the duplicate or multiple element(s) will be given a separate evidence number(s) (i.e., BP001) and recorded on the Assessment of Body Parts Form (MA45).

Occasionally, there will not be element duplication, but MNI may be inferred from other factors. Differences in the biological profile of elements is an indication that more than one individual is represented. All diagnostic elements should be examined for age and sex indicators. Clear differences suggest that there may be multiple individuals present. Gross differences in size are also potentially useful indicators, and antimeres will be examined to determine consistencies in dimensions and broad symmetry in the location, size, and character of anatomical landmarks and features. If paired elements are asymmetrical, beyond the usual boundaries of symmetry or the presence of an obvious pathological condition, it is suggestive that more than one individual is present. Incompatibility in articulation also suggests more than one individual. However, some elements within the human skeleton are unreliable indicators in this respect (e.g., the bodies of lumbar vertebrae 5 and sacral vertebrae 1, or the head of the humerus and the glenoid fossa), but others are more reliable (e.g., the talo-tibial and the ulna-humeral articulations). These techniques may also be used to identify consistencies with paired, or articulating, bones, and reassociations may be made.

Metrical methods can also be used to reassociate individuals (e.g., Byrd and Adams, 2003) but are potentially time consuming when dealing with large numbers of individuals. An assessment of what is 'normal asymmetry' within a population needs to be established for this method to be meaningful. Where it is known that a well-defined number of individuals exists within a case, there is a good chance that an experienced anthropologist can make considerable progress with reassociation. However, because this is rarely the case in mass grave investigations, reassociation of all skeletal remains may never be achieved.

The use of genetic sequence data is the only sure method of reassociating body parts, but it is expensive and generally not readily available as a resource. Differences in DNA sequence obviously suggest more than one individual and multiple sequences indicate that there are multiple individuals present in an assemblage. However, although rare, it is possible for single individuals to have more than one mtDNA sequence – heteroplasmy (James and Nordby, 2003).

Anthropological analysis of commingled and reassociated human skeletal elements should be undertaken on the relevant recording forms (MA46). These forms consist of several independent pages that must be collated and bound with the appropriate 'cover and summary page' (MA41–MA46). Most pages have at least one alternative; for example, the inventory has an adult version and a nonadult version. It is at the discretion of the anthropologist analyzing the case to decide which pages are required in the completed form.[2]

7.2.5   Application of population-specific methods

It is increasingly recognised that analytical methods developed on particular subsets of populations with known demographic characteristics have limited applicability to other populations (Byers, 2002). This is particularly the case when the population subset on which a method was developed is genetically, temporally, or environmentally distinct from the population subset being investigated. Further to this, concern exists that the range of possible variation within a population may not be characterised within a subset, which may exclude some outliers of the population. Population-specific methodologies for estimations of ancestry, age, sex, and stature are ideally required to determine the biological profile of human skeletal material with confidence. It is as important to be aware of the variation within a population and subset as it is to be aware of the variation between populations (e.g., phenotype, genotype, environmental factors, secular trends). If possible, it is advisable to test existing methods for appropriateness and determine the margin of error prior to, or during, the mortuary process. This can only be undertaken for such criteria as age determination if some of the group are of known age. It may be possible to develop population-specific standards, especially in the cases of atrocity crimes, when several hundreds or thousands of individuals will be analysed. It is the responsibility of the MMT to identify which existing population-specific methodologies should be

---

[2] This allows flexibility, especially in cases where remains are either very fragmentary (in which case only basic information can be gathered and less of the form can be completed) or in highly complex cases when several extra pages may be required.

applied and the processes used to test their appropriateness. The problem with this approach is that usually the time scale involved in developing population-specific methods is not available within the confines of a particular operation. Exceptions are where long-term identification projects are undertaken, such as that in progress in the Former Yugoslavia by the International Committee for Missing Persons or in Guatemala or Argentina by their national forensic teams. Some areas of analysis, such as stature and age at death estimation, have large confidence limits, and to some extent, these broad ranges can obviate the need to develop population-specific standards for small, and short-term projects.

Where test results indicate a significant systemic bias, demographic parameters may not be accurately reflected in the results (e.g., under- or overageing). Two options are available to the MMT, either to modify existing methods or to develop new methods. Both can only be achieved through the development of population-specific standards for the sample under analysis using cases of known biological profile. This brings with it significant ethical considerations (see 1.9) because it can only be achieved via the use of the remains of individuals identified by way of other means such as DNA. Under no circumstances must samples of tissue be taken for such research without appropriate consents. These must be from the relevant local authorities, community leaders, religious leaders, and/or family members as appropriate (referred to as 'relevant authority' in this discussion). It is implicit that consent from the most relevant authority must be obtained and that all consents must be 'informed'[3] by written agreement and fully documented.

The first step in determining which anthropological methods should be applied to a target population is to undertake a background or desktop study to find peer-reviewed, population-specific research. It may be necessary to consult local scientists, academics, and literature within the following fields of research: biological or physical anthropology, human biology, health and nutrition, and growth and development. Population-specific methods should have been tested on a statistically significant skeletal sample of individuals with known[4] age, sex, ancestry, and stature. This population must have the same genetic background and similar environmental conditions as the target group. Such methods must be easy to use, with known inter- and intraobserver error, must have known percentage accuracy, and must have useful ranges that help determine presumptive identifications or construct shortlists. Although it is sometimes the case that the range of variation within any particular method is too wide to provide specific information, it is worth considering that seriation may have value as a mechanism to determine relative differences between individuals and groups of individuals. For example, that person x appears taller or shorter, or older or younger, than persons y and z.

---

[3] Informed consent relies on all parties having a clear and full understanding of the matter in question and of the ramifications of their decision.

[4] 'Known' means criteria established by reliable documentation, not by other biological methods. This is particularly important for age determination.

Developing population-specific methods is a time-consuming, difficult process and may not be feasible. It is not appropriate to attempt to define new standards on small samples because they will generate misleading indicators. Neither is it appropriate to develop methods on cases where such criteria as age and sex have been assessed using other anthropological methods. Permissions to sample or collect data sets may not be easy or possible to obtain. Also, time and resources can be a limiting factor. However, despite these difficulties and limitations, the value of such research cannot be underestimated. Because an anthropologically developed biological profile is frequently used to narrow down the number of possibilities on which to base a match to other identification techniques (e.g., DNA or dental), the more appropriate the foundation on which such methods are developed, the more useful they become.

To develop population-specific standards, it is necessary to establish the variable to be tested; the example given here is the estimation of age at death in adult males. Next, it is necessary to identify the criteria of the study sample, which needs to mirror the target group (e.g., adult males of the same ancestral group living in similar conditions). Furthermore, the study sample needs to be of an adequate size to be statistically significant and exhibit a 'normal' (i.e., not skewed) age range distribution. Outliers within the study sample that may potentially skew results can only be excluded from the final study sample if they are caused by such variables as the presence of a preexisting pathological condition (e.g., paralysis of the lower limbs may affect the expression of observable traits on the pubic symphysis).

Once the parameters of the study population have been established, the method, the variables to be observed/measured and how they will be recorded/measured must be defined. For example, a descriptive observation may record the attribute as absent or present. In contrast, an attribute may be given a nominal or ordinal value. Because a standardised approach to the method being developed must be taken throughout (and subsequently), drawings, photos, or exemplars may be consulted or developed for observable or nominal attribute descriptions. For the developed methodology to be useful, it must be tested for intra- and interobserver error, which can be achieved by blind retesting on the same study sample using the original and different observers. The results need to be examined statistically by an experienced biostatistician. An appropriate correlation between the attribute and the variable under investigation may validate the results or lead to the development of a formula or tables. These correlations or formulae need to be tested on a second suitable study sample to establish whether the original study sample is an accurate representation of the target population. Ultimately, the methodology results and conclusions need to be submitted for publication in a peer-reviewed journal for general acceptance within the discipline and wider application. This will, of course, take several years, and in the meantime, it is essential to seek appropriate peer review of the approach under consideration before using it for analysis. Exemplars (casts, x-rays, photographs, drawings), tables, and formulae should be available for relevant application.

Where population-specific methods are established during the set-up phase of an investigation, these may not accord with the recording forms recommended in this text. In such cases, a specific form will need to be created along the lines of those provided on the accompanying CD.

7.3 Assessment of taphonomic change

The assessment of taphonomic change to skeletal remains can reveal information about peri- and postmortem influences, whether natural or anthropogenic (Haglund and Sorg, 2002b). In a forensic context, taphonomic change can inform about such variables as pre- and postburial environments, treatment of victims after death (e.g., dismemberment; destruction of skeletal remains via explosive force, burning, or sharp trauma) and evidence of bodies being moved from primary to secondary locations (Skinner et al., 2002). The types of taphonomic change discussed here are those that are likely to reflect alterations to the bone that result from human (e.g., deliberate or accidental breakage, thermal alteration, excavation damage), faunal (e.g., scavenging, gnawing, disbursement), avian (e.g., scavenging, disbursement), and environmental activity (e.g., sediment abrasion) (Loe and Cox, 2005). The level of taphonomic change that is relevant to most forensic contexts may be broadly classified as surface change rather than that penetrating the bony cortex or medullary cavity of long bones. However, this classification does not preclude change that penetrates the bone (e.g., gnawing may include tooth punctures).

Taphonomy can be defined as the investigation of those processes that affect an organism from the point of death until the time at which study commences (Buikstra and Ubelaker, 1994). This includes certain perimortem processes and all post-mortem factors. Taphonomic change includes environmentally induced weathering, and has been described as the decomposition and destruction of bone that is part of the normal process of nutrient recycling in and on various substrates (Behrensmeyer, 1978). However, it is important to remember that weathering will vary according to context and locality (Brickley and McKinley, 2004), and recording must allow for this. Taphonomy is the process by which the original microscopic organic and inorganic components of bone are separated from each other and destroyed by physical and chemical agents operating on the bone *in situ*, either on the surface or within the burial environment (ibid.). Typically, taphonomic processes on bone are visible as changes in colour, surface texture, microstructure, and morphology, due to chemical, physical, and biological processes such as temperature, erosion, rootlets, mycorrhiza, birds, insects, or animals (Buikstra and Ubelaker, 1994). In the mass grave context, changes may also reflect the postmortem treatment or processing of skeletal remains, activities that are evidence of illicit destruction and concealment.

The main types of analysis of taphonomic factors are macroscopic and micro-scopic examination of bone and tooth surfaces and their internal microstructure. A general macroscopic description of surface change should be recorded in the appro-priate section of the anthropology recording form. Anthropologists and archaeolo-gists without the experience to interpret their observations should not attempt to do so; descriptions and photographs will facilitate specialist interpretation at a later

Table 7–1. *Bone weathering stages*

Stage	Description
0	Bone surface shows no sign of cracking or flaking due to weathering.
1	Bone shows cracking, normally parallel to the fibre structure (e.g., longitudinal in long bones). Articular surfaces may show mosaic cracking.
2	Outermost concentric thin layers of bones show flaking, usually associated with cracks, in that the bone edges along the cracks tend to separate and flake first. Long, thin flakes, with one or more sides still attached to the bone, are common in the initial part of stage two. Deeper and more extensive flaking follows, until most of the outermost bone is gone. Cracked edges are usually angular in cross section.
3	Bone surface is characterised by patches of rough, homogeneously weathered compact bone, resulting in a fibrous texture. In these patches, the external, concentric layers of bone have been removed. Gradually, the patches extent to cover the entire bone surface. Weathering does not penetrate deeper than 1.0–1.5 mm at this stage, and bone fibres are still firmly attached to each other. Cracked edges are usually rounded in cross section.
4	The bone surface is coarsely fibrous and rough in texture; large and small splinters occur and may be loose enough to fall away from the bone if it is moved. Weathering penetrates into inner cavities. Cracks are open and have splintered or rounded edges.

Source: Adapted from Buikstra and Ubelaker, 1994.

date. A useful guide to detailed recording of taphonomic change to the subperiosteal surface of the cortex can be found in Loe and Cox (2005).

During the excavation phase, significant anomalies may be encountered (e.g., adjacent bodies are all missing their lower legs). This is vitally important information in understanding the significance of the condition and completeness of skeletal remains during subsequent analysis. The archaeological evidence will contribute to the interpretation of such patterns, and the description and documentation from the excavation must be conveyed to the mortuary team to ensure that misinterpretation is prevented and that evidence is not lost. An example is the exemplary recovery and interpretation of skeletal remains from a karstic cave near Hrgar, Bosnia, conducted by Simmons and colleagues (Simmons, 2002). Such understanding is crucial if anthropologists are to be able to differentiate between perimortem trauma that might have contributed to death and that caused by a particular burial environment.

The taphonomic alteration of skeletal remains has many causes and variations in expression. Nevertheless, a quantification of these changes is shown in Table 7–1. The stages described in Table 7–1 should be used to score surface features, which will then be recorded on the relevant section of the recording form. All taphonomic changes should be recorded.

7.3.1   Types of taphonomic change

Six types of characteristics are recorded, including colour change (staining and bleaching), postmortem breaks and deformation (excavation and depositional), erosion (weathering, dissolution), rootlet and mycorrhizal etching, animal scavenging, and heat modification. Bone colour may reflect multiple variables, including

Figure 7–1. Effects of freeze–thaw flux on human bone, Western Desert, Egypt. *Source:* Margaret Cox.

exposure to heat, staining by metal objects (e.g., zips, press studs, projectiles, shrapnel), contact with certain soil minerals, or biological factors such as fungal activity. A specific colour on its own will rarely provide conclusive evidence for any one causal agent because different combinations of variables may result in the same colour change. Colour variations should be described, and consistency in recording can be ensured by using appropriate Munsell colour charts (Munsell Color Co, 2000) or complex paint colour charts. It must also be recorded and photographed. Interpretation should only be attempted in light of all contextual and other relevant information. If an obvious contextual cause for the colour change can be established, for example, an *in situ* ring on a finger resulting in a localised stain, this context should be described and documented. There may be instances where the cause of a localised stain is no longer *in situ*, and field notes may be particularly useful here (e.g., a bullet found *in situ* at the time of excavation may have been seized as an exhibit in the field).

Exposure to sunlight causes bone to bleach, becoming white in colour and sometimes presenting a 'chalky' texture. Bone from a surface that has been exposed to sunlight should be recorded and interpreted as such. Desert conditions exact extremes of temperature (very hot and cold) on exposed bone, and the resultant flux can cause fracturing similar to that observed on cremated bone (Figure 7–1). For more detailed information of heat modification on bone, see 8.5.

Prolonged stress or pressure on bones can lead to temporary and permanent deformation without actually fracturing the bone. Temporary deformation can be reversed (elastic deformation), but if the level of stress breaches the yield strength, the change is permanent (plastic deformation) (Correia, 1997). To distinguish taphonomic deformation from possible antemortem deformation pathology or trauma, it is advisable to support the anthropological findings with contextual evidence from the excavation and to maintain a cultural awareness. This pressure can be of a temporary nature caused by heavy machinery used to backfill a grave or permanent pressure caused by the backfilled soil itself. If the stress on a bone exceeds its maximum tensile strength, the bone will fracture.

Distinguishing postmortem damage from perimortem trauma requires identification of taphonomic signatures and potential actors and effectors on the bony surface, as well as an understanding of perimortem trauma signatures. Taphonomy is a dynamic and multifactorial process; therefore, alteration on a single bone can display more than one causal agent, and one taphonomic signature may overlay or compound another. These may include evidence of colour differences between a break margin and the surrounding bony surface; generalised erosion or weathering surrounding the break; the softness or brittleness of the bone; the lack of sharp edges, angle, and outline of the fracture in relation to its longitudinal axis; and evidence of scavenging including teeth, beak, or claw marks. When it is not possible to distinguish the mechanism or timing of bone modification, it must be recorded as 'unknown'.

Bone fracture is perhaps the most commonly recognised type of taphonomic change. Although there is no constant rate at which a bone loses its organic component and changes from 'green' to 'dry' or becomes mineralised, the differences in the way in which green and dry bone fracture are key discriminators in determining the timing of such events. Bone that fractures while still green (and therefore possibly ante-, peri-, or postmortem) tends to fracture along smooth lines with sharp, linear edges (White and Folkens, 2005). Dry bone (always postmortem) usually fractures with rougher, jagged edges and may not follow a smooth line. If damage is relatively recent, the fracture surface is usually a different colour that the adjacent surfaces. Each skeletal element will fracture according to its own inherent biomechanical properties that reflect their physiological and mechanical functions. These properties affect the manner and form of fracture morphology whether ante-, peri-, or postmortem.

In most environments, bone will be subject to varying degrees of sedimentary abrasion or 'weathering'. Material either moves over bone, often associated with hydrological activity, or the bone moves over static or moving material. The resulting friction and abrasion will cause bone modification. This can be microscopic or macroscopic. Modification caused by the dissolution of bone matrix by water or acids is commonly referred to as erosion and is recorded as 'present', unless there is evidential value in interpretation of an obvious pattern when more detail should be provided. The severity of erosion should be noted as slight, moderate, or severe and images and descriptions must be available to provide guidance and criteria as to what comprises slight, moderate or severe erosion for quality control purposes.

Plant rootlets and mycorrhizae (a symbiotic association of a fungus and the roots of a plant) in contact with bone will leach trace elements such as calcium (Schultz, 1997). The resulting etched grooves often appear whiter than the unaffected surface due to decalcification (Buikstra and Ubelaker, 1994). Such changes should be recorded as slight, moderate, or severe, and the affected area should be described. This evidence is important because it reflects the burial environment, and the relationship to plant root systems and associated fungi can be useful to link primary to secondary deposition sites as well as providing information about the burial environment.

The direct impact of insects or their larvae on the bone matrix is relatively limited (Schultz, 1997). Most insects, especially fly puparia, consume soft tissue and do not damage bone. Beetles, however, are reported to colonise skeletal remains (Kulshrestha and Satpathy, 2001), and evidence of beetle boring from the atrocity crimes in Rwanda and Guatemala has been observed by two of the authors of this chapter. If evidence of insect scavenging is present, it should be photographed, the affected area described, and bore-hole dimensions recorded for possible interpretation by a forensic entomologist. Where such lesions in bone are roughly uniform, they are less likely to be misinterpreted as pseudopathology by the anthropologist. Furthermore, the presence of insects on human remains will attract small birds that will feed off the larvae and may thus contribute to the taphonomic process with damage caused by their beaks or claws.

Human remains that are left on the surface for any length of time may be subject to scavenging, dismemberment, and disbursement by birds, rodents, or other animals. The direct impact of such scavengers on bone is often proportional to their size, but smaller animals and birds may gather in larger numbers and, as a group, cause significant damage. If signs of scavenging are present on bone, and it can be ascertained that those marks did not occur during or after excavation, they have significant evidential value in terms of understanding events between death and burial. Therefore, a specialist should be consulted and the circumstances of the scavenging should be recorded and documented in as much detail as possible. If a specialist cannot be present during the analysis, the anthropologist should record the general presence of the marks and describe their appearance. Detailed photographs and/or micrographs should be taken for possible later evaluation because tooth marks can be characteristic of species, which can in turn indicate environment. Faunal scavenging and nonscavenging activity such as dispersement and burrowing can also move or remove bones from, and into, supposedly sealed contexts (Figure 7–2). Insect and rodent activity can draw smaller skeletal elements through the sward (vegetation layer and root zone) into the undisturbed horizon below (Cole, 2000). The impact of scavengers on skeletal remains in terms of surface taphonomy and dispersement patterns, and our ability to discern patterns of species specific activity and coscavenging relationships, is ill researched other than in an anecdotal way.

Figure 7–2. Impact of burrowing on boundaries and contextual security as seen in a grave in Guatemala. *Source:* Caroline Barker.

Anthropogenic alteration to skeletal remains encountered in forensic contexts can reflect postmortem treatment of the dead. These might include: attempts to mutilate bodies to prevent identification, transportation and interment processes, disinterment and removal to a secondary grave, and/or other factors. Human remains may be subject to deliberate mutilation either by handheld implements (e.g., machetes) or machinery. An example alleged to have taken place in Kosovo involved the use of a machine bucket. Grenades may be exploded in graves, or an incendiary liquid or device may be used and the human remains burned. Because bone will still retain much of its organic matrix shortly after death, it will be extremely difficult to differentiate between immediate postmortem activity and circumstances that relate to the manner of death. In such cases, archaeological evidence reflecting context may prove crucial in determining the timing of the modification event.

7.3.2   Water and taphonomic change

Water plays an important role in taphonomic change to bone (Goffer, 1980), depending on the context and its contact with the bone. It is important to have an understanding of these processes because atrocity crimes can involve the dumping of bodies into lakes and rivers (e.g., Rwanda, Bosnia) or at sea (e.g., Armenia, Argentina). Relatively static lake water has a very different effect on bodies than a fast-flowing, melt-water ravine. Groundwater hydrology also plays a significant role, reflecting the particular hydrological regime (e.g., recharge). There are several useful chapters on the impact of immersion in water on decomposition in Haglund and Sorg (2002b), particularly in Haglund and Sorg's chapter (2002a) and that by Ebbesmeyer and Haglund (2002).

There are three phases by which bone is affected by fluvial transport. The first is the impact of the body entering the water, which can potentially cause fractures; this can be unpredictable and is not easily classified. A body that enters water from a great height will obviously show greater impact than a body that was carefully lowered into the water. Phase two is the effect of transport on the body in the water. Depending on the condition of the body on entering the water, it will either be transported whole or in parts. With time, the impact of the water and its kinetic energy on a (fleshed) body will cause it to be separated into body parts, and later into single bones. This process may also be exacerbated or caused by fish or marine mammals such as crocodiles. Such impacts will also depend on the stage of decomposition at the outset. Individual body parts or bones will react differently to fluvial transport, depending on their density and whether gas can be trapped inside. Body parts may float on the top or be dragged over the bottom of the river. During transport, bone can encounter aquatic fauna (that may leave stains and cause damage and/or disintegration), aquatic flora (that may damage the surface), or matrices such as rocks and sediments (that may abrade, percuss, or fracture the bone matrix). The third phase is the final deposition of the skeletal remains where individual bones or body parts are deposited on the banks of a river, on the shores or bottom of a lake, or at an artificial structure (e.g., a dam). During deposition, various amounts of kinetic energy may be administered to the bone or body part. This may result in fractures, erosion, and fragmentation (ibid.). As with terrestrial and subterranean contexts (discussed previously), allocating specific taphonomic damage to individual phases is unlikely to be possible but should be considered. The circumstance of the deposition of the body into the water will determine which phase will apply (e.g., a body that is already skeletonised when entering the water will not be subject to phase two) (after Nawrocki et al., 1997).

Waterlogged environments also impact the condition of a body in buried soils and other substrates. Graves in soil with a high percentage of clay or other waterlogged sediments will hold large amounts of ground- and rainwater as well as decomposition fluids. This can often lead to some, or all, bodies being submerged permanently with little oxygen. Such conditions will affect the decomposition process and may cause saponification of soft tissues[5] and ultimately affect the condition of the bone. If the body is partly submerged, distinctively different stages of taphonomy may be encountered on the same body. A grave may be periodically or seasonally submerged in anaerobic flux, which may accelerate decomposition and taphonomic change. Factors such as water temperature, oxygen, and pH will determine the level and type

---

[5] Saponification forms adipocere from adipose tissues. Adipocere is the waxy substance caused by the processes of hydrolysis and hydrogenation of body fats. Triglycerides are hydrolysed by intrinsic tissue lipases and bacteria soon after death to the corresponding saturated and unsaturated fatty acids. The unsaturated fatty acids may then be hydrogenated by bacterial enzymes to form the corresponding saturated compound. The conjugation of these fatty acids with bivalent metallic ions forms insoluble soaps such as calcium salts of fatty acids. Bacteria may also transform the saturated fatty acids into hydroxy-fatty acids that may be oxidised to form small amounts of oxo-fatty acids. The major constituents of adipocere are often palmitic, stearic, oleic, and myristic acids, which will vary in concentration based on the degree of hydrolysis and hydrogenation (Stuart et al., 2005).

of impact on both soft and hard tissues. Seawater will affect a body differently than freshwater (Sorg et al., 1997) and with it the extent of contact with sediments and rocks at the bottom. The temperature of sea- and freshwater will influence the rate of decay directly (the rate of putrefaction and autolysis) and indirectly through its influence on the ecosystem (aquatic flora and fauna). Current is another important factor because the associated kinetic energy will speed up the disarticulation of a body and cause greater erosion to hard tissue in some sedimentary contexts. In both marine and freshwater contexts, scavengers can include fish, reptiles, gastropod molluscs, crustaceans, and echinoderms (Sorg et al., 1997). If any investigation encounters evidence of aquatic mammal or fish scavenging, expert advice should be sought.

Soil minerals, in combination with water, form the soil solution. This soil solution causes the dissolution of the inorganic bone matrix, even if the level of acidity is very weak. The remaining organic bone matrix is then at risk of being leached (Henderson, 1987). Certain soil minerals (e.g., copper and manganese) protect bone from bacterial decay (e.g., copper is a bactericide) (Schultz, 1997). In addition to eroding the bone, minerals can also cause staining. Some elements can denature DNA in bone.[6] Both erosion and colour change must be documented on the appropriate recording form.

7.3.3   Assessing and recording bone surface changes

At the point of recovery, it is essential to record the context and environment and to describe the locale in terms of observed climate, vegetation, faunal, avian, and insect activity. It is also important to record the proximity of water, if there is, for example, a possibility of gradient run-off, flood plain, or fen- or mire-related redeposition. A detailed photographic record should be made of the environmental context of the site prior to beginning an excavation. If this is not possible, a scale schematic drawing must be made, accompanied by a GIS or map bearing and a written description.

When physically lifting human skeletal material, standard excavation methods should be used as described in 5.6. Care should be taken when trowelling or using metal objects to excavate, as this may obliterate macro- and microscopic features such as cut marks, or create pseudopathology. The potential for excavation damage or pseudotrauma is unknown, but can be significant, and therefore caution is advised. Similarly, chemical consolidants must be avoided other than in exceptional circumstances. After appropriate cleaning and drying (7.2.1), surface changes to bones need to be examined macroscopically and, where cut marks are evident, using a hand lens with appropriate magnification. More detailed work can progress using microscopy, if appropriate. The distribution of changes may then be recorded onto a skeletal diagram (see MA41F for adults or MA42F for subadults) accompanied by relevant images. If necessary, examination using environmental scanning electron microscopy (SEM) should be considered. Such an instrument allows whole

---

[6] For example, DNA does not survive in skeletal remains interred in lead coffins.

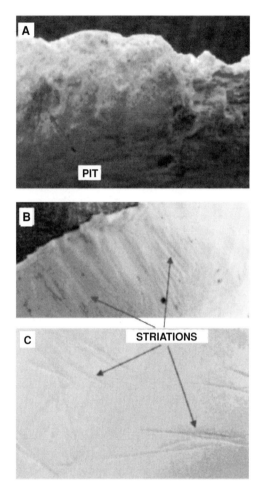

Figure 7–3. Experimentally produced pits and striations resulting from (a) carnivore gnawing, (b) rodent gnawing, and (c) defleshing. *Source:* Louise Loe.

bones to be placed directly into the chamber without pretreatment or gold coating, but this will require samples being sent to specialist laboratories. Where this is not possible, a good quality casting material should be used to replicate the changes either directly or by making a positive cast.

Surface features may be broadly classified as pits and striations (Figure 7–3) because these are the most frequently observed alterations on bone that has been modified by human, animal, and environmental agencies (Shipman, 1981). Criteria for their identification are summarised in Tables 7–2 and 7–3. Methods employed to study surface features derive from the forensic and zoo-archaeological literature (Loe and Cox, 2005 – from which much of the rest of this section is taken). These primarily aim to identify the agent (e.g., human, animal, or environmental) and timing; that is, features will display characteristic changes, depending on whether they occurred when the bone was fresh (i.e., collagen phase extant) or mineralised (i.e., collagen largely absent). It is also important to identify the actor (e.g., human or animal) and the effector (e.g., a weapon or a tooth).

Table 7–2. *The main characteristic features to score when recording striations*

Trait	Feature
Location	Zone and aspect (anterior/posterior/superior/inferior/medial/lateral)
Frequency	Multiple/single
Concentration	Isolated/clustered/disparate
Orientation	Parallel to the long axis of the bone/transverse to the long axis of the bone
Direction of multiple striations	Unidirectional/multidirectional
Travelling direction	Indeterminate/superior-inferior/medial-lateral, etc.
Shape in profile	'V'-shaped, 'U'-shaped, stepped, other
Depth	Cuts the bone/follows the contour of the bone
Margin texture	Rough/smooth/sharp/abraded/jagged/polished/flaked
Margin appearance in plan	Straight/uneven
Relationship of striations	Parallel/subparallel/nonparallel/criss-cross/clustered/disparate
Internal appearance	Microstriations/crushing
Colour of exposed surface	Clean/same colour as the surrounding bone

Source: Adapted from Blumenschine et al., 1996; Blumenschine and Selvaggio, 1988; O'Sullivan, 2001; Shipman, 1981; Shipman and Rose, 1983.

It is essential to record taphonomic alteration to bone using a method that describes characteristics qualitatively and quantitatively. This then forms the basis of subsequent interpretation. Examination should be undertaken under a bright artificial light with a $10\times$ hand lens. All elements should be inspected by slowly rotating them relative to a light source (Blumenschine et al., 1996). Where possible, a light stereomicroscope with a range of magnifications (up to at least $\times 40$) is recommended for scanning surfaces. The degree to which elements are scanned microscopically will vary, depending on the objectives of the investigation and the material being examined. In some cases, SEM may be appropriate.

Quantitative analysis involves measuring (to the nearest millimetre) the length, width, and, where appropriate, depth of a feature, as well as its distance in relation to

Table 7–3. *The main characteristic features to score when recording pits*

Trait	Feature
Location	Zone and aspect (anterior/posterior/superior/inferior/medial/lateral)
Frequency	Multiple/single
Concentration	Isolated/clustered/disparate
Shape in profile	Bowl-shaped, 'U'-shaped, stepped, other
Depth	Deep/shallow
Margin texture	Rough/smooth/sharp/abraded/jagged/polished/flaked
Margin appearance in plan	Straight/uneven
Relationship of pits	Clustered/interconnected/disparate
Internal appearance	Microstriations/crushing
Colour of exposed surface	Clean/same colour as the surrounding bone

Source: Adapted from Blumenschine et al., 1996; Blumenschine and Selvaggio, 1988; O'Sullivan, 2001; Shipman, 1981; Shipman and Rose, 1983.

any other surface features or modifications that may be present (O'Sullivan, 2001; Loe and Cox, 2005). This aids the characterisation of different surface features and the relationship between modified areas, when they occur on the same element. Different modifications that occur on the same element and are within a certain distance from each other may be related to the same event (Blumenschine and Selvaggio, 1988).

Qualitative analysis involves recording factors such as the location, orientation, frequency, concentration, direction, profile, texture, plan, internal appearance, and colour of features (see Tables 7–2 and 7–3). It is important not only to record location of features in terms of the proximal, middle, or distal portions of the bone and their concentration, direction, orientation, texture, and so on (Blumenschine and Selvaggio, 1988; Blemenschine et al., 1996) but also their relationship to areas of muscle attachment and other anatomical landmarks, which may have significant implications for their interpretation (Knüsel and Outram, 2004; Loe and Cox, 2005). For example, striations caused by cut marks as a result of disarticulation tend to occur on and around joints (Hurlbut, 2000). Some researchers consider that striations caused by animal gnawing tend to occur on prominent surfaces of bones (Buikstra and Ubelaker, 1994), but two of the authors of this chapter have seen evidence of gnawing focussed on the end of long bones (access to marrow is easier once bones are disarticulated). In fact, the location of gnawing in itself provides postdepositional information. With this in mind, location should be recorded with reference to the anatomical zone (Knüsel and Outram, 2004) in which the feature occurs in addition to its location within a zone (e.g., anteromedial/anterolateral; posteromedial/posterolateral; and proximal, middle, or distal portions of the zone) (Loe and Cox, 2005).

Based on these qualitative and quantitative observations, features may be classified according to the most likely actor and effector using the criteria described in Table 7–4. Not all features will fulfil every criterion; therefore, a differential diagnosis of actor and effector by an expert in this field is recommended. The matter of intentionality in interpreting taphonomic signatures is a complex matter (see Shipman and Rose, 1983; Loe and Cox, 2005), and it should be remembered that the marks left on bone are the unintentional artefacts of motivation, intentions, and activities.

Features may over time become abraded and lose their defining characteristics through further weathering (Loe and Cox, 2005). Research has demonstrated that cut marks can appear flatter and wider after being abraded (Shipman and Rose, 1983). The effects of abrasion on preexisting features are not yet understood, but it is logical to suppose that features will become increasingly obscured with increased exposure to damaging processes. Furthermore, we are not yet able to discern when a bone has been modified to the extent and in such a way that previous modifications have been obscured.[7] This 'taphonomic overprinting' (ibid.) means that in order to interpret these cases, taphonomic characters must be analysed at the assemblage level and not in isolation.

---

[7] The same is the case for recognising and interpreting perimortem trauma.

Table 7–4. *Criteria for identifying actor and effector*

Actor	Effector	Feature	Characteristic features
Human	Blade	Cut marks	'V'-shaped cross section, internal longitudinal microstriations (flint knife), no internal crushing, cut into surface of the bone, tend to be transverse to long axis, often occur in subparallel groups
Human	Blade	Scrape marks	Shallow 'V'-shaped cross section, occur in broad shallow fields, frequently parallel to long axis
Faunal	Tooth	Scores/furrows	'U'-shaped cross section, broad, shallow, frequently occur in parallel groups, generally perpendicular orientation, occur on thickness of the bone and/or cortical and medullary surfaces, furrows that have a relatively uniform pitch extending from outer to inner tables of bone (rodent gnaw marks)
Environmental	Sediment	Scores	Multidirectional, shallow, 'V'-shaped cross section, uneven thickness and depth
Faunal	Tooth	Pits/punctures	Bowl-shaped interiors, 'U'-shaped cross section, evidence for internal crushing, occur on cortical and medullary surfaces

Source: Adapted from Loe and Cox, 2004, Blumenschine et al., 1996; Blumenschine and Selvaggio, 1988; Haglund et al., 1988, O'Sullivan, 2001; Shipman, 1981.

An alteration to bone may be considered to be perimortem if the bony response is typical of fresh (i.e., bone that has an intact organic matrix) bone, or postmortem, if the response is typical of mineralised bone (Wakely, 1997). However, although it is relatively straightforward to identify postmortem features that have occurred on mineralised bone as a result of excavation and recovery, it is much harder to distinguish features that occur prior to excavation and recovery but after the bone has mineralised (O'Sullivan, 2001). Attention to location and other associated features are therefore essential to address this problem (Loe and Cox, 2005). Equally, our understanding of the time frame and rate of progress for green bone to lose its organic matrix is poor; it most certainly will reflect a multiplicity of interrelated intrinsic and extrinsic variables. Bone will retain its organic matrix to varying degrees for various amounts of time, so determination of what is perimortem and what is postmortem is very difficult, if not impossible, to determine in many cases. With this in mind, any recording form for taphonomic change must have 'unknown' as a recording category.

7.4 Estimation of ancestry

The issue of determination of ancestry is much discussed in the literature (e.g., Woo and Morant, 1934; Katz and Suchey, 1989; Brace, 1995; Gill, 1995; Kennedy, 1995; Tyrell, 2000). Ancestry is defined as the biogeographic population to which a particular individual belongs, by virtue of his or her genetic heritage. This definition acknowledges that ancestry neither bears a direct relationship to the culturally defined categories of ancestry, ethnicity, or religion, nor is it an accurate predictor of the soft tissue phenotype of an individual. The assessment of ancestry should not be carried out unless one or more of the following situations apply. It should be undertaken when the assessment of ancestry is deemed of critical importance to facilitate the identification of a particular individual or group of individuals for return to their families for humanitarian reasons. It should also be undertaken when individuals or groups of individuals must be linked to a particular ancestry for judicial reasons, as well as to facilitate a more accurate estimate of sex (Franklin et al., 2006), age, or stature than would otherwise be possible. This will be determined by the MMT in conjunction with legal advisors, and with reference to the wishes of appropriate community leaders and family representatives. In many forensic situations, it has to be acknowledged that the fact that ancestry can be inferred from skeletal remains may be potentially inflammatory for those still embroiled in conflict or its resultant aftermath (Simmons and Haglund, 2005). This section sets out routine procedures for the assessment of ancestry.

Any reconstruction of skeletal elements should be undertaken in accordance with 7.2.3. Standard anthropometric sliding and spreading callipers are required for the assessment of ancestry. Computer programmes may be used to assist with this assessment, and the programme used will be dependent on the population subset. FORDISC 3.0 (2005) and CRANID (Wright, 2005) should be available, and the decision as to which programme will be used should be made by the MMT.

If an assessment of ancestry is deemed critical to the analysis, the process is undertaken after skeletal remains have been determined to be human, after cleaning and appropriate reconstruction, and after the inventory and the MNI have been established. Assessment of ancestry should be undertaken prior to further analysis. Both visual and metric analysis can be undertaken. Primary nonmetric traits in skeletal and dental remains can also assist the assessment of ancestry in adults and nonadults.

Ancestry may also be assessed through mitochondrial DNA sequencing in comparison to extant references for different ancestral populations (general sampling and storage techniques are outlined in 9.3.8). If the MMT decides to follow this route and a sample is taken, then this should be explained in the analytical notes.

The anthropologist's visual and/or metric assessment will be recorded, where appropriate, in the analytical notes as an assessment of ancestry in the Anthropology Recording Form. The results will be presented in the final report.

7.4.1 Visual assessment of ancestry

Very broad classification of ancestry may be assessed through a visual inspection of cranial and mandibular characteristics (e.g., Gill, 1986), where the skull exhibits a suite of previously documented traits that are strongly correlated with a sample of a specific biogeographic origin. As different sample populations within an investigation may be encountered, the reference material for traits will vary according to

Table 7–5. *Craniofacial traits for the visual assessment of ancestry*

Characteristics	East Asian	American Indian	White	Polynesian	Black
Cranial form	Broad	Medium-broad	Medium	Highly variable	Long
Sagittal outline	High, globular	Medium-low sloping frontal	High, rounded	Medium	Highly variable postbregmatic depression
Cranial sutures	Complex	Complex	Simple	Complex	Simple
Nose form	Medium	Medium	Narrow	Medium	Broad
Nasal bone size	Small	Medium/large	Large	Medium	Medium/small
Nasal bridge form	Flat	Medium/tented	High/steeple-like	Medium	Low/Quonset hut
Nasal profile	Concave	Concavo-convex	Straight	Concave/Convexo-concave	Straight/concave
Interorbital projection	Very low	Low	High-prominent	Low	Low
Nasal spine	Medium	Medium, tilted	Prominent, straight	Highly variable	Reduced
Nasal sill	Medium	Medium	Sharp	Dull/absent	Dull/absent
Incisor form	Shovelled	Shovelled	Blade	Blade/shovelled	Blade
Facial prognathism	Moderate	Moderate	Reduced	Moderate	Extreme
Alveolar prognathism	Moderate	Moderate	Reduced	Moderate	Extreme
Malar form	Projecting	Projecting	Reduced	Projecting	Reduced
Zygomatic-maxillary suture	Angled	Angled	Curved	Curved/angled	Curved/angled
Palatal form	Parabolic/elliptic	Elliptic/parabolic	Parabolic	Parabolic	Hyperbolic/parabolic
Palatine suture	Straight/jagged	Straight	Jagged	Highly variable	Arched/jagged
Orbital form	Round	Rhomboid	Rhomboid	Rhomboid	Round
Mastoid form	Wide	Wide	Narrow, pointed	Wide	Oblique posterior tubercle
Mandible	Robust	Robust	Medium cupped below incisors	Rocker form	Oblique gonial flare
Chin projection	Moderate	Moderate	Prominent	Moderate	Reduced
Chin form	Median	Median	Bilateral	Median	Median

Source: Buikstra and Ubelaker, 1994.

the region. Where they exist, it is essential to use regionally appropriate lists of characteristics and their contrasting expression in each ancestral group (Buikstra and Ubelaker, 1994).

The morphological assessment of ancestry should, at present, only be applied to adults because there is a lack of peer reviewed material about the determination of ancestry in nonadults. That said, anthropologists with extensive experience of working internationally and/or with human remains from various ancestral groups, are aware of distinguishing features. Presently, it is only considered acceptable to

Table 7–6. *Nonmetric traits*

Primary nonmetric trait

Metopic suture	Pterygospinous bridge/spur	Sutural bones
Supraorbital notch/foramina	Pterygoalar bridge/spur	Epipteric bone
Infraorbital suture	Tympanic dehiscence	Coronal ossicle
Infraorbital foramen	Auditory exostosis	Bregmatic bone
Zygomatic facial foramina	Mastoid foramen	Sagittal ossicle
Parietal foramen	Mental foramen number	Apical bone
Inca bone	Mandibular torus	Lambdoid ossicle
Condylar canal	Mylohyoid bridge	Asterionic bone
Divided hypoglossal canal	Atlas bridging	Ossicle in occipitomastoid
Superior sagittal sulcus flexure	Septal aperture (humerus)	Parietal notch bone
Foramen ovale incomplete	Accessory transverse foramen C7	
Foramen spinosum incomplete		

Supplemental nonmetric trait

Fontal grooves	Rocker mandible	Glenoid fossa extension
Ethmoidal foramina	Suprameatal pi/spine	Circumflex sulcus
Supratrochlear notch/foramen	Divided parietal bone	Sternal foramen
Trochlear spine	Os japonicum	Supratrochlear spur
Double occipital condylar facet	Marginal tubercle	Trochlear notch form
Paracondylar process	Retroarticular bridge (C1)	Allen's fossa (femur)
Jugular foramen bridging	Accessory transverse foramen	Poirier's facet
Pharyngeal tubercle	Vertebral number shift	Third trochanter
Clinoid bridges/spurs	Accessory sacroiliac articulation	Vastus notch (patella)
Accessory lesser palatine foramen	Suprascapular foramen/notch	Squatting facets (tibia)
Palatine torus	Accessory acromial articular facet	Squatting facets (talus)
Maxillary torus	Unfused acromial epiphysis	Talus articular surface (calcaneus)

Source: Buikstra and Ubelaker, 1994.

determine the ancestry of infants and juveniles by using appropriate DNA analysis (Graham, 2006). The relevant standards for the assessment of ancestry will be determined by the MMT (7.2.5). If appropriate, the anthropologist will document the expression of each trait observed on the skull (see Table 7–5) and evaluate the results. In the case of damaged or fragmentary skulls, at least 50 percent of landmarks corresponding to traits on the list must be observable on the skull in order for ancestry to be assessed. Assessment should not be undertaken on skulls exhibiting plastic deformation, pathology, or major reconstruction. A skull exhibiting a preponderance of traits of a single ancestral population should be classified as being of that ancestry. Skulls exhibiting a mixture of traits will be classified as displaying mixed ancestry. The anthropologist will include documentation of their final assessment in analytical notes. For craniofacial trait variations, see Table 7–5. The list of nonmetric traits in Tables 7–6 and 7–7 can be used to assist the assessment of

Table 7–7. *Nonmetric variation of teeth*

Nonmetric variation	Description
Shovelling	Prominent marginal ridges of incisors (and occasionally canines) enclosing a deep fossa in the lingual surface
Double shovelling	Crowns have prominent marginal ridges on labial surface (not necessary to have ridging on lingual surface)
Tuberculum dentale	Free cusp with a deep pit located on upper incisors and canines, may extend as ridges into the concave lingual surface
Canine ridges	Canine distal accessory ridge usually found on lingual surface of upper canines between central buttress and marginal ridge
Uto-Aztecan upper premolar	Buccal cusp of upper permanent first premolar may bulge out with a marked fossa in its distal shoulder
Upper molar main cusp variations	Distobuccal cusp may be prominent, reduced, or absent
Metaconule of upper molars	Ranges from a tiny cuspule to a prominent cusp on the distal marginal ridge in permanent upper molars
Carabelli's cusp	*Tuberculus anomalus*: small additional cusp on the mesiolingual corner of upper molars
Parastyle of upper molar	*Tuberculum paramolare*: on the messiobuccal side of upper molars, ranging from a pit near the buccal groove to large, well-separated cusp, most common in third molar
Lower premolar cusp	Variable number of permanent molar lingual cusps (1–3)
Main cusp of lower molar	Variable number of cusps (usually 5) may have 4 (no distobuccal), 3 (no distobuccal or distolingual), or 6 or 7 (rare)
Groove and fissure patterns of lower molar	Mesial margin is deeply indented by a groove extending from the mesial branching fissure, or the marginal ridge runs continuously and encloses a well-defined mesial fossa
Deflecting wrinkle	Fold in the distal side of the mesiolingual cusp of permanent fist molars and deciduous lower second molars forming an L
Trigonid crest	High ridge that unites the mesiobuccal and mesiolingual cusps, which is not cut by the mesial fissure, and therefore isolates the mesial fossa
Protostyloid of lower molars	Ranges from a pit in the buccal groove through a furrow to a prominent cusp; affects the buccal side of the crown below the mesiobuccal cusp of permanent lower molars or deciduous second molars
Enamel extensions	Cervical crown margins may extend down at a root furcation as a small lobe or a long tongue of enamel running between the roots, affects multirooted teeth
Enamel pearl	Separate nodule of dentine covered by an enamel cap is present on the root surface, may be associated with enamel extensions, affects upper premolars and molars
Taurodontism	Cheek teeth having tall root trunk enclosing a large pulp chamber, and has short free roots, most visible radiographically, most pronounced in molars
Root number in cheek teeth	Varying root number, especially in premolars

Source: Hillson, 1998.

Table 7–8. *Craniofacial traits for metric assessment of ancestry needed for computation*

Cranial Vault

Maximum cranial length	g-op	Nasal height	n-ns
Maximum cranial breadth	eu-eu	Nasal breadth	al-al
Bizygomatic diameter	zy-zy	Orbital breadth	d-ec
Basion–bregma height	ba-b	Orbital height	
Cranial base length	ba-n	Biorbital breadth	ec-ec
Basion–prosthion length	ba-pr	Interorbital breadth	d-d
Maxilloalveolar breadth	ecm-ecm	Frontal chord	n-b
Maxilloalveolar length	pr-alv	Parietal chord	b-l
Biauricular breadth	au-au	Occipital chord	l-o
Upper facial height	n-pr	Foramen magnum length	ba-o
Minimum frontal breadth	ft-ft	Foramen magnum breadth	
Upper facial breadth	fmt-fmt	Mastoid length	

Mandible

Chin height	id-gn	Minimum ramus breadth	
Height of mandibular body		Maximum ramus breadth	
Breadth of mandibular body		Maximum ramus height	
Bigonial width	go-go	Mandibular length	
Bicondylar breadth	cdl-cdl	Mandibular angle	

Source: White, 1991.

ancestry of adult skeletal and dental remains. These traits will be recorded as simply present or absent, and in some cases, the number of occurrences will be noted or a description may be required. Postcranial skeletal remains have to date proved of little value in determining ancestry with the exception of the femur (Trudell, 1999; Gill, 2001). Those of Negroid descent tend to have straight femoral shafts, while most others tend to exhibit anterior curvature. However, the degree of curvature of the femur can vary enormously in non-Negroid samples and this diminishes the value of this method.

7.4.2 Osteometric assessment of ancestry

Metrical assessment of ancestry from the skull was first undertaken in the 1960s by Giles and Elliot (1962) and Howells (1989). If used, measurements will be taken in millimetres using apparatus described in 8.8. All measurements will be undertaken by anthropologists familiar and experienced with these techniques and methods. All measurements will be documented in the recording forms (see 8.9) and the anthropologist's analytical notes.

Useful cranial measurements with potential ancestral significance are described in Table 7–8, and postcranial measurements are given in Table 7–9. In practice, cranial measurements are most often used for ancestry assessment. Once collected, the data can be subject to discriminant function analysis. Measurements can be undertaken on cranial and postcranial elements of the human skeleton to identify

Table 7–9. *Postcranial traits for metric assessment of ancestry needed for computation*

Element	Measurement
Scapula	Maximum breadth
	Maximum length
Clavicle	Maximum length of clavicle
	Midclavicular circumference
	Maximum clavicular length
Humerus	Maximum length of humerus
	Least circumference of shaft
Radius and ulna	Maximum length of radius
	Least circumference
	Physiological length
Pelvis	Pubis length
	Ischium length
Sacrum	Maximum anterior breadth at S1
	Maximum anterior height

Source: Bass, 1995.

variations or similarities between regionally or genetically exclusive samples without necessarily assigning an ancestral group. Although some indices described here are not genetically acquired, they may provide information about population isolation, or regionally varied samples. If no advantage is identified in undertaking metrical assessment of ancestry for a particular investigation, this section and the appropriate page of the recording form can be bypassed and this fact recorded.

Ancestry and some group differences can be assessed through the size and shape of the cranium according to the procedures outlined in Moore-Jansen et al. (1994) and Ousley and Jantz (2004). They should be undertaken using the method considered most appropriate to the global region (such determination will be made by the MMT). CRANID (Wright, 2005) is a formula for determining ancestry that draws on a larger world sample than FORDISC, and its use is recommended for that reason. Summary worldwide results derived from the canonical variates analysis of the CRANID sample are shown in Figure 7–4. The CRANID system requires 29 measurements be obtained for each cranium. Descriptions and diagrammatic representations of these are located in 8.8. Cranial and facial indices are useful in assessment of ancestry and are described in Table 7–10 (Bass, 1995).

7.5   Assessment of biological sex

Biological sex is the quality that distinguishes males from females, reflecting chromosomal differences, which are manifested in bone morphology (Mays and Cox, 2000). *Gender* is a cultural construct and a reflection of a society's perception of feminine and masculine attributes. In forensic cases, determination of gender would be undertaken by collating biological characteristics with associated clothing and

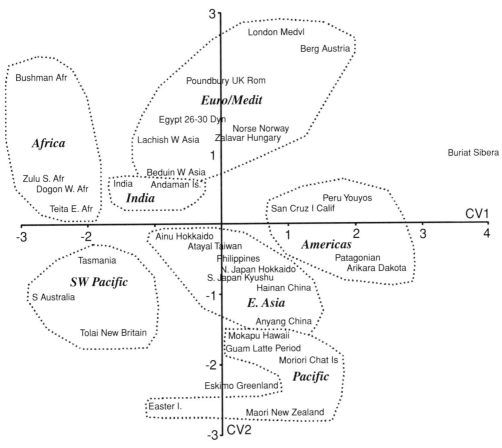

Figure 7–4. Summary worldwide results derived from the canonical variate analysis of the CRANID sample. *Source:* Wright, 2007.

other material evidence. This section is concerned with assessment of biological sex and not gender. For simplicity, we use the word sex in this chapter rather than biological sex.

The assessment of sex of skeletal remains is a prerequisite for individual identification, and the inclusion or exclusion of a presumed identity or shortlist. It is also of value in the separation of skeletal elements of differing sex within a commingled set of skeletal remains. Furthermore, sex may be used to provide, in part, a demographic profile of groups of skeletal remains recovered during the investigation of atrocity crimes or mass fatalities. The estimation of stature (see 8.2), some age estimation techniques (see 7.7), and the assessment of parity status in females (see 7.6) are sex specific and, therefore, require the prior estimation of sex before they can be applied. Equally, the degree of sexual dimorphism in skeletal characteristics indicative of sex, particularly cranial and facial differences, differs between racial

Table 7–10. *Cranial and facial indices used for assessing ancestry*

Index and description		Formula	
Cranial Index: the ratio as a percentage of the breadth to length of the skull	Cranial Index	$\dfrac{\text{Maximum cranial breadth} \times \textbf{100}}{\text{Maximum cranial length}}$	Dolichocrany X – 74.99 Mesocrany 75.00 – 79.99 Brachycrany 80.00 – 84.99 Hyperbrachycrany 85.00 – X
Cranial Module: a value for skull size	Cranial Module	$\dfrac{\text{Length} + \text{breadth} + \text{height}}{\text{Maximum length}}$	
Cranial Length–Height Index: the ratio (as a percentage) of the height to length of the skull	Length–Height Index	$\dfrac{\text{Basion–bregma height} \times \textbf{100}}{\text{Maximum length}}$	Chamaecrany X – 78.99 Orthocrany 79.0 – 85.99 Hypsiocrany 86.0 – X
Cranial Breadth–Height Index: the ratio (as a percentage) of the height to breadth of the skull	Breadth–Height Index	$\dfrac{\text{Basion–bregma height} \times \textbf{100}}{\text{Maximum breadth}}$	Tapeinocrany X – 91.99 Metriocrany 92.00 – 97.99 Acrocrany 98.00 – X
Mean Height Index: alternative measurement	Mean Height Index	$\dfrac{\text{Basion–bregma height} \times \textbf{100}}{[\text{Cranial length} + \text{breadth}] \div \textbf{2}}$	Low X – 80.49 Medium 80.50 – 83.49 High 83.50 – X
Mean Porion–Height Index: height of the cranial vault	Mean Height Index	$\dfrac{\text{Porion–bregma} \times \textbf{100}}{[\text{Cranial length} + \text{breadth}] \div \textbf{2}}$	Low X – 66.99 Medium 67.00 – 71.99 High 72.00 – X
Flatness of the Cranial Base: the basion–porion distance	Cranial Base Index	$\dfrac{\text{Basion–porion height} \times \textbf{100}}{\text{Basion–bregma height}}$	
Frontoparietal Index: the ratio between frontal and parietal breadth of skull	Frontoparietal Index	$\dfrac{\text{Minimum frontal breadth} \times \textbf{100}}{\text{Maximum cranial breadth}}$	Stenometopic X – 65.99 Metriometopic 66.0 – 69.99 Eurmetopic 70.00 – X
Total Facial Index: the ratio of the height to breadth of the face and teeth	Total Facial Index	$\dfrac{\text{Total facial height} \times \textbf{100}}{\text{Bizygomatic breadth}}$	Hypereuryprosopy X – 79.99 Euryprosopy 80.00 – 84.99 Mesoprosopy 85.00 – 89.99 Leptoprosopy 90.00 – 94.99 Hyperleptoprosopy 95.00 – X
Upper Facial Index: the ratio of the face height to breadth (without mandibular teeth)	Upper Facial Index	$\dfrac{\text{Upper facial height} \times \textbf{100}}{\text{Bizygomatic breadth}}$	Hypereuryeny X – 44.99 Euryeny 45.00 – 49.99 Meseny 50.00 – 54.99 Lepteny 55.00 – 59.99 Hyperlepteny 60.00 – X
Nasal Index: the ratio of the anterior nasal aperture	Nasal Index	$\dfrac{\text{Nasal breadth} \times \textbf{100}}{\text{Nasal height}}$	Leptorrhiny X – 47.99 Mesorhinny 48.00 – 52.99 Platyrrhiny 53.00 – X
Orbital Index: the height-to-breadth ratio of the orbit	Orbital Index	$\dfrac{\text{Orbital height} \times \textbf{100}}{\text{Orbital breadth}}$	Chamaeconchy X – 82.99 Mesoconchy 83.00 – 89.99 Hypsioconchy 89.00 – X

Index and description		Formula	
Maxilloalveolar Index: the height-to-breadth ratio of the orbit	Maxilloalveolar Index	$$\frac{\text{Maxilloalveolar breadth} \times \mathbf{100}}{\text{Maxilloalveolar length}}$$	Dolichurany X – 109.99 Mesurany 110.00 – 114.99 Brachyurany 115.00 – X
Palatal Index: the breadth-and-length ratio of the palate	Palatal Index	$$\frac{\text{Maximum palatal breadth} \times \mathbf{100}}{\text{Maximum palatal length}}$$	Leptostaphyline X – 79.99 Mesostaphyline 80.00 – 84.99 Brachystaphyline 85.00 – X

Source: Bass, 1995.

groups. Specifically, the typically robust male skull characteristic of a Negroid male and many Caucasoid males is at one end of a spectrum of robusticity and gracility, while males from Asian and Mongoloid ancestral groups, where male skulls are typically more gracile in appearance, are at the other end. Consequently, it is sensible to determine ancestry before sex.

Assessment of sex in skeletal material can only be reliably undertaken on the skeletal remains of those who have reached puberty, except by the use of DNA analysis. Macroscopic and osteometric methods exist for use on infant and juvenile skeletal remains (e.g., Weaver, 1980; Mittler and Sheridan, 1992; Schutkowski, 1993; Holcomb and Konigsberg, 1995), but these are generally not used because they are not considered reliable enough to be meaningful (Byers, 2002). DNA can also be used on fragmentary and commingled skeletal remains as a useful means of differentiating skeletal remains into groups.

There are three main modes of application involved in determining sex in adult skeletons: macromorphological, metrical, and genetic. These are described in this section. Sex assessment using macromorphological methods does not rely on any special equipment or apparatus. Estimation of sex using metrical analysis requires specialised measuring equipment, such as sliding callipers, spreading callipers, and an osteometric board. Genetic assessment of sex can only be undertaken in a DNA laboratory.

Assessment of sex will be undertaken on those skeletal remains identified as human, and where suitable cleaning and reconstruction has been undertaken. If the skeletal remains are identified as those of a single individual, the procedure is carried out while the skeleton is in anatomical position, after inventory of the skeletal elements present has been recorded, and after ancestry has been assessed (if appropriate, see 7.4). In cases of commingled skeletal remains, where a direct association or relationship to other bone elements or fragments within the assemblage cannot be made (see 7.2.4), the areas for potential sex assessment will be analysed. Skeletal remains that have been extensively fragmented or subject to other taphonomic processes (see 7.3) that render analysis impossible will be recorded as unidentifiable. The anthropologist's observations will be recorded in the analytical notes as an assessment of sex or as determined in accordance with the appropriate method. When applicable, the anthropologist will record the sex attribution in accordance with the recording forms (see 8.10). The results will be presented in the final report.

7.5.1   Morphological methods for estimating biological sex

Examination of sexually dimorphic morphological characteristics is the most common approach to assessment of sex in forensic cases. The attribution of sex based on morphological techniques relies on the analysis of the pelvic girdle, cranium, and mandible. Analysis involves the physical handling of the bone element(s) and a visual assessment of the morphological expression of each individual dimorphic characteristic. Right and left characters are recorded separately in paired traits. The pelvis is the most reliable indicator of sex, is more strongly dimorphic at an earlier age than cranial features, and should be weighted more than the cranium. Sex estimation using pelvic features can be undertaken on individuals for whom tripartite pelvic fusion is complete. Triradiate ilioischial and triradiate puboischial ossification are considered to be complete by about 15 years of age (Scheuer and Black, 2000), and Frazer (1948) indicated that by the time ossification of this element is complete most people are mid puberty. It is important to remember that sexually dimorphic changes to the cranium occur over a period of time, extending from puberty into the early twenties; therefore, it is not uncommon to encounter young adults (i.e., c. 15 years to early twenties) displaying 'male' pelvic and 'female' cranial traits simultaneously. In such cases, the pelvic indicators carry most weight. This is an issue to be mindful of, particularly when examining skeletal remains that include combatants that are usually young adult males. In such cases, it is important to estimate age at death prior to making a final judgment about sex determination.

Traits available for potential morphological analysis of the pelvic girdle are described in Table 7–11. The pelvic girdle is defined as the paired left and right innominatum and the sacrum. Traits available for potential morphological analysis of the cranium and mandible are described in Table 7–12. All of the morphological indicators of sex listed within this section are to be assessed and recorded where available.

The morphological traits of the pelvic girdle, cranium, and mandible must also be considered in relation to the overall appearance of the available skeleton. It is generally considered that males tend to be more robust with more pronounced muscle attachments than females who are relatively gracile. However, because robusticity generally reflects load-bearing activity, this difference may not pertain to areas where females also or exclusively undertake physically arduous work and where trends in robusticity and gracility could be reversed. Cultural norms for the target population must be established prior to undertaking analysis to avoid such errors of understanding.

To score and record morphological sex indicators, the assessment of each trait is placed in one of the six categories listed in Table 7–13. The accuracy and precision of

Table 7–11. *Morphological analysis of the pelvic girdle*

Pelvic elements	Typical male expression	Typical female expression
Subpubic concavity: located along the medial edge of the ischiopubic ramus, viewed from the dorsal surface of the bone	Slight to no concavity	Concavity present
Ventral arc: located on the pubis, viewed from the ventral aspect of the bone the pubic symphysis orientated anterior-posterior	Absent	Present as an elevated ridge of bone extending inferolaterally across ventral pubis
Medial aspect of ischiopubic ramus: located on medial ischiopubic ramus, viewed along medial aspect of bone	Broad, flat, and blunt, slightly everted	Ridged, sharp edge, everted
Subpubic angle: located between inferior pubic rami immediately inferior to the inferior border of the pubic symphysis, viewed from ventral aspect of the paired innominates	V shaped, narrow angle	U shaped, wide angle
Greater sciatic notch: located on the inferior border of the ilium, viewed from medial aspect of bone	Narrow, deep	Broad, shallow
Obturator foramen: located ventrally, viewed ventrally	Large and ovoid	Smaller and triangular
Pelvic inlet: pelvic girdle in anatomical position, viewed superiorly	Heart shaped, narrow mediolaterally	Circular, elliptical, wide mediolaterally
Preauricular sulcus: located along inferoposterior border of auricular surface of innominate, viewed from medial aspect	Not present or illusionary (i.e., created by bone deposition not resorption)	Sulcus caused by bone resorping and remodelling can be smooth and shallow or deep and rugged
Blade of ilium: ilium, viewed anteriorly paired or singularly	More vertical orientation	Flared, laterally divergent
Shape of sacrum: viewed anteriorly and laterally	Narrower, more curved, alae narrower than promontory of S1	Wider, less curved, alae wider than promontory
Pubic pitting: on the dorsal aspect of the pubic symphysis	Not present	Pitting present: female Pitting absent: not determinable

Source: Adapted from Bass, 1995; Buikstra and Ubelaker, 1994; White, 1991.

techniques used to determine sex depend on the availability and postmortem preservation of the skeletal elements used. In general, the more characteristics present, the greater the accuracy and precision attained. The accuracy and precision of morphological analytical methods can only be quantified if a systematic population-based study is undertaken. Morphological analysis of discrete skeletal remains is the most frequently used method due to the ease and speed of application and their accuracy in sex estimation (see Cox, 2001b). Morphological analysis will be used in preference to all methods unless otherwise stated.

Table 7–12. *Morphological analysis of the cranium and mandible*

Cranial elements	Typical male expression	Typical female expression
Angle of frontal: viewed laterally	Slanting anterior-posterior	Vertical and globular
Frontal and parietal: bossing located on midportions of **sided** frontal squama and parietals; viewed anteriorly, laterally, and superiorly, and felt using palm of hand	Absent or not pronounced	Pronounced
Nuchal crest: located on squamous portion of the occipital, viewed posteriorly and lateral profile	More rugose and pronounced	Less rugose and pronounced
Mastoid process: located on temporal, viewed laterally	Larger volume, more pronounced	Lesser volume, less pronounced
Suprameatal crest: posterior end of the zygomatic process	Extends as a crest past the auditory meatus	Crest does not extend past the auditory meatus
Orbital outline	Squared	Circular
Supraorbital margin: located on superior border of orbit, the borders are felt between the fingers to feel the shape and thickness of the region	Rounded, blunt margins	Sharper, thinner margins
Prominence of glabella: located on frontal, viewed anteriorly and laterally	Prominent and rounded	Not prominent
Gonial angle: located on posterior inferior border of ascending ramus of mandible, viewed anteriorly and laterally, and felt with fingers	Flared laterally	Not flared laterally
Shape of medial portion of mandible: located on inferior border of anterior medial portion of mandible, viewed anteriorly and superiorly	More squared	Pointed midline
Mental eminence: located on anterior medial portion of mandible, viewed anteriorly and felt with fingers	Marked projection of area above surrounding bone	Little or no projection of areas above surrounding bone
Palate	Larger	Smaller
Flexture of the mandibular ramus: at the level of the third molar	Present	Absent

Source: Adapted from Bass, 1995; Buikstra and Ubelaker, 1994; White, 1991.

The ultimate assessment of sex should be based on the convergence of the overall characteristics. For example, where all traits are present and are scored 'female', the final sex estimation will be 'female'. Where the result is a more or less equal mixture of 'probable female' and 'female', the final result should be 'female'. In cases where more 'probable female' traits are present than 'female', the final result will be 'probable female'. The same rules apply for 'male' characteristics. A mixture of characteristics of sexes, multiple ambiguous trait expressions, or probable trait determinations should be recorded as 'ambiguous'. If no characteristics are available for examination, this should be recorded as 'Not Examined'.

Table 7–13. *Categories of biological sex*

Male	Where the expression of a trait is within the range expected for male
Probable Male	Where the expression of a trait is within the outer limits of the range expected for male
Ambiguous	Where the expression of a trait does not correspond to that within the expected range for that of male or female
Female	Where the expression of a trait is within the range expected for female
Probable Female	Where the expression of a trait is within the outer limits of the range expected for female
Not Examined	Where the bone element or area for analysis is nonadult, not present, or not well enough preserved to make a determination

Source: Inforce Foundation.

7.5.2 Metrical analysis for estimating biological sex

The accuracy and precision of metrical analysis can be quantified through the use of associated confidence intervals. In osteometric analysis, the accuracy and precision of equipment is determined and quantified by the supplier. Regular calibration should be undertaken as recommended by the manufacturer. Measurements between specific anatomical landmarks in regions of the cranial and postcranial skeleton can be taken to assess sex. Comparisons can then be made to previously determined standards. Discriminant function analysis (Giles and Elliot, 1963) can be used to determine sex from craniometry and is described in Table 7–14. Application of this method to the sample population must only be made with appropriate and suitable discriminant functions. For the assessment of sex using the measurements of the

Table 7–14. *Discriminant functions (in millimetres) for metrical sex determination of the skull for blacks and whites*

Variable	Whites		Blacks	
	Coefficient	Constant	Coefficient	Constant
Maximum cranial breadth	−0.10646		−0.23287	
Bizygomatic diameter	0.40376		0.40358	
Basion–bregma height	–		0.15754	
Upper facial breadth	–	−76.2942	0.20526	−84.6585
Orbital height	0.37828		–	
Nasal height	−0.29159		–	
Frontal chord	0.19283		–	
Parietal chord	0.08209		0.26434	
D2	5.9387		6.4741	
Male mean	2.9694		3.2395	
Female mean	−2.9694		−3.2395	
Males misclassified	15/125 (12%)		4/38 (10.5%)	
Females misclassified	11/91 (12.1%)		2/27 (7.4%)	

Source: Jantz and Moore-Jansen, 1988.

cranium listed in Tables 7–14 and 7–15, the anthropologist must multiply the measurement by the appropriate discriminate coefficient and add the constant. A value greater than zero (>0) is classified as male, and a value less than zero (<0) is classified as female. Several bones are used for metrical analysis of sexual dimorphism and the most commonly used are described here. Descriptions of these measurements are shown in 8.7.2, as are the postcranial measurements used to assess the sex of skeletal remains.

Several skeletal elements have been shown to be sexually dimorphic in specific samples. Work began in this area in the 1940s with Washburn's (1948) efforts using the pelvis. An example is the humerus head, which is dimorphic in some sample populations (e.g., Christchurch, Spitalfields) (Molleson and Cox, 1993). When seeking to apply this method (as with the femoral head diameter), it should be evaluated for accuracy on individuals where sex can confidently be established using secondary sex characteristics. Only if it is demonstrably dimorphic on known sex individuals can it be applied to cases that cannot be assigned a sex by any other means (see Table 7–16). The femoral head is dimorphic in some sample populations, and for descriptions of the coefficients to apply, see Tables 7–17 and 7–18. To use these coefficients, multiply each measurement by the appropriate coefficient and add to the constant. A value greater than zero (>0) is classified as male, and a value less than zero (<0) is classified as female. The measurements for the assessment of sex using the tibia (Holland, 1991) are described in (Table 7–19). The measurements described should be multiplied by the appropriate coefficient and added to the constant. In this case, a value greater than 5 is classified as male, and a value less than 5 as female. Research by Franklin et al. (2006) has shown that it is possible to determine sex by discriminant function analysis of mandibular dimensions in black South African. FORDISC 3.0 can be used for the assessment of sex; all appropriate measurements should be taken as listed in section (Tables 7–20 and 7–21). Any metric analysis undertaken within a geographical region or population group must be appropriate in its application and will be cited during the analysis phase. The conclusions, associated confidence intervals, probability, and typicality are to be recorded in the analytical notes and given in the final report. When recording the determination of sex, it must be expressed within the parameters of the technique used (Table 7–22).

7.5.3   Disorders of sexual differentiation

Disorders of sexual differentiation can reflect abnormalities of chromosomal (normal female = 46,XX; normal male = 46,XY), gonadal (requiring the correct embryonic development of the ovaries or testes), phenotypic (physical appearance and characteristics), and endocrine development. Normal sexual development requires normal gonadal differentiation and development of the hypothalamic-pituitary-adrenal-gonadal axis (Vilain and McCabe, 1998). These conditions are present in most communities at various levels, and where they are either recorded in medical

Table 7–15. *Sex determination using the vertical diameter of the humeral head*

Females	Intermediate	Males
<43 mm	44–46 mm	>47 mm

Source: Stewart, 1979.

Table 7–16. *Sex discriminants of the humerus for whites (measurements in millimetres)*

Variable	Coefficient	Constant
Minimum diameter at midshaft	0.38574	
Epicondylar breadth	0.68813	66.85608
Vertical diameter of head	0.72249	
Male mean	5.215	
Female mean	−5.215	

Source: Jantz and Moore-Jansen, 1988.

Table 7–17. *Sex determination using the maximum diameter of the femoral head for American whites*

Female	Female?	Indeterminate	Male?	Male
<42.5 mm	42.5–43.5 mm	43.5–46.5 mm	46.5–47.5 mm	>47.5 mm

Source: Stewart, 1979.

Table 7–18. *Sex discriminants of the femur for whites (measurements in millimetres)*

Variable	Coefficient	Constant	Coefficient	Constant
Maximum length	−0.38292		–	
Bicondylar length	0.39079		–	
		55.34004		−50.90889
Epicondylar breadth	0.28839		0.25583	
Maximum head diameter	0.66200		0.66912	
Male mean	3.742		3.367	
Female mean	−3.742		−3.367	

Source: Jantz and Moore-Jansen, 1988.

Table 7–19. *Regression coefficients for the tibia*

Variation	Coefficient	Constant	Male mean	Female mean
Biarticular breadth	0.075	−4.92	0.857	0.144
Medial condyle articular width	−0.119	−3.21	0.776	0.224
Medial condyle articular length	0.078	−3.08	0.713	0.287
Lateral condyle articular width	0.83	−2.78	0.752	0.248
Lateral condyle articular length	0.125	−3.54	0.792	0.208
Medial condyle articular width × medial condyle articular length	0.002	−1.68	0.791	0.209
Lateral condyle articular length × lateral condyle articular width	0.002	−1.46	0.792	0.208

Source: Holland, 1991.

Table 7–20. *Craniometric measurements for metrical assessment*

Measurement	Ancestry	Sex	Stature	FORDISC	CRANID
Maximum cranial length	√			g-op	GOL
Nasio-occipital length	√				NOL
Maximum cranial breadth	√	√		eu-eu	XCB
Bizygomatic diameter	√	√		zy-zy	
Basion–bregma height	√	√	√	ba-b	BBH
Cranial base length	√			ba-n	BNL
Basion–prosthion length	√			ba-pr	BPL
Maxilloalveolar breadth	√			ecm-ecm	MAB
Maxilloalveolar length	√			pr-alv	
Bimaxillary breadth	√				ZMB
Zygomaxillary subtense	√				SSS
Cheek height	√				WMH
Biauricular breadth	√			au-au	AUB
Upper facial height	√			n-pr	NPH
Maximum frontal breadth	√				XFB
Biasterionic breadth	√				ASB
Minimum frontal breadth	√			ft-ft	
Upper facial breadth	√	√		fmt-fmt	FMB*
Nasion–frontal subtense	√				NAS
Nasion–bregma subtense	√				FRS
Bregma–lambda subtense	√				PAS
Lambda–opisthion subtense	√				OCS
Nasal height	√	√		n-ns	NLH
Nasal breadth	√			al-al	NLB
Orbital breadth	√			d-ec	OBB
Orbital height	√	√		√	OBH
Biorbital breadth	√			ec-ec	EKB
Interorbital breadth	√			d-d	DKB
Bijugal breadth	√				JUB
Frontal chord	√	√		n-b	FRC
Parietal chord	√	√		b-l	PAC
Occipital chord	√			l-o	OCC
Foramen magnum length	√			ba-o	
Foramen magnum breadth	√			√	
Mastoid length	√			√	
Chin height	√			√ id-gn	
Height of mandibular body	√			√	
Breadth of mandibular body	√			√	
Bigonial width	√			go-go	
Bicondylar breadth	√			cdl-cdl	
Minimum ramus breadth	√			√	
Maximum ramus breadth	√			√	
Maximum ramus height	√			√	
Mandibular length	√			√	
Mandibular angle	√			√	

* Howells' FMB differs from Wright's by approximately 6 mm. See Table 8.22 for definitions.

Table 7–21. *Postcranial measurements for metric assessment*

Measurement	Ancestry	Sex	Age	Stature	FORDISC	SOP code
Clavicle						
Maximum length	✓				✓	α
Anterior diameter at midshaft (sagittal-posterior)					✓	β
Superior diameter at midshaft (vertical-inferior)					✓	χ
Midclavicular circumference	✓					δ
Scapula						
Maximum length	✓				✓	α
Maximum breadth	✓				✓	β
Spine length						χ
Supraspinous length						δ
Infraspinous length						
Glenoid cavity breadth						φ
Glenoid cavity height						γ
Sternum						
Manubrium length						α
Body (mesosternum) length						β
Sternebra 1 width						χ
Sternebra 3 width						δ
Humerus						
Maximum length	✓		✓	✓	✓	α
Epicondylar breadth		✓			✓	β
Vertical diameter of head		✓			✓	χ
Maximum diameter at midshaft					✓	δ
Minimum diameter at midshaft		✓			✓	
Proximal epiphysis breadth						φ
Least circumference shaft	✓					γ
Radius						
Maximum length	✓		✓	✓	✓	α
Diameter at midshaft: anterior-posterior (sagittal)					✓	β
Diameter at midshaft: medial-lateral (transverse)					✓	χ
Maximum head diameter						δ
Neck circumference						
Ulna						
Maximum length				✓	✓	α
Anterior-posterior diameter (dorsovolar)					✓	χ
Medial-lateral (transverse)					✓	δ
Physiological length	✓		✓	✓	✓	
Minimum circumference	✓				✓	

(cont.)

Table 7–21 (*cont.*)

Measurement	Ancestry	Sex	Age	Stature	FORDISC	SOP code
Metacarpal						
Metacarpal length						α
Vertebra						
Vertebral body height				✓		α
Sacrum						
Anterior superior breadth	✓			✓	✓	α
Maximum transverse diameter of base					✓	β
Transverse breadth of S1	✓				✓	χ
Pelvis						
Height				✓	✓	α
Iliac breadth					✓	β
Pubis length	✓				✓	χ
Ischium length	✓				✓	δ
Femur						
Maximum length		✓		✓	✓	α
Bicondylar length		✓	✓	✓	✓	β
Epicondylar breadth		✓			✓	χ
a-p diameter medial condyle						δ
a-p diameter lateral condyle						
Sagittal (a-p) midshaft diameter					✓	φ
Transverse (m-l) midshaft diameter					✓	γ
Midshaft circumference					✓	η
Sagittal (a-p) subtrochanteric diameter					✓	ι
Transverse (m-l) subtronchanteric diameter					✓	φ
Minimum vertical diameter neck						κ
Maximum head diameter		✓			✓	λ
Upper breadth of femur				✓		μ
Lateral condyle height				✓		ν
Vertical head diameter						ο
Horizontal head diameter						π
Tibia						
Length		✓		✓		α
Maximum proximal epiphyseal breadth					✓	β
Maximum distal epiphyseal breadth					✓	χ
Medial lateral (transverse) diameter at the nutrient foramen					✓	δ
Maximum diameter at the nutrient foramen					✓	
Circumference at the nutrient foramen					✓	φ
Maximum length				✓	✓	γ
Biarticular breadth		✓		✓		η
Medial condyle articular width		✓		✓		ι
Medial condyle articular length		✓		✓		φ
Lateral condyle articular length		✓		✓		κ
Lateral condyle articular width		✓				λ

Measurement	Ancestry	Sex	Age	Stature	FORDISC	SOP code
Fibula						
Maximum length			✓	✓	✓	α
Maximum diameter at midshaft					✓	β
Calcaneus						
Maximum length				✓	✓	α
Middle breadth					✓	β
Posterior length				✓		χ
Talus						
Maximum length of talus				✓		α
Ankle height				✓		β
Metatarsal 1–4						
Length				✓		α
Metatarsal 5						
Length				✓		α

notes or commented on as 'differences' by surviving family members, they can play a role in determining presumptive identification. Identification of individuals based on genetic sex determination can never be considered conclusive because there are approximately 1 in 20,000 phenotypic males who possess an XX (female) genotype – where there has been translocation of part of the Y chromosome (the testis-determining fragment) onto an X chromosome (Guellaen et al., 1984; Page et al., 1985). In addition, although extremely rare, approximately 1 in 100,000 phenotypic females display an XY genotype (Swyer's syndrome) (Imai et al., 1997). In such cases, use of the STR amelogenin typing system, although producing correct identification of the genotype, would result in false sex identification. Although the likelihood of encountering such conditions in forensic cases is low, awareness of skeletal indicators of such conditions is warranted. A study by Stevens (2000) and O'Connell et al. (2003) examined some of these conditions and their potential impact on accurate sex determination from the skeleton. Two of these conditions are relevant to this discussion: Turner's syndrome (1:2,500 live births), which is caused by the absence of all or part of the second X chromosome in females (Gilbert, 1993)

Table 7–22. *Final sex attribution*

Male	Final measurement or calculation falls within the expected range for males
Female	Final measurement or calculation falls within the expected range for females
Not Determined	Final measurement or calculation falls within the overlap between male and female ranges

Source: Inforce Foundation.

and Klinefelter's syndrome or male hypogonadism (1:500–1,000 newborn males) (Gilbert, 1993). The skull of individuals with Turner's syndrome retains female characteristics, but the pelvis exhibits a more android (male) morphology. Consequently, there is the possibility that a Turner's female could be incorrectly sexed as a male. In individuals with Klinefelter's syndrome, the skull demonstrates female traits despite a relatively male phenotype. There is no documented effect on the pelvis, and examination of the skull in an isolated context could lead to incorrect assignment of female sex.

7.6   Assessment of parturition

Assessment of parity status has the potential to contribute to the determination of presumptive identification of adult female skeletal remains recovered from forensic contexts. Where no soft tissue survives, such assessment from skeletal remains is highly desirable but has to be based on a credible and scientifically proven and tested methodology. A recent review of methods of parity assessment was undertaken by Cox (2000b), to which the reader is referred for further detail. Because many practitioners still undertake parity assessment using inappropriate criteria, this section requires more detailed discussion of rationale than other sections.

In summary, the use of the presence/absence of preauricular sulci and pitting of the dorsal pubis, as indicators of parturition, is still undertaken by some practitioners. This approach is based on the early work of such researchers as Angel (1969), Stewart (1970), Houghton (1974), and Ullrich (1975), who extrapolated significance from its sexually dimorphic distribution. Work on the Hamann-Todd and Terry collections (see Holt, 1978; Kelley, 1979) affirmed the assumed significance of these characteristics but was based on individuals, many of whose parity status was determined by soft tissue analysis, much of which was spurious because it can be associated with variables other than parturition. Subsequent research on samples where parity status was more reliably determined (e.g., Bergfelder and Hermann, 1980; Spring et al., 1989; Cox and Scott, 1992) showed that there was no relationship between parturition and the presence and severity of preauricular sulci or pubic pitting. Both types of characteristics are, in fact, seen on male skeletal remains, and neither should be used as an indicator of sex. Studies of samples of known sex, age, and parity status have indicated that these characteristics reflect biomechanical stress relating to pelvic instability and overall body size rather than childbirth (e.g., Cox, 1989; MacLaughlin and Cox, 1989; Galloway et al., 1998). Consequently, the presence of the preauricular sulcus and of pubic pitting should *not* be used to infer parity status.

The only characteristic that has been demonstrated to be positively related to both childbirth and the number of births, and has no correlation with pelvic size, is the extended pubic tubercle (Bergfelder and Herrmann, 1980; Cox and Scott, 1992). These conclusions have been based on analysis of two different samples

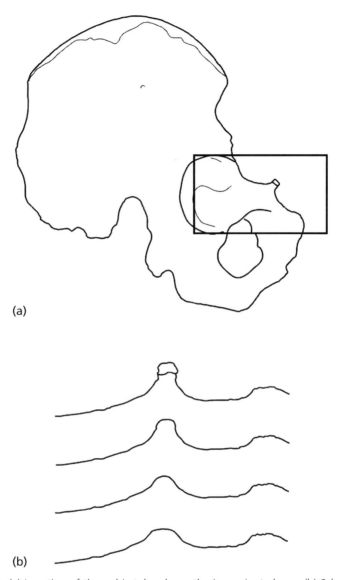

(a)

(b)

Figure 7–5. (a) Location of the pubic tubercle on the innominate bone. (b) Schematic example of different stages of extension to the pubic tubercle. *Source:* Inforce Foundation.

of known parity status. In essence, the greater the extension of the tubercle, the greater the number of births. The work of Hirschberg et al. (1998) demonstrates that extension to tubercles reflects longitudinal stress on the attachment site. The extension of the pubic tubercle reflects stresses associated with the partial attachment of rectus abdominus. Rectus abdominus is one of a group of muscles that is responsible for anterior containment and compression of the abdominal viscera, a task that is particularly important during the later stages of pregnancy when loading is exacerbated by the enlarging fetus and uterus. Extension reflects stresses associated with pregnancy, rather than the process of childbirth, and this should pertain to females whose infants have been delivered via caesarean section or vaginally.

7.6.1   Methodology and recording

The limiting factor when using this characteristic to determine parity status is that the tubercle, particularly when extended, is extremely fragile and can easily be damaged or removed by *in situ* erosion and by inappropriate handling during recovery, cleaning, and storage. Furthermore, there are no casts to aid assessment of the degree of extension; hence, the presence and degree of extension should be determined in the laboratory on a comparative and relative basis within the sample being examined, from which casts and photographic exemplars can be produced. Figure 7–5 is offered as guidance in this process. As always, it is essential to begin by ensuring that the innominate bone, particularly the pubic bone, has been gently cleaned. The innominate must be free from adhering material, but it is imperative that the cleaning process is passive to eliminate the possibility of damaging the bone. This method can only be used if the tubercle is intact and not eroded. Once clean, the pubic tubercle should be scored as (a) present but not extended, (b) slightly extended, (c) moderately extended, or (d) severely extended. Results should be tested for both intra- and interobserver error. Once scored, then it is possible to extrapolate from the score as follows: a = probably nulliparous, b = possibly parous, c = probably parous, and d = probably multiparous. Where the pubic tubercle is used to contribute to a presumptive identification, it is essential to fully record and photograph each case. It is important that the lack of an extended tubercle should not be used as exclusionary characteristic because its absence does not necessarily infer nulliparous status (Cox and Scott, 1992). It is also essential to ensure that photographs are taken illustrating exemplars exhibiting the stages described here.

The anthropologist's observations will be recorded in the analytical notes as an assessment of parity status; the rationale for the assessment will be explained and recorded photographically. When applicable, the anthropologist will record parity status on the anthropology recording form (see 8.9). The results will be presented in the final report.

7.7   Estimation of age at death

The assessment of age at death of adults and nonadults is essential when constructing the biological profile of an individual. Anthropologically assessing biological age at death (hereafter, 'ageing') of human skeletal remains from forensic contexts is typically confined to techniques developed on skeletal collections with documented ages at death (i.e., not assessed using subjective biological criteria). It must be kept in mind that the levels of accuracy of assessment of age at death vary enormously and are generally better in juveniles than for adults. The problem in determining age at death in calendric terms (i.e., gestational age, ante/peri/postnatal status, days, weeks, months, years) is that one is attempting to correlate a progressive linear state with a discontinuous and saltatory biological process that is subject to the influence of numerous intrinsic and extrinsic variables (Lampl et al., 1992). Further to this, as White and Folkens (2005) pointed out, it is necessary to arbitrarily divide the continuum of growth and remodelling into artificial stages and phases that are not based on scientific principles but on general macroscopic characteristics.

The standard ageing techniques described in this section are divided into nonadult and adult ageing techniques. They are based on relative stages of dental and skeletal development and maturation, degenerative changes in synarthroses, and ossification of cartilaginous regions. Age is estimated by macroscopically comparing a skeletal element or fragment of unknown age with a tested exemplar of known age. Methods based on seriation of data from archaeological populations (e.g., dental attrition) (Miles, 1963; Brothwell, 1981) are not considered appropriate to forensic cases.

Other techniques may be applied where necessary (e.g., the microstructural and chemical analysis of dentition), but only techniques deemed appropriate to specific populations by the MMT should be used (see 7.2). If microstructural or biochemical methods are to be used, an appropriate vital tooth will need to be extracted for analysis (see Whittaker, 2000, and Soomer et al., 2003, for useful overviews). Most such methods (e.g., cementum annulation, root dentine transparency, amino acid racemisation) require analysis in a specialist laboratory, and for that reason, these methods are not described in this text. The two-criteria method of Lamendin et al. (1992) is an exception. As always, appropriate consents for such sampling must be obtained.

Three-dimensional photographic and diagrammatic exemplars and printed reference materials should be made available to facilitate the ageing of skeletal remains. None of the exemplars requires calibration, but periodic checks of general usability and condition are required. The recording system described here ensures that all techniques used are recorded to include pertinent data and methodological detail. The final assessment of age from macroscopic skeletal indicators is the responsibility of the anthropologist and must be made on the basis of observations described in analytical notes. The conclusion must acknowledge the confidence intervals associated with the methods used.

7.7.1 Ageing nonadults

As a rule, consideration of the population specificity of standards and methods applies as much to the analysis of nonadults as it does to adults. Where possible, methods developed and tested on a relevant sample population should be used and tested for accuracy on the sample being analysed. However, when this is not possible, the most appropriate existing method should be used. Results should be recorded using the nonadult recording form (Individual Non-adult Skeleton Form, MA42F).

Scheuer and Black (2000, 2004) defined two approaches to estimating the age of juveniles. Both are techniques developed through studies that monitor the development and maturation of infants and juveniles. The first is expressed in terms of the mineralisation and eruption of dentition (deciduous and permanent), and the second is the development and maturation of skeletal elements from the time of appearance and fusion of ossification centres and the size and morphology of individual elements. The estimation of age at death for juveniles is more accurate than for adults because it is based on developmental criteria occurring relatively quickly, over a shorter time frame. However, it is still an estimate and skeletal maturation, in particular, is subject to the influences of both intrinsic and extrinsic variables. Dentition is less affected by adverse environmental circumstances such as nutrition, endocrine disturbance, and disease processes. The development of dentition and bone varies between males and females (ibid.), and where sex cannot be determined (i.e., most cases where remains are skeletonised), this is a problem that reduces the accuracy of results using some methods. However, several of the following tables contain separate age estimations for males and females. When sex cannot be determined, both ages should be combined to produce an age range. The standard deviations of both male and female age estimations must be included when producing the combined age range. In some forensic cases, soft tissue will survive, and in such cases, sex may be determined on the basis of soft tissue characteristics by the pathologist. The pathologist may require anthropological and/or odontological input into assessment of age at death.

Dental age. Each child has two sets of dentition: deciduous and permanent. In the analysis of nonadult dentition, development of mineralisation and eruption of both sets are assessed using observations and radiographs. Individual *ex situ* teeth can also be used to estimate age through observation of their mineralisation and resorption phases (Moorrees et al., 1963a, 1963b). The deciduous dentition start to mineralise at about 14 to 16 weeks *in utero* (Hillson, 1996) and are roughly half formed by birth, erupting through the hard and soft tissues during the next 2 to 3 years. Permanent dentition, which starts to form 28 to 32 weeks *in utero* (ibid.), gradually replaces the deciduous dentition. The last tooth, the third molar, is completely formed between the age of 17 and the early twenties. Numerous studies of dental development and eruption have been made (e.g., Moorrees et al., 1963a, 1963b; Haavikko, 1970; Demirjian et al., 1973, Gustafson and Koch, 1974; Anderson et al., 1976; Demirjian and Goldstein, 1976; Demirjian and Levesque,1980; Ubelaker, 1987; Smith, 1991) on samples of documented age at death.

For standardisation of recording and continuity between adult and deciduous dentition, the international recording system (Fédération Dentaire International or FDI) (see Table 7–23 and Figure 7–6) that divides dentition into quadrants should

Table 7–23. *Two-digit system of designating deciduous teeth – the FDI system (1971)*

Maxilla			Mandible	
Right	Left	Tooth	Right	Left
51	61	Central incisor	81	71
52	62	Lateral incisor	82	72
53	63	Canine	83	73
54	64	Premolar	84	74
55	65	First molar	85	75

be used in forensic cases. Observations and radiographs of the dentition being analysed can be compared to the skeletal atlas provided in this section (Schour and Massler, 1941; Figure 7–7). It combines observations of mineralisation and eruption of deciduous and permanent dentition and divides the development into broad stages (Table 7–24), to which ages are loosely attached. This method was based on seriation of First Nation skeletons from North America, and although it is easy to use (Hillson, 1996), its appropriateness to many forensic samples is questionable. Because there is no comparable option, it is used; however, the results must be presented with caution.

Tooth mineralisation stages for permanent dentition, recorded by radiographs and combined with eruption stages for deciduous and permanent dentition (Scheuer and Black, 2000), can be used in conjunction with dental development. Mineralisation stages of the crown and roots of permanent mandibular dentition (Moorrees et al., 1963b) are summarised in Figure 7–8 and Table 7–25; age is estimated in years. Figure 7–8 provides codes for recording mineralisation stages for crowns and roots. The appropriate codes must be recorded in the analytical notes when estimating age at death of nonadult individuals. This method has proven more reliable than age estimation based on tooth eruption (Tables 7–26 and 7–27).

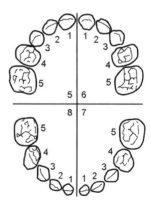

Figure 7–6. FDI two-digit system of designating teeth.
Source: FDI, 1971.

Table 7–24. *Developmental stages of teeth from 5 months antenatal to 35 years*

Stage	Schour and Massler (1941)	Ubelaker (1989)
1	5 months *in utero*	5 months *in utero* (±2 months)
2	7 months *in utero*	7 months *in utero* (±2 months)
3	Birth	Birth (±2 months)
4	6 months (±2 months)	6 months (±3 months)
5	9 months (±2 months)	9 months (±3 months)
6	1 year (±3 months)	1 year (±4 months)
7	18 months (±3 months)	18 months (±16 months)
8	2 years (±6 months)	2 years (±8 months)
9	3 years (±6 months)	3 years (±12 months)
10	4 years (±9 months)	4 years (±12 months)
11	5 years (±9 months)	5 years (±16 months)
12	6 years (±9 months)	6 years (±24 months)
13	7 years (±9 months)	7 years (±24 months)
14	8 years (±9 months)	8 years (±24 months)
15	9 years (±9 months)	9 years (±24 months)
16	10 years (±9 months)	10 years (±30 months)
17	11 years (±9 months)	11 years (±30 months)
18	12 years (±6 months)	12 years (±36 months)
19	15 years (±6 months)	15 years (±36 months)
20	21 years	21 years
21	35 years	35 years

Source: Schour and Massler, 1941; Ubelaker, 1989.

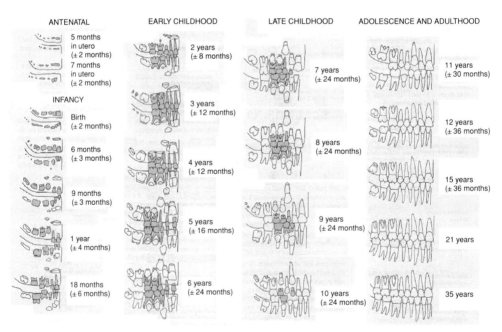

Figure 7–7. Stages of development of dentition from the ages of 5 months antenatal to 35 years. *Source:* Schour and Massler, 1941.

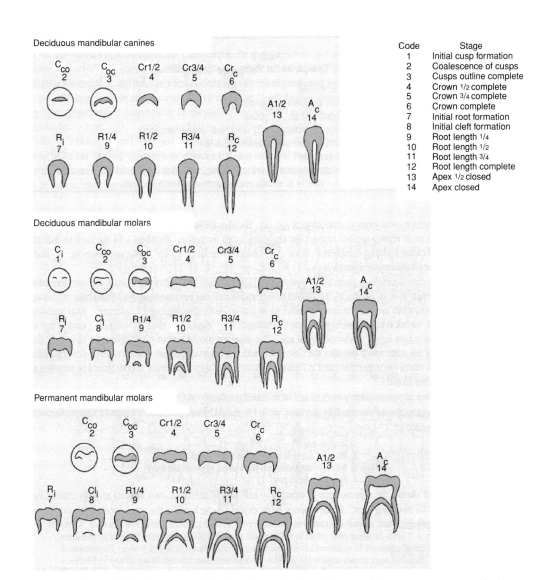

Deciduous mandibular canines

Deciduous mandibular molars

Permanent mandibular molars

Code	Stage
1	Initial cusp formation
2	Coalescence of cusps
3	Cusps outline complete
4	Crown 1/2 complete
5	Crown 3/4 complete
6	Crown complete
7	Initial root formation
8	Initial cleft formation
9	Root length 1/4
10	Root length 1/2
11	Root length 3/4
12	Root length complete
13	Apex 1/2 closed
14	Apex closed

Figure 7–8. Codes used for the stages of mineralisation of the permanent mandibular dentition. *Source:* After Moorrees et al., 1963.

Deciduous incisors, canines, and molars erupt in a predictable sequence (Hillson, 1996). Table 7–26 presents these stages (Scheuer and Black, 2000), providing an estimated age range of alveolar tooth eruption in monthly units. Similarly, age at death ranges (in years) for eruption of permanent dentition have been estimated; the age ranges are summarised in Table 7–27.

Skeletal age. The second method for estimating the age at death for nonadults is undertaken using the appearance of primary and secondary ossification centres, the

Table 7–25. *Age estimation (in years) for nonadults using tooth mineralisation*

Female	I1	I2	C	PM1	PM2	M1	M2	M3
Ci	–	–	0.6	2.0	3.3	0.2	3.6	9.9
Cco	–	–	1.0	2.5	3.9	0.5	4.0	10.4
Coc	–	–	1.6	3.2	4.5	0.9	4.5	11.0
Cr$\frac{1}{2}$	–	–	3.5	4.0	5.1	1.3	5.1	11.5
Cr$\frac{3}{4}$	–	–	4.3	4.7	5.8	1.8	5.8	12.0
Crc	–	–	4.4	5.4	6.5	2.4	6.6	12.6
Ri	–	–	5.0	6.1	7.2	3.1	7.3	13.2
Cli	–	–	–	–	–	4.0	8.4	14.1
R$\frac{1}{2}$	4.8	5.0	6.2	7.4	8.2	4.8	9.5	15.2
R$\frac{1}{2}$	5.4	5.6	7.7	8.7	9.4	5.4	10.3	16.2
R	5.9	6.2	–	–	–	–	–	–
R$\frac{3}{4}$	6.4	7.0	8.6	9.6	10.3	5.8	11.0	16.9
Rc	7.0	7.9	9.4	10.5	11.3	6.5	11.8	17.7
A$\frac{1}{2}$	7.5	8.3	10.6	11.6	12.8	7.9	13.5	19.5
Ac	–	–	–	–	–	–	–	–

Male	I1	I2	C	PM1	PM2	M1	M2	M3
Ci	–	–	0.6	2.1	3.2	0.1	3.8	9.5
Cco	–	–	1.0	2.6	3.9	0.4	4.3	10.0
Coc	–	–	1.7	3.3	4.5	0.8	4.9	10.6
Cr$\frac{1}{2}$	–	–	2.5	4.1	5.0	1.3	5.4	11.3
Cr$\frac{3}{4}$	–	–	3.4	4.9	5.8	1.9	6.1	11.8
Crc	–	–	4.4	5.6	6.6	2.5	6.8	12.4
Ri	–	–	5.2	6.4	7.3	3.2	7.6	13.2
Cli	–	–	–	–	–	4.1	8.7	14.1
R$\frac{1}{2}$	–	5.8	6.9	7.8	8.6	4.9	9.8	14.8
R$\frac{1}{2}$	5.6	6.6	8.8	9.3	10.1	5.5	10.6	15.6
R	6.2	7.2	–	–	–	–	–	–
R$\frac{3}{4}$	6.7	7.7	9.9	10.2	11.2	6.1	11.4	16.4
Rc	7.3	8.3	11.1	11.2	12.2	7.0	12.3	17.5
A$\frac{1}{2}$	7.9	8.9	12.4	12.7	13.5	8.5	13.9	19.1
Ac	–	–	–	–	–	–	–	–

Source: Smith, 1991.

observed patterns of fusion of ossification centres, and the metrical analysis of skeletal elements, including the pars basilaris, pars lateralis, and long bone measurements. The methods for osteometric analysis are dealt with separately later in this section. These approaches should be applied where condition and completeness of skeletal remains permit. Extensive reference in this section is made to the excellent and comprehensive texts of Scheuer and Black (2000, 2004), to which the reader is referred for further detail.

The appearance of primary and secondary ossification centres is a developmental method of ageing that uses the appearance of skeletal elements to determine a minimum or maximum age (Scheuer and Black, 2000). However, caution must be taken with this method because all ossification centres may not be retrieved on

Table 7–26. *Age estimation (in months) from deciduous tooth eruption*

Tooth	Mean	Range ±1 SD
Maxilla		
Central incisor	10	8–12
Lateral incisor	11	9–13
Canine	19	16–22
First molar	16	13–19♂
		14–18♀
Second molar	29	25–33
Mandible		
Central incisor	8	6–10
Lateral incisor	13	10–16
Canine	20	17–23
First molar	16	14–18
Second molar		23–31♂
	27	24–30♀

Source: Scheuer and Black, 2000.

Table 7–27. *Age estimation (in years) from permanent tooth eruption*

	Mandibular		Maxillary	
Female tooth	**Median**	**±1 SD**	**Median**	**±1 SD**
Incisor 1	6.1	0.35	5.8	0.43
Incisor 2	7.0	0.90	6.5	0.55
Canine	9.3	1.25	8.8	0.63
Premolar 1	9.0	1.09	9.1	0.90
Premolar 2	9.5	1.37	9.2	1.64
Molar 1	5.3	0.47	5.0	0.39
Molar 2	10.3	0.90	9.9	1.06
Molar 3	17.2	2.46	17.7	2.34
Male tooth	**Median**	**±1 SD**	**Median**	**±1 SD**
Incisor 1	6.2	0.86	5.9	0.74
Incisor 2	7.3	1.29	6.9	0.78
Canine	11.2	1.21	9.8	1.09
Premolar 1	9.8	1.41	9.6	1.29
Premolar 2	11.1	1.60	10.3	1.72
Molar 1	5.3	0.74	5.3	0.35
Molar 2	11.4	1.09	10.8	1.02
Molar 3	17.7	1.52	18.1	2.15

Source: Scheuer and Black, 2000.

Table 7–28. *Age estimation for nonadults through the appearance of primary and secondary cranial ossification centres*

Element		Age
Occipital	Pars squama	7–8 fetal weeks
	Pars lateralis	8–10 fetal weeks
	Pars basilaris	11–12 fetal weeks
Ear	Malleus	16–17 fetal weeks
	Incus	16 fetal weeks
	Stapes	18–19 fetal weeks
Temporal	Pars squama	7–8 fetal weeks
	Pars petrosa	By mid antenatal
	Tympanic ring	9 fetal weeks
Sphenoid	Presphenoid	12–14 fetal weeks
	Postsphenoid	13 fetal weeks
	Lesser wing	12 fetal weeks
	Greater wing	9–10 fetal weeks
Parietal		7–8 fetal weeks
Frontal		6–7 fetal weeks
Nasal		9–10 fetal weeks
Ethmoid		5 lunar months
Lacrimal		10 fetal weeks
Vomer		9–10 fetal weeks
Zygomatic		8 fetal weeks
Maxilla		6 fetal weeks
Palatine		7–8 fetal weeks
Mandible		6 weeks

Source: Scheuer and Black, 2000.

collection or exhumation. Therefore, where not all ossification centres are present, this method should be used as a guide to the minimum age only. This information is presented in two tables: the first for cranial ossification centres (Table 7–28), and the second for postcranial ossification centres (Table 7–29).

Age estimates have been developed for the fusion of primary and secondary ossification centres, based on their appearance and development (ibid.). In some instances, elements fuse at an earlier or later age than the standard, and it is also possible for elements to fail to fuse at all. These age ranges are most useful when elements are in the process of fusing that can be seen both macroscopically and, of course, radiographically. This can be deduced by the fact that fusion is incomplete, which can be to varying degrees. However, unless population-specific tests have been undertaken and provide confirmation of accuracy, this method should only be used as a guide.

Estimates for the fusion of cranial and postcranial elements are summarised in Tables 7–30 and 7–31. The various stages of maturation of bones in the hand and foot are a useful guide to age at death and where soft tissues survive, can be most easily observed using radiographs (Greulich and Pyle, 1959).

Table 7–29. *Age estimation for nonadults through the appearance of primary and secondary postcranial ossification centres*

Element		Age	
		Female	Male
Sternum	Manubrium		5 lunar months
	Sternebra 1		5–6 lunar months
	Sternebra 2		7–8 lunar months
	Sternebra 3		7–8 lunar months
	Sternebra 4		1 year
	Xiphoid		3–6 years
Clavicle	Medial epiphysis		12–14 years
	Shaft		5–6 weeks
	Lateral epiphysis		19–20 years
Scapula	Body		7–8 weeks
	Acromial epiphysis		13–16 years
	Coracoid		1 year
	Subcoracoid		8–10 years
	Glenoid epiphysis		13–16 years
	Inferior angle epiphysis		15–17 years
Hyoid	Body		Birth
	Greater horn		Birth
Atlas	Anterior arch		1–2 years
	Lateral mass		2 lunar months
Axis	Centrum		4–5 lunar months
	Apex		4–6 lunar months
	Dens		2 years
	Neural arch		7–8 fetal weeks
Ribs	1		By fetal week 12
	2		By fetal week 12
	3		By fetal week 12
	4		By fetal week 12
	5		8–9 fetal weeks
	6		8–9 fetal weeks
	7		8–9 fetal weeks
	8		By fetal week 12
	9		By fetal week 12
	10		By fetal week 12
	11		By fetal week 12
	12		By fetal week 12
Cervical 3	Centrum		4 lunar months
	Neural arch		2 lunar months
Cervical 4	Centrum		3 lunar months
	Neural arch		2 lunar months
Cervical 5	Centrum		3 lunar months
	Neural arch		2 lunar months
Cervical 6	Centrum		3 lunar months
	Neural arch		2 lunar months
Cervical 7	Centrum		3 lunar months
	Neural arch		2 lunar months
Thoracic 1	Centrum		3 lunar months
	Neural arch		2 lunar months

(cont.)

Table 7–29 (*cont.*)

Element		Age	
		Female	Male
Thoracic 2	Centrum		3 lunar months
	Neural arch		2 lunar months
Thoracic 3	Centrum		3 lunar months
	Neural arch		3 lunar months
Thoracic 4	Centrum		3 lunar months
	Neural arch		3 lunar months
Thoracic 5	Centrum		3 lunar months
	Neural arch		3 lunar months
Thoracic 6	Centrum		3 lunar months
	Neural arch		3 lunar months
Thoracic 7	Centrum		3 lunar months
	Neural arch		3 lunar months
Thoracic 8	Centrum		3 lunar months
	Neural arch		3 lunar months
Thoracic 9	Centrum		3 lunar months
	Neural arch		3 lunar months
Thoracic 10	Centrum		3 lunar months
	Neural arch		3 lunar months
Thoracic 11	Centrum		3 lunar months
	Neural arch		3 lunar months
Thoracic 12	Centrum		3 lunar months
	Neural arch		3 lunar months
Lumbar 1	Centrum		3 lunar months
	Neural arch		3 lunar months
Lumbar 2	Centrum		3 lunar months
	Neural arch		3 lunar months
Lumbar 3	Centrum		3 lunar months
	Neural arch		4 lunar months
Lumbar 4	Centrum		3 lunar months
	Neural arch		4 lunar months
Lumbar 5	Centrum		3 lunar months
	Neural arch		4 lunar months
Sacral segment 1	Centrum		3 lunar months
	Neural arch		4 lunar months
	Lateral element		6 lunar months
Sacral segment 2	Centrum		3 lunar months
	Neural arch		4 lunar months
	Lateral element		6 lunar months
Sacral segment 3	Centrum		4 lunar months
	Neural arch		4 lunar months
	Lateral element		6 lunar months
Sacral segment 4	Centrum		4 lunar months
	Neural arch		5 lunar months
Sacral segment 5	Centrum		5 lunar months
	Neural arch		5 lunar months
Coccyx	Co 1		8 lunar months
	Co 2		3–4 years

Element			Female	Male
		Co 3	10 years	
		Co 4	Puberty	
Humerus		Diaphysis	7 lunar weeks	
		Greater tubercle	1–2 years	
		Proximal epiphysis	2–6 months	
		Capitulum	1–2 years	
		Medial epicondyle	4 years +	
		Trochlea	8 years	
		Lateral epicondyle	10 years	
Radius		Diaphysis	7 fetal weeks	
		Proximal epiphysis	5 years	
		Tubercle flake	1–2 years	
Ulna		Diaphysis	7 weeks	
		Olecranon	8–10 years	
		Distal epiphysis	5–7 years	
Carpal		Scaphoid	5 years	6 years
		Lunate	3 years	4 years
		Triquetral	1–2 years	
		Pisiform	8 years	10 years
		Trapezium	4 years	5 years
		Trapezoid	5 years	6 years
		Capitate	2–3 months	3–4 months
		Hamate	3–4 months	4–5 months
Metacarpal	MC 1	Shaft	8–10 fetal weeks	
		Base	2 years	2–3 years
	MC 2–5	Head	16–19 months	22–26 months
		Shaft	8–10 fetal weeks	
Proximal phalanges	1	Shaft	9–11 fetal weeks	
		Epiphysis	2 years	2–3 years
	2–5	Shaft	9–11 fetal weeks	
		Epiphysis	10–17 months	14–24 months
Intermediate phalanges	2–4	Shaft	10–12 fetal weeks	
		Epiphysis	19 months	2.5 years
Distal phalanges	5	Shaft	10–12 fetal weeks	
		Epiphysis	2.5 years	2.3 years
	1	Shaft	7–9 fetal weeks	
		Epiphysis	22 months	17 months
	2–4	Shaft	7–9 fetal weeks	
		Epiphysis	2 years	2–3 years
	5	Shaft	7–9 fetal weeks	
Sesamoids		Epiphysis	2.5 years	2.3 years
			11–15 years	13–18 years
Pelvis		Ilium	2–3 lunar months	
		Ischium	4–5 lunar months	
		Pubis	5–6 lunar months	
		Acetabular epiphysis	10–11 years	
		Ischial tuberosity epiphysis	13–16 years	
		Iliac crest	12–14 years	14–17 years
		Anterior inferior iliac spine	10–13 years	
		Pubic symphysis	15–23 years	
		Pubic tubercle	23–27 years	

(cont.)

Table 7–29 (*cont.*)

Element			Age	
			Female	Male
Femur		Diaphysis	7–8 fetal weeks	
		Distal epiphysis	36–40 fetal weeks	
		Proximal epiphysis	By 1 year	
		Greater trochanter	2–5 years	
		Lesser trochanter	7–12 years	
Patella			3–6 years	
Tibia		Diaphysis	7–8 fetal weeks	
		Proximal epiphysis	36–40 fetal weeks	
		Distal epiphysis	3–10 months	
		Tuberosity	8–12 years	9–14 years
Fibula		Diaphysis	8 fetal weeks	
		Distal epiphysis	9–22 months	
		Proximal epiphysis	4th year	5th year
Tarsals		Calcaneus	5–6 fetal months	
		Calcaneus epiphysis	5–6 years	7–8 years
		Talus	6–7 fetal months	
		Talus epiphysis	8 years	11 years
		Cuboid	1–3 months	
		Navicular	2–3 years	4–5 years
		Navicular epiphysis	9–10 years	12–13 years
		Lateral cuneiform	3–6 months	
		Middle cuneiform	24–36 months	36–48 months
		Medial cuneiform	12–24 months	24–36 months
Metatarsal	MT 1	Shaft	12 fetal weeks	
		Base	18–20 months	26–31 months
	MT 2	Head	19–24 months	27–34 months
		Shaft	8–10 fetal weeks	
	MT 3	Head	2 years, 5 months	3 years, 5 months
		Shaft	8–10 fetal weeks	
	MT 4	Head	2 years, 8 months	4 years
		Shaft	8–10 fetal weeks	
		Head	2–3 years	4–5 years
	MT 5	Shaft	8–10 fetal weeks	
		Epiphysis	9–10 years	12–13 years
Proximal phalanges 1–5		Shaft	14–16 fetal weeks	
		Epiphysis	11–20 months	18–28 months
Intermediate phalange	1 & 5	Shaft	16–20 fetal weeks	
	2–4	Shaft	16–20 fetal weeks	
		Base	11–14 months	14–24 months
Distal phalange	1	Shaft	9–12 fetal weeks	
	Base	9 months	14 months	
	2–5	Shaft	9–12 fetal weeks	
		Epiphysis	2–3 years	4–5 years
Sesamoids for MT 1			9 years	12 years

Source: Scheuer and Black, 2000.

Table 7–30. *Age estimation for nonadults from the fusion of cranial ossification centres*

Cranial Element		Age	
		Female	Male
Occipital	Median sagittal suture and sutura mendosa	Birth–1 year	
	Hypoglossal canal complete	2–4 years	
	Pars lateralis to squama	1–3 years	
	Pars basilaris to lateralis	5–7 years	
	Spheno-occipital synchondrosis	11–16 years	13–18 years
	Closure of jugular growth plate	22–34 years	
Ear	Malleus to goniale	Week 19 antenatal	
Temporal	Pars squama to tympanic ring	Week 35 antenatal	
	Petromastoid to squamotympanic parts	1st year	
	Foramen of Huschke complete	1–5 years	
Sphenoid	Lesser wing to body sutura mendosa sutura mendosa sutura mendosa	5 months antenatal	
	Pre- to postsphenoid	8 months antenatal	
	Pterygoid to greater wings	8 months antenatal	
	Greater wings to body	1st year	
	Foramen ovale complete	1st year	
	Foramen spinosum complete	By 2nd year	
	Sphenoidal conchae to ethmoid	4 years–puberty	
Frontal	Anterior fontanelle closed	1–2 years	
	Metopic suture closed	2–4 years	
Ethmoid	Cribriform plate and crista galli to labyrinths	1–2 years	
	Ethmoid to vomer	20–30 years	
Palatal process		18 weeks antenatal	
Mandible	Coronoid to main mass	8 weeks antenatal	
	Fusion at symphysis	At year 1	

Source: Scheuer and Black, 2000.

Metrical analysis. Metrical analysis used in the estimation of age for nonadult skeletal remains uses rates of growth and development of ossification centres. The rate of growth and maturation prior to fusion is highly dependent on environmental, nutritional, and genetic factors. Consequently, any secular change and variation will be specific to the sample on which the observations were made. However, these age ranges can be used as a rough guide to differentiate between individuals of similar ages within a group, as long as it is considered that individual circumstances such as periods of poor health may have affected growth. The approach taken will, of course, depend on the condition and completeness of the skeletal remains. Where the sample size on which the data were derived is known, it is indicated as 'n'. Small sample sizes will reduce the reliance that can be placed on these data. Descriptions

Table 7–31. *Age estimation for nonadults from the fusion of postcranial ossification centres*

Postcranial Element		Age	
		Female	Male
Sternum	Sternebra 3 to 4	4–10 years	
	Sternebra 2 to sternebrae 3–4	11–16 years	
	Epiphyses begin to fuse	11–16 years	
	Sternebra 1 to mesosternum	15–20 years	
	Sternum complete	21 years	
	Xiphoid to mesosternum	40+ years	
Clavicle	Medial epiphyseal flake	Begins fusing 16–21 years, most are fused by c. 24 years, completes fusion by 29+ years	
	Lateral epiphyseal flake	19–20 years	
Scapula	Coracoid and subcoracoid to body	Begins 13–16 years Completes 15–17 years	
	Glenoid epiphysis	17–18 years	
	Acromial and coracoid epiphyses	By 20 years	
	Inferior angle and medial border	By 23 years	
Hyoid	Fusion of some elements	In adult life	
Atlas	Transverse foramen complete	3–4 years	
	Posterior synchondrosis	4–5 years	
	Anterior arch	5–6 years	
Axis	Intradental fusion	8 months antenatal to birth	
	Posterior synchondrosis	3–4 years	
	Dentoneural synchondrosis	3–4 years	
	Dens to centrum	4–6 years	
	Neural arches to centrum	4–6 years	
	Ossiculum terminale to dens	12 years	
Cervical vertebrae 3–7	Posterior synchondrosis	1–2 years	
	Transverse foramen complete	3–4 years	
	Neural arches to centrum	3–4 years	
	Annular rings	17–25 years	
Thoracic	Posterior synchondrosis	1–2 years	
	All primary centres fused	5–6 years	
	Annular rings	16–19 years	
Lumbar	Posterior synchondrosis upper lumbar	1–2 years	
	Lamina of L5	4–5 years	
	All primary centres fused	5–6 years	
	Annular rings	17–24 years	
Sacrum	Neural arch to lateral element S1–3	2–5 years	
	Neural arch to centrum to S1–2	2–6 years	
	All primary centres fused	5–6 years	
	Posterior synchondroses	Begins fusing 6–8 years Completes fusion 10–15 years	
	Lateral elements (to each other)	Begins fusing 12 years	
Ribs	Epiphyses of heads	17–25 years	
Humerus	Centres for head, lesser and greater tubercles fuse as composite epiphysis	2–6 years	
	Distal composite epiphysis to shaft	11–15 years	12–17 years
	Medial epicondyle to shaft	13–15 years	14–16 years
	Composite proximal epiphysis to shaft	13–17 years	16–20 years

Postcranial Element		Age	
		Female	Male
Radius	Proximal epiphysis	11½–13 years	14–17 years
	Distal epiphysis	14–17 years	16–20 years
Ulna	Proximal epiphysis	12–14 years	13–16 years
	Distal epiphysis	15–17 years	17–20 years
Hand	Base of MC1	14–14½ years	16½ years
	Head of MC2–5	14½–15 years	16½ years
	Distal phalangeal epiphyses	13½ years	16 years
	Proximal and distal epiphyses	14–14½ years	16½ years
Pelvis	Ischiopubic ramus	5–8 years	
	Acetabulum (tripartite fusion)	11–15 years	14–17 years
	Iliac crest	Begins fusing 17–20 years	
		Completes fusion 20–23 years	
	Anterior inferior iliac spine epiphysis	Begins fusing 20 years	
	Ischial epiphysis	20–23 years	
Femur	Proximal epiphysis	12–16 years	14–19 years
	Distal epiphysis	14–18 years	16–20 years
	Greater trochanter	14–16 years	16–18 years
	Lesser trochanter	16–17 years	
Tibia	Proximal epiphysis	13–17 years	15–19 years
	Distal epiphysis	14–16 years	15–18 years
	Tuberosity	12–14 years	
Fibula	Proximal epiphysis	12–17 years	15–20 years
	Distal epiphysis	12–15 years	15–18 years
Tarsal	Calcaneal epiphysis	Begins fusing 10–12 years	Begins fusing 11–14 years
		Completes fusion 15–16 years	Completes fusion 18–20 years
	Talar epiphysis	9 years	12 years
	Base of metatarsal 5	9–12 years	12–15 years
	Head of metatarsal 2–5	11–13 years	14–16 years
	Distal and middle phalangeal epiphyses	11–13 years	14–16 years

Source: Scheuer and Black, 2000.

of the measurements used for ageing juveniles and infants are described in Tables 7–32 to 7–43, which cover the skeletal elements listed in Table 7–32.

For determining whether an infant is pre- or postnatal, the pars basilaris is particularly useful (Scheuer and MacLaughlin-Black, 1994). The sagittal length is greater than the width in individuals younger than 28 weeks *in utero*. Furthermore, the maximum length is less than the width if the individual is more than 5 months postnatal (Table 7–33). Pars lateralis is also useful in this respect (ibid.) when correlated against the development of pars basilaris. When both the pars basilaris and the pars lateralis are available, and they are approximately the same length, then the age is younger than 7 months *in utero*. In the perinatal period, pars lateralis has a faster growth rate and is longer than pars basilaris, and at this time pars basilaris

Table 7–32. *Nonadult skeletal elements used for the metrical analysis for the estimation of age*

Skeletal element	Age group
Occipital	Ante- and postnatal
Temporal	Antenatal
Maxilla	Antenatal
Clavicle	Ante- and postnatal
Humerus	Ante- and postnatal
Ulna	Ante- and postnatal
Femur	Ante- and postnatal
Sphenoid	Antenatal
Zygomatic	Antenatal
Mandible	Antenatal
Scapula	Ante- and postnatal
Radius	Ante- and postnatal
Pelvis	Antenatal
Tibia and fibula	Ante- and postnatal

Source: Derived from Scheuer and Black, 2000.

Table 7–33. *Dimensions (in millimetres) of the pars basilaris in individuals of documented age*

Documented age	n	Mean maximum width WB	Mean length LB (F&K)	Mean length LB (R)
2 weeks	3	14.5	11.3	15.6
3 weeks	1	16.9	12.7	17.0
4 weeks	1	15.6	12.6	16.8
7 weeks	1	15.5	11.6	15.9
3 months	1	15.4	13.8	16.7
5 months	1	18.4	13.4	18.1
8 months	2	21.0	13.8	20.5
9 months	3	20.5	13.9	19.6
11 months	1	22.3	14.0	19.7
1 year	1	18.3	13.9	17.9
1 year, 1 month	2	22.1	14.8	19.8
1 year, 2 months	3	22.7	15.8	21.3
1 year, 3 months	1	23.6	16.8	22.7
1 year, 4 months	1	18.6	14.0	18.6
1 year, 6 months	3	21.9	15.5	20.8
1 year, 8 months	1	22.8	15.7	21.7
1 year, 9 months	1	22.7	16.8	21.3
2 years, 3 months	2	24.4	18.1	23.5
2 years, 5 months	2	25.8	17.5	24.2
2 years, 6 months	1	24.6	17.5	22.4
2 years, 7 months	4	25.9	17.4	24.2
2 years, 9 months	2	24.2	16.4	23.3
3 years, 2 months	1	23.2	16.6	22.7
3 years, 4 months	1	27.6	16.6	24.6
3 years, 5 months	1	26.1	18.1	24.1
3 years, 7 months	1	27.8	17.5	24.8
3 years, 8 months	1	27.3	15.5	24.0
4 years, 3 months	2	25.9	16.4	24.2
4 years, 7 months	1	26.2	15.3	23.9

Source: Scheuer and Black, 2000.

Table 7–34. *Dimensions (in millimetres) of the antenatal sphenoid bone*

Age (weeks)	Body		Lesser wing		Greater wing	
	Length	Width	Length	Width	Length	Width
12	–	–	–	–	5.0	1.5
14	–	–	–	–	5.1	2.3
16	2.7	4.5	4.7	4.0	10.3	5.7
18	3.7	5.5	5.9	4.8	13.1	7.0
20	5.1	9.6	6.3	5.2	15.3	8.5
22	5.9	10.5	7.9	6.0	17.1	9.2
24	6.1	11.7	9.0	6.4	19.0	10.1
26	7.4	12.2	10.5	7.0	19.7	10.5
28	7.9	12.5	12.5	7.6	21.6	11.7
30	8.1	13.5	13.7	8.2	22.0	12.6
32	8.5	14.5	14.7	8.5	24.5	13.7
34	9.1	15.0	15.1	9.3	25.4	14.8
36	9.5	16.0	15.8	10.3	26.4	15.4
38	10.9	17.2	17.1	11.0	28.7	16.1
40	11.7	17.9	19.4	12.4	31.0	17.4

Source: Scheuer and Black, 2000.

Table 7–35. *Dimensions (in millimetres) of the pars petrosa and the tympanic ring*

Age (weeks)	Pars petrosa	
	Length	Width
12	–	–
14	–	–
16	10.5	5.3
18	12.3	5.7
20	14.4	8.7
22	17.3	9.7
24	18.8	10.2
26	19.9	10.6
28	21.4	10.9
30	22.5	13.1
32	27.7	13.5
34	29.7	15.4
36	33.0	16.1
38	35.1	17.0
40	38.1	17.5

Source: Scheuer and Black, 2000.

Table 7–36. *Dimensions (in millimetres) of the antenatal zygomatic bone*

| Age (weeks) | Zygomatic bone | |
	Length	Width
12	4.5	4.0
14	5.8	4.9
16	9.0	7.1
18	11.5	9.6
20	13.5	10.3
22	14.2	11.2
24	15.0	12.1
26	16.5	13.4
28	17.5	14.1
30	18.5	14.8
32	19.5	15.6
34	20.9	16.6
36	21.8	17.2
38	24.6	18.4
40	25.8	20.2

Source: Scheuer and Black, 2000.

Table 7–37. *Dimensions (in millimetres) of the antenatal maxilla*

| Age (weeks) | Maxilla | | | |
	Length	Height	Width	Oblique length
12	4.2	3.1	–	6.0
14	6.3	5.6	5.6	9.3
16	8.9	8.9	9.8	14.0
18	10.6	10.0	11.6	15.3
20	12.6	12.3	13.0	18.8
22	13.5	13.4	14.2	20.0
24	15.1	14.1	15.4	21.6
26	15.9	15.6	15.9	22.3
28	17.3	17.1	17.7	23.3
30	17.8	18.2	18.7	23.8
32	19.4	19.6	20.0	26.0
34	20.0	20.9	21.2	28.2
36	22.0	21.9	22.3	28.9
38	24.1	24.1	24.2	32.1
40	24.1	24.5	25.1	34.3

Source: Scheuer and Black, 2000.

Table 7–38. *Dimensions (in millimetres) of antenatal mandible*

| Age (weeks) | Antenatal mandible | | |
	Body length	Width	Longest length
12	8.0	–	10.7
14	9.6	3.2	12.6
16	13.0	6.5	17.9
18	14.2	6.9	21.4
20	17.6	8.0	25.6
22	19.2	9.0	27.3
24	21.5	10.2	30.1
26	22.6	10.9	31.9
28	24.2	11.3	34.0
30	26.0	13.0	35.9
32	27.7	14.1	39.0
34	30.0	15.1	40.2
36	31.7	16.4	42.7
38	34.7	17.0	47.5
40	36.5	18.0	49.7

Source: Scheuer and Black, 2000.

Table 7–39. *Maximum clavicular length (in millimetres) for antenatal measurements*

| Age (weeks) | Antenatal clavicle | |
	Fazekas and Kósa (1978)	Yarkoni et al. (1985)
12	8.2	–
14	11.1	–
16	16.3	17.0
18	19.4	19.0
20	22.7	21.0
22	24.5	23.0
24	26.9	25.0
26	28.3	27.0
28	30.3	29.0
30	31.3	31.0
32	35.6	33.0
34	37.1	35.0
36	37.7	37.0
38	42.6	39.0
40	44.1	41.0

Source: Scheuer and Black, 2000.

Table 7–40. *Maximum clavicular length (in millimetres) for nonadult measurements*

| Documented age | | Postnatal clavicle | |
	n	Mean	Range
0–6 months	11	44.4	38.8–54.5
7–12 months	9	54.1	48.0–60.9
1–1½ years	11	59.5	54.3–66.0
1½–2 years	4	63.0	61.4–64.6
2–3 years	13	66.5	58.5–72.6
3–4 years	7	73.4	69.1–77.0
4–5 years	8	74.4	65.3–82.0
5–6 years	2	75.9	74.7–77.0
6–7 years	4	86.5	85.4–88.8
7–8 years	1	89.5	–
8–9 years	3	89.0	78.5–98.7
9–10 years	0	–	–
10–11 years	2	103.7	103.0–104.0
11–12 years	2	105.0	104.5–105.0
12–13 years	3	106.4	102.5–111.3
13–14 years	2	118.6	117.0–120.1
14–15 years	2	118.5	113.5–123.5
15–16 years	3	137.7	127.0–154.0

Source: Scheuer and Black, 2000.

Table 7–41. *Dimensions (in centimetres) of the antenatal scapula*

| Age (weeks) | Antenatal scapula | | |
	Length	Width	Spine
12	0.45	0.30	0.35
14	0.71	0.51	0.58
16	1.16	0.90	1.02
18	1.50	1.15	1.24
20	1.72	1.39	1.54
22	1.88	1.54	1.70
24	2.09	1.75	1.84
26	2.23	1.85	1.95
28	2.31	1.94	2.12
30	2.45	2.05	2.22
32	2.66	2.23	2.38
34	2.81	2.33	2.53
36	2.93	2.44	2.60
38	3.31	2.58	2.91
40	3.55	2.95	3.16

Source: Scheuer and Black, 2000.

Table 7–42. *Dimensions (in centimetres) of the nonadult scapula*

Documented age	n	Postnatal scapula Length	n	Width
0–6 months	1	3.93	7	3.11
6–12 months	15	4.92	16	3.70
1–2 years	19	6.04	19	4.33
2–3 years	10	6.78	8	5.98
3–4 years	5	6.39	5	5.60
4–5 years	3	8.10	3	5.68
5–6 years	3	9.17	3	6.18
6–7 years	6	9.73	7	6.61
7–8 years	1	9.40	2	6.33
8–9 years	1	11.70	1	8.25
9–10 years	2	12.00	2	7.73
10–11 years	1	12.10	2	8.73
11–12 years	1	12.10	1	8.20

Source: Scheuer and Black, 2000.

Table 7–43. *Dimensions (in millimetres) of the antenatal ilium, ischium, and pubis*

Age (weeks)	Antenatal ilium Length	Width	Ischium Length	Width	Pubis Length
12	4.8	3.2	–	–	–
14	5.7	3.8	–	–	–
16	9.7	7.8	3.1	2.2	–
18	12.0	9.8	3.8	2.9	–
20	15.6	12.6	5.5	3.5	3.6
22	16.5	14.2	6.4	4.3	4.5
24	18.3	15.6	7.5	5.6	5.5
26	19.6	17.1	8.7	6.0	6.0
28	21.3	19.1	9.7	6.6	6.6
30	22.1	20.1	10.3	7.6	8.0
32	25.1	22.2	12.1	8.1	9.9
34	26.8	24.6	13.2	9.3	12.4
36	28.7	26.0	16.2	10.4	14.1
38	32.1	28.5	17.2	11.6	15.0
40	34.5	30.4	18.5	12.4	16.6

Source: Scheuer and Black, 2000.

Table 7–44. *Humeral diaphyseal length (in millimetres) of nonadults from 1.5 months to 12 years*

Age (years)	Male			Female		
	n	Mean	SD	*n*	Mean	SD
0.125	59	72.4	4.5	69	71.8	3.6
0.25	59	80.6	4.8	65	80.2	3.8
0.50	67	88.4	5.0	78	86.8	4.6
1.00	72	105.5	5.2	81	103.6	4.8
1.5	68	118.8	5.4	84	117.0	5.1
2.0	68	130.0	5.5	84	127.7	5.8
2.5	72	139.0	5.9	82	136.9	6.1
3.0	71	147.5	6.7	79	145.3	6.7
3.5	73	155.0	7.8	78	153.4	7.1
4.0	72	162.7	6.9	80	160.9	7.7
4.5	71	169.8	7.4	78	169.1	8.3
5.0	77	177.4	8.2	80	176.3	8.7
5.5	73	184.6	8.1	74	182.6	9.0
6.0	71	190.9	7.6	75	190.0	9.6
6.5	72	197.3	8.1	81	196.7	9.7
7.0	71	203.6	8.7	86	202.6	10.0
7.5	76	210.4	8.9	83	209.3	10.5
8.0	70	217.3	9.8	85	216.3	10.4
8.5	72	222.5	9.2	82	221.3	11.2
9.0	76	228.7	9.6	83	228.0	11.8
9.5	78	235.1	10.7	83	234.2	12.9
10.0	77	241.0	10.3	84	239.8	13.2
10.5	76	245.8	11.0	75	245.9	14.6
11.0	75	251.7	10.7	76	251.9	14.7
11.5	76	257.4	11.9	75	259.1	15.3
12.0	73	263.0	12.8	71	265.6	15.6

Source: Sheuer and Black, 2000.

is either longer than it is wide, or square in shape. After the perinatal period, pars lateralis is always longer than pars basilaris, and pars basilaris has greater width than it has length.

Long bone measurements are undertaken on the complete shaft of unfused skeletal elements. In cases where the proximal or distal epiphyses are fused, methods using long bone measurements cannot be performed. The tables adapted from Maresh (1970) are used to estimate age from 1.5 months postnatal to 12 years (see Tables 7–44, 7–45, 7–46, 7–47, 7–48, and 7–49). For ages 10 to 18 years, refer to Tables 7–50, 7–51, 7–52, 7–53, 7–54, and 7–55 (ibid.). Where measurements are too small for this method to be applied, the regression formulae can be used (refer to Tables 7–56, 7–57, 7–58, 7–59, 7–60 and 7–61). These regressions equations can only be used on skeletal elements of 24 weeks *in utero* to 6 weeks postnatal. Because development does not proceed in a linear fashion in the third trimester, the logarithmic regression should be used for skeletal remains likely to fall within that phase.

Table 7–45. *Radial diaphyseal length (in millimetres) of nonadults from 1.5 months to 12 years*

Age (years)	Male			Female		
	n	Mean	SD	n	Mean	SD
0.125	59	59.7	3.3	69	57.8	2.8
0.25	59	66.0	3.3	65	63.4	2.8
0.50	67	70.8	3.5	78	67.6	3.4
1.00	72	82.6	4.0	81	78.9	3.4
1.5	68	91.4	4.4	83	87.5	4.0
2.0	68	98.6	4.7	84	95.0	4.5
2.5	71	105.2	4.8	82	101.4	5.0
3.0	71	111.6	5.3	79	107.7	5.2
3.5	73	116.9	6.2	78	113.8	5.5
4.0	72	123.1	5.6	80	119.2	5.7
4.5	71	128.2	5.6	78	125.2	6.6
5.0	77	133.8	6.1	80	130.2	6.9
5.5	73	138.9	6.4	74	134.6	7.2
6.0	71	143.8	5.9	75	140.0	7.4
6.5	72	148.3	6.4	81	144.7	7.8
7.0	71	153.0	6.7	86	149.3	8.0
7.5	76	157.9	6.9	83	154.3	8.4
8.0	70	162.9	7.1	85	158.9	8.7
8.5	72	166.8	6.6	82	162.8	8.8
9.0	76	171.3	7.4	83	167.6	9.3
9.5	78	176.1	7.7	83	172.2	10.2
10.0	77	180.5	7.9	84	176.8	10.4
10.5	76	184.4	8.4	75	181.8	11.8
11.0	75	188.7	8.5	76	186.0	11.7
11.5	76	193.0	9.2	75	192.0	12.1
12.0	74	197.4	9.5	71	196.9	12.7

Source: Scheuer and Black, 2000.

7.7.2 Ageing adults

There are many methods of age determination for adults discussed in the literature (Cox, 2001a, 2001b), and not all are considered particularly relevant to forensic work because of their large margins of error. Some methods are applied less frequently because of their restricted application (i.e., fusion of the medial clavicle), but these can serve to indicate a minimum age, and some only work when some soft tissues survive. The two most commonly used approaches are described here in greater detail. These are the final stages of maturation, and degeneration, with their associated remodelling of skeletal elements. Maturation is particularly useful for identifying young adults. Degeneration and remodelling are suitable for individuals who have reached full skeletal maturity. The most commonly applied methods in the latter category are age-related changes to the pubic symphysis, the auricular surface, and the sternal rib ends (ibid.).

Final stages of skeletal maturation. Several areas of the skeleton complete maturation during the late second and third decades of life and, consequently, have value in

Table 7–46. *Ulna diaphyseal length (in millimetres) of nonadults from 1.5 months to 12 years*

Age (years)	Male			Female		
	n	Mean	SD	n	Mean	SD
0.125	59	67.0	3.5	69	65.3	3.1
0.25	59	73.8	3.4	65	71.2	3.1
0.50	67	79.1	3.7	78	75.7	3.8
1.00	71	92.6	4.4	81	89.0	4.0
1.5	68	102.3	4.6	83	98.9	4.4
2.0	68	109.7	4.9	84	107.1	4.8
2.5	71	116.6	5.2	82	113.8	5.2
3.0	71	123.4	5.6	79	120.6	5.4
3.5	73	129.1	6.4	78	127.2	5.7
4.0	72	135.6	5.6	80	133.1	5.8
4.5	71	141.0	5.6	78	139.3	6.6
5.0	77	147.0	6.1	80	144.6	7.1
5.5	73	152.6	6.7	74	149.1	7.2
6.0	71	157.5	6.2	75	154.9	7.4
6.5	72	162.2	6.8	81	159.9	7.9
7.0	71	167.3	7.0	86	164.8	8.3
7.5	76	172.2	7.4	83	170.1	8.5
8.0	70	177.3	7.4	85	174.9	8.7
8.5	72	181.6	7.1	82	179.1	8.8
9.0	76	186.4	7.9	83	184.3	9.5
9.5	78	191.7	8.3	83	189.7	10.4
10.0	77	196.2	8.5	84	194.4	10.6
10.5	76	200.4	8.8	75	200.0	12.4
11.0	75	205.1	9.2	76	204.7	12.0
11.5	76	209.8	9.9	75	211.3	13.1
12.0	74	214.5	10.2	70	216.4	13.3

Source: Scheuer and Black, 2000.

identifying those dying in early adulthood. These include the iliac crest, ventral (or annular) rings of the vertebrae, fusion of the medial clavicle, and petroexoccipital articulation.

A study by Scoles et al. (1988) suggested that iliac crest fusion occurs in females by 18 years and 1 month (SD 12 months) and in males by 18 years and 6 months (SD 7 months). Consequently, complete fusion indicates someone older than 20 years. The patterns of fusion of annular (ventral or epiphyseal) rings to their respective vertebral bodies can also be used to estimate the age of individuals. Albert and Maples (1995) developed this method to distinguish between four phases: children, late teenagers, young adults, and older adults. The age groups and descriptions are illustrated in Table 7–62.

Although there are other studies, Black and Scheuer's (1996) evaluation of a five-phase system of medial epiphyseal fusion is particularly useful. Based on a large sample, it demonstrates that complete fusion of the medial clavicle occurs by 28 years in whites and 34 years in blacks. Fusion of the jugular growth plate (petroexoccipital articulation) was examined by Maat and Mastwijk (1995) and Hershkovitz et al.

Table 7–47. *Femoral diaphyseal length (in millimetres) of nonadults from 1.5 months to 12 years*

Age (years)	Male			Female		
	n	Mean	SD	n	Mean	SD
0.125	59	86.0	5.4	68	87.2	4.3
0.25	59	100.7	4.8	65	100.8	3.6
0.50	67	112.2	5.0	78	111.1	4.6
1.00	72	136.6	5.8	81	134.6	4.9
1.5	68	155.4	6.8	84	153.9	6.4
2.0	68	172.4	7.3	84	170.8	7.1
2.5	72	187.2	7.8	82	185.2	7.7
3.0	71	200.3	8.5	79	198.4	8.7
3.5	73	212.1	11.4	78	211.1	10.0
4.0	72	224.1	9.9	80	223.2	10.1
4.5	71	235.7	10.5	78	235.5	11.4
5.0	77	247.5	11.1	80	247.0	11.5
5.5	73	258.2	11.7	74	257.0	12.2
6.0	71	269.7	12.0	75	268.9	13.5
6.5	72	280.3	12.6	81	279.0	13.8
7.0	71	291.1	13.3	86	288.8	13.6
7.5	76	301.2	13.5	83	299.8	15.2
8.0	70	312.1	14.6	85	309.8	15.6
8.5	72	321.0	14.6	82	318.9	15.8
9.0	76	330.4	14.6	83	328.7	16.8
9.5	78	340.0	15.8	83	338.8	18.6
10.0	77	349.3	15.7	84	347.9	19.1
10.5	76	357.4	16.2	75	356.5	21.4
11.0	75	367.0	16.5	76	367.0	22.4
11.5	76	375.8	18.1	75	378.0	23.4
12.0	74	386.1	19.0	71	387.6	22.9

Source: Scheuer and Black, 2000.

(1997). Bilateral fusion in females is usually complete by 34 years and in males by 36 years. However, this method must be applied with caution because fusion can occur up to the age of 50 years, and in 9 percent of cases, fusion does not occur at all.

Further methods can be used to identify the skeletal remains of young adults, and these are documented in further detail in Scheuer and Black (2000). Of particular interest is complete epiphyseal fusion of the flakes at the head of ribs. Although there does not seem to be a pattern to the age of appearance of the flakes, fusion is complete between 17 and 25 years. Fusion of the epiphyseal suprasternal flakes of the manubrium can occur from ages 12 to 19 years, and the first costal notch on the manubrium fuses between 18 and 24 years. Finally, the epiphysis of the sacroiliac joint appears at 15 to16 years and fuses by age 18 years (ibid.).

Degeneration and remodelling. The following techniques are only suitable for ageing skeletal elements that have reached full skeletal maturity. Full skeletal maturity differs for each skeletal element and occurs at the point when all the epiphyses on the particular bone have fused. It is for this reason that methods based on

Table 7–48. *Tibiae diaphyseal length (in millimetres) of nonadults from 1.5 months to 12 years*

Age (years)	Male			Female		
	n	Mean	SD	n	Mean	SD
0.125	59	70.8	5.4	69	70.3	4.6
0.25	58	81.9	5.3	65	80.8	4.6
0.50	67	91.0	5.2	78	88.9	5.3
1.00	72	110.3	5.2	81	108.5	4.8
1.5	68	126.1	6.0	84	124.0	5.6
2.0	68	140.1	6.5	84	138.2	6.5
2.5	72	152.5	6.8	82	150.1	7.0
3.0	72	163.5	7.7	79	161.1	8.2
3.5	73	172.8	9.8	78	171.2	8.7
4.0	72	182.8	9.0	80	180.8	9.5
4.5	71	191.8	9.2	78	190.9	10.5
5.0	77	201.4	9.9	80	199.9	11.4
5.5	73	210.3	10.7	74	207.9	12.5
6.0	71	218.9	10.0	75	217.4	12.6
6.5	72	227.8	11.6	81	226.3	13.6
7.0	71	236.2	11.8	86	234.1	14.1
7.5	76	244.2	12.4	83	243.2	15.0
8.0	70	253.3	12.9	85	251.7	15.6
8.5	72	260.6	12.3	82	259.1	15.6
9.0	76	268.7	13.4	83	265.5	17.1
9.5	78	276.9	14.4	83	276.6	18.7
10.0	77	284.9	14.2	84	284.3	19.3
10.5	76	292.0	15.1	75	292.4	21.4
11.0	75	298.8	15.0	76	300.8	21.2
11.5	76	306.8	16.5	75	310.5	21.4
12.0	73	315.9	17.0	71	318.2	21.7

Source: Scheuer and Black, 2000.

morphological change to the pubic symphyses, sternal rib ends, and auricular surface of the ilium may be useful for slightly different ages. The casts for each of the former two methods can be used to assist in the estimation of age at death. Ideally, they should only be used where the individuals subject to analysis are similar to those on which the method was developed (7.2.5). There is an inherent problem with the use of casts, in that inexperienced practitioners are often assessing visual characteristics without any in-depth understanding of the underlying biological processes involved. Consequently, when a case does not 'fit' the predicted stage exactly, they lack the understanding to extrapolate from them. For that reason, it is suggested that the use of accurate and detailed descriptions of age-related changes to articular surfaces is more beneficial to inexperienced practitioners.

Pubic symphysis. The age-related changes that are manifest on the symphyseal surface of the pubis of the os coxae have been recognised for many years and are widely used. For a detailed discussion of the reliability of this method, see Cox (2000a). Although

Table 7–49. *Fibula diaphyseal length (in millimetres) of nonadults from 1.5 months to 12 years*

Age (years)	Male			Female		
	n	Mean	SD	n	Mean	SD
0.125	590	68.1	5.3	69	66.8	4.4
0.25	58	78.6	4.9	65	77.1	4.1
0.50	67	87.2	4.8	78	84.9	5.2
1.00	72	107.1	5.5	81	105.0	5.1
1.5	68	123.9	6.2	84	121.3	5.9
2.0	68	138.1	6.7	84	136.0	6.8
2.5	72	150.7	7.1	82	147.9	7.1
3.0	72	162.1	7.7	79	159.4	7.9
3.5	73	171.6	9.6	78	169.6	8.3
4.0	72	181.8	8.7	80	179.5	9.1
4.5	71	190.8	8.8	78	189.4	10.2
5.0	77	200.4	9.6	80	198.6	11.1
5.5	73	209.0	10.2	74	206.5	11.7
6.0	71	217.5	9.6	75	216.0	12.2
6.5	72	226.0	10.5	81	224.3	13.4
7.0	71	234.2	11.3	86	232.1	13.4
7.5	76	242.1	11.8	83	240.8	14.5
8.0	70	251.0	12.4	85	248.8	14.8
8.5	72	257.7	11.8	82	256.1	15.2
9.0	76	265.6	13.0	83	263.7	16.3
9.5	78	273.8	13.8	83	272.2	17.6
10.0	77	281.3	13.9	84	279.4	18.3
10.5	76	287.8	14.6	75	287.2	20.4
11.0	75	294.9	14.6	76	294.4	19.8
11.5	76	301.7	16.0	75	303.8	20.7
12.0	73	310.1	16.4	71	311.1	20.8

Source: Maresh, 1970.

Table 7–50. *Humeral total length including epiphyses (in millimetres) of nonadults from 10 to 18 years*

Age (years)	Male			Female		
	n	Mean	SD	n	Mean	SD
10.0	76	258.3	11.2	83	256.1	14.6
10.5	76	263.7	11.6	75	262.9	16.1
11.0	75	270.0	11.5	76	269.6	16.4
11.5	77	276.3	12.7	75	278.5	17.3
12.0	76	282.0	13.8	75	287.5	18.2
12.5	67	289.2	13.1	65	294.0	17.7
13.0	69	296.6	15.3	69	301.0	17.5
13.5	69	305.0	16.6	62	305.7	17.4
14.0	69	313.3	16.8	64	311.7	16.1
14.5	64	321.4	17.6	42	314.9	17.1
15.0	60	329.0	16.7	57	315.6	17.0
15.5	52	336.5	16.5	12	323.2	19.6
16.0	60	341.0	14.5	40	316.5	18.5
16.5	38	343.4	15.3	03	–	–
17.0	50	347.1	14.6	18	315.4	17.3
18.0	28	350.6	15.6	4	–	–

Source: Maresh, 1970.

Table 7–51. *Radial total length including epiphyses (in millimetres) of nonadults from 10 to 18 years*

Age (years)	Male			Female		
	n	Mean	SD	n	Mean	SD
10.0	76	193.0	8.1	83	189.3	11.4
10.5	76	197.7	8.9	75	195.0	13.0
11.0	75	202.6	8.9	76	200.0	13.0
11.5	77	207.3	9.7	75	206.7	13.5
12.0	77	212.3	10.3	75	213.5	14.2
12.5	71	218.0	10.2	67	218.8	14.2
13.0	73	223.7	11.8	70	223.6	13.1
13.5	73	230.2	12.9	63	227.8	12.7
14.0	75	236.9	13.5	64	231.4	11.8
14.5	69	242.8	14.1	42	233.5	11.7
15.0	61	248.7	13.4	57	234.5	11.7
15.5	52	255.0	12.8	12	237.4	15.2
16.0	61	257.7	11.7	40	235.0	11.8
16.5	38	259.8	11.3	03	–	–
17.0	50	261.8	11.12	18	233.8	11.8
18.0	28	263.2	12.8	04	–	–

Source: Maresh, 1970.

Table 7–52. *Ulna total length including epiphyses (in millimetres) of nonadults from 10 to 18 years*

Age (years)	Male			Female		
	n	Mean	SD	n	Mean	SD
10.0	76	202.2	9.0	83	203.8	12.3
10.5	76	208.0	9.7	75	210.2	13.8
11.0	75	213.3	20.2	76	215.5	13.3
11.5	77	219.5	11.3	75	222.6	13.8
12.0	77	224.9	11.7	75	229.7	14.7
12.5	71	231.5	11.8	67	235.4	14.4
13.0	73	237.9	13.2	70	240.0	13.3
13.5	73	245.1	13.9	63	244.4	13.1
14.0	75	252.3	14.6	65	248.1	12.1
14.5	69	259.0	14.7	42	250.2	11.8
15.0	61	265.1	14.0	57	251.0	12.2
15.5	52	271.9	13.1	12	255.0	15.1
16.0	61	274.8	12.2	40	252.3	12.0
16.5	38	277.3	12.1	03	–	–
17.0	50	279.4	11.7	17	250.2	12.3
18.0	28	281.6	13.5	04	–	–

Source: Maresh, 1970.

Table 7–53. *Femoral total length including epiphyses (in millimetres) of nonadults from 10 to 18 years*

Age (years)	Male			Female		
	n	Mean	SD	n	Mean	SD
10.0	76	385.1	17.0	83	382.8	21.1
10.5	76	394.2	17.9	75	392.6	23.7
11.0	75	405.2	17.9	76	403.5	24.8
11.5	77	414.8	19.4	75	415.4	25.2
12.0	77	425.6	20.6	74	427.9	25.2
12.5	71	437.1	19.6	67	437.9	23.9
13.0	73	447.4	21.5	69	447.2	24.1
13.5	73	458.4	24.0	63	453.1	22.0
14.0	75	470.8	24.1	64	459.9	22.5
14.5	69	478.9	25.2	41	464.5	20.8
15.0	61	489.0	23.5	57	464.4	21.4
15.5	52	498.5	23.4	12	471.5	26.0
16.0	60	502.8	22.8	40	466.7	24.0
16.5	38	504.5	24.9	03	–	–
17.0	50	508.9	23.2	18	462.9	26.2
18.0	28	511.7	24.4	04	–	–

Source: Maresh, 1970.

Table 7–54. *Tibiae total length including epiphyses (in millimetres) of nonadults from 10 to 18 years*

Age (years)	Male			Female		
	n	Mean	SD	n	Mean	SD
10.0	76	320.0	15.7	83	321.1	21.7
10.5	76	328.9	17.0	75	330.9	23.7
11.0	75	338.6	17.5	76	340.1	23.1
11.5	77	347.4	18.5	75	350.4	23.2
12.0	76	357.3	19.1	75	360.9	23.8
12.5	67	367.5	18.6	65	367.3	23.0
13.0	69	376.7	20.6	69	374.5	22.2
13.5	69	388.2	22.0	62	379.0	21.8
14.0	69	397.4	21.9	64	384.3	21.4
14.5	64	306.0	23.1	42	386.9	20.5
15.0	60	412.2	21.5	57	385.7	20.8
15.5	52	420.5	22.3	12	390.5	28.5
16.0	60	422.6	21.8	40	386.8	22.6
16.5	38	425.1	24.2	03	–	–
17.0	50	426.5	23.2	18	380.7	23.6
18.0	28	429.5	25.6	04	–	–

Source: Maresh, 1970.

Table 7–55. *Fibula total length including epiphyses (in millimetres) of nonadults from 10 to 18 years*

Age (years)	Male			Female		
	n	Mean	SD	n	Mean	SD
10.0	76	310.4	15.2	83	307.9	19.5
10.5	76	318.0	16.2	75	316.7	21.8
11.0	75	326.2	15.9	76	324.7	21.5
11.5	77	334.0	17.6	74	334.6	22.1
12.0	76	342.8	18.0	75	344.6	22.7
12.5	67	351.9	16.8	65	351.0	22.2
13.0	69	360.2	19.8	69	358.5	21.9
13.5	69	371.1	21.4	62	363.4	21.4
14.0	69	380.3	21.3	64	367.9	20.6
14.5	64	388.5	22.5	42	368.9	21.5
15.0	60	395.3	21.5	57	370.2	20.0
15.5	52	404.4	22.1	12	375.7	25.8
16.0	60	406.3	21.7	40	372.4	21.5
16.5	38	408.6	22.8	03	–	–
17.0	50	410.4	22.6	18	366.8	24.2
18.0	28	412.8	24.2	04	–	–

Source: Maresh, 1970.

Table 7–56. *Regression equations of age on maximum humeral length (in millimetres) from 24 antenatal weeks to 6 weeks postnatal*

Linear	$(0.4585 \times \text{humerus}) + 8.6563$	= Age (weeks)	±2.33
Logarithmic	$(25.069 \log_e \times \text{humerus}) - 66.4655$	= Age (weeks)	±2.26

Source: Scheuer and Black, 2000.

Table 7–57. *Regression equations of age on maximum radial length (in millimetres) from 24 antenatal weeks to 6 weeks postnatal*

Linear	$(0.5850 \times \text{radius}) + 7.7100$	= Age (weeks)	±2.29
Logarithmic	$(25.695 \log_e \times \text{radius}) - 63.6541$	= Age (weeks)	±2.24

Source: Scheuer and Black, 2000.

Table 7–58. *Regression equations of age on maximum ulna length (in millimetres) from 24 antenatal weeks to 6 weeks postnatal*

Linear	$(0.5072 \times \text{ulna}) + 7.8208$	= Age (weeks)	±2.20
Logarithmic	$(26.078 \log_e \times \text{ulna}) - 68.7222$	= Age (weeks)	±2.24

Source: Scheuer and Black, 2000.

Table 7–59. *Regression equations of age on maximum femoral length (in millimetres) from 24 antenatal weeks to 6 weeks postnatal*

Linear	$(0.3303 \times \text{femur}) + 13.5583$	$= \text{Age (weeks)}$	± 2.08
Logarithmic	$(19.7271 \log_e \times \text{femur}) - 47.1909$	$= \text{Age (weeks)}$	± 2.04

Source: Scheuer and Black, 2000.

Table 7–60. *Regression equations of age on tibiae length (in millimetres) from 24 antenatal weeks to 6 weeks postnatal*

Linear	$(0.4207 \times \text{tibia}) + 11.4724$	$= \text{Age (weeks)}$	± 2.12
Logarithmic	$(21.2071 \log_e \times \text{tibia}) - 50.2331$	$= \text{Age (weeks)}$	± 2.11

Source: Scheuer and Black, 2000.

Table 7–61. *Length (in millimetres) of the antenatal fibula diaphysis*

Age (weeks)	Length
12	6.0
14	9.9
16	16.7
18	22.7
20	27.8
22	31.1
24	34.3
26	36.5
28	40.0
30	42.8
32	46.8
34	50.5
36	51.6
38	57.6
40	62.0

Source: Scheuer and Black, 2000.

Table 7–62. *Ageing characteristics of the vertebral body*

Age category	Description of ageing characteristic
Child: Younger than 16 years	The epiphyseal ring is completely absent. Note the regular undulations on the edges of the vertebral body.
Late teenager: 16–20 years	The epiphyseal ring is in the process of fusing. Note the line of fusion on the lateral view and the slight chipping of the ring on the superior view.
Young adult: 20–29 years	The epiphyseal ring is fused, but no osteoarthritis is visible. The bone is smooth and solid.
Older adult: Older than 30 years	Osteoarthritis is obvious, and the vertebral body is beginning to degenerate. Note the osteophytes at the vertebral edges and the porous nature of the bone.

Source: Scheuer and Black, 2000.

Table 7–63. *Scoring system for male and female pubic symphysis*

Phase	Female age (years)	Male age (years)	Description
1	15–24	15–23	The symphyseal face has a billowing surface composed of ridges and furrows, which includes the pubic tubercle. The horizontal ridges are well marked. Ventral bevelling may be commencing. Although ossific nodules may occur on the upper extremity, a key feature of this phase is the lack of delimitation for either extremity (upper or lower).
2	19–40	19–34	The symphyseal face may still show ridge development. Lower and upper extremities show early stages of delimitation with or without ossific nodules. The ventral rampart may begin formation as extension from either or both extremities.
3	21–53	21–46	The symphyseal face shows lower extremity and ventral rampart in process of completion. Fusing ossific nodules may form upper extremity and extend along ventral border. The symphyseal face may either be smooth or retain distinct ridges. Dorsal plateau is complete. No lipping of symphyseal dorsal margin or bony ligamentous outgrowths.
4	26–70	23–57	The symphyseal face is generally fine grained, although remnants of ridge and furrow system may remain. Oval outline usually complete at this stage, although a hiatus may occur in upper aspect of ventral circumference. Pubic tubercle is fully separated from the symphyseal face through definition of upper extremity. The symphyseal face may have a distinct rim. Ventrally, bony ligamentous outgrowths may occur in inferior portion of pubic bone adjacent to symphyseal face. Slight lipping may appear on dorsal border.
5	25–83	27–66	A slight depression of the face relative to a completed rim is present. Moderate lipping is usually found on the dorsal border, with prominent ligamentous outgrowths on the ventral border. Little or no rim erosion, although breakdown possible on the superior aspect of ventral border.
6	42–87	34–86	The symphyseal face shows ongoing depression as rim erodes. Ventral ligamentous attachments are marked. The pubic tubercle may appear as a separate bony knob. The face may be pitted or porous, giving an appearance of disfigurement as the ongoing process of erratic ossification proceeds. Crenulation may occur, with the shape of the face often irregular.

Source: Brooks and Suchey, 1990.

all methods perform poorly when tested on known age samples, that of Brooks and Suchey (1990) is considered most useful, although age ranges for each phase are extremely large and, as such, limit its value especially for those older than 30 years. The Brooks and Suchey (1990) scoring system for males and females should be undertaken primarily using the descriptions, with appropriate cast sets available as backup. The descriptions provided in Table 7–63 (ibid.) should be applied to symphyseal faces of males or females as indicated.

Rib end morphology. Iscan and Loth (1986) developed a method of estimating age at death from age-related change to the sternal end of the fourth rib; the application

Table 7–64. *Characteristics of the adult rib end morphology as an age indicator*

Stage	Age category	Description of characteristics
0	Child: Younger than mid teens	The rib end begins as a fairly flat surface. The edges are smoothly rounded, and the surface is only slightly undulating.
1–2	Teenager+: Mid teens to early twenties	The edges are sharper and have a scalloped appearance. The inner surface is beginning to look V shaped.
3–4	Young adult: Mid twenties to early thirties	The edges are less regular, and the centres project further than the superior and inferior edges. The V is deepening.
5–6	Older adult: Mid thirties to mid fifties	The superior and inferior edges have grown to the length of centres. The V has expanded into a cup-shaped centre.
7–8	Elderly adult: Older than mid fifties	The edges are elongated, ragged, and sometimes have a "crab claw" appearance. The centre is porous and irregular.

Source: Burns, 1999.

of their method is also facilitated by the use of associated casts. Their study indicates that the stages of change corresponds broadly to age, but varies for the sexes, and for those of different ancestry. A series of phases was identified for the rim, walls, and pit shape; depth; and form. These are defined by form, shape, texture, and overall quality, and are described in Table 7–64. As with all methods, this method is least useful with older individuals (see Cox, 2000a) who are underaged and is difficult to use on fragmented material. Assessment of the value of this method on other samples of known age has illustrated large margins of error except for those 40 to 49 years of age (Loth, 1995). This method should be used with caution.

Auricular surface of the ilium. Auricular surface change is a method that can be applied regardless of sex and ancestry. Lovejoy et al. (1985) first described the changes of the auricular surface through eight phases of granulation, microporosity, macroporosity, density, and billowing. More effective subdivisions are made using secondary characteristics such as apical and retroauricular activity. Both the left and the right auricular surfaces should be recorded. It is recommended that rather than relying on the photographic aids that accompany this method, the use of the detailed written descriptions of Osbourne et al. (2004) and Buckberry and Chamberlain (2002) are far more useful (see Tables 7–65 and 7–66). As with all methods, reliability decreases with age, although tests indicate that this approach is more reliable than the pubic symphysis (Bedford et al., 1993). The usefulness of this method is, however, limited by the tendency for males older than 50 years to exhibit ankylosis of the sacroiliac joint, and some aspects are impaired when a deep preauricular sulcus is present. Furthermore, it can be prone to interobserver error (Saunders et al., 1992), and many researchers do not use this method because they find it difficult to apply with any confidence. It should never be used when the joint surface is damaged or abraded because this can mimic degenerative changes. The reader is referred to the work of Osbourne et al. (2004) for a more detailed discussion of the changes.

Table 7–65. *Description of characteristics used to derive a composite score for the auricular surface*

Phase	Age (years)	Description
1	20–24	Transverse billowing and very fine granularity. The auricular surface displays fine granular texture and marked transverse organisation. There is no porosity, retroauricular, or apical activity. The surface appears youthful because of broad and well-organised billows, which impart the definitive transverse organisation. Raised transverse billows are well defined and cover most of the surface. Any subchondral defects are smooth edged and rounded.
2	25–29	Reduction of billowing but retention of a youthful appearance. Changes from the previous phase are not marked and are mostly reflected in slight to moderate loss of billowing, with replacement by striae. There is no apical activity, porosity, or retroauricular activity. The surface still appears youthful owing to marked transverse organisation. Granulation is slightly coarser than previously.
3	30–34	General loss of billowing with replacement by striae and distinct coarsening of granularity. Both demifaces are largely quiescent, with some loss of transverse organisation. Billowing is much reduced and replaced by striae. The surface is more coarsely and recognisably granular than in the previous phase, with no significant changes at apex. Small areas of microporosity may appear. Slight retroauricular activity may occasionally be present. In general, coarse granulation supersedes and replaces billowing. Note smoothing of surface by replacement of billows with fine striae but distinct retention of slight billowing. Loss of transverse organisation and coarsening of granularity is evident.
4	35–39	Uniform, coarse granularity. Both faces are coarsely and uniformly granulated, with marked reduction of both billowing and striae, but striae may still be present. Transverse organisation is present but poorly defined. There is some activity in the retroauricular area, but this is usually slight. Minimal changes are seen at the apex, microporosity is slight, and there is no macroporosity.
5	40–44	Transition from coarse granularity to dense surface. No billowing is seen. Striae may be present but are very vague. The face is still partially (coarsely) granular, and there is a marked loss of transverse organisation. Partial densification of the surface with commensurate loss of granularity. Slight to moderate activity in the retroauricular area. Occasional macroporosity is seen, but this is not typical. Slight changes are usually present at the apex. Some increase in macroporosity, depending on the degree of densification.
6	45–49	Completion of densification with complete loss of granularity. Significant loss of granulation is seen in most cases, with replacement by dense bone. No billows or striae are present. Changes at the apex are slight to moderate but are almost always present. There is a distinct tendency for the surface to become dense. No transverse organisation is evident. Most or all of the microporosity is lost to densification. There is increased irregularity of margins, with moderate retroauricular activity and little or no macroporosity.
7	50–59	Dense irregular surface of rugged topography and moderate to marked activity in the periauricular areas. This is a further elaboration of the previous morphology, in which marked surface irregularity becomes the paramount feature. Topography, however, shows no transverse or other form of organisation. Moderate granulation is only occasionally retained. The inferior face is generally lipped at the inferior terminus. Apical changes are almost invariable and may be marked. Increasing irregularity of margins is seen. Macroporosity is present in some cases. Retroauricular activity is moderate to marked in most cases.
8	60+	Breakdown with marginal lipping, macroporosity, increased irregularity, and marked activity in the periauricular areas. The paramount feature is a nongranular, irregular surface with distinct signs of subchondral destruction. No transverse organisation is seen, and there is a distinct absence of any youthful criteria. Macroporosity is present in about one-third of all cases. Apical activity is usually marked but is not requisite. Margins become dramatically irregular and lipped, with typical degenerative joint change. The retroauricular area becomes well defined with profuse osteophytes of low to moderate relief. There is clear destruction of subchondral bone, absence of transverse organisation, and increased irregularity.

Source: Osborne et al., 2004.

Table 7–66. *Description of the locations of the auricular surface*

Definition	Description of locations
Apex	Portion of auricular surface that articulates with posterior aspect of the arcuate line
Superior demiface	Portion of auricular area above apex
Inferior demiface	Portion of auricular area below apex
Retro-auricular area	Region between auricular surface and posterior inferior iliac spine

Source: Buikstra and Ubelaker, 1994.

Buckberry and Chamberlain (2002) adapted Lovejoy's method of scoring the auricular surface (Table 7–67), and this method is preferred because it facilitates more objective scoring and treats individual components as independent variables. The definitions of the individual components are described in Table 7–68. This method is also particularly useful for establishing seriation across an assemblage.

To estimate the age of an individual using Buckberry and Chamberlain's (2002) method, a composite score must be obtained. This is the sum of the scores of all five features. An estimated age can be obtained by consulting Table 7–69, in which the composite score is allocated a stage, standard deviation, and age range.

Table 7–67. *Definitions for characteristics used to derive a composite score for the auricular surface*

Characteristic	Definition
Transverse organisa- tion	The observed billows and striae that run horizontally from the medial to the lateral margins of the auricular surface have been referred to as transverse organisation (Lovejoy et al., 1985; Buckberry and Chamberlain, 2002). The proportion of the surface exhibiting transverse organisation is calculated as a visually estimated percentage of the auricular surface covered by horizontally organised billows and striae. The scoring system for this category is provided in Table 7–68.
Surface texture	Surface texture, or granularity, can be scored, depending on the proportions of the auricular surface that appears finely granular (grains less than 0.5 mm), and the proportion of the surface that is observed visually as coarsely granular (grains over 0.5 mm) (Lovejoy et al., 1985; Buckberry and Chamberlain, 2002). As an individual matures, the granularity becomes more coarse and dense. Surface density refers to the smooth, compact areas of bone. The scoring system for this category is provided in Table 7–68.
Microporosity	The presence of pores or perforations of subchondral bone less than 1 mm in diameter is termed microporosity (Lovejoy et al., 1985; Buckberry and Chamberlain, 2002). Microporosity can be either localised or more spread out. The scoring system is described in Table 7–68.
Macroporosity	The presence of perforations, where the pores are more than 1 mm in diameter, is termed macroporosity (Lovejoy et al., 1985; Buckberry and Chamberlain, 2002). The presence of macroporosity on the demiface of the auricular surface can be either localised or more widely spread. The scoring system is described in Table 7–68.
Apical changes	Osteophytes developing on the apex of the ilium can be scored using the system described in Table 7–68. This 'lipping' becomes more severe with age (Lovejoy et al., 1985; Buckberry and Chamberlain, 2002).

Source: Buckberry and Chamberlain, 2002.

Table 7–68. *Scoring system for the auricular surface*

Score	Description
Transverse Organisation	
1	90% or more of surface is transversely organised
2	50–89% of surface is transversely organised
3	25–49% of surface is transversely organised
4	Transverse organisation is present on less than 25% of surface
5	No transverse organisation is present
Surface Texture	
1	90% or more of surface is finely granular
2	50–89% of surface is finely granular; replacement of finely granular bone by coarsely granular bone in some areas; no dense bone is present
3	50% or more of surface is coarsely granular, but no dense bone is present
4	Dense bone is present but occupies less than 50% of surface; this may be just one small nodule of dense bone in very early stages
5	50% or more of surface is occupied by dense bone
Microporosity	
1	No microporosity is present
2	Microporosity is present on one demiface only
3	Microporosity is present on both demifaces
Macroporosity	
1	No macroporosity is present
2	Macroporosity is present on one demiface only
3	Macroporosity is present on both demifaces
Apex	
1	Apex is sharp and distinct; auricular surface may be slightly raised relative to adjacent bone surface
2	Some lipping is present at apex, but shape of articular margin is still distinct and smooth (shape of outline of surface at apex is a continuous arc)
3	Irregularity occurs in contours of articular surface; shape of apex is no longer a smooth arc

Source: Buckberry and Chamberlain, 2002.

Table 7–69. *Age estimates from composite scores and age stages*

Composite score	Auricular surface stage	No. of specimens	Mean age	Standard deviation	Median age	Range
5–6	I	3	17.33	1.53	17	16–19
7–8	II	6	29.33	6.71	27	21–38
9–10	III	22	37.86	13.08	37	16–65
11–12	IV	32	51.41	14.47	52	29–81
13–14	V	64	59.94	12.95	62	29–88
15–16	VI	41	66.71	11.88	66	39–91
17–19	VII	12	72.25	12.73	73	53–92

Source: Buckberry and Chamberlain, 2002.

Other methods. Most researchers consider that the capricious nature of suture closure precludes any precise estimation of age from being undertaken (Dwight, 1890; von Lenhössek, 1917; Hrdlicka, 1939; von Singer, 1953; McKern and Stewart, 1957; Perizonius, 1984; Masset, 1989; Saunders et al., 1992; Molleson and Cox, 1993; Key et al., 1994). Consequently, we do not recommend that it is used in forensic cases.

Ossification of hyaline cartilage is best observed on skeletal remains with surviving soft tissues using radiographs. Ossification of the laryngeal cartilages (i.e., thyroid, cricoid, and arytenoid) have been examined macroscopically, histologically, and radiographically (Keen and Wainwright, 1985) on samples of different racial groups and both sexes (Hately et al., 1965). It is a potentially useful indicator of an age range. Roentgenograms of the plastron (chest plate; comprising the first to seventh costal cartilages, terminal ends of the sternal ribs, sternum, and sternal clavicles) have been examined for assessment of age-related change. This method is particularly useful for forensic cases and where some soft tissues survive, and may be undertaken by the forensic pathologist; it does not require defleshing before analysis can take place (McCormick and Stewart, 1988). This method ages to within 25 percent of real age in 95 percent of cases. Its use is more limited in older individuals, and it is not applicable for use on skeletonised remains where such tissues do not survive.

Various multifactorial approaches to ageing have been examined using different combinations of skeletal elements and approaches (Walker and Lovejoy, 1985; Stout and Paine, 1992; Macchiarelli and Bondioli, 1994; Wallin et al., 1994; Cool et al., 1995; Feik et al., 1997). The perceived advantages of using multifactorial approaches in assigning age at death rest on the minimisation of errors of individual indicators (see Jackes, 1992). However, not all researchers accept that view (Cox, 2000a) because it could also arguably compound errors. The value of this approach to forensic cases remains to be demonstrated. That aside, it is generally recommended that all possible age indicators are used, and the overall assessment should reflect this. When such an approach is used, the final estimated age has to be a combination of all individual results. This can be assessed statistically when following a particular multifactorial method, but because condition and completeness of skeletal remains rarely permit a consistent combination of methods to be used, we suggest that the lowest minimum age of all methods applied becomes the minimum age, and the highest maximum age becomes the highest. This approach must consider the confidence interval applicable to each method.

Two-criteria dental method. Of the various dental methods available, only the two-criteria dental method of Lamendin et al. (1992) is described here. This method was developed on a sample of 274 teeth from 135 males and 92 from 73 females. It requires no specialist facilities or training and is reasonably accurate for those in the 40- to 80-year bracket with a mean error of estimation of ±10 years (White and Folkens, 2005). The method should be applied to noncarious and undamaged upper incisors and seems to apply equally well to both males and females.

This method scores translucency of the root of the tooth and periodontosis or gingival regression and requires the tooth to be *ex situ* but not sectioned. Periodontosis is the maximum distance on the labial surface between the cemento-enamel junction and the line of soft tissue attachment. It appears as a smooth, yellowish area below the enamel and is darker than the rest of the root. Translucency reflects the deposit within the dentin tubuli of crystals of hydroxyapatite. It can be measured on the labial surface of the entire tooth using a negatoscope and is measured from the apex of the root to its maximum height. Root height is also measured from the apex of the root to the cemento-enamel junction. A calliper square and a millimetric ruler are required. Multiple regression analysis is used to establish an estimation of age based on the measurement of the variables. The equation to be used is Age $=$ $(0.18 \times P) + (0.42 \times T) + 25.53$. ($P =$ (periodontosis height $\times$ 100)/root height; $T =$ (transparency height $\times$ 100)/root height.)

7.7.3 Recording

Where a method for assessment of age at death is used in forensic analysis, all aspects of the data should be included in the subsequent report, including detail of phase, age range, and confidence interval (where such data are not available, that too should be recorded). In all cases, the anthropologist's observations will be recorded in the analytical notes as an estimated mean age or age bracket as determined in accordance with the appropriate method. Where a combination of methods is used, even where they comprise a designated multivariate approach with appropriate statistical applications, the details of the results of each method should be recorded.

When applicable (i.e., pubic symphysis, auricular surface, and/or sternal rib ends), the phase number and all relevant data (including range, standard deviation, etc.) will be recorded. Original analytical notes and forms will be retained with the case file. The final report will include the technique used, the mean age and age bracket (e.g., 20–28 years), the standard error, and the standard deviation (minimum should be two standard deviations to obtain the 95 percent confidence interval for the sample population's variation).

8

Mortuary procedures III – Skeletal analysis 2: Techniques for determining identity

Caroline Barker, Margaret Cox, Ambika Flavel, Joanna Laver, Mary Lewis, and Jacqueline McKinley

8.1 Introduction

In this chapter, we discuss further approaches that are of value in determining the identity of individuals and that contribute to the determination of cause and manner of their death. These methods can be applied equally to forensic and human rights cases and should be used alongside those described in Chapter 7. The degree to which any of these applications is useful will often be both individual and project specific. The mortuary management team (MMT) will determine the applicability of the various methods to an investigation. There are some methods that we have not included because the present state of research in those areas does not support their confident application in either a judicial or a humanitarian context. An example of the latter includes the estimation of body weight. The application of the methods advocated by researchers in this field produces large standard errors with estimates of range that are so imprecise as to be unusable (Byers, 2002; Klepinger, 2006). Deciding which techniques to apply while following a certain logic may be a fluid and often innovative enterprise, requiring anthropologists to liaise with other specialists and keep up to date with the literature. Returning to cases when new research is published may be an option, but rarely. The desired outcome that skeletal remains will have been returned to their families after analysis means that the anthropologist must thoroughly record all observations using as many mediums as are appropriate (e.g., photography, illustrations, casting). Forms MA41F–MA46F for use in this recording can be found on the accompanying CD. Guidance for the use of these forms and logs is located in 1.11.

8.2 Estimation of stature

This section sets out routine procedures for the estimation of living stature from complete skeletal remains and from individual bones. The limitations of the procedures associated with the estimation of living stature are discussed elsewhere (White, 1991; Buikstra and Ubelaker, 1994; Jantz et al., 1995; Simmons and Haglund, 2005). These include individual and population variability, error in the reported measurement of stature of living individuals by relatives and in documents, errors in measuring cadavers, intra- and interobserver error in measuring individual skeletal elements (particularly the tibia), secular changes that can affect stature and thus reduce the reliability of the regression equations and tables developed from archaeological samples, bias between reported versus measured stature, the reduction in stature known to occur in older individuals, and the reduction in bone lengths and dimensions due to intrinsic and extrinsic taphonomic variables (see 7.3). All of these factors must be taken into consideration when estimating living stature from skeletal remains.

Where possible, population-specific techniques should be applied. The regression equations provided in this chapter cater mainly for American black and American white populations. The reliability of these methods cannot be assured when applied to other populations or samples, and this must be considered when assessing stature. Other population-specific methods exist, including for northern Chinese males (Stevenson, 1929), South Korean males (Choi et al., 1997), and Mexican Amerindian males and females (Genovés, 1967). All are based on long bone measurements.

So that the most suitable regression formulae, standard errors, and correction factors are selected, ancestry (where appropriate), biological sex (referred to as sex in this chapter), and age must also be established before stature (see 7.4, 7.5, and 7.7). Instruments required for the estimation of stature include an osteometric board, sliding callipers (mm), digital callipers (mm), and flexible tape measure. Spreading callipers will be needed if the calculation of skull height (basion–bregma) is utilised. Stature estimation is only undertaken after remains have been determined to be human, and after any cleaning and reconstruction that may be required has been completed (7.2). The measurement of each skeletal element is generally taken from the left side of the body, and recorded in centimetres (to the nearest millimetre). Skeletal elements from the right side of the body may be used as substitutes if the left side is not available or measurable. In such cases, this should be noted on the recording form by placing an 'R' in parentheses next to the measurement.

After epiphyseal fusion is complete, long bones are deemed suitable for measurement. In cases where minor reconstruction has taken place or minor erosion is present, a single asterisk '*' should be placed next to the measurement in the recording form (see 8.9). Where the specific skeletal element is considered to be significantly reconstructed, eroded, or affected by pathology, stature will not be estimated. Where there is marked asymmetry, unless this results from pathology or trauma, it is recommend that the average of the two be taken, and in such cases, this should be noted during recording using two asterisks '**'. Stature estimates can be based on complete skeletons, partial skeletons, complete bones, and/or fragmented, but not badly eroded, bones. The most useful of these methodologies are described in the following sections. The order in which they appear does not represent their suitability for a specific population. All bone measurements referred to in this chapter are explained in 8.8.

Estimation of living stature from fragmented bones is generally considered inappropriate for forensic applications. Although it is possible to estimate stature from partial skeletons using methods such as that of Fully (1956; Fully and Pineau, 1960), such approaches bring a considerable measure of error, and their application is highly questionable, particularly in sample populations with a significant measure of homogeneity. Further to that, they have not been assessed for accuracy on samples other than that on which they were developed (skeletons exhumed from a German concentration camp post–World War II; their height was documented [Klepinger, 2006]). Estimating stature from fragmented long bones such as the femur and tibia (Simmons et al., 1990) assumes that various parts of the bone correlate with stature in much the same way as whole long bones. As would be expected, the standard error of stature estimates derived from fragmented limb bones is larger than for complete bones, and consequently, this method is of little practical value.

The programme FORDISC 3.0 (Ousley and Jantz, 2005) can be used to estimate the stature of complete long bones of adult individuals where epiphyseal fusion is complete. The elements and the measurements that are used in FORDISC 3.0 are described in Table 8–23 (8.8). Trotter and Gleser's (1952) equations are designed for use on intact long bones and samples comprising American white and black males and females, however, this method is often applied to other samples.

8.2.1   Stature estimation from the complete skeleton

The technique to establish living stature from the complete skeleton (Fully, 1956) is based on calculating the following measurements (see 8.8): the height of the skull (basion–bregma), the maximum height of the body of each vertebra from the second cervical to the fifth lumbar (inclusive), the anterior height of the first sacral vertebra, the bicondylar length of the femur, the length of the tibia (excluding the intercondylar eminence), and the height of the calcaneus and talus. These measurements are summed, and a correction factor is then added for soft tissue thicknesses (also documented in Stewart, 1979), as described in Table 8–1. This technique was developed using white males from France, but it is considered equally

Table 8–1. *Soft tissue correction factors for the Fully method*

Calculated height (cm)	Male (cm)	Female (cm)
153.5 or less	10.0	9.2
Over 153.5 and less than 165.4	10.5	9.7
165.5 or above	11.5	10.6

Source: Fully, 1956, cited by Stewart, 1979.

applicable to blacks, Asians, and Hispanic males (ibid.). Female values have been estimated to be 92 percent of male values. It is generally believed to be an accurate method for the estimation of living stature of those of Northern European ancestry when the required skeletal elements are all present and complete. Typically, results are believed to come within 1 cm (i.e., approximately 0.4 in.) of true stature. This method requires the skeleton to be complete and in good condition.

8.2.2 Stature estimation from complete long bones

Some individual long bones are known to have a strong positive correlation to stature, and those of the lower limbs are more closely correlated than those of the upper limbs. Primarily, the long bones measured for stature estimation include the humerus (length), radius (length), ulna (maximum and physiological length), femur (maximum length and bicondylar length), tibia (maximum length and length), and fibula (length). A guide to the correct measurement techniques and anatomical landmarks is located in 8.8. Once the length of the bone has been correctly measured, the result is multiplied by the factor in the regression formula and added to the constant (Tables 8–2 and 8–3). The stature range is obtained by applying Trotter's (1970) formulae for those dying prior to the 1960s and Ousley's (1995) for those dying more recently (Simmons and Haglund, 2005). This reflects the changing contribution of the tibia and femur to stature over recent decades (ibid.). We do not advocate using the earlier Trotter and Gleser (1952, 1958) formulae for reasons expounded elsewhere (Simmons and Haglund, 2005; White and Folkens, 2005). Trotter (1970) found that the regression formulae using multiple bones (i.e., femur + tibia) increased the accuracy of stature estimation. Ousley's (1995) prediction intervals are given in inches; to convert this to centimetres, multiply by 2.55. All measurements and calculations should be taken and recorded in millimetres.

In the absence of limb bones, regression equations for metacarpals (Musgrave and Harneja, 1978; Meadows and Jantz, 1992), metatarsals (Byers et al., 1989) calcaneus, and talus (Holland, 1995) have been established to estimate living stature. Although the resultant standard errors associated with these elements are large, this is considered a more reliable method than that provided by fragmented long bone measurements (Meadows and Jantz, 1992). The measurements to be obtained for the metacarpal are described and illustrated in 8.8. The resulting measurement is then entered into a regression formula for an estimation of living stature. The formula

Table 8–2. *Regression equations and standard error (in centimetres) to estimate stature from long bones in individuals between 18 and 30 years*

Bone	Equation: Stature =	±	Bone	Equation: Stature =	±
White males			**Black males**		
Humerus	3.08 (length cm) + 70.45	4.05	Humerus	3.26 (length cm) + 62.10	4.43
Radius	3.78 (length cm) + 79.01	4.32	Radius	3.42 (length cm) + 81.56	4.30
Ulna	3.70 (length cm) + 74.05	4.32	Ulna	3.26 (length cm) + 79.29	4.42
Femur	2.38 (length cm) + 61.41	3.27	Femur	2.11 (length cm) + 70.35	3.94
Fibula	2.68 (length cm) + 71.78	3.29	Fibula	2.19 (length cm) + 85.65	4.08
White females			**Black females**		
Humerus	3.36 (length cm) + 57.97	4.45	Humerus	3.08 (length cm) + 64.67	4.25
Radius	4.74 (length cm) + 54.93	4.24	Radius	2.75 (length cm) + 94.51	5.05
Ulna	4.27 (length cm) + 57.76	4.30	Ulna	3.31 (length cm) + 75.38	4.83
Femur	2.47 (length cm) + 54.74	3.72	Femur	2.28 (length cm) + 59.76	3.41
Fibula	2.93 (length cm) + 59.61	3.57	Fibula	2.49 (length cm) + 70.90	3.80
East Asian males			**Mexican males**		
Humerus	2.68 (length cm) + 83.19	4.25	Humerus	2.92 (length cm) + 73.94	4.24
Radius	3.54 (length cm) + 82.00	4.60	Radius	3.55 (length cm) + 80.71	4.04
Ulna	3.48 (length cm) + 77.45	4.66	Ulna	3.56 (length cm) + 74.56	4.05
Femur	2.15 (length cm) + 72.57	3.80	Femur	2.44 (length cm) + 58.67	2.99
Fibula	2.40 (length cm) + 80.56	3.24	Fibula	2.50 (length cm) + 75.44	3.52

Note: When utilizing the femur, use maximum femoral length.
Source: Trotter, 1970.

Table 8–3. *Stature estimation in recent forensic cases (L = length)*

	Factor	Bone measurement (mm)	Constant	90%PI (in.)
White males	0.05566	Femur Max L + Tibia L	21.64	±2.5
	0.05552	Femur Max L + Fibula L	22.00	2.6
	0.10560	Femur Max L	19.39	2.8
	0.10140	Tibia L	30.38	2.8
	0.15890	Ulna L	26.91	3.1
	0.12740	Humerus L	26.79	3.3
	0.16398	Radius L	28.35	3.3
White females	0.06524	Femur Max L + Tibia L	12.94	2.3
	0.06163	Femur Max L + Fibula L	15.43	2.4
	0.11869	Femur Max L	12.43	2.4
	0.11168	Tibia L	24.65	3.0
	0.11827	Humerus L	28.30	3.1
	0.13353	Ulna L	31.99	3.1
	0.18467	Radius L	22.42	3.4
Black females	0.11640	Femur Max L	11.98	2.4
	0.16997	Ulna L	21.20	3.3
Black males	0.10521	Tibia L	26.26	3.8
	0.08388	Femur Max L	28.57	4.0
	0.07824	Humerus L	43.19	4.4

Source: Ousley, 1995.

Table 8–4. *Equations for stature estimation (in millimetres) from metacarpal bones*

| Bone and side (mm) | Slope | Intercept | | | | ± |
		White male	White female	Black male	Black female	
Left hand						
Metacarpal 1	1.674	91.89	89.52	88.81	85.33	5.57
Metacarpal 2	1.311	81.96	79.86	78.05	73.36	5.10
Metacarpal 3	1.298	84.90	82.81	80.28	75.79	5.19
Metacarpal 4	1.355	90.41	88.11	86.93	82.01	5.27
Metacarpal 5	1.468	90.64	88.52	87.17	82.97	5.47
Right hand						
Metacarpal 1	1.659	91.77	90.02	89.15	85.45	5.52
Metacarpal 2	1.261	85.51	82.52	81.60	76.11	5.15
Metacarpal 3	1.279	85.98	83.44	81.61	76.80	5.36
Metacarpal 4	1.375	89.54	86.44	85.44	81.07	5.33
Metacarpal 5	1.433	93.16	89.95	89.35	81.41	5.67

Source: Meadows and Jantz, 1992.

is: Slope × (Metacarpal length in mm) + Intercept = Stature ± SE. The slope, intercept, and standard deviation can be taken from Table 8–4. It is necessary to be aware that these equations were developed on the Terry Collection. Evaluation of the equations on modern American black and white samples suggests estimation of stature will be correct to within one standard deviation in 50 percent of the modern population, and the other 50 percent will be correct to within three standard deviations. This is achievable if the distribution of data is normal (Meadows and Jantz, 1992).

An estimation of stature from metatarsals can be made by applying the regression equation described in Table 8–4 (Meadows and Jantz, 1992). Multiple regression equations are reported to have better standard errors than individual metatarsal formulae, and these are reproduced in Table 8–5. Holland (1995) suggested that the correlation between measurements of the heel and stature is strong irrespective of sex and ancestry. Multiple regression equations for black and white males and Euro-American females are reproduced in Table 8–6.

From the age of approximately 45 years, a decrease in standing height with advancing age has been noted, particularly in females (Giles, 1991). Reduction in standing height is due to a decrease in soft tissue thickness and in some cases reduction of vertebral height due to osteoporotic change (Galloway, 1988). To make adjustments in stature estimates for the loss of stature in older individuals, the correction shown in Table 8–7 should be used. If the exact age of the individual is known, subtract the figure located next to the appropriate age from the maximum stature estimated using any method. If an age range is used, average the appropriate figures for the age range. The applicability of these results to populations other than white Americans is assumed, but remains untested. When using the total body

Table 8–5. *Simple linear regression of stature calculated from metatarsal measurements (in millimetres)*

Bone and group	Equation: Stature =	N	R	SE (±)
First metatarsal				
Combined data	634 + 16.8 (mt 1)	130	0.79	65.4
All males	815 + 14.3 (mt 1)	70	0.72	64.2
All females	783 + 13.9 (mt 1)	58	0.71	56.1
Euro-American males	768 + 15.2 (mt 1)	57	0.72	63.2
Euro-American females	656 + 16.3 (mt 1)	49	0.79	49.6
Afro-American males	556 + 17.6 (mt 1)	11	0.87	51.0
Afro-American females	796 + 12.8 (mt 1)	7	0.70	50.8
Second metatarsal				
Combined data	675 + 13.4 (mt 2)	129	0.78	65.4
All males	873 + 11.1 (mt 2)	69	0.66	69.8
All females	791 + 11.5 (mt 2)	58	0.73	54.8
Euro-American males	868 + 11.3 (mt 2)	57	0.63	70.1
Euro-American females	712 + 12.8 (mt 2)	49	0.77	52.0
Afro-American males	605 + 14.0 (mt 2)	10	0.86	56.8
Afro-American females	783 + 10.9 (mt 2)	7	0.83	39.9
Third metatarsal				
Combined data	720 + 13.6 (mt 3)	128	0.76	67.6
All males	909 + 11.2 (mt 3)	69	0.66	68.1
All females	836 + 11.6 (mt 3)	57	0.67	59.7
Euro-American males	862 + 12.0 (mt 3)	57	0.65	68.9
Euro-American females	732 + 13.3 (mt 3)	48	0.71	57.5
Afro-American males	706 + 13.3 (mt 3)	10	0.89	42.2
Afro-American females	904 + 9.9 (mt 3)	7	0.78	44.9
Fourth metatarsal				
Combined data	715 + 14.0 (mt 4)	126	0.76	68.5
All males	910 + 11.6 (mt 4)	68	0.67	68.0
All females	835 + 11.9 (mt 4)	56	0.67	59.9
Euro-American males	863 + 12.3 (mt 4)	57	0.65	68.5
Euro-American females	719 + 13.8 (mt 4)	47	0.72	57.5
Afro-American males	759 + 13.0 (mt 4)	9	0.88	46.5
Afro-American females	961 + 9.3 (mt 4)	7	0.76	46.5
Fifth metatarsal (functional)				
Combined data	782 + 14.7 (mt 5f)	128	0.69	76.0
All males	989 + 11.8 (mt 5f)	68	0.59	73.8
All females	953 + 11.3 (mt 5f)	58	0.61	63.3
Euro-American males	938 + 12.8 (mt 5f)	57	0.60	72.2
Euro-American females	900 + 12.3 (mt 5f)	49	0.63	63.3
Afro-American males	761 + 14.7 (mt 5f)	9	0.72	68.0
Afro-American females	979 + 10.2 (mt 5f)	7	0.75	47.4
Fifth metatarsal (total)				
Combined data	768 + 12.8 (mt 5)	128	0.73	71.2
All males	952 + 10.6 (mt 5)	68	0.63	70.9
All females	922 + 10.2 (mt 5)	58	0.61	63.6
Euro-American males	912 + 11.2 (mt 5)	57	0.63	70.3
Euro-American females	905 + 10.6 (mt 5)	49	0.60	64.9
Afro-American males	846 + 11.5 (mt 5)	9	0.76	64.2
Afro-American females	891 + 10.2 (mt 5)	7	0.78	45.2

Source: Byers et al., 1989.

Table 8–6. *Multiple regression equations for stature calculated from metatarsal measurements (in millimetres)*

Metatarsal group	Equation: Stature =	SE (±)
Combined data	573 + 10.9 (mt 1) + 6.3 (mt 4)	61.8
All males	737 + 10.4 (mt 1) + 4.6 (mt 4)	61.3
Euro-American females	558 + 9.1 (mt 1) + 7.4 (mt 4)	48.4

Source: Byers et al., 1989.

method for estimating stature, it should be considered that individuals of Negroid descent, particularly females, do not experience osteoporotic changes to the extent that whites do (Creager, 1992; Aufderheide and Rodriguez-Martin, 1998; Lau, 2002). Caution should be applied in such cases.

8.2.3   Relative stature

In some contexts, measured stature is not something that has a place culturally. It also has to be recognised that in some relatively remote and/or closed communities, heterogeneity is noticeably absent, and homogeneity is marked. Despite this trend, there will still be a small proportion of adults who are either relatively short or tall in stature compared to the rest of the community. This information (i.e., relative stature among male and female groups) should be gleaned from informants during

Table 8–7. *Stature correction (in millimetres) for males and females ages 46 to 85 years*

Age (years)	Male	Female	Age (years)	Male	Female
46	2.5	0	66	17.5	14.2
47	2.9	0	67	18.6	15.6
48	3.3	0.1	68	19.8	17.1
49	3.8	0.2	69	21.0	18.6
50	4.3	0.4	70	22.2	20.2
51	4.8	0.7	71	23.4	21.8
52	5.4	1.1	72	24.7	23.5
53	6.1	1.6	73	25.9	25.2
54	6.7	2.1	74	27.2	27.0
55	7.4	2.8	75	28.6	28.8
56	8.2	3.5	76	29.9	30.7
57	8.9	4.2	77	31.3	32.6
58	9.8	5.1	78	32.7	34.5
59	10.6	6.0	79	34.2	36.5
60	11.5	7.0	80	35.6	38.5
61	12.4	8.0	81	37.1	40.5
62	13.4	9.2	82	38.6	42.6
63	14.4	10.3	83	40.1	44.7
64	15.4	11.6	84	41.7	46.8
65	16.4	12.9	85	43.2	49.0

Source: Giles, 1991.

antemortem data collection (see 10.2) in contexts where measured stature does not feature. In such cases, it is recommended that stature is estimated by the most appropriate population-specific method and that those who deviate from the average significantly are recorded as such. These data should then be used to denote those of both relatively tall and relatively short stature. This can only take place once all individuals are analysed and appropriate statistical tests have been applied to identify those who are significantly different. Where such an approach is undertaken, it must be indicated on the recording form. If resources are constrained, an experienced anthropologist will be able to identify those who are anomalous to the group based on their observations of the sample, but this is more prone to error than applying statistics to stature estimates. Where the more subjective approach is adopted, the first cases assessed must be reexamined once the anthropologist has established a sense of what is normal within the sample.

The anthropologist will record the measurements of individual skeletal elements and the appropriate equations used to determine stature in each case in the recording form. This form caters for three types of information: measurements from complete skeletons, partial skeletons, and whole bones (see MA 41F–MA46F). Each section has a tick box option that must be completed, regardless of whether the method is used, but only the appropriate section needs to be completed. For example, sections 1 and 2 will require all relevant bones to be recorded; computation can be made on the recording form in the area provided. Section 3 allows measurements to be made of all or some of the appropriate bones; formula computation can be undertaken in the space provided. FORDISC 3.0 measurements (Ousley and Jantz, 2005) should be entered into the computer programme and manually on the 'measurements' section of the recording form. Reference to this section will be necessary for equations and measurement details. An analytical notes box is provided; however, any other calculations, notes, or information can be recorded on an 'additional notes page', which should be attached to the recording form.

8.3 Assessment of skeletal pathology and trauma

The analysis of perimortem trauma is sometimes the only possible means of interpreting cause and, therefore, manner of death, and can add further evidence to assessments made from any soft tissue that may be present. Although it is one of the duties of the forensic pathologist to determine the cause and manner of death, when remains are skeletonised, the anthropologist contributes significantly to this process. Assessment of pathology is also undertaken, specifically to assist with determining the identification of individuals (Figure 8–1)[1]. This is possible where skeletal pathology may reflect disease, trauma, or lifetime condition that would have been recorded

---

[1] The images used in this chapter from Rwanda were taken from displays of human remains at genocide memorial sites within Rwanda. Such public displays infer no moral objection to such images being used in publications such as this. Permission to take photographs for educational purposes was granted by the relevant curating authorities.

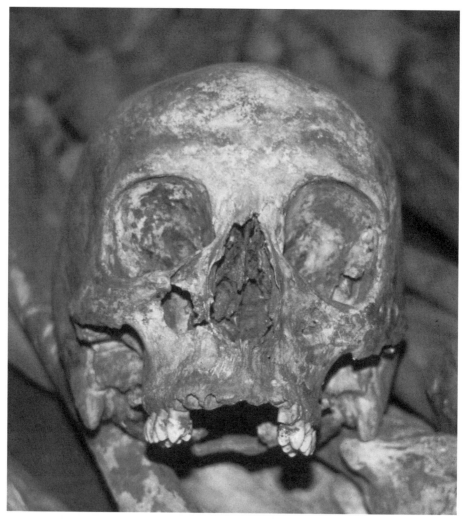

Figure 8–1a. This case from Rwanda exhibits significantly asymmetric orbit size and shape. The shape of the left orbit appears abnormal, and the bone within this feature appears to exhibit cortical remodeling. It is possible that this individual suffered from damage to, or loss of, this eye; therefore, that information might be forthcoming from antemortem data collection and/or medical records. *Source:* Margaret Cox.

on any medical notes and images. Equally, it could be a condition that was known or observed by informants. Consequently, conditions that are unusual within the sample population (including congenital disorders or genetic disease) are likely to be more useful than those that are commonplace (i.e., degenerative joint disease or trauma relating to common occupations or hazards). An alternative approach is to identify an outsider, who may be distinguished due to the absence of 'normal' conditions present in the population in question (such as nonmetric traits e.g., double articulating facets or spina bifida occulta). Recording more commonplace

Figure 8–1b. Severe arthritic conditions, such as those exhibited on this left femur, would undoubtedly cause much discomfort and probably affect the gait of the individual. Such information may be gleaned from medical records and radiographs or antemortem data and could be critical in ruling an individual in or out of the identification process. *Source:* Margaret Cox.

conditions will have particular merit in a developed region where detailed medical records and images, such as magnetic resonance imaging or computed tomography scans and radiographs, are likely to exist and be available for comparison. Unless such records or observations are accessible, recording the minutiae of commonplace degenerative change or asymptomatic conditions is likely to be of little value and can be a waste of resources. Determination of which conditions should be recorded and to what level of detail will be undertaken by the MMT and will be based on an understanding of the epidemiological and cultural context of the region as well as the availability of adequate resources and permissions to permit a very detailed assessment of the remains, which is the ideal but often not possible in the investigation of atrocity crimes. When analysis of skeletal pathology and trauma is not carried out, the anthropologist should indicate why. Interpretation of pathology and trauma at appropriate levels will be undertaken using the principle of differential diagnosis on complete, incomplete, and disarticulated remains. The following textbooks should be available for consultation: Aufderheide and Rodriguez-Martin (1998), Brogdon (1998), Di Maio (1999), Brogdon et al. (2003), and Ortner (2003). The six volumes by Resnick (1995) are also highly recommended. It is beyond the remit of this text to describe pathology and trauma in detail. Antemortem data of various types are also crucial to this exercise, but, whatever the source of information, it must be considered that only a subset of the chronic diseases to which humans are susceptible affects the skeleton.

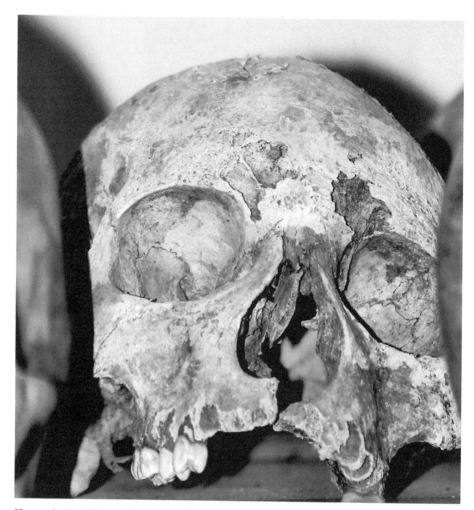

Figure 8–1c. This case from Rwanda exhibits changes characteristic of a cleft lip and palate. Although there is much postmortem damage, it is possible the individual also experienced infection of the frontal sinuses as a consequence of these conditions. Data collected during the anthropologists' analysis can be crucial in the identification process. *Source:* Margaret Cox.

Skeletal trauma and pathology should be described macroscopically, and where necessary, recorded with the aid of a binocular microscope and radiographs. In some cases, it may ultimately be necessary to use a scanning electron microscope to undertake histological assessment of a lesion. In such cases, this will require remains or samples to be taken to an accredited laboratory (subject to necessary consents for sampling). All lesions should be described in detail using standard terminology (Table 8–8), measured using sliding callipers, photographed, radiographed, and compared to anatomical and photographic exemplars. They must be described in detail and photographed.

Table 8–8. *Terminology for describing pathological lesions on bone*

Terminology	Description
Lytic	Bone removed by osteoclast (osteoclastic)
Blastic	Bone deposited by osteoblasts (osteoblastic)
Hypertrophy	Abnormal bone enlargement
Hypotrophy (atrophy)	Decrease in size (paralysis or disuse atrophy)
Ankylosis	Abnormal fusion of usually separate bones
Necrosis	Death of bone or element
Lamellar bone	Denotes healed (remodelled) lesion
Fibre (woven) bone	Denotes active lesion
Subperiosteal new bone formation	Either fibre or lamellar bone
Osteitis	Thickening of the cortex
Osteomyelitis	Infection within the medullary cavity, with evidence of these features: sequestrum (necrotic original cortex), cloaca(e) (draining sinuses), and involucrum (new sheath of bone)
Eburnation	Polishing of the joint surface
Osteophytes	Bony projections or spicules on or around the joint
Porosity	Pitting of the outer cortex

Source: Adapted from Ortner and Putschar, 1981.

To determine the presence and nature of skeletal pathology (e.g., neoplastic disease) and/or trauma, a tertiary radiographic survey can be requested (6.5). Where antemortem data are available, it may be necessary to radiograph specific skeletal elements or anatomical areas, such as frontal sinuses, as well as defining the sites of antemortem trauma or pathologies to assist with determination of presumptive identification. Preexisting radiographs of individuals may show trabeculae patterns that can also assist with identification. The results of the tertiary radiographic survey must be documented with the radiograph number on the recording forms (also see 6.7).

All observations and interpretations made during analysis must be recorded on the relevant recording forms. Unless a diagnosis can be made with confidence, the lesion or condition must only be described, and its location and extent detailed. Incorrect diagnoses may lead to misidentification or nonidentification. In these forms, trauma is divided into three sections: ante-, peri-, and postmortem. Each section has a skeletal diagram and codes for the most common descriptive terminology. This diagram must be annotated with the relevant code or description, including shading out absent bones. Any additional observations, notes, and interpretations should be made on the analytical notes page attached to the appropriate section. Additional notes pages may be used. However, these pages must be clearly marked with the section name and number. It is recommended that interpretation of lesions should be made after discussion with the radiographer and forensic pathologist. It may be necessary to illustrate (and describe) the location and distribution of all pathology and trauma as sketches. Diagrams are provided separately and may be used for this purpose as required. It should be possible to retrospectively determine the location and nature of all perimortem defects and pathological/traumatic lesions from the analytical notes. All pathology and trauma must be photographed (include the case number and a scale). Descriptions of the photographs taken (and the film and frame number or digital file number) must also be logged. Where helpful, casts can be made of the pathology or trauma for evidential purposes. In such cases, the cast(s) will be given an evidence number supplied by the scene of crime examiner (SCE). An alternative approach is to use a laser scanner to record surface change in combination with stereolithographic output to digitally record the surfaces (Mafart and Delingette, 2002).

8.3.1   Skeletal pathology

It is imperative when working on forensic missions that the anthropologist possesses an adequate knowledge and understanding of disease processes and congenital disorders that are both prevalent within particular geographic regions (e.g., leprosy, yaws) and within particular genetic groups. For example, thalassaemia major causes notable changes to bone and is a genetic condition generally affecting those originating from areas bordering the Mediterranean Sea and parts of Southeast Asia, while sickle cell anaemia occurs in blacks of African origin (Aufderheide and Rodriguez-Martin, 1998). It should, of course, be remembered that people migrate, and thus these conditions may be found in people outside these regions. Antemortem data collections must be designed to incorporate the acquisition of pertinent data about health and disease in a manner that is meaningful to survivor groups and helpful to the anthropologist.

The depth of detail required from this analysis will be decided by the MMT. Time-consuming attempts to provide many differential diagnoses of unusual conditions, including nonmetric traits, need to be justified. Many traits that affect the skeleton, but that are asymptomatic or invisible to close friends and relatives in life (e.g., spina bifida occulta, mandibular tori), may be of limited value in a society with no medical records and/or where radiography is not routine. In such cases, it may be decided that detailed analysis of such conditions is not undertaken. Nevertheless, all such lesions should be recorded briefly in the anthropologist's analytical notes. In some regions where widespread cultural practice may affect either teeth or bone, the fact that a person was unusual in that he or she did not indulge in the particular practice may be useful in determining identity. For example, betel nut chewing stains the teeth and helps protect against caries, but causes extreme periodontal disease, making this practice identifiable and comparable to antemortem data. Consequently, in areas where betel nut chewing is common, an individual with no staining, but with evidence of dental caries may be an outsider.

The initial assessment of a lesion will be to determine whether it is ante-, peri-, or postmortem. This is discussed in detail in 7.3. To recap, differentiating between antemortem and perimortem trauma is difficult because both contain collagen (a triple helix protein), which imparts resilience to trauma and determines how bone responds to force. Collagen can survive in deceased individuals for a considerable amount of time, reflecting both intrinsic and extrinsic factors; consequently,

Table 8–9. *Classifications for describing pathological lesions on bone*

Classification	Examples
Joint disease	Osteoarthritis, gout, diffuse idiopathic skeletal hyperostosis, rheumatoid arthritis
Nonspecific infection	Osteitis (or non-sclerosing osteomyelitis), osteomyelitis, septic arthritis
Specific infection	Tuberculosis, treponemal disease, leprosy
Congenital	Club foot, cleft palate, dwarfism
Neoplastic	Benign tumour, metastatic carcinoma, ivory (button) osteoma
Endocrine	Goitre, acromegaly, pituitary dwarfism
Metabolic	Osteoporosis, rickets, osteomalacia, scurvy, anaemia
Circulatory	Aneurysm, osteochondritis desiccans, Osgood-Schlatter's disease
Miscellaneous idiopathic	Paget's disease

Source: Ortner and Putschar, 1981.

determining when trauma occurs in relation to the point of death is imprecise. Antemortem trauma is indicated by the presence of healing, but it takes at least a week for bone to exhibit microscopic changes that can be observed radiographically and histologically (Sauer, 1998; Moraitis and Spiliopoulou, 2006).

In general, postmortem lesions have irregular breaks, sharp trabeculae, and may be a lighter colour (although this is not a conclusive indicator) than the surrounding cortex. The absence of any osteoblastic or microscopic osteoclastic activity could suggest a pseudopathology as opposed to a true pathology, although some cancers will produce entirely lytic lesions. However, as many pathological lesions are fragile in nature, care should be taken to assess whether an antemortem lesion underlies any postmortem damage.

Pathological lesions should be described in the following order. First, the anatomical location of the lesion must be recorded. It is important to specify which bone and side (if relevant) has been affected, indicate the precise position of the lesion(s) (referring to anatomical landmarks), and indicate whether the lesion is diffuse (widespread) or localised. Second, a description of the lesion is essential, and this must use terminology that is unambiguous and descriptive rather than diagnostic (Table 8–8) and include measurements where appropriate. Next, it is necessary to record the distribution of the lesion. If the lesion is specific to one bone, or affects more than one skeletal or dental element, this needs to be noted and described in the analytical notes. Relationships to other pathology and/or trauma should also be discussed. This is followed by classification of the lesion as described in Table 8–9. Finally, interpretation of pathology may be undertaken in consultation with the pathologist and radiographer. All interpretation will be described and justified in the analytical notes; they may also form part of the pathologist's final report.

8.3.2 Skeletal trauma

The analysis of skeletal trauma should be geared towards assisting in personal identification and providing information for determining cause and manner of death. The MMT will decide the depth of detail required for this analysis. Where soft tissue

Table 8–10. *Terminology for describing antemortem trauma on bone*

Terminology	Description
Bony callous	Sclerotic reaction, lamellar bone
Bone remodelling	Lamellar bone formation by osteoclastic and osteoblastic activity
Nonunion	When a fractured bone fails to reunite: the areas that fail to unite have a dense and rounded appearance, possibly resulting in a pseudoarthrosis (Adams and Hamblen, 1992)
Malunion	When a fractured bone heals but not in its original/anatomical orientation, uniting with angulation, rotation, loss of end–end apposition, or overlap (resulting in shortening of the bone)
Infection	Complication arising from trauma, mostly compound (open) fracture, untreated may develop into osteomyelitis
Necrosis	Bone dies due to lack of blood supply, may result in disabling osteoarthritis or joint disorganisation
Shortening	Malunion (i.e., overlap); crushing of bone (i.e., compression facture); interference with unfused epiphyses
Dislocation	Usually affecting the ligaments of a joint; however, in some cases, avulsion of bone at insertion site is possible

Table 8–11. *Classifications for describing antemortem trauma on bone*

Classification	Examples
Pathological	Disease or disorder. See section 8.3
Traumatic	Fracture, amputation, trephination, dislocation

Table 8–12. *Direct and indirect fractures*

Direct fractures	Indirect fractures
Tapping fracture: small force of low momentum on a small area of the body producing transverse fractures, some obliquely transmitted; in the lower leg, the weakest or most exposed bone is fractured	**Linear fracture**: out-bending of large thin portions of bone, usually in the skull; result from direct blows of high velocity; frequently extend from impact site; production is very rapid
	Avulsion fracture: small fragments detached from bony prominences by tension produced by attached ligaments or tendons
Crushing fracture: large force over large area; damage ranges from transverse to severely comminuted; usually lower arm and leg bones both break	**Traction or tension fracture**: an expansion of avulsion fractures; perpendicular to direction of pull; usually in patella, olecranon process, and medial medulla
	Angulation fracture: combined transverse and oblique fracture resulting in butterfly section at the compression side
	Rotational fracture: initiates as small vertical cracks that widen and become spiral fractures
	Compression fracture: in long bones, longitudinal fractures expand the length of diaphysis and terminate with a 'Y' or 'T' at the metaphysis; compression of vertebrae results in collapse of the anterior portions of the body; burst fractures involve extensive fragmentation of the centrum as the intervertebral disc is crushed

Source: Galloway, 1999.

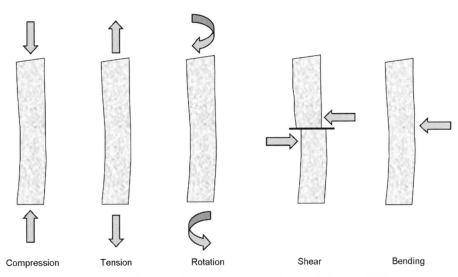

Figure 8–2. Schematic of forces acting on long bone. *Source:* Galloway, 1999.

survives, radiographs can be used as a means of assessing the presence of skeletal trauma. They can also be used on skeletal remains to provide more information than may be visible macroscopically, and in fleshed and skeletonised remains, radiographs can indicate foreign objects such as bullet fragments.

Antemortem trauma. Differentiating between ante- and perimortem trauma uses the criterion of presence or absence of healing (i.e., osteoclastic and osteoblastic activity), morphological characteristics of fracture lines, and characteristics of the cancellous bone (if appropriate). Antemortem lesions should be described as set out in this section. The anatomical location of lesions must be stated; specify which bone and side (if relevant) has been affected, and the precise position and size of the lesion(s) in relation to anatomical landmarks. Description of the lesion should use terminology that is unambiguous and descriptive rather than diagnostic (see Table 8–10), including measurements where appropriate. It is essential to record the distribution of a lesion, stating whether the lesion is specific to one bone or affects several bones; this should be discussed in the analytical notes. Possible relationships with other pathology and/or trauma should also be discussed. After the descriptive phase of the assessment is complete, a classification should be attributed to the lesion if possible (Table 8–11). Finally, any interpretation of trauma must be justified in the analytical notes. Where no interpretation is possible, this too must be recorded.

Perimortem trauma. Distinguishing perimortem from postmortem trauma requires the anthropologist to identify sharp margins, class morphology, uniformity of colour, and taphonomic signatures on the surrounding bony surfaces. This will require interpreting observed characteristics according to the context in which the remains were recovered. Perimortem lesions should be described, specifying which bone and side (if relevant) has been affected and indicating the precise position of the lesion(s) referring to anatomical landmarks, including measurements where appropriate (triangulation may be necessary). The lesion is described using terminology that is unambiguous and descriptive rather than diagnostic. The possible causal force and agents need to be described and interpreted (see Figure 8–2), where possible. The force involved can be described as direct (localised at the point of impact) or indirect (beyond the point of impact) (see Table 8–12). Perimortem injury can have two basic classifications: pathological or traumatic (e.g., projectile including ballistics) (Figure 8–3), or blunt force (Figure 8–4) or sharp force trauma (Figure 8–5) (Galloway, 1999).

After the descriptive phase of the assessment is complete, a classification should be attributed to the pathology if this is possible with confidence. Interpretation of perimortem lesions requires several considerations. First, it is important to determine the sequence of events. An injury may result in lesions affecting more than one bone. Second, injury to several bones may have resulted from a single event. Ordering events on single elements (e.g., the cranium) requires the anthropologist to sequence intercepting fractures. All interpretations must be supported by relevant observations. Detailed photography and annotated illustrations should be made.

Perimortem trauma can be loosely separated into sharp force, blunt force, and projectile trauma. Sharp force trauma encompasses wounds caused by blade instruments. These modifications will display sharp margins, V-shaped profile, and often some degree of polishing. Microscopic analysis of the margins may be necessary to identify the weapon type used (i.e., machete/cleaver) (Tucker et al., 2001). The length, depth, and direction of the wound must be recorded, describing the start and end points in relation to nearby bony landmarks (Kurosaki et al., 2005). Puncture (stab/penetrating) wounds are characteristically deeper than the entrance wound. They can be caused by a bladed (e.g., a knife) or pointed instrument (e.g., a pen or piece of wood) (Mason, 1993). Blunt force trauma includes injury resulting when a relatively large surface area comes into contact with the body. Weapons can range from blunt instruments (e.g., axe handles) to fists. Trauma includes injuries caused by impact at high velocities such as a moving vehicle, or falling from a building and landing on a hard surface. The range of possible fracture patterns is immense and requires careful interpretation (see Table 8–13).

Projectiles entering the body may be bullets or other objects (e.g., spears) that either perforate (enter and exit) or penetrate (enter only) the body (Di Maio, 1985). They have highly variable results, depending on the velocity of the projectile, firing distance and weapon used. Unusual patterns are encountered when modification of the projectile or weapon is undertaken and when projectiles ricochet off other objects. Subject-specific texts should be consulted for further information (e.g., Berryman and Symes, 1998; Whiting and Zernicke, 1998; Di Maio, 1999).

Penetration of a projectile may produce an entrance and exit wound. The shape, size, and direction of any bevelling (internal, external, or both) must be described.

Table 8–13. *Complete and incomplete bone fractures*

Complete fracture	Incomplete fracture
Transverse fracture: runs at right angles to the long axis; combination of tension and compression forces	**Bow fracture**: (plastic deformation): bone has an exaggerated curvature; can occur during longitudinal compression
Oblique fracture: runs diagonally along the diaphysis at 45-degree angle; angulation and compression forces	**Bone bruise**: (occult intraosseous fracture): an area of extensive trabecular bone microfracturing; produced by compression or impaction forces
Spiral fracture: circles the shaft and includes a vertical step; low-velocity rotational force; direction of spiral reflects the direction of tensile forces	**Torus fracture**: (buckling): a rounded expansion of bone where the cortical bone has been outwardly displaced around the circumference; usually at the end of long bones and junction of metaphysic and epiphysis; may combine with incomplete transverse fracture of one cortex while the other buckles; produced by compression force
Comminuted fracture: more than two fragments are generated:	
Butterfly fragment: elongated triangular fragment formed on the concave side of an angulation fracture, resulting from oblique-transverse fractures produced when angulation is combined with compression, resulting in a second oblique fracture	**Greenstick fracture**: incomplete transverse fracture travelling midway around the bone and then converting to a longitudinal split at right angles; produced by bending or angulation force
Segmental fracture: when multiple fractures have diaphyseal segments separated from the distal and proximal ends; may result from multiple simultaneous fractures	**Vertical fracture**: runs along the axis of long bones; as the fracture reaches trabecular bone, it may branch; produced by axial compression or a direct blow
Epiphyseal fracture:	**Depressed fracture**: cave-in of the outer table, usually of the cranium; produced by a direct blow; size depends on impacted area and velocity of force
Type i: complete separation of epiphyseal plate without associated fracture of diaphysis	
Type ii: separation that extends through the bony plate into the metaphysic; most common type; results from shearing or avulsion forces	
Type iii: intraarticular fracture from joint surface to weak zone of plate: shearing forces	
Type iv: as type iii but extends to metaphysic	
Type v: crushing of plate due to compression of epiphysis	

Source: Galloway, 1999.

A projectile will usually bevel bone in the direction in which it travels. Entrance wounds characteristically display a circular defect with bevelling on the internal table. This must not be mistaken for chips of bone that can flake off the edge of an entrance wound. Contact wounds can produce bevelling on the external as well as internal table, but to a lesser degree. The entrance is usually smaller than the exit, although exceptions can occur. An example of an entrance wound with external bevelling is shown in Figure 8–3a. Other examples can include a ricochet

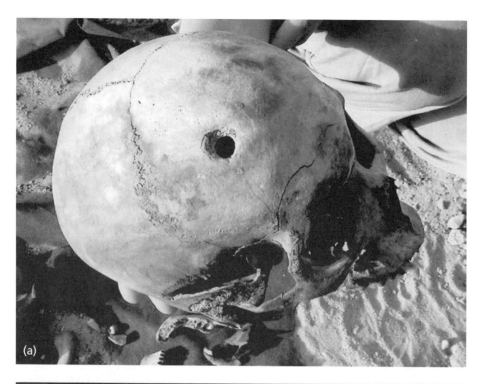

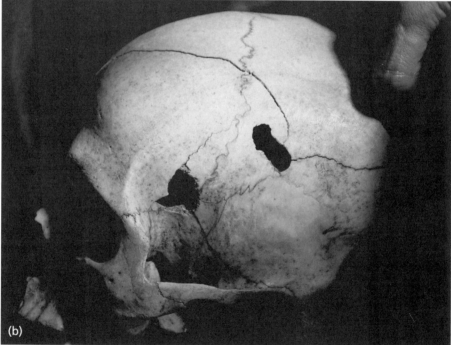

Figure 8–3. Ballistics trauma to crania. (a) An entrance wound with unusual external bevelling (Iraq). *Source:* Inforce. (b) A keyhole lesion (on the right) with radiating fractures (South Africa). The cause of the lesion on the left cannot be attributed with confidence; it exhibits radiating fractures. *Source:* Alan McClue.

402

Figure 8–4. Blunt force trauma to crania. (a) Characteristic lesion demonstrating flaking of the outer table (Rwanda). *Source:* Margaret Cox. (b) Close-up of depression fracture to the left frontal region (Rwanda). *Source:* Margaret Cox. (c) A depression fracture caused by a blow to the cranium with a hammer (South Africa). Analysis of the unusual outline of the lesion was verified by witness testimony. Note the radiating fracture extending from the inferior margin. *Source:* Alan McClue. (d) Extreme trauma to the cranium, the mechanics of which are uncertain (Rwanda). *Source:* Alan McClue. (e) Major blunt force trauma to a child's cranium. This might reflect the type of damage incurred by an allegedly common method of killing babies and children in the Rwandan genocide. Many were apparently picked up by their feet and their heads swung against a hard surface (e.g., a wall or tree). *Source:* Alan McClue.

entrance (the projectile is yawing [tumbling] due to contact with another object before entering), if a projectile fragments internally and exits as small pieces, and tangential entrances causing avulsion of bone. The calibre of the projectile cannot be estimated from the diameter of the entrance. Exit wounds characteristically display irregular defects with cone-shaped bevelling on the external table (see also Mason, 1993; Quatrehomme and Iscan, 1997, 1999; Di Maio, 1985; 1999; di Maio and Di Maio, 1993) (see Figure 8–6).

Tangential wounds are observed when a projectile enters at an angle. If they perforate, the entrance and exit may be at close proximity and undistinguishable from one another. Keyhole entrances are identified when the projectile enters the bone at an angle and fragments, resulting in bevelling on the internal table where the fragment enters and external bevelling where the fragment exits. A projectile can reenter the body once it has passed through and exited another area (e.g., through the arm and then into the thorax). Similarly, when a projectile passes through an

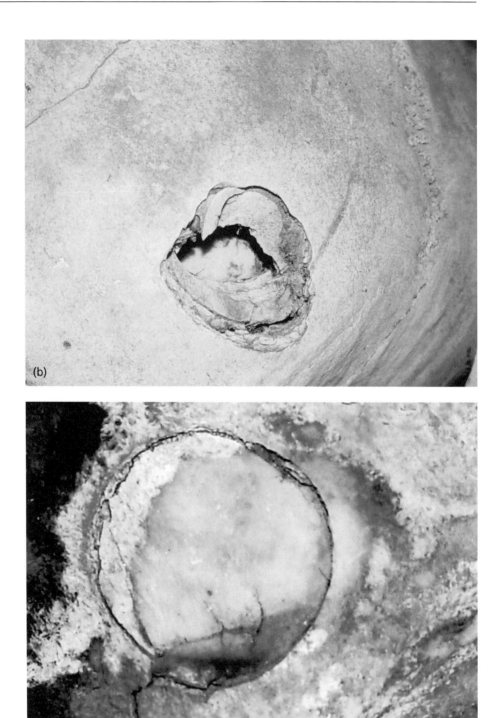

Figure 8–4 (*cont.*)

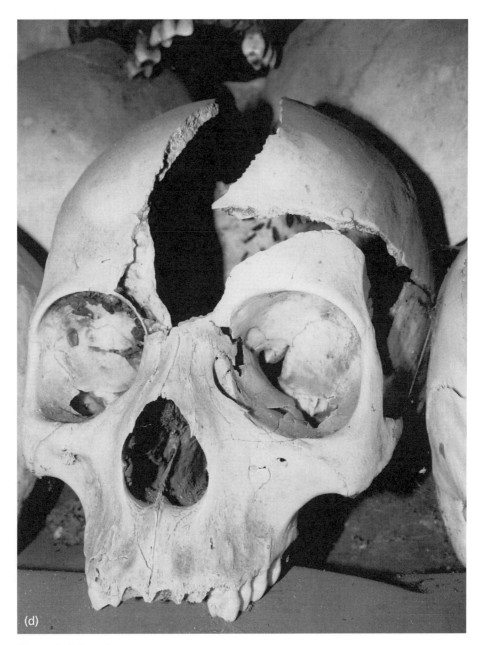

Figure 8–4 (*cont.*)

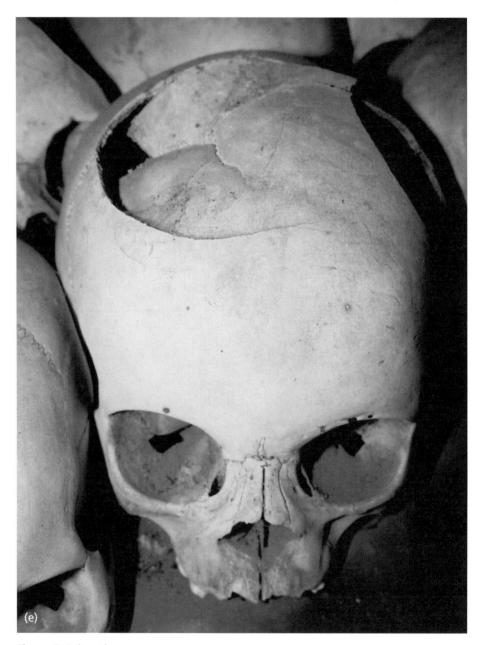

Figure 8–4 (*cont.*)

Figure 8–5. Sharp force trauma to crania. (a) The impact of three blows to the face and skull with a blade instrument (Rwanda). It appears that the blow to the left side of the face removed most of the zygomatic region. Note the radiating fracture extending from the right parietal anteriorly down the right frontal that reflects further trauma. *Source:* Margaret Cox. (b) This example of a male cranium illustrates blade trauma horizontally across the frontal bone with radiating fractures inferiorly (Rwanda). This blade lesion is intercepts by a radiating fracture associated with blade trauma across the right coronal suture (note the associated flaking). This demonstrates that the trauma to the frontal bone was inflicted first. *Source:* Alan McClue. (c) An example of blade trauma and associated radiating fractures (Rwanda). The blows were directed across the top of the skull, and the most anterior lesion, in particular, was inflicted with considerable force. *Source:* Alan McClue. (d) The limits of the blade lesion are from the coronal suture at midpoint traversing posteriorly around and crossing the sagittal suture, stopping at approximately midpoint on the right parietal bone (Rwanda). *Source:* Alan McClue.

intermediate target (e.g., a window or other object) and then hits the body, the lesion characteristics will be altered, usually more severely. When a projectile does not penetrate an object but ricochets (e.g., water or a smooth stone) it becomes unstable and tumbles, entering the body in a disorganised manner causing a large irregular entrance. The shape and size of the entrance and exit wounds must be described, and the central point of the lesion must be measured to pinpoint its location in relation to nearby bony landmarks (Di Maio, 1993). Secondary fractures (radiating and concentric) should be numbered and described, noting the areas or bones affected and the fracture termination points (Shuman and Wright, 1999; De la Grandmaison et al., 2001; Fenton et al., 2005).

Radiographs (preferably of two planes) can be of assistance in identifying bullets and fragments (Mason, 1993). If it is possible to ascertain the trajectory (direction

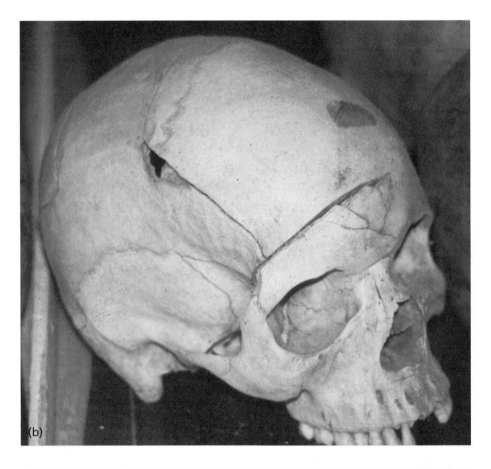

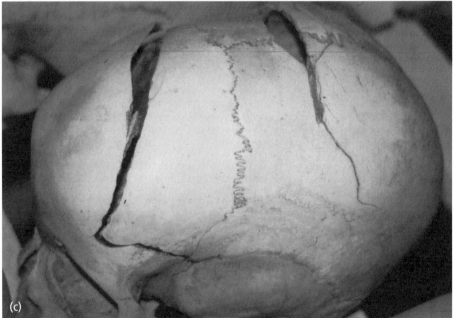

Figure 8–5 *(cont.)*

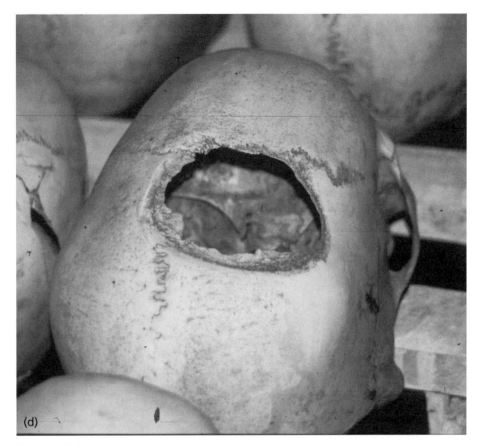

Figure 8–5 *(cont.)*

and angle) of a projectile or force, this should be recorded in detail, noting the direction and angle of entry/exit. An inspection of any clothing for associated damage can be made.

Explosive injury often results in severe mutilation of the body, the severity depending on the proximity to and force of the blast (Mason, 1993; Clasper et al., 2002). Bone can be fragmented and the pattern of fragmentation will affect force, distance, and biomechanics of each bone. The explosion can cause foreign objects to penetrate the body either as a direct result of the explosion (i.e., shrapnel) or secondary (i.e., wood, metal, or plastics), and both have the capacity to behave as projectiles. Blunt force injury may also be experienced due to larger objects (e.g., masonry) impacting the body. Antipersonnel mines can cause either comminute fracture of the heel or amputation at midcalf level. The impact of blast force on human bone is inadequately understood and researched.

Secondary complications such as infection often result from contaminated wounds; evidence suggesting infection (e.g., periosteal reaction) should be described and recorded.

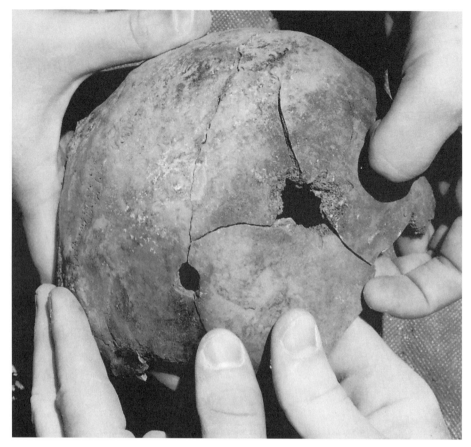

Figure 8–6. Ballistics trauma to the right parietal of a male (Iraq). This acutely angled trajectory exhibits external beveling on the left side of the entrance wound (left). The opposite side of this lesion exhibits internal bevelling. The uneven bevelling reflects the acute angle of fire. The exit wound (right) exhibits characteristic external bevelling. Interestingly, the radiating fracture associated with the exit wound is intercepted by a radiating fracture created by the entrance wound. Thus, there is no uncertainty that these two lesions are associated. The green colour of the bone reflects the proximity of copper-based metal objects in the burial environment. *Source:* Inforce.

8.4 Examination of dentition

The examination of dentition will be undertaken by the forensic odontologist whenever present. The odontologist will examine teeth using specialist methods and recording systems as specified in 9.4. However, in cases where an odontologist is not present, an anthropologist can undertake the examination. This section includes the procedures to be used by the anthropologist and should only be applied in the absence of an odontologist.

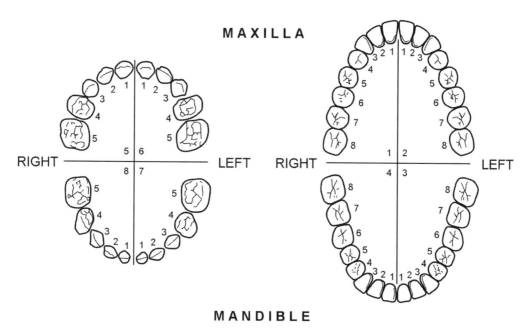

MAXILLA

MANDIBLE

Figure 8–7. FDI system for labelling deciduous and permanent dentition. *Source:* FDI, 1971.

All individuals with unerupted or erupting dentition will be radiographed to assist with the estimation of age at death, using dental development and eruption of both deciduous and permanent dentition (see 7.7.1). Additional radiographs can be taken to provide evidence of disease and dental anomalies of the teeth and roots, and may assist with the interpretation of alveolar absorption, congenital absence, and nonerupted and impacted teeth. Radiographs can be requested by the anthropologist and will be recorded accordingly. Where dental records exist, radiographs of adult dentition could prove valuable in determining identification.

When recording the dentition for both nonadults and adults, the FDI (Fédération Dentaire International, 1971) system should be used. Figure 8–7 gives an example of the system in which the dentition is divided into quadrants and where each tooth has a two-digit number beginning with the right then left maxilla and left then right mandible (1-4). This labelling is identical for the nonadult dentition however, the numbers of the quadrants are five to eight. The second digit denotes the tooth where the numbering begins at the midline (medial/sagittal plane) for each quadrant. For each tooth, the status column on the anthropology recording form must be completed as either present or absent. When the tooth is absent, its status must be recorded, for example, as ante- or postmortem. Congenital absence of teeth is difficult to assign, and care must be taken during analysis (Bass, 1995). When teeth are confidently identified as congenitally absent through radiographic examination, this must be recorded in the analytical notes. When dentition is present, each tooth will undergo examination for the presence of anomalies, pathology, trauma,

Table 8–14. *Coding for dental analysis by anthropologists*

Status		Modification	
P	Present	Dc	Discolouration
A	Absent	Dr	Decoration
		At	Attrition
Time		As	Abrasion
Am	Antemortem	Er	Erosion
Cm	Perimortem		
Pm	Postmortem	**Malformation**	
		Rt	Rotation
Location		Tn	Transportation
M	Mesial	Cr	Crowding
D	Distal	Mo	Malocclusion
Lg	Lingual	Ds	Diastema
Lb	Labial		
B	Buccal	**Pathology**	
O	Occlusal	Ab	Abscess
R	Root	Ca	Caries
C	Crown	Pq	Plaque
		Rp	Resorption
Anomaly		Rd	Remodelling
Ue	Unerupted	Ed	Enamel defects
Im	Impacted		
Sp	Supernumerary	**Bite**	
Ec	Extra cusp	Ob	Overbite
Pt	Peg tooth	Eb	Edge-to-edge bite
Rd	Retained deciduous	Ub	Underbite
Trauma			
Ch	Chip		
Fx	Fracture		

modification, malformation, and restoration. The maxilla and mandible should be united at the temporomandibular joint to assess bite. Recording bite, for example, can be useful where tooth alignment is unusual because it may be described by relatives or be seen on photographs if they show the missing person smiling. Specific enquiry must be made about the visual appearance of teeth during antemortem data collection (see 10.2).

The codes for recording these variables are described in Table 8–14. Anthropologists must record the location of anomalies or lesions on individual teeth and associated bone structures. Location should be described, as appropriate, as primarily on the root or crown, and then with further detail of location (e.g., mesial) (see Figure 8–8). They must also note the relative chronology at which these variations are believed to have manifested themselves. These can be recorded as ante-, peri-, or postmortem. If a tooth is absent, it should be determined if that loss was ante-, peri-, or postmortem. This will be based on the degree of alveolar remodelling, if any, that has taken place. Recent but antemortem tooth loss will be indicated by active remodelling and resorption of the alveolus, while long-standing tooth loss

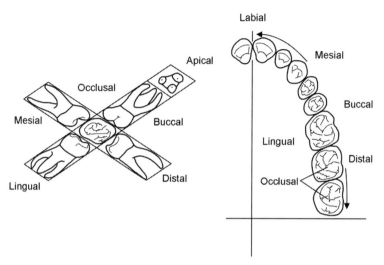

Figure 8–8. Descriptive aspects of an individual tooth and palatal quadrant. *Source:* Hillson, 1998.

will be evident by the alveolus and associated crypt being completely remodelled and smooth.

Potential anomalies that might affect teeth are recorded using the following conventions. Additional comments such as the location of the anomaly will be recorded by codes (see 8.9) on the drawing within the recording form and in the analytical comments. Anomalies might include (i) the presence of unerupted teeth (confirmed through radiography). This may occur for different reasons. (ii) Congenitally absent teeth (partial agenesis) (confirmed through radiography). (iii) Impacted teeth – are those that may not have erupted and remain within the alveolus (confirmed through radiography), or that may have erupted sideways into the mouth. (iv) Supernumerary teeth – are extra teeth (not always erupted and these will be confirmed through radiography); these teeth may take on the form of neighbouring teeth on the lingual aspect (Hillson, 1996) and can occur as permanent and, more rarely, deciduous dentition (Bass, 1995). (v) Extra cusps on teeth – should be recorded in terms of the affected tooth and the location at which it occurs. (vi) A peg tooth develops as a single-rooted tooth with a dome shaped crown that is conical in appearance and lacks normal morphological features. (vii) Mulberry molars – have prominent plane-form defects around the cusps, with a marked step at their base, below which the crown side is normal (Karnosh, 1926, taken from Hillson, 1998); they usually are associated with those suffering from congenital syphilis. (viii) Retained deciduous teeth – occur where there is either no permanent tooth, or where the permanent tooth has erupted in an abnormal position negating the absorption and shedding of the preceding tooth (Hillson, 1996).

The following dental pathologies and conditions will be recorded by their occurrence using the relevant code (see Table 8–14), and their position by using location codes and the diagram. Additional comments can be made within the analytical notes. The degree of progress of these conditions should be recorded as outlined here for each category, and all should be fully described and photographed.

Caries may be located within either the crown or the root of the tooth. Evidence of dental pathology can also be seen within the bone of the alveolus. Caries should be recorded in terms of the tooth affected, position, and size of the lesion. Location on the tooth is described as follows: Coronal caries can either be on the occlusal surface of the tooth, the approximal crown surface (mesial or distal), and other smooth surfaces (i.e., buccal or labial). Root surface caries are usually located at the cemento–enamel junction (CEJ) (the junction between the root and the crown), or above the gingival margin (Hillson, 2001). The severity of the lesion can be described as a pit/fissure, less than half a crown destroyed, more than half a crown destroyed, and the crown totally destroyed. Cavities in the bone can be on the maxilla or the mandible, can be buccal or, more rarely, lingual, and can be caused by cysts or dental abscesses. The location and the size of the cavity should be recorded (small: <3 mm, medium: 3–7 mm, and large: >7 mm). The cause of these cavities cannot be confirmed without consulting an odontologist (Hillson, 1996), and radiography is advised if there is any doubt.

Calculus is the most common condition affecting teeth. Created by the accumulation of microorganisms on the tooth surface, calculus is mineralised plaque (Hillson, 1996). There are two forms of calculus; that above the CEJ and that below. The affected tooth and the site of the calculus should be recorded, as should the surface extent and thickness of the calculus (e.g., slight, medium, severe). Hypercementosis of tooth roots is, in our experience, often encountered in regions with poor oral health and should be recorded. It is suggestive of the presence of periodontal disease.

Resorption of dental tissue in nonadults is the demineralisation of the roots of deciduous dentition to allow the permanent dentition to grow (White, 2000). The dentine and the cementum of the tooth can also undergo resorption in adult dentition and the line of reversal may be identified (Hillson, 1996). The alveolar bone can be resorbed in response to periodontal disease. In addition, *periodontal disease* often results in macroscopic porosity and periostitis of the alveolar bone. The resorption can be horizontal and/or vertical. The site and extent of the resorption should be recorded. Extent can be divided into five grades: crater (one side of tooth), trench (two or three sides of tooth), moat (all sides), ramp (one side), or plane (all sides). These can also be graded as slight, moderate, or severe. Diagnosis of periodontal disease should only be made in consultation with an odontologist. Remodelling of the alveolar can reflect tooth loss, trauma, infection, and metabolic diseases such as scurvy. The location and extent of remodelling should be described and recorded. Diagnosis of any pathology should be made in consultation with the odontologist and/or pathologist.

Enamel defects usually comprise areas of decreased enamel thickness on the tooth crown as a result of a disruption in enamel formation (amelogenis) during periods of fever and malnutrition in childhood. In addition, areas of opacity (hypocalcification), which is caused by a disruption to mineralisation at the maturation stage of the tooth may also be observed. Dental enamel hypoplasias are usually evident macroscopically as pits or furrows that extend around the surface of the affected tooth and are initiated during secretion of the enamel matrix (Hillson, 1996). The location and type of defect should be recorded as opacity, pits, furrows, or missing enamel. The number (i.e., single, multiple or diffuse) and size of defects should also be recorded. If enamel hypoplasia is unusual within a sample population, then it should be recorded, and its position assessed against age of occurrence by using microscopic analysis as a possible aid in the identification process (Lewis, 2007). It can be used to indicate a period(s) of severe stress (e.g., illness) during childhood and can inform the identification process (Hillson, 1996). It should be remembered that severe hypoplasia might be visible on photographs, and this should be considered during the antemortem data collection.

The same is true for *discolouration*, which can be caused by developmental enamel defects where deposits of pigment reflect metabolic disorders, or by later staining, reflecting deficiencies in mineralisation (Buikstra and Ubelaker, 1994). Care must be taken when identifying the timing of any discoloration because ante- (tobacco, caffeine), peri-, or postmortem staining (weathering) may also discolour teeth. A more unusual defect is fluorosis (Ferguson, 1999), which can present as stained opacities or pitted hypoplastic defects. This should be recorded in the analytical notes and photographed, for possible correlation with antemortem data.

Dental trauma must be noted and recorded appropriately. The timing (ante, peri-, or postmortem) at which it occurred can be difficult to assign as occasionally, taphonomic processes, including extreme heat, can cause postmortem damage and fracture of teeth. That said, dentition is generally fairly robust and suffers less from taphonomic agents than bone. A chipped tooth is defined as the loss of enamel and/or a section of the tooth and antemortem damage should be apparent by wear causing rounding of the chipped edge. Fissuring of the tooth enamel and fracturing of the tooth root, dentine, or enamel should be recorded using appropriate coding.

Dentition can also be modified both incidentally (i.e., reflecting habitual activity in an occupational or recreational context) or by deliberate ornamentation. *Decoration of teeth* is modification undertaken for aesthetic or cultural reasons and differs between cultural groups. Decoration can include carving the teeth and jewellery on teeth, such as gold crowns and the insertion of gems (Hillson, 1998). The location, type, and colour of the decoration should be recorded, and additional comments and sketches made in the analytical notes. Photographs should be taken. When applicable, the classifications of Romero (1958, 1970) should be used.

Attrition is wear caused by friction or rubbing and can reflect chewing, grinding, and tapping of the teeth. It can be useful in identification where attrition is unusual for the sample in question. It only merits recording in such circumstances. The degree of attrition can be graded in stages using the modified scoring method of Smith (1984), as recommended by Buikstra and Ubelaker (1994). This method scores the left incisor, canine, and premolars from the mandible and the maxilla in eight stages. In forensic cases, attrition should not be used for ageing individuals (7.7.2). Assessment of the significance of attrition must also consider the occlusion of mandibular and maxillary dentition. A preferred methodology for grading the stage of wear may be recommended by the odontologist. Unusual patterns of attrition should be noted in the analytical notes. Malocclusion can lead to unusual attrition patterns and merits recording because it can affect facial appearance.

Abrasion of enamel (sometimes also affecting dentine or roots) occurs through an unusual or abnormal mechanical process, such as toothbrushing, and the use of foreign objects, including toothpicks, smoking equipment, blades, and oral jewellery (Harnett and To, 2002). This may be sited in a specific place caused by habitual practice such as pipe smoking or the use of teeth in industry or occupation (Figure 8–9). *Enamel etching or erosion* is caused by acidic chemical application and can result from the application of acidic tooth cleansers, reflex stomach disorders, and stomach acid from vomiting in conditions such as anorexia or bulimia. The location and dimensions of types of abrasion and etching should be recorded (Hillson, 1996) because this can contribute to identification.

Malformation should be recorded and photographed, particularly where it affects anterior teeth and has the potential to assist with identification. *Rotation* is the displacement of teeth along the axis of the tooth. The second molars are reportedly the teeth most often rotated (Bass, 1995), but our observations suggest that it is in fact more common in canines and premolars. The location and direction of the rotation should be recorded. 'Winging' is rotation of adjacent teeth, particularly the central incisors, either mesially or distally. *Transposition* is where neighbouring teeth 'swap' positions and is generally related to rotation or some other positional irregularity (Hillson, 1996). *Crowding* is caused when there is insufficient space in the jaws for the teeth, with one or more teeth consequently pushed out of their normal position (Bass, 1995). This should be described in the dental section of the relevant recording form and photographed. Where anterior teeth are affected, this might be visible on relevant family photographs.

Malocclusion is defined as poor positioning or inappropriate contact between teeth on closure. In cases where it is possible, the character of occlusion or bite can be recorded as edge-to-edge bite, where the top teeth line up with the bottom teeth; overbite, where the upper teeth are anterior of the lower teeth; or underbite, where the lower teeth are anterior of the upper teeth (Hillson, 1996). Variants on these should be recorded in the analytical notes. *Diastema* is the presence of a gap between two teeth that is more common in the upper dentition than in the lower (Hillson, 1996). The location of the gap should be recorded and measured.

Restorations can be fillings, a false tooth or teeth, or a crown. All restoration is to be recorded, including the location, extent, and material of the restoration (e.g., metal, ceramic, plastic). It may be necessary to remove a small sample of restoration material for elemental analysis in an appropriate laboratory. Photographs should be taken when anterior teeth are affected. Dental plates should be recorded and

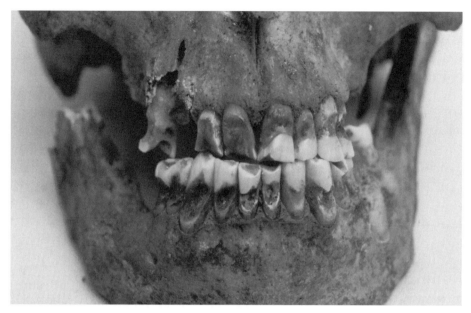

Figure 8–9. Anterior view of the dentition of an adult male exhibiting enamel erosion of anterior dentition reflecting the use of a tartaric-based tooth cleansing substance. *Source:* P. Rowley.

examined for manufacturer's details and unique marks. These can be useful in identification in regions where dentures are uniquely marked, and even something as generic as a manufacturer's mark can be useful, particularly if it is unusual.

When considered necessary (see 9.3), teeth may be extracted for DNA sampling and isotope analysis. In such cases, it is preferable to use single-rooted, noncarious teeth.

If an odontologist recommends changes to be made to the standard recording form because of the requirements of an investigation, these should be made before the analytical process begins. All dental pathology should be described and interpreted in the Anthropology Recording Form (MA41F–MA46F). If present, an odontologist can confirm the dental pathology that will be recorded in the pathologist's report. All dentition, including disassociated teeth, should be photographed. Further photographic records can be made of specific details as necessary. All photographs and radiographs will be listed on the relevant anthropology recording form. If undertaking the examination, the anthropologist will record the dental examination in the Dental Recording Section using the relevant forms.

The details obtained during the dental examination can be compared with antemortem data where clinical records exist. Comparisons of dental postmortem and antemortem data for identification should be made by the odontologist. Once individual loose teeth have been classified using the FDI numbering system, they can

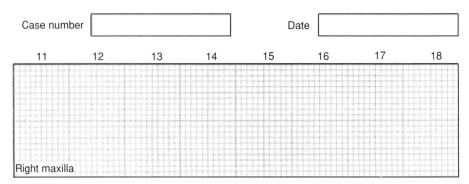

Figure 8–10. Quadrant of the suggested background for dental photography. *Source:* Inforce Foundation.

be placed on the appropriate section of (millimetre) graph paper (Figure 8–10); the case number and date must be noted on the page. If appropriate, the absence of teeth can be illustrated by writing 'A' in the appropriate place, and the entire page can then be photographed. This system is also useful for deciduous or mixed dentition. All anomolies affecting anterior dentition must be photographed for comparison with family photographs and other antemortem data if such exists.

8.5 Assessment of heat-modified remains

This section discusses the analysis of human bone that has been subject to extensive heat modification or burning, with the consequent removal of all or most of the recognisable soft tissue. Even where the bone is largely calcined, some charred soft tissue may remain attached. Connective tissue, muscle fibres, and some of the denser organs may survive as charred masses; analysis of these is not discussed here. The methods described in this section are specifically intended for cases where little soft tissue survives and the remains consist wholly or largely of burnt bone. Basic analysis can be undertaken with sliding callipers. If it is considered appropriate to assess the fragmentation levels, a set of sieves of 10-, 5-, and 2-mm fraction size will be required (1-mm fraction sieves are required for obtaining burnt skeletal remains and other material remains from the recovery scene).

The analysis of burnt human bone shares many of the aims common to that of other human bone. The methods are largely the same; however, their effectiveness is limited by the degree and impact of heat alteration (fragmentation, shrinkage, and distortion) and proportion of the skeletal remains available for examination (only part may be present). In forensic contexts, attempts to dispose of remains via burning are often only partially successful, and in individual cases a wide variation in the impact of heat on both hard and soft tissues frequently occurs. Consequently, it is not always appropriate to weigh remains from such a contexts unless for purely descriptive purposes. Analysis may also include the recording of taphonomic and other data that could potentially indicate site formation processes acting on the remains before, during, and subsequent to burning.

Much can be done to maximise the preservation of burnt skeletal remains at the recovery and pre-analysis processing stages. Deposits comprising or containing burnt bone should be subject to whole earth recovery where possible, although where remains overlie one another it may not be. Details of the recovery procedure are dictated by the size and form of the deposit. The burnt bone, including any excavated from intact contained deposits by the forensic archaeologist or anthropologist must be cleaned prior to analysis. Where bone is robust and in good condition, this is best effected by careful wet sieving to 1-mm mesh size, and all extraneous material (e.g., stones and other coarse components) within the larger fraction residues (5 mm and above) should have been removed. The small fraction residues (<5 mm) should be retained for scanning by the anthropologist to enable recovery of fragments of dental tissue or human bone identifiable to a skeletal element, animal bone, or other class and type of material evidence (the quantity and quality of extraneous material in these smaller fractions is generally of limited evidentiary value). Further to this, they should be collected so the maximum amount of remains can be returned to the next of kin.

Although additional techniques may be required, in the vast majority of cases macroscopic examination of the remains will be sufficient to accomplish analysis. Burnt bone will not necessarily be fully calcined. The degree of burning depends on the conditions under which the body was burnt and the level of oxidation of the organic components of the bone. The term 'calcined' should only be applied to fully oxidised bone, which will display, among other attributes, a uniform white colour (Holden et al., 1995a, 1995b). Bone showing lesser degrees of oxidation should be referred to as 'burnt' or 'heat modified'. The terms 'cremated bone', 'cremains', and 'cremation' imply the ritual burning of the body as part of a mortuary rite and will generally not be appropriate in forensic circumstances. A special consideration should be made to not misinterpret post-depositional changes creating the appearance of burning. Such changes as blackening and 'thinning' of bone can occur when bone is in contact with certain soils, materials (e.g., tar), dyes, moulds, soil bacteria, and so on.

The specific questions asked within any individual forensic situation are likely to vary, depending on the circumstances. As a minimum, the recovery of demographic and other specific data with the potential to assist with the identification of the individual (pathology/morphology) will be recorded to the highest standard. The recovery of data pertaining to the formation processes affecting the remains themselves, and the deposits from which they are recovered may not routinely be requested, but may be of evidentiary value in the interpretation of the sequence of events. Therefore, such data should also be systematically collected (see 5.6).

The various types of data required to fulfil (as far as possible) the aims of a minimum analysis are establishing a minimum number of individuals (MNI); assessment of each individual's biological profile (ancestry, sex and age); details of pathology and trauma of nonmetric variation; and information pertaining to formation processes (taphonomy). The form and integrity of the deposit from which remains were recovered is of vital importance with respect to the interpretation of the results from several categories of data, particularly those relevant to the formation processes of the deposit itself and interpretation of how the remains were modified. Information on the levels of obvious disturbance to the deposit, its form (e.g., from a positive or negative feature, or a surface deposit), and the method of recovery all need to be considered during interpretation, and should be made available to the anthropologist before analysis commences. The anthropologists working on the grave site are best placed to record this.

It is essential to record a number of factors when analysing burnt remains. These may include the total weight of bone, which can provide a basic unit of quantification of material and may indicate manipulation of remains if the weight is not commensurate with that anticipated from individual bodies (exclusive of extraneous material and attached soft tissue). Assessment of the skeletal elements represented also indicates pre- or postburning manipulation of the body/remains. The degree and pattern of fragmentation and warping may indicate the speed and intensity of the heat source acting on the bone (as distinct from the entire body), the condition of bone at the time of burning (green or dry), stresses on the bone, and manipulation of the remains during or subsequent to burning. The colour of the bone reflects the levels of oxidation, which in turn indicates factors affecting the process of burning (temperature, oxygen supply, length of time). Coloured staining to bone or adhering substances may further indicate materials that were in contact with the body during burning and cooling of the remains and could be of assistance with identification. If possible, colour should be assigned using a coded colour chart (e.g., Munsell chart; Munsell Color Co, 2000) for consistency and reduction of interobserver error.

In the following outline of procedures, other sections of this document are referred to, such as methods for determining the MNI, attribution of sex, and estimation of age. Some areas and aspects of analysis outlined elsewhere, such as reconstruction, inferred ancestry, and analysis of trauma, are likely to be limited where remains are incomplete or survive in poor or distorted condition. Appropriate records of morphology should be made wherever practicable, and a degree of reconstruction may be possible in some cases. Estimation of living stature from burnt bone (e.g., Rösing, 1977) is fraught with difficulties and is open to a relatively large margin of error, due to the effects of shrinkage, fracturing, and incomplete representation of skeletal elements. It is not generally recommended (Wahl, 1982; Holck, 1986; McKinley, 2000).

8.5.1 Analytical techniques

Analysis of burnt bone can be undertaken in a series of steps that will allow the recovery of data without the necessity of repeated handling. Bone from each context or subcontext may first be weighed (quantified) if considered appropriate. However, where bone has burnt tissue associated with it in various ratios the value of weighing materials for comparative purposes is limited. Where only bone is present, fragmentation levels may be recorded using bone from 10-, 5-, and 2-mm sieve fractions (calculated as a percentage of the total weight), the total weight may be obtained by summing those from the sieve fractions. Measures of maximum fragment size from each context or subcontexts should be recorded at this stage. The weight of bone from a context should be recorded to the nearest tenth of a gram. The weight of bone from a context, or group of associated contexts, may be reflective of the number of individuals represented, or the relative proportion of the remains of one individual present (McKinley, 1993).

Every fragment of bone, however small, will need to be examined at least once. Identifiable material may be present among even the 1-mm sieve residue. Bone fragments identifiable to skeletal element should be separated into four anatomical regions – skull, axial skeleton, upper limb, and lower limb – for further detailed recording and analysis. A skeletal inventory should be made on all fragments within the four anatomical regions. Because bone fragments will often be very small, this must be as precise as possible to avoid confusion or errors in the determination of the minimum number of individuals (in case a different fragment from the same bone is recovered in another associated subcontext). The number of fragments from individual skeletal elements (e.g., six fragments of radius shaft) should be recorded. The description should include any morphological observations that may pertain to age, sex, or assessment of identity, such as pathological lesions or morphological variations. Any variation in colour should be noted, together with observation of fragmentation and warping (see MA43F and MA44F).

Analysis will record a standard set of data as follows: case number, anthropologist, date of analysis, context number, context description, skull, axial skeleton, upper limb, lower limb, approximate age, assessment of sex, pathology and trauma summary, fragmentation summary, and oxidation summary. If the remains are weighed, the weight of bone within each of the four skeletal areas should be presented as a percentage of the total weight of bone recovered. This will help illustrate any bias towards or omission of remains from individual skeletal areas. Photographs should be taken of pathological lesions or morphological variations that may assist in the identification of the individual. Radiographs should be used as deemed necessary to investigate and assist in the diagnosis of pathological conditions.

When large quantities of material likely to represent the remains of several individuals are being examined, it is helpful to construct a table to record the numbers of morphologically distinctive, discrete, skeletal elements from which counts can be made. Such a table is provided in Anthropology Recording form MA43 and includes detailed breakdowns, particularly of elements of the skull that are easy to recognise, even as small fragments. As with all fragmentary and commingled assemblages, extreme care must be exercised to ensure that fragmentary parts of individual elements are clearly defined to avoid errors (e.g., recording 'anterior fragment of left petrous temporal' rather than 'left petrous temporal', if the former is all that is present).

Burnt bone, as with all skeletal material, may be greatly affected by the nature of the deposit from which it is recovered and taphonomic processes (including postdepositional disturbance, excavation, and postexcavation processing). Levels of potential truncation and disturbance will have been noted during excavation, together with observations on the form of the deposit. This information should be passed on to the anthropologist because these processes may, for example, have affected the weight of bone present (if undertaken) and degree of fragmentation.

The overall degree of bone fragmentation may be measured in a variety of ways, but the weight of fragments within specific size ranges (calculated as a percentage of the overall weight of bone from the context) gives a relatively quick, representative, and quantifiable measure of degree of fragmentation. The use of sieve stacks of varying fraction size (10, 5, and 2 mm), although not 100 percent representative, allows for rapid recovery of data. A measure (mm) of the maximum bone fragment within a context should be taken, and where possible a preexcavation maximum fragment size should also be recorded by the archaeologist or anthropologist, in the unlikely event that an intact contained deposit has been excavated.

The size of surviving bone fragments may be related to a number of intrinsic and extrinsic factors (Wahl, 1982; McKinley, 1994). Interpretation requires consideration of the degree of fragmentation expected as a result of intrinsic factors (McKinley, 1993), as well as the possible extrinsic ones that may have been brought to bear on the material. For example, deliberate breakage in an attempt at further concealment; accidental breakage due to trampling; manipulation of the remains during burning, as in stirring a fire to reoxygenate; or repeated redeposition. Interpretation will require consideration of the place of deposition (e.g., material from a pit is less likely to be trampled *in situ* than that in a surface spread) and the level of disturbance (e.g., if the site has been used for repeat fires).

Fleshed and green bone dehydrates during high temperature burning, causing shrinkage, fissuring, and sometimes warping of the bone. Dehydration produces distinctive patterns of fissuring, characteristically curved in long bone shafts and concentric fissuring in articular heads, but with small bones frequently remaining almost intact (McKinley, 2000, fig. 1; McKinley and Bond, 2000, fig. 21.1). Dry bone that is burnt will not display this type of fissuring, but is limited to angular fractures and surface cracking, although the latter may also be observed to some extent in green bone (Baby, 1954; Thurman and Wilmore, 1981; Buikstra and Ubelaker, 1994, fig. 66). Any abnormal warping should be recorded (skeletal element, side, and description of warping), as should any surface cracking or longitudinal/transverse cracking.

The degree of oxidation may indicate the temperature acting on the individual bone in an oxidising atmosphere. This is reflected macroscopically in the colour of the bone (Holden et al., 1995a, 1995b), ranging from brown/orange (not burnt) to black (charred, c. 300°C), through hues of blue and grey (incompletely oxidised, up to c. 600°C) to the fully oxidised white (>c. 600°C). Any variation should be fully described, noting the following: (a) the skeletal element affected and, where possible, the side; (b) which part or parts of the bone (e.g., exo/endocranial, diploe, cortical, medullary, central section); (c) the colour or combination of colours (they commonly vary across and through the bone); (d) a summary of the percentage of the remains affected within an individual deposit; and (e) such zones as anatomical areas.

The degree of oxidation may be of significance as an indicator of the temperature attained over various parts of the body and the length of time over which the heat was applied (allowing full removal of the soft tissues and exposure of the bone to oxidation), both of which may be influenced by the size and intensity of the heat source, and the oxidising/reducing conditions. Patterns in colour variation across different skeletal elements may indicate the conditions under which burning occurred. However, normal variations across the body related to degree of soft tissue coverage and infiltration by other organic components must be considered. Such information can then be examined alongside witness testimony.

If available, transmission electron microscopy can detect the occurrence of low heat modification of bone (i.e., cooked). Unlike burnt bone, 'cooking' leaves no trace on the surface of the bone and is difficult to determine macroscopically (Koon et al., 2003). Further information about temperature, if required, may be obtained from microscopic examination of the crystal structure of the bone (Shipman et al., 1984; Lange et al., 1987; Holden et al., 1995a, 1995b). However, to date there is no consensus on the nature and timing of the changes (see McKinley, 2000). Such analysis is not routinely undertaken at present and should not be considered unless agreed by the MMT, who will decide if it has relevance to a specific investigation.

Generally, it will not be possible to identify every bone fragment to a specific skeletal element. Many small fragments of trabecular bone and long bone shaft may be difficult to distinguish, and only where a fragment can be placed to element (e.g., 'radius shaft' rather than 'upper limb', 'cervical vertebra' rather than just 'vertebra') should it be considered 'identifiable'. The distinctive appearance of parts of the skull, even as very small fragments, invariably leads to a bias in the amount of skull identified. A record should be made of the skeletal element, side (where possible), part of the bone (e.g., vertebral body, spinal or transverse, or articular process) and whether it is whole (e.g., complete head of radius) or part (e.g., fragment of head of radius). The weight of bone from each skeletal area (skull, axial skeleton, upper limb, lower limb) and the percentage of the total weight of identifiable bone represented should be presented. Quantities of both long and trabecular bone fragments remaining among the fragments not identifiable to skeletal element should be quantified (by weight), together with observations on variations in colour, patterns of fracturing, and degree of warping. It is not advisable to quantify material by the number of fragments, as they may become further fragmented post primary analysis. Material should be photographed (with an appropriate scale measurement) to record the condition, state of preservation, degree of fragmentation, and the amount of burnt remains. When packaging burnt bone after identifying fragments of elements, it is

essential to put all identified fragments together and not to mix them with unidentified fragments. It is recommended that they should be bagged by skeletal region
(i.e., skull, axial skeleton, upper limb, lower limb). Any fragment that has particular value for identification, biological profile, or cause of death should be bagged
separately, especially if not individually numbered, so that they can be more easily
identified if required for further analysis, photography, or radiography.

The range of skeletal elements identified from any one individual will help indicate whether an entire body, or only part of it, was subject to burning. Alternatively,
it may help distinguish if only part of the burnt remains were placed within the
deposit. The interpretation must take into consideration the nature of the deposit,
evidence for disturbance, distribution of skeletal elements within the deposit, quantity of bone recovered, and ease of identifying small fragments of bone to skeletal
element.

8.5.2   Assessment of demography, pathology, and trauma in burnt bone

The MNI will be assessed using the criteria outlined in 7.2.4. The often highly
fragmented condition of burnt bone is likely to lead to a reliance on elements of
the skull, which are easily identified even as very small fragments (McKinley, 2000,
figures 2–3). Skeletal indicators of age and sex (7.7 and 7.5) will also be applied to
burnt bone. The entire skeleton is not usually available for analysis after a period of
heat alteration because post burning dispersal of fragments will affect completeness
and, consequently, analysis. Metric methods used for bone that is not heat modified
(e.g., ranges for femoral or humeral head diameters presented in Bass, 1995) cannot
reliably be applied to burnt bone due to the problems of variable shrinkage rates
both between the burnt remains of different individuals and within the remains of
one individual (Wahl, 1982; Holck, 1986; McKinley, 2000).

With large-scale assemblages (comprising > 10 individuals), it is advised, where
possible, to collect a series of measurements potentially relevant to sexual dimorphism in accordance with the methods of Gejvall (1969, 1981), Van Vark (1974,
1975), and Wahl (1982). Although there are often limitations to the applicability of these methods, particularly in small assemblages (<10), and other potential
discrepancies related to variable shrinkage (McKinley, 2000; McKinley and Bond,
2000), the maximisation of data recovery is strongly encouraged. The use of broad
adult age ranges should be applied where possible. Similarly, where the data available
are not conclusive, the attribution of 'probable' or 'possible' sex is preferable to the
overconfident and potentially erroneous attribution of sex.

Successful DNA analysis of burnt material depends on the temperatures reached
during the burning process. Temperatures greater than 300°C will result in loss of the
organic components of the bone necessary for such analysis to be undertaken. Not
all ostensibly burnt bone, even from one individual, will necessarily have attained
this temperature and, in some cases, DNA analysis may be possible (see 9.3). DNA

can survive higher temperatures in dental pulp, where the enamel (as well as the soft tissues and alveolar bone) protects the pulp from the heat (Duffy et al., 1991). Generally speaking, DNA survives reasonably well until after the insulator-conductive transmission, which occurs at around 350°C, after which degradation begins to occur (Reyes-Gasga et al., 1999).

Evidence for pathology and trauma should be recorded as detailed in 8.2. The detail with which this can be undertaken will vary widely because it is largely dependent on the amount of the skeleton available and the degree of fragmentation and warping. Evidence for trauma can be particularly difficult to discern in burnt material, which will tend to fracture further along lines of weakness already present, and careful examination of all fragments will be necessary (Pope and Smith, 2004). Cut marks on the cortex do, however, tend to survive and can be clearly seen in burnt bone. With such material, disease processes resulting in bone proliferation (hypertrophic changes) are more likely to survive than those that result in loss of bone density (atrophic changes); the weakening of the bone structure renders it more likely to collapse under the stresses of burning.

Some materials (e.g., glass, copper alloy) may fuse to bone fragments during cooling following burning. The bone fragment should be examined to identify the skeletal element and side. The original proximity of some materials to bone may be indicated by coloured staining (e.g., blue or green staining from copper alloy). Any abnormal coloured staining should be described in terms of colour, extent, and location on the recording form.

In all cases, the anthropologist's observations will be recorded in the analytical notes in accordance with the applicable method. In the case of component systems, the individual component scores and the total component score will be recorded in the relevant recording form.

8.6 Assessment of handedness

Human skeletal tissues respond to stresses placed on them. Hence, preferential use of a limb on one side of the body over the other will inevitably contribute to a difference in the bone mass, contours, and dimension of key elements within that limb. Handedness is the preference for the use of one hand in skilled tasks (e.g., writing, needlework, carpentry). The natural dominance of the left hand over the right is assessed variously at between 5 and 10 percent (Steele, 2000; Byers, 2002), and there is often secular change in preferred use, reflecting the influence of cultural preference over natural handedness. For example, traditional Catholicism deems the use of the left hand to be a 'mark of the devil'. Such contexts pressure individuals to use their right hand for skilled tasks, even though they have a natural preponderance for the left. In such cases, it is impossible to know if this pressure translates from skilled to manual tasks that require a lot of force. As with all variables assessed, it is imperative to determine if there is a cultural preference that might reduce the incidence of natural left-hand dominance within a population before commencing a mission.

Generally speaking, hand dominance is reflected in asymmetry of the long bones of the upper limb and pectoral girdle. Byers (2002) advocated the use of six criteria. Those that we recommend are (a) glenoid bevelling (the amount of excess bone outside the surrounding edge of the glenoid cavity – assessed visually); (b) glenoid posterior deflection (the amount by which this structure angles backward from the infraspinous plane – assessed visually by comparing the left and right); (c) the combined lengths of the upper limb bones; (d) the width of the distal humerus (for details of these measurements see 8.8); (e) the size of the deltoid tuberosity; and (different from Byers, 2002) (f) the length of the clavicle. We would not recommend the use of Byers' sixth criterion, osteoarthritic changes to the elbow, because the arthropathies can also reflect genetic predisposition and trauma (Ortner, 2003). Once these measurements and observations have been made, the side that manifests the greatest glenoid bevelling and posterior deflection and that has the greatest combined length of the long bones of the arm is considered to be dominant. Where results of observations are ambiguous, no conclusion can be drawn, and similarly, if the metrical data are not statistically different, then no conclusion can be drawn. In all cases, the anthropologist's observations and conclusions will be recorded in the analytical notes of the relevant recording form.

8.7   Sampling tissue for analysis by external laboratories

During the planning phase of an investigation, it will be necessary to establish sampling requirements and to arrange for specialist laboratories to be on standby to receive samples. This is the responsibility of the MMT, and must be made after consultation with relevant authorities and with necessary permissions. This decision will depend on several factors. Consideration should be made of the specific requirements of the investigation and cultural sensitivities (especially concerning destructive methods and disassociation of remains). It is important to consider the relevance of sample taking for the specific population and investigation (e.g., availability of antemortem records and comparative material). Logistical requirements, such as access to specialist laboratories and adequate storage facilities, have to be considered, and resources made available.

If it is considered appropriate to take samples, an accredited laboratory should be involved. Each laboratory will have specific requirements, protocols, and procedures that should be communicated to the MMT during the planning phase of an investigation. These requirements should be met in the sampling processes and during subsequent treatment and packaging.

By definition, sampling involves the assessment and analysis of a representative part of an entity; it may only be a small part of the entity and may involve physical alteration of the original specimen (DeGusta and White, 1996). Where sample extraction will significantly alter the element (e.g., a tooth or small bone), the element must first be photographed, analysed, and recorded. Photographing all bones to be sampled prior to taking the sample is recommended. A sample derived during anthropological analysis might be one or more of the following: a thin section of bone or tooth, a bone core, a tooth, a small bone, part of a bone, soft tissue, hair, a fingernail, or a toenail. The technology for biomolecular and chemical analyses is constantly improving in accuracy and in scope. Consequently, it would be inappropriate to attempt to provide an all-inclusive outline of possible techniques and applications for samples. Rather, the aim is to outline the important considerations.

Samples may be taken for genetic, histological, chemical, biological, or micro/macroscopic analysis. These examinations can assist the investigation in determining the cause and/or manner of death of an individual, assessing the biological profile of an individual, genetic relationships between individuals and groups, personal identification, provenance, and dietary information. Samples may also be taken of materials adhering to skeletal remains or evidence, including plant material, soil, organic or inorganic residues, and entomological samples. This may enhance understanding of circumstances surrounding preburial, burial, and postdepositional activities.

No samples of human tissue may be taken without the informed consent of the relevant authorities, community, or families concerned. Depending on the nature of the sample, it may be taken by the anthropologist or APT during or after analysis of the remains. For example, hair, plant, soil, and other residual samples (including blood) may be found on the clothing of an individual and therefore sampled by the SCE prior to removal and cleaning of clothing. The collection of hair, soft tissue, blood, and other liquids will usually be undertaken by a pathologist or APT during postmortem analysis. Bone and tooth samples can only be taken by an anthropologist or odontologist after analysis. A record (in analytical notes) must be made to show that teeth/bones have been removed for sampling.

Several elements of the body may be sampled to collect genetic information that can be used for personal identification of remains. The technology for extraction of DNA is ever changing and improving; it is therefore recommended that the laboratory undertaking the sequencing of DNA be consulted on their preferred sample types, quantities, and storage requirements. If no specification has been given, general guidelines on storage are given in 9.3.8. Extreme care must be taken to avoid contamination of such samples and methods to ensure this will be prescribed by the laboratory in question. The reader is referred to 9.3.4 for detail of methods of DNA sampling.

As noted previously, possible elements to sample during the anthropological analysis include hair, bone, teeth, or nails. When a hair sample is taken, it should comprise a hair follicle or a small clump of hair. Bone must never be removed for sampling until after the anthropological examination has been completed. A complete small bone (e.g., metatarsal or metacarpal) or 2.5- to 3.0-cm window section of long bone, preferably from midshaft, can be an appropriate bone sample. Care should be taken to avoid cutting landmarks or areas affected by trauma or pathology (unless this is the objective of the analysis). With dentition, two healthy (i.e., noncarious) canines or molars (with the apex closed) should be collected, but only after the dental examination is complete. If nails are to be used, those from either fingers or toes will suffice. Once the samples have been taken, they should be packaged and sent to the laboratory as soon as possible. Where this is not possible, they should be allowed to dry naturally (not in direct sunlight) and stored at room temperature in low humidity. Long-term storage treatment requirements must follow the specifications of the laboratory.

Histological studies can provide information on the structure of the bone matrix and may assist in cases where radiographs are inconclusive (Aaron and Shore, 2003). They are particularly useful for providing information about disease processes. Although the need for histological analysis is not likely to be great, it has value in some cases. Histological analysis may give insight into growth patterns, bone healing, bone loss, diagenesis, infective, metabolic and neoplastic disease processes, analysis of bone–cement and cement–metal interfaces, estimating the age at death of skeletal remains, and, occasionally, analysis of burnt skeletal remains.

A thin section of bone is required for analysis; this can be taken from small amounts of frozen or dry bone. The nature of the specimen and the specific requirements of the analysis will determine the most appropriate methods of fixation, embedding, sectioning, and staining undertaken at the laboratory. When sampling bone for histological analysis, most questions posed can be addressed using a combination of decalcified and nondecalcified sections, along with photography and histomorphometry (Bauer and Mahovlic, 2003). Histological analysis can be undertaken using a light microscope. If further analysis is required, it will be necessary to use a higher-powered microscope in an external laboratory. Such analysis could comprise scanning electron microscopy, back-scattered electron microscopy, transmission electron microscopy, confocal laser scanning microscopy, and atomic force microscopy. All types of analysis, sample pretreatment, and short- and long-term storage treatment requirements must follow the specifications of the relevant laboratory.

Stable light isotope analysis can be undertaken on samples of bone, hair, nail, and flesh. Studies on samples from bone collagen, which is more suitable than its mineral component, can reconstruct a dietary profile for up to 10 years prior to death. The childhood diet of adults may be ascertained by examination of dental hard tissues (Mays et al., 2002); this can be useful in determining movement of people after childhood. The most commonly analysed isotopes include nitrogen, carbon, strontium, and oxygen. For isotope analysis of diet or provenance that reflects the months prior to death, hair and a fingernail or toenail are the most appropriate mediums for analysis.

If a child is breast-fed, then this also can be determined from their ^{15}N levels, with a decline in ^{15}N suggesting recent weaning (Katzenberg and Pfeiffer, 1995; Wright and Schwarcz, 1998; Mays et al., 2002; Richards et al., 2002; Humphrey et al., 2004). Caution is advised as a lag in this decreased nitrogen signal has been noticed in modern hair samples. As such, the most recently weaned infants may not be identifiable (O'Connell T. and Hedges R., 2001; Lewis, 2007).

Carbon can provide information on the ratios of marine foods in the diet compared to terrestrial proteins such as grains, bread, meat, and milk. Nitrogen can provide ratios between animal foods (e.g., meat, milk) and plant foods. Elevated nitrogen levels in hair, for example, can also indicate starvation in the period prior to death. Isotope analysis may also identify dietary differences (within and between groups) relating to socioeconomic status or religious practice. Oxygen (^{18}O), lead (mass ^{204}Pb, ^{206}Pb, ^{207}Pb, and ^{208}Pb), and strontium ($^{87/86}$S) isotopes (radioisotopes) can be used to assess an individual's geographical provenance (White et al., 1998; Beard and Johnson, 2000; Schutkowski et al., 2006). Following the work of Fricke et al. (1995), it has been shown that ^{18}O levels in rainwater vary with climate. Such analysis could be potentially valuable when dealing with suspected cases of people being forcibly transported from one region of a country to another. For example, this method could be used as one of the techniques to discern the remains of Iraqi Kurds from the North buried in mass graves in the south of Iraq.

A sample of approximately 4 to 5 cm of diaphyseal cortical bone, preferably from the femur, will be enough to obtain accurate results from isotope analysis. Contamination when sampling for isotope analysis must be avoided by following guidelines from the assigned laboratory. It is not advisable to use any organic solvents, glues, consolidants, or varnishes at any stage. These will ultimately contaminate the isotope signatures stored in bone collagen and teeth, particularly for oxygen, carbon, and nitrogen. Similar provisos apply for other chemical elements, such as strontium and lead. As a rule, distilled water is the safest cleaning solution, followed by gentle drying. If any pretreatment has been used, regardless of the purpose, cleaning methods must be annotated on the recording forms that accompany the individual skeleton (or part) (MC14L). If isotope analysis is to be undertaken, it is imperative to seek specialist advice about sampling, storage, and transport.

Microstructural (e.g., Stott et al., 1982; Condon et al., 1986; Whittaker, 2000) and chemical (e.g., Gillard et al., 1990; Ohtani, 1995) ageing of dentition may be useful in a forensic context. For such analysis, a left mandibular canine with an intact root that is noncarious and without restoration is required; if the left is not available, then use the right. If it is not be possible to collect a canine tooth, a premolar is acceptable. To determine if infants survived the birth process, the neonatal line can be assessed. Deciduous teeth are generally used for this analysis (Skinner and Dupras, 1993; Kodaka et al., 1996), although the neonatal line can be seen in the first permanent molar (Scheuer and Black, 2000). In neonates, the cusps are friable and have not coalesced, making them difficult to identify (out of the crypt) and collect. Instead, the first and second deciduous molar is preferred. Any tooth removed or any sampling must be recorded (using the FDI system). When possible, such analysis should be referred to the forensic odontologist.

Other samples can be collected from residues, such as cement from implants or metals. In addition, plant material (see 9.2 for further details) or insect remains (see 9.1) may be sampled to provide evidence of the associated burial environments, aiding the reconstruction of circumstances surrounding death. The flowering stage of vegetation can indicate month or season of activity, collection of soil samples for pollen, seeds, macrofossils, and spores may also be useful (see 9.2). It is possible that some specialists will prefer to take samples personally. This will depend on factors such as the nature of the investigation, the difficulty of collecting the specimens, and the storage facilities available. Ideally, the collection, treatment, and storage of all samples will be the responsibility of the appropriate scientist (e.g., DNA specialist, entomologist, botanist). In situations where the specialist is not present, samples can be collected following the specific standard operating procedure (SOP) provided by the external organisation. All samples will be appropriately packaged, labelled, and entered into the chain of custody (see 4.3.2).

All samples taken are given a sample and/or an evidence number and will be recorded on the evidence log by the SCE. Where necessary, the samples will be photographed. The sample number(s) and description will also be recorded on the anthropologist's recording form. Several different fields of information must be recorded beginning with the evidence number (allocated by the SCE, the name of the person who took the sample, and the date the sample was taken). This must be followed by a note of the reason for taking the sample, the sample type (e.g., bone, hair, tooth, or nail), its origin (e.g., skeletal element, facial or pubic hair, digit), and, if appropriate, side. Finally, any treatments such as cleaning must be recorded, as must the storage conditions (temperature, humidity), packaging information, and location where the sample can be found (packaging and storage is the responsibility of the SCE). This must be completed and handed to the SCE. A copy of form MC14F will accompany samples when sent for analysis. Any documentation completed by an external specialist will be in addition to the mortuary record.

8.8 Metrical analysis

This section is designed to provide the anthropologist with details of the measurements necessary for metric analysis of the skeleton. Excellent diagrams depicting the precise location of skeletal landmarks and points from which measurements should be taken can be found in such texts as Scheuer and Black (2000) and White and Folkens (2000). In this text, we describe the measurements (adult and nonadult) and provide schematic indications of them (adult). In some cases, where variations in a single measurement are available in the literature (e.g., femoral length), distinctions between these are made. This discussion is divided into two subsections: nonadult and adult measurements. These are further divided into cranial and postcranial measurements. Most sections refer to measurements on illustrations by allocating Greek letters (α, β, χ) to standardise nomenclature within the document. Exceptions include Buikstra and Ubelaker's (1994) and Wright's (CRANID) cranial measurements. Figure 8–11 shows directional terms and sections used to locate features during assessment.

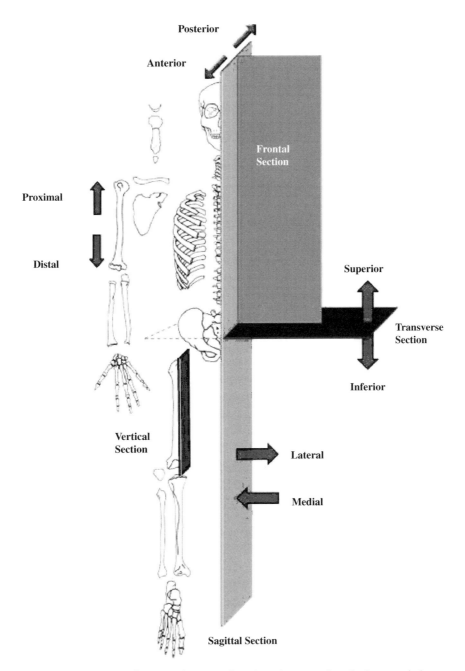

Figure 8–11. Directional terms, planes, and sections for recording the human skeleton. *Source:* Burns, 1999.

8.8.1   Measurement of nonadult skeletons

Metrical analysis of the nonadult skeleton may be used for age and developmental estimations. Great care must be taken when handling fetal and neonate bones because they are often fragile and may be damaged when using metal sliding callipers. In this section, the measurements are based on those described by Buikstra and Ubelaker (1994, fig. 21) and Scheuer and Black (2000, 2004). Cranial measurements for nonadults are summarized in Tables 8–15 to 8–17 and postcranial measurements for nonadults are in Tables 8–18 to 8–20.

Nonadult cranial measurements

Measurement of the nonadult sphenoid

Table 8–15. *Measurement of nonadult sphenoid bone*

Code	Measurement	Description of measurement
Sphenoid		
α	Length of lesser wing	Distance from the lateral tip of the lesser wing to the midline of the synchondrosis intersphenoidalis. In a very immature foetus, measure the distance between the tip and the medial end of the lesser wing
β	Width of lesser wing	Greatest width of the lesser wing measured across the optic canal
χ	Length of greater wing	Greatest distance between the medial pterygoid plate and the lateral tip of the greater wing
δ	Width of greater wing	Greatest distance between the sphenoidal spine and the anterior end of the pterygoid plate
ε	Length of body	Distance measured in the midline between synchondrosis intersphenoidalis and synchondrosis spheno-occipitalis
Φ	Width of body	Greatest distance measured transversely in the plane of the middle part of the hypophyseal fossa

Measurement of the nonadult temporal, basilar, and zygomatic

Table 8–16. *Measurement of the nonadult temporal, pars basilaris, and zygomatic bones*

Code	Measurement	Description of measurement
Temporal Bone		
α	Length	Greatest distance between the apex of the petrous portion and the superior posterior end of the mastoid portion
β	Width	Greatest distance measured in the vertical plane of the posterior surface of the petrous bone
Pars Basilaris		
α	Length	Minimum distance measured in the sagittal plane between foramen magnum and the spheno-occipital synchondrosis
β	Maximum length	Maximum distance, measured perpendicular to width
	Width	Greatest distance perpendicular to length
Zygomatic Bone		
α	Length	Distance between the anterior end of the infraorbital margin and the posterior end of the temporal process
β	Width	Distance between the anterior end of the infraorbital margin and the frontosphenoidal process

Source: Adapted from Buikstra and Ubelaker, 1994.

Measurement of the nonadult maxilla and mandible

Table 8–17. *Measurement of the nonadult maxilla and mandible*

Code	Measurement	Description of measurement
Maxilla		
α	Length	Distance between the anterior nasal process and posterior border of palatal process in the sagittal plane
β	Height	Distance measured in the vertical plane between the alveolar part and the frontal process
χ	Width	Distance between the posterior end of the palatal process and the end of the zygomatic process
Mandible		
α	Length of body	Distance from the tuberculum mentale to the angle
β	Width of arc	Distance between the coronoid and the condyloid processes
χ	Full length of half mandible	Distance between the tuberculum mentale and the articular condyle

Source: Adapted from Buikstra and Ubelaker, 1994.

Nonadult postcranial measurements

Measurement of the nonadult clavicle, scapula, humerus, radius, and ulna

Table 8–18. *Measurement of the nonadult clavicle, scapula, humerus, radius, and ulna*

Code	Measurement	Description of measurement
Clavicle		
α	Length	Maximum distance between the sternal and acromial ends
β	Diameter	Maximum diameter at midshaft
Scapula		
α	Length/height	Distance between the medial and inferior angles of the scapula
β	Width	Distance between the margin of the glenoid fossa and the medial end of the spine
χ	Length of spine	Distance between the medial end of the spine and the tip of the acromion
Humerus		
α	Length	Maximum length of diaphysis
β	Width	Maximum width of distal extremity
χ	Diameter	Maximum diameter at midshaft
Radius and ulna		
α	Length	Maximum length of diaphysis
β	Diameter	Maximum diameter at midshaft

Source: Adapted from Buikstra and Ubelaker, 1994.

Measurement of the nonadult ilium, ischium, and pubis

Table 8–19. *Measurement of the nonadult ilium, ischium, and pubis*

Code	Measurement	Description of measurement
Ilium		
α	Length	Distance between the anterior superior and posterior superior spines
β	Width	Distance between the middle point of the iliac crest and the farthest point on the acetabular extremity
Ischium		
α	Length	Greatest distance between the acetabular extremity and the most ventral portion of the ischial tuberosity
β	Width	Greatest distance of the acetabular portion
Pubis		
α	Length	Greatest distance between the symphyseal end and acetabular portion

Source: Adapted from Buikstra and Ubelaker, 1994.

Measurement of the nonadult femur, tibia, and fibula

Table 8–20. *Measurement of the nonadult femur, tibia, and fibula*

Code	Measurement	Description of measurement
Femur		
α	Length	Maximum length of diaphysis
β	Width	Maximum width of distal extremity
γ	Diameter	Maximum diameter at midshaft
Tibia and fibula		
α	Length	Maximum length of diaphysis
β	Diameter	Maximum diameter at midshaft

Source: Adapted from Buikstra and Ubelaker, 1994.

8.8.2   Measurement of adult skeletons

Adult cranial measurements. Cranial measurements in this section are summarised in Table 8–21. The following descriptions are the keys to the craniometric points (see Figures 8–12 to 8–15). The descriptions set out in Tables 8–21 and 8–22 feature the code, points, measurement, and description for the determination of ancestry using CRANID and FORDISC (Ousley and Jantz, 2005) are based on Howells (1989) and Wright (2005). Where the point is not present, refer to the code on the illustrations.

Table 8–21. *Cranial measurements*

Measurement	Howells	FORDISC 2.0	FORDISC 3.0	CRANID
Basion radius	BAR			
Basion–bregma height	BBH	ba-b	BBH	BBH
Basion–prosthion length	BPL	ba-pr	BPL	BPL
Biasterionic breadth	ASB		ASB	ASB
Biauricular breadth	AUB	au-au	AUB	AUB
Bicondylar breadth		cdl-cdl	CDB	
Bigonial width		go-go	GOG	
Bijugal breadth	JUB			JUB
Bimaxillary breadth	ZMB			ZMB
Biorbital breadth	EKB	ec-ec	EKB	EKB
Bistephanic breadth	STB			
Bizygomatic diameter	ZYB	zy-zy	ZYB	
Breadth of mandibular body		√	TMF	
Bregma radius	BRR			
Bregma–lambda subtense (parietal subtense)	PAS			PAS
Cheek height	WMH			WMH
Chin height		id-gn	GNI	
Cranial base length (basion–nasion length)	BNL	ba-n	BNL	BNL
Dacryon radius	DKR			
Dacryon subtense	DKS			
Ectoconchion radius	EKR			
Foramen magnum breadth	FOB	√	FOB	
Foramen magnum length	FOL	ba-o	FOL	
Frontal chord	FRC	n-b	FRC	FRC
Frontal fraction	FRF			
Frontomalar radius	FMR			
Glabella projection	GLS			
Height of mandibular body		√	HMF	
Interorbital breadth	DKB	d-d	DKB	DKB
Lambda radius	LAR			
Lambda–opisthion subtense (occipital subtense)	OCS			OCS
Malar length inferior	IML			
Malar length maximum	XML			
Malar subtense	MLS			
Mandibular angle		√	MAN	
Mandibular length		√	MLN	
Mastoid height	MDH	√	MDH	
Mastoid width	MDB			
Maxillo-alveolar breadth (external palate breadth)	MAB	ecm-ecm	MAB	MAB
Maxillo-alveolar length (external palate length)	MAL	pr-alv	MAL	
Maximum cranial breadth	XCB	eu-eu	XCB	XCB
Maximum cranial length (glabello-occipital length)	GOL	g-op	GOL	GOL
Maximum frontal breadth	XFB			XFB
Maximum ramus breadth		√	XRB	
Maximum ramus height		√	XRH	
Midorbital width			MOW	
Minimum cranial breadth	WCB			
Minimum frontal breadth	WFB	ft-ft	WFB	
Minimum ramus breadth		√	WRB	
Molar (first) alveolus radius	AVR			
Nasal breadth	NLB	al-al	NLB	NLB
Nasal height	NLH	n-ns	NLH	NLH
Nasion radius	NAR			
Nasion–bregma subtense (frontal subtense)	FRS			FRS
Nasion–frontal subtense	NAS			NAS
Nasio-occipital length	NOL			NOL

(cont.)

Table 8–21 (*cont.*)

Measurement	Howells	FORDISC 2.0	FORDISC 3.0	CRANID
Nasodacryal subtense	NDS			
Occipital chord	OCC	l-o	OCC	OCC
Occipital fraction	OCF			
Opisthion radius	OSR			
Orbital breadth	OBB	d-ec	OBB	OBB
Orbital height	OBH	√	OBH	OBH
Parietal chord	PAC	b-l	PAC	PAC
Parietal fraction	PAF			
Prosthion radius	PRR			
Simotic chord	WNB			
Simotic subtense	SIS			
Stephanic subtense	STS			
Subspinale radius	SSR			
Supraorbital projection	SOS			
Upper facial breadth (bifrontal breadth)	FMB	fmt-fmt	UFBR	FMB*
Upper facial height	NPH	n-pr	UFHT	NPH
Vertex radius	VRR			
Zygomaxillare radius	ZMR			
Zygomaxillary subtense	SSS			SSS
Zygo-orbitale radius	ZOR			

* Howells' FMB differs from Wright's by approximately 6 mm. See Table 8–22 for definitions.
Source: Adapted from Howells, 1973; Buikstra and Ubelaker, 1994; Moore-Jansen, Ousley and Jantz, 1994; Wright, 2007.

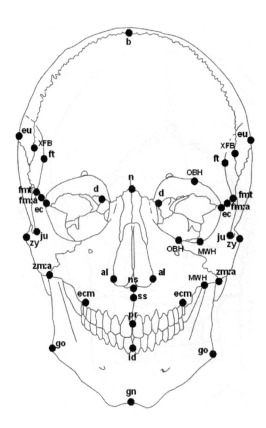

Figure 8–12. Anterior aspect of the cranium showing cranial landmarks for use in craniometric analysis. *Source:* Adapted from Buikstra and Ubelaker (1994: Fig. 34) by Wright, 2005.

436

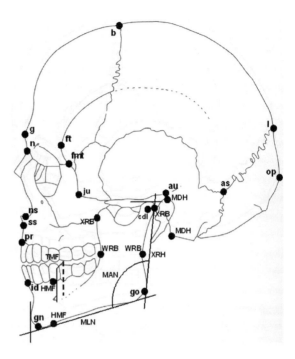

Figure 8–13. Lateral aspect of the cranium showing cranial landmarks for use in craniometric analysis. *Source:* Adapted from Buikstra and Ubelaker (1994; Fig. 35 and Fig. 46) by Wright, 2005.

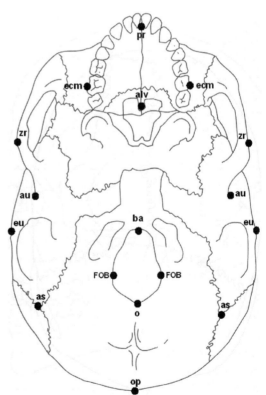

Figure 8–14. Basilar view of the cranium showing cranial landmarks for use in craniometric analysis. *Source:* Adapted from Buikstra and Ubelaker (1994: Fig. 36) by Wright, 2005.

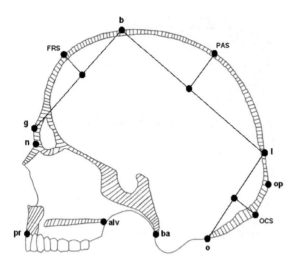

Figure 8–15. Cranial measurements in the sagittal plane showing cranial landmarks for use in craniometric analysis. *Source:* Adapted from Buikstra and Ubelaker (1994: Fig. 37 and Fig. 42) by Wright, 2005.

Table 8–22. *Definitions for adult cranial measurements used in CRANID and FORDISC*

Code	Points	Measurement	Description of measurement	Programme
ASB	as-as	Biasterionic breadth	Direct measurement from one asterion to the other	CRANID
AUB	au-au	Biauricular breadth	Least exterior breadth across the roots of the zygomatic processes, wherever found	CRANID
AUB	au-au	Biauricular breadth	Last exterior breadth across the roots of the zygomatic processes, wherever found. With the skull resting on the occiput and with the base towards the observer, measure to the outside of the roots of the zygomatic processes at their deepest incurvature, generally slightly anterior to the external auditory meatus, with the sharp points of the calliper	FORDISC
BBH	ba-b	Basion–bregma height	Distance from basion to bregma, as defined	CRANID
BBH	ba-b	Basion–bregma height	Direct distance from the lowest point on the anterior margin of the foramen magnum to bregma	FORDISC
BNL	eu-eu	Basion–nasion length	Direct length between basion and nasion	CRANID
BNL	ba-n	Cranial base length	Direct distance from nasion to basion	FORDISC
BPL	ba-pr	Basion-prosthion length	Facial length from basion to prosthion, as defined	CRANID
CDB	cdl-cdl	Bicondylar breadth	Direct distance between the most lateral points on the two condyles	FORDISC
DKB	d-d	Interorbital breadth	Breadth across the nasal space from dacryon to dacryon	CRANID
DKB	d-d	Interorbital breadth	Direct distance between right and left dacryon	FORDISC
EKB	ec-ec	Biorbital breadth	Breadth across the orbits from ectoconchion to ectoconchion	CRANID

Code	Points	Measurement	Description of measurement	Programme
EKB	ec-ec	Biorbital breadth	Direct distance between right and left ectoconchion	FORDISC
FMB	fm:a-fm:a	Bifrontal breadth	Breadth across the frontal bone between frontomalar anterior on each side (i.e., the most anterior point on the frontomalar suture). Buikstra and Ubelaker (1994) measured between the most laterally positioned points on the frontomalar suture; this distance is perhaps 6 mm longer than Howells' FMB	CRANID
FOB		Foramen magnum breadth	Direct distance between the lateral margins of foramen magnum at the points of greatest lateral curvature	FORDISC
FOL	ba-o	Foramen magnum length	Direct distance from basion to opisthion. Calliper tips should rest precisely on opposing edges of the foramen magnum border	FORDISC
FRC	n-b	Frontal chord	Direct distance from nasion to bregma taken in the midsagittal plane	FORDISC
FRC	n-b	Nasion–bregma chord, frontal chord	Frontal chord, or direct distance from nasion to bregma, is taken in the midplane and at the external surface	CRANID
FRS		Nasion–bregma subtense, frontal subtense	Maximum subtense, at the highest point on the convexity of the frontal bone in the midplane, to the basion–bregma chord	CRANID
GNI	id-gn	Chin height	Direct distance from infradentale to gnathion.	FORDISC
GOG	go-go	Bigonial width	Direct distance between right and left gonion. Place the blunt points of the calliper to the most prominent external points at the mandibular angles.	FORDISC
GOL	g-op	Glabello-occipital length	Greatest length, from the glabellar region, in the median sagittal plane	CRANID
GOL	g-op	Maximum cranial length	Distance between glabella and opisthocranion in the midsagittal plane, measured in a straight line. Place the skull on its side, holding one end of the calliper at the glabella and extending the calliper until the maximum diameter at posterior aspect of the skull is obtained	FORDISC
HMF		Height of mandibular body	Direct distance from the alveolar process to the inferior border of the mandible perpendicular to the base at the level of the mental foramen	FORDISC
JUB	ju-ju	Bijugal breadth	External breadth across the malars at the jugalia (i.e., at the deepest points in the curvature between the frontal and temporal process of the malars)	CRANID
MAB	ecm-ecm	Maxillo-alveolar breadth	Maximum breadth across the alveolar borders of the maxilla measured on the lateral surfaces at the location of the second maxillary molars	FORDISC

(cont.)

Table 8–22 (*cont.*)

Code	Points	Measurement	Description of measurement	Programme
MAB	ecm-ecm	Palate breadth, external	Greatest breadth across the alveolar borders, wherever found, perpendicular to the median plane	CRANID
MAL	pr-alv	Maxillo-alveolar length	Direct distance from prostheon to alveon. Position skull with basilar portion facing up; apply a thin wooden rod to the posterior borders of the alveolar arch and measure the distance from prosthion to the middle of the rod (on the midsagittal plane)	FORDISC
MAN		Mandibular angle	Angle formed by the inferior border of the corpus and the posterior border of the ramus	FORDISC
MDH		Mastoid height	Vertical projection of the mastoid process below and perpendicular to the eye-ear (Frankfort) plane. Rest skull on its right side and apply the calibrated bar of the calliper just behind the mastoid process, with the fixed flat arm tangent to the upper border of the external auditory meatus and pointing to the lower border of the orbit. Slide the measuring arm until it is level with the tip of the mastoid process	FORDISC
MLN		Mandibular length	Distance of the anterior margin of the chin from a centre point on the projected straight line placed along the posterior border of the two mandibular angles. Apply movable board of the mandibulometer to the posterior borders of the mandibular rami and the fixed board against the most anterior point of the chin; stabilise the mandible by applying gentle pressure to the left second molar	FORDISC
NAS		Nasiofrontal subtense	Subtense from nasion to the bifrontal breadth	CRANID
NLB	al-al	Nasal breadth	Distance between the anterior edges of the nasal aperture at its widest extent	CRANID
NLB	al-al	Nasal breadth	Maximum breadth of the nasal aperture	FORDISC
NLH	n-ns	Nasal height	Average height from nasion to the lowest point on the border of the nasal aperture on either side	CRANID
NLH	n-ns	Nasal height	Direct distance from nasion to the midpoint of a line connecting the lowest points of the inferior margin of the nasal notches	FORDISC
NOL		Nasio-occipital length	Greatest cranial length in the median sagittal plane, measured from nasion	CRANID
NPH	n-pr	Nasion–prosthion height	Upper facial height from nasion to prosthion, as defined	CRANID
OBB	d-ec	Orbit breadth, left	Breadth from ectoconchion to dacryon, as defined, approximating the longitudinal axis which bisects the orbit into equal upper and lower parts	CRANID

Code	Points	Measurement	Description of measurement	Programme
OBB	d-ec	Orbital breadth	Laterally sloping distance from dacryon to ectoconchion. *Note*: Measure the left side unless damaged, pathological or absent	FORDISC
OBH		Orbit height, left	Height between the upper and lower borders of the left orbit, perpendicular to the long axis of the orbit and bisecting it	CRANID
OBH		Orbital height	Direct distance between the superior and inferior orbital margins, avoiding any orbital notches	FORDISC
OCC		Lambda–opisthion chord, occipital chord	External occipital chord, or direct distance from lambda to opisthion, taken in the midplane and at the external surface	CRANID
OCC	l-o	Occipital chord	Direct distance from lambda to opisthion taken in the midsagittal plane	FORDISC
OCS		Lambda–opisthion subtense, occipital subtense	Maximum subtense, at the most prominent point on the basic contour of the occipital bone in the midplane	CRANID
PAC		Bregma–lambda chord, parietal chord	External parietal chord, or direct distance from bregma to lambda, taken in the midplane and at the external surface	CRANID
PAC	b-l	Parietal chord	Direct distance from bregma to lambda taken in the midsagittal plane	FORDISC
PAS		Bregma–lambda subtense, parietal subtense	Maximum subtense, at the highest point on the convexity of the parietal bones in the midplane, to the bregma–lambda chord	CRANID
PBL	ba-pr	Basion–prosthion length	Direct distance from basion to prosthion	FORDISC
TMF		Breadth of mandibular body	Maximum breadth measured in the region of the mental foramen perpendicular to the long axis of the mandibular body	FORDISC
UFBR	fmt-fmt	Upper facial breadth	Direct distance between the two external points on the frontomalar suture	FORDISC
UFHT	n-pr	Upper facial height	Direct distance from nasion to prosthion	FORDISC
WFB	ft-ft	Minimum frontal breadth	Direct distance between the two frontotemporale	FORDISC
WMH		Cheek height	Minimum distance, in any direction, from the lower border of the orbit to the lower margin of the maxilla, mesial to the masseter attachment, on the left side	CRANID
WRB		Minimum ramus breadth	Least breadth of the mandibular ramus measured perpendicular to the height of the ramus	FORDISC
XCB	eu-eu	Maximum cranial breadth	Maximum cranial breadth perpendicular to the median sagittal plane (above the supramastoid crests)	CRANID
XCB	eu-eu	Maximum cranial breadth	Maximum width of skull perpendicular to midsagittal plane wherever it is located, with the exception of the inferior temporal lines and the area immediately surrounding them	FORDISC

(cont.)

Table 8–22 (*cont.*)

Code	Points	Measurement	Description of measurement	Programme
XFB		Maximum frontal breadth	Maximum breadth at the coronal suture, perpendicular to the medial plane	CRANID
XRB		Maximum ramus breadth	Distance between the most anterior point on the mandibular ramus and a line connecting the most posterior point on the condyle and the angle of the jaw	FORDISC
XRH		Maximum ramus height	Direct distance from the highest point on the mandibular condyle to gonion	FORDISC
ZMB	zm:a-zm:a	Bimaxillary breadth	Breadth across the maxillae, from one zygomaxillare to the other	CRANID
ZYB	zy-zy	Bizygomatic diameter	Direct distance between most lateral points on the zygomatic arches	FORDISC
XMB		Zygomaxillary breadth	Distance from left to right zygomaxillare	CRANID
SSS		Zygomaxillary subtense	Projection or subtense from subspinale to the bimaxillary width (ZMB)	CRANID

Source: Adapted from Howells, 1973; Buikstra and Ubelaker, 1994; Moore-Jansen, Ousley and Jantz, 1994; Wright, 2007.

Adult postcranial measurements. All measurements listed here are summarised in Table 8–23, the 'tick' indicates its usefulness for the particular area. Some of these measurements can be placed into the computer programme FORDISC 3.0 (Ousley and Jantz, 2005) for assessment of sex, stature, and ancestry. The SOP code refers to the codes used in this document; the descriptions and diagrams follow.

Table 8–23. *Standard postcranial measurements*

Measurement	Ancestry	Sex	Age	Stature	FORDISC	SOP Code
Clavicle						
Maximum length	√				√	α
Anterior diameter at midshaft (sagittal-posterior)					√	β
Superior diameter at midshaft (vertical-inferior)					√	χ
Midclavicular circumference	√					δ
Scapula						
Maximum length	√				√	α
Maximum breadth	√				√	β
Spine length						χ
Supraspinous length						δ
Infraspinous length						ε
Glenoid cavity breadth						φ
Glenoid cavity height						γ
Sternum						
Manubrium length						α
Body (mesosternum) length						β
Sternebra 1 width						χ
Sternebra 3 width						δ

Measurement	Ancestry	Sex	Age	Stature	FORDISC	SOP Code
Humerus						
Maximum length	✓		✓	✓	✓	α
Epicondylar breadth		✓			✓	β
Vertical diameter of head		✓			✓	χ
Maximum diameter at midshaft					✓	δ
Minimum diameter at midshaft		✓			✓	ε
Proximal epiphysis breadth						φ
Least circumference shaft	✓					γ
Radius						
Maximum length	✓		✓	✓	✓	α
Diameter at midshaft: anterior-posterior (sagittal)					✓	β
Diameter at midshaft: medial-lateral (transverse)					✓	χ
Maximum head diameter						δ
Neck circumference						ε
Ulna						
Maximum length			✓		✓	α
Anterior-posterior diameter (dorsovolar)					✓	χ
Medial-lateral (transverse)					✓	δ
Physiological length	✓		✓	✓	✓	β
Minimum circumference	✓				✓	ε
Metacarpal						
Metacarpal length						α
Vertebra						
Vertebral body height				✓		α
Sacrum						
Anterior superior breadth	✓			✓	✓	β
Maximum transverse diameter of base					✓	α
Transverse breadth of S1	✓				✓	χ
Pelvis						
Height				✓	✓	α
Iliac breadth					✓	β
Pubis length	✓				✓	χ
Ischium length	✓				✓	δ
Femur						
Maximum length		✓		✓	✓	α
Bicondylar length	✓	✓	✓	✓	✓	β
Epicondylar breadth	✓				✓	χ
a-p diameter medial condyle						δ
a-p diameter lateral condyle						ε
Sagittal (a-p) midshaft diameter					✓	φ

(cont.)

Table 8–23 (*cont.*)

Measurement	Ancestry	Sex	Age	Stature	FORDISC	SOP Code
Transverse (m-l) midshaft diameter					√	γ
Midshaft circumference					√	η
Sagittal (a-p) subtrochanteric diameter					√	ι
Transverse (m-l) subtronchanteric diameter					√	φ
Minimum vertical diameter neck						κ
Maximum head diameter		√			√	λ
Upper breadth of femur				√		μ
Lateral condyle height				√		ν
Vertical head diameter						o
Horizontal head diameter						π
Tibia						
Length			√	√		α
Maximum proximal epiphyseal breadth					√	β
Maximum distal epiphyseal breadth					√	χ
Medial-lateral (transverse) diameter at the nutrient foramen					√	δ
Maximum diameter at the nutrient foramen					√	ε
Circumference at the nutrient foramen					√	φ
Maximum length				√	√	γ
Biarticular breadth		√		√		η
Medial condyle articular width		√		√		ι
Medial condyle articular length		√		√		φ
Lateral condyle articular length		√		√		κ
Lateral condyle articular width		√				λ
Fibula						
Maximum length		√	√		√	α
Maximum diameter at midshaft					√	β
Calcaneus						
Maximum length				√	√	α
Middle breadth					√	β
Posterior length				√		χ
Talus						
Maximum length of talus				√		α
Ankle height				√		β
Metatarsal 1–4						
Length				√		α
Metatarsal 5						
Length				√		α

Source: Adapted from Buikstra and Ubelaker, 1994; Moore-Jansen, Ousley and Jantz, 1994.

Table 8–24. *Measurement of the adult clavicle, scapula, and sternum*

Code	Measurement	Description of measurement
Clavicle		
α	Maximum length	Maximum distance between the most extreme ends of the clavicle (Buikstra and Ubelaker, 1994)
β	Anterior diameter at midshaft, sagittal-posterior	Distance from the anterior to the posterior surface at the midshaft (ibid.)
χ	Superior diameter at midshaft, vertical-inferior	Distance from the superior to the inferior surface at the midshaft (ibid.)
δ	Circumference at midshaft	Circumference at the level of the midshaft diameter (ibid.)
Scapula		
α	Maximum length	Direct distance from the most superior point of the cranial angle to the most inferior point on the caudal angle (Buikstra and Ubelaker, 1994)
β	Maximum breadth	Distance from the midpoint on the dorsal border of the glenoid fossa to the midway between the two ridges of the scapular spine on the vertebral border (ibid.)
χ	Spine length	Distance from the end of the spinal axis on the vertebral border to the most distal point on the acromion process (Bass, 1995)
δ	Supraspinous length	Distance from the end of the spinal axis on the vertebral border to the top of the anterior angle (ibid.)
ε	Infraspinous length	Distance from the end of the spinal axis on the vertebral border to the tip of the posterior angle (ibid.)
φ	Glenoid cavity breadth	Maximum breadth of the articular surface from the anterior aspect to the inferior aspect (ibid.)
γ	Glenoid cavity height	Distance from the sharp inferior border to the elevated point of the superior aspect of the glenoid cavity on the articular surface (ibid.)
Sternum		
α	Manubrium length	Distance from the jugular notch to the facet of articulation with the body of the sternum (Schwartz, 1995)
β	Mesosternum length	Distance from facet for articulation with the manubrium to facet for articulation with the xiphoid process (ibid.)
χ	Sternebra 1 width	Minimum distance from side to side across first sternebra. Measure the lowest point between the facet for the second and the third costal cartilage, one each side (ibid.)
δ	Sternebra 3 width	Minimum distance from side to side across the first sternebra. Measure the lowest point between the facet for the fourth and fifth costal cartilage, one each side (ibid.)
ε	Manubrium breadth	Distance between midpoints of the right and left facet for the first costal cartilage taken perpendicular to the long axis (ibid.)

Source: Adapted from Buikstra and Ubelaker, 1994; Bass, 1995; Schwartz, 1995.

Descriptions of the measurements of the adult clavicle, scapula, and sternum can be found in Table 8–24 and Figures 8–16 to 8–18; those of the upper limb in Table 8–25 and Figures 8–19 to 8–23; the vertebrae in Table 8–26 and Figure 8–24; the pelvis in Table 8–27 and Figures 8–25 and 8–26; the lower limb in Table 8–28 and Figures 8–27 to 8–31; and the foot in Table 8–29 and Figures 8.32 to 8–34.

Measurement of the adult clavicle, scapula, and sternum

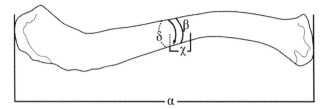

Figure 8–16. A guide to measurements of the left clavicle, superior aspect. *Source:* Bass, 1995.

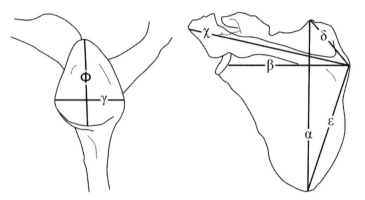

Figure 8–17. A guide to measurements of the left scapula. *Source:* Bass, 1995.

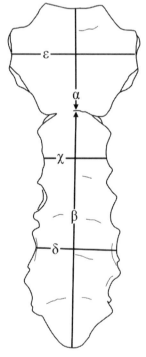

Figure 8–18. A guide to measurements of the sternum. *Source:* Bass, 1995.

Table 8–25. *Measurement of the adult humerus, radius, and ulna*

Code	Measurement	Description of measurement
Humerus		
α	Maximum length	The direct distance from the most superior point on the head of the humerus to the most inferior point on the trochlea. Place the humerus on the osteometric board so that its long axis parallels the instrument. Place the head against the vertical end board and press the movable upright against the trochlea. Move the bone vertically and laterally to determine the maximum distance (Moore-Jansen et al., 1994).
β	Epicondylar breadth	The distance of the most laterally protruding point on the lateral epicondyle from the corresponding projection of the medial epicondyle (Buikstra and Ubelaker, 1994).
χ	Vertical diameter of head	Measuring the vertical diameter of the head of the humerus from the most superior boarder of the articular surface to the most inferior boarder of the articular surface (ibid.).
δ	Maximum diameter at midshaft	Locate the midpoint of the shaft on the osteometric board and measure the maximum diameter at that point (Bass, 1995).
⬜	Minimum diameter at midshaft	Taken at the right angle to the maximum diameter at the midshaft measurement, it is the minimum diameter of the midshaft (ibid.).
φ	Proximal epiphyseal breadth	Measuring the transverse diameter of the proximal epiphyses at right angles to the shaft. If relevant, include the ridge at the end of the articular surface (Bass, 1995).
γ	Minimum circumference of the shaft	The measurement is taken approximately at the second third of the shaft distal to the deltoid tuberosity (ibid.).
Radius		
α	Maximum length	The distance from the most proximally positioned point on the head of the radius to the tip of the styloid process without regard to the long axis of the bone. Place the proximal end against the vertical upright of the osteometric board and press the movable upright against the distal end. Move the bone up, down, and sideways to obtain the maximum length (Moore-Jansen et al., 1994).
β	Diameter at midshaft: anterior-posterior (sagittal)	The distance between the anterior and posterior surfaces at the midshaft. The midpoint of the diaphysis is determined by using an osteometric board and measure the sagittal diameter at that point (Buikstra and Ubelaker, 1994).
χ	Diameter at midshaft: medial-lateral (transverse)	The distance between the medial and lateral surface at the midshaft, perpendicular to the anterior-posterior diameter (ibid.).
δ	Maximum head diameter	The maximum distance on the surface of the head.
⬜	Neck circumference	The minimum circumference just below the head.
Ulna		
α	Maximum length	The distance between the most superior point on the olecranon and the most inferior point on the styloid process. Place the proximal end of the ulna against the vertical end board. Press the movable upright against the distal end while moving the bone up, down, and sideways to obtain the maximum length (Moore-Jansen et al., 1994).
β	Physiological length	The distance between the deepest point on the surface of the coronoid process and the lowest point on the inferior surface of the distal head of the ulna. Use spreading callipers and do not include the styloid process or the groove between the styloid process and the distal surface of the head (ibid.).
χ	Anterior-posterior diameter (dorso-volar)	The maximum diameter of the diaphysis where the crest exhibits the greatest development in anterior-posterior plane (ibid.).
δ	Medial-lateral (transverse)	The distance between the medial and lateral surfaces at the level of the greatest crest development (Buikstra and Ubelaker, 1994).
⬜	Minimum circumference	This point is located slightly above the distal epiphysis, where the shaft becomes nearly cylindrical because of the reduction of the muscular ridges and crest (Bass, 1995).

Source: Adapted from Moore-Jansen, Ousley, and Jantz, 1994; Buikstra and Ubelaker, 1994; Bass, 1995; Meadows and Jantz, 1992.

Measurement of the adult humerus, radius, ulna, and metacarpal

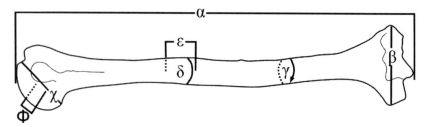

Figure 8–19. A guide to measurements of the left humerus. *Source:* Bass, 1995.

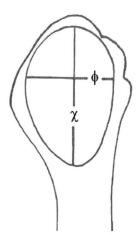

Figure 8–20. A guide to measurements of the proximal left humerus. *Source:* Bass, 1995.

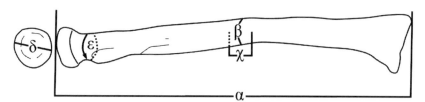

Figure 8–21. A guide to measurements of the left radius, anterior view. *Source:* Bass, 1995.

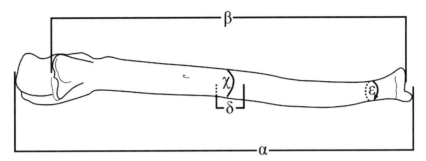

Figure 8–22. A guide to measurements of the left ulna. *Source:* Bass, 1995.

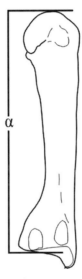

Figure 8–23. A guide to measurement of the metacarpal. *Source:* Bass, 1995.

Measurement of the adult vertebra

Table 8–26. *Measurement of the adult vertebra*

Code	Measurement	Description of measurement
Vertebra		
α	Vertebral body height	Maximum height of the vertebral body from superior to the inferior surface checking across the body (Fully, 1956; Fully and Pineau, 1960)

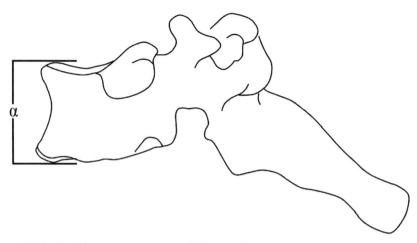

Figure 8–24. A guide to measurement of the vertebra. *Source:* Bass 1995.

Measurement of the adult pelvis

Table 8–27. *Measurement of the adult pelvis*

Code	Measurement	Description of measurement
Sacrum		
α	Maximum transverse diameter of base	Direct distance between the two most laterally projecting points on the sacral base measured perpendicular to the midsagittal plane (Buikstra and Ubelaker, 1994)
β	Anterior length	Distance from a point on the promontory in the midsagittal plane to a point on the anterior border of the tip of the sacrum measured in the midsagittal plane. Place the pointed tips of the sliding calliper on the promontory and the anterior inferior border of the fifth sacral vertebra (Moore-Jansen et al., 1994). If a sacrum exhibits more than five segments, do not use this measurement
χ	Anterior superior breadth	Maximum traverse breadth of the sacrum at the level of the anterior projection of the auricular surface (ibid.)
Innominate		
α	Height	Height is the distance from the most superior point on the iliac crest to the most inferior point on the ischial tuberosity. Place the ischium against the vertical end board of the osteometric board and press the movable upright against the iliac crest. Move the ilium sideways and up and down to obtain the maximum distance (Moore-Jansen et al., 1994)
β	Iliac breadth	Distance between the anterior-superior iliac spine to the posterior iliac spine (Bass, 1995)
χ	Pubis length	Distance from the point in the acetabulum where the three elements of the pelvis meet to the upper end of the pubic symphysis. The measuring point in the acetabulum may be identified in the adult by an irregularity, changes in thickness or the presence of a notch (Buikstra and Ubelaker, 1994)
δ	Ischium length	Distance from the point in the acetabulum where the three elements meet to the deepest point on the ischial tuberosity (ibid.)

Source: Adapted from Buikstra and Ubelaker, 1994; Moore-Jansen, Ousley and Jantz, 1994; Bass, 1995.

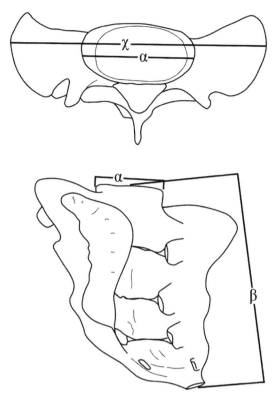

Figure 8–25. A guide to measurements of the sacrum. *Source:* Bass, 1995.

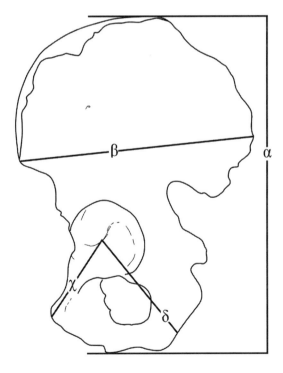

Figure 8–26. A guide to measurements of the pelvis. *Source:* Bass, 1995.

Measurement of the adult femur, tibia, and fibula

Table 8–28. *Measurement of the adult femur, tibia, and fibula*

Code	Measurement	Description of measurement
Femur		
α	Maximum length	Distance from the most superior point on the head of the femur to the most inferior point on the distal condyles. Place the femur parallel to the long axis of the osteometric board and resting on its posterior surface. Press the medial condyle against the vertical end board while applying the movable upright to the femoral head. Raise the bone up and down and shift sideways until the maximum length is obtained (Moore-Jansen et al., 1994)
β	Bicondylar length	Distance from the most superior point on the head of the femur to a plane drawn along the inferior surfaces of the condyles. Place the femur on the osteometric board so the bone is resting on its posterior surface. Press both distal condyles against the vertical end board while applying the movable upright to the head of the femur (ibid.). This measurement is also known as 'oblique' length
χ	Epicondylar breadth	Distance between the two most laterally projecting points of the epicondyles (Buikstra and Ubelaker, 1994)
δ	Anterior-posterior diameter (lateral condyle)	Distance from the most anterior point of the joint surface of the lateral condyle to the most posterior point of the joint surface (Moore-Jansen et al., 1994)
ε	Anterior-posterior diameter (medial condyle)	Distance from the most anterior point of the joint surface of the medial condyle to the most posterior point of the joint surface (ibid.)
φ	Anterior-posterior (sagittal) midshaft diameter	Locate the midpoint of the shaft on the osteometric board and at that point measure the maximum anterior-posterior diameter (Bass, 1995)
γ	Medial-lateral (transverse) midshaft diameter	Distance between the medial and lateral surface at the mid-shaft measures perpendicular to the anterior-posterior diameter (Buikstra and Ubelaker, 1994)
η	Midshaft circumference	Measure the circumference at the level of the midshaft diameters. If the linear aspera exhibits a strong projection that is not evenly expressed across a large portion of the diaphysis, then this measurement is recorded approximately 10 mm above the midpoint (ibid.)
ι	Anterior posterior (sagittal) subtrochanteric diameter	Distance between the anterior and posterior surfaces at the proximal end of the diaphysis, measured perpendicular to the medial-lateral diameter, gluteal lines, and/or tuberosities should be avoided (ibid.)
φ	Medial-lateral (transverse) subtronchanteric diameter	Distance between medial and lateral surfaces of the proximal end of the diaphysis at the point of its greatest lateral expansion below the base of the lesser trochanter (ibid.)
κ	Minimum vertical diameter neck	Shortest distance between the upper and lower surfaces of the neck (Moore-Jansen et al., 1994)
λ	Maximum head diameter	Measured on the periphery of the articular surface of the head. Rotate the bone until the maximum distance is obtained (Bass, 1995)
μ	Upper breadth	Distance from the apex of the head of the femur to the lateral side of the diaphysis. Using sliding callipers, place

Code	Measurement	Description of measurement
		the fixed jaw on the most prominent point on the femoral head. Place the movable jaw on the lateral margin of the diaphysis so the line formed between the two points splits the neck into two equal portions (Simmons et al., 1990)
ν	Lateral condyle height	Situated on the lateral condyle of the distal femur, it is the distance from the most superior point on the condyle to the most inferior point. Holding the femur in anatomical position with the distal condyles facing the observer, place the fixed jaw of the sliding calliper on the top of the condyle and place the movable jaw on the most inferior point on the condyle. The femur should be held so it is possible to accurately judge the location of the most inferior point (ibid.)
o	Vertical head diameter	Greatest distance obtained from a point on the inferior edge to the margin of the articular surface of the head to a point on the superior edge of the margin (Schwartz, 1995)
π	Horizontal head diameter	Greatest distance obtained from the anterior margin to the posterior margin of the articular surface of the femoral head

Tibia

Code	Measurement	Description of measurement
α	Length of the tibia	When using the method published by Trotter and Gleser (1952), note that Trotter measured the tibial length without the malleolus, by allowing it to curve around the end of the osteometric board, bringing the distal articular surface to rest flat against the end. FORDISC 3.0 automatically corrects for this problem when estimating stature from the tibial length
β	Maximum proximal epiphyseal breadth	Maximum distance between the two most laterally projecting points on the medial and lateral condyles of the proximal articular region (Buikstra and Ubelaker, 1994)
χ	Maximum distal epiphyseal breadth	Maximum distance between two most laterally projecting points on the medial malleolus and the lateral surface of the distal articular region (ibid.)
δ	Medial-lateral transverse	Diameter at the nutrient foramen. The straight line distance of the medial margin from the interosseous crest at the level of the nutrient foramen (ibid.)
ϵ	Maximum diameter at the nutrient foramen	Distance between the anterior crest and the posterior surface at the level of the nutrient foramen (ibid.)
Φ	Circumference at the nutrient foramen	Circumference measured at the level of the nutrient foramen (ibid.)
η	Maximum length of the tibia	Distance from the superior articular surface of the lateral condyle of the tibia to the tip of the medial malleolus. Place the tibia on the osteometric board, resting on its posterior surface with the longitudinal axis of the bone parallel to the board. Place the lip of the medial malleolus on the vertical end board and press the movable upright against the proximal articular surface of the lateral condyle (Moore-Jansen et al., 1994). This measurement should be used with FORDISC 3.0

(cont.)

Table 8–28 (*cont.*)

Code	Measurement	Description of measurement
τ	Biarticular breadth	Maximum breadth of the proximal articular surface of the tibia as measured from the lateral edge of the lateral condyle to the medial edge of the medial condyle. This is not the maximum breadth of the proximal tibia, but rather the maximum breadth of the articular surface. Holding the tibia so the proximal articular surface is in plain view, place the fixed jaw of the digital calliper on the most lateral edge of the lateral condyle. Extend the movable jaw to what appears to be the most medial edge of the medial condyle. Pivot the movable jaw slightly to ensure that the maximum is recorded (Holland, 1995)
φ	Medial condyle articular width	Maximum transverse width of the medial condyle as measured from lateral to medial edges. The surface of the condyle generally is circumscribed by a slight rim, and points of the calliper should be placed on this rim. Hold the tibia so you can look directly down on the proximal articular surface. Place the fixed jaw of the digital calliper on the medial edge of the condyle. Extend the movable jaw to the lateral edge of the medial condyle. Move the calliper to the anterior and then to the posterior, adjusting the jaws so they always contact the opposing edges of the condyle. Find the maximum in this manner (ibid.)
κ	Medial condyle articular length	Similar but perpendicular to width. Measurement should record maximum length from the anterior edge of the medial condyle to the posterior margin. Hold the tibia so you can look directly down on the proximal articular surface. Place the fixed jaw of the digital calliper on the anterior edge of the medial condyle. Extend the movable jaw to the posterior edge of the condyle. Move the calliper medially and then laterally, adjusting the jaws so they always contact the opposing edges of the condyle. Find the maximum in this manner (ibid.)
λ	Lateral condyle articular length	Maximum length of the lateral condyle as measured in a manner similar to that for medial condyle articular length (ibid.)
μ	Lateral condyle articular width	Maximum width of the lateral condyle as measured in the same manner as that for medial condyle articular width

Fibula

Code	Measurement	Description of measurement
α	Maximum length	Maximum distance between the most superior point on the fibula head and the most inferior point on the lateral malleolus. Place the fibula on the osteometric board, and place the tip of the lateral malleolus against the vertical end board. Press the movable upright against the proximal end of the bone while moving it up and down and sideways to obtain the maximum length (Moore-Jansen et al., 1994)
β	Maximum diameter at midshaft	Determine the midpoint of the shaft using an osteometric board; at the midpoint, measure the maximum diameter (Buikstra and Ubelaker, 1994)

Source: Adapted from Buikstra and Ubelaker, 1994; Moore-Jansen, Ousley and Jantz, 1994; Bass, 1995; Simmons et al., 1990; Schwartz, 1995; Holland, 1995.

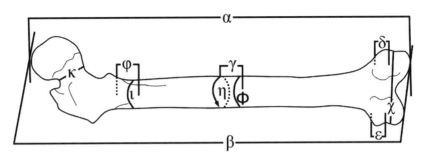

Figure 8–27. A guide to measurements of the left femur. *Source:* Bass, 1995.

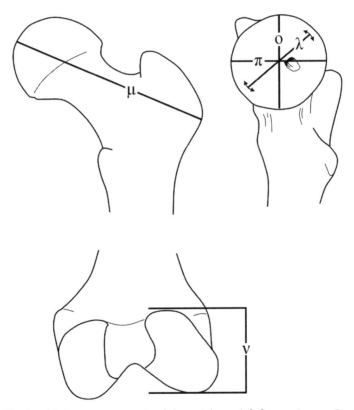

Figure 8–28. A guide to measurements of the epiphyses left femur. *Source:* Bass, 1995.

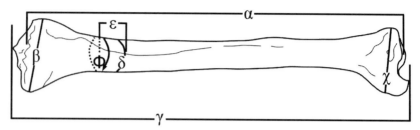

Figure 8–29. A guide to measurements of the left tibia. *Source:* Bass, 1995.

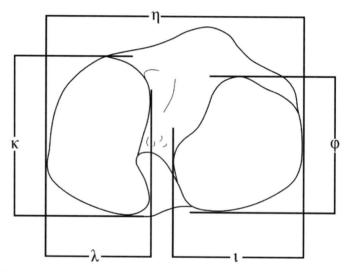

Figure 8–30. A guide to measurements of the proximal left tibia. *Source:* Bass, 1995.

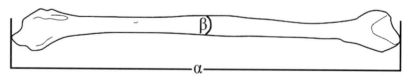

Figure 8–31. A guide to measurements of the fibula. *Source:* Bass, 1995.

Measurement of the adult tarsals and metatarsals

Table 8–29. *Measurement of the adult tarsals and metatarsals*

Code	Measurement	Description of measurement
Calcaneus		
α	Maximum length of the calcaneus	Maximum length of the calcaneus as taken parallel to the long axis. Hold the calcaneus in anatomical position so that you are looking down on the articular surface. Place the fixed jaw of the digital callipers on the anterior-most point of the articular surface. Extend the movable jaw to the posterior surface of bone in a line parallel to the long axis. Move the callipers medially and laterally while maintaining an orientation parallel to the long axis of the bone and pivot them slightly up and down until the maximum is found (Holland, 1995)
β	Middle breadth	Distance between the most laterally projecting point on the dorsal articular facet and the most medial point on the superior margin of the articular facet for the cuboid. Measured in the sagittal plane and projected onto the underlying surface (Buikstra and Ubelaker, 1994)
χ	Posterior length of the calcaneus	Maximum length between the most anterior point of the posterior talar articular surface and the most posterior point of the calcaneus on the tuberosity ignoring any extensive exostoses). Hold the calcaneus in anatomical position so that you are looking down on the articular surface. Place the fixed jaw of the callipers on the posterior margin of the talar articular surface and extend the movable jaw to the posterior surface of the bone. Move the callipers slightly up and down and medially and laterally to find the maximum. Avoid any exostoses (Holland, 1995)
Talus		
α	Maximum length of the talus	Maximum length between the most anterior point of the head and the posterior tubercle. Place the fixed jaw of the digital callipers on the anterior-most point on the head. Extend the movable jaw to the tip of the tubercle. Pivot the bone slightly in the jaws of the callipers to find the maximum (ibid.)
β	Ankle height	Measured from the superior surface of the talus to the most inferior part of the plantar surface of the calcaneus when both elements are articulated in anatomical position (Fully, 1989)
Metatarsals 1–4		
α	Length, functional	Length from the apex of the capitulum to the midpoint of the articular surface of the base parallel to the longitudinal axis of the bone. Hold the metatarsal with the proximal end up. Place the fixed jaw of the callipers on the midpoint of the proximal articular surface and extend the movable jaw to the surface of the capitulum. Move the capitulum slightly back and forth to find its apex (Byers et al., 1989)
Metatarsal 5		
α	Length, total	Length from the apex of the capitulum to the tip of the tuberosity at the proximal end. Place the fixed jaw of the callipers on the tip of the tuberosity and extend the movable jaw to the capitulum. Move the capitulum slightly back and forth to find the apex (ibid.)

Source: Adapted from Buikstra and Ubelaker, 1994; Holland, 1995; Fully, 1956; Byers et al., 1989.

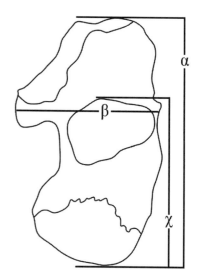

Figure 8–32. A guide to measurements of the calcaneus. *Source:* Bass, 1995.

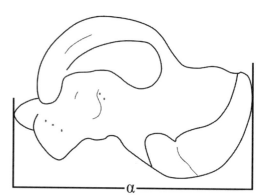

Figure 8–33. A guide to measurements of the talus. *Source:* Bass, 1995.

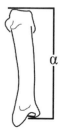

Figure 8–34. A guide to measurement of the fifth metatarsal. *Source:* Bass, 1995.

8.9 Documentation and quality control

8.9.1 Recording and documentation

Results of all comparisons, estimations, assessments, and interpretations are recorded in the anthropologist's analytical notes, including the techniques used, traits recorded, scores given, measurements taken, discriminant functions used, and any associated confidence intervals. The analytical notes will include all observations that were deemed relevant to the analysis of the skeletal remains in a case, and also to the formulation of any professional opinion expressed in the final report. There must be no opinion in a final report that does not have a basis in observations recorded in the analytical notes. All apparatus and equipment used during the investigation must be noted, including detail of the make, model, and manufacturer. Where equipment requires regular calibration, a record of this must be also be logged. This must be recorded in the final report, as must the storage location of the apparatus (e.g., the organisational headquarters).

Interpretations of the cause and manner of death, as well as presumptive or positive identification of skeletal remains, will ultimately form part of the forensic pathologist's report and notes when working in a judicial context. It may also be part of the anthropologist's report in humanitarian cases. However, it is imperative that discussion between the two specialists takes place to avoid inconsistencies and contradictions in final results and the specialists' report. Where appropriate, anthropologists may record descriptions, dimensions, and distributions within anthropological recording forms. If the grave has yielded the remains of a large number of individuals, although each case will have its own report compiled by the anthropologist in question (checked by the senior anthropologist), the senior anthropologist will produce an overall report, including summary statistics based on all cases. The legal statement concerning the assessment of cause and manner of death and identification is one of the duties of the forensic pathologist.

Results of all steps of the anthropological assessment will be recorded using the relevant forms. These are described in 8.9.3 to assist anthropologists in deciding which recording form is most appropriate.

8.9.2 Quality control

The results of each stage of the anthropological assessment will be peer reviewed. This may include reanalysis of the case materials and analytical notes. Quality assessment plays an important role in all operations and must reflect a transparent, considered, and structured process that is documented. Quality control ensures that all stages of anthropological assessment and report writing are reviewed as a matter of course by a senior anthropologist.

The recording forms should be checked for accuracy by the senior anthropologist, while the skeletal remains are laid out in anatomical position. The senior anthropologist must check that summary and conclusions are backed up by diagrams, photographic and radiographic records, descriptions, and appropriate samples. These records should also be double-checked for quality assurance. If there is disagreement or disparity in observations, allocation or 'scores', or any aspect of recording and reporting, the senior anthropologist will review the case in full and discuss the results with the anthropologist as necessary. The senior anthropologist must sign the designated location on the front page of each anthropology recording form on completion of the review.

Assessment is complete when all aspects of analysis deemed necessary have been completed. This includes verifying (a) that all necessary sections of the appropriate recording form are complete (if sections have not been completed, this should be noted and explained); (b) that all interpretations and notes on the analytical notes pages have been recorded; (c) that any extra notes and drawings are attached; (d) that all necessary photographs have been taken and recorded; (e) that all necessary radiographs have been taken, reviewed, and recorded; (f) that any necessary casts have been made; (g) that appropriate samples have been taken; and (h) that the case summary pages have been completed. Finally, it is important to undertake a final evidence check with the SCE for such materials as samples and clothing. When this has been completed, the skeletal remains can be returned to storage. Bones can be replaced in the packaging in which they arrived at the mortuary if this is in good and clean condition; otherwise, new materials should be used (e.g., coffins and shrouds for handover to next-of-kin or communities, or materials conducive to long-term storage of bone, if this is envisaged). All dry bones (i.e., not green) that were not packaged in individual bags can now be separated by body part (if appropriate). For long-term storage they should be packaged in acid-free paper bags, within acid-free cardboard boxes.

All bags and the skull box should be labelled with an indelible marker in the centre so as not to be obscured when sealed. Information to be labelled includes the site code and case number, the date of packaging, and the person's name recording the information. The content of all bags needs to be briefly described (e.g., 'left arm and hand'), and the number of each bag written within a circle in the right-hand corner (e.g., '1 of 10'). Completed reports will be checked by the senior anthropologist for confirmation of completion. All (and only) bags and boxes associated with a single individual will then be placed into a body box for storage. The box can be sealed as determined by the SCE. The senior pathologist may request an individual case report from the anthropologist; this may be appropriate in investigations where only skeletonised remains are recovered. This report will contain all the results of the anthropological analyses, including an inventory and all methods, including statistical tests and results. Documentation must be given to the SCE for data entry. If appropriate, on the completion of all analysis, the human remains may be placed directly into a coffin or shroud, depending on the religious or cultural context, for return to the next of kin.

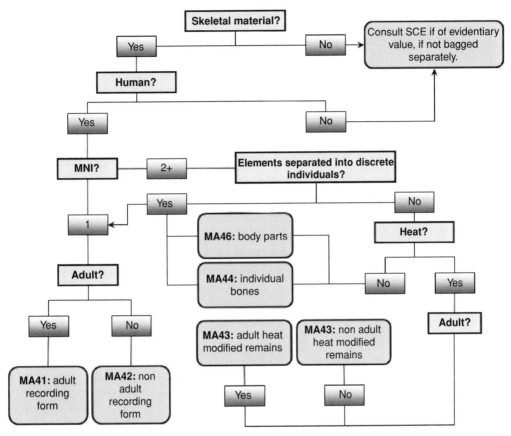

Figure 8–35. Flow chart to determine which forms should be used when recording human skeletal remains.

8.9.3   Recording forms

The following flowchart (Figure 8–35) should be consulted for selecting the most appropriate recording form (all recording forms are listed on Table 8–30 and can be found on the accompanying CD). Note that the recording forms are designed, when used in paper (rather than electronic) format, as individual pages that are collated in booklet form and then bound with a cover page. This approach allows flexibility. Additional pages (e.g., *analytical notes*) or pages from other recording forms (e.g., *fusion of primary ossification centres*) can be included, and pages not required (e.g., *additional nonhuman elements*) can be omitted, saving resources on several levels. This will also allow modification of the form if population-specific standards (i.e., for stature) have been produced. These modifications can be made as policy decisions by the MMT, and any such decision and the reason for it must be specified. These decisions can also be made on a case-by-case basis, such as

Table 8–30. *Anthropology and odontology recording forms*

Code	Forms and logs
MA41F	Individual Adult Skeleton
MA42F	Individual Non-Adult Skeleton
MA43F	Multiple Heat Modified Adult Remains
MA44F	Multiple Heat Modified Non-Adult Remains
MA45F	Skeletonised Body Parts Recording Form
MA46F	Individual and Commingled Skeletonised Remains
MO33F	Dental Chart

when remains are highly fragmented and no measurements can be made. The total number of pages must be written on the cover page. Each page should be signed and dated by the anthropologist. All sections of the recording forms have prepared tables or tick boxes for analysis. However, it is implied that for each conclusion, detailed descriptions and calculations will be written/illustrated in the areas provided or on additional notes pages. As many additional pages as are required should be used.

9

Forensic sciences

Martin Hall, Tony Brown, Peter Jones, and Derek Clark

The range of forensic sciences that crime scene investigators can call on is now considerable, with expertise being available in many disciplines, including ballistics, knots, and trace elements such as fibres, toxins, and blood splatter analysis. The number of areas of science involved in investigating the scenes of atrocity crimes where victims' remains have been deposited is still limited but growing. In this section, we focus on the areas of science most often used in atrocity crime investigations, particularly those that involve field or laboratory sampling. These are entomology (e.g., Byrd and Castner, 2001), environmental sampling (e.g., Ruffell and McKinley, 2005), DNA (e.g., Gibson and Muse, 2002), and forensic odontology (e.g., Bowers, 2004). Sampling and analysis of ballistics is widely discussed elsewhere in the literature and is not included here (e.g., Di Maio, 1985, 1999; Di Maio and Di Maio, 1993; Glattstein et al., 2000).

9.1 Forensic entomology

9.1.1 Introduction

Forensic entomology involves the interpretation of entomological evidence to help resolve a criminal investigation (Keh, 1985; Smith, 1986; Catts and Haskell, 1990; Greenberg, 1991; Turner, 1991; Catts and Goff, 1992; Erzinçlioglu, 1996, 2000; Goff, 2000; Byrd and Castner, 2001; Greenberg and Kunich, 2002; Amendt et al., 2004; 2007). This investigation might be related to an isolated domestic crime or an atrocity crime. In all cases, whether small or large in scale, knowledge of the distribution, biology, and behaviour of insects found at a crime scene can provide

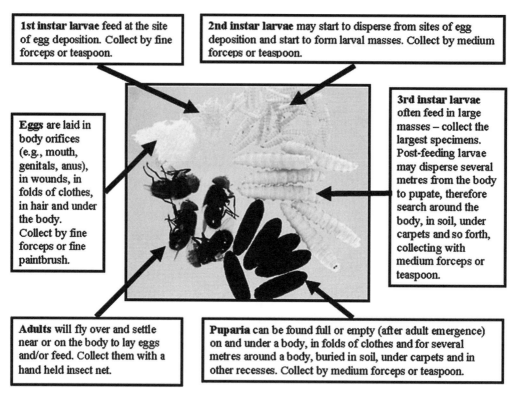

1st instar larvae feed at the site of egg deposition. Collect by fine forceps or teaspoon.

2nd instar larvae may start to disperse from sites of egg deposition and start to form larval masses. Collect by medium forceps or teaspoon.

3rd instar larvae often feed in large masses – collect the largest specimens. Post-feeding larvae may disperse several metres from the body to pupate, therefore search around the body, in soil, under carpets and so forth, collecting with medium forceps or teaspoon.

Eggs are laid in body orifices (e.g., mouth, genitals, anus), in wounds, in folds of clothes, in hair and under the body. Collect by fine forceps or fine paintbrush.

Adults will fly over and settle near or on the body to lay eggs and/or feed. Collect them with a hand held insect net.

Puparia can be found full or empty (after adult emergence) on and under a body, in folds of clothes and for several metres around a body, buried in soil, under carpets and in other recesses. Collect by medium forceps or teaspoon.

Figure 9–1. Life cycle of a typical blowfly – summary of where and how to collect each stage. *Source:* Martin Hall.

information on when, where, and how a crime was committed. The insects that have been most studied in relation to their forensic value in investigations of suspicious deaths are those in the fly family *Calliphoridae*, commonly known as blowflies (e.g., bluebottle flies or *Calliphora* sp.; greenbottle flies or *Lucilia* sp.) and, in particular, their larvae (maggots). This family is studied because (a) they are the insects most commonly associated with corpses and are present in far greater numbers than most other insect groups, and (b) they are usually the first group to colonise the body after death and, consequently, often provide the most accurate information regarding the latest possible time of death (minimum postmortem interval), a major objective of forensic entomology. This section therefore concentrates on a discussion of blowflies.

Some basic entomological terminology must be explained to facilitate discussion of the basic principles underlying forensic entomology. The larva is one of the four developmental stages of blowflies (i.e., egg, larva, pupa, and adult) (see Figure 9–1). This stage is divided into three substages called 'instars', and between each instar, the larva sheds its skin (cuticle) to allow for growth in the next instar. The pupa is the transition stage between larva and adult. It is found inside the barrel-shaped puparium, which is actually the hardened and darkened skin of the final, third instar larva.

The essential first step in estimating the time of death from fly larvae or other insects found on a body is to identify them. There are a number of identification keys to mature larvae of forensically important flies (Smith, 1986; Greenberg and Kunich, 2002). However, morphological identification of fly larvae is not easy because only about 2 percent of the species known to science have been described in their immature stages (Smith, 1989). Therefore, it is sometimes necessary to rear larvae to adults to confirm a tentative identification.

Having identified the species, the next step is to estimate their age, which will indicate the minimum postmortem interval. The basic information needed to age larvae is a measure of their size (length or, less often, weight) or developmental stage and an estimate of the temperatures to which they were exposed during their growth. The latter are necessary because insects develop at a rate that is largely dependent on environmental factors, the most important of which is temperature. The relationship between temperature and larval development has been established for a number of blowfly species (Kamal, 1958; Reiter, 1984; Greenberg, 1991; Wall et al., 1992; Greenberg and Tantawi, 1993; Davies and Ratcliffe, 1994; Wells and Kurahashi, 1994; Byrd and Butler, 1996; Wells and LaMotte, 1995; Byrd and Allen, 2001; Grassberger and Reiter, 2001, 2002; Grassberger et al., 2003; Donovan et al., 2006). Therefore, if accurate temperature data can be determined for the period of development of blowfly stages on the body, a good estimate of the age of those stages can be made.

It is important to be aware that ageing larvae or other stages will not determine the actual time of death; instead, it will estimate the time that blowflies, or other insects, first colonised the body. If the body is lying outdoors, then the first blowfly infestation could be initiated within just a few hours of death in the summer. However, establishment of insects on a body could be delayed for many reasons, such as initial concealment of a body in a sealed room or in a freezer, wrapping the body in a tight-fitting cover, burial, or nonavailability of flies due to cold weather. To accurately identify and age insect specimens, it is essential for them to be collected in optimal conditions (Catts and Haskell, 1990; Amendt et al., 2007). The following sections provide guidance on best practices for insect specimen collection.

9.1.2   Equipment for insect collecting

The basic items of equipment needed for collection of insect samples are standard-size forceps for larvae, puparia, and beetles, and fine forceps or a paintbrush for eggs. A teaspoon can be used to collect larvae when they are abundant. For storage of samples, standard clear glass or plastic 8 × 2.5-cm specimen tubes are ideal; they should have leak-proof screw tops.

To maximise the forensic value of larvae, it is necessary to divide them into three main batches at the scene and then follow several processes. As a record of their size at the time of collection, one batch should be killed promptly at the scene to prevent any further development. To do this, a source of near-boiling water ($>80°C$) is needed (e.g., a thermos of boiling water or a heater powered by a car lighter socket), and for preservation of all stages, 80 percent ethanol. The remaining two batches should be taken live back to the laboratory, one batch for subsequent rearing to adulthood and the other for immediate killing and measurement. If needed, a small number of live specimens can be prepared for toxicological analysis and molecular identification (see Section 9.1.4 for details). The live samples should be kept cool after collection, ideally in a cooler bag with ice packs, but this is not essential. However, a record of the time in transit and transit temperatures should be made. The live samples should be placed in larger specimen tubes, with air holes and with sawdust or tissue paper lining the bottom or, if these are not available, some substrate from the site such as leaf litter or dry soil. As a simple alternative to large specimen tubes, large (e.g., 25×35 cm) resealable plastic bags can be used. Labelling all samples is essential, with a label placed inside the specimen tube. Labels should be written in pencil because many inks will fade or run in water and ethanol. Where appropriate, samples for molecular identification or toxicological analysis can be collected.

A range of other equipment is needed for entomological sampling and site analysis. A handheld net is essential for the capture of flying insects. A small spade or trowel will be needed for searching through soil samples for migrating larvae and for puparia. Soil samples can be sorted at the site on a white or clear plastic sheet, or strong plastic bags can be used to store soil samples to take back to the laboratory (Figure 9–2). A set of soil sieves can be useful for separating insect remains from soil, depending on the soil moisture content and texture. Standard protective clothing (e.g., disposable overalls, gloves, shoe covers) should be worn (Figure 9–2). A digital camera should be available to record insect activity *in situ* (ideally including a measurement scale in the image), and a digital temperature data logger for measuring site temperatures. An infrared or probe thermometer should be used to record larval mass temperatures (Figure 9–3). Contaminated equipment should be cleansed with a disinfectant solution.

In summary, the equipment needed is as follows:

Essential: tool box; medium forceps; fine forceps; fine paintbrush; a range of standard storage tubes (e.g., 8×2.5 cm, 6×3.5 cm, 10×5 cm); freshly boiled water ($>80°C$); 80 percent ethanol (ethyl alcohol); specimen labels; handheld insect capture net; handheld trowel; strong plastic bags (c. 25×35 cm); protective clothing (disposable overalls, gloves, shoe covers and/or boots); digital camera; measurement scale for inclusion in photographs (e.g., 10×10 cm); digital temperature data logger (e.g., Gemini Dataloggers Tinytag Plus); tape measure; disinfectant wipes or solution (e.g., Trigene).

Desirable: sawdust or tissue paper; cooler bag; reusable ice packs; teaspoon; set of soil sieves

Figure 9–2. Searching soil samples from a grave site for insect specimens. The search is made on a plastic sheet before bagging the samples for further analysis in the laboratory. Note the use of all-over protective clothing. *Source:* Martin Hall.

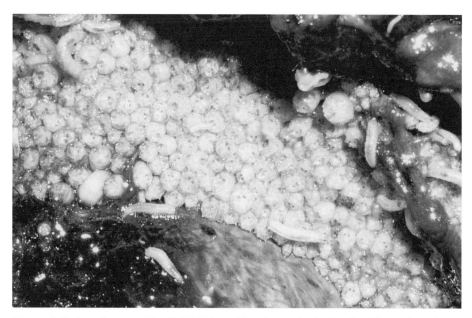

Figure 9–3. Larval mass of *Lucilia/Calliphora* blowfly species in the shoulder region of a human corpse. The temperature of the larval mass was 36°C in an ambient temperature of 24°C. *Source:* Martin Hall.

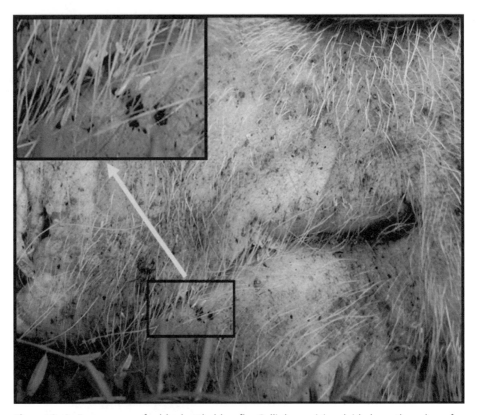

Figure 9–4. Egg masses of a bluebottle blowfly, *Calliphora vicina*, laid along the edge of the mouth of a pig, a typical body orifice site. *Source:* Martin Hall.

9.1.3   Collection of insect samples

Collection from the body. On an uninjured body, blowfly eggs are usually laid at the openings of body orifices (e.g., mouth, nose, ears, eyes, anus, genitalia), and it is in those areas that the hatched larvae start to feed (Figure 9–4). However, eggs can also be laid at sites of traumatic wounding that might be associated with, and therefore indicate, the manner of death. Consequently, it is important to keep a record of the position on the body where the larvae were collected, backed up by photography at the scene of the body's discovery and from the postmortem. Collections of larvae made at different sites should be kept separate with detailed labelling. Photographic evidence should ideally include a measurement scale (e.g., 10 × 10 cm, calibrated in millimetres).

The oldest larvae (i.e., those deposited first on the body) are usually the largest, so collection should concentrate on these. However, a reasonably large sample should be collected that is representative of the complete range of larval sizes present. This is necessary because there may be several species present, and a small larva of one species might be older than a large larva of another species. The sample size will vary, depending on the number of larvae found; however, as a rough guide, it should range from all of the larvae where fewer than 100 are available to 1 to 10 percent of the larvae where thousands are available. If a body is discovered relatively soon after death or after subsequent exposure to adult flies, then it is possible that only eggs will be available for collection. Samples of these should be collected and treated as for larvae, except that eggs to be killed and preserved do not need to be boiled before immersion in 80 percent ethanol. Where eggs and larvae are present on the same body, both should be collected because they may represent a different species and give some additional information on species succession. Any empty blowfly puparia collected will probably be the only traces recoverable of the oldest specimens from the insect infestation because the emerging adults will have dispersed. This is only excepted when some of the adults that emerged from these puparia can also still be collected, alive or dead, as is possible at indoor sites, especially those with closed windows and doors.

Although the developmental stages of blowflies are the most important insect specimens in forensic investigations, other insects should not be overlooked, particularly on or in a body in an advanced state of decomposition, because their presence can be considered in relation to the expected succession of insects on a body. Of course, some insects may be on the body merely because it is an object in the environment on which to rest or gain shelter (adventitious colonisation), and these will not normally provide any useful information regarding postmortem interval. But many other flies, beetles, and moths will be on the body because they were attracted to it for feeding and/or egg laying, and these can provide useful information. For example, the observation and capture of adult blowflies on a body might help determine the flight period for these flies at the time of discovery. It would also indicate the availability of that particular species in the locality, information that is especially important if there are no immature stages of the same species on the body.

Collection from wrapped and buried bodies. Particular care needs to be taken in collecting specimens from wrapped or buried remains. The entomologist should not proceed with uncovering the body or removing clothing and other wrapping materials until all other forensic specialists are also ready to begin their analysis and recording because crucial evidence could be disturbed. With wrapped remains, a detailed record should be kept of the different insect evidence revealed as the wrapping is removed. Some species of blowfly pupariate on the body, especially in the lining of clothing; therefore, a careful check should be made for puparia (full or empty) on and around the body and clothing. With buried remains, soil samples above the body should be checked for evidence of insects either moving towards the body or dispersing away from it.

Collection from around the body. When they have completed feeding on the body, larvae of some blowfly species will pupariate on or immediately around the body,

Figure 9–5. Larvae of a greenbottle blowfly, *Lucilia* species, recovered in loose soil from a depth of about 3 to 5 cm at a distance of 1.4 m from a human corpse. *Source:* Martin Hall.

but larvae of other species can disperse for several metres in search of a suitable site for pupariation (Greenberg, 1991). Therefore, it is important to search the area up to about 5 m around the body for insects that might be or have been associated with the body, especially under stones, rocks, and fallen logs (Figure 9–5). Care should be taken to ensure that other possible competing sources of carrion insects (e.g., dead wildlife) are taken into account; specifically, insects that are found at a distance from a body might not have developed on that body. A control sample taken at a distance of 10 to 20 m from the body will indicate the background levels of insect activity in the soil. (When soil samples are taken, this should be coordinated with the senior archaeologist to ensure that crucial information in the grave is not lost.) After the body has been removed, the soil under and around it should be inspected for larvae and puparia of larvae that might have migrated from the body. The puparia could be full or, following adult emergence, empty. Using a trowel, soil should be sampled down to a depth of about 15 cm. A standard set of soil sieves could be used to separate insect specimens from the soil, providing the soil is of the right consistency. This could be carried out in a laboratory if the soil samples are bagged and labelled on site. In a building, larvae and puparia might be found under nearby furniture, rugs, carpets, and so on. The distance of the insect samples from the body should be recorded. It has to be remembered that if puparia are overlooked and not recovered, then the oldest specimens may not have been collected, and the minimum postmortem interval could be incorrectly estimated.

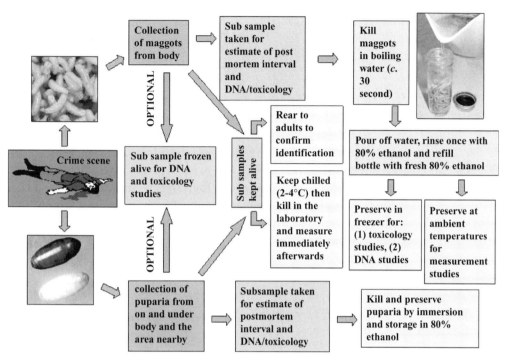

Figure 9–6. Summary of sampling techniques for fly larvae and puparia. *Source:* Martin Hall.

Collection from the postmortem. The collection of insects at a postmortem should proceed in the same general way as collection at the crime scene (i.e., with regard to sampling technique and recording the site of infestation on the body). In addition, particular attention should be paid to recording the period that the body has spent at various temperatures that might be different to those at the site of the body's discovery because these can influence larval development. For example, at a temperature of 3°C to 4°C, common in a morgue's cold storage chamber, the development of the bluebottle blowfly is effectively suspended for short periods of up to 24 hours (Johl and Anderson, 1996). However, a large mass of larvae on a body can generate sufficient metabolic heat ('maggot mass' effect; Turner and Howard, 1992) that the expected retardation of larval development under short-term refrigeration is less evident. A summary of sampling techniques for recovering fly larval and puparial evidence is depicted in Figure 9–6.

9.1.4   Killing and preservation of insect specimens

Direct immersion of live larvae into ethanol and other killing fluids causes larvae to contract as they die (Adams and Hall, 2003). This makes it difficult to see some diagnostic features and, equally important, causes errors in the estimation of larval age based on larval length (Tantawi and Greenberg, 1993; Adams and Hall, 2003). However, good quality, extended specimens can be obtained if larvae are first killed by brief immersion (30 seconds) in freshly boiled water (>80°C) and then transferred to 80 percent ethanol (Adams and Hall, 2003). Boiled water can be taken to the site of an investigation in a thermos flask, or it can be prepared on site using a water heater (e.g., operated from a car cigarette lighter socket). Because these larvae will be used to estimate postmortem interval, it is vital to record the time when they were killed. Boiled larvae placed into 80 percent ethanol can lengthen by about 5 percent within 24 hours, making them appear longer and, therefore, older than they actually are (Adams and Hall, 2003).

Although not always essential, if possible, four further samples of larvae should be collected: one kept alive for rearing studies in the laboratory; one frozen alive (−20°C) and kept frozen for potential use in toxicological studies; one killed as before in boiling water followed by storage in 80 percent ethanol at −20°C for molecular studies (Sperling et al., 1994); and one kept alive, ideally as cool as possible but not frozen (e.g., in a cool box or domestic refrigerator at 2°C–4°C), for killing and immediate measurement of larval length in the laboratory. The lengths of the latter group can then be compared directly with published tables of rates of development (e.g., Reiter, 1984; Donovan et al., 2006), which are usually based on measurement of experimental specimens that were killed by boiling and then measured immediately.

In summary, the larval samples needed are, in order of importance, (a) a sample killed on-site in boiling water, and then transferred to 80 percent ethanol and stored at ambient temperature for ageing studies; (b) a sample kept alive at 2°C to 4°C for killing in the laboratory as soon as possible, followed by immediate length measurement for ageing studies; (c) a sample kept alive for rearing to adulthood for confirmation of identification; (d) a sample killed in a freezer and then stored without preservative in a freezer for potential toxicological studies; and (e) a sample killed on-site in boiling water, and then transferred to 80 percent ethanol and stored in a freezer for potential molecular identification studies.

Puparia should be killed by direct immersion in 80 percent ethanol, in which they can then be kept for preservation. A pinprick in the puparial cuticle will enhance preservation by facilitating the entry of preservative. Adult flies can be killed by placing them in a deep freezer for 1 hour. When newly emerged from their puparium, adults should only be killed after first allowing them to fully harden their wings and develop their colouring (after c. 6 hours) (Figure 9–7). Once dead, they can be thawed and packed between paper tissue for storage or mailing in a crush-proof container. Care should be taken not to keep dead, wet insects out of preservative at room temperature, especially in an airtight container, because they will quickly decompose if they cannot dry out. Dry insects will keep well without preservative for decades, as long as their storage container prevents the entry of small beetles (e.g., *Anthrenus* sp., the museum or carpet beetles) that feed on dead insects. For taxonomic study, pinned adults are the ideal. Where there are problems with maintaining dry

Figure 9–7. Newly emerged adults of a bluebottle blowfly, *Calliphora vicina*, with their empty puparia. Note the crumpled wings of the adults and the dislodged anterior ends of the puparia. *Source:* Martin Hall.

storage conditions, adults, as for eggs, larvae, and puparia, can be preserved in a storage tube in 80 percent ethanol, but this can sometimes make identification more difficult.

9.1.5 Maintenance of living larvae

Adult flies are usually easier to identify than immature stages, especially the younger immature stages. In addition, there is an alternative method of calculating the age of blowflies that can be used with live larvae, based on the period taken to reach critical stages of development, such as the time periods to third instar, to pupariation, and to adult emergence (e.g., Greenberg, 1991). Therefore, it can be valuable to keep some larvae alive in two batches: one for killing and immediate length measurement in the laboratory, and the other to rear to adulthood. Those to be killed later should be cooled to about 4°C as soon as possible after removal from the corpse, and then kept without food in a container in a domestic refrigerator at about 2°C to 4°C, until being handed over to an entomologist at the earliest opportunity. The container should be punched with small holes that allow air to enter but do not allow larvae to escape. It should be lined with coarse sawdust or tissue paper to absorb fluids associated with the larvae. Details of how long they were maintained at low temperature should be recorded. Those larvae to be reared to adulthood should be kept in the same manner. If, however, it is not possible to pass them quickly on to an entomologist, they should be removed from the refrigerator and transferred to a clean jar lined with sawdust or paper tissue and a perforated lid. They should then be maintained at room temperature, with a record of that temperature. If the larvae are immature and still in their feeding phase, then some meat (e.g., liver, minced meat, or canned dog food) should be added to enable them to feed and complete their development.

9.1.6 Recording

To determine the influence of temperature on the development of larvae on the body, it is important at the time of discovery to take the temperature of the air, the ground, the body (on, in, and under the corpse) and, if possible, the 'larval mass'. If the latter is not possible, some measure of the numbers of larvae in the 'larval mass' should be recorded, including a photographic record. Previous weather data for the general area of discovery of the body should be collected from the nearest meteorological station. The period for which these data should be collected depends on the likely period that the body has been at the site. To correlate the meteorological station data with the conditions at the actual site of discovery of the body, temperatures should be recorded at the site for 5 to 10 days and compared to those at the nearest meteorological station over the same period. For preference, these measurements should be made hourly, using an automated digital temperature data logger. If this is not possible, daily maximum and minimum temperature records should be obtained by leaving one or several maximum/minimum temperature thermometers at the crime scene.

It is essential to record from where all samples are collected, both photographically and by written record, a copy of the data being inserted into the relevant specimen tubes. If sampling is undertaken in the field, then the observer should record the sampling position in question. All forms and logs associated with entomological analysis (e.g., Sample Recording Form [FA13F], Field Sample Log [FA14R], Mortuary Sample Recording Form [MC14F], Mortuary Sample Log [MC14L]), must be logged by the scene of crime examiner (SCE) or scene of crime manager (SCM). All recording forms and logs mentioned in this chapter are located on the accompanying CD; guidance for their use in located in 1.11. All samples must be allocated a number by the SCE or SCM and dealt with as for any type of evidence in terms of evidential integrity and chain of custody both in terms of storage and analysis.

9.1.7 Summary points

1. Entomology can make an important contribution to forensic investigations, especially in determining a minimum postmortem interval.
2. The lack of insect activity can be important; sampling that considers the presence and absence of entomological evidence must form part of a sampling strategy.
3. Do not place fly larvae live into preservative; kill them first by boiling.
4. Do not keep live fly larvae in conditions that are unknown, especially with regard to temperature.
5. Do not overlook the possibility that larvae and puparia could be found at some distance from the body.

6. Do not make direct assumptions about site temperatures from temperatures at the nearest meteorological station – ensure that a good regression analysis of scene and meteorological station data are undertaken.

7. If an entomologist cannot attend the scene, do not forget to pass on as much evidence as possible by way of photography and written description of the scene.

9.2   Environmental sampling

This section details the use of techniques associated with environmental materials and draws on two specialist areas: environmental archaeology and forensic geosciences (Ruffell and McKinley, 2005). The subject can be broadly divided into (a) geological techniques for the analysis of soils and sediments, and (b) biological techniques, which includes plants, insects (see 9.1), and animal remains and microfossils.

9.2.1   Introduction

Prior to the deployment of an environmental specialist to a grave or potential grave site, it must be clear what kind of information is required by the investigating authorities from the scene of crime, or exhibits. There are three questions most commonly asked of environmental forensic specialists:

1. *Can the soil or sediment in a grave, within clothing, on a body, etc., be linked back to a scene of crime, or link scenes of crime, and with what degree of evidential strength?* This may be done by determining an "environmental profile" for the sample (Brown et al., 2002; Wiltshire, 2004; Brown, 2006).

2. *Does the soil or sediment contain any evidence pertinent to the crime?* This could include evidence related to the location of a site of incarceration or capture.

3. *Does the soil or sediment suggest the postmortem transport of a body (i.e., from a primary to a secondary grave), and if so, can the former location(s) be identified?*

Each crime scene will have unique aspects to which environmental analyses may contribute. In general, this will require sampling from both within graves and the surrounding soil or sediment for control. The procedures outlined here have been derived from palaeoenvironmental standards (Berglund, 1986) and amended by experience of both civilian scenes of crime and mass grave work (Brown et al., 2002; Brown, 2006).

9.2.2   Soil and sediment

Although soil type is not a unique descriptor of the constitution of any soil or sediment, it can be valuable in comparison and elimination. In theory, because soils are made up of multiple components and have evolved over time in different locations, they are unique and can be matched to their original location or source. However, in practise, analytical limits and natural variation restrict our ability to provenance soil and sediment. The distinction between 'soil' and 'sediment', which is based on organic activity, is not deemed relevant to forensic work, and so the same procedures can often be applied to both. Indeed, the key distinction is generally between the A horizons of soil (loosely referred to as *topsoil*) and the B and C horizons (or *subsoil*). In most cases, the excavation of mass graves will have been undertaken by a mechanical excavator into flat or gently sloping and relatively soft ground. In practise, this means into relatively soft sediments such as those found on floodplains and colluvial toe slopes or into river gravel terraces or areas of unconsolidated geological sands or clays. The exception to this is where preexisting excavations or depressions are used, such as old quarries, mines, or dolines (closed depressions in limestone), and these are backfilled. Indeed, in most cases, there are many constraints on the excavation of mass graves in addition to the geological and geomorphological, including access, vegetation, and distance/time. The result is that with the aid of geographical information systems, the location of sites is at least semipredictable.

Due to the biochemical activity that occurs in graves associated with decomposition, soil chemistry is unlikely to reflect the source material, so standard chemical descriptors such as pH, Eh, N, P, K, or Fe would be of little value. Instead, most analyses concentrate on nontransient properties and constituents.

In the field, all grave or pit faces and exposures (e.g., cliff) should be described using a standard soil and sediment system. One of the most widely used is the United Kingdom Soil Survey System (Hodgson, 1976), and this is the recommended source for description of soil for forensic missions. However, this system is not comprehensive and so can be replaced by the United States Soil Taxonomic System (Soil Survey Staff, 1999) or the Food and Agriculture Organization of the United Nations (FAO) system (FAO, 1990). Sediments can be described with the addition of sedimentological characteristics as described by Tucker (1988).

When taking profiles within and at the edges of the grave, the following descriptions are suggested: colour – use the Munsell colour chart system; texture – describe as clay, silt, sand, or gravel; stone content – lithology and shape; organic fragments; soil/sediment structure; and soil/sediment stratigraphy. The same information as described previously should be collected from auger samples derived from around a grave site, although structure and stone characteristics are difficult to define from these samples. The geomorphological context of any site must also be described because this may have a direct bearing on the distinction between natural and transported soils or sediment. The geology (lithology) of the area should also be known. Although geological maps are useful in most cases, field observation will have to be made. Further details of these field techniques can be found in recently published volumes on geoarchaeology and environmental archaeology (French, 2003; Wilkinson and Stevens, 2003; Branch et al., 2005). A particularly useful summary is provided by Ayala et al. (2004).

Table 9–1. *Sample sizes and storage for plant, soil, pollen, spore, and diatom analysis methods*

Analyses	Volume required	Sample storage	Analytical methods
Plant macrofossils and charcoal	Ideally, 5 kg or 150 cm^3 from cores, but in practice whatever can be recovered	Cold store or frozen	Separation, sieving, and identification. Flotation can be used for charcoal
Grain size analysis	In theory, this depends on the mean grain size (sand 50 g, silt/clay 10 g)	Dried, frozen or cold store	Sand and coarser: dry sieving
			Silt wet sieving, silt and clay: sedigraph, Coulter counter, or mastersizer
Carbonate content	Generally, fine sediment/soil so 10 g	Dried, frozen, or cold store	Calcimeter
Organic matter	Generally, fine sediment/soil so 10 g	Dried, frozen or cold store	Loss on ignition (if not clay rich) or a C:N analyser or wet oxidation
Pollen and spores	1 g or even the washings of clothes	Frozen or cold store best, but dried is possible	Chemical procedures (see text)
Diatoms	1 g or possibly even a smear	Frozen or cold store best, but dried is possible	Chemical procedures (see text)

Source: Adapted from Clark, 1994.

9.2.3 Sampling

Different analyses require different quantities of soil (Table 9–1). In most cases, sampling procedures can be combined so only a single sample is necessary. Sampling at scenes of crimes and graves is almost invariably judgemental (i.e., samples are taken from specific points or locations). The only exception to this can be control sampling, which may be done systematically or from a grid or transect. With samples for microfossils (e.g., pollen), mineralogy, and elemental chemistry, care must be taken to avoid any contamination. If possible, sampling should not be undertaken in the rain. Tools should be cleaned using distilled or deionised water before and after each sample is taken.

All samples should be kept in sealed plastic bags, in a dark and cool environment, and ideally in a refrigerator, mortuary container, or freezer. The high levels of anaerobic bacteria and fungi in mass graves complicates sample storage because continued growth has been observed in cold stores if the temperatures even briefly rise above 2°C. If cold storage is not available, then samples can be dried, but this may damage pollen. Samples for mineralogy and elemental analysis may also be dried or freeze-dried and stored. Ideally, samples should be split on-site with retention of one-half in the field or at the mortuary. For transport, small samples should be packed into padded bags and sealed, while larger samples may require crating. It should be noted that the importation of soil into many countries requires specific permissions and licences. In the United Kingdom, it can only be undertaken with an appropriate licence to import, move, and keep prohibited plants, plant pests, soil or growing medium, and plant material for scientific or trialling purposes. This also applies to work as provided for in derogations from Council Directive 77/93/EEC, or for changes to an existing licence requiring scientific or technical assessment (Document PHI 3). For details, see http://www.defra.gov.uk/corporate/regulat/forms/ phealth/phi3.htm. Similar schemes may exist in other countries and must be observed. All sampling must be recorded both spatially (by the surveyor) and descriptively (including photographically) on appropriate forms (see 5.10 for Field Sample Log [FA13L] and Sample Recording Form [FA13F]) and must be logged by the SCE, who will allocate numbers as appropriate. All such samples must be stored, transported, and 'handed over' in accordance with scene of crime procedures.

9.2.4   Analytical methodology: Macroscopic

The range of environmental techniques currently available for soil analysis is extremely broad, and it is not possible to cover them here in any detail. However, standard procedures can be applied to the main categories described in this section.

Soil and sediment bulk characteristics are techniques that analyse the macroscopic characteristics of soil or sediment. They are adversely affected by the physical process of sample accumulation (e.g., by vehicle, by clothing) but can nevertheless be used to discount matches. The main properties are particle grain size distribution, calcium carbonate content, and organic matter content. These are all covered by British Standards or equivalent standards. For analytical procedures, see Goudie (1981) and Canti (1991).

A further field of analysis is of macroscopic plant remains. The inclusion of unusual elements or a skewed suite of plant remains can be used to provenance soils, or material adhering to surfaces, or on clothing. For the extraction methodology, see Wasylikowa (1986). There are standard keys for nonwoody plants (e.g., Beijerinck, 1947; Martin and Barkley, 1961), wood, and charcoal (Schweingruber, 1978), which can be used in conjunction with local floras. However, access to an extensive reference collection by a trained specialist is essential. They can also be used to infer season of deposition as used by the War Crimes Court in the Radislav Krstic trial in The Hague in 2004 (International Criminal Tribunal for the Former Yugoslavia, 2001) by virtue of their flowering or other developmental stage. Plant macrofossils and wood can also give additional and corroborative evidence to that provided by mineralogy and palynology (Brown et al., 2002).

9.2.5   Analytical methodology: Palynomorphs

The analysis of microfossils is a further source of potential forensic information and the main advantage of these, especially pollen, is that they are not adversely affected by the accumulation process. This is because they are practically unalterable in the grave and can be used to provenance to soil, or sediment type, and location given favourable circumstances. Microfossils are also retained in small traps within the body (including intestines, turbinates, and teeth), on and within clothing, and on exhibits, especially vehicles. They can even be accumulated and transported on clothing with little or no soiling (P. Wiltshire, personal communication, March 2003). With the exception of internal organs and teeth, and on textiles, the microfossils are invariably held within a matrix of soil or sediment, and there must be enough to allow processing. The main microfossils that have been used forensically are pollen (Bryant et al., 1990; Mildenhall, 1990; Stanley, 1991; Horrocks and Walsh, 1998, Horrocks et al., 1998; Brown et al., 2002; Wiltshire, 2004; Brown, 2006), spores, and diatoms (Cameron, 2004). After processing and along with pollen, many other resistant microfossils can be found, including fern, moss, fungal, and algal spores; as a result, they are often referred to collectively as palynomorphs. In addition to being a standard method of establishing death due to drowning (Pollanen, 1998), diatoms can indicate whether the body or sediment has come from an aquatic source and its characteristics (e.g., freshwater, marine, brackish, or polluted water) (Cameron, 2004).

Pollen has only recently been used extensively in forensic analysis (see previous references), although the history of its occasional use extends to before the 1960s (Erdtman, 1969). It is the most applicable microfossil partly because the upper 1 to 2 cm of most soils are rich in pollen, and this pollen is retained year on year (Horrocks and Walsh, 1999). The most common approach is to identify unusual pollen or spore types, which are poorly dispersed and come from a limited number of locations. The standard methodologies are specific to each technique, but all processing must be undertaken in a clean laboratory with either positive pressure or an air filtration system. Processing samples for palynomorphs involves removing carbonates (usually with hydrochloric acid), silicates (generally with hydrofluoric acid), and less resistant organic materials (generally using an acetylation mixture). Details of the standard chemical procedures can be found in Moore et al. (1991) and Branch et al. (2005). However, other less hazardous methods have been developed, including density separation (Nakagawa et al., 1998). The sample residue is then mounted under silicon oil or glycerine. Although the identification of palynomorphs is easier under silicon oil, they are prone to move and so it is less suitable for forensic work that glycerine. Identification takes place under plane-transmitted light using oil immersion and phase contrast at x400–1000 magnification. The identification must be undertaken by a suitably trained specialist, and in most cases, access to a comprehensive reference collection is essential.

The forensic interpretation of palynomorphs is not straightforward because the biases encountered in all environmental work are not only present but are also typically exaggerated by the complexity of pollen accumulation mechanisms and the superlocal nature of forensic 'sites'. The potential complexity of accumulation may have an affect on the sampling strategy employed, as is shown in a case from Bosnia (Figure 9–8). Possible accumulating mechanisms are listed in Table 9–2.

All microfossil sampling is statistical in nature. It follows that even the same sample counted twice but to different levels will have slightly different spectra. In practice, no two samples from the same location or vegetation will have exactly the

Table 9–2. *Typical and forensic inputs of palynomorphs to a site*

Natural accumulating mechanisms	Additional forensic case mechanisms
• Local airborne: from plants on the site itself • Extralocal airborne: from plants surrounding the site • Regional and long-distance airborne pollen • Waterborne: from the site's catchment	• Clothing • Body and hair • Artefacts (tools, etc.) • Extraneous organic material and soil imported with the bodies • Incorporation from perpetrator's feet

same palynomorph spectra. Matching samples therefore requires considerable experience and consideration of the site peculiarities. There are basically three elements of comparison:

1. Identification of rare types in both control and forensic samples
2. Consideration of the similarities of the control and forensic samples in terms of the types present
3. Consideration of the similarities of the control and forensic samples in terms of the values of types present in both samples

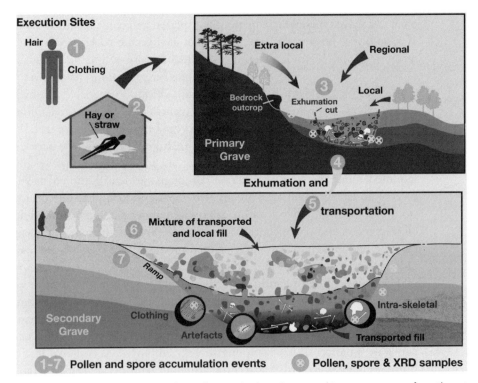

Figure 9–8. Sampling contexts for pollen and mineralogy used in mass graves of northeast Bosnia. *Source:* Anthony Brown.

This is done in all reports, and in effect, the analyst is comparing the rarity of the match to how common the match is in nature (likelihood ratio). This has been described in greater detail by Horrocks and Walsh (1998). Although there is not enough data to be sure, it is likely that the major problems in matching based on palynomorphs come from a lack on knowledge as to how common a 'rare' type is in areas where little data may exist. The largest study of mass graves using palynomorphs was conducted as part of the investigation of the International Tribune for the Former Yugoslavia in northeast Bosnia by Brown from 1999 to 2003 (Brown, 2006).

The processing of samples for diatoms is simpler than for palynomorphs, involving the removal of carbonates and salts, removal of organic matter using hydrogen peroxide, and dilution (Branch et al., 2005). Identification takes place under plane-transmitted light using oil immersion and phase contrast at ×400–1000 magnification. The identification must be undertaken by a suitably trained specialist with access to the standard and local diatom identification keys (Battarbee, 1986).

Other microfossils could be used including phytoliths (plant silica), ostracods, and foraminifera, and details of these techniques can be found in Lowe and Walker (1997) and Branch et al. (2005). The microfossils that are present will depend on the chemistry and origin of the sediment and soil, and in general, they are likely to be of only occasional value.

9.2.6 Analytical methodology: Mineralogy and geochemistry

The most unchangeable soil and sediment characteristic is its mineralogy. This is largely the result of its geological history and cannot be altered by organic decomposition in the short term (i.e., within the effectively forensic time scale). There are, however, some soil minerals that can be formed due to decomposition processes (e.g., vivianite, a blue iron phosphate mineral), but these can either be removed before analysis or discounted. The most time and cost-effective, as well as robust, method is x-ray diffraction (see Herz and Garrison, 1998, and James and Nordby, 2002, for details of this technique). Standard procedures are followed with crushing pelletisation and glycolation if required for detailed analysis of clay mineralogy (http://www.xraydiffrac.com/soilandclaymineralanalysis.html). In many areas, soils will be separable due to the regional geology into quartz, quartz-calcite, or quartz-clay dominated and organic soils. Rare minerals may also be present, derived from particular sediments or lithologies such as tourmaline. In most cases, the underlying lithology of the source site can be determined. In Bosnia, the forensic samples could be split into those that had derived from soils with and without swelling clay minerals (Brown, 2006).

An allied technique is the characterisation of mineral grain surfaces using a scanning electron microscope, referred to as surface texture analysis (Bull, 1981). Approximately forty different surface textures have been recognised that can be attributed to particular geological conditions, and so, in some cases, to particular locations or geological units. The identification of a particularly unusual marker grain texture on a forensic sample and control can be used to support a match.

Elemental chemistry can also be used, particularly where a rare earth element may be able to give a locational match due to an industrial process, pollution source, or spatial variation in geology. The most commonly used method is x-ray fluorescence (James and Nordby, 2002). However, the most precise analyses will be obtained using inductively coupled plasma mass spectrometry (James and Nordby, 2002). A new approach with considerable promise is the automated combination of scanning electron microscopy and x-ray technology (or QEMSCAN), originally designed for the rapid characterisation of particles for the mineral exploration industry. One of these machines at Camborne School of Mines, UK, has recently been used in a number of forensic cases (D. Pirrie, personal communication, September 2006).

At each subsampling stage, material should be retained that allows the material to be reprocessed or analysed. Samples must be held for use by defence or prosecution teams, and the count sheets must be archived. Evidence is normally submitted in the form of a witness statement or specialist report.

9.2.7   Conclusions

Mass graves or the sites of atrocities should be treated in just as much depth as civil forensic cases or archaeological sites. The forensic identification of the chain of events is often valuable evidence, which may have to stand alone or be corroborated by witness evidence. Mass execution and grave sites are not randomly located and, in many cases, have a complex history. Although they may seem chaotic, detailed excavation and environmental analyses can often reveal the location of previous interment or execution sites; time of year; and sequence of excavation, use, and backfilling. However, like all forensic evidence, the interpretation of environmental evidence has strong statistical elements and is best combined with as many other techniques as possible.

9.3   DNA analysis

9.3.1   Introduction

The subject of DNA appears in a number of different places throughout this text, and the purpose of this section is to expand on all the relevant sections dealing with DNA under one heading. It also seeks to expand on the uses of DNA in the investigation of atrocity crimes and to consider ethical issues. Samples for DNA analysis collected during forensic investigations must always and only be analysed by an internationally accredited DNA laboratory, preferably accredited to ISO 9001:2000 and ideally ISO 17025:2000. As such, this text does not discuss aspects of DNA extraction, analysis and associated methodologies, or laboratory practice (Lewin, 1996; Butler, 2005).

The collection of samples from human remains for destructive analysis can be a delicate and politically charged subject. The following section assumes that all appropriate permissions have been obtained for the collection, storage, and analysis of human remains from the country of origin, the national or provisional authority, and, if appropriate, the country to which the samples are to be exported (Merz and Sankar, 1998). The latter is not usually a problem. At the beginning of the project, due consideration should be given to the ultimate fate of the sampled remains. A number of factors will need to be taken into account. For instance, do all used samples and or DNA have to be returned for burial, or should they be destroyed at the end of the project? In all cases, it is strongly recommended that the decision on how to proceed is reached via informed consent from the local community and relevant authorities rather than on a person-by-person basis. If it is desirable to keep extracted DNA for future analysis, excess tissue could be returned, kept, or destroyed. From a practical storage point of view, it would be desirable to retain the option to incinerate excess samples, but only if that is acceptable to the community in question.

9.3.2   Rationale

The use of DNA-based profiling is a powerful method of determining relatedness. It should always be kept in mind that genetic relatedness is not the same as evidence of a family group (Rothstein et al., 2006). It is therefore important that the DNA-based evidence is used in conjunction with other forms of evidence to either establish relatedness or the identity of an individual (Wiesner et al., 2000). DNA has two primary functions: (a) to aid in the identification of individuals or groups of individuals based on obtaining a unique genetic profile, and (b) to aid in the repatriation of the individuals' remains to their relatives. A third and much more difficult task is the assignment of ancestry or culture based purely on genetic evidence without the involvement of relatives (Harding and McVean, 2004; Bonilla et al., 2005; Salas et al., 2005; Shriver et al., 2005).

In the first two examples, the DNA profile of the unknown individual under investigation must be compared to examples of verifiable sources of DNA. The sources of DNA can be obtained directly from items belonging to the individual, such as hospital samples, hair from brushes or combs, toothbrushes, envelopes sealed with saliva, or other personal items (Alonso et al., 2005). This route leads to a direct comparison of profiles and is unambiguous for that individual. It does not rely on the genetic parentage of the individual. The second and indirect method involves matching the genetic profile of the individual with that of his or her relatives. Samples of saliva or blood of the relatives are collected in small family units of close genetic relatives (Wenk, 2004). The availability of relatives and victim will inevitably be determined by circumstances. However, the general rule of thumb is that the greater the number of close relatives within one generation of the victim, the greater the probability of finding a match (ibid.). That is not to say that second- or even third-generation relatives cannot be used; in fact, in some circumstances, this may be the only option available. The advantage of using this method is that it operates as a screen whereby a large number of people can be processed and the degree of relatedness determined computationally. It does, however, have some drawbacks that need to be considered.

Within the western European population, the cases of nonpaternity (i.e., the ostensible father is not in fact the biological father) run at 7 to 15 percent (Brock and Shrimpton, 1991), and this can rise as high as 30 percent in some specific groups (Lucassen and Parker, 2001; Collins et al., 2003). There is, therefore, the possibility of having the correct profile data and family members but not finding a match. There is also the possibility of matching the victim to the incorrect family but the correct genetic relative. Using DNA profiling will expose cases of nonpaternity. In such circumstances, it is essential to consider the resulting ethical dilemma. Should we consider not reporting these matches to the family concerned and instead report that no match was found? Alternatively, do we report the match with the ensuing consequences and disruption of the community involved?

In the case of mass graves, it is likely that there will be individuals that are related to others within the same grave. One of the first tasks is to produce a genetic profile of all individuals and then check for relatedness between all victims. This will reveal the extent of genetic relatedness; it does not, however, signify a family group for reasons of nonpaternity, as mentioned previously. The data on the relatedness of individuals should be retained until corroborating evidence has been gathered from surviving relatives and considered. This is to avoid cases of, for example, informing a surviving father that his son and daughter have been found, whereas the family group was only aware of the daughter. In some extremely genetically similar populations, this can become a difficult problem to resolve. Establishing paternity should always be done on the basis that there is no other close relative, such as a brother, who could also have been the father. This is why, wherever possible, it is always desirable to confirm paternity using both family relatives and direct DNA from the contemporary genetic artefacts (e.g., hair, saliva) (Smith, 2003).

The reliance on genetic data alone may be sufficient to complete the picture for repatriation purposes. The DNA data should be used in conjunction with the recovery of articles found on a body such as papers or other identifying features (e.g., false teeth, morphology) and/or anthropological data. DNA may either confirm or disprove the artefacts found on an individual. It is not unknown for the perpetrators of crimes against humanity to deliberately remove, swap, or insert papers or other means of identification. DNA-based profiling should be regarded as one strand of the complete investigation and not the panacea for identification (Budowle et al., 2005).

9.3.3   DNA quality and quantity

The quality of DNA obtained from the samples is of ultimate importance. Generally, if DNA can be extracted from a sample of sufficient quality, then there will be enough DNA present to perform profiling. In this context, 'sufficient quality' refers to DNA of which 50 percent will have a mean size 200 bp. As an example, approximately 1 g of fresh soft tissue will yield 2 mg of DNA. However, only 250 pg to 1 ng is required to produce a profile, which is more than 1 million-fold in excess of that required for a profile. Provided there is at least 250 pg of sufficient quality of intact DNA, a profile can be produced (Budimlija et al., 2003).

9.3.4   Sampling from bodies

Sample collection in the field will be determined by the circumstances surrounding the site and the availability of collection and storage facilities. Following is a list of a number of collection and storage conditions. The exact one to be followed will need to be determined at the time of collection, based on the availability of equipment, personnel, the overall strategy for performing the DNA profiling, and the requirements of the DNA laboratory. Samples for DNA analysis can be derived, theoretically, from any hard or soft tissue. However, practical circumstance and the condition of the human remains usually tend to determine which tissues are taken. In cases where there are extensive commingled remains, it may not be possible to make a reliable identification of the individuals concerned using DNA profiling alone (Budimlija et al., 2003).

The degree of DNA preservation is determined by factors such as temperature during burial, duration of burial, degree of moisture, and pH of the surrounding soil (Chung et al., 2004). It is therefore useful to sample the surrounding soil in the area of the inhumation and determine the physical characteristics of the site to include temperature, pH, and moisture content (Horswell et al., 2002). Although these data have no direct bearing on the ultimate DNA profile, it will help design the sample preparation protocols and guide future efforts. Unfortunately, there is no totally accurate way of predicting whether a particular sample will produce a reliable profile. However, techniques such as 'flash pyrolysis' followed by gas chromatography and mass spectroscopy (see James and Norby, 2002, for details of these techniques) (Stankiewicz et al., 1997; Poinar and Stankiewicz, 1999) look promising. It is therefore a case of taking a number of different samples and processing them to determine whether DNA can be obtained and then profiling the DNA to determine if it is of sufficient quality and human in origin (Swango et al., 2005). Samples taken should include, wherever possible, at least two of the following, listed in order of importance: intact molar or incisor teeth (Gaytmenn and Sweet, 2003); a small complete bone either tarsal or metatarsal; a piece of muscle c. 1 to 4 cm²; or a small bundle (c. 0.5 cm in diameter) of hair (with root, so pulled, not cut) (Holland et al., 2003).

Care should be taken to obtain samples that are not too heavily contaminated with soil or other material. If this cannot be avoided, then no attempt should be made to 'clean' the sample in the field. Instead, a note should be made regarding the nature of the contamination, and the sample should be frozen as soon as possible, without the addition of any preserving agents such as formaldehyde. Samples should be stored in 14-ml or 50-ml Falcon tubes, labelled, security tagged, and cross-referenced to the body ID. The best way of storing samples is in a freezer at –20°C. At this temperature, samples will remain stable for about a month (Atmadja et al., 1995). If, however, they are intended to be kept for longer in an unprocessed form, then they will need to be stored at –70°C to –196°C (liquid nitrogen) (Mitchell et al., 2005). The availability of sufficient, and adequately cold, freezer space in the field may well be a serious consideration. It should be considered whether it is better to process the tissue samples to DNA in the field or to ship them frozen, back to the country of analysis, in as short a period as possible. Practical considerations will dictate the most appropriate route.

9.3.5   Field preservation of samples

If freezing facilities are not available, then the alternative is to place the samples in a preserving solution such as 20% PEG, 20% ethylene glycol-propylene glycol (E/P20) (Leal-Klevezas et al., 2000). This solution needs to be made before use, and samples need to be stored.

An alternative that does not need storage at –20°C is TNES (6 M urea; 10 mM Tris-HCl, pH 7.5; 125 mM NaCl; 10 mM EDTA; 1% SDS) (Asahida et al., 1996). This solution needs to be made up prior to shipping but has the advantage of being less hazardous than 4 M guanidine thiocyanate, 0.5% sarcostyle, which has traditionally been used. The solution should be stored in dark glass bottles. Sufficient solution should be added to totally cover the sample. This will partly dissolve soft tissue, but more important, it will neutralise all nucleases, thus preserving the sample from further deterioration (Asahida et al., 1996). Samples can then be stored at room temperature in the dark until shipped back for processing. The advantage of this method is that it avoids requiring freezing facilities, and samples can be stored at ambient temperature. It does suffer from the drawback that the preserving solution is corrosive and needs to be handled with care; appropriate Control of Substances Hazardous to Health procedures must to be followed. Shipping large quantities of this solution will require special containment conditions to prevent leakage during transport. An alternative preservation solution is 4 M guanidine thiocyanate, and 0.5% sarcostyle (Muralidharan and Wemmer, 1994). This solution needs to be made up prior to shipping but is more hazardous than TNES. However, it is useful if the samples are going to be processed on-site.

As an alternative to the liquid method, soft tissue may also be preserved by desiccating the samples either by simply drying them in a hot environment or alternatively by the addition of solid NaCl to the sample. Salt will do no harm to the DNA (Kilpatrick, 2002). This method is usually performed in the presence of 20% DMSO; however, it works satisfactorily if samples are then frozen. Once the samples are returned to the laboratory, they are washed and the DNA extracted. This method has obvious advantages over the liquid method. However, the NaCl does not afford any protection against the action of nucleases, particularly if the sample has residual moisture.

A quick method to preserve samples can be used when field conditions dictate a rapid response and all other methods are unavailable. The samples can be packed in dry or liquid laundry detergent. This may seem a dubious method, but laundry detergents are one of the most intensely researched products on the market. Although their exact make up is only known to a few, they are stated as containing EDTA, proteases, and lipases, which will help preserve DNA and neutralise the effect of nucleases (ibid.). The advantage of this method is that in most parts of the world laundry detergent is readily available in quantity and cheaply (Drabek and Petrek, 2002). This method may well be the most appropriate in the field.

9.3.6 Sample verification

Once an exhumation begins, a representative number of samples (as determined statistically) should be transported to the designated laboratory for analysis as soon as possible. This material will be processed, and the quality and quantity of DNA determined. From this material, a sample set of DNA profiles will be determined. This is done to ensure that the sampling and preservation methods are optimal, therefore resulting in a high proportion of usable profiles, and avoids the nightmare scenario of collecting hundreds of thousands of samples only to discover 6 to 12 months later that the material does not produce usable profiles. This is also the reason for collecting multiple samples and using multiple preservation techniques.

In cases of burnt remains, the choice of available material will be determined by what survives, as has been described in 8.5.2. In such circumstances, material from a selection of sources should be collected and taken to the laboratory for processing and analysis. Even unpromising material can retain enough DNA to produce a profile. As stated in 8.5.2, DNA in dental pulp generally survives better at high temperatures than bone because the temperature within the tooth is significantly lower than without (Duffy et al., 1991; Gaytmenn and Sweet, 2003).

9.3.7 Contamination issues

Throughout the duration of field activities, archaeologists, anthropologists, and pathologists involved in collection of samples should be aware of the importance of keeping their instruments, containers, and reagents clean (Rutty et al., 2000; Aslanzadeh, 2004) This is crucial to prevent cross-contamination from one body to the next, or from the collecting member of staff to the sample (Sullivan et al., 2004). The use of commercial protective suits is compulsory (Rutty et al., 2003). Dissecting instruments should be cleaned in a DNA removing solution, such as DNAaway,[1] between bodies. If storage of samples in the same container is unavoidable, polyethylene sacks or similar may be used to separate individual samples.

An attempt should be made at the time of sample collection to remove all dirt and contaminating organisms (e.g., epiphytes, fungi, ectoparasites) from the bone or tissue sample. It will not be possible to remove all such organisms (e.g., endoparasites, gut flora), but this problem can be circumvented by judicious tissue choice. Mites and other small relevant insects are a particularly problematic contaminant of field-collected samples. Not only can these arthropods destroy specimens, they can also cross-contaminate a collection as they move about. In addition, the removal of contaminating organisms is important for preventing the introduction of foreign organisms across international borders. Once the majority of contaminating organisms is removed, the sample can be preserved using one of the methods outlined previously (Kilpatrick, 2002). The process of preservation will kill or render inactive all residual microorganisms, parasites, and fungi. Even though the sample can appear badly contaminated with DNA from a number of sources other than the individual under investigation, this will not significantly affect the DNA profile because the DNA markers will have been chosen to be human specific (Borst et al., 2004).

Inevitably, proximity in a mass grave context, especially in a secondary or subsequent grave where bodies will be commingled and body parts become detached, can lead to cross-contamination of DNA and potentially mistaken reassociation of body parts. It is therefore important to ensure that samples are taken in a manner that ensures continuity (Sullivan et al., 2004). If there is a genuine mix-up at the time of sample collection, then this will be revealed during the profiling process by the presence of a spurious profile. This can be minimised by the collection of hair root samples wherever possible because this has been shown to be less susceptible to cross-contamination (Gilbert et al., 2006).

Contamination of samples by personnel who have handled the body postmortem is a concern but generally of practically little significance unless a gross contamination event occurs. From the time of death until the sample is collected, up to 20 people may have come in contact with the body. Some of these will be field personnel, while others may have been perpetrators of the crime. It is virtually impossible to eliminate accidental contamination of the samples with small quantities of exogenous DNA from hair, sweat, saliva, blood, or other bodily fluids (Torres et al., 2003). When such contaminations occur, the DNA profile will produce a ghost profile in the background of the victim profile. When this occurs, the profile

---

[1] Made by Molecular BioProducts, Inc. Phone: 800-995-2787; Fax: 858-453-4367.

is repeated with a new sample, and identification of the victim can proceed. The question arises as to the source of the ghost profile. Personnel involved in fieldwork can easily be eliminated by comparing their profile with the ghost profile. If the profile is still not eliminated, then the ghost profile may be potential evidence linking a perpetrator with the victim. Mission personnel may be asked to give a DNA sample for elimination purposes (Rutty, 2000).

Samples will be contaminated from insect and microbial sources. This will then be processed to DNA and form part of the DNA pool, which will then be used in the DNA profiling process. The primers used in the profiling process have been designed to specifically amplify human DNA. There is, however, the possibility that DNA may be amplified from a nonhuman source. This type of anomaly will be picked up in the profiling process.

9.3.8 Recording, packing, labelling, and transporting

As with all forensic evidence from mass disposal sites, the handling of DNA samples, including storage and handover, must be undertaken in collaboration with the mortuary SCE who will allocate numbers to samples and ensure that all due process is followed to ensure continued evidential integrity. A recording form must be completed recording all details of the evidence number, location of sample, sample collection method, treatment, and processing (for further details, see Mortuary Sample Recording Form [MC14F]). Sturdy, internally padded packaging should be used when transporting tissue samples. All external labels should be clearly marked with permanent ink and covered with a plastic sheet. A list of materials included, with relevant names, addresses, and telephone numbers, should be enclosed for the benefit of customs officials and to help recipients determine whether the package has been tampered with.

When transporting conventional field-gathered samples, the outside of the package should be marked 'BIOMEDICAL SAMPLES FOR SCIENTIFIC RESEARCH – PLEASE RUSH', although for most packages, the words 'SCIEN-TIFIC SPECIMENS FOR RESEARCH' will suffice. Also customs forms should clearly indicate that the contents have 'NO COMMERCIAL VALUE'. The choice of words here may need to be modified according to specific circumstances. Before transportation of samples, ensure that holidays (civic and religious) will not impede or delay the delivery of packages. It is also prudent to avoid weekends. These considerations are especially critical for frozen samples. Recipients should be called, faxed, or contacted via e-mail on the date of dispatch and notified of the expected arrival of the package and the air bill or tracking number. Recipients should be informed as to whether they can expect delivery or should collect their samples, and are advised to bring multiple copies of any permits or documentation necessary for collection. If transporting across international boundaries, colleagues on both sides should be intimately involved in the process (Nederhand et al., 2003).

DO NOT USE IN DISSERTATION

9.4 Forensic odontology

9.4.1 Introduction

The use of dentition in identifying victims in atrocity crimes and in mass disaster incidents is considerable, especially when such victims come from a society with formal dental treatment where detailed dental records are kept (see Clement, 1998, for a good overview). The presence of restorations (e.g., fillings, crowns) is a major factor in identification, and this varies according to the incidence of dental disease in different ancestral groups and the standard and availability of dental treatment. However, in atrocity crime investigations, antemortem records may be difficult to obtain or may have been destroyed (Strinovic et al., 1994). It is also useful to compare dentition with recent family photographs in which the individual is smiling and revealing his or her teeth. This is helpful when an individual had a marked over- or underbite, or with juveniles where the presence of mixed deciduous and permanent dentition is present. With the aid of good antemortem intraoral photographs and radiographs, it is possible to undertake a full mouth charting (Clark, 1994). Dimensions, spacing, restorations, discolouration, or even misalignment provide characteristics useful for comparison, or it may be possible to superimpose the two different images of the teeth. This form of comparison, if applicable and appropriate, is an easy, inexpensive, and quick method of contributing to identification. In mass disaster recoveries, some regions and countries have their own dental identification teams (Bowers, 2004), some of which form a component of larger multidisciplinary identification teams.

9.4.2 Personnel

The forensic odontologist is a qualified dental practitioner with additional formal training and relevant experience in the medicolegal aspects of dentistry. The decision to use forensic odontology in a given context should be agreed on by the mortuary management team, taking into account the advice of the forensic odontologist involved. Clearly, unless detailed and current dental records exist for victims and are accessible, the potential of odontological evidence to assist in determining identification is limited. Nonforensic dentists, dental specialists, or dental auxiliary who might take part in the examination should, whenever possible, receive appropriate training in forensic odontology. A distinction has to be made between a dentist and a forensic odontologist. That is, although all qualified dentists throughout the world are capable of carrying out a detailed examination of the mouth, they are not all experienced in carrying out this function on the dead. Note that the term 'qualified dentists' has been used. In some countries, dentistry is undertaken by unqualified 'dentists', and experience has shown that there will be no antemortem records for comparison purposes in these countries. When only a nonforensic dentist is available, he or she should be capable of undertaking the same level of postmortem examination as the pathologist (*vide infra*), but caution needs to be exercised due to the lack of relevant experience. Although nonforensic dentists are useful for assessing antemortem records of their country of residence, they may need instruction on how to obtain international records, and they may be unfamiliar with a computer disaster victim identification (DVI) program. Training should be provided where necessary. If positive identification of human remains is to be based solely on odontology, the involvement of a forensic odontologist is essential. If the dental evidence is only a contributory part of the identification, involvement of a forensic odontologist is desirable but not essential. A good dental DVI software programme will eliminate a considerable amount of manual checking, producing a list of the most likely matches in order of probability. The computer does not make an identification but reduces the number of records to be compared. The dental team makes the final decision.

Pathologists will, as part of their routine postmortem examination, carry out an examination of the mouth. In normal circumstances, this will be mainly for the purposes of examining for injuries or pathology and will not be a detailed examination of the dentition. Anthropologists can normally collect and record dental data to a standard equivalent to a dentist. The level of experience of anthropologists in antemortem data collection depends entirely on the individual and his or her professional background. It can vary between none and that equivalent to a forensic odontologist. An experienced anthropologist is capable of collating different data. The anthropologist should be able to carry out a comparison of an antemortem record with postmortem findings. In small numbers, up to one hundred bodies, comparison of ante- and postmortem dental records is possible without a computer by sifting into groups such as male and female, adults and children, and those with and without fillings, bridges, dentures, and so on. In larger groups, the use of a computer dental identification program is essential. Such a program will require a trained operator to input the data and an anthropologist who is familiar with the program. Where a tentative positive identification is obtained, the anthropologist should be capable of interpreting the result. However, this information should then be compared with other biological and evidential indicators of identity and, of course, DNA where undertaken.

The next section describes what may be reasonably expected of the odontologist, pathologist, or anthropologist in carrying out (a) the forensic odontological examination, (b) the collection of antemortem records, and (c) the interpretation of ante- and postmortem records and any ensuing identification.

9.4.3 Procedure for dental identification

Positive identification is possible by dental comparison alone. This is because every human normally has thirty-two teeth comprising up to five surfaces, thereby giving rise to a possible total of 160 surfaces. The number of combinations with restored (or decayed) surfaces, missing teeth, misaligned or rotated teeth, anomalous teeth, supernumerary teeth, prosthesis, restorations, surgical procedures, and root canal treatment makes one's dentition virtually unique. This can facilitate conclusive identification of the individual, where reliable, detailed, and current antemortem dental records exist.

The procedures of dental identification are credible because of a number of factors. These include the fact that human dentition has good postmortem preservation, and that dental restorations and prostheses are also extremely resistant to physical and chemical deterioration and to changes to the environment. The unique morphological characteristics of human teeth and dental restorations have great individuality, and the availability of routine dental treatment records, especially radiographs and models, provide useful and detailed evidence for comparison. In some regions, prostheses are marked with the deceased's identification numbers or name, and these can contribute to identification. However, denture marking is not routine and has been found to be of limited use (Ayton et al., 1985).

The forensic odontologist should always have his or her own basic equipment. This is described in Table 9–3.

9.4.4 Age assessment in neonates and infants

Age estimation of neonates, infants, and juveniles can be reasonably accurate. Although radiographic survey of calcifying dental cusps and stages of dental development can be extremely useful in those older than 3 years, for younger infants it is necessary to use histological techniques to examine the mineralised cusps of the dentition. There is a marked time lag between the initial stages of cusp calcification as apparent between histological and radiographic methods. Early mineralisation is detectable up to 12 weeks before it becomes apparent on a radiograph. These require removal of the mandible and maxilla to facilitate scientific analysis, but radiographs should be taken before beginning any such dissection. In a dry skeletonised jaw of a neonate, the small developing mineralised tooth cusps will be found lying loose in their dental crypts and will require careful retrieval. For older juveniles (older than 3 years), radiography alone may be sufficient. Lateral oblique radiographic views of both sides have proved to be the most effective views for age assessment. There are several dental development surveys published (Schour and Massler, 1941; Ubelaker, 1987), and subject to their originating from an appropriate reference sample, they can provide excellent comparison charts for assessment purposes (Ciapparelli, 1992).

9.4.5 Forensic odontological examination and recording

The procedure for dental identification includes the forensic postmortem odontological examination, collection of antemortem records, interpretation of ante- and postmortem records, comparison, and identification or exclusion.

Table 9–3. *Equipment for forensic odontology*

Lighting

- Illuminated* mouth mirror
- Illuminated* retractor
- Head light

Examination

- Swann Morton PM40 scalpel blades and handles
- Small screwdriver for changing blades
- Stainless steel autopsy saw for sawing through maxilla and ascending rami
- Rongeurs for trimming sharp bone from the sawn maxilla
- Skull keys (to gain access by placing in the retromolar fossae)
- Mouth props and mouth gaga
- Surgical scissors and large haemostats for freeing soft tissue
- Large rat-teeth tweezers
- Self-retaining lip retractors
- At least three dental mirrors (not plastic handles); the type used in surgery are best
- Dental mouthy mirrors
- Dental probes
- Tweezers
- Spatula
- Small sponges
- Toothbrushes, including interproximal brushes
- Small garden sprays
- Upper and lower forceps
- Elevators
- Alginate

For taking impressions

- Water and powder measures
- Disposable impression trays of various dentate sizes

Stationary (much of this may not be needed if data are entered directly into an electronic database)

- Dental charts
- Interpol charts
- Consent forms
- Clipboard
- Ballpoint and felt-tip pens, pencils
- Fluid correction pen
- Bite mark rulers
- Adhesive scales
- Self-adhesive labels
- Tie-on labels and string
- Notebook and paper
- Paper clips and rubber bands
- Dictaphone

Miscellaneous

- Self-sealing plastic bags
- Specimen pots
- Concentrated air deodorant
- Illuminated magnifying glass
- Small illuminated radiographic viewer
- Cyanoacrylate glue or similar product for securing brittle burnt teeth
- Etching brushes for handling and applying glue
- Spare batteries
- Cotton wool rolls
- Throat packs
- Plastic food box with an airtight lid

* Must be battery operated.
Source: Adapted from Clark, 1994.

It is desirable to conduct the following examinations: postmortem dental charting, intra- and extraoral photography, and radiography. The first stage of the dental identification process is the dental examination of each recovered victim and the preparation of the postmortem record (MO33F). The information recorded is then transferred to the computer.

Because it may not be known what records will be found, the postmortem examination must be very thorough and complete, often with radiographs, photographs, and models. Portable dental x-ray units should be available if possible. Self-processing films can be used if no darkroom or processing facilities are available. This can also be a time-saving process, although caution must be expressed because the quality of these self-processing films is poor, and the image will deteriorate rapidly with time (Whaites, 1992). In other situations, the intraoral video camera system can be used to provide excellent multi-image displays of the dentition. In addition, such equipment can also provide excellent hard copy printouts for documentation and future presentation in courts.

Discussion of recording dentition by anthropologists is found in 8.4. As stipulated there, the Fédération Dentaire International or FDI system (1971) will be used. However, odontologists generally favour the use of the Interpol recording form, which can be located at on the Interpol web pages. See http://www.interpol.com. The features and pathologies that are generally recorded for comparison in a dental identification process are also further described in 8.4. Additional detail includes that, where observed, it is essential to record the partial deficit of the tooth caused by dental caries, detachment of restorations, or tooth fracture. This should be indicated on the recording form (MO33F) by highlighting the surface, but not blocking it out. Because the deficit of a front tooth might occur because of externally caused injury, it should be careful examined. Each geometric square on the chart (Figure 9–9) should be completed to show the surfaces covered by restorations. Restorations may be fillings, crowns, or bridges; each type should also be described in the appropriate descriptive box. Because materials for tooth restoration are made of metal or materials with tooth colour, they must also be described. Dental restorations that are made of metal are shown by black, and the type of metal should be described, if known. Those with tooth colour are shown by oblique lines. An alternative method is the use of colour felt-tip pens, indicating amalgam restorations in black, gold in red, and tooth colour restorations in green. Where a gold crown has a tooth colour facing, the lingual (back) part of the box is marked in red and the buccal (front) surface in green. The method used for the restorations should be recorded at the same time. When a material is not known, the colour should be indicated. Where radiography is available, root canal treatment, implants, and embedded teeth may be described and the x-rays attached to the form for any antemortem or postmortem comparison. Any abnormality of the occlusion or arch, crowding of the front teeth, or soft tissue abnormality or damage should be recorded and described in detail. Crowned or unusual anterior dentition should be photographed because this may aid the process of identification. Intraoral photography of the dentition is valuable but not essential.

Radiographs provide excellent diagnostic and treatment guides during dental procedures. As with photographs, radiographs also provide excellent records for the identification process (Kerr and Murray, 1971). Dental radiographs are usually in the form of intraoral bitewing, periapical, and occlusal views. Useful extraoral

BINDING HOLES

P ost M ortem *(pink)* **VICTIM IDENTIFICATION FORM** **F2**

DEAD BODY

Nature of disaster :	**No** :
Place of disaster :	*Sex unknown* ☐
Date of disaster : ☐☐ *Day* ☐☐ *Month* ☐☐☐☐ *Year*	*Male* ☐ *Female* ☐

86	**DENTAL FINDINGS in permanent teeth (Notify temporary teeth specifically)**		
11	Tooth fracture	Tooth fracture	**21**
12	Intact	Porcelain facing crown, Root canal filling	**22**
13	Intact	Resin filing (O)	**23**
14	Resin filling (O)	Amalgam filing (O)	**24**
15	Inlay (MOD), silver in colour	Inlay (OD), silver in colour	**25**
16	Crown, silver in colour	Crown, silver in colour, Root canal filling	**26**
17	Decayed tooth (OM)	Intact	**27**
18	Intact	Missing	**28**

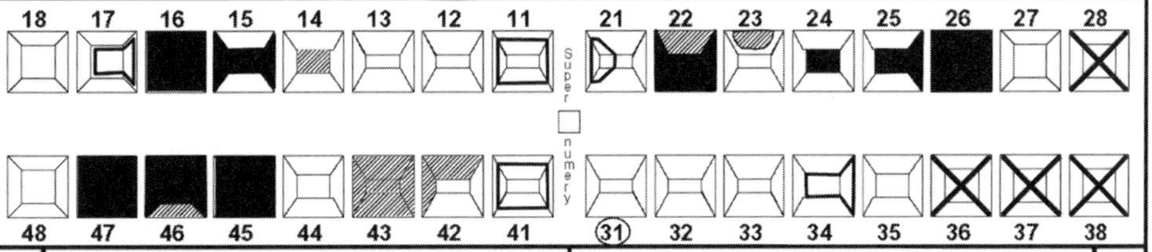
18 17 16 15 14 13 12 11
21 22 23 24 25 26 27 28
Super numerary
48 47 46 45 44 43 42 41
31 32 33 34 35 36 37 38

48	Partially erupted	Missing	**38**
47	Crown, silver in colour	Missing, Denture (resin tooth)	**37**
46	Intact	Missing, Denture (resin tooth)	**36**
45	Pontic (resin facing), silver in colour	Intact	**35**
44	Inlay (MOD), silver in colour	Under root canal treatment	**34**
43	Crown, silver in colour	Intact	**33**
42	Decayed tooth (OM)	Intact	**32**
41	Intact	Missing	**31**

87	**Specific description of** Crowns, bridges, dentures and implants	47-45: Bridge with resin facing pontic 37, 36, 44: Denture with lingual bar, castclasp at 43 and 45, and wire clasp at 35
88	**Further findings** Occlusion, attrition, anomalies, smoker, periodontal status, etc.	Normal occlusion 11, 12, 41: tooth fracture
89	**X-rays taken of** Type and region	11, 21, 22: Dental x-ray 25-27: Dental x-ray
90	**Supplementary examination**	
91	**Estimated age**	*Method ?*

BINDING HOLES

[(GB) Version 2002]

Figure 9–9. Example of recording forensic odontological examination on an Interpol recording form.

radiographs include the various maxillofacial views, oblique lateral jaw views, and dental panoramic radiographs. The maxillofacial views also provide comparison of the frontal sinuses, which is considered unique to every individual and may be of significant value in establishing identification (Harris et al., 1987a, 1987b; Kullman et al., 1990; Reichs, 1993). Furthermore, extraoral radiographs can offer additional information, particularly where there is evidence that the individual had received orthodontic or other dental therapy prior to death. The matching potential of the teeth, maxilla, and mandible – particularly tori, sinuses and configuration of the base and vault of the skull are extremely useful. Maxillary sinus configuration is also usually visible in upper molar periapical x-rays. The medullary bone of the mandible and maxilla may possess a characteristic trabecular pattern, which will be recorded on x-ray. In addition, root shape and angulation, crown morphology, bone loss due to periodontitis, interproximal caries, and specific changes in pulp cavity outline may also be assessed.

Impacted teeth, anomalous and supernumerary teeth, dilacerated or retained roots, developmental or other cysts, and nutrient canals may also be evident through radiography. Because root anatomy and bone structure will not change significantly with age, they will not impede identification. Apart from fine details of anatomy and disease, dental restorations, root canal fillings, and bases under fillings can be recorded accurately. Dental materials are also usually radiodense. Metallic restorations and other intracoronal techniques such as retentive pins, endodontic posts, cements, and obturation materials contribute to a wealth of fine discriminatory features that support the use of dental radiographs in identification (Maclean et al., 1994). The location, shape, size, and unique characteristics of each restoration can be compared with great accuracy when examining ante- and postmortem dental radiographs. If possible, take two lateral oblique radiographs. These will indicate most root treatments and impacted teeth, and can also contribute to age estimation.

9.4.6   Collection of antemortem records

Information sources that may be available for constructing antemortem dental records include a clinical dental record, x-rays (dental and panoramic x-ray), models or casts, and intraoral photographs of the deceased. These may be obtainable from the relevant dentist whose name should be available from the next of kin. Such records must be sued with some caution because there can be problems with them, including notation variability, incompleteness, inaccuracy, misinterpretation, and fraud (discussed in Clement, 1998). As noted previously, a recent photograph supplied by the family and showing the person in question smiling, in addition to hospital records, may also be helpful. If the relatives indicate that the missing person had previously been investigated in the hospital for a head injury, then there is a strong possibility that one of the radiographic views of the skull will demonstrate the frontal sinuses, which are themselves almost as unique to individuals as fingerprints

(Clement, 1998). They are particularly useful once the third molars have erupted (Feik and Glover, 1998).

Involvement of forensic odontology in antemortem data collection is not essential, but is desirable. If antemortem data are to be extracted from dental records this work must be undertaken by someone with knowledge of dental recording. This could be a dentist or dental specialist, appropriately trained dental auxiliary or dental nurse. Forensic odontologists are in the best position to provide such training. If antemortem data relevant to dental identification is to be collected from other sources (e.g., interviews with the families of the Missing), it is important to liaise with psychosocial workers undertaking such interviews to ensure that all relevant data are collected in a useful form for the odontologist.

10

Antemortem data collection: Interaction with families and communities

Margaret Samuels

10.1 Introduction

To provide a context for the reactions and needs of families with missing persons, as well as the reactions of forensic and mental health professionals, it is important to understand the ways in which war and atrocity crime trauma, and traumatic grief, affect survivors and impact the antemortem data (AMD) and identification process. It has to be stressed that those undertaking psychosocial work in any context, particularly in such a traumatic and complex context as the investigation of atrocity crimes, must have had relevant professional training and experience.

'Helping professionals' (in this chapter referred to as 'psychosocial workers',) may need to initiate contact with the families of missing people and be responsible for assisting families in the AMD collection process. This may take place at a viewing of clothes or other recovered artefacts, or at an exhumation site. Where possible, it is important for forensic teams to engage local psychosocial assistance when forensic work is being undertaken in a community affected by postconflict issues. International forensic teams will ideally include or work with a mental health consultant to assist the team in supporting families and identifying local capacity to engage in the process. Families need to know that psychosocial professionals can be a bridge to the forensic/exhumation teams and will assist families with the events. Psychosocial professionals are in a good position to collect and record antemortem information, and let families know how they can help identify bodies by providing detailed information about their loved ones. Families will have many questions that must be addressed. Perhaps the forensic team is the first independent organization in the area, and so there is a need to offer a supportive intervention.

Psychosocial workers may need to both offer and provide support to families with missing family members. In one example, such a professional learned from a group of family members waiting at an exhumation site that they were all worried about one particular woman. They reported that this woman had lost three close family members. Away from the others, the psychosocial worker sat beside the woman and asked her whom she lost and how it happened. For the next 2 hours, the social worker listened as the woman told her story. As the woman talked, the psychosocial worker gently urged her to continue, and when the woman cried, the psychosocial worker held her hand but did not attempt to stop the tears. The psychosocial worker visited the woman several times after that day. Eventually, the woman's family members were identified and reburied. In this way, the woman was able to go through the grieving process.

If children are present, it may be helpful for the psychosocial worker to provide them with paper and markers. Children can be invited to draw whatever they want. The psychosocial worker should be prepared for children's drawings to reflect the events of the day, or the events that led to the killing of their family members. Afterwards, children may be asked to talk about their drawings. Their feelings and fears should be validated, and their courage in the face of such danger should be highlighted. Follow-up visits to the child and his or her family might be necessary. In one instance, a 12-year-old saw his father and ten other family members killed. He was asked to be a witness for an international tribunal investigation. The psychosocial worker was able to assist by talking to the young boy after he was interviewed by a forensic investigator, and they used this as an opportunity to develop rapport with the child. A few days later, the psychosocial worker visited the child at home to continue talking about his tragedy; subsequent visits followed.

10.2 Antemortem data collection

AMD consists of detailed information describing a missing person or a person believed to be dead. Those family members who were the last to see the missing person may be asked questions about that person during his or her life and at the time of disappearance. This information will be compared with findings from the recovered bodies (postmortem data collected by forensic pathologists and anthropologists) to determine whether any of the information coincides. An illustrative guide to how AMD fit into the broader investigative and identification process can be see in Figure 10–1. Antemortem data recording forms are usually designed by the organisation responsible and reflect the mission in hand and its context. No such recording form is presented with this book.

Interviewers should always remember that participation in AMD collection is completely *voluntary* for informants and/or families. Families with missing must be

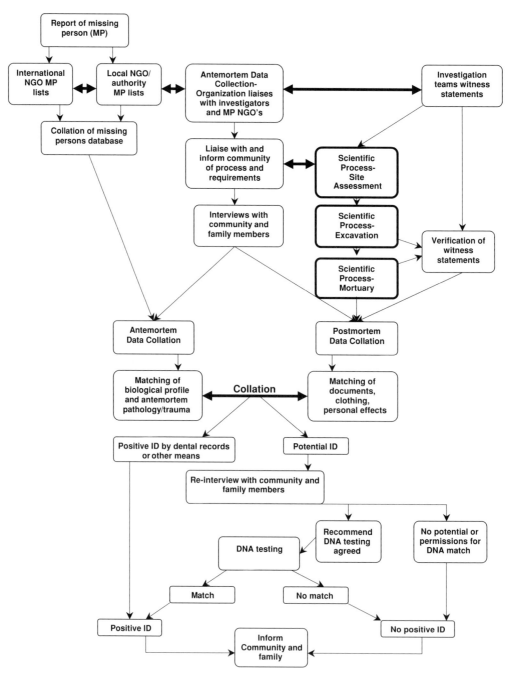

Figure 10–1. Relationship between the scientific process and AMD collection. *Source:* Adapted from Keough et al., 2004.

assisted in understanding the purposes of the AMD collection and how it relates to possible identifications. In other cases, informants may be too upset to participate, or may have mental or physical conditions that could be exacerbated by answering questions about their missing loved ones. In such circumstances, attempts should be made to locate another family member who may be able to give information about the missing person. The informant's wishes should be thoroughly respected by the interviewer, and the psychosocial worker must refrain from trying to persuade the family to give information. Organizations involved in AMD collection may organize and deliver a community education process prior to actually collecting data; this will help ensure 'community buy-in'.

10.2.1 Engaging informants

Clear demonstration of the psychosocial worker's sincerity and genuine interest in the informant and their situation will be important in establishing rapport. Following is an example of an appropriate introduction of the AMD process for families:

We are working in collaboration with forensic scientists and medical doctors to assist with the identification of bodies exhumed from mass graves. The information we collect will be compared with the data which the expert teams of forensic doctors find on the bodies. If the data from our questionnaire and the data obtained through postmortem examination of bodies match, this will be only the first step toward identification of the missing person. We don't know if we will find your missing person through the process, but if a body is recovered, antemortem information provides us the best chance for identification. We do not know the identity of the bodies found and exhumed from mass graves. Obtaining as much information as possible from the families will increase the possibility for the identification of the exhumed bodies. Your information will help begin the process of identifying bodies. We do not know what condition we will find the bodies in. If the grave is very big it may take much time to identify all the bodies. If the burial conditions have been severe, it may be quite difficult to identify individuals. The questions we will ask will include information about the physical appearance of your loved one, his or her medical and dental history, and personal belongings and clothing the missing had with them at the time of disappearance. The information you give today will be treated as confidential. We will not discuss this information with others unless we have your informed permission to do so. Do you have any questions before we begin the survey? Are you ready to begin?

Sometimes families may have difficulty beginning their story or organizing their thoughts. The data collector may use the following: 'You heard they were soldiers, but you don't know what happened?' Or the data collector might want to approach a family in an information-seeking role, for example, 'Can you help us in completing our files? Can you go back before the war, just a little bit before the war?' If the family member is confused, stop him or her, and if he or she is not speaking about the dead person, bring him or her back to the topic. Ask the family about their feelings, perceptions, and experiences during the conflict. For example: 'Was it cold or not, were you hungry?', 'Were you threatened by someone?', 'Did you hear something? When and where?' Keep bringing the informant back to the discussion, back to the difficult topics. Remember that survivors do need to talk about these topics and may avoid doing so with family members. However, do not forget to empathize with them. Never force them to talk about things that they do not want to discuss or demand that they talk when they do not want to.

10.2.2 Data collection tool

AMD questionnaires are designed to collect the most useful information from informants to aid in identifying mortal remains recovered as a result of exhumations. It is imperative that collaboration with forensic anthropologists and pathologists informs their design. A basic guideline for administering any survey instrument is to use standardized techniques in asking questions. Standardization requires that all interviewers ask a question in the same way and read the question as written. In some cases, the respondent will jump ahead in telling his or her story. It is important to both listen and follow the flow of the survey to ensure that no questions are missed and that all data are collected. AMD collection surveys will differ from country to country and event to event. Interpol has a basic AMD form (see http://www.interpol.int/Public/DisasterVictim/Forms/AMFormEng.pdf) that can be adapted for various events and cultural contexts (Keough and Samuels, 2004). The Interpol AMD form is available in English, French, Spanish, and Arabic, and was used in 1999 by the Belgian DVI Team working in Cikatova, Kosovo. For Kosovo, the form required several translation revisions, and was adapted for the culture and region in which it was to be used. Color charts and various prompt forms were also designed locally to enhance the form.

Questions and answers should be written in a format that is easy to 'code', and for compatibility, it is recommended that the Interpol codes should be used where possible. Any code used should facilitate easy data entry into a database designed for AMD. As much as possible, prompts should be used with corresponding codes that can be entered into a computer program for analysis. This should include colour charts and illustrations of clothing types. Shoes and body diagrams should be used, measuring tapes for determining height should be available, and a recent photograph should be requested (Keough et al., 2000). Regional clothing and personal effects diagrams need to be prepared beforehand. Knowledge of whether hair dyes, tattoos, or dental jewellery is common in the particular community is essential.

10.2.3 Engaging appropriate staff

It may be necessary to use translators when conducting interviews because fully trained/qualified psychosocial workers with working knowledge of local dialects may not be available. In these cases, it is essential to use translators who will not influence the responses of the witness. In cases when impartial translators (who are removed emotionally or politically from the events) cannot be found, it may be necessary to try alternative methods of conducting interviews. For example, both questions and answers can be recorded on video- or audiotape. To assist in clarification and to make sure the witnesses are answering the questions adequately, a translator can be made available. The tapes themselves can be translated later. Obviously, however, questions must be translated before the interviews commence. Training on using the data collection tool and how to perform a standardized interview are essential. Staff conducting AMD interviews should be very familiar with the form and coding characteristics.

Cultural anthropologists and religious and/or community leaders may be interviewed before a major data collecting operation is undertaken to ensure that the correct questions are asked. For example, in Muslim communities where a man may have several wives, it may be necessary to ask for names of, and interview, all wives. If time and conditions permit, interviews maybe audio- or videotaped. This allows the information to be double-checked at a later date; however, issues of informant comfort level, confidentiality, and data protection must be considered before any taping occurs.

10.2.4 Elements of an antemortem data tool

The interviewer's name and place of location, as well as the date, name, and contact information of the informant, should be noted. It is critical to obtain a date of birth and to record any official documents identifying the missing person and the last known address or location of the missing person. Attempts should be made to ascertain if there may have been other individuals, or groups of individuals, who disappeared together and that, therefore, may be found together. Knowing in whose custody the Missing were being held may provide information on how people disappeared. There are two types of information that might be yielded by an interviewee: 'firsthand' and 'secondhand' information. Firsthand information is effectively a primary source of information that the informant either saw or experienced him- or herself. Informants should be asked when the person disappeared and when they last saw the missing person. If the information does not qualify as firsthand, it should be collected as secondhand information in another area of the data form. Secondhand information is effectively a secondary source of information and can be that which has been told to or passed on to the informant by another person. Essentially, the informant did not experience any of the information him- or herself. The relationship of the interviewee to the missing person may indicate the reliability of the information. All the dates and location for when the secondhand informant last saw the missing person should be recorded in the same way as for firsthand information. This information will be used as leads and contacts for follow-up. As with firsthand information, if the informants saw others who disappeared at the same time, this will be useful in helping identify groups or cohorts who might have disappeared together.

Attempting to determine possible information on death and burial is particularly difficult, but questions need to be asked to determine a number of issues. These include determining the precise location of where the person died and where the body might have been buried or disposed of, as well as the date that the informant saw the body. Corroborating detail regarding witnesses' names, contacts, and phone numbers is important, as is information about the burial site.

Obtaining detailed information on all types of clothing, including outer clothes, underwear, shoes, hats, and gloves, is essential. Many personal items, such as necklaces, cigarette cases, compact mirrors, and earrings, found during exhumation and in postmortem examination have aided in identifying people. Information that can be clearly and thoroughly described by informants should be recorded. Always ask the respondent to estimate the size and shape of the item and, if there is something special or unique about it, to draw a picture of it.

It is critical to have as much firsthand information about the physical characteristics of the missing person as possible. Ask the informant if he or she saw the person at the time of disappearance. Height can be estimated during postmortem examination (see 8.2), and it is therefore important information in assisting with the determination of identification. If the informant knows exactly how tall the person is (i.e., from a recent measurement), record it as such. If the informant is not sure and can give only an estimate or approximate height, ask the person to stand with you and point out how tall the missing person is compared to you. Ask the informant to estimate the difference in height between you and the Missing to determine how much taller or shorter the missing person is. Record the final standard measured height. Another useful comparator is an estimate of the height of the missing person against others within the community. Were they particularly tall or short? When no formal measurement of height is standard practice, this can be useful in comparing metrical data from different individuals and determining the identity of those of unusual height (see 8.2.3).

Hair is a body component that remains intact during decomposition, although oxidation can occur (makes dark hair red) and should be considered. However, it is one of the first components to separate from the body and can sometimes be difficult to assign to a particular body. It is important to determine colour and type (i.e., straight, wavy, curly) for those cases where hair is still detectable at time of postmortem. If the missing person is a woman, or in cultures where men also dye or perm their hair, include questions regarding perms, dye, and colouring. Also ask about facial hair (i.e., type, location, thickness, length, colour, style). It is important to ask the family about the colour of the missing person's eyes as part of the physical description. This can be useful information, even though eyes do not survive well postmortem and eye colour changes during the early stages of decomposition (i.e., blue eyes turn brown/black) (Jackson, 2001; Gomez, 2005). Eyeglasses may be found among personal effects, so a description of the frames from the family will be helpful. Diopter measurement of contact lenses would also be useful because both soft and hard contact lenses can survive burial and close proximity to decomposing soft tissues (Jackson, 2001), and still retain their diopter qualities. If the missing person wore contact lenses, then details of his or her prescription is also a valuable tool.

In some cases, skin is discernible on postmortem examination. If skin is intact at postmortem, large moles or discolouration from birthmarks may be visible. Skin can also be modified. Tattoos can be visible or invisible,[1] and evidence of what may be sites of removed tattoos[2] should also be noted. Informants should be asked whether the Missing had any tattoos, and if so, then it is important to record the position and design of them. When determining the size of the tattoo, use a probe by asking the informant to estimate size based on a familiar object, such as a coin or a person's hand. The interviewer should then estimate the measurement based on this comparison. Branding, or decorative scars made using heat, may also be evident on remains in some cultures.

Subject to the survival of skin, large or wide scars on the body should also be noted. This would indicate healing from some sort of injury or surgery. This information is potentially important for two reasons. In a minority of cases, the scar itself may still be apparent on postmortem examination. More likely, is that the injury resulting in the scar could be visible on the bones. For example, if an accident with farming equipment resulted in a severe cut on the forearm of the Missing and a broken bone, the damaged bone underneath may still be visible. Healed bones can often be detected from remains subject to the timing of the accident. In cultures where hand preference is not stigamatised, asking for information about left- or right-handedness can also provide useful AMD for comparison with measurements from the arm and shoulder (see 8.6).

Medical history can be very important (e.g., operations on the brain for tumours or other conditions are sometimes apparent in postmortem examinations). Operations that affect bones also leave indicators, and prosthetic implants such as pins will survive decomposition and interment (Ubelaker and Jacobs, 1995; Simmons and Haglund, 2005). The location of any such operations and implants must be recorded. Broken bones and healed fractures provide one of the most important clues in antemortem–postmortem comparison. When a person breaks or fractures a bone during his or her life, the natural healing of the bone results in a change in both the colour and texture of the bone, although this does disappear with time. However, if the break occurs at the moment of death, or shortly before death, the bones would have had no time to heal and would not show those particular characteristics common to healed fractures. If the person did have a broken bone, it is important to ask whether the person ever went to the doctor. Often, when a bone heals without a doctor's intervention and without a cast, there is a permanent deformity of the broken bone after it heals (see Figure 10–2). This may also be apparent on postmortem examination. Also, the doctor may have arranged for radiographs to

---

[1] Tattoos may be performed using normal and visible inks or reactive inks. The latter are a fluorescent dye that is openly visible under ultraviolet light. These are popular in nightclub cultures.

[2] Removal of tattoos may be undertaken using excision, dermabrasion, and laser salabrasion.

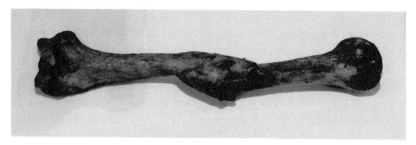

Figure 10–2. Permanent shortening and deformity of the left humerus of an adult male where a midshaft fracture has not been effectively treated. *Source:* Inforce Foundation.

be taken, and these may be available for comparative purposes. When talking to a relative, use a body diagram to record the appropriate location of the fracture.

Interviewers should also ask about congenital conditions a person may have been born with or developed during his or her life, such as limp arising from a congenital dislocation of the hip or a club foot, a hair lip or cleft palette, or other visible deformities. The postmortem examination may reveal missing body parts, especially arm, leg, foot, hand, finger, and toe. Many amputees have prostheses or artificial replacement limbs. If prostheses are found during postmortem examinations, they would provide excellent leads and matching criteria. Ask the informant for details concerning the presence and location of prostheses.

Frequently, bodies are recovered with the mandible, face, and skull still intact. Diagrams and visual aids can be used to determine whether the person has any significant dental history, including missing teeth or dental prostheses. When an informant can provide reliable information about *specific* teeth, use a simplified numbered dental chart. Recent photographs depicting an open smile can be useful in identification (see 9.4.6); alternatively, description of teeth can often be very specific. Because teeth are less prone to decomposition and damage than bone, they often remain intact more than any other element, especially in skeletonised remains. It is worth the effort of correctly recording this information with the assistance of dental diagrams. Ask if the relative had dental treatment.

Pregnancy can obviously be a distinguishing characteristic at postmortem and is, therefore, key information if the missing person is a female. Similarly, it is important to establish a woman's obstetric history because child birth can be determined skeletally, and both pregnancy and childbirth can be ascertained from soft tissues (see 7.6) (Cox and Scott, 1992; Cox, 2000b). Record all hospitalizations, and ask if there may be medical records.

DNA blood samples for mitochondrial DNA (see 9.3) can only be obtained through maternal relationships of the missing person. All possible living maternal relatives should be recorded, along with their contact information, to assist in follow-up should DNA become a possibility. Maternal relatives include the missing person's mother, any brothers and sisters with the same mother, and the mother's brothers and sisters.

Sometimes, medication, or the containers for medication, and personal medical equipment are found with remains. To optimize the value of these, ask the informant whether the missing person had any specific medical problems for which he or she took medication. Of special note would be asthma, skin conditions, high blood pressure, and diabetes, for which the person might be carrying medicines.

10.2.5 Informant rights and terminating the interview

Informants should be given an opportunity to add any additional information and to ask the data collector any questions. It is also important to leave contact information when possible, so the informant can provide additional information at a later date. Those collecting the data should acknowledge that participating in the interview is stressful for most families. The family should be thanked for their participation. Informants have rights, including data protection rights, and you can reinforce these by describing that care is taken with all personal information and by indicating how the AMD will be used in the identification process.

10.3 Viewing human remains and clothing

Eventually, some families may be invited to view clothes or pictures of clothes to assist with identification. It is important to warn family members that clothes will not look precisely as they did in life. They will be soiled and may be damaged. It is also necessary to warn families that recognition of a garment is not a guarantee of a person's identity because the captors sometimes switch the clothing of their victims. However, because clothing can be a strong clue to identity, it would then be linked to other clues, such as AMD given by the families. When the time comes, psychosocial workers can accompany family members as they view the clothing and be available if they are in need of support. Psychosocial staff can acknowledge how difficult it is for the person making the identification. In some cases, families have already been exposed to what is usually a pungent odour at excavation sites. Because the clothes themselves may give off a strong odour, families need to know what to expect. Typically, families have mixed feelings about the pending identification; that is, they do and do not want the final answer (Keough et al., 2004). Even when they say they know the loved one is dead and hope to find clothing they recognize, it will be difficult for them to confront the truth. The moment of recognition is typically the 'moment of death.' Sometimes, family members desire to touch the clothes, whereas others want to take pictures. These wishes may or may not be allowed, depending on the forensic team and judicial requirements. Psychosocial workers may need to advocate for the family's wishes, preferably discussing such issues in advance.

At one site in Kosovo in 1999, psychosocial workers were asked to accompany family members as they walked past clothing that had been laid out on large plastic sheets by the exhumation team. The psychosocial workers were asked to record which items the families recognized. This information was then given to the exhumation team to help with identification.

If the family wants to see the body or the remains, it is usually advisable that some support work is provided prior to the viewing. Families must know that their loved one will not look the same as he or she did in life. They may have been buried and have often decomposed to become virtually unrecognizable. In some situations, staff have found it helpful to suggest that families may want to keep the picture of their loved one in their mind, as he or she was when they last saw him or her, rather than to always have a picture of the horror of the mass grave remains associated with their memory. Often this helps the family member make the choice not to view the body. In the end, however, if a family member insists on a viewing and the forensic experts (i.e., pathologists, investigators) agree, it should ultimately be the family's right to see the remains (see 6.4.3 for further detail on how to manage viewings). This process must be established prior to the start of the exhumation so there is no confusion for team members or families. Families should be as prepared as possible to view remains, and if the situation permits, should view photos or any personal effects (as clean as possible) prior to seeing the actual remains.

The psychosocial worker should take the opportunity to support the family after the viewing of clothes. If identification is made, supportive comments regarding the family's strength and showing appreciation for the difficult emotion may be offered. At an appropriate point in time, the family could be reminded that now they can take the body and undertake funeral ceremonies as they would if their loved one had died normally. Now, he or she can stay in their memories.

In some cases, identification is not possible, and this can often be a more difficult situation for the family. Missing persons may be detained, in hiding, or not in the particular grave exhumed, and as such, it is not unrealistic for the families to hope for a safe return. Families may be directed to advocacy groups, but teams should never give 'false hope' to families. Certainly, every person is different, and reactions will vary according to the time elapsed since the event, age, gender, personality, degree of prior trauma, how closely related the person was, and, of course, cultural norms. Reactions witnessed in the field can be intense and may require additional resources.

10.4 Traumatic events and reactions

The basis for dealing with survivors of conflict and those with missing relatives is an understanding of the complexity of human reactions to trauma. Traumatic events generally involve threats to life or to body. They can involve close personal encounters with violence and death, including witnessing the death of others. The common denominator of psychological trauma is the feeling of intense fear, help-lessness and loss of control, and threat of annihilation (Yehuda, 2002). Traumatic events overpower the ordinary physical and psychic systems that give people a sense of control, connection, and meaning, and that help them through the adaptations of the life cycle. At the moment of exposure to a traumatic event, the victim is rendered helpless by overwhelming force. Traumatic reactions occur when the threat is so extreme that human action is of no avail. When neither resistance nor escape is possible, the human system of self-defence becomes overwhelmed and disorganized. Traumatic events produce profound and sometimes lasting changes in emotion, cognition, and memory. Studies have shown that this may be especially true for children, whose brains are still developing.

Traumatic events must be examined within their context. For example, in Kosovo (which is not dissimilar to many postconflict regions), as a result of ethnic conflict, approximately 4,000 people were missing (United Nations, 1999). Much of the population of Kosovo had been living for years with discrimination and despair, and many stresses had prevailed long before intervention by NATO forces in April 1999 (Physicians for Human Rights, 1999). Over time, consequences of oppression can create an environment of chronic tension and stress. Thus, the events of the war occurred against this backdrop, and the result may be described as cumulative trauma (Herman, 1992).

Physical reactions to trauma can include nausea, sleep disturbance, or rapid heartbeat. Emotional reactions can include fear, anger, guilt, memory lapses, difficulty concentrating, loss of faith, questioning of the meaning of life, and loss of purpose. There are many other very common reactions for those living in postconflict societies. These can include those described in the following sections (National Centre for PTSD, 2001b).

Hyperarousal. After traumatic experiences, the human system seems to go on permanent alert. The traumatized person startles easily, may react to small provocations, and may sleep poorly. Often, these reactions will subside over time, assuming a semblance of safety and 'normalcy' can be restored and that the victims are no longer exposed to traumatic events.

Intrusion/Re-experiencing. Long after the danger is past, traumatized persons relive the event as though it were continually recurring in the present. It can be seen as an attempt to 'master' the original experience where one felt so helpless. For children, traumatic play is repetitive play.

Search for meaning. Trauma permanently alters an individual's understanding of the world around him or her. Individuals constantly try to fit the traumatic events into a mental picture so they can understand and process the events. In one example of a family from Kosovo, an adult child was in a paramilitary force and was executed by opposing forces. She assumed a martyred position within the family and community. In this way, the family constructed a 'schema' whereby her death had meaning. This was an attempt at 'reframing' the event (Dziegielewski and Sumner, 2005). Many times, this assists families in resolving some of their traumatic feelings. However, in many cases, this can also lead to denial and an inability to accept the circumstances surrounding the traumatic event.

Shattered assumptions. Traumatic events may destroy the survivor's fundamental assumptions about the safety of the world, the positive value of the self, and the meaningful order of creation. It may destroy basic trust, leading to a sense of alienation, disconnection, and even aggression.

Vulnerability and resilience. In catastrophic events, the greater the exposure to the event, the greater is the chance of suffering symptoms of traumatic stress.

It can be assumed that anyone exposed to such horrors would normally have 'symptoms'. What is important is to look at the extremity of those reactions, the potential danger to self or others, and the longevity of symptoms. Each individual is different in his or her adaptation. Posttrauma studies (Kaul and Welzant, 2005) have shown that many people can reduce the stress they feel and the symptoms they experience due to their own resiliency. Yet, some people may need varying degrees of assistance and intervention. Some may develop posttraumatic stress disorder (PTSD), a psychological disorder characterized by exposure to a stress-inducing event (e.g., war, atrocity crimes, natural disasters) that leads to a series of symptoms that may include flashbacks, nightmares, anxiety, and depression.

Traumatic events, such as witnessing the death of family members, being threatened with bodily harm, and the loss of one's home, affect the entire family. Children and the elderly are particularly vulnerable. Because children, especially younger children, do not have the language skills to enable them to speak about what happened to them, they may hold feelings inside. This can result in poor concentration in school, nightmares, sleep problems, bedwetting, and other behaviours that are normal in much younger children. Children affected by trauma and grief may also 'act out' their feelings through aggressive behaviour. Traumatic events and traumatic grief may also be particularly stressful for the elderly, who are at a stage in life where they may be feeling vulnerable or their physical health may be failing. Children and the elderly are often present in the field when the forensic professional conducts their work. It is important to know how the events of the conflict and the events of the exhumations impact upon them. Often adults forget that children are taking everything in and have witnessed events along with the adults.

Upon recognition of clothing, some people feel numb and may go into shock. For example, one young wife identified her husband at the exhumation site. She became withdrawn and unable to respond to the crying and hugs of her two young children. The psychosocial worker acknowledged how difficult the process had been for the woman, how hard it had been for her to go through the identification process, and asked if she believed the experience might have also been difficult for her children. As the woman gradually became able to speak and then cry, the psychosocial worker encouraged the woman to comfort her children. Eventually, the young woman allowed herself to hold and kiss her children. She later said that she realized how much her children needed her.

Some people react with anger when first confronted with issues of exhumation or identification. This anger may be directed at the individuals who committed the crime, at society or the government, or even at friends and other family members. Some people feel guilty about their anger, but it can be a normal phase of grief. As with any reaction, the extremity of the feeling, and the intent to carry out aggressive thoughts, should be assessed. Some people's emotions fall into turmoil. They may become physically ill or be unable to stop crying. They may become very nervous and unable to concentrate on anything the professional is saying. In these cases, it is often best to convey information about burial, death certificates, and other concrete matters. Some people may be unable to sleep at night or to keep food down. The psychosocial worker can let the family know that these reactions are normal releases of pain. As time goes on, these feelings should subside. If they do not subside, the person may need professional medical or psychological help. Survivors often live with 'if only': 'If only we had left for safety when we had the chance.', 'If only I had made my son and husband leave the night before, as I had the desire to do.', or 'If only they took me instead of my son.' This is often referred to as survivor's guilt (Hass, 1995) and can be a normal reaction. Psychosocial workers should be prepared to help support the survivor, offering that no one can predict the future or change the events that took place. Guilt may be a normal reaction to traumatic loss, but blaming oneself for such catastrophic events is destructive and should be discouraged. Many survivors find themselves for the first time in their lives thinking about revenge or killing the person who committed the crime. This is a normal reaction, and almost every survivor has these thoughts at one time or another. Having these feelings does not mean the person will act on them. Cultural norms and personal choices regarding forgiveness should be respected.

10.5   What can the forensic team and helping professional do?

In the short term, a supportive response from other people may mitigate the impact of the event, while a hostile or negative response may compound the damage and aggravate the traumatic syndrome (Stover and Shigekane, 2002). In the immediate aftermath of the trauma, rebuilding of some minimal form of trust is the primary task. Restoration of a sense of personal control and self-esteem is also vital. Preserving connections to the community and stimulating an individual's ability to cope may protect them against the development of PTSD.

Recognition that a person or family has been harmed and a sense of resulting justice are necessary to rebuild the survivor's sense of order and justice. This is why forensic efforts are crucial. It is important for the forensic expert or investigator to acknowledge that they are gathering more than just 'evidence'. These are the bodies of men, women, and children, whose families love them and yearn for the chance to retrieve them (Stover et al., 2003). This may be the first time that the person has allowed him- or herself to tell the story. Your response must be one of acceptance, empathy, and acknowledgment of the experience. These are mechanisms for establishing trust. Often people believe that their stories are so horrific that listeners will run away or reject them. Forensic teams and psychosocial workers do not run away or gasp in horror. They do not say 'stop crying' or 'don't worry'. Professionals should always allow a full expression of the survivor's feelings. A survivor's courage should be recognized, and they should not feel judged. Forensic and psychosocial professionals should set the stage for healing.

Families, at the time of AMD collection and/or exhumation, are suffering from the trauma of war and atrocities. These can include experience of physical threat, rape, witnessing the death of loved ones, and witnessing the destruction of home and property. This is all complicated by what we call 'traumatic grief'. They have lost family members and may desperately hope that a loved one is in the grave to be exhumed. They may have missing family members whom they believe are still alive. Living with missing relatives is a complex task.

A professional may help validate a survivor's feeling regarding their missing loved one. Statements such as 'you had a hard time', 'you have much pain', or 'it must be hard to live with those feelings inside of you' are acceptable when a person has lost a loved one. Sometimes a person can feel bad about feeling bad, believing that he or she must be able to take care of him- or herself without help. The psychosocial or forensic professional may be able to reframe these feelings for this type of person; for example, he or she should be encouraged not call him- or herself sick, but stressed.

No matter how long the family may have been missing their loved one, and even if they 'know' the body is buried at a particular site, the moment that the family sees an article of clothing or a personal effect they recognize is the real 'moment of death.' It can be anticipated that their reactions will be extreme. Visible and audible expression of grief may be expected. If the person exhibits physical problems, he or she should be assisted appropriately. In the field, this may mean anything from helping the person sit or lie down to finding medical attention. The forensic and psychosocial professionals should be prepared with regional and local resources to assist in the event of a health emergency. If, however, the person is crying, it is usually more helpful to support his or her expression of feelings than to cut the feelings off. In fact, an important 'task of mourning' is to help the survivor identify and express his or her feelings. Psychosocial and forensic professionals should be aware of these interactions. The psychosocial worker may inadvertently stop the healthy expression of feelings by saying something like 'Don't cry, now, it will be all right'. This is inappropriate. The person may need to cry, and it is not certain that 'everything will be alright.' That kind of remark may be the professional's way of feeling better, but it will not serve the suffering family members. A more facilitative approach is to listen attentively to the person or family, and to help the person put their feelings into words and be compassionate. The restoration of trust at this stage is very important. Sometimes just being with the family during these painful moments is a helpful intervention. At some point, the family will have a need for information. For example, they will ask to see the body, want to retrieve the remains, ask how they can get a coffin, or where will they may get a death certificate. These issues will have been clarified prior to any exhumation, and at least one or two members of the forensic/family support team should be prepared to convey the needed information, when possible, in written and verbal formats. The community often decides on questions of reburial, and advance preparation with the community is, therefore, optimal.

Trauma is characterized by a loss of control for the survivors. Therefore, it becomes critical for the forensic and psychosocial professional to look for small opportunities to restore some control and dignity to the family (e.g., asking the family if they would like to sit or stand, acknowledging their wish to view the clothing). It must be stated, however, that bodies are often in badly decomposed states, and some families will insist on viewing them. The psychosocial or forensic professional should attempt to inform the family about the condition of the body to dispel the myth that the loved one may look just as he or she had in life. If the family insists despite such caveats, then the family's wishes must be respected, and the family must be fully prepared for what they will see and smell. It may be that the families will be at the exhumation sites all day. In such instances, forensic and family support professionals may have the opportunity to establish relationships with the families so follow-up visits will be welcome. It may be that during such visits, families will reveal additional difficulties, such as problems obtaining humanitarian aid, or even acknowledge that a family member was raped and may need medical assistance. In these instances, the psychosocial worker should assist the family by being supportive and 'networking' with other organizations to help ensure that the person gets in touch with the proper resources.

10.6 The professionals' own reactions

This work can also be a very stressful process for the forensic and psychosocial professionals who are working with families trying to identify their missing loved ones. Professionals want to help. This can be very frustrating at times when little can be done. There is a gap between the desire to help and the realities of how much a forensic and psychosocial professional can actually do. It is important for the professional to be aware of his or her own feelings about death and grieving (Regehr, 2005).

Such work can be stressful for a variety of reasons. When on-site at a grave or in the process of taking data, forensic and psychosocial professionals are tasked with multiple roles, whether perceived or actual. These may include interviewer, community liaison, medical/scientific expert, and country representative. As a result, the professional may find workdays long and intense. Constant work with victims exposed to violence; the drain from continually empathizing, working, and compromising with a traumatized and desperate population for long hours and with few resources; and concern for personal safety can lead to compassion fatigue, secondary traumatic stress, or vicarious trauma (National Center for PTSD, 2001). Normal cognitive or emotional changes when working with trauma survivors are expected. Secondary trauma or symptoms of PTSD that mirror those experienced by the survivors who are searching for their missing loved ones is a more serious condition and may require intervention. These symptoms can include anxiety, hyperarousal, intrusive symptoms, avoidance, substance abuse, and depression.

Who is at greatest risk? Those who are assisting in the forensic effort must be aware of this impact in order to be helpful to others (Dunning, 1990). Professional staff and those who assist the professionals, including staff that may be hired from the affected population, are at greatest risk of stressful reactions. Exposure to dead or maimed bodies; violence and destruction; searching for missing persons or interacting with bereaved family members; loss of community and support; and any type of health impairment all put professionals at the greatest risk of developing stress symptoms. Many of the psychosocial and forensic professionals, and locally hired paraprofessional staff employed to work on exhumations in countries that have suffered great loss, have also been victims of loss and deprivation. Often, forensic professionals believe that with their experience in the field they are immune to the emotional effects of missing persons, exhumations, and identifications. However, this is frequently not the case. Observing family members attempting identifications, particularly those of civilians, and especially children, can have an impact on the stress level of the forensic professional (Keough and Samuels, 2004).

What can employers and field personnel do? Whenever possible, a clear, concise mission that all staff buy into and a plan for work with graves and families that is flexible and adaptable to change in the field should be shared with staff before engaging in the work. Camaraderie and clear direction and input, along with creating teams, acknowledging natural relationships to development, and facilitating group and individual processing, may reduce stress reactions in staff.

Agencies employing and working in the area of forensic data collection and exhumations should provide pre-event training and stress screening for those who will be working on this issue. International staff responding to international disaster training should have a full awareness of the cultural context of the country affected and the possible stressors related to forensic work in a mass disaster context. Employers or contracting organisations should institute a way of measuring current stress levels of staff through self-reporting scales that can assist in helping staff identify triggers for their own emotional reactions. For national staff responding to the crisis, there should be education around secondary trauma and ways of combating stress within the cultural context. Management and colleagues must work together to provide a safe and caring environment (see 3.4 and 3.5) within which symptoms of stress can be monitored. At the end of service, an exit interview, as well as post event screening and education processes, should be implemented that focus on integrating and processing experiences in the field.

Forensic and psychosocial professionals must take time to care for themselves, including eating and sleeping properly, taking breaks during long workdays, and talking to their supervisor if they are experiencing symptoms of trauma or stress. It is crucial that a workplace culture where this is possible is facilitated and managed. Self-monitoring, peer interaction, and relaxation exercises and activities are often highlighted as avenues by which professional staff can deal with the effects of stress-related reactions (National Child Traumatic Stress Network, 2005). Establishing a strong connection with coworkers and the ability to take breaks and unwind after particularly troubling incidents is strongly recommended.

Bibliography

Aaron, J. E. and Shore, P. A. 2003. 'Bone histomorphometry: concepts and common techniques', in An, Y. H. and Martin, K. L. (eds.), *Handbook of Histological Methods for Bone and Cartilage*. pp. 331–52. Totowa, NJ: Humana Press.

ActionAid International. 2006. *About Us: Impact Assessment – Understanding the Changes Brought About by Our Work*. Accessed: http://www.actionaid.org/471/impact_assessment.html

Adams, J. C. and Hamblen, D. L. 1992. *Outline of Fractures*. Edinburgh: Churchill Livingstone.

Adams, Z. J. O. and Hall, M. J. R. 2003. 'Methods used for the killing and preservation of blowfly larvae, and their effect on post-mortem larval length', *Forensic Science International* 138: 50–61.

Albert, A. M. and Maples, W. R. 1995. 'Stages of epiphyseal union for thoracic and lumbar vertebral centra as a method of age determination for teenage and young adult skeletons', *Journal of Forensic Sciences* 40(1): 623–33.

Allen, J. L. and St John Holt, A. 1997. *Health and Safety in Field Archaeology*. London: Standing Conference of Archaeological Unit Managers.

Alonso, A., Martin, P., Albarran, C., Garcia, P., Fernandez de Simon, L., Jesus Iturralde, M., Fernandez-Rodriguez, A., Atienza, I., Capilla, J., Garcia-Hirschfeld, J., Martinez, P., Vallejo, G., Garcia, O., Garcia, E., Real, P., Alvarez, D., Leon, A. and Sancho, M. 2005. 'Challenges of DNA profiling in mass disaster investigations', *Croatian Medical Journal* 46(4): 540–8.

Amendt, J., Krettek, R. and Zehner, R. 2004. 'Forensic entomology', *Naturwissenschaften* 91(2): 51–65.

Amendt, J., Campobasso, C. O., Gaudyry, E., Reiter, C., LeBlanc, H. N. and Hall, M. J. R. 2007. Best practice in forensic entomology – standards and guidelines. *International Journal of Legal Medicine* 121: 90–104.

Anderson, D. L., Thompson, G. W. and Popovich, F. 1976. 'Age of attainment of mineralization stages of the permanent dentition', *Journal of Forensic Sciences* 21(1): 191–200.

Angel, J. 1969. 'The bases of paleodemography', *American Journal of Physical Anthropology* 30(3): 427–37.

Asahida, T., Kobayashi, T., Saitoh, K. and Nakayama, I. 1996. 'Tissue preservation and total DNA extraction from fish stored at ambient temperature using buffers containing high concentration of urea', *Fisheries Science* 62(5): 727–30.

Aslanzadeh, J. 2004. 'Preventing PCR amplification carryover contamination in a clinical laboratory', *Annals of Clinical and Laboratory Science* 34(4): 389–96.

Association of Chief Police Officers (ACPO) and Centrex. 2005. *Guidance to Missing Persons*. ACPO and Centrex. Accessed:

http://www.missingpersons.police.uk/docs/MissingPersonsInteractive.pdf

Atmadja, D. S., Tatsuno, Y., Ueno, Y. and Nishimura, A. 1995. 'The effect of extraction methods. The kind of organ samples and the examination delay on the DNA yields and typing', *The Kobe Journal of Medical Sciences* 41(6): 197–211.

Aufderheide, A. C. and Rodriguez-Martin, C. 1998. *The Cambridge Encyclopedia of Human Palaeopathology*. Cambridge: Cambridge University Press.

Ayala, G., Canti, M., Heathcote, J., Sidell, J. and Usai, R. 2004. *Geoarchaeology: Using Earth Sciences to Understand the Archaeological Record*. London: English Heritage.

Ayton, F. D., Hill, C. M. and Parfitt, H. N. 1985. 'The dental role in the identification of victims of the Bradford City Football Ground fire', *British Dental Journal* 159: 262–4.

Babic, J., Cupkovic, T. and Bosiocic, N. 2000. *The Application of Remote Sensing and IT in Research of Mass Graves in the System of Jasenovac Ustasha Camps*. Accessed: http://www.balkan-archive.org.yu/Jasenovac/pdf/rsgis_jasenovac_eng1.pdf

Baby, R. S. 1954. *Hopewell Cremation Practices Papers in Archaeology: 1–7*. Columbus: Ohio Historical Society.

Ball, P. 2005. *Mass Graves Not Necessary for Tsunami Victims*. Accessed: http://www.nature.com/news/2005/050103/pf/050103-10_pf.html

Banning, E. B. 2002. *Archaeological Survey*. New York: Kluwer Academic/Plenum.

Banos Smith, H. 2006. 'International NGOs and impact assessment. Can we know we are making a difference?' *Research in Drama Education* 11(2): 157–74.

Barker, P. 1987. *Techniques of Archaeological Excavation*. London: Batsford.

Bass, W. M. 1995. *Human Osteology: A Laboratory and Field Manual* (3rd ed.). Columbia: Missouri Archeological Society.

Battarbee, R. W. 1986. 'Diatom analysis', in Berglund, B., (ed.), pp. 527–70.

Bauer, W. and Mahovlic, D. 2003. 'Cutting and grinding methods for hard-tissue histology', in An, Y. H. and Martin, K. L. (eds.), *Handbook of Histological Methods for Bone and Cartilage*, pp. 233–42. Totowa, NJ: Humana Press.

Bazyler, M. J. 2002. 'Using civil litigation to achieve some justice', in Rittner, C., Roth, J. K. and Smith, J. (eds.), pp. 151–7.

Beard, B. L. and Johnson, C. M. 2000. 'Strontium isotope composition of skeletal material can determine the birth place and geographic mobility of humans and animals', *Journal of Forensic Sciences* 45(5): 1049–61.

Bedford, M. E., Russell, K. F., Lovejoy, C. O., Meindl, R. S., Simpson, S. W. and Stuart-Macadam, P. I. 1993. 'Test of the multifactoral aging method using skeletons of known ages-at-death from the Grant Collection', *American Journal of Physical Anthropology* 91(3): 287–97.

Behrensmeyer, A. K. 1978. 'Taphonomic and ecologic information from bone weathering', *Paleobiology* 4(2): 150–62.

Beijerinck, W. 1947. *Zadenatlas der Nederlandsche flora*. Wageningen: H. Veenman and Zonen.

Bergfelder, T. and Hermann, B. 1980. 'Estimating fertility on the basis of birth traumatic changes in the pubic bone', *Journal of Human Evolution* 9: 611–13.

Berglund, B. 1986. *Handbook of Holocene Palaeoecology and Palaeohydrology*. Chichester: John Wiley and Sons.

Berryman, H. E. and Symes, S. A. 1998. 'Recognizing gunshot and blunt cranial trauma through fracture interpretation', in Reichs, K. J. (ed.), *Forensic Osteology: Advances in the Identification of Human Remains* (2nd ed.). Springfield, IL: Charles C Thomas, pp. 333–52.

Bevan, D. 1994. *A Case to Answer, the Story of Australia's First European War Crimes Prosecution*. Adelaide: Wakefield Press.

Bhalla, V. 1968. 'Comment on: a survey of the evidence for intrahuman killing in the

Pleistocene, by M. K. Roper', *Current Anthropology* 10(4): 427–59.

Black, S. and Scheuer, L. 1996. 'Age changes in the clavicle: from the early neonatal period to skeletal maturity', *International Journal of Osteoarchaeology* 6(5): 425–34.

Blumenschine, R. J. and Selvaggio, M. M. 1988. 'Percussion marks on bone surfaces as a new diagnostic of hominid behaviour', *Nature* 333: 763–5.

Blumenschine, R. J., Marean, C. W. and Capaldo, S. D. 1996. 'Blind tests of interanalyst correspondence and accuracy in the identification of cut marks, percussion marks, and carnivore tooth marks on bone surfaces', *Journal of Archaeological Science* 23: 493–507.

Bonilla, C., Gutierrez, G., Parra, E. J., Kline, C. and Shriver, M. D. 2005. 'Admixture analysis of a rural population of the state of Guerrero, Mexico', *American Journal of Physical Anthropology* 128(4): 861–9.

Borst, A., Box, A. T. and Fluit, A. C. 2004. 'False-positive results and contamination in nucleic acid amplification assays: suggestions for a prevent and destroy strategy', *European Journal of Clinical Microbiology and Infectious Diseases: Official Publication of the European Society of Clinical Microbiology* 23(4): 289–99.

Bowers, C. M. 2004. *Forensic Dental Evidence: An Investigator's Handbook.* San Diego: Elsevier/Academic Press.

Brace, C. L. 1995. *The Stages of Human Evolution.* Englewood Cliffs, NJ: Prentice Hall.

Brady N. C. and Weil R. R. 2002. *The Nature and Properties of Soils.* Upper Saddle River, NJ: Prentice Hall.

Branch, N., Canti, M., Clark, P. and Turney, C. 2005. *Environmental Archaeology: Theoretical and Practical Approaches.* London: Hodder Arnold.

Brearley, M. 2001. 'The persecution of Gypsies in Europe', *American Behavioural Scientist* 45(4): 588–99.

Brickley, M. and McKinley, J. I. (eds.). 2004. *Guidelines to the Standards for Recording Human Remains.* Reading: IFA Publication.

Brock, D. J. H. and Shrimpton, A. E. 1991. 'Non-paternity and prenatal genetic screening', *Lancet* 338: 1151.

Brogdon, B. G. 1998. *Forensic Radiology.* Boca Raton, FL: CRC Press.

Brogdon, B. G., Vogel, H. and McDowell, J. 2003. *A Radiologic Atlas of Abuse, Terrorism and Inflicted Trauma.* Boca Raton, FL: CRC Press.

Brooks, S. and Suchey, J. M. 1990. 'Skeletal age determination based on the os pubis: a comparison of the Acsádi-Nemeséri and Suchey-Brooks methods', *Human Evolution* 5(3): 227–38.

Brothwell, D. R. 1981. *Digging Up Bones.* London: British Museum (Natural History).

Brown, A. G. 2006. 'The use of forensic botany and geology in war crimes investigations in NE Bosnia', *Forensic Science International* 163(3):204–10.

Brown, A. G., Smith, A. and Elmhurst, O. 2002. 'The combined use of pollen and soil analyses in a search and subsequent murder investigation', *Journal of Forensic Sciences* 47(3): 614–18.

Brown, T. 1999. *The Science and Art of Tracking.* New York: Berkeley Book.

Bryant, V. M., Jr., Jones J. G. and Mildenhall, D. C. 1990. 'Forensic palynology in the United States of America', *Palynology* 14(1): 193–208.

Buchli, V. and Lucas, G. (eds.). 2001. *Archaeologies of the Contemporary Past.* London: Routledge.

Buckberry, J. L. and Chamberlain A. T. 2002. 'Age estimation from the auricular surface of the Ilium: a revised method', *American Journal of Physical Anthropology* 119(3): 231–9.

Budimlija, Z. M., Prinz, M. K., Zelson-Mundorff, A., Wiersema, J., Bartelink, E., MacKinnon, G., Nazzaruolo, B. L., Estacio, S. M., Hennessey, M. J. and Shaler, R. C.

2003. 'World Trade Center human identification project: experiences with individual body identification cases', *Croatian Medical Journal* 44(3): 259–63.

Budowle, B., Bieber, F. R. and Eisenberg, A. J. 2005. 'Forensic aspects of mass disasters: strategic considerations for DNA-based human identification', *Legal Medicine* 7(4): 230–43.

Buikstra, J. E. and Ubelaker, D. H. 1994. *Standards for Data Collection from Human Skeletal Remains*. Fayetteville, AR: Arkansas Archaeological Survey Research Series 44.

Bull, P. A. 1981. 'Surface textures of individual particles (scanning electron microscope analysis)', in Goudie, A. S. (ed.), *Geomorphological Techniques*. pp. 90–3. London: Routledge.

Burnett, B. R. 1991. 'Detection of bone and bone-plus-bullet particles in backspatter from close range shots to the heads', *Journal of Forensic Sciences* 36(6): 1745–52.

Butler, J. M. 2005. *Forensic DNA Typing: Biology, Technology, and Genetics of STR Markers* (2nd ed.). San Diego: Elsevier/Academic Press.

Byers, S. N. 2002. *Introduction to Forensic Anthropology: A Textbook*. Boston: Allyn and Bacon.

Byers, S., Akoshima, K. and Curran, B. 1989. 'Determination of adult stature from metatarsal length', *American Journal of Physical Anthropology* 79(3): 275–9.

Byrd, J. E. and Adams, B. J. 2003. 'Osteometric sorting of commingled human remains', *Journal of Forensic Sciences* 48(4): 717–24.

Byrd, J. H. and Allen, J. C. 2001. 'Computer modeling of insect growth and its application to forensic entomology', in Byrd, J. H. and Castner, J. L. (eds.), *Forensic Entomology: The Utility of Arthropods in Legal Investigations*, pp. 303–30. Boca Raton, FL: CRC Press.

Byrd, J. H. and Butler, J. F. 1996. 'Effects of temperature on *Cochliomyia macellaria* (Diptera: Calliphoridae) development', *Journal of Medical Entomology* 33(6): 901–5.

Byrd, J. H. and Castner, J. L. (eds.). 2001. *Entomological Evidence: The Utility of Arthropods in Legal Investigations*. Boca Raton, FL: CRC Press.

Cameron, N. 2004. 'The use of diatom analysis in forensic geoscience', in Pye, K. and Croft, D. J. (eds.), *Forensic Geoscience: Principles, Techniques and Applications*. Bath: Geological Society, pp. 277–89.

Canti, M. 1991. *Soil Particle Size Analysis: A Revised Interpretive Guide for Excavators*. English Heritage Ancient Monuments Laboratory Reports 1(91. Unpublished report, English Heritage.

Catts, E. P. and Goff, M. L. 1992. 'Forensic entomology in criminal investigations', *Annual Review of Entomology* 37: 253–72.

Catts, E. P. and Haskell, N. H. (eds.). 1990. *Entomology and Death: A Procedural Guide*. Clemson, SC: Joyce's Print Shop.

Central Identification Laboratory (CIL). 2002/2003. *Standard Operating Procedures*. Hickam AFB, HI: CIL.

Chalk, F. and Jonassohn, K., 1990. *The History and Sociology of Genocide: Analyses and Case Studies*. London: Yale University Press.

Chapman, J., Miller, V., Soares A. C. and Samuel, J. 2005. *Rights-Based Development: The Challenge of Change and Power*. Advocacy Action Research Project. Working Paper No 2. ActionAid International. Accessed: http://www.gprg.org/pubs/workingpapers/pdfs/gprg-wps-027.pdf

Charny, I. W. (ed.). 1999. *The Encyclopedia of Genocide*. Oxford: ABC Clio.

Cheetham, P. 2005. 'Forensic geophysical survey', in Hunter, J. R. and Cox, M. (eds.), pp. 62–95.

Chisum W. J. and Turvey, B. E. 2002. *Criminal Profiling*. London: Academic Press.

Choi, B. Y., Chae Y. M., Chung I. H. and Kang H. S. 1997. 'Correlation between the postmortem stature and the dried limb-bone lengths of Korean adult males', *Yonsei Medical Journal* 38(2): 79–85.

Christensen, A. M. 2004. 'The impact of Daubert: implications for testimony and research in forensic anthropology (and the use of frontal sinuses in personal identification)', *Journal of Forensic Sciences* 49(3): 1–4.

Chung, D. T., Drabek, J., Opel, K. L., Butler, J. M. and McCord, B. R. 2004. 'A study on the effects of degradation and template concentration on the amplification efficiency of the STR Miniplex primer sets', *Journal of Forensic Sciences* 49(4): 733–40.

Ciapparelli, L. 1992. 'The chronology of dental development and age assessment', in Clark, D. H. (ed.), *Practical Forensic Odontology*. Oxford: Butterworth-Heinemann, pp. 22–42.

Clark, D. H. 1994. 'An analysis of the value of forensic odontology in ten mass disasters', *International Dental Journal* 44(3): 241–50.

Clasper, J. C., Hill, P. F. and Watkins, P. E. 2002. 'Contamination of ballistic fractures: an in vitro model', *Injury* 33(2): 157–60.

Clement, J. G. 1998. 'Dental identification', in Clement, J. G. and Ranson, D. L., (eds.), *Craniofacial Identification in Forensic Medicine*. London: Arnold, pp. 63–81.

Cloutier, G. 2005. *U-2 Aids in Katrina Relief.* Accessed: http://www.globalsecurity. org/ intell/library/news/2005/intell-050913-afpn02.htm

Cole, M. 2000. *An Investigation into the Type and Nature of Post-Mortem Change to Sus Srofa Exposed Over Winter in the UK.* Unpublished master's dissertation, School of Conservation Sciences, Bournemouth University, UK.

Collins, R. A., Wu, W. S., Xing, J., Lau. L., and Yu, A. C. H. 2003. 'Parentage testing anomalies in Hong Kong SAR of China', *Chinese Medical Journal* 116(5): 708–11.

Committee on Conscience. 2001. *Genocide Warning on Sudan*. Washington DC: Holocaust Museum.

Condon, K., Charles, K. D., Cheverud, J. M. and Buikstra, J. E. 1986. 'Cementum annulation and age determination in *Homo sapiens*. II. Estimates and accuracy', *American Journal of Physical Anthropology* 71(3): 321–30.

Connor, M. A. and Scott, D. D. 2001a. 'Paradigms and perpetrators'. *Historical Archaeology* 35(1): 1–6.

Connor, M. A. and Scott, D. D. 2001b. 'Archaeologists as forensic investigators: defining the role', *Historical Archaeology* 35(1).

Cool, S. M., Hendrikz, J. K. and Wood, W. B. 1995. 'Microscopic age changes in the human occipital bone', *Journal of Forensic Sciences* 40(5): 789–96.

Correia, P. M. M. 1997. 'Fire modification of bone: a review of the literature', in Haglund, W. D. and Sorg, M. H. (eds.), *Forensic Taphonomy: The Postmortem Fate of Human Remains*, pp. 275–93. Boca Raton, FL: CRC Press.

Cox, M. 1989. *An Evaluation of the Significance of 'Scars or Parturition' in the Christ Church, Spitalfields Sample.* Unpublished doctoral thesis, University College, London.

Cox, M. and Scott, A. 1992. 'Evaluation of the obstetric significance of some pelvic characters in an 18th century British sample of known parity status', *American Journal of Physical Anthropology* 89(4): 431–40.

Cox, M. J. 1995. 'Crime scene archaeology is one of the most frightening areas of archaeology in which to practice', *The Field Archaeologist* 23:14–16.

Cox, M. J. 2000a. 'Aging adults from the skeleton', in Cox, M. J. and Mays, S. (eds.), *Human Osteology in Archaeology and Forensic Science*. London: Greenwich Medical Media, pp. 61–81.

Cox, M. J. 2000b. 'Assessment of parturition', in Cox, M. and Mays, S. (eds.), *Human Osteology in Archaeological and Forensic Science*. London: Greenwich Medical Media, pp. 131–42.

Cox, M. J. 2001a. 'Forensic archaeology in the UK: questions of socio-intellectual context and socio-political responsibility', in Buchli, V. and Lucas, G. (eds.), pp. 145–57.

Cox, M. J. 2001b. 'Forensic archaeology: a United Kingdom perspective', in Godwin,

M. (eds.), *Criminal Psychology and Forensic Technology: A Collaborative Approach to Effective Profiling*. Boca Raton, FL: CRC Press, pp. 1–14.

Cox, M. J. 2003. 'A multidisciplinary approach to the investigation of crimes against humanity, war-crimes and genocide: the Inforce Foundation', *Science and Justice* 43(4): 225–8.

Cox, M. J. in press 2008. 'The history of forensic archaeology and anthropology: a UK perspective', in Blau, S. and Ubelaker, D. (eds) *World Archaeological Congress Handbook of Forensic Anthropology and Archaeology*. California: Left Coast Press.

Creager, J. G. 1992. *Human Anatomy and Physiology* (2nd ed.). Dubuque, IA: Wm. C. Brown.

Cronyn, J. M. 1990. *The Elements of Archaeological Conservation*. London: Routledge.

Cutler, B. L. and Penrod, S. D. 1995. *Mistaken Identification: The Eyewitness, Psychology and the Law*. Cambridge: Cambridge University Press.

Daubert v. Merrell Dow Pharmaceuticals, 1993. (92–102), 509 US 579.

Davies, L. and Ratcliffe, G. G. 1994. 'Development rates of some pre-adult stages in blowflies with reference to low temperatures', *Medical and Veterinary Entomology* 8: 245–54.

De la Grandmaison, G. L., Brion, F. and Durigon, M. 2001. 'Frequency of bone lesions: an inadequate criterion for gunshot wound diagnosis in skeletal remains', *Journal of Forensic Sciences* 46(3): 593–5.

Declaration of Helsinki. 1996. *British Medical Journal*, World Medical Organization 313(7070): 1448–9.

DeGusta, D. and White, T. D. 1996. 'On the use of skeletal collections for DNA analysis', *Ancient Biomolecules* 1: 89–92.

Demirjian, A. and Goldstein, H. 1976. 'New systems for dental maturity based on seven and four teeth'. *Annals of Human Biology* 3: 129–134.

Demirjian, A. and Levesque, G. Y. 1980. 'Sexual differences in dental development and prediction of emergence'. *Journal of Dental Research*. 59(7): 1110–22.

Demirjian, A., Goldstein, H. and Tanner, J. M. 1973. 'A new system of dental age assessment', *Human Biology* 45: 211–28.

Department for Culture, Media and Sport. 2005. *Guidance for the Care of Human Remains in Museums*. London: HMSO.

Di Maio, D. J. and Di Maio, V. J. M., 1993. *Forensic Pathology*. Boca Raton, FL: CRC Press.

Di Maio, V. J. M. 1985. *Gunshot Wounds: Practical Aspects of Firearms, Ballistics, and Forensic Techniques*. New York: Elsevier.

Di Maio, V. J. M. 1999. *Gunshot Wounds: Practical Aspects of Firearms, Ballistics and Forensic Techniques* (2nd ed.). Boca Raton, FL: CRC Press.

Dirkmaat, D. C. and Adovasio, J. M. 1997. 'The role of archaeology in the recovery and interpretation of human remains from an outdoor setting', in Haglund, W. D. and Sorg, M. H. (eds.), *Forensic Taphonomy: The Postmortem Fate of Human Remains*. Boca Raton, FL: CRC Press. pp. 39–64.

Donovan, S. E., Hall, M. J. R., Turner, B. D. and Moncrieff, C. B. 2006. 'Larval growth rates of the blowfly, *Calliphora vicina*, over a range of temperatures', *Medical and Veterinary Entomology* 20(1): 1–9.

Doretti, M. and Fondebrider, L. 2001. 'Science and human rights: truth, justice, reparation and reconciliation, a long way in third world countries', in Buchli, V. and Lucas, G. (eds.), London: Routledge. pp. 138–44.

Dorries, C. 1999. *Coroner's Court: A Guide to Law and Practice*. Chichester: John Wiley.

Drabek, J. and Petrek, M. 2002. 'A sugar, laundry detergent, and salt method for extraction of deoxyribonucleic acid from blood', *Biomedical Papers of the Medical Faculty of the University Palacky, Olomouc, Czechoslovakia* 146(2): 37–9.

Duffy, J. B., Waterfield, J. D. and Skinner, M. F. 1991. 'Isolation of tooth pulp cells for sex chromatin studies in experimental dehydrated and cremated remains', *Forensic Science International* 49(2): 127–41.

Dunning, C. 1990. 'Mental health sequelae in disaster workers: Prevention and intervention', *International Journal of Mental Health* 19: 91–103.

Dwight, T. 1890. 'The closure of the cranial sutures as a sign of age', *Boston Medical and Surgical Journal* 122(17): 389–92.

Dziegielewski, S. and Sumner, K. 2005. 'An examination of the US response to bioterrorism: Handling the threat and aftermath through crisis intervention', in Roberts, A. R. (ed.), *Crisis Intervention Handbook: Assessment Treatment and Research*. Oxford: Oxford University Press, pp. 262–78.

Ebbesmeyer, C. C. and Haglund, W. D. 2002. 'Floating remains on Pacific Northwest waters', in Haglund, W. D. and Sorg, M. H. (eds.), pp. 219–42.

Erdtman, G. 1969. *Handbook of Palynology. Morphology, Taxonomy, Ecology*. Copenhagen: Munsgaard.

Erzinçlioglu, Z. 1996. 'Entomological investigation of the scene', in Vanezis, P. and Busuttil, A. (eds.), *Suspicious Death Scene Investigation*. London: Arnold, pp. 89–101.

Erzinçlioglu, Z. 2000. *Maggots, Murder and Men: Memories and Reflections of a Forensic Entomologist*. Colchester: Harley Books.

Fagles, R. 1984. *Aeschylus' Oresteia*. London: Penguin Classics.

Fazekas, I. G. and Kósa, F. 1978. *Forensic Fetal Osteology*. Budapest: Akadémiai Kiadó.

Fédération Dentaire International. 1971. Two-digit system of designating teeth, *International Dental Journal* 21: 104–106.

Feik, S. A. and Glover, J. E. 1998. 'Growth of children's faces', in Clement, J. G. and Ranson, D. L. (eds.), *Craniofacial Identification in Forensic Medicine*. New York: Oxford University Press, pp. 204–24.

Feik, S. A., Thomas, C. D. L. and Clement, J. G. 1997. 'Age-related changes in cortical porosity of the midshaft of the human femur', *Journal of Anatomy* 191: 407–16.

Fenton, T. W., Stefan, V. H., Wood, L. A. and Sauer, N. J. 2005. 'Symmetrical fracturing of the skull from midline contact gunshot wounds: reconstruction of individual death histories from skeletonized human remains', *Journal of Forensic Sciences* 50(2): 247–85.

Fenton, T., Birkby, W. and Cornelison, J. 2003. 'A fast and safe non-bleaching method for forensic skeletal preparation', *Journal of Forensic Sciences* 48(2): 274–6.

Ferguson, D. B. (ed.). 1999. *Oral Bioscience*. Edinburgh: Churchill Livingstone.

Food and Agriculture Organization of the United Nations (FAO). 1990. *Soil Map of the World: Revised Legend*. World Soil Resources Report 60. Rome: FAO.

Forensic Science Service (FSS). 2004. *The Scenes of Crime Handbook*. Chorley: FSS.

Fox, F. 1999. *God's Eye: Aerial Photography and the Katyn Forest Massacre*. West Chester, PA: West Chester University Press.

France, D. L., Griffin, T. J., Swanburg, J. G., Lindemann, J. W., Deavenport, G. C., Trammel, V., Armbrust, C. T., Kondratieff, B., Nelson, A., Castellano, K. and Hopkins, D. 1992. 'A multidisciplinary approach to the detection of clandestine graves', *Journal of Forensic Sciences* 37: 1435–750.

Franklin, D., O'Higgins, P., Oxnard, C. E. and Dadour, I. 2006. 'Determination of sex in South African Blacks by discriminant function analysis of mandibular linear regression'. *Forensic Science, Medicine and Pathology* 2(4): 263–8.

Frazer, J. E. 1948. *The Anatomy of the Human Skeleton* (4th ed.). London: Churchill.

French, C. 2003. *Geoarchaeology in Action*. London: Routledge.

Fricke, H. C., O'Neil, J. R. and Lynnerup, N. 1995. 'Oxygen isotope composition of human tooth enamel from medieval

Greenland: linking climate and society', *Geology* 23: 869–72.

Fully, G. 1956. 'Une nouvelle méthode de détermination de la taille', *Annales de Médecine Légale et de Criminologie* 36: 266–73.

Fully, G. and Pineau, H. 1960. 'Détermination de la stature au moyen du squelette', *Annales de Médecine Légale et de Criminologie* 60:145–53.

Gaffney, C. and Gater, J. 2003. *Revealing the Buried Past: Geophysics for Archaeologists.* Stroud, UK: Tempus.

Galloway, A. 1988. 'Estimating actual height in the older individual'. *Journal of Forensic Sciences* 33: 126–36.

Galloway, A. (ed.). 1999. *Broken Bones: Anthropological Analysis of Blunt Force Trauma.* Springfield, IL: Charles C Thomas.

Galloway, A., Snodgrass, J. and Suchey, J. 1998. 'Markers of childbirth? Effect of body size and pubic morphological change', *American Journal of Physical Anthropology* 26(suppl): 102–3.

Galloway, A., Walsh-Haney, H. and Byrd, J. H. 2001. 'Recovering buried bodies and surface scatter: the associated anthropological, botanical and entomological evidence', in Byrd, J. and Castner, J. (eds.), *Forensic Entomology.* Boca Raton, FL: CRC Press, pp. 223–62.

Gamble, C. 2001. *Archaeology: The Basics.* London: Routledge.

Gaytmenn, R. and Sweet, D. 2003. 'Quantification of forensic DNA from various regions of human teeth', *Journal of Forensic Sciences* 48(3): 622–5.

Gejvall, N. G. 1969. 'Cremations', in Brothwell, D. and Higgs, E. (eds.), *Science in Archaeology* (2nd ed.). London: Thames and Hudson, pp. 468–79.

Gejvall, N. G. 1981. 'Determination of burned bones from prehistoric graves: observations on the cremated bones from the graves at Horn', *Ossa.Letters, 2.*

Geneva Convention. 1949. Part III, Section IV, Chapter XI, Article 130.

Genovés, S. 1967. 'Proportionality of the long bone and their relation to stature among Mesoamericans', *American Journal of Physical Anthropology* 26(1): 67–77.

Gerberth, V. J. 1996. *Practical Homicide Investigation: Tactics, Procedures and Forensic Techniques* (3rd ed.). Boca Raton, FL: CRC Press.

Gibson, G. and Muse, S. V. 2002. *A Primer of Genome Science.* New York: Sinauer Associates/Academic Press.

Gibson, P. J. 2000. *Introductory Remote Sensing: Principles and Concepts.* London: Routledge.

Gilbert, M. T., Menez, L., Janaway, R. C., Tobin, D. J., Cooper, A. and Wilson, A. S. 2006. 'Resistance of degraded hair shafts to contaminant DNA', *Forensic Science International* 156(2–3): 208–12.

Gilbert, P. 1993. *The A–Z Reference Book of Syndromes and Inherited Disorders. A Manual for Health, Social and Education Workers.* London: Chapman and Hall.

Gilbert, S. 2003. *Interviewing and Interrogation: The Discovery of Truth.* New York: Thomson Wadsworth.

Giles, E. 1991. 'Corrections for age in estimating older adults' stature from long bones', *Journal of Forensic Sciences* 36(3): 898–901.

Giles, E. and Elliot, O. 1962. 'Race identification from cranial measurements', *Journal of Forensic Sciences* 7: 147–157.

Giles, E. and Elliot, O. 1963. 'Sex determination by discriminant function analysis of crania'. *American Journal of Physical Anthropology* 21: 53–68.

Gill, G. W. 1986. 'Craniofacial criteria in forensic race identification', in Reichs, K. J. (ed.), *Forensic Osteology: Advances in the Identification of Human Remains.* Springfield, IL: Charles C Thomas, pp 293–318.

Gill, G. W. 1995. 'Challenge on the frontier: discerning American Indians from whites osteologically', *Journal of Forensic Sciences*, 40(5): 783–8.

Gill, G. W. 2001. 'Racial variation in the proximal and distal femur: heritability and forensic utility', *Journal of Forensic Sciences* 46(4): 791–9.

Gillard, R. D., Pollard, A. M., Sutton, P. A. and Whittaker, D. 1990. 'An improved method for age at death determination from the measurement of daspartic acid in dental collagen', *Archaeometry* 32: 61–70.

Glattstein, B., Zeichner, A., Vinokurov, A., Levin, N., Kugel, C. and Hiss, J. 2000. 'Improved methods for shooting distance estimation. I. Bullet holes in clothing items', *Journal of Forensic Sciences* 45(6):1243–9.

Godwin, G. M. 2001. *Criminal Psychology and Forensic Technology.* New York: CRC Press.

Goff, M. L. 2000. *A Fly for the Prosecution: How Insect Evidence Helps Solve Crimes.* Cambridge: Harvard University Press.

Goffer, Z. 1980. *Archaeological Chemistry.* New York: John Wiley & Sons.

Goldstone, R. and Fritz, N. 2002. 'War crimes trials', in Rittner, C., Roth, J. K. and Smith, J. (eds.), pp. 183–6.

Gomez, E. A. 2005. *An Evaluation of Post–mortem Iris Colour Change in the Eyes of Sus Scrofa.* Unpublished bachelor's dissertation, Bournemouth University, UK.

Goudie, A. S. 1981. *Geomorphological Techniques.* London: British Geomorphological Research Group, Allen and Unwin.

Graham, E. 2006. 'Sex determination'. *Forensic Science, Medicine, and Pathology* 2(4): 283–6.

Grassberger, M. and Reiter, C. 2001. 'Effect of temperature on *Lucilia sericata* (Diptera: *Calliphoridae*) development with special reference to the isomegalen- and isomorphen-diagram', *Forensic Science International* 20(1): 32–6.

Grassberger, M. and Reiter, C. 2002. 'Effect of temperature on development of the forensically important holarctic blow fly *Protophormia terraenovae* (R.-D.) (Diptera *Calliphoridae*)', *Forensic Science International* 128(3): 177–82.

Grassberger, M., Friedrich, E. and Reiter, C. 2003. 'The blowfly *Chrysomya albiceps*

(Wiedemann) (Diptera: *Calliphoridae*) as a new forensic indicator in Central Europe', *International Journal of Legal Medicine* 117: 75–81.

Greenberg, B. and Kunich, J. C. 2002. *Entomology and the Law: Flies as Forensic Indicators.* Cambridge: Cambridge University Press.

Greenberg, B. and Tantawi, T. I. 1993. 'Different developmental strategies in two boreal blow flies (Diptera: *Calliphoridae*)', *Journal of Medical Entomology* 30(2): 481–4.

Greenberg, B. 1991. 'Flies as forensic indicators', *Journal of Medical Entomology* 28: 565–77.

Greulich, W. W. and Pyle, S. I. 1959. *Radiographic Atlas of Skeletal Development of the Hand and Wrist.* Palo Alto, CA: Stanford University Press.

Guellaen, G., Casanova, M., Bishop, C., Geldwerth, D., Andre, G., Fellous, M. and Weissenbach, J. 1984. 'Human XX males with Y single-copy DNA fragments', *Nature* 307: 172–3.

Gustafson, G. and Koch, G. 1974. 'Age estimation up to 16 years of age based on dental development', *Odontologisk Revy* 25(3): 297–306.

Haavikko, K. 1970. 'The formation and the alveolar and clinical eruption of the permanent teeth. An orthopantomographic study', *Suom Hammaslaak Toim* 66: 103–70.

Haglund, W. D. 2002. 'Recent mass graves: an introduction', in Haglund, W. D. and Sorg, M. H. (eds.), pp. 243–62.

Haglund, W. D. and Sorg, M. H. 2002a. 'Human remains in water environments', in Haglund, W. D. and Sorg, M. H. (eds.), pp. 219–42.

Haglund, W. D. and Sorg, M. H. (eds.). 2002b. *Advances in Forensic Taphonomy: Method, Theory and Archaeological Perspectives.* Boca Raton, FL: CRC Press.

Hamshaw-Thomas, H. 1916. *The Interpretation of Aeroplane Photographs.* London, Office of the General Staff.

Hanson, I. 2004. 'The importance of stratigraphy in forensic investigation', in Pye, K.

and Croft, D. (eds.), *Forensic Geoscience: Principles, Techniques and Applications.* pp. 39–48. London: Conference Abstracts, Geological Society of London.

Harding, R. M. and McVean, G. 2004. 'A structured ancestral population for the evolution of modern humans', *Current Opinion in Genetics and Development* 14(6): 667–74.

Harnett, K. M. and To, D. 2002. 'Modern oral piercing: the application of their dental wear patters for forensic anthropology', *Proceedings of the American Academy of Forensic Sciences* Vol 8 (Atlanta) H25: 227.

Harris, E. 1979. *Principles of Archaeological Stratigraphy.* London and New York, Academic Press.

Harris, A. M. P., Wood, R. E., Nortjé, C. J. and Thomas, C. J. 1987a. 'Gender and ethnic differences of the radiographic image of the frontal region', *Journal of Forensic Odontostomatology* 5: 51–7.

Harris, A. M. P., Wood, R. E., Nortjé, C. J. and Thomas, C. J. 1987b. 'The frontal sinus: forensic fingerprint? A pilot study', *Journal of Forensic Odontostomatology* 5: 9–15.

Hass, A. 1995. 'Survivor guilt in Holocaust survivors and their children', in Lemberger, J. (ed.), *A Global Perspective on Working with Holocaust Survivors and the 2nd Generation.* pp. 163–83. Jerusalem: AMCHA.

Hately, W., Gordon, E. and Samuel, E. 1965. 'The pattern of ossification in the laryngeal cartilages: a radiological study', *The British Journal of Radiology* 38: 585–91.

Health and Safety Executive (HSE). 1997. *First aid at work. The Health and Safety (First Aid) Regulations. 1981.* London: HSE Books.

Health and Safety Executive (HSE). 2003. *Safe Working and Prevention of Infection in the Mortuary and Post-mortem Room* (2nd ed.). London: HSE Books.

Henderson, J. 1987. 'Factors determining the state of preservation of human remains', in Boddington, A., Garland, A. N. and Janaway, R. C. (eds.), *Death, Decay and Reconstruction.* Manchester: Manchester University Press, pp. 43–54.

Herman, J. 1992. *Trauma and Recovery: The Aftermath of Violence – From Domestic Abuse to Political Terror.* New York: Basic Books.

Hershkovitz, I., Latimer, B., Dutour, O., Jellema, L. M., Wish-Baratz, S., Rothchild, C. and Rothchild, B. M. 1997. 'The elusive petro-exoccipital articulation', *American Journal of Physical Anthropology* 103(3): 365–73.

Herz, N. and Garrison, E. G. 1998. *Geological Methods for Archaeology.* New York: Oxford University Press.

Hillson, S. 1996. *Dental Anthropology.* Cambridge: Cambridge University Press.

Hillson, S. 1998. *Dental Anthropology* (2nd ed.). Cambridge: Cambridge University Press.

Hillson, S. 2001. 'Recording dental caries in archaeological human remains', *International Journal of Osteoarchaeology* 11(4): 249–89.

Hirschberg, J., Milne, N. and Oxnard, C. 1998. 'The interface between muscle and bone: biomechanical implications', *Annual meeting of the American Association of Physical Anthropologists*, Supplement 26, p. 96.

Hodgson, J. M. 1976. 'Soil survey field handbook: describing and sampling soil profiles', *Soil Survey Technical Monograph* No. 5. Harpenden.

Holck, P. 1986. 'Cremated bones: A medical-anthropological study of an archaeological material on cremation burials', *Anthropologiske Skrifter 1.* Oslo: Anatomisk Institute University of Oslo.

Holcomb, S. M. C. and Konigsberg, L. W. 1995. 'Statistical study of sexual dimorphism in the human fetal sciatic notch', *American Journal of Physical Anthropology* 97(2): 113–25.

Holden, J. L., Phakey, P. P. and Clement, J. G. 1995a. 'Scanning electron microscope observations of heat-treated human bone', *Forensic Science International* 74(1–2): 29–45.

Holden, J. L., Phakey, P. P. and Clement, J. G. 1995b. 'Scanning electron microscope observations of incinerated human femoral bone: a case study', *Forensic Science International* 74(1–2): 17–28.

Holland, M. M., Cave, C. A., Holland, C. A. and Bille, T. W. 2003. 'Development of a quality, high throughput DNA analysis procedure for skeletal samples to assist with the identification of victims from the World Trade Center attacks', *Croatian Medical Journal* 44(3): 264–72.

Holland, T. D. 1991. 'Sex assessment using the proximal tibia', *Journal of Physical Anthropology* 85(2): 221–7.

Holland, T. D. 1995. 'Brief communication: estimation of adult stature from the calcaneus and talus', *American Journal of Physical Anthropology* 96(3): 315–20.

Holt, C. A. 1978. A re-examination of parturition scars on the human female pelvis', *American Journal of Physical Anthropology* 49 (1): 91–94.

Horrocks, M. and Walsh, K. A. J. 1998. 'Forensic palynology: assessing the value of the evidence', *Review of Palaeobotany and Palynology* 103(1): 69–74.

Horrocks, M. and Walsh, K. A. J. 1999. 'Fine resolution of pollen patterns in limited space: differentiating a crime scene and alibi scene seven meters apart', *Journal of Forensic Sciences* 44(2): 417–20.

Horrocks, M., Coulson, S. A. and Walsh, K. A. J. 1998. 'Forensic palynology: variation in the pollen content of soil surface samples', *Journal of Forensic Sciences* 43(2): 320–3.

Horswell, J., Cordiner, S. J., Maas, E. W., Martin, T. M., Sutherland, K. B., Speir, T. W., Nogales, B. and Osborn, A. M. 2002. 'Forensic comparison of soils by bacterial community DNA profiling', *Journal of Forensic Sciences* 47(2): 350–3.

Hoshower, L. M. 1998. 'Forensic archaeology and the need for flexible excavation strategies: a case study', *Journal of Forensic Sciences* 43(1): 53–6.

Houck, M. M. and Siegel, J. A. 2006. *Fundamentals of Forensic Science*. Burlington, MA: Academic Press.

Houghton, P. 1974. 'The relationship of the pre-auricular groove of the ilium to pregnancy', *American Journal of Physical Anthropology* 41(3): 381–89.

Howells, W. W. 1989. 'Skull shapes and the map: craniometric analyses in the dispersion of modern homo', *Peabody Museum of Archaeology and Ethnology*, Vol. 79. Cambridge, MA: Harvard University Press.

Hrdlicka, A. 1939. *Practical Anthropometry*. Philadelphia: Wistar Institute of Anatomy and Biology.

Human Rights Watch. 2004. *Iraq: State of the Evidence, Part IV, The Forensic Evidence*. Accessed: http://www.hrw.org/reports/2004/iraq1104/4.htm

Humphrey, L., Jeffries T. and Dean, M. 2004. 'Investigation of age at weaning using Sr/Ca ratios in human tooth enamel', *American Journal of Physical Anthropology* 38(suppl): 117.

Hunter, J. R. 2000. 'Forensic archaeology', in Siegel, J. A., Saukko, P. J. and Knupfer, G. C. (eds.), *Encyclopaedia of Forensic Sciences*. London: Academic Press, pp. 206–12.

Hunter, J. R. and Cox, M. 2005. *Forensic Archaeology: Advances in Theory and Practice*. London: Routledge.

Hunter, J. R., Roberts C. A. and Martin A. L. (eds.). 1996. *Studies in Crime: An Introduction to Forensic Archaeology*. London: Batsford.

Hurlbut, S. A. 2000. 'The taphonomy of cannibalism: a review of anthropogenic bone modification in the American Southwest', *International Journal of Osteoarchaeology* 10(1): 4–26.

Imai, T., Sugawara, T., Nishiyama, A., Shimada, R., Ohki, R., Seki, N., Sagara, M., Ito, H., Yamauchi, M. and Hori, T. 1997. 'The structure and organization of the human NPAT gene', *Genomics* 42(3): 388–92.

Industrial Rope Access Trade Association (IRATA). 2001. *International Guidelines on the use of Rope Access Methods for Industrial Purposes.* Hampshire: IRATA

Inforce Foundation. 2003. *Report on the Feasibility of Providing Forensic Training for Rwanda 2003.* Unpublished. Bournemouth, Inforce Foundation.

Inforce Foundation. 2004a. *Inforce Scientific and Scene of Crime Protocols for the Investigation of Mass Graves, Version 4.* Unpublished. Bournemouth, Inforce Foundation.

Inforce Foundation. 2004b. *Standard Operating Procedures for Use in Investigating Mass Graves, Version 1.* Unpublished. Bournemouth, Inforce Foundation.

Institute of Field Archaeologists (IFA). 2004. *Codes, Guidelines and Standards.* Reading, UK: IFA. http://www.archaeologists.net/modules/icontent/index.php?page=15

International Atomic Energy Agency (IAEA) 1996. International Basic Safety Standards for Protection against Ionising Radiation and for the Safety of Radiation Sources. Safety Series No. 115. Vienna (http://www-pub.iaes.org/MTCD/publications/PDF/SS-115-Web/start.pdf).

International Atomic Energy Agency (IAEA). 2004. *International Basic Safety Standards for Protection Against Ionizing Radiation and for the Safety of Radiation Sources.* Vienna: IAEA. 115(CD.

International Committee of the Red Cross (ICRC). 1987. *Basic Rules of the Geneva Conventions and Their Additional Protocols.* 2nd ed (1988) available online: http://www.icrc.org/WEB/ENG/siteeng0.nsf/htmlall/p0365?OpenDocument&style=Custo_Final.4&View=defaultBody2. Geneva: ICRC Publication.

International Court of Justice. 1951. *The Trial of Adolf Eichmann: Judgment. Article 1.* Accessed: http://www.nizkor.org/hweb/people/e/eichmann-adolf/transcripts/Judgment/Judgment-003.html

International Criminal Tribunal for the Former Yugoslavia (ICTY). 2001, August 15. *Prosecutor v. Radislav Krstic.* Case No. IT-98-33.

International Criminal Tribunal for the Former Yugoslavia (ICTY). 2003. *Blagojevic, Jokic and Obrenovic ICTY Trial Transcripts.* Accessed: http//www.un/org/icty/transe60/030519IT.htm

International Criminal Tribunal for the Former Yugoslavia (ICTY). 2004. *Blagojevic and Jokic ICTY Trial Transcripts.* Accessed: http//www.un/org/icty/transe60/040205IT.htm

İşcan, M. Y. and Loth, S. R. 1986. 'Estimation of age and determination of sex from the sternal rib', in Reichs, K. J. (ed.), *Forensic Osteology: Advances in the Identification of Human Remains.* Springfield, IL: Charles C Thomas, pp. 68–89.

Jackes, M. 1992. 'Paleodemography: Problems and techniques', in Saunders, S. R. and Katzenberg, M. A. (eds.), *Skeletal Biology of Past Peoples: Research Methods.* New York: Wiley-Liss, pp. 189–224.

Jackson A. R. W. and Jackson, J. M. 2004. *Forensic Science.* Harlow: Pearson-Prentice Hall.

Jackson, R. 2001. *An Investigation into the Forensic Potential of Soft Contact Lenses and an Identification Tool for Victims of Crime.* Unpublished master's dissertation, Bournemouth University, UK.

James, S. H. and Nordby, J. J. 2003. *Forensic Science: An Introduction to Scientific and Investigation Techniques.* 2nd Edition. Boca Raton, FL: CRC Press.

Janaway, R. C. 1996. 'The decay of buried human remains and their associated materials', in Hunter, J. R., Martin, A. L. and Roberts, C. A. (eds.), pp. 58–65.

Jantz, R. L., Hunt, D. R. and Meadows, L., 1995. 'The measure and mismeasure of the tibia: implications for stature estimation', *Journal of Forensic Sciences* 40(5): 758–61.

Jessee, E. and Skinner, M., 2005. 'A typology of mass grave and mass grave-related sites', *Forensic Science International* 152(1): 55–9.

Johl, H. K. and Anderson, G. S., 1996. 'Effects of refrigeration on development of the blow fly, *Calliphora vicina* (Diptera: *Calliphoridae*) and their relationship to time of death', *Journal of the Entomological Society of British Columbia* 93(0): 93–98.

Juhl, K. 2005. '*The Contribution by (Forensic) Archaeologists to Human Rights of Investigations of Mass Graves*', Amsnett no. 5. Stavanger. Accessed: http://www.ark.museum.no/AmS-NETT/Mass_Graves2.pdf

Kamal, A. S. 1958. 'Comparative study of thirteen species of sarcosaprophagous *Calliphoridae* and *Sarcophagidae* (Diptera) I. Bionomics', *Annals of the Entomological Society of America* 51: 261–71.

Karnosh, L. J. 1926 'Enamel hypoplasia,' in Hillson, S. (ed.), *Dental Anthropology* (2nd ed.). Cambridge: Cambridge University Press.

Katz, D. and Suchey, J. M., 1989. 'Race differences in pubic symphyseal aging patterns in the male', *American Journal of Physical Anthropology* 80(2): 167–72.

Katzenberg, M. A. and Pfeiffer, S. 1995. 'Nitrogen isotope evidence for weaning age in a nineteenth century Canadian skeletal sample', in Grauer. A. L. (ed.), *Bodies of Evidence: Reconstructing History Through Skeletal Analysis*. New York: Wiley-Liss, pp. 221–35.

Kaul, R. E. and Welzant, V., 2005. 'Disaster mental health: a discussion of best practices as applied after the Pentagon attack', in Roberts, A. R. (ed.), *Crisis Intervention Handbook: Assessment, Treatment, and Research*. New York: Oxford University Press, pp. 200–20.

Keen, J. A. and Wainwright, J. 1985. 'Ossification of the thyroid, cricoid and arytenoid cartilages', *South African Journal of Laboratory and Clinical Medicine* 4: 83–108.

Keh, B., 1985. 'Scope and applications of forensic entomology', *Annual Review of Entomology* 30: 137–54.

Kelley, M., 1979. 'Parturition and pelvic changes', *American Journal of Physical Anthropology* 51(4): 541–6.

Kennedy, K. A. R., 1995. 'But professor, why teach race identification if races don't exist?', *Journal of Forensic Sciences* 40(5): 797–800.

Kennedy, P., 1998. *Naismith Rules? Actual Versus Predicted Route Times in the Scottish Highlands and English Lake District*. Accessed: http://www.gillean.demon.co.uk/Naismith/Naismith.htm

Keough, M. E. and Samuels, M. 2004. 'The Kosovo Family Support Project: offering psychosocial support for families with missing persons', *Social Work* 49(4): 587–94.

Keough, M. E., Kahn, S. and Andrejevic, A., 2000. 'Disclosing the truth: informed participation in the Antemortem Database Project for survivors of Srebrenica', *Health and Human Rights* 5(1): 68–87.

Keough, M. E., Simmons, T. and Samuels, M. 2004. 'Missing persons in post-conflict settings: best practices for integrating psychosocial and scientific approaches', *The Journal of the Royal Society for the Promotion of Health* 124(6): 271–5.

Keppel, R. D. and Weis, J. G. 1994. 'Time and distance as solvability factors in murder cases', *Journal of Forensic Sciences* 39(2): 386–401.

Kerr, N. W. and. Murray, J. M. 1971. 'An identification by means of forensic odontology: the Mearns (Garvie) murder', *Journal of Forensic Sciences* 11(4): 223–5.

Key, C. A., Aiello, L. C. and Molleson, T. 1994. 'Cranial suture closure and its implications for age estimation', *International Journal of Osteoarchaeology* 4(3): 193–207.

Killam, E. W. 1990. *The Detection of Human Remains*. Springfield, IL, Charles C. Thomas.

Kilpatrick, C. W. 2002. 'Noncryogenic preservation of mammalian tissues for DNA extraction: an assessment of storage methods', *Biochemical Genetics* 40(1–2): 53–62.

Kittichaisaree, K. 2001. *International Criminal Law*. Oxford: Oxford University Press.

Klepinger, L. L. 2006. *Fundamentals of Forensic Anthropology*. Hoboken, NJ: Wiley-Liss.

Kneller, P. 1998. 'Health and safety in church and funerary archaeology', in Cox, M. J. (ed.), *Grave Concerns: Death and Burial in Post-Medieval England 1700 to 1850*. York: CBA, pp. 181–9.

Kneller, P. 1999. 'Health and safety in church archaeology', *The Safety and Health Practitioner* 17(11): 12–15.

Knüsel, C. J. and Outram, A. K. 2004. 'Fragmentation: the zonation method applied to fragmented human remains from archaeological and forensic contexts', *The Journal of Human Palaeoecology* 9(1): 85–97.

Kodaka, T., Sano, T. and Higashi, S. 1996. 'Structural and calcification patterns of the neonatal line in the enamel of human deciduous teeth', *Scanning Microscope* 10(3): 737–43.

Koon, H. E. C., Nicholson, R. A. and Collins, M. J. 2003. 'A practical approach to the identification of low temperature heated bone using TEM', *Journal of Archaeological Science* 30(11): 1393–9.

Kullman, L., Eklund, B. and Grundin, R., 1990. 'The value of frontal sinus in identification of unknown persons', *Journal of Forensic Odontostomatology* 8: 3–10.

Kulshrestha, P. and Satpathy, D. K. 2001. 'Use of beetles in forensic entomology', *Forensic Science International* 120(1–2): 15–17.

Kurosaki K., Wang L., Tang J., Wang W., Saitou N., Endo T. and Ueda S. 2005. 'Identification of a bronze weapon based on an embedded fragment in a 3000-year-old skull', *Forensic Science International* 151(1): 105–8.

Lamendin, H., Baccino, E., Humbert, J. F., Tavernier, J. C., Nossintchouk, R. M. and Zerilli, A. 1992. 'A simple technique for age estimation in adult corpses: the two criteria dental method', *Journal of Forensic Sciences* 37(5): 1373–9.

Lampl, M., Veldhuis, J. D. and Johnson, M. L. 1992. 'Saltation and stasis: a model of human growth', *Science* 258: 801–3.

Lange, M., Schutkowski, H., Hummel, S. and Herrmann, B. 1987. *A Bibliography on Cremation*. Strasbourge: Council of Europe, PACT 19, p. 168.

Lau, E. M. C. 2002. 'Osteoporosis: a worldwide problem and the implications in Asia,' *Annals of the Academy of Medicine* 31(1): 67–8.

Leal-Klevezas, D. S., Martinez-Vazquez, I. O., Cuevas-Hernandez, B., and Martinez-Soriano, J. P. 2000. 'Antifreeze solution improves DNA recovery by preserving the integrity of pathogen-infected blood and other tissues', *Clinical and Diagnostic Laboratory Immunology* 7(6): 945–6.

Legal Information Institute, Cornell Law School. 2006. *Ethics*. Accessed: http://www.law.cornell.edu/wex/index.php/Ethics

Lemkin, R. 1944. *Axis Rule in Occupied Europe: Laws of Occupation, Analysis of Government, Proposals for Redress*. Washington, DC: Carnegie Endowment for International Peace. Reprinted 2005 by The Lawbook Exchange.

Lewin, P. K. 1996. 'Current technology in the examination of ancient man', in Spindler, K., Wilfing, H., Rastbichler-Zissernig, E., ZurNedden, D. and Nothdurfter, H. (eds.), *Human Mummies: A Global Survey of Their Status and the Techniques of Conservation. (The Man in the Ice)*. New York: Springer, pp. 9–14.

Lewis. M. 2007. *The Bioarchaeology of Children. Perspectives from Biological and Forensic Anthropology*. Cambridge: Cambridge University Press.

Loe, L. and Cox, M. 2005. 'Peri- and post-mortem surface features on archaeological human bone: why they should not be ignored and a protocol for their identification and interpretation', in Zakrzewski, S. R. and Clegg, M. (eds.), *Proceedings of the Fifth Annual Conference for the British Association for Biological Anthropology*. BAR International Series 1383. Oxford: Archaeopress, pp. 11–21.

Loth, S. R. 1995. 'Age assessment of the Spitalfields cemetery population by rib phase analysis', *American Journal of Human Biology* 7: 465–71.

Lovejoy, C. O., Meindl, R. S., Mensforth, R. P. and Barton, T. J. 1985. 'Multifactorial determination of skeletal age-at-death: a method and blind tests of its accuracy', *American*

Journal of Physical Anthropology 68(1): 1–14.

Lowe, J. J. and Walker, M. J. C. 1997. *Reconstructing Quaternary Environments*. London: Harlow.

Lucassen, A. and Parker, M. 2001. 'Revealing false paternity: some ethical considerations', *Lancet* 357: 1033–5.

Lundrigan, S. and Canter, D. 2001a. 'Spatial patterns of serial murder: an analysis of disposal site location choice', *Behavioural Sciences and the Law* 19(4): 595–610.

Lundrigan, S. and Canter, D. 2001b. 'A multivariate analysis of serial murderers' disposal site choice', *Journal of Environmental Psychology* 21(4): 423–32.

Lyman, R. L. 1979. 'Available meat from faunal remains: A consideration of techniques'. *American Antiquity* 44: 536–46.

Maat, G. R. and Mastwijk, R. W. 1995. 'Fusion status of the jugular growth plate: an aid for age at death determination', *International Journal of Osteoarchaeology* 5(2): 163–7.

Macchiarelli, R. and Bondioli, L. 1994. 'Linear densitometry and digital image processing of proximal femur radiographs: implications for archaeological and forensic anthropology', *American Journal of Physical Anthropology* 93(1): 109–22.

MacLaughlin, S. and Cox, M. 1989. 'The relationship between body size and parturition scars', *Journal of Anatomy* 164: 256–7.

Maclean, D. F., Kogan, S. L. and Sitt, L. W. 1994. 'Validation of dental radiographs for human identification', *Journal of Forensic Sciences* 39(5): 1195–200.

Mafart, B. and Delingette, H. (eds.). 2002. 'Three dimensional imaging in paleoanthropology and prehistoric archaeology', *Proceedings of the 14th Congress of the International Union of Prehistoric and Protohistoric Sciences*, BAR International Series 1049. Oxford: Archaeopress, pp. 93–9.

Manhein, M. H., Listi, G. and Leitner, M. 2003. 'The landscape's role in dumped and scattered remains,' *Proceedings of the American Academy of Forensic Sciences* Vol 9 (Chicago) H32: 256.

Mant, A. K. 1950. *A Study in Exhumation Data*. Unpublished doctoral thesis in Medicine, University College London.

Mant, A. K. 1987. 'Knowledge acquired from post-war exhumations', in Boddington, A., Garland, A. N. and Janaway, R. C. (eds.), *Death, Decay and Reconstruction: Approaches to Archaeology and Forensic Science*. Manchester: Manchester University Press, pp. 65–78.

Maresh, M. M. 1970. 'Measurement from Roentgenograms', in McCammon, R. W. (ed.), *Human Growth and Development*. Springfield, IL: Charles C Thomas, pp. 157–200.

Martin, A. C. and Barkley, W. D. 1961. *Seed Identification Manual*. Berkley: University California Press.

Martin, R. B., Sharkey, N. A. and Burr, D. B. 1998. *Skeletal Tissue Mechanics*. New York: Springer-Verlag.

Mason, J. 1993. *The Pathology of Trauma* (2nd ed.). London: Edward Arnold.

Masset, C. 1989. 'Age estimation on the basis of cranial sutures', in İşcan, M. Y. (ed.), *Age Markers in the Human Skeleton*. Springfield, IL: Charles C Thomas, pp: 71–103.

Mays, S. and Cox, M. 2000. 'Sex determination in skeletal remains', in Cox, M. and Mays, S. (eds.), *Human Osteology: In Archaeology and Forensic Science*. London: Greenwich Medical Media, pp. 117–30.

Mays, S., Richards, M. P. and Fuller, B. 2002. 'Bone stable isotope evidence for infant feeding in mediaeval England', *Antiquity* 76: 654–6.

McCormick, W. F. and Stewart, J. H. 1988. 'Age related changes in the human plastron: a roentgenographic and morphologic study', *Journal of Forensic Sciences* 33(1): 100–20.

McKern, T. W. and Stewart, T. D. 1957. *Skeletal Age Changes in Young American Males Analysed From the Standpoint of Age Identification*.

Technical Report EP-45. Natick, MA: Headquarters, Quartermaster Research and Development Command.

McKinley, J. and Brickley, M. 2004. *Guidelines to the Standards for Recording Human Remains.* Reading: IFA Publication.

McKinley, J. and Roberts, C. 1993. *Excavation and Post-excavation Treatment of Cremated and Inhumed Human Remains.* Technical Paper 13. Institute of Field Archaeologists. Reading: IFA Publication, pp. 1–12

McKinley, J. I. 1993. 'Bone fragment size and weights of bone from modern British cremations and the implications for the interpretation of archaeological cremations', *International Journal of Osteoarchaeology* 3(4): 283–7.

McKinley, J. I. 1994. 'Bone fragment size in British cremation burials and its implications for pyre technology and ritual', *Journal of Archaeological Science* 21: 339–42.

McKinley, J. I. 2000. 'The analysis of cremated bone', in Cox, M. and Mays, S. (eds.), *Human Osteology in Archaeological and Forensic Science.* London: Greenwich Medical Media, pp. 403–21.

McKinley, J. I. and Bond, J. M. 2000. 'Cremated bone', in Brothwell, D. R. and Pollard, A. M. (eds.), *Handbook of Archaeological Sciences.* Chichester: Wiley, pp. 281–92.

McLaughlin, J. E. 1974. *The Detection of Buried Bodies.* Yuba City, CA: Andermac.

Meadows, L. and Jantz, R. L. 1992. 'Estimation of stature from metacarpal lengths', *Journal of Forensic Sciences* 37(1): 147–54.

Melvern, L. R. 2000. *A People Betrayed: The Role of the West in Rwanda's Genocide.* London: Zed Books.

Melvern, L. R. 2004. *Conspiracy to Murder: Planning the Rwandan Genocide.* London: Verso Books.

Merz, J. F. and Sankar, P. 1998. 'DNA banking: an empirical study of a proposed consent form', in Merz, J. F. and Sankar, P. (eds.), *Stored Tissue Samples: Ethical, Legal, and Public Policy Implications.* Iowa City: University of Iowa Press, pp. 198–225.

Micozzi, M. S. 1991. *Postmortem Change in Human and Animal Remains: A Systematic Approach.* Springfield, IL: Charles C Thomas.

Miethe T. D. and Drass K. A. 2002. 'Classifying crime scene behaviour: new directions', in Godwin, G. M. (ed.), *Criminal Psychology and Forensic Technology: A Collaborative Approach to Effective Profiling.* Boca Raton, FL: CRC Press, pp. 105–66.

Mildenhall, D. C. 1990. 'Forensic palynology in New Zealand', *Review of Palaeobotany and Palynology* 64: 227–34.

Miles, A. E. W. 1963. 'The dentition in the assessment of individual age in skeletal material: dental anthropology', in Brothwell, D. R. (ed.), *Dental Anthropology.* Oxford: Pergaman Press, pp. 191–209.

Mitchell, D., Willerslev, E. and Hansen, A. 2005. 'Damage and repair of ancient DNA', *Mutation Research* 571(1–2): 265–76.

Mittler, D. M. and Sheridan, S. G. 1992. 'Sex determination in subadults using auricular surface morphology: a forensic science perspective'. *Journal of Forensic Sciences* 37(4): 1068–75.

Molleson, T. and Cox, M. 1993. *The Spitalfields Project Volume 2: The Anthropology* Research Report 86. York: Council for British Archaeology.

Moore, P. D., Webb, J. A. and Collinson, M. E. 1991. *Pollen Analysis* (2nd ed.). Oxford: Blackwell Scientific.

Moore-Jansen, P. H., Ousley, S. D. and Jantz, R. L. 1994. *Data Collection Procedures for Forensic Skeletal Material* (3rd ed.). Knoxville: University of Tennessee, Department of Anthropology. Report of Investigations No. 48.

Moorrees, C. F., Fanning, E. A. and Hunt, E. E. 1963a. 'Formation and resorption of three deciduous teeth in children', *American Journal of Physical Anthropology* 21: 205–13.

Moorrees, C. F., Fanning, E. A. and Hunt, E. E. 1963b. 'Age variation of formation stages for ten permanent teeth', *Journal of Dental Research* 42: 1490–502.

Moraitis, K. and Spiliopoulou, C. 2006. 'Identification and differential diagnosis of perimortem blunt force trauma in tubular long bone'. *Forensic Science, Pathology and Medicine* 2(4)221–9.

Munsell Color Co. 2000. *Munsell Soil Color Charts* (2nd Ed.). Baltimore, Munsell Color Company.

Muralidharan, K. and Wemmer, C. 1994. 'Transporting and storing field-collected specimens for DNA without refrigeration for subsequent DNA extraction and analysis', *Biotechniques* 17(3): 420–2.

Museum of London Archaeological Service (MoLAS). 1994. *Archaeological Site Manual*. London: MoLAS.

Musgrave, J. H. and Harneja, N. K. 1978. 'The estimation of adult stature from metacarpal bone length', *American Journal of Physical Anthropology* 48(1): 113–19.

Mynors, R. A. B. 1998. *William of Malmesbury: Gesta Regum Anglorum (Deeds of the English Kings) Vol. 1*. Oxford: Oxford University Press.

Naismith, W. W. 1892. *Naismith's Rule*. Accessed: http://en.wikipedia.org/wiki/Naismith%27s_Rule

Nakagawa, T., Brugiapaglia, E., Digerfeldt, G., Reille, M., De Beaulieu, J.-L. and Yasuda, Y. 1998. 'Dense-media separation as a more efficient pollen extraction method for use with organic sediment samples: comparison with the conventional method', *Boreas* 27: 15–24.

National Center for Post Traumatic Stress Disorder. 2001a. *Effects of Traumatic Stress in a Disaster Situation*. A National Center for Post Traumatic Stress Disorder Fact Sheet. Parramatta: The NSW Institute of Psychiatry.

National Centre for Post Traumatic Stress Disorder. 2001b. *How is Post Traumatic Stress Disorder Measured?* Los Angeles, CA. National Centre for Post Traumatic Stress Disorder.

National Child Traumatic Stress Network (NCTSN). 2005. *Provider Self Care During Relief Work*. Los Angeles, CA: National Center for Child Traumatic Stress, Terrorism and Disaster Branch.

Nawrocki, S. P., Pless, J. E., Hawley, D. A. and Wagner, S. A. 1997. 'Fluvial transport of human crania', in Haglund, W. D. and Sorg, M. H. (eds.), *Forensic Taphonomy: The Postmortem Fate of Human Remains*. Boca Raton, FL: CRC Press, pp. 529–52.

Nederhand, R. J., Droog, S., Kluft, C., Simoons, M. L. and de Maat, M. P. 2003. 'Logistics and quality control for DNA sampling in large multicenter studies', *Journal of Thrombosis and Haemostasis* 1(5): 987–91.

O'Connell T. and Hedges R (2001) 'Isolation and isotopic analysis of individual amino acids from archaeological bone collagen: a new method using RP-HPLC'. *Archaeometry* 43: 421–438.

O'Connell, L. E., Stevens, J. S. and Cox, M. J. 2003. 'Sex size and genetic mistakes: identifying disorders of sexual differentiation in human skeletal remains', *Proceedings of the American Academy of Forensic Sciences* Vol 9 (Chicago) H6: 242.

O'Connor, T. and Evans, J. 2005. *Environmental Archaeology: Principles and Methods* (2nd ed.). Stroud, UK: Sutton.

O'Sullivan, M. I. 2001. *An Analysis of Possible Anthropogenic Alteration of Human Bones Recovered from Eton Rowing Lake, South Buckinghamshire, UK*. Unpublished master's dissertation, University of Bournemouth, UK.

Office of the United Nations Security Coordinator. 1998. *Security in the Field*. New York: United Nations.

Office of the United Nations. n.d. *UN Volunteers Handbook*. Accessed: http://www.unvolunteers.org/volunteers/Safety/UNVH.pdf

Ohtani, S. 1995. 'Estimation of age from the teeth of unidentified corpses using the amino acid racemization method with reference to actual cases', *American Journal of Forensic Medicine and Pathology* 16(3): 238–42.

Ortner, D. J. 2003. *Identification of Pathological Conditions in Human Skeletal Remains* (2nd ed.). Washington, DC: Smithsonian Institution Press.

Ortner, D. J., and Putschar, W. G. J., 1985. *Identification of Pathological Conditions in Human Skeletal Remains*. Smithsonian Institute Press, Washington, D.C.

Osborne, D., Simmons, T. L. and Nawrocki, S. P. 2004. 'Reconsidering the auricular surface as an indicator of age at death', *Journal of Forensic Sciences* 49(5): 905–11.

Ousley, S. 1995. 'Should we estimate biological or forensic stature?', *Journal of Forensic Sciences* 40(5): 768–73.

Ousley, S. D. and Jantz, R. L. 2005. *FORDISC 3.0: Personal Computer Forensic Discriminant Functions*. Knoxville: Forensic Anthropology Centre, University of Tennessee.

Owsley, D. W. 1995. 'Techniques for locating burials, with emphasis on the probe', *Journal of Forensic Sciences* 40(5): 735–40.

Oxlee, D. D. 1997a. *Air Reconnaissance Overflights: Abbeystead Trial Report*. Forensic Search Advisory Group. (Unpublished)

Oxlee, G. 1997b. *Aerospace Reconnaissance*. London: Brassey.

Page, D. C., Chapelle, A. and Weissenbach, J. 1985. 'Chromosome Y-specific DNA in related human XX males'. *Nature* 315: 224–6.

Perizonius, W. R. K. 1984. 'Closing and non-closing sutures in 256 crania of known age and sex from Amsterdam (AD 1883–1909)', *Journal of Human Evolution* 13: 201–16.

Physicians for Human Rights. 1999. *War Crimes in Kosovo, A Population based assessment of Human Rights Violations against Kosovo Albanians*. A report by Physicians for Human Rights in conjunction with Program on Forced Migration and Health, Center for Population and Family Health, The Joseph L. Mailman School of Public Health, Columbia University, Boston.

Poinar, H. N. and Stankiewicz, B. A. 1999. 'Protein preservation and DNA retrieval from ancient tissues', *Proceedings of the National Academy of Sciences of the United States of America* 96(15): 8426–31.

Pollanen, M. S. 1998. *Forensic Diatomology and Drowning*. Amsterdam: Elsevier.

Pope, E. J. and Smith, O. C. 2004. 'Identification of traumatic injury in burned cranial bone: an experimental approach', *Journal of Forensic Sciences*, 49(3): 431–40.

Quatrehomme, G. and İşcan, M. 1997. 'Bevelling in exit gunshot wounds in bones', *Forensic Science International* 89(1–2): 93–101.

Quatrehomme, G. and İşcan, M. Y. 1999. 'Characteristics of gunshot wounds in the skull', *Journal of Forensic Sciences* 44(3): 568–76.

Rackham, O. 1994. 'Trees and woodland in Anglo-Saxon England: the documentary evidence,' in Rackham, J. (ed.), *Environment and Economy in Anglo-Saxon England*. Council for British Archaeology Research Report. 89: 7–11. York: Council for British Archaeology.

Rebmann, A., David, E. and Sorg, M. H. 2000. *Cadaver Dog Handbook*. Boca Raton, FL: CRC Press.

Regehr, C. 2005. 'Crisis support for families of emergency responders,' in Roberts, A. R. (ed.), *Crisis Intervention Handbook: Assessment, Treatment, and Research*. New York: Oxford University Press, pp. 246–61.

Reichs, K. J. 1993. 'Quantified comparison of the frontal sinus by means of computed tomography', *Forensic Science International* 61(2–3): 141–68.

Reid, M. C., 2003. *Methods of Defleshing Human Remains and their Utilisation in Forensic Anthropological Analysis*. Unpublished master's dissertation, Bournemouth University, UK.

Reiter, C. 1984. 'Zum wachstumsverhalten der maden der blauen schmeißfliege', *Calliphora vicina. Zeitschrift für Rechtsmedizin* 91: 295–308.

Resnick, D. 1995. *Diagnosis of Bone and Joint Disorders*. Philadelphia: WB Saunders.

Reyes-Gasga, J., García, R., Alvarez-Fregoso, O., Chávez-Carvayar, J. A. and Vargas-Ulloa, L. E. 1999. 'Conductivity in human tooth enamel', *Journal of Material Science* 34(9): 2183–8.

Rezendes, P. 1999. *Tracking and the Art of Seeing*. New York: Harper Collins.

Richards, M. P., Mays, S. and Fuller, B. 2002. 'Stable carbon and nitrogen isotope values of bone and teeth reflect weaning age at the mediaeval Wharram Percy site, Yorkshire, UK', *American Journal of Physical Anthropology* 199: 205–10.

Rittner, C. 2002. 'Using rape as a weapon of genocide', in Rittner, C., Roth, J. K. and Smith, J. (eds.), pp. 91–9.

Rittner, C., Roth, J. K. and Smith, J. 2002. *Will Genocide Ever End?* St. Paul, MN: Paragon House Publishers.

Roberts, D. L. (1999) *Staying Alive: Safety and Security Guidlines for Humanitarian Volunteers in Conflict Areas*. Geneva, International Committee of the Red Cross.

Roche, C. 1999. *Impact Assessment for Development Agencies*. Oxford: Oxfam.

Rohde, D. 1997. *Endgame: The Betrayal and Fall of Srebrenica, Europe's Worst Massacre Since World War II*. New York: Farrar, Straus and Giroux.

Romero, J. 1958. *Mutilaciones dentarias prehispánicas de México y América en general*. México City: Instituto Nacional de Antropología e Historia.

Romero, J. 1970. 'Dental mutilation, trephination, and cranial deformation,' in Stewart, T. D. (ed.), *Handbook of Middle American Indians, Vol. 9: Physical Anthropology*. Austin: University of Texas Press, pp. 50–67.

Roper, M. K. 1969. 'Survey of the evidence for intrahuman killing in the Pleictocene', *Current Anthropology* 10(4): 427–59.

Rösing, F. W. 1977. Methoden und assagemöglichkeiten der anthropologischen leichenbrandbearbeitung', *Archäologie und Naturwissenschaeften* 1: 53–80.

Roskam, S. 2001. *Excavation*. Cambridge: Cambridge University Press.

Rossmo, K. D. 1999. *Geographic Profiling*. Boca Raton, FL: CRC Press.

Roth, J. K. 2002. 'The politics of definition', in Rittner, C., Roth, J. K. and Smith, J. M. (eds.), pp. 23–30.

Rothstein, M., Murray, T., Kaebnick, G. and Majumder, M. (eds.). 2006. *Genetic Ties and the Family: The Impact of Paternity Testing on Parents and Children*. Baltimore: The Johns Hopkins University Press.

Rowe, W. F. 1997. 'Biodegradation of hairs and fibres,' in Haglund, W. D. and Sorg, M. H. (eds.), *Forensic Taphonomy: The Postmortem Fate of Human Remains*. Boca Raton, FL: CRC Press, pp. 337–52.

Royal College of Pathologists. Sept. 2002. *Guidelines on Autopsy Practice*. Appendices A1–A3. http://www.rcpath.org/index.asp?Pagel.

Ruffell, A. and McKinley, J. 2005. 'Forensic geoscience: applications of geology, geomorphology and geophysics to criminal investigations', *Earth Science Review* 69: 235–47.

Rummel, R. J. 1997. *Statistics of Democide: Genocide and Mass Murder Since 1900*. Charlottesville: Centre for National Security Law, School of Law, University of Virginia.

Russell, M. A., Atkinson, R. D., Klatt, E. C. and Noguchi, T. T. 1995. 'Safety in bullet recovery procedures: a study of the Black Talon bullet'. *American Journal of Forensic Medicine and Pathology* 16(2): 120–3.

Rutty, G. N. 2000. 'Human DNA contamination of mortuaries: does it matter?', *The Journal of Pathology* 190(4): 410–1.

Rutty, G. N., Byard, R. and Toskos, M. 2005. 'The tsunami: an environmental mass disaster', *Forensic Science, Medicine and Pathology* 1: 3–8.

Rutty, G. N., Hopwood, A. and Tucker, V. 2003. 'The effectiveness of protective clothing in the reduction of potential DNA contamination of the scene of crime', *International Journal of Legal Medicine* 117(3): 170–4.

Rutty, G. N., Watson, S. and Davison, J. 2000. 'DNA contamination of mortuary instruments and work surfaces: a significant problem in forensic practice?', *International Journal of Legal Medicine* 114(1–2): 56–60.

Saferstein, R. 2004. *Criminalistics – An Introduction to Forensic Sciences*. Upper Saddle River, NJ: Pearson/Prentice Hall.

Salas, A., Phillips, C. and Carracedo, A. 2005. 'Ancestry vs physical traits: the search for ancestry informative markers (AIMs)', *International Journal of Legal Medicine* 120(3): 188–9.

Sanford, V. 2003. *Buried Secrets: Truth and Human Rights in Guatemala*. New York: Macmillan.

Sauer, N. J. 1998. 'The timing if injuries and manner of death: distinguishing among antemortem, perimortem and postmortem trauma,' in Reichs, K. J. (ed.), *Forensic Osteology: Advances in the Identification of Human Remains* (2nd ed.). Springfield, IL: Charles C Thomas, pp. 321–32.

Saukko, P. J. and Knight, B. 2004. *Knight's Forensic Pathology*. London: Arnold.

Saunders, S. R., Fitzgerald, C., Rogers, T., Dudar, C. and McKillop, H. 1992. 'A test of several methods of skeletal age estimation using a documented archaeological sample', *Canadian Society of Forensic Science Journal* 25: 97–117.

Save the Children. 2003. *Toolkits: A Practical Guide to Planning, Monitoring, Evaluation and Impact Assessment* (2nd ed). London: Save the Children.

Schabas, W. A. 2000. *Genocide in International Law*. Cambridge: Cambridge University Press.

Scheffer, D. 2001, June 13. *Fiftieth Anniversary of the Genocide Convention*. Accessed: http://www.iccnow.org/documents/USScheffer_Genocide13June01.pdf?PHPSESSID/dacc676a5cc797c9970bbf3fe0096253

Scheuer, J. L. and Black, S. 2000. *Developmental Juvenile Osteology*. London: Elsevier/Academic Press.

Scheuer, J. L. and MacLaughlin-Black, S. M. 1994. 'Age estimation from the pars basilaris from the fetal and juvenile occipital bone', *International Journal of Osteoarchaeology* 4: 377–80.

Scheuer, L. and Black, S. 2004. *The Juvenile Skeleton*. London: Academic Press.

Schofield, D. 2004. Health and safety in genocide investigations. *Journal of the Royal Society for the Promotion of Health* 124(6): 257–8.

Scholtz, H. J. 2005. *Manual for Forensic Medical Practice in South Africa*. Johannesburg, South Africa: Department of Health.

Scholtz, H. J. and the National Forensic Pathology Services Committee: Academic Subcommittee members. 2007. *National Code of Guidelines for Forensic Pathology in South Africa*. Johannesberg, National Department of Health, South Africa.

Schour, I. and Massler, M. 1941. 'The development of human dentition', *Journal of American Dental Association* 28: 1153–60.

Schultz, M. 1997. 'Microscopic investigation of excavated skeletal remains: a contribution to paleopathology and forensic medicine,' in Haglund, W. D. and Sorg, M. H. (eds.), *Forensic Taphonomy: The Postmortem Fate of Human Remains*. Boca Raton, FL: CRC Press, pp. 201–22.

Schutkowski, H., Hansen, B., Wormuth, M. and Herrmann, B. 2006. *Signatures of Stable Strontium Isotopes in Human Hard Tissue – Applications to Forensic Identification*. Poster for American Association of Physical Anthropologist annual meeting. Accessed: www.physanth.org

Schutkowski, W. W. 1993. 'Sex determination in infant and juvenile skeletons using morphological features in mandible and ilium'. *American Journal of Physical Anthropology* 90: 199–205.

Schwartz, J. H. 1995. *Skeleton Keys*. New York: Oxford University Press.

Schweingruber, F. H. 1978. *Microscopic Wood Anatomy*. Teufen: Fluk-Wirth.

Scoles, P. V., Salverno, R., Villalba, K. and Riew, D. 1988. 'Relationship of the iliac crest to skeletal and chronological age', *Journal of Pediatric Orthopaedics* 8: 639–44.

Sheaff, M. T. and Hopster, D. J. 2005. *Post Mortem Technique Handbook*. 2nd Ed. London, Springer-Verlag.

Shipman, P. 1981. 'Application of scanning electron microscopy to taphonomic problems,' in Cantwell, A. E., Griffin, J. B. and Rotherschild, N. A. (eds.), *The Research Potential of Anthropological Museum Collection*. New York: Annals of the New York Academy of Science, pp. 357–85.

Shipman, P., Foster, G. and Schoeninger, M. 1984. 'Burnt bones and teeth: an experimental study of colour, morphology, crystal structure and shrinkage', *Journal of Archaeological Sciences* 11: 307–25.

Shipman, P. and Rose, J. 1983. 'Early hominid hunting, butchering, and carcass processing behaviours: approaches to the fossil record', *Journal of Anthropological Archaeology* 2: 57–98.

Shriver, M. D., Mei, R., Parra, E. J., Sonpar, V., Halder, I., Tishkoff, S. A., Schurr, T. G., Zhadanov, S. I., Osipova, L. P., Brutsaert, T. D., Friedlaender, J., Jorde, L. B., Watkins, W. S., Bamshad, M. J., Gutierrez, G., Loi, H., Matsuzaki, H., Kittles, R. A., Argyropoulos, G., Fernandez, J. R., Akey, J. M. and Jones, K. W. 2005. 'Large-scale SNP analysis reveals clustered and continuous patterns of human genetic variation', *Human Genomics* 2(2): 81–9.

Shuman, M. and Wright, R. 1999. 'Evaluation of clinician accuracy in describing gunshot wound injuries', *Journal of Forensic Sciences*, 44(2): 339–42.

Simmons, T. 2002. 'Taphonomy of a karstic cave execution site at Hrgar, Bosnia-Herzegovina', in Haglund, W. and Sorg, M. (eds.), pp. 263–75.

Simmons, T. and Haglund. W. 2005. 'Anthropology in a forensic context,' in Hunter, J. and Cox, M. (eds.), pp. 159–76.

Simmons, T., Jantz, R. L. and Bass, W. M. 1990. 'Stature estimation from fragmentary femora: a revision of the Steele method', *Journal of Forensic Sciences* 35(3): 628–36.

Simmons, T. and Skinner, M. F. 2006, February 20–25. 'The accuracy of ante-mortem data and presumptive identification: appropriate procedures, applications and ethics', *Proceedings of the American Academy of Forensic Sciences* Vol 12 (Seattle) H51: 303.

Simonett, D. S. 1983. *Manual of Remote Sensing* (2nd ed.). Sheridan: American Society of Photogrammetry.

Simpson, B. 2005. *Forensic Archaeology in an Urban Setting: Preliminary Research – An Under-used Resource*. Unpublished master's dissertation, Bournemouth University, UK.

Skinner, M. and Dupras, T. 1993. 'Variation in birth timing and location of the neonatal line in human enamel', *Journal of Forensic Sciences*, 38(6): 1383–90.

Skinner, M. and Lazenby, R. A. 1983. *Found! Human Remains: A Field Manual for the Recovery of the Recent Human Skeleton*. Vancouver: Simon Fraser University Archaeology Press.

Skinner, M. F. 1987. 'Planning the archaeological recovery of evidence from recent mass graves', *Forensic Science International* 34(4): 267–87.

Skinner, M. F., York, H. P. and Connor, M. A. 2002. 'Postburial disturbance of graves in Bosnia-Herzegovina', in Haglund, W. D. and Sorg, M. H. (eds.), pp. 293–308.

Smith, A. 2003. 'Disaster victim identification of military aircrew, 1945–2002', *Aviation, Space, and Environmental Medicine* 74(11): 1198–200.

Smith. B. H. 1984. 'Patterns of molar wear in hunter-gatherers and agriculturalists', *American Journal of Physical Anthropology* 63: 39–56.

Smith, B. H. 1991. 'Standards of human tooth formation and dental age assessment', in Kelley, M. A. and Larsen, C. S. (eds.), *Advances in Dental Anthropology*. New York: Wiley-Liss, pp. 143–68.

Smith, J. D. 2001. 'Patrolling the boundaries of race: motion picture censorship and Jim Crow in Virginia, 1922–1932', *Historical Journal of Film, Radio and Television* 21(3): 273–91.

Smith, K. G. V. 1986. *A Manual of Forensic Entomology*. London: British Museum (Natural History)/Ithaca, NY: Cornell University Press.

Smith, K. G. V. 1989. 'An introduction to the immature stages of British flies: Diptera larvae, with notes on eggs, puparia and pupae', *Handbooks for Identification of British Insects* 10(14): 1–280.

Snow, C. P. 1982. 'Forensic anthropology', *Annual Review of Archaeology* 11: 97–191.

Soil Survey Staff. 1999. *Soil Taxonomy: A Basic System of Soil Classification for Making and Interpreting Soil Surveys* (2nd ed.). Agricultural Handbook 436. Washington, DC: U.S. Department of Agriculture Soil Conservation Service.

Soomer, H., Ranta, H., Lincoln, M. J., Penttilä, A. and Leibur, E. 2003. 'Reliability and validity of eight dental age estimation methods for adults', *Journal of Forensic Sciences* 48(1): 149–52.

Sorg, M. H., Dearborn, J. H., Monahan, E. I., Ryan, H. F., Sweeney, K. G. and David, E. 1997. 'Forensic taphonomy in marine contexts', in Haglund, W. D. and Sorg, M. H. (eds.), *Forensic Taphonomy: The Postmortem Fate of Human Remains*. Boca Raton, FL: CRC Press, pp. 567–604.

Speiser, A. E. 1969. 'Enuma Elish', in Prichard, J. (ed.), *Near Eastern Texts Relating to the Old Testament* (3rd ed.). Princeton, NJ: Princeton University Press, pp. 60–119.

Sperling, F. A. H., Anderson, G. S. and Hickey, D. A. 1994. 'A DNA-based approach to the identification of insect species used for postmortem interval estimation', *Journal of Forensic Sciences* 39(2): 418–27.

Spring, D., Lovejoy, C., Bende, G. and Duerr, M. 1989. 'The radiographic preauricular groove of pregnancy: its non-relationship to past parity', *American Journal of Physical Anthropology* 79(2): 247–52.

Stankiewicz, B. A., Hutchins, J. C., Thomson, R., Briggs, D. E. and Evershed, R. P. 1997. 'Assessment of bog-body tissue preservation by pyrolysis-gas chromatography/mass spectrometry', *Rapid Communications in Mass Spectrometry* 11(17): 1884–90.

Stanley, E. A. 1991. 'Forensic palynology. Federal Bureau of Investigation International', in *Symposium on Trace Evidence*. Washington, DC: US Government Printing Office, pp. 17–30.

Steele, J. 2000. 'Skeletal indicators of handedness', in Cox, M. and Mays, S. (eds.), *Human Osteology*. London: Greenwich Medical Media, pp. 307–23.

Sterenberg, J. 2001. *The Archaeology of Mass Graves*. Unpublished master's dissertation, Bournemouth University, UK.

Stevens, J. S. 2000. *An Evaluation of the Skeletal Manifestations of Disorders of Sexual Differentiation and Their Potential Use in Individuation*. Unpublished master's dissertation, Bournemouth University, UK.

Stevenson, P. H. 1929. 'On racial differences in stature long bone regression formulae, with special reference to stature reconstruction formulae for the Chinese', *Biometrika* 21: 303–18.

Stewart, T. 1970. *Personal Identification in Mass Disasters*. Washington, DC: National Museum of History.

Stewart, T. D. 1979. *Essentials of Forensic Anthropology*. Springfield, IL: Charles C Thomas.

Stott, G. G., Sis, R. F. and Levy, B. M. 1982. 'Cemental annulation as an age criterion in forensic dentistry', *Journal of Dental Research* 61(6): 814–17.

Stout, S. D. and Paine, R. R. 1992. 'Histological age estimation using rib and clavicle',

American Journal of Physical Anthropology 87(1): 111–15.

Stover, E. and Shigekane, R. 2002. 'The missing in the aftermath of war: when do the needs of victims' families and international war crimes tribunals clash?', *International Review of the Red Cross* 848: 845–65.

Stover, E., Haglund, W. D. and Samuels, M. 2003. 'Exhumation of mass graves in Iraq: consideration for forensic investigations, humanitarian needs, and the demands of justice', *Journal of the American Medical Association* 290(5): 663–6.

Strinovic, D., Skavi, J., Kostovic, I., Henigsberg, N., Judas, M. and Clark, D. 1994. 'Identification of war victims in Croatia', *Medical Science Law* 34(3): 207–12.

Stuart, B. H., Craft, L., Forbes, S. L. and Dent, B. B. 2005. 'Studies of adipocere using attenuated total reflectance infrared spectroscopy', *Forensic Science, Medicine and Pathology* 1(3): 197–202.

Sullivan, K., Johnson, P., Rowlands, D. and Allen, H. 2004. 'New developments and challenges in the use of the UK DNA Database: addressing the issue of contaminated consumables', *Forensic Science International* 146: S175–6.

Swango, K. L., Timken, M. D., Chong, M. D. and Buoncristiani, M. R. 2005. 'A quantitative PCR assay for the assessment of DNA degradation in forensic samples', *Forensic Science International* 158(1): 14– 26.

Tantawi, T. I. and Greenberg, B. 1993. 'The effect of killing and preservative solutions on estimates of maggot age in forensic cases', *Journal of Forensic Sciences* 38(3): 702–7.

Taylor, T. 1996. *The Prehistory of Sex*. London: Fourth Estate.

The College of Radiographers. 1999. *Guidance for the Provision of Forensic Radiography Services*. London: The College of Radiographers.

The Eagle. 2004. U.S. Army Space and Missile Defence Command, 11(4):10

'The Nuremberg Code (1947)' in Mitscherlich, A. and Mielke, F. (eds.), *Doctors of Infamy: The Story of the Nazi Medical Crimes*. New York: Schuman, 1949: xiii–xxv.

The Prosecutor v. Akayesu, 1998, September 2, Case No. ICTR-96–4-T, ICTR TC.

Thorpe, I. J. N. 2003. 'Anthropology, archaeology, and the origin of warfare', *World Archaeology* 35(1): 145–65.

Thurman, M. D. and Wilmore, L. J. 1981. 'A replicative cremation experiment', *North American Archaeologist* 2: 275–83.

Torres, Y., Flores, I., Prieto, V., López-Soto, M., Farfan, M. J., Carracedo, A. and Sanz, P. 2003. 'DNA mixtures in forensic casework: a 4-year retrospective study', *Forensic Science International* 134(2–3): 180–6.

Trotter, M. 1970. 'Estimation of stature from intact limb bones', in Stewart, T. D. (ed.), *Personal Identification in Mass Disasters*. Washington, DC: National Museum of Natural History, Smithsonian Institution.

Trotter, M. and Gleser, G. C. 1952. 'Estimation of stature from long bones of American whites and Negroes', *American Journal of Physical Anthropology* 10(4): 463–514.

Trotter, M. and Gleser G. 1958. 'A re-evaluation of estimation of stature based on measurements of stature taken during life and of long bones after death', *American Journal of Physical Anthropology* 16(1): 79–123.

Trudell, M. B. 1999. 'Anterior femoral curvature revisited: race assessment from the femur', *Journal of Forensic Sciences* 44(4): 700–7.

Trueman, C. N. 2004. 'Forensic geology of bone mineral: geochemical tracers for postmortem movement of bone remains', in Pye, K. and Croft, D. J. (eds.), *Forensic Geoscience: Principle, Techniques and Applications*. Special Publication 232. London: Geological Society, pp. 249–56.

Tucker, B. K., Hutchinson, D. L., Gilliland, M. F. G., Charles, T. M., Daniel, H. J. and Wolfe, L. D. 2001. 'Microscopic characteristics of hacking trauma', *Journal of Forensic Sciences* 46(2): 234–40.

Tucker, M. E. 1988. *Techniques in Sedimentology*. Oxford: Blackwell.

Tuller, H. and Duric, M. 2006. 'Keeping the pieces together: comparison of mass grave excavation methodology', *Forensic Science International* 156(2–3): 192–200.

Turner, B. D. 1991. 'Forensic entomology', *Forensic Science Progress* 5: 129–52.

Turner, B. D. and Howard, T. 1992. 'Metabolic heat generation in dipteran larval aggregations: a consideration for forensic entomology', *Medical and Veterinary Entomology* 6: 179–81.

Tyrrell, A. 2000. '*Corpus saxonum*: early medieval bodies and corporeal identity', in Frazer, W. O. and Tyrrell A. (eds.), *Social Identity in Early Medieval Britain*. London and New York: Leicester University Press. pp. 137–55.

Ubelaker, D. H. 1987. 'Estimating age at death from immature human skeleton: an overview', *Journal of Forensic Sciences* 32: 1254–63.

Ubelaker, D. H. 1989. *Human Skeletal Remains* (2nd ed.). Washington, DC: Taraxacum Press.

Ubelaker, D. H. and Jacobs, C. H. 1995. 'Identification of orthopedic device manufacturer', *Journal of Forensic Sciences* 40(2): 168–70.

Ullrich, H. 1975. 'Estimation of fertility by means of pregnancy and childbirth alterations at the pubis, the ilium and the sacrum', *Ossa* 2: 23–39.

United Nations. 1991. *Manual on the Effective Prevention and Investigation of Extra-Legal, Arbitrary and Summary Executions (Minnesota protocols)*. UN Doc. ST/CSDHA/12. New York: United Nations.

United Nations. 1999. *Briefing by War Crimes Tribunal Prosecutors*. Accessed: http://www.un.org/News/briefings/docs/1999/19991110.delponte.brf.doc.html

United Nations. 1999. *Report of the Secretary General Pursuant to General Assembly Resolution 53.35, the Fall of Srebrenica*. New York: UN General Assembly.

United Nations' International Covenant on Civil and Political Rights. 1966. *Article 7*. Accessed: http://www.ohchr.org/english/law/ccpr.htm

Van Vark, G. N. 1974. 'The investigation of human cremated skeletal material by multivariate statistical methods: I methodology', *Ossa* 1: 63–95.

Van Vark, G. N. 1975. 'The investigation of human cremated skeletal material by multivariate statistical methods: II methodology', *Ossa* 2: 47–68.

Vass, A. A., Bass, W. M., Wolt, J. D., Foss, J. E. and Ammons, J. T. 1992. 'Time since death determinations of human cadavers using soil solution', *Journal of Forensic Sciences* 37(5): 1236–53.

Vilain, E. and McCabe, E. R. 1998. 'Mammalian sex determination: from gonads to brain', *Molecular Genetics and Metabolism* 65(2): 74–84.

von Lenhössek, M. 1917. 'Über Nahtverknocherung im Kindesalter', *Arch für Anthropol* 15: 164–80.

von Singer, R. 1953. 'Estimation of age from cranial suture closure', *Journal of Forensic Medicine* 1: 52–9.

Wahl, J. 1982. 'Leichenbranduntersuchungen. Ein überblick über die bearbeitungs- und aussagemöglichkeiten von Brandgräbern', *Prähistorische Zeitschrift* 57: 1–125.

Wakely, J. 1997. 'Identification and analysis of violent and non-violent head injuries in osteoarchaeological material', in Carman, J. (ed.), *Material Harm: Archaeological Studies of War and Violence*. Glasgow: Cruithne Press, pp. 24–46.

Walker, R. A. and Lovejoy, C. O. 1985. 'Radiographic changes in the clavicle and proximal femur and their use in the determination of skeletal age at death', *American Journal of Physical Anthropology* 68(1): 67–78.

Wall, R., French, N. P. and Morgan, K. L. 1992. 'Effects of temperature on the development and abundance of the sheep blowfly *Lucilia sericata* (Diptera: *Calliphoridae*)', *Bulletin of Entomological Research* 82: 125–31.

Wallace, T. and Kaplan, A. 2003. *The Taking of the Horizon: Lessons from ActionAid Uganda's Experiences of Changes in Development Practice.* Working Paper No. 4. London: ActionAid International.

Wallin, J. A., Tkocz, I. and Kristensen, G. 1994. 'Microscopic age determination of human skeletons including an unknown but calculable variable', *International Journal of Osteoarchaeology* 4(4): 353–62.

Walsh, J. 1996. 'Unearthing evil', *Time Magazine* January 29.

Washburn, S. L. 1948. 'Sex differences in the pubic bone', *American Journal of Physical Anthropology* 6(2): 199–208.

Wasylikowa, K., 1986. 'Analysis of fossil fruits and seeds', in Berglund, B. E. (ed.), *Handbook of Holocene Palaeoecology and Palaeohydrology.* Chichester: John Wiley and Sons, pp. 571–90. (Reprinted by Blackburn Press, 2004.)

Watters, W. and Hunter, J. R. (2004). *Forensic Geoscience: Principles, Techniques and Application.* Geological Society of London Special Publication. Bath: Geological Society Publishing House, pp. 21–31.

Weaver, D. S. 1980. 'Sex differences in the ilia of a known sex and age sample of fetal and infant skeletons', *American Journal of Physical Anthropology* 52(2): 191–5.

Wells, J. D. and Kurahashi, H. 1994. '*Chrysomya megacephala* (Fabricius) (Diptera: *Calliphoridae*) development: rate, variation and the implications for forensic entomology', *Japanese Journal of Sanitary Zoology* 45(4): 303–9.

Wells, J. D. and LaMotte, L. R. 1995. 'Estimating maggot age from weight using inverse prediction', *Journal of Forensic Sciences* 40(4): 585–90.

Wenk, R. E. 2004. 'Testing for parentage and kinship', *Current Opinion in Hematology* 11(5): 357–61.

Whaites, E. 1992. *Essentials of Dental Radiography and Radiology.* London: Churchill Livingstone.

White, C. D., Spence, M. W., Stuart-Williams, H. L. Q. and Schwartz, H. P. 1998. 'Oxygen isotopes and the identification of geographical origins: the valley of Oaxaca versus the valley of Mexico', *Journal of Archaeological Science* 25: 643–55.

White, P. C. 1998. *Crime Scene to Court: The Essentials of Forensic Science.* London/Cambridge: The Royal Society of Chemistry.

White, P. C. 2004. *Crime Scene to Court – The Essentials of Forensic Science* (2nd ed.). London: The Royal Society of Chemistry.

White, T. D. 1991. *Human Osteology.* London: Academic Press.

White, T. D. 2000. *Human Osteology* (2nd ed.). New York: Academic Press.

White, T. D. and Folkens, P. A. 2000. *Human Osteology* (2nd ed). London: Academic Press.

White, T. D. and Folkens, P. A. 2005. *The Human Bone Manual.* Burlington, MA: Elsevier/Academic Press.

Whiting, W. C. and Zernicke, R. F. 1998. *Biomechanics of Musculoskeletal Injury.* Champaign, IL: Human Kinetics.

Whittaker, D. 2000. 'Aging from the dentition', in Cox, M. and Mays, S. (eds.), *Human Osteology: In Archaeology and Forensic Science.* London: Greenwich Medical Media, pp. 83–100.

Wiesner, G. L., Lewis, S. and Scott, J. 2000. 'Human subjects research, ethics, family, and pedigree studies', in Murray, T. H. and Mehlman, M. J. (eds.), *Encyclopedia of Ethical, Legal, and Policy Issues in Biotechnology.* New York: John Wiley and Sons, vol 2, pp. 595–611.

Wilkinson, K. N. and Stevens, C. J. 2003. *Environmental Archaeology: Approaches, Techniques and Applications.* Stroud, UK: Tempus.

Willey, P. and Heilman, A. 1987. Estimating time since death using plant roots and stems. *Journal of Forensic Sciences* 32(5): 1264–70.

Wilson, D. R. 1982. *Air Photo Interpretation for Archaeologists.* London: Batsford.

Wilson, D. R. 2000. *Air Photo Interpretation for Archaeologists.* (2nd edition). Stroud, UK: Tempus.

Wiltshire, P. E. J. 2004. 'Pollen and related botanical evidence – its recent contribution to forensic investigations', in Pye, K. and Croft, D. (eds.), *Forensic Geoscience: Principles, Techniques and Applications.* London: Conference Abstracts, Geological Society of London, p. 232.

Wisner, B. and Adams, J. 2002. *Environmental Health in Emergencies and Disasters.* Geneva: World Health Organization.

Woo, T. L. and Morant, G. M. 1934. 'A biometric study of the 'flatness' of the facial skeleton in man', *Biometrika* 26(1–2): 196–250.

World Health Organization (WHO). 2004. *International Travel and Health.* Geneva: WHO.

Wright, L. E. and Schwarcz, H. P. 1998. 'Stable carbon and oxygen isotopes in human tooth enamel: identifying breastfeeding and weaning in prehistory', *American Journal of Physical Anthropology* 106(1): 1–18.

Wright, R. V. S. 7 Sept 2005. '*Guide to Using the CRANID program CR5Ind.EXE*'. Unpublished manual. richwrig@tig.com.au. Note: this is an updated version of the 2005 CRANID manual cited for the scattergram Fig. 7–4, and cranial diagrams Figs. 8–12 to 8–15.

Wright, R., Hanson, I. and Sterenberg, J. 2005. 'Mass grave excavation', in Hunter, J. and Cox, M. (ed.), pp. 137–58.

Wright, R. and Hanson, I. in press 2008. 'How to do forensic archaeology under the auspices of large organisations like the United Nations', in Blau, S. and Ubelaker, D. (eds) *World Archaeological Congress of Forensic Anthropology and Archaeology*, California. Left Coast Press.

Yarkoni, S., Schmidt, W., Jeanty, P., Reece, E. A. and Hobbins, J. C. 1985. 'Clavicular measurement: a new biometric parameter for fetal evaluation', *Journal of Ultrasound Medicine* 4(9): 467–70.

Yehuda, R. 2002. 'Current status of cortisol findings in post-traumatic stress disorder', *The Psychiatric Clinics of North America* 25(2): 341–68.

Zipf, G. 1950. *The Principle of Least Effort.* Reading, MA: Addison Wesley.

Index